Lecture Notes in Computer Science   9583

Commenced Publication in 1973
Founding and Former Series Editors:
Gerhard Goos, Juris Hartmanis, and Jan van Leeuwen

Advanced Research in Computing and Software Science

Subline of Lecture Notes in Computer Science

More information about this series at http://www.springer.com/series/7407

Barbara Jobstmann · K. Rustan M. Leino (Eds.)

Verification, Model Checking, and Abstract Interpretation

17th International Conference, VMCAI 2016
St. Petersburg, FL, USA, January 17–19, 2016
Proceedings

 Springer

Editors
Barbara Jobstmann
EPFL IC-DO
Lausanne
Switzerland

K. Rustan M. Leino
Microsoft Research
Redmond, WA
USA

ISSN 0302-9743 ISSN 1611-3349 (electronic)
Lecture Notes in Computer Science
ISBN 978-3-662-49121-8 ISBN 978-3-662-49122-5 (eBook)
DOI 10.1007/978-3-662-49122-5

Library of Congress Control Number: 2015958744

LNCS Sublibrary: SL1 – Theoretical Computer Science and General Issues

This Springer imprint is published by SpringerNature
The registered company is Springer-Verlag GmbH Berlin Heidelberg

Preface

This volume contains the papers presented at VMCAI 2016, the 17th International Conference on Verification, Model Checking, and Abstract Interpretation, held during January 17–19, 2016, in St. Petersburg, FL, USA, co-located with POPL 2016 (the annual ACM SIGPLAN/SIGACT Symposium on Principles of Programming Languages). Previous meetings were held in Port Jefferson (1997), Pisa (1998), Venice (2002), New York (2003), Venice (2004), Paris (2005), Charleston (2006), Nice (2007), San Francisco (2008), Savannah (2009), Madrid (2010), Austin (2011), Philadelphia (2012), Rome (2013), San Diego (2014), and Mumbai (2015).

VMCAI provides a forum for researchers from the communities of verification, model checking, and abstract interpretation, facilitating interaction, cross-fertilization, and advancement of hybrid methods that combine these and related areas. VMCAI topics include: program verification, model checking, abstract interpretation and abstract domains, program synthesis, static analysis, type systems, deductive methods, program certification, debugging techniques, program transformation, optimization, hybrid and cyber-physical systems.

This year the conference attracted 89 abstract submission leading to 67 full-paper submissions. Each submission was reviewed by at least three Program Committee members. The committee decided to accept 24 papers. The principal selection criteria were relevance, quality, and originality. We are glad to include in the proceedings the contributions of three invited keynote speakers: Peter Müller on "Viper — A Verification Infrastructure for Permission-based Reasoning," Bryan Parno on "Ironclad — Full Verification of Complex Systems," and Thomas Reps on "Automating Abstract Interpretation." We would like to thank them for sharing their insights with us through their talks and articles contributed to the proceedings.

We thank our wonderful Program Committee members and reviewers for their reviews and discussions. Our gratitude goes to the Steering Committee members for their helpful advice and support, in particular to Lenore Zuck and Dave Schmidt for their assistance and invaluable experience with the organization of VMCAI. We would like to thank Annabel Satin for the great help in coordinating the events co-located with POPL 2016. We are indebted to EasyChair for providing us with an excellent conference management system. Finally, we thank our sponsors, Facebook and Microsoft Research, as well as NSF for providing travel grants for students.

November 2015

Barbara Jobstmann
K. Rustan M. Leino

Organization

Program Committee

Bor-Yuh Evan Chang	University of Colorado Boulder, USA
Hana Chockler	King's College London, UK
Eva Darulova	MPI for Software Systems, Germany
Rayna Dimitrova	MPI for Software Systems, Germany
Javier Esparza	Technical University of Munich, Germany
Aarti Gupta	Princeton University, USA
Arie Gurfinkel	Software Engineering Institute, CMU, USA
Barbara Jobstmann	EPFL, Switzerland
Rustan Leino	Microsoft Research, USA
Francesco Logozzo	Facebook, USA
Madhavan Mukund	Chennai Mathematical Institute, India
Peter Müller	ETH Zürich, Switzerland
David Parker	University of Birmingham, UK
Andreas Podelski	University of Freiburg, Germany
Nadia Polikarpova	MIT CSAIL, USA
Philipp Rümmer	Uppsala University, Sweden
Roopsha Samanta	Institute of Science and Technology, Austria
Martina Seidl	Johannes Kepler University Linz, Austria
Sanjit A. Seshia	UC Berkeley, USA
Sharon Shoham	The Academic College of Tel Aviv Yaffo, Israel
Tachio Terauchi	Japan Advanced Institute of Science and Technology, Japan
Caterina Urban	ETH Zürich, Switzerland
Thomas Wies	New York University, USA
Lenore Zuck	University of Illinois in Chicago, USA

Steering Committee

Agostino Cortesi	Ca Foscari University of Venice, Italy
Patrick Cousot	CNRS and ENS and Inria, France and New York University, USA
E. Allen Emerson	University of Texas at Austin, USA
Andreas Podelski	University of Freiburg, Germany
Thomas W. Reps	University of Wisconsin at Madison, USA
David Schmidt	Kansas State University, USA
Lenore Zuck	University of Illinois at Chicago, USA

Additional Reviewers

Avni, Guy
Backeman, Peter
Bucur, Stefan
Cai, Xiaojuan
Chistikov, Dmitry
Christakis, Maria
Daca, Przemyslaw
Darais, David
Davies, Jessica
Donzé, Alexandre
Ehlers, Rüdiger
Feret, Jerome
Ferrara, Pietro
Ferrere, Thomas
Fremont, Daniel J.
Furia, Carlo A.
Garoche, Pierre-Loic
Gjomemo, Rigel
Hahn, Ernst Moritz
Hoffmann, Philipp
Itzhaky, Shachar
Kim, Eric
Kincaid, Zachary
Komuravelli, Anvesh
Krishna, Siddharth
Kupriyanov, Andrey
Lahav, Ori
Lammich, Peter
Meshman, Yuri
Meyer, Philipp J.
Milicevic, Aleksandar
Miné, Antoine

Mover, Sergio
Mukherjee, Suvam
Namjoshi, Kedar
Navas, Jorge A.
Ngo, Tuan Phong
Padon, Oded
Pavlinovic, Zvonimir
Pavlogiannis, Andreas
Prasad, Sanjiva
Rabe, Markus N.
Raghothaman, Mukund
Reynolds, Andrew
Rinetzky, Noam
Sadigh, Dorsa
Schilling, Christian
Schwerhoff, Malte
Schäf, Martin
Shenoy R., Gautham
Shoukry, Yasser
Sickert, Salomon
Sinha, Rohit
Srivathsan, B.
Summers, Alexander J.
Suresh, S.P.
Suwimonteerabuth, Dejvuth
Tarrach, Thorsten
Totla, Nishant
Unno, Hiroshi
Van Horn, David
Zeljić, Aleksandar
Zhai, Ennan

Ironclad: Full Verification of Complex Systems (Invited Talk)

Bryan Parno

Microsoft Research

The Ironclad project at Microsoft Research is using a set of new and modified tools based on automated theorem proving to build Ironclad services. An Ironclad service guarantees to remote parties that every CPU instruction the service executes adheres to a high-level specification, convincing clients that the service will be worthy of their trust. To provide such end-to-end guarantees, we built a full stack of verified software. That software includes a verified kernel; verified drivers; verified system and cryptography libraries including SHA, HMAC, and RSA; and four Ironclad Apps [1]. As a concrete example, our Ironclad database provably provides differential privacy to its data contributors. In other words, if a client encrypts her personal data with the database's public key, then it can only be decrypted by software that guarantees, down to the assembly level, that it preserves differential privacy when releasing aggregate statistics about the data.

We've also recently expanded the scope of our verification efforts to distributed systems, which are notorious for harboring subtle bugs. We have developed IronFleet [2], a methodology for building practical and provably correct distributed systems. We demonstrated the methodology on a complex implementation of a Paxos-based replicated state machine library and a lease-based sharded key-value store. We proved that each obeys a concise safety specification, as well as desirable liveness requirements. Each implementation achieves performance competitive with a reference system.

In this talk, we describe our methodology, formal results, and lessons we learned from building large stacks of verified systems software. In pushing automated verification tools to new scales (over 70K lines of code and proof so far), our team has both benefited from automated verification techniques and uncovered new challenges in using them.

By continuing to push verification tools to larger and more complex systems, Ironclad ultimately aims to raise the standard for security- and reliability-critical systems from "tested" to "correct".

References

1. Hawblitzel, C., Howell, J., Lorch, J.R., Narayan, A., Parno, B., Zhang, D., Zill, B.: Ironclad apps: end-to-end security via automated full-system verification. In: Proceedings of the USENIX Symposium on Operating Systems Design and Implementation (OSDI), October 2014
2. Hawblitzel, C., Howell, J., Kapritsos, M., Lorch, J.R., Parno, B., Roberts, M.L., Setty, S., Zill, B.: Ironfleet: proving practical distributed systems correct. In: Proceedings of the ACM Symposium on Operating Systems Principles (SOSP), October 2015

Contents

Hybrid and Timed Systems

Dynamic and Static Verification

Probabilistic Systems

Concurrent Programs

Parameterized and Component-Based Systems

Solver Improvements

Invited Talks

Automating Abstract Interpretation

Thomas Reps[1,2](✉) and Aditya Thakur[3]

[1] University of Wisconsin, Madison, WI, USA
reps@cs.wisc.edu
[2] GrammaTech, Inc., Ithaca, NY, USA
[3] Google, Inc., Mountain View, CA, USA

Abstract. Abstract interpretation has a reputation of being a kind of "black art," and consequently difficult to work with. This paper describes a twenty-year quest by the first author to address this issue by raising the level of automation in abstract interpretation. The most recent leg of this journey is the subject of the second author's 2014 Ph.D. dissertation. The paper discusses several different approaches to creating correct-by-construction analyzers. Our research has allowed us to establish connections between this problem and several other areas of computer science, including automated reasoning/decision procedures, concept learning, and constraint programming.

1 Introduction

Establishing that a program is correct is undecidable in general. Consequently, program-analysis and verification tools typically work on an *abstraction* of a program, which over-approximates the original program's behavior. The theory underlying this approach is called *abstract interpretation* [18]. Abstract interpretation provides a way to create program analyzers that obtain information about the possible states that a program reaches during execution, but without actually running the program on specific inputs. Instead, the analyzer executes the program using finite-sized descriptors that represent *sets* of states. For example, one can use descriptors that represent only the *sign* of a variable's value: neg, zero, pos, or unknown. If the abstract state maps variables x and y as follows, $[x \mapsto \text{neg}, y \mapsto \text{neg}]$, the product "$x * y$" would be performed as "neg $*$ neg," yielding pos. This approximation discards information about the specific *values* of x and y; $[x \mapsto \text{neg}, y \mapsto \text{neg}]$ represents all concrete states in which x and y hold negative integers. By using such descriptors to explore the program's behavior for *all* possible inputs, the analyzer accounts for all possible states that the program can reach.

The tar-pit of undecidability is sidestepped via two concepts:

- **Abstraction.** In this context, abstraction means "representing an information space by a smaller space that captures its essential features." (The smaller

---

Portions of this work appeared in [26,35,45,63,64,66,70,76,78,81,82]. T. Reps has an ownership interest in GrammaTech, Inc., which has licensed elements of the technology reported in this publication.

B. Jobstmann and K.R.M. Leino (Eds.): VMCAI 2016, LNCS 9583, pp. 3–40, 2016.
DOI: 10.1007/978-3-662-49122-5_1

space is called an *abstract domain*; an example of an abstract domain is the set of all descriptors that record the signs of variables, as used above.)

– **One-Sided Analysis.** Whenever the analyzer says "no" it means "no," but whenever it says "yes" it means "maybe-yes/maybe-no"—i.e., the property might or might not hold.

When the analyzer reports "no, a bad state is not reachable," one is guaranteed that only good states can arise—and hence that the program is correct with respect to the property being checked. If the analyzer reports "yes, a bad state might be reachable," it must try other techniques to attempt to establish the desired property (e.g., refining the abstraction in use).

However, there is a glitch: abstract interpretation has a reputation of being a kind of "black art," and consequently difficult to work with. This paper describes a twenty-year quest to make abstract interpretation easier to work with by (i) raising the level of discourse for specifying abstract interpreters, and (ii) automating some of abstraction interpretation's more difficult aspects, thereby making it possible to create correct-by-construction analyzers.

A major focus of the work has been how to automate the construction of the functions to transform abstract states—also known as *abstract transformers.*

The motivation came from our experience with two challenging analysis contexts:

Analysis of Programs Manipulating Linked Data Structures: When analyzing such programs, the number of fine-grained details that one needs to track causes the abstractions to be inherently complex.

Analysis of Stripped Machine Code: Here an analyzer needs to use multiple (separate and cooperating) abstract interpretations [6,45], and we also had the goal of creating machine-code-analysis tools for multiple instruction sets.

In both cases, our experience with hand construction of abstract transformers [6,69] was that the process was tedious, time-consuming, and a source of errors.

The paper summarizes three major milestones of our research, based on different approaches that we explored.

1. The TVLA system [12,42,70] introduced a way to create abstractions of systems specified in first-order logic, plus transitive closure (Sect. 3). To construct abstract transformers in TVLA, we developed a non-standard approach to weakest precondition based on a finite-differencing transformation [63].
2. The TSL system [45] supports the creation of correct-by-construction implementations of the abstract transformers needed in tools that analyze machine code (Sect. 4). From a single specification of the concrete semantics of an instruction set, TSL can generate abstract transformers for static analysis, dynamic analysis, symbolic analysis, or any combination of the three.
3. Our work on symbolic methods for abstract interpretation [64,78,82] aims to bridge the gap between (i) the use of logic for specifying program semantics and program correctness, and (ii) abstract interpretation. Many of the issues, including the construction of abstract transformers, can be reduced to the problem of *symbolic abstraction* (Sect. 5):

> Given formula φ in logic $\mathcal{L}$, and abstract domain $\mathbb{A}$, find the most-precise descriptor $a^\sharp$ in $\mathbb{A}$ that over-approximates the meaning of φ.

A particularly exciting aspect of the work on symbolic abstraction is the number of links the problem has with other research areas that one would not normally think of as being connected to static program analysis. Our investigations have established connections with such areas as automated reasoning/decision procedures (Sect. 5.4), concept learning (Sect. 6.1), and constraint programming (Sect. 6.2).

Section 7 discusses related work. Section 8 concludes with a few final insights and takeaways.

2   Problem Statement

2.1   What Can Be Automated About Abstract Interpretation?

A static-analysis system can have many components, including

(i) construction and use of abstract transformers
  - an algorithm to construct sound abstract transformers to model the actions of language primitives and/or user-defined functions
  - an algorithm to apply or compose abstract transformers
(ii) state-space exploration
  - state-space-exploration algorithms (i.e., equation/constraint solvers)
  - methods to enforce termination via widening policies
  - containment algorithms (for determining whether state-space exploration should terminate)
(iii) mechanisms for improving precision
  - narrowing
  - reduced product
  - semantic reduction
  - construction of best transformers
  - determination of the best inductive invariant
(iv) abstraction refinement (enabled by (i))

While the first author has also done a lot of work on state-space-exploration algorithms [62,65,67] and some on widening policies [29,30], because so many of the other aspects of the problem of automating abstract interpretation are enabled by automating the construction (and use) of abstract transformers, the paper will focus on work he and his collaborators have carried out on that topic. In Sect. 5, we discuss recent work on a uniform mechanism to construct abstract transformers that also provides a way to address reduced product, semantic reduction, and (for some abstract domains) finding the best inductive invariant.

To create sound abstract transformers that use a given abstract domain, we need to have some way to create the abstract analogs of

(I) each constant that can be denoted in the programming language
(II) each primitive operation in the programming language
(III) each user-defined function in every program to be analyzed.

Task **(I)** is related to defining the *abstraction function* α; to create the abstract analog $k^\sharp$ of concrete constant k, apply α; i.e., $k^\sharp = \alpha(\{k\})$. By an abstract analog of a concrete operation/function f, we mean an abstract operation/function $f^\sharp$ that satisfies

$$\alpha(\tilde{f}(V_1, \ldots, V_k)) \sqsubseteq f^\sharp(\alpha(V_1), \ldots, \alpha(V_k)), \tag{1}$$

where $\tilde{f}$ denotes the lifting of f to operate on a set of values, i.e., $\tilde{f}(V_1, \ldots, V_k) = \{f(v_1, \ldots, v_k) \mid v_1 \in V_1, \ldots, v_k \in V_k\}$, and $\sqsubseteq$ denotes an ordering on abstract values that respects concrete containment; i.e., $a_1^\sharp \sqsubseteq a_2^\sharp$ implies $\gamma(a_1^\sharp) \subseteq \gamma(a_2^\sharp)$, where γ denotes the *concretization function* for the abstract domain.

The effort that has to go into task **(II)** is bounded—the language has a fixed number of primitive operations—and task **(II)** only has to be done once for a given abstract domain. However, task **(III)** needs automation, because it will be performed for all functions in all users' programs, which are not known *a priori*.

2.2   Non-Compositionality

Unfortunately, abstract interpretation is *inherently non-compositional*—meaning that one cannot create abstract analogs of operations/functions separately, and put them together without losing precision (see below). The non-compositionality property is the essence of what makes it hard to automate the construction of abstract transformers. This message is an uncomfortable one for computer scientists because compositionality is so ingrained in our training—e.g., our programming languages are defined using context-free grammars; many concepts and properties are defined using inductive definitions, and recursive tree traversals are a basic workhorse.

Syntax-Directed Replacement. A compositional approach to constructing sound abstract transformers is relatively easy to implement. In particular, Eq. (1) makes possible a simple, compositional approach—namely, syntax-directed replacement of the concrete constants and concrete primitive operations by their abstract analogs. For instance, consider the following function: $f(x_1, x_2) = x_1 * x_2 + 1$. First, hoist f to $\tilde{f}$, i.e., $\tilde{f}(X_1, X_2) = X_1 \tilde{*} X_2 \tilde{+} \{1\}$. Then, by Eq. (1), we have

$$\alpha(\tilde{f}(X_1, X_2)) = \alpha(X_1 \tilde{*} X_2 \tilde{+} \{1\}) \sqsubseteq \alpha(X_1 \tilde{*} X_2) +^\sharp \{1\}^\sharp \sqsubseteq \alpha(X_1) *^\sharp \alpha(X_2) +^\sharp \{1\}^\sharp.$$

Thus, one way to ensure that we have a sound $f^\sharp$ is to define $f^\sharp(x_1, x_2)$ by

$$f^\sharp(x_1, x_2) \stackrel{\text{def}}{=} x_1 *^\sharp x_2 +^\sharp \{1\}^\sharp.$$

Drawbacks of Syntax-Directed Replacement. Although syntax-directed replacement is simple and compositional, it can be quite myopic because it focuses solely on what happens at a single production in the abstract syntax tree. The approach can lead to a loss of precision by not accounting for correlations between operations at far-apart positions in the abstract syntax tree.

To illustrate the issue, consider the function $h(x) \stackrel{\text{def}}{=} x + (-x)$. Obviously, $h(x)$ always returns 0. Now suppose that we apply syntax-directed replacement, $h^\sharp(x) \stackrel{\text{def}}{=} x +^\sharp (-^\sharp x)$, and evaluate $h^\sharp$ over the *sign abstract domain*, which consists of six values: $\{\text{neg}, 0, \text{pos}, \text{nonpos}, \text{nonneg}, \top\}$. In particular, the abstract unary-minus operation is defined as follows:

x	$\top$	nonneg	nonpos	pos	zero	neg
$-^\sharp x$	$\top$	nonpos	nonneg	neg	zero	pos

Consider evaluating $h^\sharp(x)$ with the abstract value pos for the value of x. (Abstract values at leaves and internal nodes of the AST of $h^\sharp$'s defining expression are shown within square brackets in the tree in Fig. 1.) Because $\text{pos} +^\sharp \text{neg} = \top$, we obtain no useful information from the abstract interpretation. In contrast, the concrete value is always 0, and therefore the most-precise abstract answer is zero (because $\alpha(\{0\}) = \text{zero}$).

Artificially imposing compositionality on an abstract interpreter has a number of drawbacks:

- compositionality at expression granularity may not produce the best abstraction, even if all abstract program primitives are best abstract primitives
- compositionality at statement or basic-block level may not produce the best transformer, even if each abstract transformer being composed is a best transformer

Fig. 1. Abstract subtraction when leaves are correlated.

Moreover, if an analyzer loses precision at one point in a program, it can provoke a cascade of precision loss throughout the program.

2.3 What Does It Mean to Automate the Construction of Abstract Transformers?

We sometimes describe our work by saying that we are working on "a yacc for automating the construction of abstract transformers," by which we mean a tool that automates the task to an extent similar to the automation of the construction of parsers achieved by yacc [36]. As a model for what we would like to achieve, consider the problem that yacc addresses:

- An instance of a parsing problem, Parse(L,s), has two parameters: L, a context-free language; and s, a string to be parsed. String s changes more frequently than language L.
- Context-free grammars are a formalism for specifying context-free languages.
- Create a tool that implements the following specification:
  - Input: a context-free grammar that describes language L.
  - Output: a parsing function, `yyparse()`, for which executing `yyparse()` on string s computes Parse(L,s).

Thus, we would like to follow a similar scheme.

- An abstract interpreter $\text{Interp}^\sharp(M_s, \mathbb{A}, a^\sharp)$ has three inputs
  - M_s = the meaning function for a programming-language statement s
  - $\mathbb{A}$ = an abstract domain
  - $a^\sharp$ = an abstract-domain value (which represents a set of pre-states) $a^\sharp$ changes more frequently than M_s and $\mathbb{A}$.
- Find appropriate formalisms F_1 and F_2 for specifying M_s and $\mathbb{A}$.
- Create a tool that implements the following specification:
  - Input:
    * an F_1 specification of the programming language's semantics
    * an F_2 specification that characterizes the abstraction that $\mathbb{A}$ supports
  - Output: a function $I_{s,\mathbb{A}}(\cdot)$ such that $I_{s,\mathbb{A}}(a^\sharp)$ computes $\text{Interp}^\sharp(M_s, \mathbb{A}, a^\sharp)$

An alternative goal for the tool's output is as follows:

Output: a *representation* of the function $I_{s,\mathbb{A}}(\cdot)$ that can be used in the function-composition operations performed by interprocedural dataflow analyzers [74].

Relationship to Partial Evaluation. Readers who are familiar with partial evaluation [28,37] may be struck by how similar the problem statement above is to the specification of partial evaluation, which suggests that partial evaluation could play a role in automating abstract interpretation. However, we believe that this observation is a red herring: whereas partial evaluation provides a mechanism to speed up computations by removing interpretive overhead, the key question in automating the construction of abstract transformers is *"Given the specification of an abstraction, how does one create an execution engine for an analyzer that performs computations in an over-approximating fashion?"*

2.4 Four Questions

The above discussion suggests four questions to ask about methods for automating the construction of abstract transformers:

Q1. What formalism is used to specify M_s?

Q2. What formalism is used to specify $\mathbb{A}$?

Q3. What is the engine at work that applies/constructs abstract transformers?

    (a) What method is used to create $I_{s,\mathbb{A}}(\cdot)$?

    (b) Can it be used to create a representation of $I_{s,\mathbb{A}}(\cdot)$?

Q4. How is the non-compositionality issue discussed in Sect. 2.2 addressed?

The answers given in Sects. 3, 4, and 5 explain how these issues are addressed in the three approaches described in the paper.

3 TVLA: 3-Valued Logic Analyzer

In 1999, Sagiv, Reps, and Wilhelm devised an abstraction method, called *canonical abstraction* [70], for analyzing the properties of evolving logical structures. The original motivation for developing canonical-abstraction domains was the desire to apply abstract interpretation to imperative programs that manipulate linked data structures, to check such properties as

- when the input to a list-insert program is an acyclic list, the output is an acyclic list, and
- when the input to a list-reversal program that uses destructive-update operations is an acyclic list, the output is an acyclic list.

Such analysis problems are known generically as *shape-analysis* problems. In programs that manipulate linked data structures, storage cells can be dynamically allocated and freed, and structure fields can be destructively updated. Data structures can thus grow and shrink, with no fixed upper bound on their size or number. In the case of thread-based languages, such as Java, the number of threads can also grow and shrink dynamically [84]. The challenge in shape analysis is to find a way to create finite-sized descriptors of memory configurations that (i) abstract away certain details, but (ii) retain enough key information so that an analyzer can identify interesting node-linkage properties that hold.

    A *logical structure* is a set of *individuals* together with a certain collection of relations over the individuals. (In shape analysis, individuals represent entities such as memory locations, threads, locks, etc.; unary and binary relations encode the contents of variables, pointer-valued structure fields, and other aspects of memory states; and first-order formulas with transitive closure are used to specify properties such as sharing, cyclicity, reachability, etc.) Because canonical abstraction is a general method for abstracting logical structures, it actually has much broader applicability for analyzing systems than just shape-analysis problems. It is relevant to the analysis of any system that can be modeled as an evolving logical structure [11, 12, 34, 42].

    The concrete semantics of a system—such as the concrete semantics of programs written in a given programming language—is defined using a fixed set of *core relation symbols* $\mathcal{C}$. (Different kinds of systems, such as different programming languages, are defined by varying the symbols in $\mathcal{C}$.) The concrete semantics expresses how a program statement st causes the core relations to change. The semantics of st is specified with formulas in first-order logic plus transitive closure over the client-defined core relations in $\mathcal{C}$.

Different abstract domains are defined using canonical abstraction by

- Defining a set of *instrumentation relations* $\mathcal{I}$ (also known as *derived relations* or *views*). Each instrumentation relation $p(v)$ is defined by a formula $\psi_p(v)$ over the core relations.
- Choosing a set of unary *abstraction relations* $\mathcal{A}$ from among the unary relations in the vocabulary $\mathcal{R} \stackrel{\text{def}}{=} (\mathcal{C} \uplus \mathcal{I})$.

$\mathcal{I}$ controls what information is maintained (in addition to the core relations); $\mathcal{A}$ controls what individuals are indistinguishable. The two mechanisms are connected because it is possible to declare unary instrumentation relations as abstraction relations. An *abstract logical structure* is the quotient of a concrete logical structure with respect to the sets of indistinguishable individuals.

The TVLA (Three-Valued-Logic Analyzer) system [12, 42] automates some of the more difficult aspects of working with canonical-abstraction domains. However, the initial version of TVLA failed to meet our goal of automating abstract interpretation because not all aspects of abstract transformers were derived automatically from the specification of a given abstraction. The analysis designer had to supply a key portion of every abstract transformer manually.

The introduction of instrumentation relations causes auxiliary information to be recorded in a program state, such as whether an individual memory location possesses (or does not possess) a certain property. The concrete semantics expresses how a program statement st causes the core relations to change; the challenge is how one should go about updating the instrumentation relations. Canonical-abstraction domains are based on 3-valued logic, where the third truth value $(1/2)$ arises when it is not known whether a property holds or not. Suppose that $p(v) \in \mathcal{I}$ is defined by $\psi_p(v)$. Reevaluating $\psi_p(v)$ almost always yields $1/2$, and thus completely defeats the purpose of having augmented logical structures with instrumentation relation p.

To overcome this effect, the initial version of TVLA required an analysis designer to specify a *relation-maintenance formula* for each instrumentation relation, for each kind of statement in the language being analyzed. This approach could obtain more precise results than that of reevaluating $\psi_p(v)$, but placed the onus on the analysis designer to supply a key part of every abstract transformer, which was both burdensome and a source of errors.

Table 1. Core relations for shape analysis of programs that manipulate linked lists.

Relation	Intended meaning
$eq(v_1, v_2)$	Do v_1 and v_2 denote the same memory cell?
$x(v)$	Does pointer variable x point to memory cell v?
$n(v_1, v_2)$	Does the n-field of v_1 point to v_2?

In 2002, we developed a way to create relation-maintenance formulas—and thereby abstract transformers—fully automatically [63]. Our solution to the problem is based on a finite-differencing transformation. Finite-differencing turns out to be a natural way to identify the "footprint" of statement st on an instrumentation relation p, which reduces the number of tuples in p that have to be reevaluated (compared to reevaluating *all* of p's tuples using $\psi_p(v)$).

2-Valued Logical Structures. A concrete state is a *2-valued logical structure*, which provides an interpretation of a vocabulary $\mathcal{R} = \{eq, p_1, \ldots, p_n\}$ of relation symbols (with given arities). $\mathcal{R}_k$ denotes the set of k-ary symbols.

Definition 1. *A 2-**valued logical structure** S over $\mathcal{R}$ is a pair $S = \langle U, \iota \rangle$, where U is the set of **individuals**, and ι is the **interpretation**. Let $\mathbb{B} = \{0, 1\}$ be the domain of truth values. For $p \in \mathcal{R}_i$, $\iota(p) \colon U^i \to \mathbb{B}$. We assume that $eq \in \mathcal{R}_2$ is the identity relation: (i) for all $u \in U$, $\iota(eq)(u, u) = 1$, and (ii) for all $u_1, u_2 \in U$ such that u_1 and u_2 are distinct individuals, $\iota(eq)(u_1, u_2) = 0$.*
*   The set of 2-valued logical structures over $\mathcal{R}$ is denoted by $\mathcal{S}_2[\mathcal{R}]$.*

A concrete state is modeled by a 2-valued logical structure over a fixed vocabulary $\mathcal{C} \subseteq \mathcal{R}$ of *core relations*. Table 1 lists the core relations that are used to represent a program state made up of linked lists. The set of unary core relations, $\mathcal{C}_1$, contains relations that encode the pointer variables of the program: a unary relation of the form $x(v) \in \mathcal{C}_1$ encodes pointer variable $\mathsf{x} \in \mathit{Var}$. The binary relation $n(v_1, v_2) \in \mathcal{C}_2$ encodes list-node linkages.

$\mathcal{R}$ does not include constant or function symbols. Constant symbols are encoded via unary relations, and k-ary functions via $k + 1$-ary relations. In both cases, we use *integrity rules*—i.e., global constraints that restrict the set of structures considered to ones that we intend. The following integrity rules restrict each unary relation x, for $\mathsf{x} \in \mathit{Var}$, to serve as a constant, and restrict binary relation n to encode a partial function:

$$\text{for each } \mathsf{x} \in \mathit{Var}, \forall v_1, v_2 : x(v_1) \wedge x(v_2) \Rightarrow eq(v_1, v_2)$$
$$\forall v_1, v_2, v_3 : n(v_3, v_1) \wedge n(v_3, v_2) \Rightarrow eq(v_1, v_2)$$

3-Valued Structures, Embedding, and Canonical Abstraction. A *3-valued logical structure* provides a finite over-approximation of a possibly infinite set of 2-valued structures. The set $\mathbb{T} \overset{\text{def}}{=} \{0, 1, 1/2\}$ of 3-valued truth values is partially ordered under the *information order*: $l \sqsubseteq 1/2$ for $l \in \{0, 1\}$. 0 and 1 are *definite* values; $1/2$, which denotes uncertainty, is an *indefinite* value. The symbol $\sqcup$ denotes the least-upper-bound operation with respect to $\sqsubseteq$.

Definition 2. *A 3-**valued logical structure** $S = \langle U, \iota \rangle$ is almost identical to a 2-valued structure, except that ι maps each $p \in \mathcal{R}_i$ to a 3-valued function $\iota(p) \colon U^i \to \mathbb{T}$. In addition, (i) for all $u \in U$, $\iota(eq)(u, u) \sqsupseteq 1$, and (ii) for all $u_1, u_2 \in U$ such that u_1 and u_2 are distinct individuals, $\iota(eq)(u_1, u_2) = 0$. (An individual u for which $\iota(eq)(u, u) = 1/2$ is called a **summary individual**.)*

The set of 3-valued logical structures over $\mathcal{R}$ is denoted by $\mathcal{S}_3[\mathcal{R}] \supsetneq \mathcal{S}_2[\mathcal{R}]$.
Given $S = \langle U, \iota \rangle, S' = \langle U', \iota' \rangle \in \mathcal{S}_3[\mathcal{R}]$, and surjective function $f: U \to U'$, f
embeds S in S', *denoted by $S \sqsubseteq^f S'$, if for all $p \in \mathcal{R}$ and $u_1, \ldots, u_k \in U$,*
$\iota(p)(u_1, \ldots, u_k) \sqsubseteq \iota'(p)(f(u_1), \ldots, f(u_k))$ If, in addition, for all $u'_1, \ldots, u'_k \in U'$,

$$\iota'(p)(u'_1, \ldots, u'_k) = \bigsqcup_{u_1, \ldots, u_k \in U, s.t. f(u_i) = u'_i, 1 \le i \le k} \iota(p)(u_1, \ldots, u_k)$$

*then S' is the **tight embedding of** S **with respect to** f, denoted by $S' = f(S)$.*

The relation $\sqsubseteq^{\text{id}}$, abbreviated as $\sqsubseteq$, reflects the tuple-wise information order between structures with the same universe. We have $S \sqsubseteq^f S' \Leftrightarrow f(S) \sqsubseteq S'$.

The Embedding Theorem [70, Theorem 4.9] says that if $S \sqsubseteq^f S'$, then every piece of information extracted from S' via a formula φ is a conservative approximation of the information extracted from S via φ:

Theorem 1. (Embedding Theorem [simplified]). *If $S = \langle U, \iota \rangle, S' = \langle U', \iota' \rangle \in \mathcal{S}_3[\mathcal{R}]$ such that $S \sqsubseteq^f S'$, then for every formula φ, $[\![\varphi]\!]_3^S \sqsubseteq [\![\varphi]\!]_3^{S'}$.*

However, embedding alone is not enough. The universe U of 2-valued structure $S = \langle U, \iota \rangle \in \mathcal{S}_2[\mathcal{R}]$ is of *a priori* unbounded size; consequently, we need a method that maps U to an abstract universe $U^\sharp$ of bounded size. The idea behind canonical abstraction is to choose a subset $\mathcal{A} \subseteq \mathcal{R}_1$ of *abstraction relations*, and to define an equivalence relation $\simeq_{\mathcal{A}^S}$ on U that is parameterized by S itself:

$$u_1 \simeq_{\mathcal{A}^S} u_2 \Leftrightarrow \forall p \in \mathcal{A} : \iota(p)(u_1) = \iota(p)(u_2).$$

This equivalence relation defines the surjective function $f_{\mathcal{A}}^S: U \to (U/\simeq_{\mathcal{A}^S})$, which maps an individual to its equivalence class. We have the Galois connection

$$\wp(\mathcal{S}_2[\mathcal{R}]) \xrightleftharpoons[\alpha]{\gamma} \wp(\mathcal{S}_3[\mathcal{R}])$$

$$\alpha(X) = \{f_{\mathcal{A}}^S(S) \mid S \in X\} \qquad \gamma(Y) = \{S \mid S^\sharp \in Y \wedge S \sqsubseteq^f S^\sharp\},$$

where $f_{\mathcal{A}}^S$ in the definition of α denotes the tight-embedding function for logical structures induced by the node-embedding function $f_{\mathcal{A}}^S: U \to (U/\simeq_{\mathcal{A}^S})$. The abstraction function α is referred to as *canonical abstraction*. Note that there is an upper bound on the size of each structure $\langle U^\sharp, \iota^\sharp \rangle \in \mathcal{S}_3[\mathcal{R}]$ that is in the image of α: $|U^\sharp| \le 2^{|\mathcal{A}|}$—and thus the power-set of the image of α is a finite sublattice of $\wp(\mathcal{S}_3[\mathcal{R}])$. The ordering on $\wp(\mathcal{S}_3[\mathcal{R}])$ is the Hoare ordering: $SS_1 \sqsubseteq SS_2$ if for all $S_1 \in SS_1$ there exists $S_2 \in SS_2$ such that $S_1 \sqsubseteq^f S_2$.

Maintaining Instrumentation Relations. The technique used to create abstract transformers for canonical-abstraction domains works as follows. The post-state structures for statement st are determined using four primitives: (i) partial concretization (or partial model enumeration) via the *focus* operation [70], [Sect. 6.3]; (ii) formula evaluation, using (a) for a core relation $c \in \mathcal{C}$, the relation-update formula $\tau_{c,st}$ from the concrete semantics, evaluated in 3-valued logic: $[\![\tau_{c,st}]\!]_3$, and (b) for an instrumentation relation $p \in \mathcal{I}$, a finite-differencing-based relation-maintenance formula $\mu_{p,st}$ created by the technique described below [63, Sects. 5 and 6]; (iii) lightweight logical reasoning via the *coerce* operation [70, Sect. 6.4], which repeatedly performs semantic-reduction steps [19] on the post-state structure to increase the precision of the result; and (iv) a final application of canonical abstraction with respect to abstraction relations $\mathcal{A}$. Due to space limitations, we will only discuss step (ii).[1] Step (ii) transforms a 3-valued pre-state structure $S_1^\#$ that arises just before step (ii), into post-state structure $S_2^\#$ just after step (ii). The structure that consists of just the core relations of $S_2^\#$ is called a *proto-structure*, denoted by $S_{proto}^\#$. The creation of core relation c in $S_{proto}^\#$ from $S_1^\#$ can be expressed as follows:

$$\text{for each } u_1, \ldots, u_k \in U^{S_1^\#}, \iota^{S_{proto}^\#}(c)(u_1, \ldots, u_k) := [\![\tau_{c,st}(u_1, \ldots, u_k)]\!]_3^{S_1^\#} \quad (2)$$

We now come to the crux of the matter: Suppose that instrumentation relation p is defined by formula ψ_p; how should the analysis engine obtain the value of relation p in $S_2^\#$? From the standpoint of the concrete semantics, p is just cached information that could always be recomputed by reevaluating the defining formula ψ_p, and thus the Embedding Theorem tells us that it is sound to perform

$$\text{for each } u_1, \ldots, u_k \in U^{S_{proto}^\#}, \iota^{S_2^\#}(p)(u_1, \ldots, u_k) := [\![\psi_p(u_1, \ldots, u_k)]\!]_3^{S_{proto}^\#}. \quad (3)$$

In practice, however, this approach loses too much precision.

An alternative approach is to create a relation-maintenance formula for p with respect to st via a weakest-liberal-precondition (WLP) transformation,

$$\mu_{p,st} \stackrel{\text{def}}{=} \psi_p[c \leftharpoondown \tau_{c,st} \mid c \in \mathcal{C}], \quad (4)$$

where $\varphi[q \leftharpoondown \theta]$ denotes the formula obtained from φ by replacing each occurrence of relation symbol q by formula θ. Formula $\mu_{p,st}$ is evaluated in $S_1^\#$:

$$\text{for each } u_1, \ldots, u_k \in U^{S_1^\#}, \iota^{S_2^\#}(p)(u_1, \ldots, u_k) := [\![\mu_{p,st}(u_1, \ldots, u_k)]\!]_3^{S_1^\#}. \quad (5)$$

However, Eqs. (3) and (5) turn out to be equivalent—and hence equivalently imprecise—because the steps of creating $S_{proto}^\#$ and evaluating $[\![\psi_p]\!]_3^{S_{proto}^\#}$ *mimic exactly* those of evaluating $[\![\psi_p[c \leftharpoondown \tau_{c,st} \mid c \in \mathcal{C}]]\!]_3^{S_1^\#}$.

Relation Maintenance via Finite Differencing. The algorithm for creating a relation-maintenance formula $\mu_{p,st}$, for $p \in \mathcal{I}$, uses an incremental-computation

---

[1] It is interesting to note that the roles of steps (i), (iii), and (iv) are close to the steps of splitting, propagation, and join, respectively, in our generalization of Stålmarck's algorithm to perform symbolic abstraction [82]. See Sect. 5.

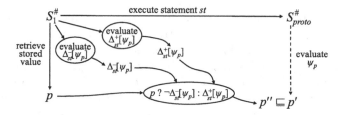

Fig. 2. How to maintain the value of ψ_p in 3-valued logic in response to changes in the values of core relations caused by the execution of structure transformer st.

φ	$\Delta^+_{st}[\varphi]$	$\Delta^-_{st}[\varphi]$
1	0	0
0	0	0
$p(w_1,\ldots,w_k)$, $p \in \mathcal{C}$, and $\tau_{p,st}$ is of the form $p\ ?\ \neg\delta^-_{p,st} : \delta^+_{p,st}$	$(\delta^+_{p,st} \wedge \neg p)(w_1,\ldots,w_k)$	$(\delta^-_{p,st} \wedge p)(w_1,\ldots,w_k)$
$p(w_1,\ldots,w_k)$, $p \in \mathcal{C}$, and $\tau_{p,st}$ is of the form $p \vee \delta_{p,st}$ or $\delta_{p,st} \vee p$	$(\delta_{p,st} \wedge \neg p)(w_1,\ldots,w_k)$	0
$p(w_1,\ldots,w_k)$, $p \in \mathcal{C}$, and $\tau_{p,st}$ is of the form $p \wedge \delta_{p,st}$ or $\delta_{p,st} \wedge p$	0	$(\neg\delta_{p,st} \wedge p)(w_1,\ldots,w_k)$
$p(w_1,\ldots,w_k)$, $p \in \mathcal{C}$, but $\tau_{p,st}$ is not of the above forms	$(\tau_{p,st} \wedge \neg p)(w_1,\ldots,w_k)$	$(p \wedge \neg\tau_{p,st})(w_1,\ldots,w_k)$
$p(w_1,\ldots,w_k)$, $p \in \mathcal{I}$	$((\exists v: \Delta^+_{st}[\varphi_1]) \wedge \neg p)(w_1,\ldots,w_k)$ if $\psi_p \equiv \exists v: \varphi_1$ $\quad$ $\Delta^+_{st}[\psi_p](w_1,\ldots,w_k)$ $\quad$ otherwise	$((\exists v: \Delta^-_{st}[\varphi_1]) \wedge p)(w_1,\ldots,w_k)$ if $\psi_p \equiv \forall v: \varphi_1$ $\quad$ $\Delta^-_{st}[\psi_p](w_1,\ldots,w_k)$ $\quad$ otherwise
$\neg\varphi_1$	$\Delta^-_{st}[\varphi_1]$	$\Delta^+_{st}[\varphi_1]$
$\varphi_1 \vee \varphi_2$	$(\Delta^+_{st}[\varphi_1] \wedge \neg\varphi_2) \vee (\neg\varphi_1 \wedge \Delta^+_{st}[\varphi_2])$	$(\Delta^-_{st}[\varphi_1] \wedge \neg\mathbf{F}_{st}[\varphi_2]) \vee (\neg\mathbf{F}_{st}[\varphi_1] \wedge \Delta^-_{st}[\varphi_2])$
$\varphi_1 \wedge \varphi_2$	$(\Delta^+_{st}[\varphi_1] \wedge \mathbf{F}_{st}[\varphi_2]) \vee (\mathbf{F}_{st}[\varphi_1] \wedge \Delta^+_{st}[\varphi_2])$	$(\Delta^-_{st}[\varphi_1] \wedge \varphi_2) \vee (\varphi_1 \wedge \Delta^-_{st}[\varphi_2])$
$\exists v: \varphi_1$	$(\exists v: \Delta^+_{st}[\varphi_1]) \wedge \neg(\exists v: \varphi_1)$	$(\exists v: \Delta^-_{st}[\varphi_1]) \wedge \neg(\exists v: \mathbf{F}_{st}[\varphi_1])$
$\forall v: \varphi_1$	$(\exists v: \Delta^+_{st}[\varphi_1]) \wedge (\forall v: \mathbf{F}_{st}[\varphi_1])$	$(\exists v: \Delta^-_{st}[\varphi_1]) \wedge (\forall v: \varphi_1)$

Fig. 3. Finite-difference formulas for first-order formulas.

strategy: $\mu_{p,st}$ is defined in terms of the stored (pre-state) value of p, along with two finite-differencing operators, denoted by $\Delta^-_{st}[\cdot]$ and $\Delta^+_{st}[\cdot]$.

$$\mu_{p,st} \stackrel{\text{def}}{=} p\ ?\ \neg\Delta^-_{st}[\psi_p] : \Delta^+_{st}[\psi_p]. \qquad (6)$$

In this approach to the relation-maintenance problem, the two finite-differencing operators characterize the tuples of relation p that are *subtracted* and *added* in response to structure transformation st. $\Delta^-_{st}[\cdot]$ has value 1 for tuples that st changes from 1 to 0; $\Delta^+_{st}[\cdot]$ has value 1 for tuples that st changes from 0 to 1. Equation (6) means that if the old value of a p tuple is 1, then its new value is 1 unless there is a negative change; if the old value of a p tuple is 0, then its new value is 0 unless there is a positive change. Figure 2 depicts how the static-analysis engine evaluates $\Delta_{st}^-[\psi_p]$ and $\Delta_{st}^+[\psi_p]$ in $S_1^\#$ and combines these values with the value of the p tuple from $S_1^\#$ to obtain the value of the p'' tuple.

The operators $\Delta_{st}^-[\cdot]$ and $\Delta_{st}^+[\cdot]$ are defined recursively, as shown in Fig. 3. The definitions in Fig. 3 make use of the operator $\mathbf{F}_{st}[\varphi]$ (standing for "Future"), defined as follows:

$$\mathbf{F}_{st}[\varphi] \stackrel{\text{def}}{=} \varphi \; ? \; \neg \Delta_{st}^-[\varphi] : \Delta_{st}^+[\varphi]. \tag{7}$$

Thus, maintenance formula $\mu_{p,st}$ can also be expressed as $\mu_{p,st} \stackrel{\text{def}}{=} \mathbf{F}_{st}[p]$. Equation (7) and Fig. 3 define a syntax-directed translation scheme that can be implemented via a recursive walk over a formula φ. The operators $\Delta_{st}^-[\cdot]$ and $\Delta_{st}^+[\cdot]$ are mutually recursive. For instance, $\Delta_{st}^+[\neg\varphi_1] = \Delta_{st}^-[\varphi_1]$ and $\Delta_{st}^-[\neg\varphi_1] = \Delta_{st}^+[\varphi_1]$. Moreover, each occurrence of $\mathbf{F}_{st}[\varphi_i]$ contains additional occurrences of $\Delta_{st}^-[\varphi_i]$ and $\Delta_{st}^+[\varphi_i]$.

Note how $\Delta_{st}^-[\cdot]$ and $\Delta_{st}^+[\cdot]$ for $\varphi_1 \vee \varphi_2$ and $\varphi_1 \wedge \varphi_2$ resemble the product rule of differentiation. Continuing the analogy, it helps to bear in mind that the "independent variables" are the core relations, whose values are changed via the $\tau_{c,st}$ formulas; the "dependent variable" is the relation defined by formula φ.

The relation-maintenance formula defined in Eq. (6) is, in essence, a non-standard approach to WLP based on *finite differencing*, rather than *substitution*. To see the relationship with WLP, consider the substitution-based relation-maintenance formula $\psi_p[c \leftrightarrow \tau_{c,st} \mid c \in \mathcal{C}]$ defined in Eq. (4), which computes the WLP of post-state instrumentation relation p with respect to statement st. In the concrete semantics, this formula is equivalent to the finite-differencing-based relation-maintenance formula, $\mathbf{F}_{st}[p] = p \; ? \; \neg\Delta_{st}^-[p] : \Delta_{st}^+[p]$ [63, Theorem 5.3]. In effect, $\mathbf{F}_{st}[p]$ is a "footprint-based" version of WLP.

Answers to The Four Questions.

Q1. The concrete semantics is specified by (i) declaring a suitable set of core relations $\mathcal{C}$ that define a system's concrete states, and (ii) writing—using first-order logic plus transitive closure over $\mathcal{C}$—the $\tau_{c,st}$ formulas that define the concrete transformers.

Q2. A canonical-abstraction domain is specified by (i) defining instrumentation relations $\mathcal{I}$ (again, using first-order logic plus transitive closure), and (ii) selecting which unary relations in $\mathcal{C}_1 \uplus \mathcal{I}_1$ to use as abstraction relations $\mathcal{A}$. $\mathcal{I}$ controls what information is maintained (in addition to the core relations); $\mathcal{A}$ controls what individuals are indistinguishable. The two mechanisms are connected because one can declare unary instrumentation relations to be abstraction relations.

Q3. (a) Abstract transformers are constructed automatically by means of the four-part construction sketched in the section "Maintaining Instrumentation Relations" above. In particular, an instrumentation relation $p \in \mathcal{I}$ is evaluated using the relation-maintenance formula $\mu_{p,st}$, created by applying a finite-differencing transformation to p's defining formula ψ_p (Eq. (6)).

(b) Representations of abstract transformers can be created by means of a principle of "pairing and then abstracting" [35, Sect. 6]. In particular, one uses (sets of) logical structures over a duplicated vocabulary $\mathcal{R} \uplus \mathcal{R}'$

to represent relations between logical structures over vocabulary $\mathcal{R}$. The relation-composition operation needed for interprocedural analysis [74], can be performed in the usual way, i.e., $R_3[\mathcal{R} \uplus \mathcal{R}''] = \exists \mathcal{R}' : R_1[\mathcal{R} \uplus \mathcal{R}'] \wedge R_2[\mathcal{R}' \uplus \mathcal{R}'']$, using three vocabularies of relation symbols, a meet operation on 3-valued structures [4], and implementing $\exists \mathcal{R}'$ by dropping all $\mathcal{R}'$ relations [35, Sect. 6.5].

Q4. For statement st, the relation-maintenance formula $\mu_{p,st}$ for instrumentation relation p is $p ? \neg \Delta^-_{st}[\psi_p] : \Delta^+_{st}[\psi_p]$ (evaluated in the pre-state structure), rather than ψ_p (evaluated in the post-state structure) or $\psi_p[c \hookleftarrow \tau_{c,st} \mid c \in \mathcal{C}]$ (evaluated in the pre-state structure). Finite-differencing addresses the non-compositionality issue because $\mu_{p,st}$ identifies the "footprint" of statement st on p, which reduces the number of tuples in p that have to be reevaluated.

4   TSL: Transformer Specification Language

In 2008, Lim and Reps created the TSL system [45], a meta-tool to help in the creation of tools for analyzing machine code. From a single specification of the concrete semantics of a machine-code instruction set, TSL automatically generates correct-by-construction implementations of the state-transformation functions needed in state-space-exploration tools that use static analysis, dynamic analysis, symbolic analysis, or any combination of the three [44,45,80].

The TSL meta-language is a strongly typed, first-order functional language with a datatype-definition mechanism for defining recursive datatypes, plus deconstruction by means of pattern matching. Writing a TSL specification for an instruction set is similar to writing an interpreter in first-order ML: the specification of an instruction set's concrete semantics is written as a TSL function

```
state interpInstr(instruction I, state S) ...;
```

where instruction and state are user-defined datatypes that represent the instructions and the semantic states, respectively. TSL's meta-language provides a fixed set of basetypes; a fixed set of arithmetic, bitwise, relational, and logical operators; and a facility for defining map-types.

TSL's most basic mechanism for creating abstract transformers is similar to the syntax-directed-replacement method described in Sect. 2.2. From the specification of interpInstr for a given instruction set, the TSL compiler creates a C++ template that serves as a common intermediate representation (CIR). The CIR template is parameterized on an abstract-domain class, $\mathbb{A}$, and a fixed set of $\mathbb{A}$ primitive operations that mainly correspond to the primitive operations of the TSL meta-language. A C++ class that can be used to instantiate the CIR is called a *semantic reinterpretation* [46,56–58]; it must implement an interface that consists of 42 basetype operators, most of which have four variants, for 8-, 16-, 32-, and 64-bit integers, as well as 12 map access/update operations and a few additional operations, such as join, meet, and widen.

The CIR can be used to create multiple abstract interpreters for a given instruction set. Each analyzer is specified by supplying a semantic reinterpretation (for the TSL primitives), which—by extension to TSL expressions and user-defined functions—provides the reinterpretation of the function interpInstr, which is essentially the desired function $I_{s,\mathbb{A}}(\cdot)$ discussed in Sect. 2.3. Each reinterpretation instantiates the same CIR template, which in turn comes directly from the specification of the instruction set's concrete semantics. By this means, the abstract transformers generated for different abstract domains are guaranteed to be mutually consistent (and also to be consistent with an instruction-set emulator that is generated from the same specification of the concrete semantics).

Although the syntax-directed-replacement method has its drawbacks, it works well for machine-code instruction sets. Using a corpus of 19,066 Intel x86 instructions, Lim and Reps found, for one abstract domain, that 96.8 % of the transformers created via semantic reinterpretation reached the limit of precision attainable with that abstract domain [45, Sect. 5.4.1]. Evidently, the semantic specifications of x86 instructions do not usually suffer from the kinds of missed-correlation effects discussed in Sect. 2.2.

Answers to The Four Questions.

Q1. The semantics of machine-code instructions are specified by writing an interpreter in the TSL meta-language.
Q2. To define an abstract domain and its operations, one needs to supply a C++ class that implements a semantic reinterpretation.
Q3. (a) The common intermediate representation (CIR) generated for a given TSL instruction-set specification is a C++ template that can be instantiated with multiple semantic-reinterpretation classes to create multiple reinterpretations of the function interpInstr.
    (b) Representations of abstract transformers can be created via the approach discussed below in the section "Relational Abstract Domains."
Q4. One predefined reinterpretation is for quantifier-free formulas over the theory of bitvectors and bitvector arrays (QF_ABV). One can avoid the myopia of operator-by-operator reinterpretation illustrated in Sect. 2.2 by using the QF_ABV reinterpretation on basic blocks and loop-free fragments. The formula so obtained has a "long-range view" of the fragment's semantics. One can then employ the symbolic-abstraction techniques described in Sect. 5.

Relational Abstract Domains. An interesting problem that we encountered with TSL was how to perform reinterpretation for relational abstract domains, such as polyhedra [21], weakly relational domains [49], and affine equalities [27,40,55]. With such domains, the goal is to create a *representation* of an abstract transformer that over-approximates the concrete transformer for an instruction or basic block. Clearly state should be redefined as a relational-abstract-domain class whose values represent a relation between input states and output states; however, it was not immediately obvious how the TSL basetypes should be redefined, nor how operations such as Plus32, And32, Xor32, etc. should be handled.

The literature on relational numeric abstract domains did not provide much assistance. Most papers on such domains focus on some modeling language—typically affine programs ([21, Sect. 4], [55, Sect. 2], [49, Sect. 4])—involving only assignments and tests written in some restricted form—and describe how to create abstract transformers only for concrete transformers written in that form. For instance, for an assignment statement "x := e"

- If e is a linear expression, the coefficients for the variables in e are used to create an abstract-domain value that encodes a linear transformation.
- If e is a non-linear expression, it is modeled as "x := ?" or, equivalently, "havoc(x)." (That is, after "x := e" executes, x can hold any value.)

In contrast, with TSL each abstract-domain value must be constructed by evaluating an expression in the TSL meta-language. Moreover, the concrete semantics of an instruction set often makes use of non-linear operators, such as bitwise-and bitwise-or. There could be an unacceptable loss of precision if *every* use of a non-linear operator in an instruction's semantic definition caused a havoc. Fortunately, we were able to devise a generic method for creating abstract transformers, usable with multiple relational abstract domains, that can retain some degree of precision for some occurrences of non-linear operators [27, Sect. 6.6.4].

For relational abstract domains, the usually straightforward syntax-directed-replacement method is somewhat subtle. For a set of variables V, a value in type $\text{Rel}[V]$ denotes a set of *assignments* $V \to \text{Val}$ (for some value space Val). When V and V' are disjoint sets of variables, the type $\text{Rel}[V; V']$ denotes the set of Rel values over variables $V \uplus V'$. We extend this notation to cover singletons: if i is a single variable not in V, then the type $\text{Rel}[V; i]$ denotes the set of Rel values over the variables $V \uplus \{i\}$. (Operations sometimes introduce additional temporary variables, in which case we have types like $\text{Rel}[V; i, i']$ and $\text{Rel}[V; i, i', i'']$.)

In a reinterpretation that yields abstractions of concrete transition-relations, the type state represents a relation on pre-states to post-states. For example, suppose that the goal is to track relationships among the values of the processor's registers. The abstraction of state would be $\text{Rel}[R; R']$, where R is the set of register names (e.g., for Intel x86, $R \overset{\text{def}}{=} \{\text{eax}, \text{ebx}, \dots\}$), and R' is the same set of names, distinguished by primes ($R' \overset{\text{def}}{=} \{\text{eax'}, \text{ebx'}, \dots\}$).

In contrast, the abstraction of a machine-integer type, such as INT32, becomes a relation on pre-states to machine integers. Thus, for machine-integer types, we introduce a fresh variable i to hold the "current value" of a reinterpreted machine integer. Because R still refers to the pre-state registers, we write the type of a Rel-reinterpreted machine integer as $\text{Rel}[R; i]$. Although technically we are working with relations, for a $\text{Rel}[R; i]$ value it is often useful to think of R as a set of *independent variables* and i as the *dependent variable*.

Constants. The Rel reinterpretation of a constant c is the $\text{Rel}[V; i]$ value that encodes the constraint $i = c$.

Variable-Access Expressions. The Rel reinterpretation of a variable-access expression $\text{access}(S, v)$, where S's value is a Rel state-transformer of type $\text{Rel}[V; V']$ and $v \in V$, is the $\text{Rel}[V; i]$ value obtained as follows:

1. Extend S to be a $\mathrm{Rel}[V; V'; i]$ value, leaving i unconstrained.
2. Assume the constraint $i = v'$ on the extended S value (to retrieve v from the "current state").
3. Project away V', leaving a $\mathrm{Rel}[V; i]$ value that holds in i constraints on v's value in terms of the pre-state vocabulary V.

Update Operations. Suppose that $S \in \mathrm{Rel}[V; V']$, and the reinterpretation of expression e with respect to S has produced the reinterpreted value $J \in \mathrm{Rel}[V; i]$. We want to create $S'' \in \mathrm{Rel}[V; V']$ that acts like S, except that post-state variable $v' \in V'$ satisfies the constraints on i in $J \in \mathrm{Rel}[V; i]$. The operation $\mathrm{update}(S, v, J)$ is carried out as follows:

1. Let S' be the result of havocking v' from S.
2. Let K be the result of starting with J, renaming i to v', and then extending it to be a $\mathrm{Rel}[V; V']$ value by adding unconstrained variables in the set $V' - \{v'\}$.
3. Return $S'' \stackrel{\text{def}}{=} S' \sqcap K$.

S' captures the state in which we "forget" the previous value of v', and K asserts that v' satisfies the constraints (in terms of the pre-state vocabulary V) that were obtained from evaluating e.

Addition. Suppose that we have two $\mathrm{Rel}[V; i]$ values x and y, and wish to compute the $\mathrm{Rel}[V; i]$ value for the expression $x + y$. We proceed as follows:

1. Rename y's i variable to i'; this makes y a $\mathrm{Rel}[V; i']$ value.
2. Extend both x and y to be $\mathrm{Rel}[V; i, i', i'']$ values, leaving i' and i'' unconstrained in x, and i and i'' unconstrained in y.
3. Compute $x \sqcap y$.
4. Assume the constraint $i'' = i + i'$ on the value computed in step (3).
5. Project away i and i', leaving a $\mathrm{Rel}[V; i'']$ value.
6. In the value computed in step (5), rename i'' to i, yielding a $\mathrm{Rel}[V; i]$ value.

5   Symbolic Abstraction

Since 2002, the first author has been interested in connections between abstract interpretation and logic—in particular, how to harness decision procedures to obtain algorithms for several fundamental primitives used in abstract interpretation [64,78,79,82,85]. The work aims to bridge the gap between (i) the use of logic for specifying program semantics and performing program analysis, and (ii) abstract interpretation. In 1997, Graf and Saïdi [31] showed how to use theorem provers to generate best abstract transformers for predicate-abstraction domains (fixed, finite collections of Boolean predicates). In 2004, Reps et al. [64] gave a method that makes such a connection for a much broader class of abstract domains. That paper also introduced the following problem, which we (now) call *symbolic abstraction*:

Given formula φ in logic $\mathcal{L}$, and abstract domain $\mathbb{A}$, find the most-precise descriptor $a^\sharp$ in $\mathbb{A}$ that over-approximates the meaning of φ (i.e., $[\![\varphi]\!] \subseteq \gamma(a^\sharp)$).

We use $\widehat{\alpha}_{\mathbb{A}}(\varphi)$ to denote the symbolic abstraction of $\varphi \in \mathcal{L}$ with respect to abstract domain $\mathbb{A}$. We drop the subscript $\mathbb{A}$ when it is clear from context.

The connection between logic and abstract interpretation becomes clearer if we view an abstract domain $\mathbb{A}$ as a logic fragment $\mathcal{L}_{\mathbb{A}}$ of some general-purpose logic $\mathcal{L}$, and each abstract value as a formula in $\mathcal{L}_{\mathbb{A}}$. We say that $\widehat{\gamma}$ is a *symbolic-concretization operation* for $\mathbb{A}$ if it maps each $a^\sharp \in \mathbb{A}$ to $\varphi_{a^\sharp} \in \mathcal{L}_{\mathbb{A}}$ such that the meaning of $\varphi_{a^\sharp}$ equals the concretization of $a^\sharp$; i.e., $[\![\varphi_{a^\sharp}]\!] = \gamma(a^\sharp)$. $\mathcal{L}_{\mathbb{A}}$ is often defined by a syntactic restriction on the formulas of $\mathcal{L}$.

Example 1. If $\mathbb{A}$ is the set of environments over intervals, $\mathcal{L}_{\mathbb{A}}$ is the set of conjunctions of one-variable inequalities over the program variables. It is generally easy to implement $\widehat{\gamma}$ for an abstract domain. For example, given $a^\sharp \in \mathbb{A}$, it is straightforward to read off the appropriate $\varphi_{a^\sharp} \in \mathcal{L}_{\mathbb{A}}$: each entry $x \mapsto [c_{low}, c_{high}]$ contributes the conjuncts "$c_{low} \leq x$" and "$x \leq c_{high}$." $\qquad\square$

Thus, symbolic abstraction addresses a fundamental approximation problem:

Given formula $\varphi \in \mathcal{L}$, find the strongest consequence of φ that is expressible in a different logic $\mathcal{L}'$.

Since 2011, we (Thakur and Reps) pursued several new insights on this question. One insight was that generalized versions of an old, and not widely used, method for validity checking of propositional-logic formulas, called Stålmarck's method, provide new ways to implement $\widehat{\alpha}$. The methods that we subsequently developed [78,79,81,82] offer much promise for building more powerful program-analysis tools. They (i) allow more precise implementations of abstract-interpretation primitives to be created—including ones that attain the fundamental limits on precision that abstract-interpretation theory establishes—and (ii) drastically reduce the time needed to implement such primitives while ensuring correctness by construction. In [79], we described a method that, for a certain class of abstract domains, uses $\widehat{\alpha}$ to solve the following problem:

Given program P and abstract domain $\mathbb{A}$, find the most-precise inductive $\mathbb{A}$-invariant for P.

5.1 Abstract Transformers via Symbolic Abstraction

We now illustrate how $\widehat{\alpha}$ can be used both to apply an abstract transformer and to construct a representation of an abstract transformer.

Example 2. Consider the Intel x86 instruction $\tau \equiv$ add bh,al, which adds al, the low-order byte of 32-bit register eax, to bh, the second-to-lowest byte of 32-bit register ebx. No other register apart from ebx is modified. For simplicity, we only consider the registers eax, ebx, and ecx. The semantics of τ can be expressed in the logic QF_ABV as the formula φ_τ:

$$\varphi_\tau \overset{\text{def}}{=} \text{ebx}' = \begin{pmatrix} (\text{ebx} \;\&\; \text{0xFFFF00FF}) \\ | ((\text{ebx} + 256 * (\text{eax} \;\&\; \text{0xFF})) \;\&\; \text{0xFF00}) \end{pmatrix} \wedge \text{eax}' = \text{eax} \\ \wedge \text{ecx}' = \text{ecx}, \quad (8)$$

where "&" and "|" denote the non-linear bit-masking operations bitwise-and bitwise-or, respectively.

Suppose that the abstract domain is $\mathcal{E}_{2^{32}}$, the domain of affine equalities over the 32-bit registers eax, ebx, and ecx, and that we would like to apply the abstract transformer for τ when the input abstract value in $\mathcal{E}_{2^{32}}$ is ebx = ecx. This task corresponds to finding the strongest consequence of the formula $\psi \equiv$ (ebx = ecx$\wedge\varphi_\tau$) that can be expressed as an affine relation among eax', ebx', and ecx', which turns out to be $\widehat{a}(\psi) \equiv (2^{16}\text{ebx}' = 2^{16}\text{ecx}' + 2^{24}\text{eax}') \wedge (2^{24}\text{ebx}' = 2^{24}\text{ecx}')$. Multiplying by a power of 2 shifts bits to the left; because we are using arithmetic mod 2^{32}, bits shifted off the left end are unconstrained. Thus, the first conjunct of $\widehat{a}(\psi)$ captures the relationship between the low-order two bytes of ebx', the low-order two bytes of ecx', and the low-order byte of eax'. This example illustrates that the result of applying an abstract transformer can be non-obvious—even for a single machine-code instruction—which serves to motivate the desire for automation.

Now suppose that we would like to compute a representation of the best abstract transformer for τ in abstract domain $\mathcal{E}_{2^{32}}$. This task corresponds to finding the strongest consequence of φ_τ that can be expressed as an affine relation among eax, ebx, ecx, eax', ebx', and ecx', which turns out to be $\widehat{a}(\varphi_\tau) \equiv (2^{16}\text{ebx}' = 2^{16}\text{ebx} + 2^{24}\text{eax}) \wedge (\text{eax}' = \text{eax}) \wedge (\text{ecx}' = \text{ecx})$. □

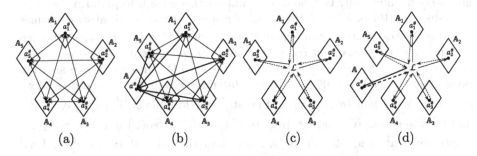

Fig. 4. Conversion between abstract domains with the clique approach ((a) and (b)) versus the symbolic-abstraction approach ((c) and (d)).

5.2   Communication of Information Between Abstract Domains

We now show how symbolic abstraction provides a way to combine the results from multiple analyses automatically (thereby enabling the construction of new, more-precise analyzers that use multiple abstract domains simultaneously).

Figures 4(a) and (b) show what happens if we want to communicate information between abstract domains *without* symbolic abstraction. Because it is necessary to create explicit conversion routines for each pair of abstract domains, we call this approach the "clique approach." As shown in Fig. 4(b), when a new abstract domain $\mathbb{A}$ is introduced, the clique approach requires that a conversion method be developed for each prior domain $\mathbb{A}_i$. In contrast, as shown in Fig. 4(d), the symbolic-abstraction approach only requires that we have $\widehat{\alpha}$ and $\widehat{\gamma}$ methods that relate $\mathbb{A}$ and $\mathcal{L}$.

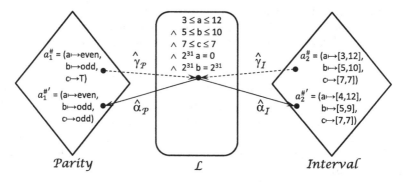

Fig. 5. Improving values from two abstract domains via symbolic abstraction.

If each analysis i is sound, each result $a_i^{\sharp}$ represents an over-approximation of the actual set of concrete states. Consequently, the collection of analysis results $\{a_i^{\sharp}\}$ implicitly tells us that only the states in $\bigcap_i \gamma(a_i^{\sharp})$ can actually occur. However, this information is only implicit, and it can be hard to determine what the intersection value really is. One way to address this issue is to perform a semantic reduction [19] of each of the $a_i^{\sharp}$ with respect to the set of abstract values $\{a_j^{\sharp} \mid i \neq j\}$. Fortunately, symbolic abstraction provides a way to carry out such semantic reductions *without the need to develop pair-wise or clique-wise reduction operators*. The principle is illustrated in Fig. 5 for the case of two abstract domains, $\mathcal{P} = Env[Parity]$ and $\mathcal{I} = Env[Interval]$. Given $a_1^{\sharp} \in \mathcal{P}$ and $a_2^{\sharp} \in \mathcal{I}$, we can improve the pair $\langle a_1^{\sharp}, a_2^{\sharp} \rangle$ by first creating the formula $\varphi \stackrel{\text{def}}{=} \widehat{\gamma}_{\mathcal{P}}(a_1^{\sharp}) \wedge \widehat{\gamma}_{\mathcal{I}}(a_2^{\sharp})$, and then applying $\widehat{\alpha}_{\mathcal{P}}$ and $\widehat{\alpha}_{\mathcal{I}}$ to φ to obtain $a_1^{\sharp\,\prime} = \widehat{\alpha}_{\mathcal{P}}(\varphi)$ and $a_2^{\sharp\,\prime} = \widehat{\alpha}_{\mathcal{I}}(\varphi)$, respectively. $a_1^{\sharp\,\prime}$ and $a_2^{\sharp\,\prime}$ can be smaller than the original values $a_1^{\sharp}$ and $a_2^{\sharp}$, respectively. We then use the pair $\langle a_1^{\sharp\,\prime}, a_2^{\sharp\,\prime} \rangle$ instead of $\langle a_1^{\sharp}, a_2^{\sharp} \rangle$. Figure 5 shows a specific example of how this approach to semantic reduction improves both the $Env[Parity]$ value and the $Env[Interval]$ value. When there are more than two abstract domains, we form the conjunction $\varphi \stackrel{\text{def}}{=} \bigwedge_i \widehat{\gamma}_i(a_i^{\sharp})$, and then apply each $\widehat{\alpha}_i$ to obtain $a_i^{\sharp\,\prime} = \widehat{\alpha}_i(\varphi)$.

5.3 Algorithms for Symbolic Abstraction

The various algorithms for computing symbolic abstraction can be seen as relying on the following two properties:

Theorem 2. *[76, Theorem 3.14]* $\widehat{\alpha}(\varphi) = \bigsqcup\{\beta(S) \mid S \models \varphi\}$ □

Theorem 3. *[76, Theorem 3.15]* $\widehat{\alpha}(\varphi) = \bigsqcap\{a \mid \varphi \Rightarrow \widehat{\gamma}(a)\}$ □

The *representation function* β returns the abstraction of a singleton concrete state; i.e., $\beta(\sigma) = \alpha(\{\sigma\})$.

RSY Algorithm. Reps et al. [64] presented a framework for computing $\widehat{\alpha}$—which we call the RSY algorithm—that applies to any logic $\mathcal{L}$ and abstract domain $\mathbb{A}$ that satisfy certain conditions. The key insight of the algorithm is the use of an SMT solver for $\mathcal{L}$ as a black-box to query for models of φ and then make use of Theorem 2. Unfortunately, Theorem 2 does not directly lead to an algorithm for computing $\widehat{\alpha}(\varphi)$, because, as stated, it involves finding *all* models of φ, which would be impractical. The RSY algorithm queries the SMT solver to compute a *finite* sequence $\sigma_1, \sigma_2, \ldots, \sigma_k$ of models of φ. This sequence is used to compute the sequence of abstract values $a_0^\sharp, a_1^\sharp, a_2^\sharp, \ldots, a_k^\sharp$ as follows:

$$
\begin{aligned}
a_0^\sharp &= \bot \\
a_i^\sharp &= a_{i-1}^\sharp \sqcup \beta(\sigma_i), \quad \sigma_i \models \varphi, \;\; 1 \le i \le k
\end{aligned}
\tag{9}
$$

Merely sampling k arbitrary models of φ would not work. In particular, it is possible that $a_{i-1}^\sharp = a_i^\sharp$, in which case step i has not made progress. To ensure progress, we require σ_i to be a model of φ such that $\sigma_i \notin \gamma(a_{i-1}^\sharp)$. In other words, σ_i should be a model that satisfies $\varphi \wedge \neg\widehat{\gamma}(a_{i-1}^\sharp)$. Equation (9) can be restated as

$$
\begin{aligned}
a_0^\sharp &= \bot \\
a_i^\sharp &= a_{i-1}^\sharp \sqcup \beta(\sigma_i), \quad \sigma_i \models \varphi \wedge \neg\widehat{\gamma}(a_{i-1}^\sharp), \;\; 1 \le i
\end{aligned}
\tag{10}
$$

Obtaining σ_i as a model of $\varphi \wedge \neg\widehat{\gamma}(a_{i-1}^\sharp)$ ensures that either $a_{i-1}^\sharp \sqsubset a_i^\sharp$ or else $a_{i-1}^\sharp = a_i^\sharp = \widehat{\alpha}(\varphi)$. Thus, if $\mathbb{A}$ has no infinite ascending chains, the sequence constructed by Eq. (10) forms a finite ascending chain that converges to $\widehat{\alpha}(\varphi)$:

$$
\bot = a_0^\sharp \sqsubset a_1^\sharp \sqsubset a_2^\sharp \sqsubset \ldots \sqsubset a_{k-1}^\sharp \sqsubset a_k^\sharp = \widehat{\alpha}(\varphi).
\tag{11}
$$

From Eq. (10), we can identify the requirements on $\mathcal{L}$ and $\mathbb{A}$:

1. There is a Galois connection $\mathbb{C} \xrightleftharpoons[\alpha]{\gamma} \mathbb{A}$ between $\mathbb{A}$ and concrete domain $\mathbb{C}$, and an implementation of the corresponding representation function β.
2. There is an algorithm to evaluate $a^\sharp \sqcup \beta(\sigma)$ for all $a^\sharp \in \mathbb{A}$.
3. There is a symbolic-concretization operation $\widehat{\gamma}$ that maps an abstract value $a^\sharp \in \mathbb{A}$ to a formula $\widehat{\gamma}(a^\sharp)$ in $\mathcal{L}$.
4. $\mathbb{A}$ has no infinite ascending chains.
5. There is a decision procedure for logic $\mathcal{L}$ that is also capable of returning a model satisfying a given formula in $\mathcal{L}$.
6. Logic $\mathcal{L}$ is closed under conjunction and negation.

Pseudo-code for the RSY algorithm can be found in [64].

Bilateral Algorithm. The bilateral algorithm [78] is a framework for computing $\widehat{\alpha}$ that is similar to the RSY algorithm in that it queries an SMT solver.
However, the nature of the queries differ in the two algorithms. Furthermore,
the bilateral algorithm makes use of both Theorems 2 and 3. While the RSY
algorithm converges to the final answer by moving up the lattice, the bilateral
algorithm converges to the final answer by both moving up the lattice starting from $\perp$ and moving down the lattice starting from $\top$. That is, the bilateral
algorithm computes a finite sequence of pairs of abstract values $(l_i^\sharp, u_i^\sharp)$ such that

$$\perp = l_0^\sharp \sqsubseteq l_1^\sharp \sqsubseteq \ldots \sqsubseteq l_k^\sharp = \widehat{\alpha}(\varphi) = u_k^\sharp \sqsubseteq \ldots \sqsubseteq u_1^\sharp \sqsubseteq u_0^\sharp = \top. \tag{12}$$

The progress guarantee for the RSY algorithm is that $a_i^\sharp \sqsubset a_{i+1}^\sharp$: on each iteration, the algorithm moves up the lattice. The progress guarantee for the bilateral
algorithm is slightly different: on each iteration, the algorithm either moves up
the lattice or moves down the lattice: *either* $l_i^\sharp \sqsubset l_{i+1}^\sharp$ *or* $u_{i+1}^\sharp \sqsubset u_i^\sharp$.

A key concept in the bilateral algorithm is the notion of an *abstract-
consequence* operation:

Definition 3. *An operation $AC(\cdot, \cdot)$ is an **acceptable abstract-consequence**
operation iff for all $l^\sharp, u^\sharp \in \mathbb{A}$ such that $l^\sharp \sqsubset u^\sharp$, $a^\sharp = AC(l^\sharp, u^\sharp)$ implies that
$l^\sharp \sqsubseteq a^\sharp$ and $a^\sharp \not\sqsupseteq u^\sharp$.* ☐

In particular, $\gamma(a^\sharp)$ does not encompass $\gamma(u^\sharp)$, and whenever $a^\sharp \neq \perp$, $\gamma(a^\sharp)$
overlaps $\gamma(u^\sharp)$.

Readers familiar with the concept of interpolation [23] might see similarities between interpolation and abstract consequence. However, as discussed in
[78, Sect. 3] there are significant differences between these two notions.

The sequence $(l_i^\sharp, u_i^\sharp)$ is computed using the following rules:

$$(l_0^\sharp, u_0^\sharp) = (\perp, \top) \tag{13}$$

$$(l_i^\sharp, u_i^\sharp) = (l_{i-1}^\sharp, u_{i-1}^\sharp \sqcap AC(l_{i-1}^\sharp, u_{i-1}^\sharp)), \; \varphi \Rightarrow \widehat{\gamma}(AC(l_{i-1}^\sharp, u_{i-1}^\sharp)), \; l_{i-1}^\sharp \sqsubset u_{i-1}^\sharp \tag{14}$$

$$(l_i^\sharp, u_i^\sharp) = (l_{i-1}^\sharp \sqcup \beta(\sigma_i), u_{i-1}^\sharp), \; \sigma_i \models \varphi \wedge \neg\widehat{\gamma}(AC(l_{i-1}^\sharp, u_{i-1}^\sharp)), \; l_{i-1}^\sharp \sqsubset u_{i-1}^\sharp \tag{15}$$

The invariant that is maintained is that $l_i^\sharp \sqsubseteq \widehat{\alpha}(\varphi) \sqsubseteq u_i^\sharp$. $l_0^\sharp$ is initialized to $\perp$,
and $u_0^\sharp$ is initialized to $\top$. Let $a_{i-1}^\sharp = AC(l_{i-1}^\sharp, u_{i-1}^\sharp)$. There are two cases: either
$\varphi \Rightarrow \widehat{\gamma}(a_{i-1}^\sharp)$ or it does not. If $\varphi \Rightarrow \widehat{\gamma}(a_{i-1}^\sharp)$, then $u_i^\sharp$ can be defined as $u_{i-1}^\sharp \sqcap a_{i-1}^\sharp$,
and $l_i^\sharp = l_{i-1}^\sharp$ (Eq. (14)). This step makes progress because $a_{i-1}^\sharp \not\sqsupseteq u_{i-1}^\sharp$ implies
that $u_i^\sharp \sqsubset u_{i-1}^\sharp \sqcap a_{i-1}^\sharp$. Otherwise, there must exist a model σ_i such that $\sigma_i \models$
$\varphi \wedge \neg\widehat{\gamma}(a_{i-1}^\sharp)$. In this case, $l_i^\sharp$ can be defined as $l_{i-1}^\sharp \sqcup \beta(\sigma_i)$ (Eq. (15)). This step
makes progress for reasons similar to the RSY algorithm. Thus, on each iteration
either $l_i^\sharp$ or $u_i^\sharp$ is updated. The values $l_i^\sharp$ and $u_i^\sharp$ are guaranteed to converge to
$\widehat{\alpha}(\varphi)$ provided $\mathbb{A}$ has neither infinite ascending chains nor infinite descending
chains.[2]

---

[2] A slight modification to the bilateral algorithm can remove the requirement of having
no infinite descending chains [78].

There can be multiple ways of defining the abstract-consequence operation. In fact, the bilateral algorithm reduces to the RSY algorithm if we define $\mathrm{AC}(l_{i-1}^\sharp, u_{i-1}^\sharp) \stackrel{\text{def}}{=} l_{i-1}^\sharp$. Other algorithms for computing abstract consequence for a large class of abstract domains are described in [78]. The choice of abstract consequence determines the cost of each query of the SMT solver as well as the rate of convergence of the bilateral algorithm.

The key advantage of the bilateral algorithm over the RSY algorithm is that the bilateral algorithm is an *anytime algorithm*, because the algorithm can return a sound over-approximation ($u_i^\sharp$) of the final answer if it is stopped at any point. This property makes the bilateral algorithm resilient to SMT-solver timeouts.

Pseudo-code for the bilateral algorithm can be found in [78] and [76, Ch. 5].

Generalizations of Stålmarck's Algorithm. In [81], we showed how Stålmarck's method [75], an algorithm for satisfiability checking of propositional formulas, can be explained using abstract-interpretation terminology—in particular, as an instantiation of a more general algorithm, Stålmarck[$\mathbb{A}$], that is parameterized on an abstract domain $\mathbb{A}$ and operations on $\mathbb{A}$. The algorithm that goes by the name "Stålmarck's method" is one instantiation of Stålmarck[$\mathbb{A}$] with a certain Boolean abstract domain. At each step, Stålmarck[$\mathbb{A}$] holds some $a^\sharp \in \mathbb{A}$; each of the proof rules employed in Stålmarck's method improves $a^\sharp$ by finding a semantic reduction of $a^\sharp$ with respect to φ.

The abstraction-interpretation-based view enables us to lift Stålmarck's method from propositional logic to richer logics by instantiating Stålmarck[$\mathbb{A}$] with richer abstract domains [82]. Moreover, it brings out a new connection between Stålmarck's method and $\widehat{\alpha}$. To check whether a formula φ is unsatisfiable, Stålmarck[$\mathbb{A}$] computes $\widehat{\alpha}_{\mathbb{A}}(\varphi)$ and performs the test "$\widehat{\alpha}_{\mathbb{A}}(\varphi) = \bot_{\mathbb{A}}$?" If the test succeeds, it establishes that $[\![\varphi]\!] \subseteq \gamma(\bot_{\mathbb{A}}) = \emptyset$, and hence that φ is unsatisfiable.

To explain the Stålmarck[$\mathbb{A}$] algorithm for $\widehat{\alpha}$, we first define the notion of $\widehat{\text{Assume}}$. Given $\varphi \in \mathcal{L}$ and $a^\sharp \in \mathbb{A}$, $\widehat{\text{Assume}}[\varphi](a^\sharp)$ returns the best value in $\mathbb{A}$ that over-approximates the meaning of φ in concrete states described by $a^\sharp$. That is, $\widehat{\text{Assume}}[\varphi](a^\sharp)$ equals $\alpha([\![\varphi]\!] \cap \gamma(a^\sharp))$.

The principles behind the Stålmarck[$\mathbb{A}$] algorithm for $\widehat{\alpha}$ can be understood via the following equations:

$$\widehat{\alpha}(\varphi) = \widehat{\text{Assume}}[\varphi](\top) \tag{16}$$

$$\widehat{\text{Assume}}[\varphi_1 \wedge \varphi_2](a^\sharp) \sqsubseteq \widehat{\text{Assume}}[\varphi_1](a^\sharp) \sqcap \widehat{\text{Assume}}[\varphi_2](a^\sharp) \tag{17}$$

$$\widehat{\text{Assume}}[\varphi](a^\sharp) \sqsubseteq \widehat{\text{Assume}}[\varphi](a^\sharp \sqcap a_1^\sharp) \sqcup \widehat{\text{Assume}}[\varphi](a^\sharp \sqcap a_2^\sharp),$$
$$\text{where } \gamma(a_1^\sharp) \cup \gamma(a_2^\sharp) \supseteq \gamma(a^\sharp) \tag{18}$$

$$\widehat{\text{Assume}}[\ell](a^\sharp) \sqsubseteq \mu\widehat{\alpha}(\ell) \sqcap a^\sharp, \text{where } \ell \text{ is a literal in } \mathcal{L} \tag{19}$$

Equation (16) follows from the definition of $\widehat{\alpha}$ and $\widehat{\text{Assume}}$. Equation (17) follows from the definition of $\wedge$ and $\sqcap$, and corresponds to the simple deductive rules used in Stålmarck's algorithm. Equation (18) is the abstract-interpretation counterpart of the Dilemma Rule used in Stålmarck's method: the current goal $a^\sharp$ is split into sub-goals using meet ($\sqcap$), and the results of the sub-goals are combined using join ($\sqcup$). The correctness of this rule relies on the condition that $\gamma(a_1^\sharp) \cup \gamma(a_2^\sharp) \supseteq \gamma(a^\sharp)$. The $\mu\widehat{\alpha}$ operation in Eq. (19) translates a literal in $\mathcal{L}$ into an abstract value in $\mathbb{A}$; that is $\mu\widehat{\alpha}(\ell) \stackrel{\text{def}}{=} \widehat{\alpha}(\ell)$. However, for certain combinations of $\mathcal{L}$ and $\mathbb{A}$, the $\mu\widehat{\alpha}$ operation is straightforward to implement—for example, when $\mathcal{L}$ is linear rational arithmetic (LRA) and $\mathbb{A}$ is the polyhedral domain [21]. $\mu\widehat{\alpha}$ can also be implemented using the RSY or bilateral algorithms when $\mathcal{L}$ and $\mathbb{A}$ satisfy the requirements for those frameworks.

The Stålmarck-based framework is based on much different principles from the RSY and bilateral frameworks for computing symbolic abstraction. The latter frameworks use an *inductive-learning approach* to learn from examples, while the Stålmarck-based framework uses a *deductive approach* by using inference rules to deduce the answer. Thus, they represent two different classes of frameworks, with different requirements for the abstract domain. In contrast to the RSY/Bilateral framework, which uses a decision procedure as a black box, the Stålmarck-based framework adopts (and adapts) some principles from decision procedures.

Answers to The Four Questions.

Q1. The semantics of a statement st are specified as a two-vocabulary formula φ_{st} in some logic $\mathcal{L}$. In our work, we have typically used quantifier-free formulas over the theory of bitvectors and bitvector arrays (QF_ABV).

Q2. The abstract domain is specified via an interface consisting of the standard operations ($\sqcup$, $\sqcap$, etc.). The RSY and bilateral frameworks for symbolic abstraction require the β operation. The Stålmarck-based framework for symbolic abstraction requires the $\mu\widehat{\alpha}$ operation.

Q3. The various algorithms for $\widehat{\alpha}$ are the engines that apply/construct abstract transformers for a concrete transformer τ.
   (a) The abstract execution of τ on $a^\sharp$ is performed via $a^{\sharp\prime} = \widehat{\alpha}(\varphi_\tau \wedge \widehat{\gamma}(a^\sharp))$.
   (b) The representation of the abstract transformer for τ is obtained via $\tau^\sharp = \widehat{\alpha}(\varphi_\tau)$.

Q4. The formula used to construct an abstract transformer can express the concrete semantics of (i) a basic block or (ii) a loop-free fragment (including a finite unrolling of a loop) à la large-block encoding [9] or adjustable-block encoding [10]. In our work, we used the TSL framework to obtain such formulas.

5.4   Automated Reasoning/Decision Procedures

Our investigation of symbolic abstraction led us to a new connection between decision procedures and abstract interpretation—namely, how to exploit abstract interpretation to provide new principles for designing decision procedures [82]. This work, which we call *Satisfiability Modulo Abstraction* (SMA), has led to new principles for designing decision procedures, and provides a way to create decision procedures for new logics. At the same time, it shows great promise from a practical standpoint. In other words, the methods for symbolic abstraction are "dual-use." In addition to providing methods for building improved abstract-interpretation tools, they also provide methods for building improved logic solvers that use abstract interpretation to speed up the search that a solver carries out.

One of the main advantages of the SMA approach is that it is able to reuse abstract-interpretation machinery to implement decision procedures. For instance, in [82], the polyhedral abstract domain—implemented in PPL [5]—is used to implement an SMA solver for the logic of linear rational arithmetic.

More recently, we created an SMA solver for separation logic [77]. Separation logic (SL) [68] is an expressive logic for reasoning about heap structures in programs, and provides a mechanism for concisely describing program states by explicitly localizing facts that hold in separate regions of the heap. SL is undecidable in general, but by using an abstract domain of shapes [70] we were able to design an unsatisfiability checker for SL.

5.5   Symbolic Abstraction and Quantifier Elimination

Gulwani and Musuvathi [32] defined what they termed the "cover problem," which addresses *approximate existential-quantifier elimination*:

> Given a formula φ in logic $\mathcal{L}$, and a set of variables V, find the strongest quantifier-free formula $\overline{\varphi}$ in $\mathcal{L}$ such that $[\![\exists V : \varphi]\!] \subseteq [\![\overline{\varphi}]\!]$.

(We use $\text{Cover}_V(\varphi)$ to denote the cover of φ with respect to variable set V.)

Both $\text{Cover}_V(\varphi)$ and $\widehat{\alpha}(\varphi)$ (deliberately) lose information from φ, and hence both result in over-approximations of $[\![\varphi]\!]$. In general, however, they yield *different* over-approximations of $[\![\varphi]\!]$.

1. The information loss from $\text{Cover}_V(\varphi)$ only involves the removal of variable set V from the vocabulary of φ. The resulting formula $\overline{\varphi}$ is still allowed to be an *arbitrarily complex* $\mathcal{L}$ formula; $\overline{\varphi}$ can use all of the (interpreted) operators and (interpreted) relation symbols of $\mathcal{L}$.
2. The information loss from $\widehat{\alpha}(\varphi)$ involves finding a formula ψ in an impoverished logic $\mathcal{L}'$: ψ must be a *restricted* $\mathcal{L}$ formula; it can only use the operators and relation symbols of $\mathcal{L}'$, and must be written using the syntactic restrictions of $\mathcal{L}'$.

One of the uses of information-loss capability 2 is to bridge the gap between the concrete semantics and an abstract domain. In particular, it may be necessary to use the full power of logic $\mathcal{L}$ to express the semantics of a concrete transformer τ (e.g., Eq. (8)). However, the corresponding abstract transformer *must* be expressed in $\mathcal{L}'$. When $\mathcal{L}'$ is something other than the restriction of $\mathcal{L}$ to a sub-vocabulary, the cover of φ_τ is not guaranteed to return an answer in $\mathcal{L}'$, and thus does not yield a suitable *abstract* transformer. This difference is illustrated using the scenario described in Ex. 2.

Example 3. In Ex. 2, the application of the abstract transformer for τ is obtained by computing $\widehat{\alpha}(\psi) \in \mathcal{E}_{2^{32}}$, where $\mathcal{E}_{2^{32}}$ is the domain of affine equalities over the 32-bit registers eax, ebx, and ecx; $\psi \equiv (\text{ebx} = \text{ecx} \wedge \varphi_\tau)$; and φ_τ is defined in Eq. (8). In particular, $\widehat{\alpha}(\psi) \equiv (2^{16}\text{ebx}' = 2^{16}\text{ecx}' + 2^{24}\text{eax}') \wedge (2^{24}\text{ebx}' = 2^{24}\text{ecx}')$.

Let R be the set of pre-state registers $\{\text{eax}, \text{ebx}, \text{ecx}\}$. The cover of ψ with respect to R is

$$\text{Cover}_R(\psi) \equiv \text{ebx}' = \begin{pmatrix} (\text{ecx}' \ \& \ \text{0xFFFF00FF}) \\ | \ ((\text{ecx}' + 256 * (\text{eax}' \ \& \ \text{0xFF})) \ \& \ \text{0xFF00}) \end{pmatrix} \qquad (20)$$

Equation (20) shows that even though the result does not contain any unprimed registers, it is not an abstract value in the domain $\mathcal{E}_{2^{32}}$. □

The notion of symbolic abstraction subsumes the notion of cover: if $\mathcal{L}'$ is the logic $\mathcal{L}$ restricted to the variables not contained in V, then $\widehat{\alpha}_{\mathcal{L}'}(\varphi) = \text{Cover}_V(\varphi)$.

6   Connections with Other Areas of Computer Science

One of the most exciting aspects of the work on symbolic abstraction and automating the creation of abstract transformers is that the problem turns out to have many connections to other areas of Computer Science. Connections with automated reasoning and decision procedures were discussed in Sect. 5.4. Other connections include concept learning (Sect. 6.1) and constraint programming (Sect. 6.2).

6.1   Concept Learning

Reps et al. [64] identified a connection between the RSY algorithm for symbolic abstraction and the problem of *concept learning* in (classical) machine learning. In machine-learning terms, an abstract domain $\mathbb{A}$ is a *hypothesis space*; each domain element corresponds to a *concept*. A hypothesis space has an *inductive bias*, which means that it has a limited ability to express sets of concrete objects. In abstract-interpretation terms, inductive bias corresponds to the image of γ on $\mathbb{A}$ not being the full power set of the concrete objects. Given a formula φ, the symbolic-abstraction problem is to find the most specific concept that explains the meaning of φ.

The RSY algorithm is related to the Find-S algorithm for concept learning [51, Sect. 2.4]. Both algorithms start with the most-specific hypothesis (i.e., $\bot$) and work bottom-up to find the most-specific hypothesis that is consistent with positive examples of the concept. Both algorithms generalize their current hypothesis each time they process a (positive) training example that is not explained by the current hypothesis. A major difference is that Find-S receives a sequence of positive and negative examples of the concept (e.g., from nature). It discards negative examples, and its generalization steps are based solely on the positive examples. In contrast, the RSY algorithm already starts with a precise

statement of the concept in hand, namely, the formula φ, and on each iteration, calls a decision procedure to generate the next positive example; the RSY
algorithm never sees a negative example.

A similar connection exists between the Bilateral algorithm and the
Candidate-Elimination (CE) algorithm for concept learning [51, Sect. 2.5]. Both
algorithms maintain two approximations of the concept, one that is an over-
approximation and one that is an under-approximation. The CE algorithm
updates its under-approximation using positive examples in the same way that
the Find-S algorithm updates its under-approximation. Similarly, the Bilateral
algorithm updates its under-approximation (via a join) in the same way that the
RSY algorithm updates its under-approximation. One key difference between the
CE algorithm and the Bilateral algorithm is that the CE algorithm updates its
over-approximation using *negative* examples. Most conjunctive abstract domains
are not closed under negation. Thus, given a negative example, there usually does
not exist an abstract value that only excludes that particular negative example.

There are, however, some differences between the problems of symbolic
abstraction and concept learning. These differences mostly stem from the fact
that an algorithm for performing symbolic abstraction already starts with a precise statement of the concept in hand, namely, the formula φ. In the machine-
learning context, usually no such finite description of the concept exists, which
imposes limitations on the types of queries that the learning algorithm can make
to an oracle (or teacher); see, for instance, [2, Sect. 1.2]. The power of the oracle
also affects the guarantees that a learning algorithm can provide. In particular,
in the machine-learning context, the learned concept is not guaranteed or even
required to be an over-approximation of the underlying concrete concept. During the past three decades, the machine-learning theory community has shifted
their focus to learning algorithms that only provide probabilistic guarantees.
This approach to learning is called *probably approximately correct learning (PAC
learning)* [39,83]. The PAC guarantee also enables a learning algorithm to be
applicable to concept lattices that are not complete lattices.

The similarities and differences between symbolic abstraction and concept
learning open up opportunities for a richer exchange of ideas between the two
areas. In particular, one can imagine situations in which it is appropriate for
the over-approximation requirement for abstract transformers to be relaxed to
a PAC guarantee—for example, if abstract interpretation is being used only to
find errors in programs, instead of proving programs correct [14], or to analyze
programs with a probabilistic concrete semantics [22,41,52].

6.2 Constraint Programming

Constraint programming [54] is a declarative programming paradigm in which
problems are expressed as conjunctions of first-order-logic formulas, called constraints. A constraint-satisfaction problem is defined by (i) a set of variables
$V_1, \ldots, V_n$; (ii) a search space S given by a domain D_i for each variable V_i;
and (iii) a set of constraints $\varphi_1, \ldots, \varphi_p$. The objective is to enumerate all variable valuations in the search space that satisfy every constraint. Different fam-

ilies of constraints come with specific operators—such as choice operators and propagators—used by the solver to explore the search space of the problem and to reduce its size, respectively. A constraint solver alternates two kinds of steps:

1. *Propagation steps* exploit constraints to reduce the domains of variables by removing values that cannot participate in a solution. The goal is to achieve *consistency*, when no more values can be removed.
2. When domains cannot be reduced further, the solver performs a *splitting step*: it makes an assumption about how to split a domain, and continues searching in the smaller search spaces.

The search proceeds, alternating propagation and splitting, until the search space contains either no solution, only solutions, or is smaller than a user-specified size. Backtracking may be used to explore other splitting assumptions.

Because the solution set cannot generally be enumerated exactly, continuous solvers compute a collection of intervals with floating-point bounds that contain all solutions and over-approximate the solution set while trying—on a best-effort basis—to include as few non-solutions as possible. In our terminology, such a constraint solver approaches $\widehat{\alpha}(\varphi)$ from above, for a conjunctive formula φ; the abstract domain is the disjunctive completion of the domain of environments of intervals; and the splitting and tightening steps are semantic reductions.

Several connections between abstract interpretation and constraint solving have been made in the past. Apt observed that applying propagators can be seen as an iterative fixpoint computation [3]. Pelleau et al. used this connection to describe a parameterized constraint solver that can be instantiated with different abstract domains [60]. Miné et al. describe a related algorithm to prove that a candidate invariant φ for a loop really is an invariant [50]. The goal is to identify a stronger invariant ψ that is both inductive and implies φ. The algorithm is parameterized on an abstract domain $\mathbb{A}$; the algorithm's actions are inspired by constraint solvers: it repeatedly splits and tightens non-overlapping elements of $\mathbb{A}$ (and therefore is searching for an inductive invariant in the disjunctive completion of $\mathbb{A}$). The algorithm works from "above" in the sense that it starts with (an under-approximation of) φ and creates descriptors of successively smaller areas of the state space as it searches for a suitable ψ.

7   Related Work

7.1   Best Abstract Transformers

In 1979, Cousot and Cousot [19] gave the specification of the best abstract transformer:

> Let $\tau : Store \to Store$ be a concrete transformer and $\mathbb{C} = \mathcal{P}(Store)$. Given a Galois connection $\mathbb{C} \xleftrightarrow[\alpha]{\gamma} \mathbb{A}$, the *best abstract transformer*, defined by
>
> $$\tau_{best}^{\sharp} \stackrel{\text{def}}{=} \alpha \circ \tilde{\tau} \circ \gamma, \tag{21}$$
>
> is the most precise abstract transformer that over-approximates τ.

$\tau_{best}^{\sharp}$ establishes the limit of precision with which the actions of τ can be tracked using a given abstract domain $\mathbb{A}$. It provides a limit on what can be achieved by a system to automate the construction of abstract transformers. However, Eq. (21) is non-constructive; it does not provide an *algorithm*, either for computing the result of applying $\tau_{best}^{\sharp}$ or for finding a representation of the function $\tau_{best}^{\sharp}$. In particular, the explicit application of γ to an abstract value would, in most cases, yield an intermediate set of concrete states that is either infinite or too large to fit into memory.

Graf and Saïdi [31] showed that theorem provers can be used to generate best abstract transformers for predicate-abstraction domains. In 2004, three papers appeared that concerned the problem of automatically constructing abstract transformers:

- Reps et al. [64] gave the method described in Sect. 5.3 for computing best transformers from below, which applies to a broader class of abstract domains than predicate-abstraction domains.
- Yorsh et al. [85] gave a method that works from above, for abstract domains based on canonical abstraction.
- Regehr and Reid [61] presented a method to construct abstract transformers for machine instructions, for interval and bitwise abstract domains. Their method is not based on logical reasoning, but instead uses a physical processor (or simulator) as a black box. To compute the abstract post-state for an abstract value $a^{\sharp}$, the approach recursively divides $a^{\sharp}$ until an abstract value is obtained whose concretization is a singleton set. The concrete semantics are then used to derive the post-state value. The results of each division are joined as the recursion unwinds to derive the abstract post-state value.

Since then, a number of other methods for creating best abstract transformers have been devised [8, 27, 40, 53, 71, 78, 82]. (Some of them are discussed in Sect. 7.3.)

7.2 Heuristics for Good Transformers

With TVLA, a desired abstraction is specified by (i) defining the set of instrumentation relations $\mathcal{I}$ to use, and (ii) selecting which unary relations to use as abstraction relations $\mathcal{A}$. The abstract transformers are then constructed automatically by means of the four-part construction sketched in the paragraph "Maintaining Instrumentation Relations" of Sect. 3. There is no expectation that the abstract transformers constructed in this way are best transformers. However, practical experience with TVLA has shown that when the abstract domain is defined by the right sets of relations $\mathcal{I}$ and $\mathcal{A}$, TVLA produces excellent results.

Four theorems at the level of the framework—one for each part of the four-part construction—relieve the TVLA user from having to write the usual "near-commutativity" proofs of soundness that one finds in papers about one-off uses of abstract interpretation.[3] These meta-level theorems are the key enabling factors

---

[3] (i) The correctness theorem for *focus* [70, Lemmas 6.8 and 6.9]; (ii) the Embedding Theorem [70, Theorem 4.9]; (iii) the correctness theorem for the finite-differencing scheme for maintaining instrumentation relations [63, Theorem 5.3]; and (iv) the correctness theorem for *coerce* [70, Theorem 6.28].

that allow abstract transformers to be constructed automatically for canonical-abstraction domains.

The finite-differencing approach is generally able to retain an appropriate amount of precision because, for a concrete transformer τ_{st}, the application of the finite-differencing operators to an instrumentation relation p's defining formula ψ_p identifies the "footprint" of st on p. Knowledge of the footprint lets the relation-maintenance formula reuse as much information as possible from the pre-state structure, and thereby avoid performing formula-reevaluation operations for tuples whose values cannot be changed by st.

The term "footprint of a statement" also appears in work on abstract interpretation using separation logic (SL) [15,24], but there it means a compact characterization of the concrete semantics of a statement in terms of the resources it accesses. In our terminology, footprints in the SL literature concern the core relations—i.e., the *independent variables* in the analogy with differentiation from Sect. 3. In this paper, when we refer to footprints, we mean the minimal effects of the concrete transformer on the instrumentation relations—which play the role of *dependent* variables.

The finite-differencing operators used in TVLA are most closely related to work on logic and databases: finite-difference operators for the propositional case were studied by Akers [1] and Sharir [73]. Work on (i) incrementally maintaining materialized views in databases [33], (ii) first-order incremental evaluation schemes [25], and (iii) dynamic descriptive complexity [59] have also addressed the problem of maintaining one or more auxiliary relations after new tuples are inserted into or deleted from base relations. In databases, view maintenance is solely an optimization; the correct information can always be obtained by reevaluating the defining formula. In the abstract-interpretation context, where abstraction has been performed, this is no longer true: reevaluating a formula in the local (3-valued) state can lead to a drastic loss of precision. Thus, the motivation for the work is completely different, although the techniques have strong similarities.

The method used in TVLA for finite differencing of formulas inspired some follow-on work using *numeric* finite differencing for program analysis [26]. That paper shows how to augment a numeric abstraction with numeric views, and gives a technique based on finite differencing to maintain an over-approximation of a view-variable's value in response to a transformation of the program state.

The idea of augmenting domains with instrumentation values has been used before in predicate-abstraction domains [31], which maintain the values of a given set of Boolean predicates. Graf and Saïdi [31] showed that decision procedures can be used to generate best abstract transformers for predicate-abstraction domains, but with high cost. Other work has investigated more efficient methods to generate approximate transformers that are not best transformers, but approach the precision of best transformers [7,16]. Ball et al. [7] use a "focus" operation inspired by TVLA's *focus*, which as noted in footnote 1, plays a role similar to the splitting step in Stålmarck's algorithm.

Scherpelz et al. [72] developed a method for creating abstract transformers for use with parameterized predicate abstraction [17]. It performs WLP of a post-state relation with respect to transformer τ, followed by heuristics that attempt to determine combinations of pre-state relations that imply the WLP value. Generating the abstract transformer for a (nullary) instrumentation relation $p \in \mathcal{I}$, defined by the nullary formula $\psi_p()$, involves two steps:

1. Create the formula $\varphi = \mathrm{WLP}(\tau, \psi_p())$.
2. Find a Boolean combination $\nu_{p,\tau}$ of pre-state relations such that if $\nu_{p,\tau}$ holds in the pre-state, then φ must also hold in the pre-state (and hence p must hold in the post-state).

The abstract transformer is a function that sets the value of p in the post-state according to whether $\nu_{p,\tau}$ holds in the pre-state.

Because WLP performs substitution on $\psi_p()$, the formula created by step (1) is related to the substitution-based relation-maintenance formula defined in Eq. (4). Step (4) applies several heuristics to φ to produce one or more strengthenings of φ; step (2) returns the disjunction of the strengthened variants of φ. In contrast, the finite-differencing algorithm discussed in Sect. 3 does not operate by trying to strengthen the substitution-based relation-maintenance formula; instead, it uses a systematic approach—based on finite differencing of p's defining formula $\psi_p()$—to identify how τ changes p's value. Moreover, the method is not restricted to nullary instrumentation relations: it applies to relations of arbitrary arity.

A special case of canonical abstraction occurs when no abstraction relations are used at all, in which case all individuals of a logical structure are collapsed to a single individual. When this is done, in almost all structures the only useful information remaining resides in the nullary core and instrumentation relations. Predicate abstraction can be seen as going one step further, retaining only the nullary instrumentation relations (and *no* abstracted core relations). However, to be able to evaluate a "Future" formula—as defined in Eq. (7)—such as $\mathbf{F}_\tau[p] \stackrel{\mathrm{def}}{=} p\,?\,\neg\Delta_\tau^-[p] : \Delta_\tau^+[p]$, one generally needs the pre-state abstract structure to hold (abstracted) core relations. From that standpoint, the finite-differencing method and that of Scherpelz et al. [72] are incomparable; they have different goals, and neither can be said to subsume the other.

Cousot et al. [20, Sect. 7] define a method of abstract interpretation based on using particular sets of logical formulas as abstract-domain elements (so-called *logical abstract domains*). They face the problems of (i) performing abstraction from unrestricted formulas to the elements of a logical abstract domain [20, Sect. 7.2] and (ii) creating abstract transformers that transform input elements of a logical abstract domain to output elements of the domain [20, Sect. 7.3]. Their problems are particular cases of $\widehat{\alpha}(\varphi)$. They present heuristic methods for creating over-approximations of $\widehat{\alpha}(\varphi)$.

7.3 Symbolic Abstraction

Work on symbolic abstraction falls into three categories:

1. algorithms for specific domains [8,13,27,40,43,47,61,77]
2. algorithms for parameterized abstract domains [31,53,71,85]
3. abstract-domain frameworks [64,78,82].

What distinguishes category 3 from category 2 is that each of the results cited in category 2 applies to a specific *family* of abstract domains, defined by a *parameterized Galois connection* (e.g., with an abstraction function equipped with a readily identifiable parameter for controlling the abstraction). In contrast, the results in category 3 are defined by an *interface*; for any abstract domain that satisfies the requirements of the interface, one has a method for symbolic abstraction. The approaches presented in Sect. 5 fall into category 3.

Some of the work mentioned above has already been discussed in Sect. 7.1.

Algorithms for Specific Domains. Brauer and King [13] developed a method that works from below to derive abstract transformers for the interval domain. Their method is based on an approach due to Monniaux [53] (see below), but they changed two aspects:

1. They express the concrete semantics with a Boolean formula (via "bit-blasting"), which allows a formula equivalent to $\forall x.\varphi$ to be obtained from φ (in CNF) by removing the x and $\neg x$ literals from all of the clauses of φ.
2. Whereas Monniaux's method performs abstraction and then quantifier elimination, Brauer and King's method performs quantifier elimination on the concrete specification, and then performs abstraction.

The abstract transformer derived from the Boolean formula that results is a guarded update: the guard is expressed as an element of the octagon domain [48]; the update is expressed as an element of the abstract domain of rational affine equalities [38]. The abstractions performed to create the guard and the update are optimal for their respective domains. The algorithm they use to create the abstract value for the update operation is essentially the King-Søndergaard algorithm for $\widehat{\alpha}$ [40], Fig. 2 which works from below. Brauer and King show that optimal evaluation of such transfer functions requires linear programming. They give an example showing that an octagon-closure operation on a combination of the guard's octagon and the update's affine equality is sub-optimal.

Barrett and King [8] describe a method for generating range and set abstractions for bit-vectors that are constrained by Boolean formulas. For range analysis, the algorithm separately computes the minimum and maximum value of the range for an n-bit bit-vector using $2n$ calls to a SAT solver, with each SAT query determining a single bit of the output. The result is the best over-approximation of the value that an integer variable can take on (i.e., $\widehat{\alpha}$).

Li et al. [43] developed a symbolic-abstraction method for LRA, called SYMBA. The scenario considered by [43] is the following: Given a formula φ in LRA logic and a *finite* set of objectives $\{t_1, t_2, \ldots, t_n\}$, where t_i is a linear-rational expression, SYMBA computes the lower and upper bounds $l_1, l_2, \ldots, l_n$ and $u_1, u_2, \ldots, u_n$ such that $\varphi \Rightarrow \left(\bigwedge_{1 \leq i \leq n} l_i \leq t_i \leq u_i\right)$. Similar to the bilateral framework described in Sect. 5, the SYMBA algorithm maintains an under-approximation and an over-approximation of the final answer.

McMillan [47] presents an algorithm for performing symbolic abstraction for propositional logic and the abstract domain of propositional clauses of length up to k. The algorithm can be viewed as an instance of the RSY algorithm: a SAT solver is used to generate samples, and a trie data structure is used to perform the join of abstract values. The specific application for which the algorithm is used is to compute don't-care conditions for logic synthesis.

Algorithms for Parameterized Abstract Domains. Template Constraint Matrices (TCMs) are a parametrized family of linear-inequality domains for expressing invariants in linear real arithmetic. Sankaranarayanan et al. [71] gave a meet, join, and set of abstract transformers for all TCM domains. Monniaux [53] gave an algorithm that finds the best transformer in a TCM domain across a straight-line block (assuming that concrete operations consist of piecewise linear functions), and good transformers across more complicated control flow. However, the algorithm uses quantifier elimination, and no polynomial-time elimination algorithm is known for piecewise-linear systems.

8   Conclusion

The algorithms developed in our research reduce the burden on analysis designers and implementers by raising the level of automation in abstraction interpretation. The work summarized in this paper focuses on the question "Given the specification of an abstraction, how does one create an execution engine for an analyzer that performs computations in an over-approximating fashion?" We know of only four systematic ways to address this question, three of which feature in our work:

1. Semantic reinterpretation and the related technique of syntax-directed reinterpretation (Sect. 4).
2. A strategy of splitting, propagation, and join à la the work on the generalized Stålmarckprocedure [82] and TVLA [63, 70].
3. The approach illustrated by our bilateral algorithm, which uses concept learning via sampling, generalization, and abstract consequence to bound the answer from below and above.
4. Heuristic methods for formula normalization, for use with abstract domains in which abstract values are formulas in some logic ([24, Sect. 5.1] and [20, Sect. 7.3]).

The availability of automated methods for creating abstract transformers provides help along the following four dimensions:

Soundness: Creation of analyzers that are correct by construction, while requiring an analysis designer to implement only a small number of operations. Consequently, one only relies on a small "trusted computing base."

Precision: In contrast to most conventional approaches to creating abstract transformers, the use of symbolic abstraction can achieve the fundamental limits of precision that abstract-interpretation theory establishes.

Resource awareness: The algorithms for applying/constructing abstract transformers that approach $\widehat{\alpha}(\varphi_\tau)$ from above can be implemented as "anytime" algorithms—i.e., an algorithm can be equipped with a monitor, and if the algorithm exhausts some time or space budget, the monitor can stop it at any time, and a safe (over-approximating) answer can be returned.

Extensibility: If an additional abstract domain is needed in an analyzer, automation makes it easy to add. In addition, for techniques 2 and 3, information can be exchanged automatically between domains via symbolic abstraction to improve the abstract values in each domain.

In terms of future research directions, we believe that because methods 2, 3, and 4 all provide a way to avoid the myopia of reinterpretation, they are all worthy of future research. In particular, for method 2, more results on partial-concretization and semantic-reduction operations are desirable, and for method 3, more results about abstract consequence are desirable. Finally, we believe that it will be fruitful to continue to explore the connections between the problems that arise in creating abstract transformers automatically and other areas of computer science.

Acknowledgments. T. Reps would like to thank the many people with whom he collaborated on the work described in the paper (as well as work that motivated the work described): for shape analysis: M. Sagiv, R. Wilhelm, a long list of their former students, as well as his own former students A. Loginov and D. Gopan; for machine-code analysis: G. Balakrishnan, J. Lim, Z. Xu, B. Miller, D. Gopan, A. Thakur, E. Driscoll, A. Lal, M. Elder, T. Sharma, and researchers at GrammaTech, Inc.; for symbolic abstraction: M. Sagiv, G. Yorsh, A. Thakur, M. Elder, T. Sharma, J. Breck, and A. Miné.

The work has been supported for many years by grants and contracts from NSF, DARPA, ONR, ARL, AFOSR, HSARPA, and GrammaTech, Inc. Special thanks go to R. Wachter, F. Anger, T. Teitelbaum and A. White.

Current support comes from a gift from Rajiv and Ritu Batra; DARPA under cooperative agreement HR0011-12-2-0012; AFRL under DARPA MUSE award FA8750-14-2-0270 and DARPA STAC award FA8750-15-C-0082; and the UW-Madison Office of the Vice Chancellor for Research and Graduate Education with funding from WARF. Any opinions, findings, and conclusions or recommendations expressed in this publication are those of the authors, and do not necessarily reflect the views of the sponsoring organizations.

References

1. Akers Jr, S.: On a theory of Boolean functions. J. SIAM **7**(4), 487–498 (1959)
2. Angluin, D.: Learning regular sets from queries and counterexamples. Inf. Comput. **75**(2), 87–106 (1987)
3. Apt, K.: The essence of constraint propagation. TCS **221**, 179–210 (1999)
4. Arnold, G., Manevich, R., Sagiv, M., Shaham, R.: Combining shape analyses by intersecting abstractions. In: Emerson, E.A., Namjoshi, K.S. (eds.) VMCAI 2006. LNCS, vol. 3855, pp. 33–48. Springer, Heidelberg (2006)
5. Bagnara, R., Hill, P.M., Zaffanella, E.: The Parma Polyhedra Library: Toward a complete set of numerical abstractions for the analysis and verification of hardware and software systems. SCP **72**(1–2), 3–21 (2008)
6. Balakrishnan, G., Reps, T.: WYSINWYX: what you see is not what you eXecute. TOPLAS **32**(6), 202–213 (2010)
7. Ball, T., Podelski, A., Rajamani, S.K.: Boolean and cartesian abstraction for model checking C programs. In: Margaria, T., Yi, W. (eds.) TACAS 2001. LNCS, vol. 2031, pp. 268–283. Springer, Heidelberg (2001)
8. Barrett, E., King, A.: Range and set abstraction using SAT. ENTCS **267**(1), 17–27 (2010)
9. Beyer, D., Cimatti, A., Griggio, A., Keremoglu, M., Sebastiani, R.: Software model checking via large-block encoding. In: FMCAD (2009)
10. Beyer, D., Keremoglu, M., Wendler, P.: Predicate abstraction with adjustable-block encoding. In: FMCAD (2010)
11. Boerger, E., Staerk, R.: Abstract State Machines: A Method for High-Level System Design and Analysis. Springer, Heidelberg (2003)
12. Bogudlov, I., Lev-Ami, T., Reps, T., Sagiv, M.: Revamping TVLA: Making parametric shape analysis competitive. In: Damm, W., Hermanns, H. (eds.) CAV 2007. LNCS, vol. 4590, pp. 221–225. Springer, Heidelberg (2007)
13. Brauer, J., King, A.: Automatic abstraction for intervals using Boolean formulae. In: Cousot, R., Martel, M. (eds.) SAS 2010. LNCS, vol. 6337, pp. 167–183. Springer, Heidelberg (2010)
14. Bush, W., Pincus, J., Sielaff, D.: A static analyzer for finding dynamic programming errors. Softw. Pract. Experience **30**, 775–802 (2000)
15. Calcagno, C., Distefano, D., O'Hearn, P.W., Yang, H.: Footprint analysis: A shape analysis that discovers preconditions. In: Riis Nielson, H., Filé, G. (eds.) SAS 2007. LNCS, vol. 4634, pp. 402–418. Springer, Heidelberg (2007)
16. Clarke, E., Kroening, D., Sharygina, N., Yorav, K.: Predicate abstraction of ANSI-C programs using SAT. FMSD **25**(2–3), 125–127 (2004)
17. Cousot, P.: Verification by abstract interpretation. In: Verification Theory and Practice (2003)
18. Cousot, P., Cousot, R.: Abstract interpretation: A unified lattice model for static analysis of programs by construction or approximation of fixpoints. In: POPL (1977)
19. Cousot, P., Cousot, R.: Systematic design of program analysis frameworks. In: POPL (1979)
20. Cousot, P., Cousot, R., Mauborgne, L.: Theories, solvers and static analysis by abstract interpretation. J. ACM **59**(6), Article No. 31 (2012)
21. Cousot, P., Halbwachs, N.: Automatic discovery of linear constraints among variables of a program. In: POPL (1978)

22. Cousot, P., Monerau, M.: Probabilistic abstract interpretation. In: Seidl, H. (ed.) Programming Languages and Systems. LNCS, vol. 7211, pp. 169–193. Springer, Heidelberg (2012)

23. Craig, W.: Three uses of the Herbrand-Gentzen theorem in relating model theory and proof theory. J. Symbolic Logic **22**(3), 269–285 (1957)

24. Distefano, D., O'Hearn, P.W., Yang, H.: A local shape analysis based on separation logic. In: Hermanns, H., Palsberg, J. (eds.) TACAS 2006. LNCS, vol. 3920, pp. 287–302. Springer, Heidelberg (2006)

25. Dong, G., Su, J.: Incremental and decremental evaluation of transitive closure by first-order queries. Inf. Comp. **120**, 101–106 (1995)

26. Elder, M., Gopan, D., Reps, T.: View-augmented abstractions. ENTCS **267**(1), 43–57 (2010)

27. Elder, M., Lim, J., Sharma, T., Andersen, T., Reps, T.: Abstract domains of affine relations. TOPLAS **36**(4), 1–73 (2014)

28. Futamura, Y.: Partial evaluation of computation process - an approach to a compiler-compiler. Higher-Order and Symb. Comp., 12(4) (1999). Reprinted from Systems · Computers · Controls 2(5) (1971)

29. Gopan, D., Reps, T.: Lookahead widening. In: Ball, T., Jones, R.B. (eds.) CAV 2006. LNCS, vol. 4144, pp. 452–466. Springer, Heidelberg (2006)

30. Gopan, D., Reps, T.: Guided static analysis. In: Riis Nielson, H., Filé, G. (eds.) SAS 2007. LNCS, vol. 4634, pp. 349–365. Springer, Heidelberg (2007)

31. Graf, S., Saïdi, H.: Construction of abstract state graphs with PVS. In: CAV (1997)

32. Gulwani, S., Musuvathi, M.: Cover algorithms and their combination. In: Drossopoulou, S. (ed.) ESOP 2008. LNCS, vol. 4960, pp. 193–207. Springer, Heidelberg (2008)

33. Gupta, A., Mumick, I. (eds.): Materialized Views: Techniques, Implementations, and Applications. The M.I.T. Press, Cambridge, MA (1999)

34. Jackson, D.: Software Abstractions: Logic, Language, and Analysis. The M.I.T. Press, Cambridge (2006)

35. Jeannet, B., Loginov, A., Reps, T., Sagiv, M.: A relational approach to interprocedural shape analysis. TOPLAS **32**(2), 5:1–5:2 (2010)

36. Johnson, S.: YACC: Yet another compiler-compiler. Technical Report Comp. Sci. Tech. Rep. 32, Bell Laboratories (1975)

37. Jones, N., Gomard, C., Sestoft, P.: Partial Evaluation and Automatic Program Generation. Prentice-Hall International (1993)

38. Karr, M.: Affine relationship among variables of a program. Acta Inf. **6**, 133–151 (1976)

39. Kearns, M.J., Vazirani, U.V.: An Introduction to Computational Learning Theory. MIT Press, Cambridge, MA, USA (1994)

40. King, A., Søndergaard, H.: Automatic abstraction for congruences. In: Barthe, G., Hermenegildo, M. (eds.) VMCAI 2010. LNCS, vol. 5944, pp. 197–213. Springer, Heidelberg (2010)

41. Kozen, D.: Semantics of probabilistic programs. JCSS **22**(3), 328–350 (1981)

42. Lev-Ami, T., Sagiv, M.: TVLA: A system for implementing static analyses. In: Palsberg, J. (ed.) Static Analysis. LNCS, vol. 1824, pp. 280–301. Springer, Heidelberg (2000)

43. Li, Y., Albarghouthi, A., Kincaid, Z., Gurfinkel, A., Chechik, M.: Symbolic optimization with smt solvers. In: POPL (2014)

44. Lim, J., Lal, A., Reps, T.: Symbolic analysis via semantic reinterpretation. STTT **13**(1), 61–87 (2011)

45. Lim, J., Reps, T.: TSL: A system for generating abstract interpreters and its application to machine-code analysis. In: TOPLAS, 35(1), (2013). Article 4
46. Malmkjær, K.: Abstract Interpretation of Partial-Evaluation Algorithms. Ph.D. thesis, Dept. of Comp. and Inf. Sci., Kansas State Univ. (1993)
47. McMillan, K.: Don't-care computation using k-clause approximation. In: IWLS (2005)
48. Miné, A.: The octagon abstract domain. In: WCRE (2001)
49. Miné, A.: A few graph-based relational numerical abstract domains. In: Hermenegildo, M.V., Puebla, G. (eds.) SAS 2002. LNCS, vol. 2477, pp. 117–132. Springer, Heidelberg (2002)
50. Miné, A., Breck, J., Reps, T.: An algorithm inspired by constraint solvers to infer inductive invariants in numeric programs. Submitted for publication (2015)
51. Mitchell, T.: Machine Learning. WCB/McGraw-Hill, Boston, MA (1997)
52. Monniaux, D.: Abstract interpretation of probabilistic semantics. In: Palsberg, J. (ed.) Static Analysis. LNCS, vol. 1824, pp. 322–339. Springer, Heidelberg (2000)
53. Monniaux, D.: Automatic modular abstractions for template numerical constraints. LMCS 6(3), 4 (2010)
54. Montanari, U.: Networks of constraints: Fundamental properties and applications to picture processing. Inf. Sci. 7(2), 95–132 (1974)
55. Müller-Olm, M., Seidl, H.: Precise interprocedural analysis through linear algebra. In: POPL (2004)
56. Mycroft, A., Jones, N.: A relational framework for abstract interpretation. In: Programs as Data Objects (1985)
57. Mycroft, A., Jones, N.: Data flow analysis of applicative programs using minimal function graphs. In: POPL (1986)
58. Nielson, F.: Two-level semantics and abstract interpretation. TCS 69, 117–242 (1989)
59. Patnaik, S., Immerman, N.: Dyn-FO: A parallel, dynamic complexity class. JCSS 55(2), 199–209 (1997)
60. Pelleau, M., Miné, A., Truchet, C., Benhamou, F.: A constraint solver based on abstract domains. In: Giacobazzi, R., Berdine, J., Mastroeni, I. (eds.) VMCAI 2013. LNCS, vol. 7737, pp. 434–454. Springer, Heidelberg (2013)
61. Regehr, J., Reid, A.: HOIST: A system for automatically deriving static analyzers for embedded systems. In: ASPLOS (2004)
62. Reps, T., Horwitz, S., Sagiv, M.: Precise interprocedural dataflow analysis via graph reachability. In: POPL (1995)
63. Reps, T., Sagiv, M., Loginov, A.: Finite differencing of logical formulas for static analysis. TOPLAS 6(32), 1–55 (2010)
64. Reps, T., Sagiv, M., Yorsh, G.: Symbolic implementation of the best transformer. In: Steffen, B., Levi, G. (eds.) VMCAI 2004. LNCS, vol. 2937, pp. 252–266. Springer, Heidelberg (2004)
65. Reps, T., Schwoon, S., Jha, S., Melski, D.: Weighted pushdown systems and their application to interprocedural dataflow analysis. SCP 58(1–2), 206–263 (2005)
66. Reps, T., Thakur, A.: Through the lens of abstraction. In: HCSS (2014)
67. Reps, T., Turetsky, E., Prabhu, P.: Newtonian program analysis via tensor product. In: POPL (2016)
68. Reynolds, J.: Separation logic: A logic for shared mutable data structures. In: LICS (2002)
69. Sagiv, M., Reps, T., Wilhelm, R.: Solving shape-analysis problems in languages with destructive updating. TOPLAS 20(1), 1–50 (1998)

70. Sagiv, M., Reps, T., Wilhelm, R.: Parametric shape analysis via 3-valued logic. TOPLAS **24**(3), 217–298 (2002)
71. Sankaranarayanan, S., Sipma, H.B., Manna, Z.: Scalable analysis of linear systems using mathematical programming. In: Cousot, R. (ed.) VMCAI 2005. LNCS, vol. 3385, pp. 25–41. Springer, Heidelberg (2005)
72. Scherpelz, E., Lerner, S., Chambers, C.: Automatic inference of optimizer flow functions from semantic meanings. In: PLDI (2007)
73. Sharir, M.: Some observations concerning formal differentiation of set theoretic expressions. TOPLAS **4**(2), 196–225 (1982)
74. Sharir, M., Pnueli, A.: Two approaches to interprocedural data flow analysis. Program Flow Analysis Theory and Applications. Prentice-Hall, Englewood Cliffs (1981)
75. Sheeran, M., Stålmarck, G.: A tutorial on Stålmarck's proof procedure for propositional logic. Formal Methods Syst. Des. **16**(1), 23–58 (2000)
76. Thakur, A.: Symbolic Abstraction: Algorithms and Applications. Ph.D. thesis, Comp. Sci. Dept., Univ. of Wisconsin, Madison, WI, Aug. 2014. Technical Report (1812)
77. Thakur, A., Breck, J., Reps, T.: Satisfiability modulo abstraction for separation logic with linked lists. In: Spin Workshop (2014)
78. Thakur, A., Elder, M., Reps, T.: Bilateral algorithms for symbolic abstraction. In: Miné, A., Schmidt, D. (eds.) SAS 2012. LNCS, vol. 7460, pp. 111–128. Springer, Heidelberg (2012)
79. Thakur, A., Lal, A., Lim, J., Reps, T.: PostHat and all that: Automating abstract interpretation. ENTCS **311**, 15–32 (2015)
80. Thakur, A., Lim, J., Lal, A., Burton, A., Driscoll, E., Elder, M., Andersen, T., Reps, T.: Directed proof generation for machine code. In: Touili, T., Cook, B., Jackson, P. (eds.) CAV 2010. LNCS, vol. 6174, pp. 288–305. Springer, Heidelberg (2010)
81. Thakur, A., Reps, T.: A generalization of Stålmarck's method. In: SAS (2012)
82. Thakur, A., Reps, T.: A method for symbolic computation of abstract operations. In: Madhusudan, P., Seshia, S.A. (eds.) CAV 2012. LNCS, vol. 7358, pp. 174–192. Springer, Heidelberg (2012)
83. Valiant, L.G.: A theory of the learnable. Commun. ACM **27**(11), 1134–1142 (1984)
84. Yahav, E.: Verifying safety properties of concurrent Java programs using 3-valued logic. In: POPL (2001)
85. Yorsh, G., Reps, T., Sagiv, M.: Symbolically computing most-precise abstract operations for shape analysis. In: Jensen, K., Podelski, A. (eds.) TACAS 2004. LNCS, vol. 2988, pp. 530–545. Springer, Heidelberg (2004)

Viper: A Verification Infrastructure for Permission-Based Reasoning

Peter Müller[✉], Malte Schwerhoff, and Alexander J. Summers

Department of Computer Science, ETH Zurich, Zurich, Switzerland
{peter.mueller,malte.schwerhoff,alexander.summers}@inf.ethz.ch

Abstract. The automation of verification techniques based on first-order logic specifications has benefitted greatly from verification infrastructures such as Boogie and Why. These offer an intermediate language that can express diverse language features and verification techniques, as well as back-end tools: in particular, verification condition generators.

However, these infrastructures are not well suited to verification techniques based on separation logic and other permission logics, because they do not provide direct support for permissions and because existing tools for these logics often favour symbolic execution over verification condition generation. Consequently, tool support for these logics (where available) is typically developed independently for each technique, dramatically increasing the burden of developing automatic tools for permission-based verification.

In this paper, we present a verification infrastructure whose intermediate language supports an expressive permission model natively. We provide tool support including two back-end verifiers: one based on symbolic execution, and one on verification condition generation; an inference tool based on abstract interpretion is currently under development. A wide range of existing verification techniques can be implemented via this infrastructure, alleviating much of the burden of building permission-based verifiers, and allowing the developers of higher-level reasoning techniques to focus their efforts at an appropriate level of abstraction.

1 Introduction

Over the last 15 years, static program verification has made wide-ranging and significant progress. Among the many theoretical and practical achievements that enabled this progress, two have been particularly influential. First, the development of widely-used common architectures for program verification tools, simplifying the development of new verifiers. Second, the development of permission logics (of which separation logic [34] is the most prominent example), simplifying the specification and verification of heap-manipulating programs and concurrent programs.

Many modern program verifiers use an architecture in which a front-end tool translates the program to be verified, together with its specification, into a simpler intermediate language such as Boogie [22] or Why [14]. The intermediate language provides a medium in which diverse high-level language features

© Springer-Verlag Berlin Heidelberg 2016
B. Jobstmann and K.R.M. Leino (Eds.): VMCAI 2016, LNCS 9583, pp. 41–62, 2016.
DOI: 10.1007/978-3-662-49122-5_2

and verification problems can be encoded, while allowing for the development of efficient common back-end tools such as verification condition generators. Developing a verifier for a new language or a new verification technique is, thus, often reduced to developing an encoding into one of these intermediate languages. For instance, Boogie is at the core of verifiers such as Chalice [26], Corral [20], Dafny [23], Spec# [25], and VCC [11], while Why powers for instance Frama-C [19] and Krakatoa [13].

This infrastructure is generally not ideal for verifiers based on permission logics, such as separation logic. Verification condition generators and automatic theorem provers support first-order logic, but typically have no support for permission logics because of their higher-order nature. Therefore, most verifiers based on these specialised logics implement their own reasoning engines, typically based on symbolic execution, for each technique independently, increasing the burden of developing general-purpose automatic tools for permission-based verification.

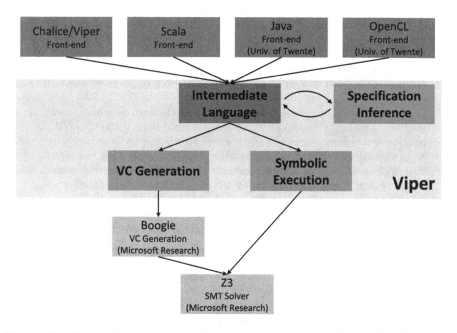

Fig. 1. The Viper infrastructure, underlying tools and currently-existing front-ends. All Viper components are implemented in Scala and can thus be used under Windows, Mac OS and Linux (Boogie and Z3 can also be compiled for these systems).

In this paper, we present Viper, a verification infrastructure whose intermediate language includes a flexible permission model, allowing for simple encodings of permission-based reasoning techniques. The Viper infrastructure provides two back-end verifiers, one using symbolic execution and one using verification condition (VC) generation (via an encoding into Boogie); a specification inference via abstract interpretation is under development. Currently, Viper is targeted by four front-end tools: we developed front-ends for a re-implementation of Chalice and for a small subset of Scala; front-ends for Java and for OpenCL [4] have been developed in the context of the VerCors project [5]. Several additional front-ends are under development. Fig. 1 gives an overview of the Viper infrastructure.

The Viper infrastructure serves three main purposes:

1. Viper facilitates the development of program verifiers based on permission logics, alleviating much of the involved burden by making a large portion of the tool chain reusable, and allowing the developers of higher-level techniques to focus their efforts at this level of abstraction. To support this purpose, Viper provides an expressive intermediate language with primitives that let front-ends encode a wide range of source languages, specifications, and verification techniques. Moreover, the Viper back-ends provide a high degree of automation, aiming to eliminate situations in which tool developers and users need to understand the internals of the back-ends in order to guide the verification effort. This automation is crucial to preserving both the abstractions provided by the Viper infrastructure and the front-ends developed on top of it.
2. Viper allows researchers to rapidly prototype and experiment with new verification techniques by encoding them manually in our intermediate language without (initially) developing a dedicated front-end. To support this purpose, Viper's intermediate language is human readable and provides high-level features such as methods and loops. A parser and type-checker allow one to write Viper code directly.
3. Viper supports the comparison and integration of different verification back-ends. To support this purpose, Viper provides two deductive verifiers and an abstract interpreter. The intermediate language is designed to cater for different reasoning techniques, for instance by providing a heap model similar to those of source languages (facilitating, for example, the use of existing heap analyses).

Outline. This paper gives an overview of the Viper intermediate language. The next section surveys key features of the language and illustrates how they are used to encode more abstract languages and verification techniques. The subsequent sections provide more details on permissions and predicates (Sect. 3), the specification of functional behaviour (Sect. 4), and the encoding of mathematical theories (Sect. 5). We present an evaluation in Sect. 6, summarise related work in Sect. 7, and conclude in Sect. 8. A comprehensive set of examples, including all examples presented in this paper, as well as manually encoded examples from verification competitions, is available in an online appendix [28].

2   Viper in a Nutshell

The Viper infrastructure is centred around a sequential, imperative, object-based intermediate language. A program in this language consists of a sequence of global declarations for fields, methods, functions, predicates, and custom domains. There is no notion of class; every object has every field declared in the program, and methods and functions have no implicit receiver. Predicates [30] can be used both to abstract over concrete assertions and to write recursive specifications of heap data structures. Custom domains are used to declare mathematical theories. Verification of Viper programs is method-modular; method calls are verified with respect to the specification of the callee and not its implementation.

In this section we illustrate the core features of the Viper language using two examples. We use an implementation of a sorted list to illustrate how Viper supports the specification and verification of heap data structures. We then use a client of the list to demonstrate how to encode language features and verification approaches which are not directly available in Viper.

2.1   Specification and Verification of Heap Data Structures

```
1   field data: Seq[Int]
2
3   define sorted(s) forall i: Int, j: Int :: 0 <= i && i < j && j < |s|
4                                         ==> s[i] <= s[j]
5
6   method insert(this: Ref, elem: Int) returns (idx: Int)
7     requires acc(this.data) && sorted(this.data)
8     ensures  acc(this.data) && sorted(this.data)
9     ensures  0 <= idx && idx <= old(|this.data|)
10    ensures  this.data == old(this.data)[0..idx] ++
11                          Seq(elem) ++ old(this.data)[idx..]
12  {
13    idx := 0
14    while(idx < |this.data| && this.data[idx] < elem)
15      invariant acc(this.data, 1/2)
16      invariant 0 <= idx && idx <= |this.data|
17      invariant forall i: Int :: 0 <= i && i < idx
18                               ==> this.data[i] < elem
19    { idx := idx + 1 }
20    this.data := this.data[0..idx] ++ Seq(elem) ++ this.data[idx..]
21  }
```

Fig. 2. A sorted list of integers, implemented via immutable sequences. We will discuss implementations based on linked lists and arrays later.

Figure 2 shows the specification and implementation of a sorted integer list. In this initial version, the list is represented using a mathematical sequence datatype. Line 1 declares an appropriate field; "Int" and "Seq" are built-in datatypes (along with booleans, references, sets and multisets). To make the example more concise, line 3 introduces a parameterised macro that expresses that the argument sequence is sorted.

Viper controls access to the program heap using permissions. Permissions simplify framing (that is, proving that an assertion is not affected by a heap modification), as well as reasoning about concurrency. Permission to a heap location may be held by a method execution or a loop iteration. A method or loop body may access the location only if the appropriate permission is held at the corresponding program point.

Permissions may be transferred between method executions and loop iterations; the permissions to be transferred are specified as part of method pre- and postconditions, and loop invariants, respectively. These specifications are based on implicit dynamic frames [24,31,36]. The most fundamental construct is the *accessibility predicate*, acc($e.f$), which represents permission to a single field location: the field f of the reference denoted by e.

Method insert in Fig. 2 adds a new element to the list. It returns the index at which the element was inserted, which is useful both programmatically (to retrieve the element later), and to simplify the specified postcondition. The precondition of insert requires that callers provide permission to access the list's data field; moreover, the list must be sorted. The first postcondition returns the permission to the caller and guarantees that the list remains sorted. The second postcondition constrains the range of the returned index, while the third postcondition specifies the functional behaviour. This postcondition uses an old expression to refer to the content of the list in the method pre-state. The specification of insert reveals implementation details by referring directly to the data field. We will discuss language features that support information hiding and data abstraction in Sect. 4.

The implementation of insert iterates over the sequence to determine where to insert the new element. Besides the expected properties, the loop invariant requires a *fractional permission* [7] to this.data, denoted by acc(this.data, 1/2). Using a half permission here serves two purposes: first, it allows the loop body to *read* this.data; second, leaving the other half permission in the method execution enclosing the loop lets the verifier conclude that the loop does not modify this.data (for which the full permission is necessary); that is, it can frame properties of this location such as sortedness of the sequence across the loop.

Viper supports a flexible permission model which includes fractional permissions, symbolic permissions via permission-typed variables (of the built-in type Perm), and an approach to constrain such symbolic permissions without using concrete fractions [16], which can be used to model counting permissions [8].

2.2 Encoding High-level Concepts

The example in the previous subsection shows that Viper can be used to manually specify and verify programs. However, the focus of the language design has mostly been on making Viper an effective intermediate language which can be targeted by a variety of front-ends. To illustrate this use of the language, this subsection presents an encoding of a small client of a sorted list, implemented in a Java-like language.

```
1   class Client {
2     @GuardedBy("this") List l;
3     @GuardedBy("this") boolean changed;
4
5     monitor invariant forall int i, j :: 0 <= i && i < j &&
6                             j < |l.data| ==> l.data[i] <= l.data[j]
7     monitor invariant old(l.data) == l.data || changed
8
9     synchronized void test(int e1, int e2) {
10      l.insert(e1);
11      l.insert(e2);
12      assert l.data[0] <= l.data[1];
13      changed = true;
14    }
15  }
```

Fig. 3. An example in a Java-like language whose Viper encoding is shown in Fig. 4. We assume here that class List has a field data whose type is a mathematical sequence. The @GuardedBy("this") annotation indicates that the receiver must be locked before accessing the decorated field. The first monitor invariant requires the list to be sorted; the second is a two-state invariant and requires the changed flag to be set whenever a thread changes the content of list l between acquiring and releasing the monitor.

Class Client in Fig. 3 stores a reference to a list in field l. We assume here that class List has a field data whose type is a mathematical sequence; we will show an alternative encoding using mutable arrays in Sect. 3.3. The client is thread-safe and uses coarse-grained locking to protect its data representation (Java's @GuardedBy("this") annotation indicates that the receiver must be locked before accessing the field). It maintains two monitor invariants: the first is a one-state invariant that requires the list to be sorted; the second is a two-state invariant which states that any thread that acquires the monitor must either leave the content of the underlying list unchanged or set the changed flag to true by the time it releases the monitor. In the latter invariant, we use an old expression to refer to the state in which the monitor was acquired. Method test acquires the monitor of its receiver (since it is declared synchronized), adds two elements to the list and asserts that the first two list elements are in order. It then sets the changed flag and implicitly releases the monitor when it terminates.

Guarded command languages such as Boogie encode high-level language features mostly via three primitives: assert statements to introduce proof obligations, assume statements to state properties which the verifier may use because they have been justified elsewhere, and havoc statements to assign non-deterministic values to variables in order to model side effects or interference. Viper provides permission-aware analogues of these primitives: the operation exhale A asserts all *pure* assertions in A (that is, assertions that do not include accessibility predicates). Any permissions specified in A via accessibility predicates are *removed* from the current program state; if no permission is left for a location then no information about its value is retained, similarly to havocking the location. Conversely, `inhale` A assumes all pure assertions in A and *adds* permissions.

```
1  field changed: Bool
2  field l: Ref
3  field held: Int
4
5  method test(this: Ref, e1: Int, e2: Int)
6    ensures [true, forperm[held] r :: false]
7  {
8    // acquire l
9    inhale acc(this.l) && acc(this.l.data) && acc(this.changed) &&
10           sorted(this.l.data)
11   inhale acc(this.held)
12   statelabel acq
13
14   var tmp: Int
15   tmp := insert(this.l, e1)
16   tmp := insert(this.l, e2)
17   assert this.l.data[0] <= this.l.data[1]
18   this.changed := true
19
20   // release l
21   exhale acc(this.l) && acc(this.l.data) && acc(this.changed) &&
22           sorted(this.l.data) &&
23           (old[acq](this.l.data) == this.l.data || this.changed)
24   exhale acc(this.held)
25 }
```

Fig. 4. A simplified Viper encoding of the source program in Fig. 3.

Figure 4 shows a simplified Viper encoding of the client from Fig. 3, using `exhale` and `inhale` to encode concurrency features, which are not supported by Viper directly. We model locks as resources which can be transferred between methods. To model this, the Viper program includes a field `held` and uses the permission to location o.`held` to represent that the monitor of object o is held by the current method execution. Consequently, acquiring the receiver's monitor at the start of method `test` is encoded by inhaling permission to `this.held` (line 11), and releasing the monitor exhales this permission (line 24). This encoding ensures that a monitor can be released only when it is held. We do not include checks for other properties such as deadlock freedom here, but they could also be encoded. Note that the only purpose of field `held` is to use its permission to represent that a monitor is held; its value and type are irrelevant.

We encode the @GuardedBy annotations by inhaling permission to the client's fields when acquiring the monitor (line 9) and exhaling them upon release (line 21). We interpret @GuardedBy deeply and include the permission to the list's data field. Finally, the encoding of acquire and release also takes into account the monitor invariants declared in the source program. Acquiring a monitor inhales its (one-state) invariant (line 10). Releasing it exhales the one-state and two-state invariants (lines 22–23). Checking a two-state invariant requires a way to access the earlier of the two states: here, the state in which the monitor was acquired. Viper provides a convenient way to refer to earlier program states: programs can declare *state labels* (line 12) and refer to these states in later assertions using labelled old expressions (line 23). This feature is also useful for encoding other comparisons across states such as termination measures.

It is often useful to assert or assume properties about the permissions currently held, without adding or removing permission. Viper supports this via two pure assertions: perm($o.f$) yields the permission amount held for location $o.f$ in the current state; forperm[f] $r :: P(r)$ expresses that all references r to which the current state has non-zero permission to $r.f$, satisfy $P(r)$. The example in Fig. 4 uses the latter feature to encode a *leak check* for monitors; this check fails if a method terminates without either releasing the monitors that it holds or explicitly transferring them back to the caller via a postcondition. The leak check is expressed by the assertion forperm[held] r :: false in line 6.

Since the leak check must be performed *after* any remaining monitors have been transferred to the caller via the method's postcondition, it cannot be placed at the end of the method body, where it would be checked *before* exhaling the postcondition. Therefore, we place it in a postcondition and encode it as *inhale-exhale assertion*. These assertions have the form $[A_1, A_2]$ and are interpreted as A_1 when the assertion is inhaled and A_2 when the assertion is exhaled. In our example, the leak check is performed during exhale, but no corresponding assumption is made by the caller when inhaling the postcondition after a call.

It is common for encodings of high-level verification techniques to contain asymmetries between the properties that are assumed and those that are checked. The leak check is an example of a property that is checked, but not assumed. It is also common to assume properties that are justified by a different (possibly weaker or even vacuous) check together with an external argument provided by a type system, soundness proof or other meta-reasoning. For instance, the following assertion allows the verifier to use a quantified property in its direct form when assuming the property, and to use the premises of the corresponding inductive argument when proving the property:

```
[forall x: Int :: 0 <= x ==> P(x) ,
 forall x: Int :: (forall y: Int :: 0 <= y && y < x ==> P(y)) &&
                                     0 <= x ==> P(x)]
```

3   Unbounded Heap Structures

Viper supports several idioms for specifying and reasoning about unbounded heap structures. There are no specific definitions built in; instead, Viper includes three features which allow one to provide the relevant definitions as part of the input program: recursive predicates (the traditional means in separation-logic-based tools), magic wands (useful for specifying data structures with "missing parts"), and quantified permissions (for writing pointwise rather than recursive specifications). We will briefly discuss each of these features in this section, with respect to variations on our example in Fig. 2. We will focus on the specification of permissions, and show how to extend these specifications with sortedness constraints and rich functional properties in Sect. 4 and the online appendix [28].

3.1   Recursive Predicates

Recursive predicates [30] are the classical means in separation logic of specifying linked data structures such as lists and trees. A predicate definition consists of a name, a list of formal parameters, and a body, which contains the assertion defining the predicate. The body is optional; omitting it results in an abstract predicate, which is useful to hide implementation details from client code. Like permissions, predicates may be held by method executions and loop iterations, and may be transferred between them. Exchanging a predicate for its body and vice versa is done via unfold and fold statements to prevent the automatic prover from unfolding a recursive definition indefinitely. In expressions, unfolding can be used to temporarily unfold a predicate.

```
1   field data: Ref // for the nodes
2   field next: Ref // for the nodes
3   field head: Ref // for the list head
4
5   predicate List(this: Ref)
6   {
7     acc(this.head) && acc(lseg(this.head, null))
8   }
9
10  predicate lseg(this: Ref, end: Ref)
11  {
12    this != end ==>
13      acc(this.data) && acc(this.next) && acc(lseg(this.next, end))
14  }
```

Fig. 5. Fields and predicates for a linked list structure. The acc syntax around predicate instances is optional, but needed when specifying fractional permissions to predicates.

As an example, we consider a variant of Fig. 2, in which the list is implemented based on a linked list of nodes. The appropriate predicate definitions can be found in Fig. 5. The List predicate provides the definition for the permissions to an entire instance of the list. It is defined in terms of the lseg predicate, which defines a list *segment* from start to end: in this case, from this.head to null.

List segment predicates can be used to specify iterative traversals of linked lists, as shown in Fig. 6. The loop invariant at lines 20-21 describes the permissions to the list nodes in terms of one lseg predicate for the nodes seen so far and one for the remainder of the list. The former explains the need for a list segment predicate; tracking permissions for the partial list already inspected is needed to reassemble the whole list after the loop (the code to do this is omitted at line 29).

Manipulating recursive predicates can be tedious. While it is easy to prepend an element to a data structure (by folding another instance of the predicate), extending a data structure at the other end requires additional work to unfold the recursive predicate until the end and then re-fold it including the new element. In Fig. 6, this operation is performed by the concat method, which plays the role of proving the lemma that from lseg(x,y) && lseg(y,z) we can obtain lseg(x,z). concat is a specification-only method, but Viper does not distinguish between regular and ghost code. In the next subsection, we will explain an approach that reduces the overhead of writing and proving such methods in many cases.

3.2   Magic Wands

The *magic wand* is a binary connective (written $A \twoheadrightarrow B$), which describes the promise that if combined with state satisfying the assertion A, the combination can be exchanged for the assertion B [29,34].

Figure 7 shows an alternative specification of the loop from Fig. 6 (lines 17-31). The alternative loop invariant uses a magic wand to represent the permissions to the partial list seen so far. These permissions are expressed indirectly, by the promise that the wand can be combined with the permission to the remainder of the list (the list segment acc(lseg(ptr,null))) to obtain permission to the full list. The permissions implicitly associated with the magic wand instance are essentially the same as those required by the acc(lseg(hd,ptr)) assertion in Fig. 6, which is replaced by the wand.

Viper's support for magic wands [35] includes heuristics to automate (in many cases) reasoning about magic wand assertions, for example, in establishing our loop invariant. Magic wands can also be manipulated manually via dedicated operations, similar to the fold and unfold statements used for predicates [35]. For example, the apply statement in line 12 of Fig. 7 instructs the verifier to exchange the magic wand assertion and its left-hand side for the right-hand-side, restoring the full list after the (partial) traversal.

Compared to the solution without magic wands in Fig. 6, we no longer require the auxiliary concat method to manage lseg predicates. In addition, we could replace lseg by a simpler predicate that describes only full lists. Magic wands provide a general means for tracking partial versions of data structures, without the need to explicitly define or manipulate these partial versions.

```
1   method insert(this: Ref, elem: Int) returns (idx: Int)
2     requires acc(List(this))
3     ensures  acc(List(this))
4   {
5     idx := 0;  var tmp: Ref
6     unfold acc(List(this))
7     if(this.head != null) { unfold acc(lseg(this.head, null)) }
8
9     if(this.head == null || elem <= this.head.data)
10    {
11      ... // allocate new node at this.head, fold predicates
12    } else {
13      var hd : Ref := this.head
14      var ptr: Ref := hd // running variable
15      idx := idx + 1
16
17      fold acc(lseg(hd, hd))  // for loop invariant
18      while(ptr.next != null &&
19          unfolding acc(lseg(ptr.next, null)) in ptr.next.data < elem)
20        invariant acc(lseg(hd, ptr)) && acc(ptr.next) && acc(ptr.data)
21        invariant acc(lseg(ptr.next, null))
22      {
23        unfold acc(lseg(ptr.next, null))
24        idx := idx + 1;  var ptrn: Ref := ptr.next
25        fold acc(lseg(ptrn, ptrn));  fold acc(lseg(ptr, ptrn))
26        concat(hd, ptr, ptrn) // add to end of list segment
27        ptr := ptrn
28      }
29      ... // allocate new node at ptr.next, fold predicates
30      concat(hd, ptr, null) // concat two lsegs to obtain full list
31    }
32    fold acc(List(this))
33  }
34
35  method concat(this: Ref, ptr: Ref, end: Ref)
36    requires acc(lseg(this, ptr)) && acc(lseg(ptr, end))
37    requires end != null ==> acc(end.next, 1/2) // not forming a cycle
38    ensures  acc(lseg(this, end))
39    ensures  end != null ==> acc(end.next, 1/2)
40  {
41    if(this != ptr) {
42      unfold acc(lseg(this, ptr));  concat(this.next, ptr, end)
43      fold acc(lseg(this, end))
44    }
45  }
```

Fig. 6. The insert method of a sorted linked list with recursive predicates.

```
1    while(ptr.next != null &&
2        unfolding acc(lseg(ptr.next, null)) in ptr.next.data < elem)
3      invariant acc(lseg(ptr, null)) --* acc(lseg(hd, null))
4      invariant acc(ptr.next) && acc(ptr.data)
5      invariant acc(lseg(ptr.next, null))
6    {
7      unfold acc(lseg(ptr.next, null))
8      idx := idx + 1;  var last: Ref := ptr
9      ptr := ptr.next
10    }
11     ... // allocate new node at ptr.next, fold predicates
12    apply acc(lseg(ptr, null)) --* acc(lseg(hd, null)) // full list
13  }
```

Fig. 7. Alternative loop specification with magic wands (cf. Fig. 6, lines 17-31).

3.3   Quantified Permissions

In addition to recursive predicates, Viper supports *quantified permissions* as a means of specifying unbounded heap structures. Quantified permissions are similar to separation logic's iterated separating conjunction [34] and allow the specification of permissions *pointwise*. The flat structure of a pointwise specification is convenient for specifying data structures that are not limited to traversals in a single, hierarchical fashion, such as cyclic lists, random access data structures such as arrays, and general graphs.

We denote quantified permissions by a universal quantifier around the usual accessibility predicates. For example, forall x: Ref :: x in S ==> acc(x.f) denotes permission to the f field of every reference in the set S. The quantified variable can be of any type, and we permit arbitrary boolean expressions to constrain its range.

Quantified permissions provide a natural way to specify properties of arrays. Arrays are not supported natively in Viper but can be encoded. As we show in Sect. 5, we can introduce a custom type Array which models the ith slot of an array a as loc(a,i).val, where loc(a: Array, i: Int): Ref is an injective function provided by the Array type. The type also provides a function len(a: Array): Int to model the length of an array. One can then denote permission to the array slots via quantified permissions ranging over the array indices.

Figure 8 applies this approach to encode an array list. The field elems stores the array, while size keeps track of the number of used array slots. The quantified permission assertion at line 9 represents permission to all array slots. These are used, for instance, to permit the array access in the while-condition in line 20. Note that the loop invariant is essentially a copy of the AList predicate body (with the additional constraint on the idx loop variable). We employ fractional permissions (including fractional quantified permissions in line 23) to specify that the loop will not modify the corresponding locations.

```
1  field val: Int       // array slots modelled by loc(this.elems,i).val
2  field elems: Array // see Array domain definition in Sec. 5
3  field size: Int      // how many array slots have been used
4
5  predicate AList(this: Ref)
6  {
7    acc(this.elems) && acc(this.size) &&
8    0 <= this.size && this.size <= len(this.elems) &&
9    (forall i: Int :: 0 <= i && i < len(this.elems) ==>
10                               acc(loc(this.elems, i).val))
11 }
12
13 method insert(this: Ref, elem: Int) returns (idx: Int)
14   requires acc(AList(this))
15   ensures  acc(AList(this))
16 {
17   idx := 0
18   unfold acc(AList(this))
19
20   while (idx < this.size && loc(this.elems, idx).val < elem)
21     invariant acc(this.elems, 1/2) && acc(this.size, 1/2)
22     invariant this.size <= len(this.elems)
23     invariant forall i: Int :: 0 <= i && i < len(this.elems) ==>
24                               acc(loc(this.elems, i).val, 1/2)
25     invariant 0 <= idx && idx <= this.size
26   { idx := idx + 1 }
27
28   ... // move the later elements forward by one, resize if necessary
29   loc(this.elems, idx).val := elem
30   this.size := this.size + 1
31   fold acc(AList(this))
32 }
```

Fig. 8. Array-list, specified using quantified permissions.

4 Functional Behaviour

The specifications shown in Sect. 3 focus on the management of permissions, but do not constrain the values stored in data structures (for instance, to require sortedness of the list) or computed by operations (for instance, to express the functional behaviour of method insert). The examples in Sect. 2 specify such properties, but in a way which exposes implementation details. In this section, we explain several ways to express functional behaviour in Viper.

A simple way to specify the values stored in data structures is to include constraints on the values in the body of a predicate, in addition to permissions. For example, we could extend the body of the lseg predicate in Fig. 5 by conjoining the following assertion:

```
unfolding acc(lseg(this.next, end)) in
  this.next != end ==> this.data <= this.next.data
```

This assertion specifies sortedness pairwise between list nodes. Maintaining the augmented predicate entails corresponding additions to the loop invariant and specification of the concat method in Fig. 6, as shown in the online appendix.

Constraining values via predicates allows one to encode representation invariants, but is not suitable to express client-visible invariants or the functional behaviour of operations. To support such specifications, Viper supports *heap-dependent functions* that may be used in program statements and assertions. Functions (as opposed to methods) have (side-effect free) expressions rather than statements as a body. A function's precondition must require sufficient permissions to evaluate the function's body; in contrast to methods, invoking a function does not consume these permissions, and they do not need to be returned via a function's postcondition.

Functions are a flexible feature which can play several different roles in a Viper program. The first major role is to encode side-effect free observer methods (*pure* methods in JML [21] and Spec# [1]), which are a part of the interface of many data structures. For instance, list-style collections typically provide observer methods such as length and itemAt to retrieve data. As an example, we extend our lseg-based specification from Sect. 3.1 with the following function definition:

```
function lengthNodes(this: Ref, end: Ref): Int
  requires acc(lseg(this, end))
{
  unfolding acc(lseg(this, end)) in
    this == end ? 0 : 1 + lengthNodes(this.next, end)
}
```

This definition enables us, whenever we hold an lseg predicate instance, to express its length via an application of lengthNodes. The Viper verifiers carefully (and automatically) control the unrolling of recursive function definitions, essentially mimicking the traversal of the corresponding lseg data structure [15].

A second major role of functions is to define *abstraction functions* [17] providing abstractions of the underlying data representation, in order to express specifications without revealing implementation details. For example, the following function abstracts the values of a list segment to a mathematical sequence:

```
function contentNodes(this: Ref, end: Ref): Seq[Int]
  requires acc(lseg(this, end))
  ensures  forall i: Int, j: Int :: 0 <= i && i < j && j < |result|
                            ==> result[i] <= result[j]
{
  this == end ? Seq[Ref]() : unfolding acc(lseg(this, end)) in
              ( Seq(this.data) ++ contentNodes(this.next, end) )
}
```

Viper verifiers reason about function applications in terms of the function's body. Nevertheless, it is sometimes useful to provide a function postcondition. In the above example, the postcondition expresses that the sequence of all values stored in the list is sorted, which is implied by the pairwise sortedness we have added to the `lseg` predicate. Note that the inductive argument required to justify this postcondition is implicit in the checking of `contentNodes`'s recursive definition.

A similar `content` function for the overall data structure (described by the `List` predicate) allows us to specify the functional behaviour of `insert`:

```
ensures  content(this) == old(content(this))[0..index] ++
                          Seq(elem) ++ old(content(this))[index..]
```

Function bodies are optional in Viper, which allows hiding details when verifying client code (similarly to predicates). Omitting the body is also useful for axiomatising a function rather than defining it (assuming the existence of the function is otherwise justified). In the array list example from Fig. 8, defining `length` and `itemAt` functions is straightforward. However, an analogous `content` function would be awkward to define recursively since our specifications for this random-access example avoid recursive definitions. Instead, we can axiomatise the function, that is, specify its meaning via a quantified postcondition. Such quantifiers are supported in Viper assertions in general, and provide another important tool for writing functional specifications:

```
function content(this: Ref): Seq[Int]
  requires acc(AList(this))
  ensures  |result| == length(this)
  ensures  forall i: Int ::  0 <= i && i < length(this)
                   ==> result[i] == itemAt(this, i)
```

The third major role of heap-dependent functions is to express refinements of existing predicate definitions. For example, instead of expressing sortedness as part of a predicate definition, we can write a boolean function (here for the array list from Fig. 8) and use it in combination with the unchanged `AList` predicate:

```
function sorted(this: Ref): Bool
  requires acc(AList(this))
{
  unfolding acc(AList(this)) in
      forall i: Int, j: Int ::  0 <= i && i < j && j < this.size
                   ==> result[i] <= result[j]
}
```

`AList(this) && sorted(this)` describes a sorted list, while `AList(this)` specifies an array list that may or may not be sorted. In this way, functions can be used to augment data-structure instances with additional invariants, without requiring many versions of a predicate definition or resorting to higher-order logic.

The combination of predicates, functions, and quantifiers supported by Viper provides the means for writing rich functional specifications in a variety of styles, which are further illustrated by examples in the online appendix [28].

5   First-Order Theories

Many specification and verification techniques provide their own mathematical vocabulary, for instance, to encode algebraic data types. To support such techniques, Viper supports the declaration of custom first-order theories via *domains*: each domain introduces a (potentially polymorphic) type and may declare uninterpreted function symbols and axioms. Organising mathematical theories into domains allows back-ends to provide dedicated support for certain theories. For instance, while both Viper verifiers let the underlying SMT solver reason about domains, an abstract-interpretation-based inference might provide specialised abstract domains for certain Viper domains.

```
1   domain Array {
2     function loc(a: Array, i: Int): Ref
3     function len(a: Array): Int
4     function loc_a(r: Ref): Array
5     function loc_i(r: Ref): Int
6
7     axiom loc_injective {
8       forall a: Array, i: Int :: {loc(a, i)} 0 <= i && i < len(a)
9         ==> loc_a(loc(a, i))) == a && loc_i(loc(a, i))) == i
10    }
11
12    axiom length_nonneg { forall a: Array :: 0 <= len(a) }
13  }
```

Fig. 9. A domain definition for arrays, as used in Sect. 3.3. The injective function `loc` maps an array and an index to a reference; in combination with a field (such as `val` in Fig. 8), an array slot `a[i]` can be encoded as `loc(a, i).val`.

Figure 9 uses a domain to model arrays, which are not natively supported in Viper. We represent the ith slot of an array a as $loc(a,i)$.val, where `loc` is a function introduced by the domain and `val` is a suitable field. Since each array slot corresponds to a dedicated memory location, `loc` must be injective; this property is expressed by the axiom `loc_injective`, which axiomatises `loc_a` and `loc_i` as the inverse functions of `loc`. Axiomatising injectivity via inverse functions improves performance of the SMT solver by reducing the number of instantiations of the axiom.

Universal quantifiers in axioms (as well as in assertions) may be decorated with triggers [27]: terms used as patterns which restrict the potential instantiations. For instance, the trigger `{loc(a, i)}` in axiom `loc_injective` lets the SMT solver instantiate the quantifier with x and y whenever it knows about a term $loc(x,y)$. When no trigger is provided, Viper attempts to infer triggers automatically. In general, however, hand-crafted triggers lead to better performance.

The online appendix [28] shows how to encode algebraic data types as domains, with functions for constructors and selectors, and with appropriate axioms. Such an encoding is useful when encoding source languages that provide ADTs (such as Scala's case classes) or for specification languages that make use of ADTs.

6 Evaluation

In this section, we evaluate the performance of the Viper verifiers on a wide variety of examples. Moreover, we give preliminary qualitative and quantitative evidence for Viper's suitability as an intermediate verification language.

6.1 Performance of the Viper Verifiers

To evaluate the performance of the Viper verifiers, we ran both our symbolic execution (SE) verifier and our verification-condition-generation (VCG) verifier on the following collections of input programs: our own Viper regression tests, Viper programs generated by the VerCors tools [4,5], and programs generated from Chalice examples via our Chalice front-end. For the Viper and VerCors programs, we split the files into those using quantified permissions (for which only our SE verifier currently provides support), and those which can be run in both verifiers. The set of VerCors examples was provided to us by the VerCors developers as representative of their Viper usage.

The results are shown in Fig. 10. Both verifiers perform consistently well in the average case, with the SE verifier being significantly faster. As the average times suggest, the maximum times are true outliers—these were typically examples designed to be complex, in order to test what the tools could handle. The Viper tests (which are mostly regression tests) tend to be shorter and less challenging than the VerCors-generated programs, which are representative of real usage of Viper as a back-end infrastructure.

Input programs	Number of programs	Average size (LOC)	Mean time (s) SE	VCG	Max. time (s) SE	VCG
Viper tests w/o QPs	208	43.8	0.23	0.81	18.36	34.17
VerCors w/o QPs	43	152.1	0.94	2.24	16.25	31.78
Chalice (no QPs)	221	122.0	0.26	0.97	21.26	29.37
Viper tests with QPs	74	34.0	0.30	-	2.00	-
VerCors with QPs	65	105.6	0.95	-	8.39	-

Fig. 10. Performance evaluation of Viper verifiers. Lines of code (LOC) measurements do not include whitespace lines and comments. All input programs were run 10 times and average times recorded. The mean and maximum times were calculated based on these averages. Timings do not include JVM start-up time: we persist a JVM across test runs using the Nailgun tool; for the VCG verifier, timings include start-up of Boogie via Mono. All timings were gathered on a Lenovo Thinkpad T450s running Ubuntu 15.04 64 bit, with 12 GB RAM; full details are available in our online appendix [28].

6.2   Viper as an Intermediate Verification Language

To assess Viper's suitability as an intermediate verification language, we provide some observations about Viper's language design and compare the performance of Viper as the back-end of the VerCors tools. to the previously-used Chalice-Boogie tool chain [26].

Language Design. The most comprehensive front-ends for Viper are the Java and OpenCL front-ends developed in the VerCors project and our own Chalice/Viper front-end. Various language features of Viper have proven essential for these different front-ends. VerCors' work on verifying concurrent Java makes use of Viper's custom domains for encoding custom ADT-like datatypes along with additional axioms, and makes heavy use of sequences, recursive functions and predicates. The VerCors OpenCL front-end instead employs quantified permissions along with domains similar to the array encoding shown in Sect. 5, and pure quantifiers to specify functional properties. Our front-end for Chalice makes extensive use of inhale and exhale statements to encode high-level features, similarly to the example in Sect. 2.2. As such, the key language features described in this paper have all been heavily used in at least one existing front-end.

There are Chalice front-ends for both Boogie and Viper, which support very similar (but not identical) versions of the Chalice language. For the Chalice programs from the previous subsection, the Boogie files were between 3.3 and 32.1 times the size of the corresponding Viper files, and on average 11.2 times larger. This significant difference illustrates the higher level of abstraction provided by the Viper language, compared with existing intermediate verification languages.

Performance of the Infrastructure. The VerCors project switched from using Chalice-Boogie as back-end infrastructure, to Viper. This switch was partly motivated by the available language features; for instance, the VerCors OpenCL front-end relies heavily on quantified permissions, which are not available in Chalice. Another reason was the performance of the Viper tools. In the following, we compare the performance of the two infrastructures on inputs generated by the VerCors tools.

Running tests through the entire alternative tool chains proved difficult due to legacy syntactic and implementation differences; however, we identified 17 VerCors examples from the test suite used in Sect. 6.1 that could be run on the alternative infrastructures. For each of these examples, we generated two (essentially equivalent) Boogie programs, one using Chalice as a VerCors back-end, and one using Viper with our VCG verifier.

Figure 11 shows the results of our comparison. In all cases, the Boogie files generated via the Viper route were smaller and verified faster. The same example was slowest via both routes, and more than 4 times faster in the Viper-generated version. Although our sample size is small, the results suggest Viper enables a more direct encoding and offers a more streamlined verification condition generator. In practice, the VerCors team typically use Viper's SE verifier, which is substantially faster still, as shown in Fig. 10.

	Average size (LOC)	Mean time (s)	Max. time (s)
Boogie file via Chalice	945.0	0.83	3.22
Boogie file via Viper (VCG)	631.1	0.53	0.73
Ratio	66.8%	64.3%	22.5%

Fig. 11. Comparison of alternative back-end infrastructures for the VerCors tools. Using Viper's VCG verifier significantly reduces the size and verification time of the generated Boogie programs compared to the Chalice/Boogie infrastructure.

7 Related Work

Boogie [22] and Why [14] are widely-used intermediate verification languages, but they do not offer native support for permission-based reasoning. Chalice [26] demonstrates that permissions can be encoded in such a first-order setting; our VCG-based back-end makes such a complex encoding reusable. Boogie and Why front-ends encode heaps as maps. In contrast, the Viper language has a built-in notion of heap, which is slightly less expressive (for instance, in Viper, heaps cannot be stored in variables), but enables the development of more-specialised back-ends, such as verifiers based on Smallfoot-style symbolic execution and inference engines based on abstract interpretation.

To our knowledge, the only other verification infrastructure for permission-based reasoning is coreStar [6], which includes an intermediate language for separation logic and a symbolic execution engine. Front-ends implemented on top of coreStar encode programs into coreStar's language and also need to provide proof rules and abstraction rules to customise the behaviour of coreStar's symbolic execution, even for fundamental concepts such as permissions (points-to predicates). In contrast, Viper has been designed to be expressive enough to capture a wide variety of languages and verification techniques out of the box, without requiring front-end developers to descend into the back-end(s). Furthermore, having a fixed language (with fixed rules) simplifies writing different back-ends, potentially with specialised handling of certain language features.

Some verifiers for separation logic such as Smallfoot [3], GRASShopper [33], Asterix [32], and the work by Chin et al. [9], achieve a relatively high degree of automation by restricting themselves to specific (classes of) theories: often those of linked lists and trees. Without support for important features such as fractional permissions or user-defined predicates and functions, they do not offer the expressiveness needed for an intermediate language which can encode a wide range of verification techniques.

VeriFast [18], a verifier for C and Java programs, supports an expressive assertion language, including user-defined higher-order predicates and function pointers, but it requires significant amounts of user annotations, in particular when reasoning about functional specifications and abstractions. This complicates the encoding of front-end languages that try to achieve a higher degree of automation.

Several verification techniques based on interactive proof assistants such as Coq or HOL4 [2,10,12,37] provide tactics that automate common proof steps in separation logic. Viper aims at a higher level of automation, such that users do not have to interact directly with the verification back-ends.

8   Conclusion and Future Work

We have presented Viper, an infrastructure which facilitates the rapid proto-typing of permission-based verification techniques and the development of verification tools. Viper's intermediate language offers a flexible permission model, supports user-defined predicates and functions, and provides advanced specification features such as magic wands and quantified permissions. It provides the necessary expressiveness to encode a wide range of language features and permission-based verification techniques. In particular, users may choose between and combine different styles of encodings, as we have demonstrated in Sects. 3 and 4. Viper includes two back-end verifiers: one based on verification condition generation and one based on symbolic execution. An abstract-interpretation-based specification inference is under development.

Viper is targeted by several front-ends, developed both inside and outside of our research group. Together with collaborators, we are currently working on encodings of verification techniques for JavaScript and for fine-grained concurrency. Viper is also being used to verify safety and security properties of a network router implemented in Python.

As future work, we plan to provide a comprehensive variety of specification inference techniques and to improve the reporting and debugging of verification failures. We are also interested in integrating alternative, possibly specialised verification back-ends.

Acknowledgements. This work has been funded in part by the Swiss National Science Foundation and by the Hasler Foundation. Viper has benefitted from the work of many people. We are especially grateful to Uri Juhasz for his contributions to the design of the Viper language, Ioannis Kassios for his work on quantified permissions and the initial Chalice front-end, and to Vytautas Astrauskas for his improvements of the latter. We are also thankful to Milos Novacek for his work on specification inference, and to Stefan Heule for the initial development of the verification condition generator. We warmly thank Stefan Blom for his extensive feedback on Viper and his help with using VerCors, and Marco Eilers for his help with our experimental evaluation.

References

1. Barnett, M., Fähndrich, M., Leino, K.R.M., Müller, P., Schulte, W., Venter, H.: Specification and verification: the Spec# experience. Commun. ACM **54**(6), 81–91 (2011)
2. Bengtson, J., Jensen, J.B., Birkedal, L.: A framework for higher-order separation logic in Coq. In: Beringer, L., Felty, A. (eds.) ITP 2012. LNCS, vol. 7406, pp. 315–331. Springer, Heidelberg (2012)

3. Berdine, J., Calcagno, C., O'Hearn, P.W.: Smallfoot: modular automatic assertion checking with separation logic. In: de Boer, F.S., Bonsangue, M.M., Graf, S., de Roever, W.-P. (eds.) FMCO 2005. LNCS, vol. 4111, pp. 115–137. Springer, Heidelberg (2006)
4. Blom, S., Darabi, S., Huisman, M.: Verification of loop parallelisations. In: Egyed, A., Schaefer, I. (eds.) FASE 2015. LNCS, vol. 9033, pp. 202–217. Springer , Heidelberg (2015)
5. Blom, S., Huisman, M.: The VerCors tool for verification of concurrent programs. In: Jones, C., Pihlajasaari, P., Sun, J. (eds.) FM 2014. LNCS, vol. 8442, pp. 127–131. Springer, Heidelberg (2014)
6. Botincan, M., Distefano, D., Dodds, M., Grigore, R., Naudziuniene, D., Parkinson, M.J.: coreStar: the core of jStar. In: Leino, K.R.M., Moskal, M. (eds.) BOOGIE 2011, pp. 65–77 (2011). http://research.microsoft.com/en-us/um/people/moskal/boogie2011/boogie_2011_all.pdf
7. Boyland, J.: Checking interference with fractional permissions. In: Cousot, R. (ed.) SAS 2003. LNCS, vol. 2694, pp. 55–72. Springer, Heidelberg (2003)
8. Boyland, J.T., Müller, P., Schwerhoff, M., Summers, A.J.: Constraint semantics for abstract read permissions. In: FTfJP 2014, pp. 2:1–2:6. ACM, New York, NY, USA (2014)
9. Chin, W.-N., David, C., Nguyen, H.H., Qin, S.: Automated verification of shape, size and bag properties via user-defined predicates in separation logic. Sci. Comput. Program. **77**(9), 1006–1036 (2012)
10. Chlipala, A., Malecha, J.G., Morrisett, G., Shinnar, A., Wisnesky, R.: Effective interactive proofs for higher-order imperative programs. In: Hutton, G., Tolmach, A.P. (eds.) ICFP, pp. 79–90. ACM (2009)
11. Cohen, E., Moskal, M., Schulte, W., Tobies, S.: Local verification of global invariants in concurrent programs. In: Touili, T., Cook, B., Jackson, P. (eds.) CAV 2010. LNCS, vol. 6174, pp. 480–494. Springer, Heidelberg (2010)
12. Dockins, R., Hobor, A., Appel, A.W.: A fresh look at separation algebras and share accounting. In: Hu, Z. (ed.) APLAS 2009. LNCS, vol. 5904, pp. 161–177. Springer, Heidelberg (2009)
13. Filliâtre, J.-C., Marché, C.: The Why/Krakatoa/Caduceus platform for deductive program verification. In: Damm, W., Hermanns, H. (eds.) CAV 2007. LNCS, vol. 4590, pp. 173–177. Springer, Heidelberg (2007)
14. Filliâtre, J.-C., Paskevich, A.: Why3 — where programs meet provers. In: Felleisen, M., Gardner, P. (eds.) ESOP 2013. LNCS, vol. 7792, pp. 125–128. Springer, Heidelberg (2013)
15. Heule, S., Kassios, I.T., Müller, P., Summers, A.J.: Verification condition generation for permission logics with abstract predicates and abstraction functions. In: Castagna, G. (ed.) ECOOP 2013. LNCS, vol. 7920, pp. 451–476. Springer, Heidelberg (2013)
16. Heule, S., Leino, K.R.M., Müller, P., Summers, A.J.: Abstract read permissions: fractional permissions without the fractions. In: Giacobazzi, R., Berdine, J., Mastroeni, I. (eds.) VMCAI 2013. LNCS, vol. 7737, pp. 315–334. Springer, Heidelberg (2013)
17. Hoare, C.A.R.: Proof of correctness of data representation. Acta Informatica **1**(4), 271–281 (1972)
18. Jacobs, B., Smans, J., Philippaerts, P., Vogels, F., Penninckx, W., Piessens, F.: VeriFast: a powerful, sound, predictable, fast verifier for C and Java. In: Bobaru, M., Havelund, K., Holzmann, G.J., Joshi, R. (eds.) NFM 2011. LNCS, vol. 6617, pp. 41–55. Springer, Heidelberg (2011)

19. Kirchner, F., Kosmatov, N., Prevosto, V., Signoles, J., Yakobowski, B.: Frama-C: a software analysis perspective. Formal Asp. Comput. **27**(3), 573–609 (2015)

20. Lal, A., Qadeer, S., Lahiri, S.K.: A solver for reachability modulo theories. In: Madhusudan, P., Seshia, S.A. (eds.) CAV 2012. LNCS, vol. 7358, pp. 427–443. Springer, Heidelberg (2012)

21. Leavens, G., Baker, A.L., Ruby, C.: JML: a notation for detailed design. In: Kilov, I., Rumpe, B., Simmonds, I. (eds.) Behavioral Specifications of Businesses and Systems, pp. 175–188. Kluwer, Dordrecht (1999)

22. Leino, K.R.M.: This is Boogie 2. Working draft (2008). http://research.microsoft.com/en-us/um/people/leino/papers.html

23. Leino, K.R.M.: Dafny: an automatic program verifier for functional correctness. In: Clarke, E.M., Voronkov, A. (eds.) LPAR-16 2010. LNCS, vol. 6355, pp. 348–370. Springer, Heidelberg (2010)

24. Leino, K.R.M., Müller, P.: A basis for verifying multi-threaded programs. In: Castagna, G. (ed.) ESOP 2009. LNCS, vol. 5502, pp. 378–393. Springer, Heidelberg (2009)

25. Leino, K.R.M., Müller, P.: Using the Spec# language, methodology, and tools to write bug-free programs. In: Müller, P. (ed.) LASER Summer School 2007/2008. LNCS, vol. 6029, pp. 91–139. Springer, Heidelberg (2010)

26. Leino, K.R.M., Müller, P., Smans, J.: Verification of concurrent programs with Chalice. In: Aldini, A., Barthe, G., Gorrieri, R. (eds.) FOSAD. LNCS, vol. 5705, pp. 195–222. Springer, Heidelberg (2009)

27. Moskal, M.: Programming with triggers. In: SMT 2009, pp. 20–29. ACM, New York, NY, USA (2009)

28. Müller, P., Schwerhoff, M., Summers, A.J.: Online appendix. http://viper.ethz.ch/VMCAI16

29. O'Hearn, P.W., Reynolds, J.C., Yang, H.: Local reasoning about programs that alter data structures. In: Fribourg, L. (ed.) CSL 2001 and EACSL 2001. LNCS, vol. 2142, pp. 1–19. Springer, Heidelberg (2001)

30. Parkinson, M., Bierman, G.: Separation logic and abstraction. In: POPL, pp. 247–258 (2005)

31. Parkinson, M.J., Summers, A.J.: The relationship between separation logic and implicit dynamic frames. Logical Methods Comput. Sci. **8**(3:01), 1–54 (2012)

32. Navarro Pérez, J.A., Rybalchenko, A.: Separation logic modulo theories. In: Shan, C. (ed.) APLAS 2013. LNCS, vol. 8301, pp. 90–106. Springer, Heidelberg (2013)

33. Piskac, R., Wies, T., Zufferey, D.: GRASShopper—complete heap verification with mixed specifications. In: Ábrahám, E., Havelund, K. (eds.) TACAS 2014 (ETAPS). LNCS, vol. 8413, pp. 124–139. Springer, Heidelberg (2014)

34. Reynolds, J.: Separation logic: a logic for shared mutable data structures. In: LICS, pp. 55–74. IEEE Computer Society (2002)

35. Schwerhoff, M., Summers, A.J.: Lightweight support for magic wands in an automatic verifier. In: Boyland, J.T. (ed.) ECOOP, vol. 37 of LIPIcs, pp. 614–638. Schloss Dagstuhl (2015)

36. Smans, J., Jacobs, B., Piessens, F.: Implicit dynamic frames: combining dynamic frames and separation logic. In: Drossopoulou, S. (ed.) ECOOP 2009. LNCS, vol. 5653, pp. 148–172. Springer, Heidelberg (2009)

37. Tuerk, T.: A formalisation of Smallfoot in HOL. In: Berghofer, S., Nipkow, T., Urban, C., Wenzel, M. (eds.) TPHOLs 2009. LNCS, vol. 5674, pp. 469–484. Springer, Heidelberg (2009)

Abstract Interpretation

Predicate Abstraction
for Linked Data Structures

Alexander Bakst[✉] and Ranjit Jhala

University of California, San Diego, USA
{abakst,jhala}@cs.ucsd.edu

Abstract. We present *Alias Refinement Types* (ART), a new approach
that uses predicate-abstraction to automate the verification of correctness properties of linked data structures. While there are many techniques for checking that a heap-manipulating program adheres to its
specification, they often require that the programmer annotate the
behavior of each procedure, for example, in the form of loop invariants
and pre- and post-conditions. We introduce a technique that lifts predicate abstraction to the heap by factoring the analysis of data structures
into two orthogonal components: (1) Alias Types, which reason about the
physical shape of heap structures, and (2) Refinement Types, which use
simple predicates from an SMT decidable theory to capture the *logical*
or semantic properties of the structures. We evaluate ART by implementing a tool that performs type *inference* for an imperative language, and
empirically show, using a suite of data-structure benchmarks, that ART
requires only 21 % of the annotations needed by other state-of-the-art
verification techniques.

1 Introduction

Separation logic (SL) [31] has proven invaluable as a unifying framework for
specifying and verifying correctness properties of linked data structures. Para-
doxically, the richness of the logic has led to a problem – analyses built upon
it are exclusively either expressive *or* automatic. To *automate* verification,
we must restrict the logic to decidable fragments, *e.g.* list-segments [4,21],
and design custom decision procedures [6,14,16,27,28] or abstract interpretations [7,23,40]. Consequently, we lose expressiveness as the resulting analyses
cannot be extended to *user*-defined structures. To *express* properties of user-
defined structures, we must fall back upon arbitrary SL predicates. We sacrifice
automation as we require programmer assistance to verify entailments over such
predicates [10,24]. Even when entailment is automated by specializing proof
search, the programmer has the onerous task of providing complex auxiliary
inductive invariants [9,30].

We observe that the primary obstacle towards obtaining expressiveness and
automation is that in SL, machine state is represented by monolithic assertions
that conflate reasoning about heap and data. While SL based tools commonly
describe machine state as a conjunction of a pure, heap independent formula,

© Springer-Verlag Berlin Heidelberg 2016
B. Jobstmann and K.R.M. Leino (Eds.): VMCAI 2016, LNCS 9583, pp. 65–84, 2016.
DOI: 10.1007/978-3-662-49122-5_3

abs :: (int) ⇒ nat[1]	
`function abs(x){`	`x:int`
`   if (0 <= x)`	$(0 \leqslant x); x{:}int$
`      return x;`	
	$r{:}\{\nu = 0 - x\};$
`   var r = 0 - x;`	
	$\neg(0 \leqslant x); x{:}int$
`   return r;`	
`}`	

absR :: (x:⟨data:int⟩) ⇒ ()/&x ↦ ⟨data:nat[2]	
`function absR(x){`	$\Gamma_0 \doteq x{:}\langle \&x \rangle$
	$\Sigma_0 \doteq \&x \mapsto \langle data{:}int \rangle$
`   var d = x.data;`	$\Gamma_1 \doteq d{:}int; \Gamma_0$
`   var t = abs(d);`	$\Gamma_2 \doteq t{:}nat[1]; \Gamma_1$
`   x.data = t;`	$\Sigma_1 \doteq \&x \mapsto \langle data{:}\nu = t \rangle$
`   return;`	
`}`	

Fig. 1. Refinement types   **Fig. 2.** Strongly updating a location

and a∗ combination of heap predicates, the heap predicates themselves conflate reasoning about links (*e.g.* reachability) and correctness properties (*e.g.* sizes or data invariants), which complicates automatic checking and inference.

In this paper, we introduce *Alias Refinement Types* (ART), a subset of separation logic that reconciles expressiveness and automation by *factoring* the representation of machine state along two independent axes: a *"physical"* component describing the basic shape and linkages between *heap cells* and a *"logical"* component describing semantic or relational properties of the *data* contained within them. We connect the two components in order to describe global logical properties and relationships of heap structures, using *heap binders* that name pure "snapshots" of the mutable data stored on the heap at any given point.

The separation between assertions about the heap's structure and heap-oblivious assertions about pure values allow ART to automatically *infer* precise data invariants. First, the program is type-checked with respect to the physical type system. Next, we generate a system of subtyping constraints over the *logical* component of the type system. Because the logical component of each type is heap-oblivious, solving the system of constraints amounts to solving a system of Horn clauses. We use predicate abstraction to solve these constraints, thus yielding precise refinements that summarize unbounded collections of objects.

In summary, this paper makes the following contributions:

- a description of ART and formalization of a constraint generation algorithm for inferring precise invariants of linked data structures;
- a novel soundness argument in which types are interpreted as assertions in separation logic, and thus typing derivations are interpreted as proofs;
- an evaluation of a prototype implementation that demonstrates ART is effective at verifying and, crucially, inferring data structure properties ranging from the sizes and sorted-ness of linked lists to the invariants defining binary search trees and red-black trees. Our experiments demonstrate that ART requires only 21 % of the annotation required by other techniques to verify intermediate functions in these benchmarks.

2   Overview

Refinements Types and Templates. A *basic* refinement type is a basic type, *e.g. int*, refined with a formula from a decidable logic, *e.g. nat* $\doteq \{\nu : int \mid \; \leqslant \nu\}$

is a refinement type denoting the set of non-negative integers, where *int* is the basic or *physical* part of the type and the refinement $0 \leqslant \nu$ is the *logical* part. A *template* is a refinement type where, instead of concrete formulas we have *variables* κ that denote the unknown to-be-inferred refinements. In the case that the refinement is simply **true**, we omit the refinement (*e.g.* $int = \{\nu : int \mid \textbf{true}\}$). We specify the behaviors of functions using refined function types: $(x_1 : t_1, \ldots, x_n : t_n) \Rightarrow t$. The input refinement types t_i specify the function's *preconditions* and t describes the *postcondition*.

Verification. ART splits verification into two phases: (1) *constraint generation*, which traverses the program to create a set of Horn clause constraints over the κ, and (2) *constraint solving*, which uses an off the shelf predicate abstraction based Horn clause solver [32] that computes a least fixpoint solution that yields refinement types that verify the program. Here, we focus on the novel step (1).

Path Sensitive Environments. To generate constraints ART traverses the code, building up an *environment* of type bindings, mapping program variables to their refinement types (or templates, when the types are unknown.) At each callsite (resp. return), ART generates constraints that the arguments (resp. return value) are a subtype of the input (resp. output) type. Consider **abs** in Fig. 1 which computes the absolute value of the integer input **x**. ART creates a template $(int) \Rightarrow \{\nu : int \mid \kappa_1\}$ where κ_1 denotes the unknown output refinement. (We write nat^1 in the figure to connect the inferred refinement with its κ.) In Fig. 1, the environment after each statement is shown on the right side. The initial environment contains a binder for **x**, which assumes that **x** may be *any int*. In each branch of the **if** statement, the environment is extended with a *guard* predicate reflecting the condition under which the branch is executed. As the type $\{\nu : int \mid \nu = \textbf{x}\}$ is problematic if **x** is mutable, we use SSA renaming to ensure each variable is assigned (statically) at most once.

Subtyping. The returns in the *then* and *else* yield subtyping constraints:

$$\textbf{x}:int, 0 \leqslant \textbf{x} \vdash \&\{\nu : int \mid \nu = \textbf{x}\} \preceq \{\nu : int \mid \kappa_1\}$$
$$\textbf{x}:int, \neg(0 \leqslant \textbf{x}), \textbf{r}:\{\nu : int \mid \nu = 0 - \textbf{x}\} \vdash \&\{\nu : int \mid \nu = \textbf{r}\} \preceq \{\nu : int \mid \kappa_1\} \tag{1}$$

which respectively reduce to the Horn implications

$$(\textbf{true} \wedge 0 \leqslant \textbf{x}) \Rightarrow \&(\nu = \textbf{x}) \Rightarrow \kappa_1$$
$$(\textbf{true} \wedge \neg(0 \leqslant \textbf{x}) \wedge \textbf{r} = 0 - \textbf{x}) \Rightarrow \&(\nu = \textbf{r}) \Rightarrow \kappa_1$$

By predicate abstraction [32] we find the solution $\kappa_1 \doteq 0 \leqslant \nu$ and hence infer that the returned value is a *nat*, *i.e.* non-negative.

References and Heaps. In Fig. 2, **absR** takes a *reference* to a structure containing an *int* valued **data** field, and updates the **data** field to its absolute value. We use κ_2 for the output refinement; hence the type of **absR** desugars to: $(\textbf{x} : \&\textbf{x})/\&\textbf{x} \mapsto \langle \textbf{data} : int \rangle \Rightarrow ()/\&\textbf{x} \mapsto \langle \textbf{data} : \kappa_2 \rangle$ which states that **absR** *requires* a parameter **x** that is a *reference* to a *location* named **&x**. in an *input heap* where **&x** contains a structure with an *int*-valued **data** field. The function

$absL :: (x : list[int]) \Rightarrow ()/\&x \mapsto list[nat^3]$	
`function absL(x){`	$\Gamma_0 \doteq x : \langle \&x \rangle, \Sigma_0 \doteq \&x \mapsto x_0 : list[int]$
`//: unfold(&x);`	$\Gamma_1 \doteq \Gamma_0$
	$\Sigma_1 \doteq \&x \mapsto x_1 : \langle data : int, next : ?\langle \&t \rangle \rangle * \&t \mapsto t_0 : list[int]$
`var d = x.data;`	$\Gamma_2 \doteq d : int, xn : \{\nu : ?\langle \&t \rangle \mid \nu = x_2.next\}, \Gamma_1$
`x.data = abs(d);`	$\Sigma_2 \doteq \&x \mapsto x_2 : \langle data : nat^1, next : ?\langle \&t \rangle \rangle * \&t \mapsto t_0 : list[int]$
`var xn = x.next;`	
`if (xn == null){`	
`//: fold(&x);`	$\Gamma_3 \doteq xn = null, \Gamma_2, \Sigma_3 \doteq \&x \mapsto list[nat^3]$
`  return;`	
`}`	
`absL(xn);`	$\Gamma_4 \doteq xn \neq null; \Gamma_2$
	$\Sigma_4 \doteq \&x \mapsto x_2 : \langle data : nat^1, next : ?\langle \&t \rangle \rangle * \&t \mapsto t_1 : list[nat^3]$
`//: fold(&x);`	$\Gamma_5 \doteq \Gamma_4 \ \Sigma_5 \doteq \&x \mapsto x_3 : list[nat^3]$
`  return;`	
`}`	

Fig. 3. Strongly updating a collection. The `fold` and `unfold` annotations are automatically inserted by a pre-analysis [3]

returns () (*i.e.* no value) in an *output heap* where the location `&x` is *updated* to a structure with a κ_2-valued `data`-field.

We extend the constraint generation to precisely track updates to locations. In Fig. 2, each statement of the code is followed by the environment Γ and heap Σ that exists after the statement executes. Thus, at the start of the function, `x` refers to a location, `&x`, whose `data` field is an arbitrary *int*. The call `abs(d)` returns a κ_1 that is bound to `t`, which is then used to *strongly update* the `data` field of `&x` from *int* to κ_1. At the `return` we generate a constraint that the return value and heap are sub-types of the function's return type and heap. Here, we get the *heap subtyping* constraint:

$$x : \langle \&x \rangle, \ d : int, \ t : \kappa_1 \ \vdash \& \ \&x \mapsto \langle data : \nu = t \rangle \preceq \&x \mapsto \langle data : \kappa_2 \rangle$$

which reduces by field subtyping to the implication: $\kappa_1[t/\nu] \Rightarrow (\nu = t) \Rightarrow \kappa_2$ which (together with the previous constraints) can be solved to $\kappa_2 \doteq 0 \leqslant \nu$ letting us infer that `absR` updates the structure to make `data` non-negative. This is possible because the κ variables denote pure formulas, as reasoning about the heap shape is handled by the alias type system. Next we see how this idea extends to infer strong updates to collections of linked data structures.

Linked Lists. Linked lists can be described as iso-recursive alias types [38]. The definition

$$type \ list[A] \ \doteq \ \exists! \ell \mapsto t : list[A].h : \langle data : A, next? \langle \ell \rangle \rangle$$

says $list[A]$ is a *head* structure with a `data` field of type A, and a `next` field that is either `null` or a reference to the *tail*, denoted by the $?\langle \ell \rangle$ type. The heap $\ell \mapsto t : list[A]$ denotes that a *singleton* $list[A]$ is stored at the location denoted by ℓ *if* it is reachable at runtime. The $\exists!$ quantification means that the tail is *distinct* from every other location, ensuring that the list is inductively defined.

Consider absL from Fig. 3, which updates each data field of a list with its absolute value. As before, we start by creating a κ_3 for the unknown output refinement, so the function gets the template

$$(x : \langle \&x \rangle)/\&x \mapsto x_0 : list[int] \Rightarrow ()/\&x \mapsto x_r : list[\kappa_3]$$

Figure 3 shows the resulting environment and heap after each statement.

The annotations unfold and fold allow ART to manage updates to collections such as lists. In ART, the user *does not* write fold and unfold annotations; these may be inferred by a straightforward analysis of the program [3].

Unfold. The location $\&x$ that the variable x refers to initially contains a $list[int]$ named with a *heap binder* x_0. The binder x_0 may be used in refinements. Suppose that x is a reference to a location containing a value of type $list[A]$. We require that before the fields of x can be accessed, the list must be *unfolded* into a head cell and a tail list. This is formalized with an unfold($\&x$) operation that unfolds the list at $\&x$ from $\&x \mapsto x_0 : list[int]$ to

$$\&x \mapsto x_1 : \langle \mathtt{data} : int, \mathtt{next} ? \langle \&t \rangle \rangle * \&t \mapsto t_0 : list[int],$$

corresponding to *materializing* in shape analysis. The type system guarantees that the head structure and (if next is not null) the newly unfolded tail structure are unique and distinct. So, after unfolding, the structure at $\&x$ can be strongly updated as in absR. Hence, the field assignment generates a fresh binder x_2 for the updated structure whose data field is a κ_1, the output of abs.

Fold. After updating the data field of the head, the function tests whether the next field assigned to xn is null, and if so returns. Since the expected output is a list, ART requires that we *fold* the structure back into a $list[\kappa_3]$ – effectively computing a *summary* of the structure rooted at $\&x$. As xn is null and xn : $\{\nu : ? \langle \&t \rangle \mid \nu = x_2.\mathtt{next}\}$, fold($\&x$) converts $\&x \mapsto x_2 : \langle \mathtt{data} : \kappa_1, \mathtt{next} : ? \langle \&t \rangle \rangle$ to $\&x \mapsto list[\kappa_3]$ *after* generating a heap subtyping constraint which forces the "head" structure to be a subtype of the folded list's "head" structure.

$$\Gamma_3 \vdash \&x \mapsto x_2 : \langle \mathtt{data} : \kappa_1, \ldots \rangle \preceq \&x \mapsto x_2 : \langle \mathtt{data} : \kappa_3, \ldots \rangle \qquad (2)$$

If instead, xn is non-null, the function updates the tail by recursively invoking absL(xn). In this case, we can inductively assume the specification for absL and so in the heap *after* the recursive call, the tail location $\&t$ contains a $list[\kappa_3]$. As xn and hence the next field of x_2 is non-null, the fold($\&x$) transforms

$$\&x \mapsto x_2 : \langle \mathtt{data} : \kappa_1, \mathtt{next} : ? \langle \&t \rangle \rangle * \&t \mapsto t_1 : list[\kappa_3]$$

into $\&x \mapsto list[\kappa_3]$, as required at the return, by generating a heap subtyping constraints for the head and tail:

$$\Gamma_5 \vdash \&x \mapsto x_2 : \langle \mathtt{data} : \kappa_1, \ldots \rangle \preceq \&x \mapsto x_2 : \langle \mathtt{data} : \kappa_3, \ldots \rangle \qquad (3)$$

$$\Gamma_5 \vdash \&\&t \mapsto t_1 : list[\kappa_3] \preceq \&t \mapsto t_1 : list[\kappa_3] \qquad (4)$$

The constraints Eqs. (2), (3) and (4) are simplified field-wise into the implications $\kappa_1 \Rightarrow \kappa_3$, $\kappa_1 \Rightarrow \kappa_3$ and $\kappa_3 \Rightarrow \kappa_3$ which, together with the previous constraints (Eq. (1)) solve to: $\kappa_3 \doteq 0 \leqslant \nu$. Plugging this back into the template for absL we see that we have automatically inferred that the function *strongly* updates the contents of the input list to make *all* the data fields non-negative.

ART *infers* the update the type of the value stored at &x at fold and unfold locations because reasoning about the shape of the updated list is delegated to the alias type system. Prior work in refinement type inference for imperative programs [33] can not type check this simple example as the physical type system is not expressive enough. Increasing the expressiveness of the *physical* type system allows ART to "lift" invariant inference to collections of objects.

Snapshots. So far, our strategy is to factor reasoning about pointers and the heap into a "physical" alias type system, and functional properties (*e.g.* values of the data field) into quantifier- and heap-free "logical" refinements that may be inferred by classical predicate abstraction. However, reasoning about recursively defined properties, such as the length of a list, depends on the interaction between the physical and logical systems.

We solve this problem by associating recursively defined properties *not* directly with mutable collections on the heap, but with immutable *snapshot values* that capture the contents of the collection at a particular point in time. These snapshots are related to the sequences of pure values that appear in the definition of predicates such as list in [31]. Consider the heap Σ defined as:

$$\&x_0 \mapsto h : \langle \text{data} = 0, \text{next} = \&x_1 \rangle * \&x_1 \mapsto t : \langle \text{data} = 1, \text{next} = \text{null} \rangle$$

We say that *snapshot of $\&x_0$ in Σ* is the value v_0 defined as:

$$v_0 \doteq (\&x_0, \langle \text{data} = 0, \text{next} = v_1 \rangle) \quad v_1 \doteq (\&x_1, \langle \text{data} = 1, \text{next} = \text{null} \rangle)$$

Now, the logical system can avoid reasoning about the heap reachable from x_0 – which depends on the heap – and can instead reason about the length of the snapshot v_0 which is independent of the heap.

Heap Binders. We use *heap binders* to name snapshots in the refinement logic. In the desugared signature for absR from Fig. 2,

$$(x : \langle \&x \rangle) / \&x \mapsto x_0 : list[int] \Rightarrow () / \&x \mapsto x_r : list[nat]$$

the name x_0 refers to the snapshot of input heap at &x. In ART, no reachable cell of a folded recursive structure (*e.g.* the list rooted at &x) can be *modified* without first *unfolding* the data structure starting at the root: references pointing into the cells of a folded structure may not be dereferenced. Thus we can soundly update heap binders *locally* without updating transitively reachable cells.

Measures. We formalize structural properties like the *length* of a list or the *height* of a tree and so on, with a class of recursive functions called *measures*,

insert :: $(A, x:?\texttt{list}[A]) \Rightarrow \{\nu:\texttt{list}[A] \mid (\texttt{len}(\nu) = 1 + \texttt{len}(x))^4\}$	
`function insert(k, x)`	$\Gamma_0 = \texttt{k}:A;\ \texttt{x}:?\langle\&\texttt{x}\rangle\ \Sigma_0 = \&\texttt{x} \mapsto x_0:list[A]$
`if (x == null) {`	
`var y =`	$\Gamma_1 \doteq \texttt{y}:\langle\&\texttt{y}\rangle; \texttt{x} = \texttt{null}; \Gamma_0$
`{data:k,next:null};`	$\Sigma_1 \doteq \&\texttt{x} \mapsto x_0:list[A] * \&\texttt{y} \mapsto y_0:\langle\texttt{data}:A, \texttt{next}:\texttt{null}\rangle$
`//: fold(&y)`	$\Gamma_2 \doteq \texttt{len}(y_1) = 1; \Gamma_1$
	$\Sigma_2 \doteq \&\texttt{x} \mapsto x_0:list[A] * \&\texttt{y} \mapsto y_1:list[A]$
`return y;`	
`}`	
`//: unfold(&x)`	$\Gamma_3 \doteq \texttt{len}(x_0) = 1 + \texttt{len}(t_0); x \neq \texttt{null}; \Gamma_0$
	$\Sigma_3 \doteq \&\texttt{x} \mapsto x_1:\langle\texttt{data}:a, \texttt{next}:?\langle\&t\rangle\rangle * \&t \mapsto t_0:list[a]$
`if (k <= x.data) {`	
`var y =`	$\Gamma_4 \doteq \texttt{y}:\langle\&\texttt{y}\rangle; \Gamma_3$
`{data:k,next:x};`	$\Sigma_4 \doteq \&\texttt{y} \mapsto y_2:\langle\texttt{data}:A, \texttt{next}:?\langle\&x\rangle\rangle * \Sigma_3$
`//: fold(&x)`	$\Gamma_5 \doteq \texttt{len}(x_2) = 1 + \texttt{len}(t_0); \Gamma_4$
	$\Sigma_5 \doteq \&\texttt{x} \mapsto x_2:list[A] * \&\texttt{y} \mapsto y_2:\langle\texttt{data}:A, \texttt{next}:?\langle\&x\rangle\rangle$
`//: fold(&y)`	$\Gamma_6 \doteq \texttt{len}(y_3) = 1 + \texttt{len}(x_2); \Gamma_5\ \Sigma_6 \doteq \&\texttt{x} \mapsto y_3:list[A]$
`return y;`	
`}`	
`var z = x.next;`	
`var u = insert(k,z);`	$\Gamma_7 \doteq u_0:\kappa_4[t_0/x_0]; \texttt{u}:\langle\&\texttt{u}\rangle; \texttt{z}:?\langle\&t\rangle; \Gamma_3$
`x.next = u;`	$\Sigma_7 \doteq \&\texttt{x} \mapsto x_1:\langle\texttt{data}:A, \texttt{next}:\langle\&u\rangle\rangle * \&\texttt{u} \mapsto u_0:list[A]$
`//: fold(&x)`	$\Gamma_8 \doteq \texttt{len}(x_2) = 1 + \texttt{len}(u_0); \Gamma_7\ \Sigma_8 \doteq \&\texttt{x} \mapsto x_2:list[A]$
`return x;`	
`}`	

Fig. 4. Inserting into a collection

which are catamorphisms over (snapshot values of) the recursive type. For example, we specify the length of a list with the measure:

$$\texttt{len}: : list[A] \Rightarrow int \qquad \texttt{len}(\texttt{null}) = 0 \qquad \texttt{len}(x) = 1 + \texttt{len}(x.next)$$

We must reason *algorithmically* about these recursively defined functions. The direct approach of encoding measures as *background axioms* is problematic due to the well known limitations and brittleness of quantifier instantiation heuristics [13]. Instead, we encode measures as uninterpreted functions, obeying the congruence axiom, $\forall x, y.x = y \Rightarrow f(x) = f(y)$. Second, we recover the semantics of the function by adding *instantiation constraints* describing the measure's semantics. We add the instantiation constraints at `fold` and `unfold` operations, automating the reasoning about measures while retaining completeness [36].

Consider `insert` in Fig. 4, which adds a key `k` of type `A` into its position in an (ordered) $list[A]$, by traversing the list, and mutating its links to accomodate the new structure containing `k`. We generate a fresh κ_4 for the output type to obtain the function template:

$$(A, \texttt{x}:?\langle\&\texttt{x}\rangle)/\&\texttt{x} \mapsto x_0:list[A] \Rightarrow \langle\&l\rangle/\&l \mapsto \{\nu:list[A] \mid \kappa_4\}$$

Here, the snapshot of the input list `x` upon entry is named with the heap binder x_0; the output list must satisfy the (as yet unknown) refinement κ_4.

Constraint generation proceeds by additionally instantiating measures at each `fold` and `unfold`. When `x` is null, the `fold(&y)` transforms the binding

$\&y \mapsto y_0 : \langle \mathtt{data} : A, \mathtt{next:null} \rangle$ into a (singleton) list $\&y \mapsto y_1 : list[A]$ and so we add the instantiation constraint $\mathsf{len}(y_1) = 1$ to the environment. Hence, the subsequent **return** yields a subtyping constraint over the output list that simplifies to the implication:

$$\mathsf{len}(x_0) = 0 \wedge \mathsf{len}(y_1) = 1 \Rightarrow \nu = y_1 \Rightarrow \kappa_4 \tag{5}$$

When x is non-null, $\mathtt{unfold(\&x)}$ transforms the binding $\&x \mapsto x_0 : list[A]$ to

$$\&x \mapsto x_1 : \langle \mathtt{data} : a, \mathtt{next?} \langle \&t \rangle \rangle * \&t \mapsto t_0 : list[A]$$

yielding the instantiation constraint $\mathsf{len}(x_0) = 1 + \mathsf{len}(t_0)$ that relates the length of the list's snapshot with that of its tail's. When $\mathtt{k <= x.data}$ the subsequent folds create the binders x_2 and y_3 with instantiation constraints relating their sizes. Thus, at the **return** we get the implication:

$$\mathsf{len}(x_0) = 1 + \mathsf{len}(t_0) \wedge \mathsf{len}(x_2) = 1 + \mathsf{len}(t_0) \wedge \mathsf{len}(y_3) = 1 + \mathsf{len}(x_2) \Rightarrow \nu = y_3 \Rightarrow \kappa_4 \tag{6}$$

Finally, in the else branch, after the recursive call to **insert**, and subsequent fold, we get the subtyping implication

$$\mathsf{len}(x_0) = 1 + \mathsf{len}(t_0) \wedge \kappa_4[\nu, x_0/u_0, t_0] \wedge \mathsf{len}(x_2) = 1 + \mathsf{len}(u_0) \Rightarrow \nu = x_2 \Rightarrow \kappa_4 \tag{7}$$

The recursive call that returns u_0 constrains it to satisfy the unknown refinement κ_4 (after substituting t_0 for the input binder x_0). Since the heap is factored out by the type system, the classical predicate abstraction fixpoint computation solves Eqs. (5), (6) and (7) to $\kappa_4 \doteq \mathsf{len}(\nu) = 1 + \mathsf{len}(x_0)$ inferring a signature that states that **insert**'s output has size one more than the input.

Abstract Refinements. Many important invariants of linked structures require us to reason about relationships *between* elements of the structure. Next, we show how our implementation of ART allows us to use *abstract refinements*, developed in the purely functional setting [37], to verify relationships between elements of linked data structures, allowing us to prove that **insertSort** in Fig. 5 returns an ordered list. To this end, we parameterize types with *abstract refinements* that describe relationships between elements of the structure. For example,

$$\mathtt{type} \; list[A]\langle p \rangle \; \doteq \; \exists! l \mapsto t : list[\{\nu : A \mid p(\mathtt{data}, \nu)\}]\langle p \rangle . h : \langle \mathtt{data} : A, \mathtt{next} : ? \langle l \rangle \rangle$$

is the list type as before, but now parameterized by an abstract refinement p which is effectively a relation between two A values. The type definition states that, if the data fields have values $x_1, \ldots, x_n$ where x_i is the ith element of the list, then *for each* $i < j$ we have $p(x_i, x_j)$.

Ordered Lists. We *instantiate* the refinement parameters with concrete refinements to obtain invariants about linked data structures. For example, increasing lists are described by the type $incList[A] \doteq list[A]\langle(\leqslant)\rangle$.

Verification. Properties like sortedness may be *automatically infered* by using liquid typing [32]. ART infers the types:

$$\mathtt{insertSort} :: (?list[A]) \Rightarrow incList[A] \quad \mathtt{insert} :: (A, ?incList[A]) \Rightarrow incList[A]$$

```
(x:?list[A]) ⇒ {ν:?incList[A] | len(ν) = len(x)}
function insertSort(x){
   if (x == null) return null;
   //: unfold(&x);
   var y = insertSort(x.next);
   var t = insert(x.data, y);
   //: fold(&t);
   return t;
}
```

Fig. 5. Insertion Sort

i.e. that `insert` and `insertSort` return sorted lists. Thus, alias refinement types, measures, and abstract refinements enable both the specification and automated verification of functional correctness invariants of linked data structures.

3   Type Inference

To explain how ART infers refinement types as outlined in Sect. 2, we first explain the core features of ART's refinement type system. We focus on the more novel features of our type system; a full treatment may be found in [3].

3.1   Type Rules

Type Environments. We describe ART in terms of an imperative language Imp with record types and with the usual call by value semantics, whose syntax is given in Fig. 6. A *function environment* is defined as a mapping, Φ, from functions f to function schemas S. A *type environment* (Γ) is a sequence of *type bindings* $x:T$ and *guard expressions* e. A *heap* (Σ) is a finite, partial map from locations (ℓ) to type bindings. We write $\Gamma(x)$ to refer to T where $x:T \in \Gamma$, and $\Sigma(\ell)$ to refer to $x:T$ where the mapping $\ell \mapsto x:T \in \Sigma$.

Type Judgements. The type system of ART defines a judgement $\Phi \vdash f :: S$, which says given the environment Φ, the function f behaves according to its pre- and post-conditions as defined by S. An auxiliary judgement $\Phi, \Gamma, \Sigma \vdash s :: \Gamma'/\Sigma'$ says that, given the input environments Γ and Σ, s produces the output environments Γ' and Σ'. We say that a program p *typechecks* with respect to Φ if, for every function f defined in p, $\Phi \vdash f :: \Phi(f)$.

Well-Formedness. We require that types T be *well formed* in their local environments Γ and heaps Σ, written $\Gamma, \Sigma \vdash T$. A heap Σ must heap be well formed in its local environment Γ, written $\Gamma \vdash \Sigma$. The rules for the judgment [3] capture the intuition that a type may only refer to binders in its environment.

Subtyping. We require a notion of subsumption, *e.g.* so that the integer 2 can be typed either as $\{\nu : int \mid \nu = 2\}$ or simply int. The subtyping relation depends on the environment. For example, $\{\nu : int \mid \nu = x\}$ is a subtype of $\{\nu : int \mid \nu = 2\}$

Expressions $e ::= n \mid \texttt{true} \mid \texttt{false} \mid \texttt{null} \mid r_\ell \mid x \mid e \oplus e$	

$$
\begin{aligned}
\textit{Expressions } e &::= n \mid \texttt{true} \mid \texttt{false} \mid \texttt{null} \mid r_\ell \mid x \mid e \oplus e \\
\textit{Statements } s &::= s; s \mid x = e \mid y = x.f \mid x.f = e \mid \texttt{if } e \texttt{ then } s \texttt{ else } s \\
&\quad \mid \texttt{return } e \mid x = \texttt{alloc } \{\overline{f : e}\} \mid x = f(\overline{e}) \\
&\quad \mid \texttt{unfold}(\ell) \mid \texttt{fold}(\ell) \mid \texttt{concr}(x) \mid \texttt{pad}(\ell) \\
\textit{Programs } \quad p &::= \texttt{function } f(\overline{x}) \, \{s\} \\
\textit{Primitive Types } b &::= \textit{int} \mid \textit{bool} \mid \alpha \mid \textit{null} \mid \langle\ell\rangle \mid ?\langle\ell\rangle \\
\textit{Types } \quad \tau &::= b \mid C[\overline{T}] \mid \langle\overline{f : T}\rangle \\
\textit{Refined Types } \quad T &::= \{\nu : \tau \mid p\} \\
\textit{Type Definition } \quad C &::= C[\overline{\alpha}] \doteq \exists! \, \Sigma. \, x : \langle\overline{f : T}\rangle \\
\textit{Contexts } \quad \Gamma &::= \varnothing \mid x : T; \Gamma \mid e; \Gamma \\
\textit{Heaps } \quad \Sigma &::= \texttt{emp} \mid \Sigma * \ell \mapsto x : C[\overline{T}] \mid \Sigma * \ell \mapsto x : \langle\overline{f : T}\rangle \\
\textit{Function Types } \quad S &::= \forall \overline{\ell, \alpha}. \, (\overline{x : T})/\Sigma \Rightarrow \exists! \overline{\ell'}. \, x' : T'/\Sigma'
\end{aligned}
$$

$n \in$ Integers, $\; r_\ell \in$ Reference Constants, $\; x, y, f \in$ Identifiers, $\; \oplus \in \{+, -, \ldots\}$

Fig. 6. Syntax of Imp programs and types

if $x : \{\nu : int \mid \nu = 2\}$ holds as well. Subtyping is formalized by the judgment $\Gamma \vdash T_1 \preceq T_2$, of which selected rules are shown in Fig. 7. Subtyping in Imp reduces to the validity of logical implications between refinement predicates. As the refinements are drawn from a decidable logic of Equality, Linear Arithmetic, and Uninterpreted Functions, validity can be automatically checked by SMT solvers [13]. The last two rules convert between non-null and possibly null references ($\langle\ell\rangle$ and $?\langle\ell\rangle$).

Heap Subtyping. The heap subtyping judgment $\Gamma \vdash \Sigma \preceq \Sigma'$ describes when one heap is subsumed by another. Figure 7 summarizes the rules for heap subsumption. Heap subtyping is *covariant*, which is sound because our type system is flow sensitive – types in the heap are updated *after* executing a statement.

Statements. When the condition x, y *fresh* appears in the antecedent of a rule, it means that x and y are distinct names that do not appear in the input environment Γ or heap Σ. We write $[y/x]$ for the capture avoiding substitution that maps x to y. The rules for sequencing, assignment, control-flow joins, and function calls are relatively straightforward extensions from previous work (*e.g.* [33]). Selected rules are given in Fig. 8. The complete set of rules may be found in [3].

Allocation. In T-ALLOC, a record is constructed from a sequence of field name and expression bindings. The rule types each expression e_f as T_f, generates a record type T, and allocates a fresh location ℓ on the heap whose type is T. To connect fields with their containing records, we create a new binder y denoting the record, and use the helper *NameFields* [3] to *strengthen* the type of each field-binding for y from $f : \{\nu_f : \tau \mid p\}$, to $f : \{\nu_f : \tau \mid p \land \nu_f = \mathsf{Field}(\nu, f)\}$. Here, Field is an uninterpreted function.

Access. T-RD and T-WR both require that non-*null* pointers are used to access a field in a record stored on the heap. As T-ALLOC strengthens each type with *NameFields*, the type for y in T-RD contains the predicate $\nu_{f_i} = \mathsf{Field}(\nu, f_i)$. Any facts established for y are linked, in the refinement logic, with the original

Subtyping $\boxed{\Gamma \vdash T_1 \leq T_2, \ \Gamma \vdash \Sigma \leq \Sigma'}$

$$\frac{Valid(\llbracket \Gamma \rrbracket \Rightarrow \llbracket p \rrbracket \Rightarrow \llbracket p' \rrbracket)}{\Gamma \vdash \{\nu : b \mid p\} \leq \{\nu : b \mid p'\}} \ \leq\text{-B}$$

$$\frac{Valid(\llbracket \Gamma \rrbracket \Rightarrow \llbracket p \rrbracket \Rightarrow \llbracket p' \wedge \nu \neq \texttt{null} \rrbracket)}{\Gamma \vdash \{\nu : ?\langle \ell \rangle \mid p\} \leq \{\nu : \langle \ell \rangle \mid p'\}} \ \leq\text{-DOWN}$$

$$\frac{Valid(\llbracket \Gamma \rrbracket \Rightarrow \llbracket p \rrbracket \Rightarrow \llbracket p' \rrbracket)}{\Gamma \vdash \{\nu : \langle \ell \rangle \mid p\} \leq \{\nu : ?\langle \ell \rangle \mid p'\}} \ \leq\text{-UP1} \quad \frac{Valid(\llbracket \Gamma \rrbracket \Rightarrow \llbracket p \rrbracket \Rightarrow \llbracket p' \rrbracket)}{\Gamma \vdash \{\nu : \texttt{null} \mid p\} \leq \{\nu : ?\langle \ell \rangle \mid p'\}} \ \leq\text{-UP2}$$

$$\frac{}{\Gamma \vdash \mathsf{emp} \leq \mathsf{emp}} \ \leq\text{-EMP} \quad \frac{\Gamma \vdash \Sigma \leq \Sigma' \quad \Gamma \vdash T \leq T'}{\Gamma \vdash \Sigma * \ell \mapsto x : T \leq \Sigma' * \ell \mapsto x : T'} \ \leq\text{-HEAP}$$

Heap Folding $\boxed{\Gamma \vdash x : T_1/\Sigma_1 \rhd x : T_2/\Sigma_2}$

$$\frac{locs(T_1) \cap Dom(\Sigma_1) = \varnothing \quad \Gamma \vdash T_1 \leq T_2}{\Gamma \vdash x : T_1/\Sigma_1 \rhd x : T_2/\Sigma_2} \ \text{F-BASE}$$

$$\frac{\Sigma_1 = \Sigma_1' * \ell \mapsto x : T \quad \Sigma_2 = \Sigma_2' * \ell \mapsto x : T'}{\Gamma \vdash \{\nu : \langle \ell \rangle \mid p\} \leq T_2 \quad \Gamma \vdash x : T/\Sigma_1' \rhd x : T'/\Sigma_2'}{\Gamma \vdash y : \{\nu : \langle \ell \rangle \mid p\}/\Sigma_1 \rhd y : T_2/\Sigma_2} \ \text{F-REF}$$

$$\frac{\Gamma \vdash \{\nu : ?\langle \ell \rangle \mid p\} \leq T_2 \\ \Sigma_1 = \Sigma_1' * \ell \mapsto y : T \quad \Sigma_2 = \Sigma_2' * \ell \mapsto y : T' \\ x : \{\nu : ?\langle \ell \rangle \mid p \wedge \nu \neq null\}; \Gamma \vdash y : T/\Sigma_1' \rhd y : T'/\Sigma_2' \\ x : \{\nu : ?\langle \ell \rangle \mid p \wedge \nu = null\}; \Gamma \vdash y : T/\Sigma_1' \rhd y : T'/\Sigma_2'}{\Gamma \vdash x : \{\nu : ?\langle \ell \rangle \mid p\}/\Sigma_1 \rhd x : T_2/\Sigma_2} \ \text{F-?REF}$$

$$\frac{\Gamma \vdash x : T_i/\Sigma_1 \rhd x : T_i'/\Sigma_2}{\Gamma \vdash y : \langle \overline{f_i : T_i} \rangle/\Sigma_1 \rhd y : \langle \overline{f_i : T_i'} \rangle/\Sigma_2} \ \text{F-HEAP}$$

Fig. 7. Selected subtyping, heap subtyping, and heap folding rules

record's field: when a record field is *mutated*, a *new* type binding is created in the heap, and each unmutated field is linked to the old record using Field.

Concretization. As heaps also contain bindings of names to types, it would be tempting to add these bindings to the *local* environment to strengthen the subtyping context. However, due to the presence of possibly null references, adding these bindings would be unsound. Consider the program fragment:

```
function f(){ return null; }
function g(){ var p = f(); assert(false) }
```

One possible type for f is $()/\mathsf{emp} \Rightarrow \exists ! \ell. \ r : ?\langle \ell \rangle/\ell \mapsto x : \{\nu : int \mid false\}$ because the location ℓ is unreachable. If we added the binding $x : \{\nu : int \mid false\}$ to Γ after the call to f, then the `assert(false)` in g would unsoundly typecheck!

Statement Typing $\boxed{\Phi, \Gamma, \Sigma \vdash s :: \Gamma'/\Sigma'}$

$$\frac{\Gamma \vdash x : \langle \ell \rangle \quad \ell \mapsto z : \langle \overline{f_i : T_i} \rangle \in \Sigma}{\Phi, \Gamma, \Sigma \vdash y = x.f_i :: y : T_i; \Gamma/\Sigma} \quad \text{T-RD}$$

$$\frac{\begin{array}{c} \Gamma \vdash x : \langle \ell \rangle \quad \Gamma \vdash e : \{\nu : \tau \mid p\} \\ T_r = \mathit{NameFields}(z, \langle f_0 : T_0, \ldots, f_i : \{\nu : \tau \mid \nu = e\}, \ldots \rangle) \quad z \text{ fresh} \end{array}}{\Phi, \Gamma, \ell \mapsto y : \langle \overline{f_j : T_j} \rangle * \Sigma \vdash x.f_i = e :: \Gamma/\ell \mapsto z : T_r * \Sigma} \quad \text{T-WR}$$

$$\frac{\text{for each } e_f, \ \Gamma, \Sigma \vdash e_f : T_f \quad T = \mathit{NameFields}(z, \langle \overline{f : T} \rangle) \quad \ell, z \text{ fresh}}{\Phi, \Gamma, \Sigma \vdash x = \texttt{alloc} \ \{\overline{f : e_f}\} :: x : \langle \ell \rangle; \Gamma/\ell \mapsto z : T * \Sigma} \quad \text{T-ALLOC}$$

$$\frac{\Gamma, \Sigma \vdash x : \langle \ell \rangle \quad T_y = \{\nu : \tau \mid p\} \quad T_z = \{\nu : \tau \mid \nu = y\} \quad z \text{ fresh}}{\Phi, \Gamma, \ell \mapsto y : T_y * \Sigma \vdash \texttt{concr}(x) :: y : T_y; \Gamma/\ell \mapsto z : T_z * \Sigma} \quad \text{T-CONCR}$$

$$\frac{\begin{array}{c} \Gamma \vdash C[\overline{\alpha}] = \exists! \ \Sigma_c. \ x_c : T_c \quad C[\overline{\alpha}] \vdash_M \mathsf{m}(x) \doteq e_m \\ \Sigma = \ell \mapsto x : \{\nu : C[\overline{T}] \mid q\} * \Sigma_0 \quad \Sigma' = \ell \mapsto x_c : \overline{[T/\alpha]}T_c * \overline{[T/\alpha]}\Sigma_c * \Sigma_0 \\ \Gamma, \Sigma \vdash \overline{T} \quad \Gamma, \Sigma' \vdash \Sigma' \quad Dom(\Sigma_c), \ Binders(\Sigma_c), \ x_c \text{ fresh} \end{array}}{\Phi, \Gamma, \Sigma \vdash \texttt{unfold}(\ell) :: (\bigwedge_m \mathsf{m}(x) = e_m); \Gamma/\Sigma'} \quad \text{T-UNFOLD}$$

$$\frac{\begin{array}{c} \Gamma \vdash C[\overline{\alpha}] = \exists! \ \Sigma_c. \ x : T_c \\ \Gamma \vdash x : T_x/\Sigma_x \triangleright x : \overline{[T/\alpha]}T_c/\overline{[T/\alpha]}\Sigma_c \quad \Gamma \vdash \ell \mapsto y : T_y * \Sigma' \quad \Gamma \vdash \Sigma \leq \Sigma' \\ C[\overline{\alpha}] \vdash_M \mathsf{m}(x) \doteq e_m \quad T_y = \{\nu : C[\overline{T}] \mid \bigwedge_m \mathsf{m}(\nu) = e_m\} \quad y \text{ fresh} \end{array}}{\Phi, \Gamma, \ell \mapsto x : T_x * \Sigma_x * \Sigma \vdash \texttt{fold}(\ell) :: \Gamma/\ell \mapsto y : T_y * \Sigma'} \quad \text{T-FOLD}$$

Fig. 8. Selected Statement Typing Rules. We assume that type definitions (and, hence, measures over these definitions) $\Gamma \vdash C[\overline{\alpha}] = \exists! \ \Sigma. \ x : T$ are α-convertible.

We thus require that in order to include a heap binder in a local context, Γ, the location must first be made *concrete*, by checking that a reference to it is definitely *not* null. Concretization of a location ℓ is achieved with the *heap annotation* $\texttt{concr}(x)$. Given a non-null reference, T-CONCR transforms the local context Γ and the heap Σ by (1) adding the binding $y : T_y$ at the location ℓ to Γ; (2) adding a *fresh* binding $z : T_z$ at ℓ that expresses the equality $y = z$.

Unfold. T-UNFOLD describes how a type constructor application $C[\alpha]$ may be unfolded according to its definition. The context is modified to contain the new heap locations corresponding to those mentioned in the type's definition. The rule assumes an α-renaming such that the locations and binders appearing in the definition of C are *fresh*, and then instantiates the formal type variables $\overline{\alpha}$ with the actual $\overline{T}$. The environment is strengthened using the thus-instantiated measure bodies.

Fold. Folding a set of heap bindings *into* a data structure is performed by T-FOLD. Intuitively, to fold a heap into a type application of C, we ensure that it is consistent with the definition of C. Note that the rules assume an appropriate α-renaming of the definition of C. Simply requiring that the heap-to-be-folded be a subtype of the definition's heap is too restrictive. Consider the first `fold` in `absL` in Fig. 3. As we have reached the end of the list $xn = \mathtt{null}$ we need to fold

$$\&\mathtt{x} \mapsto x_1 : \langle \mathtt{data} : nat, \mathtt{next}? \langle \&t \rangle \rangle * \&t \mapsto t_0 : list[int]$$

into $\&\mathtt{x} \mapsto x_2 : list[nat]$. An application of heap subtyping, *i.e.* requiring that the heap-to-be-folded is a subtype of the body of the type definition, would require that $\&t \mapsto list[int] \preceq \&t \mapsto list[nat]$, which does not hold! However, the fold *is* safe, as the `next` field is `null`, rendering $\&t$ unreachable. We observe that it is safe to fold a heap into another heap, so long as the sub-heap of the former that is *reachable from a given type* is subsumed by the latter heap.

Our intuition is formalized by the relation $\Gamma, \Sigma \vdash x : T_1 / \Sigma_1 \triangleright x : T_2 / \Sigma_2$, which is read: "given a local context Γ, Σ, the type T_1 and the heap Σ_1 may be folded into the type T_2 and heap Σ_2." F-BASE defines the ordinary case: from the point of view of a type T, any heap Σ_1 may be folded into another heap Σ_2. On the other hand, if T_1 is a reference to a location ℓ, then F-REF additionally requires the folding relation to hold at the type bound at ℓ in Σ_1.

F-?REF splits into two cases, depending on whether the reference is null or not. The relation is checked in two strengthened environments, respectively assuming the reference is in fact null and non-null. This strengthening allows the subtyping judgement to make use reachability. Recall the first fold in `absL` that happens when $\mathtt{xn} = \mathtt{null}$. To check the `fold(&x)`, the rule requires that the problematic heap subtyping $\Gamma \vdash \&t \mapsto list[int] \preceq \&t \mapsto list[nat]$ only holds when `x.next` is non-null, *i.e.* when Γ is

$$\mathtt{xn} : \{\nu :? \langle \&t \rangle \mid \nu = x_2.\mathtt{next}\}, \ \mathtt{xn} = \mathtt{null}, \ x_2.\mathtt{next} \neq \mathtt{null}$$

This heap subtyping reduces to checking the validity of the following, which holds as the antecedent is inconsistent:

$$\mathtt{xn} = x_2.\mathtt{next} \wedge \mathtt{xn} = \mathtt{null} \wedge x_2.\mathtt{next} \neq \mathtt{null} \Rightarrow 0 \leqslant \nu.$$

3.2 Refinement Inference

In the definition of the type system we assumed that type refinements were given. In order to *infer* the refinements, we replace each refinement in a program with a unique variable, κ_i, that denotes the unknown refinement. More formally, let $\hat{\Phi}$ denote a function environment as before except each type appearing in $\hat{\Phi}$ is optionally of the form $\{\nu : \tau \mid \kappa_i\}$, *i.e.* its refinement has been omitted and replaced with a unique κ variable. Given a set of function definitions p and a corresponding environment of *unrefined* function signatures $\hat{\Phi}$, to infer the refinements denoted by each κ we extract a system of Horn clause constraints C. The constraints, C, are *satisfiable* if there exists a mapping of K of κ-variables to refinement formulas such each implication in KC, *i.e.* substituting each κ_i with its image in K, is valid. We solve the constraints by abstract interpretation in the predicate abstraction domain generated from user-supplied predicate templates.

CGen : FunEnv × TypeEnv × HeapEnv × Stmt → {Constr} × TypeEnv × HeapEnv
CGen(Φ,Γ,Σ,s) = **match** s **with**

...

| y = x.f → **let** ℓ = loc(Γ(x)) **in** ({$\Gamma \vdash \Gamma$(x) $\preceq \langle\ell\rangle$}, y:TypeAt($\Sigma,\ell$);$\Gamma,\Sigma$)
| x.f = e → **let** (cs, t)   = CGEx(Γ,Σ,e)
     ℓ = Loc(t)
     (y:T_y, z) = ($\Sigma(\ell)$, FreshId())
     ht   = NameFields(z, T_y[f : Shape(t) $\sqcap$ (v = e)])
  in (cs $\cup$ {$\Gamma \vdash t \preceq \langle\ell\rangle$}, Γ, $\Sigma[\ell \mapsto$z:ht])

Fig. 9. Statement constraint generation

For more details, we refer the reader to [32]. We thus infer the refinements missing from $\hat{\Phi}$ by finding such a solution, if it exists.

Constraint Generation. Constraint generation is carried out by the procedure CGen which takes a function environment (Φ), type environment (Γ), heap environment (Σ), and statement (s) as input, and ouputs (1) a set of Horn constraints over refinement variables κ that appear in Φ, Γ, and Σ; (2) a new type- and heap-environment which correspond to the effect (or post-condition) after running s from the input type and heap environment (pre-condition).

The constraints output by CGen correspond to the well-formedness constraints, $\Gamma, \Sigma \vdash T$, and subtyping constraints, $\Gamma \vdash T \preceq T'$, defined by the type system. *Base* subtyping constraints $\Gamma \vdash \{\nu : b \mid p\} \preceq \{\nu : b \mid q\}$ correspond to the (Horn) Constraint $[\![\Gamma]\!] \Rightarrow p \Rightarrow q$, where $[\![\Gamma]\!]$ is the conjunction of all of the refinements appearing in Γ [32]. *Heap* Subtyping constraints $\Gamma \vdash \Sigma \preceq \Sigma'$ are decomposed via classical subtyping rules into base subtyping constraints between the types stored at the corresponding locations in Σ and Σ'. This step crucially allows the predicate abstraction to sidestep reasoning about reachability and the heap, enabling inference.

CGen proceeds by pattern matching on the statement to be typed. Each FreshType() or Fresh() call generates a new κ variable which may then appear in subtyping constraints as described previously. Thus, in a nutshell, CGen creates Fresh templates for unknown refinements, and then performs a type-based *symbolic execution* to generate constraints over the templates, which are solved to infer precise refinements summarizing functions and linked structures. As an example, the cases of CGen corresponding to T-RD and T-WR are show in Fig. 9.

3.3 Soundness

The constraints output by CGen enjoy the following property. Let (C,Γ',Σ') be the output of CGen($\hat{\Phi},\Gamma,\Sigma$,s). If C is satisfiable, then there exists some solution K such that $K\hat{\Phi}, K\Gamma, K\Sigma \vdash s :: K\Gamma'/K\Sigma'$ [32], that is, there is a type derivation using the refinements from K. Thus K yields the inferred program typing $\Phi \doteq K\hat{\Phi}$, where each unknown refinement has been replaced with its solution, such that $\Phi \vdash f :: \Phi(f)$ for each f defined in the program p.

To prove the soundness of the type system, we translate types, environments and heaps into separation logic *assertions* and hence, typing derivations into *proofs* by using the interpretation function $[\![\,\cdot\,]\!]$. We prove [3] the following:

Theorem 1. [Typing Translation]

- *If $\Phi, \Gamma, \Sigma \vdash s :: \Gamma'/\Sigma'$ then $[\![\Phi]\!] \vdash \{[\![\Gamma, \Sigma]\!]\}\, s\, \{[\![\Gamma', \Sigma']\!]\}$*
- *If $\Phi \vdash f :: S$ then $[\![\Phi]\!] \vdash \{Pre(S)\}\, Body(f)\, \{Post(S)\}$*

Pre(S), *Post(S)* and *Body(f)* are the translations of the input and output types of the function, the function (body) statement. As a corollary of this theorem, our main soundness result follows:

Corollary 1. [Soundness] *If $\Phi, \varnothing, emp \vdash s :: \Gamma/\Sigma$, then $[\![\Phi]\!] \vdash \{true\}\, s\, \{true\}$*

If we typecheck a program in the empty environment, we get a valid separation logic proof of the program starting with the pre-condition *true*. We can encode programmer-specified `asserts` as calls to a special function whose type encodes the assertion. Thus, the soundness result says that if a program typechecks then on *all* executions of the program, starting from *any* input state: (1) all memory accesses occur on non-*null* pointers, and (2) all assertions succeed.

4   Experiments

We have implemented alias refinement types in a tool called ART. The user provides (unrefined) function signatures, and ART infers (1) annotations required for alias typing, and (2) refinements that capture correctness invariants. We evaluate ART on two dimensions: the first demonstrates that it is *expressive* enough to verify a variety of sophisticated properties for linked structures; the second that it provides a significant *automation* over the state-of-the-art, represented by the SMT-based VCDRYAD system. VCDRYAD has annotations comparable to other recent tools that use specialized decision procedures to discharge Separation Logic VCs [11]. Our benchmarks are available at [1].

Expressiveness. Table 1 summarizes the set of data structures, procedures, and properties we used to evaluate the expressiveness of ART. The user provides the type definitions, functions (with unrefined type signatures), and refined type specifications to be verified for top-level functions, *e.g.* the top-level specification for `insertSort`. **LOC** is lines of code and **T**, the verification time in seconds.

We verified the following properties, where applicable: [Len] the output data structures have the expected length; [Keys] the elements, or "keys" stored in each data structure [Sort] the elements are in sorted order [Order] the ouput elements have been labeled in the correct order (*e.g.* preorder) [Heap] the elements satisfy the max heap property [BST] the structure satisfies the binary search tree property [Red-black] the structure satisfies the red-black tree property.

Table 1. Experimental Results (Expressiveness)

Data Structure	Properties	Procedures	LOC	T
Singly linked list	Len, Keys	append, copy, del, find, insBack, insFront, rev	73	2
Doubly linked list	Len, Keys	append, del, delMid, insBack, insMid, insFront	90	16
Cyclic linked list	Len, Keys	delBack, delFront, insBack, insFront	49	2
Sorted linked list	Len, Keys, Sort	rev, double, pairwiseSum, insSort, mergeSort, quickSort	135	10
Binary Tree	Order, Keys	preOrder, postOrder, inOrder	31	2
Max heap	Heap, Keys	heapify	48	27
Binary search tree	BST, Keys	ins, find, del	105	11
Red-black tree	Red-black, BST, Keys	ins, del	322	213

Automation. To demonstrate the effectiveness of *inference*, we selected benchmarks from Table 1 that made use of loops and intermediate functions requiring extra proof annotations in the form of pre- and post-conditions in VCDRYAD, and then used type inference to infer the intermediate pre- and post-conditions. The results of these experiments is shown in Table 2. We omit incomparable benchmarks, and those where the implementations consist of a single top-level function. We compare the number of tokens required to specify type refinements (in the case of ART) and pre- and post-conditions (for VCDRYAD). The table distinguishes between two types of annotations: (1) those required to specify the desired behavior of the top-level procedure, and (2) additional annotations required (such as intermediate function specifications). Our results suggest that it is possible to verify the correctness of a variety of data-structure manipulating algorithms without requiring many annotations beyond the top-level specification. On the benchmarks we examined, overall annotations required by ART were about 34 % of those required by VCDRYAD. Focusing on intermediate function specification, ART required about 21 % of the annotation required by VCDRYAD.

Limitations. Intuitively, ART is limited to "tree-like" ownership structures: while sharing and cycles are allowed (as in double- or cyclic-lists), there is a tree-like *backbone* used for traversal. For example, even with a singly linked list, our system will reject programs that traverse deep into the list, and return a pointer to a cell *unboundedly* deep inside the list. We believe it is possible to exploit the connection made between the SL notion of "magic wands" and the type-theoretic notion of "zippers" [18] identified in [34] to enrich the alias typing discipline to accommodate such access patterns.

Table 2. Experimental results (Inference). For each procedure listed we compare the number of tokens used to specify: **ART** Type refinements for the top-level procedure in ART; **ART** Annot manually-provided predicate templates required to infer the necessary types [32]; **VCDryad** Spec pre- and post-conditions of the corresponding top-level VCDryad procedure; and **VCDryad** Annot loop invariants as well as the specifications required for intermediate functions in VCDryad. ART Annot totals include only *unique* predicate templates across benchmarks.

Data Structure	Procedure	ART		VCDryad	
		Specification	Annotation	Specification	Annotation
Singly Linked List	(definition)	34	-	31	-
	rev	5	0	11	15
Sorted Linked List	(definition)	38	-	50	-
	rev	11	9	17	15
	double	0	4	7	54
	pairwiseSum	0	4	13	75
	insSort	5	0	20	17
	mergeSort	5	18	18	79
	quickSort	5	18	11	140
Binary Search Tree	(definition)	58	-	55	-
	del	7	32	20	33
	Total	168	63	253	428

5 Related Work

Physical Type Systems. ART infers logical invariants in part by leveraging the technique of alias typing [2,38], in which access to dynamically-allocated memory is factored into references and capabilities. In [8,29], capabilities are used to decouple references from regions, which are collections of values. In these systems, algebraic data types with an ML-like "match" are used to discover spatial properties, rather than null pointer tests. fold &unfold are directly related to roll &unroll in [38]. These operations, which give the program access to quantified heap locations, resemble reasoning about capabilities [29,35]. These systems are primarily restricted to verifying (non-)aliasing properties and finite, non-relational facts about heap cells (*i.e.* "typestates"), instead of functional correctness invariants. A possible avenue of future work would be to use a more sophisticated physical type system to express more data structures with sharing.

Logical Type Systems. Refinement types [20,25,39], encode invariants about recursive algebraic data types using indices or refinements. These approaches are limited to *purely functional* languages, and hence cannot verify properties of linked, mutable structures. ART brings logical types to the imperative setting by using [38] to structure and reason about the interaction with the heap.

Interactive Program Logics. Several groups have built interactive verifiers and used them to verify data structure correctness [12,41]. These verifiers require the programmer write pre- and postconditions and loop invariants in addition to top-level correctness specifications. The system generates verification conditions (VCs) which are proved with user interaction. [19] uses symbolic execution and SMT solvers together with user-supplied tactics and annotations to prove programs. [10,24] describe separation logic frameworks for Coq and tactics that provide some automation. These are more expressive than ART but require non-trivial user assistance to prove VCs.

Automatic Separation Logics. To automate the proofs of VCs (*i.e.* entailment), one can design decision procedures for various fragments of SL, typically restricted to common structures like linked lists. [4] describes an entailment procedure for linked lists, and [6,14,16] extend the logic to include constraints on list data. [5,21,27,28] describe SMT-based entailment by reducing formulas (from a list-based fragment) to first-order logic, combining reasoning about shape with other SMT theories. The above approaches are not extensible (*i.e.* limited to list-segments); other verifiers support user defined, separation-logic predicates, with various heuristics for entailment [9,11]. ART is related to natural proofs [26,30] and the work of Heule et al. [17], which instantiate recursive predicates using the local footprint of the heap accessed by a procedure, similar to how we insert `fold` and `unfold` heap annotations, enabling generalization and instantiation of structure properties. Finally, heap binders make it possible to use recursive functions (e.g. measures) over ADTs in the imperative setting. While our measure instantiation [20] requires the programmer adhere to a typing discipline, it does not require us to separately prove that the function enjoys special properties [36].

Inference. The above do not deal with the problem of inferring annotations like the inductive invariants (or pre- and post- conditions) needed to generate appropriately strong VCs. To address this problem, there are several abstract interpreters [22] tailored to particular data structures like list-segments [40], lists-with-lengths [23]. Another approach is to combine separate domains for heap and data with widening strategies tailored to particular structures [7,15]. These approaches conflate reasoning about the heap and data using monolithic assertions or abstract domains, sacrificing either automation or expressiveness.

Acknowledgement. This work was supported by NSF grants CCF-1422471, C1223850, CCF-1218344, and a generous gift from Microsoft Research.

References

1. https://github.com/UCSD-PL/nano-js/tree/vmcai_2016/tests/eval
2. Ahmed, A., Fluet, M., Morrisett, G.: L^3: a linear language with locations. Fundam. Inf. **77**(4), 397–449 (2007)
3. Bakst, A., Jhala, R.: Predicate abstraction for linked data structures. http://arxiv.org/abs/1505.02298
4. Berdine, J., Calcagno, C., O'hearn, P.W.: Smallfoot: modular automatic assertion checking with separation logic. In: de Boer, F.S., Bonsangue, M.M., Graf, S., de Roever, W.-P. (eds.) FMCO 2005. LNCS, vol. 4111, pp. 115–137. Springer, Heidelberg (2006)

5. Botinčan, M., Parkinson, M., Schulte, W.: Separation logic verification of c programs with an smt solver. ENTCS **254**, 5–23 (2009)
6. Bouajjani, A., Drăgoi, C., Enea, C., Sighireanu, M.: Accurate invariant checking for programs manipulating lists and arrays with infinite data. In: Chakraborty, S., Mukund, M. (eds.) ATVA 2012. LNCS, vol. 7561, pp. 167–182. Springer, Heidelberg (2012)
7. Chang, B.E., Rival, X.: Relational inductive shape analysis. In: POPL (2008)
8. Charguéraud, A., Pottier, F.: Functional translation of a calculus of capabilities. In: Hook, J., Thiemann, P. (eds.), Proceeding of the 13th ACM SIGPLAN International Conference on Functional Programming (ICFP 2008), pp. 213–224. ACM (2008)
9. Chin, W.-N., David, C., Nguyen, H., Qin, S.: Automated verification of shape, size and bag properties via user-defined predicates in separation logic. Sci. Comput. Program. **77**(9), 1006–1036 (2012)
10. Chlipala, A.: Mostly-automated verification of low-level programs in computational separation logic. In: PLDI. ACM (2011)
11. Chu, D.-H., Jaffar, J., Trinh, M.-T.: Automatic induction proofs of data-structures in imperative programs. In: Proceedings of the 36th ACM SIGPLAN Conference on Programming Language Design and Implementation, Portland, OR, USA, June 15–17, 2015, pP. 457–466 (2015)
12. Cohen, E., Dahlweid, M., Hillebrand, M., Leinenbach, D., Moskal, M., Santen, T., Schulte, W., Tobies, S.: VCC: a practical system for verifying concurrent C. In: Berghofer, S., Nipkow, T., Urban, C., Wenzel, M. (eds.) TPHOLs 2009. LNCS, vol. 5674, pp. 23–42. Springer, Heidelberg (2009)
13. Detlefs, D., Nelson, G., Saxe, J.B.: Simplify: a theorem prover for program checking. J. ACM **52**(3), 365–473 (2005)
14. Dudka, K., Peringer, P., Vojnar, T.: Predator: a practical tool for checking manipulation of dynamic data structures using separation logic. In: Gopalakrishnan, G., Qadeer, S. (eds.) CAV 2011. LNCS, vol. 6806, pp. 372–378. Springer, Heidelberg (2011)
15. Gulwani, S., McCloskey, B., Tiwari, A.: Lifting abstract interpreters to quantified logical domains. In: POPL, pp. 235–246 (2008)
16. Haase, C., Ishtiaq, S., Ouaknine, J., Parkinson, M.J.: SeLoger: a tool for graph-based reasoning in separation logic. In: Sharygina, N., Veith, H. (eds.) CAV 2013. LNCS, vol. 8044, pp. 790–795. Springer, Heidelberg (2013)
17. Heule, S., Kassios, I.T., Müller, P., Summers, A.J.: Verification condition generation for permission logics with abstract predicates and abstraction functions
18. Gérard, P.: Huet. The zipper. J. Funct. Program. **7**(5), 549–554 (1997)
19. Jacobs, B., Smans, J., Philippaerts, P., Vogels, F., Penninckx, W., Piessens, F.: VeriFast: a powerful, sound, predictable, fast verifier for C and Java. In: Bobaru, M., Havelund, K., Holzmann, G.J., Joshi, R. (eds.) NFM 2011. LNCS, vol. 6617, pp. 41–55. Springer, Heidelberg (2011)
20. Kawaguchi, M., Rondon, P., Jhala, R.: Type-based data structure verification. In: PLDI (2009)
21. Lahiri, S.K., Qadeer, S.: Back to the future: revisiting precise program verification using smt solvers. In: POPL (2008)
22. Lev-Ami, T., Sagiv, M.: TVLA: a system for implementing static analyses. In: Palsberg, J. (ed.) SAS 2000. LNCS, vol. 1824, pp. 280–301. Springer, Heidelberg (2000)

23. Magill, S., Tsai, M.-H., Lee, P., Tsay, Y.-K.: THOR: a tool for reasoning about shape and arithmetic. In: Gupta, A., Malik, S. (eds.) CAV 2008. LNCS, vol. 5123, pp. 428–432. Springer, Heidelberg (2008)
24. Nanevski, A., Morrisett, G., Shinnar, A., Govereau, P., Birkedal, L.: Ynot: reasoning with the awkward squad. In: ICFP (2008)
25. Nystrom, N., Saraswat, V., Palsberg, J., Grothoff, C.: Constrained types for object-oriented languages. In: OOPSLA. ACM (2008)
26. Pek, E., Qiu, X., Madhusudan, P.: Natural proofs for data structure manipulation in c using separation logic. In: Proceedings of the 35th ACM SIGPLAN Conference on Programming Language Design and Implementation, pp. 46. ACM (2014)
27. Navarro Pérez, J.A., Rybalchenko, A.: Separation logic+ superposition calculus = heap theorem prover. In: PLDI (2011)
28. Piskac, R., Wies, T., Zufferey, D.: Automating separation logic using SMT. In: Sharygina, N., Veith, H. (eds.) CAV 2013. LNCS, vol. 8044, pp. 773–789. Springer, Heidelberg (2013)
29. Pottier, F., Protzenko, J.: Programming with permissions in mezzo. In: ICFP (2013)
30. Qiu, X., Garg, P., Stefanescu, A., Madhusudan, P.: Natural proofs for structure, data, and separation. In: PLDI (2013)
31. Reynolds, J.C.: Separation logic: a logic for shared mutable data structures. In: LICS (2002)
32. Rondon, P., Kawaguchi, M., Jhala, R.: Liquid types. In: PLDI (2008)
33. Rondon, P., Kawaguchi, M., Jhala, R.: Low-level liquid types. In: POPL (2010)
34. Schwerhoff, M., Summers, A.J.: Lightweight support for magic wands in an automatic verifier. In: 29th European Conference on Object-Oriented Programming, ECOOP 2015, July 5–10, 2015, Prague, Czech Republic, pp. 614–638 (2015)
35. Sunshine, J., Naden, K., Stork, S., Aldrich, J., Tanter, E.: First-class state change in plaid. In: OOPSLA (2011)
36. Suter, P., Dotta, M., Kuncak, V.: Decision procedures for algebraic data types with abstractions. In: POPL (2010)
37. Vazou, N., Rondon, P.M., Jhala, R.: Abstract refinement types. In: Felleisen, M., Gardner, P. (eds.) ESOP 2013. LNCS, vol. 7792, pp. 209–228. Springer, Heidelberg (2013)
38. Walker, D., Morrisett, J.G.; Alias types for recursive data structures. In: Types in Compilation (2000)
39. Xi, H., Pfenning, F.: Dependent types in practical programming. In: POPL (1999)
40. Yang, H., Lee, O., Berdine, J., Calcagno, C., Cook, B., Distefano, D., O'hearn, P.W.: Scalable shape analysis for systems code. In: Gupta, A., Malik, S. (eds.) CAV 2008. LNCS, vol. 5123, pp. 385–398. Springer, Heidelberg (2008)
41. Zee, K., Kuncak, V., Rinard, M.C.: Full functional verification of linked data structures. In: PLDI, pp. 349–361 (2008)

An Abstract Domain of Uninterpreted Functions

Graeme Gange[1]([✉]), Jorge A. Navas[2], Peter Schachte[1], Harald Søndergaard[1], and Peter J. Stuckey[1]

[1] Department of Computing and Information Systems, The University of Melbourne, Melbourne, VIC 3010, Australia
{gkgange,schachte,harald,pstuckey}@unimelb.edu.au
[2] NASA Ames Research Center, Moffett Field, CA 94035, USA
jorge.a.navaslaserna@nasa.gov

Abstract. We revisit relational static analysis of numeric variables. Such analyses face two difficulties. First, even inexpensive relational domains scale too poorly to be practical for large code-bases. Second, to remain tractable they have extremely coarse handling of non-linear relations. In this paper, we introduce the subterm domain, a weakly relational abstract domain for inferring equivalences amongst sub-expressions, based on the theory of uninterpreted functions. This provides an extremely cheap approach for enriching non-relational domains with relational information, and enhances precision of both relational and non-relational domains in the presence of non-linear operations. We evaluate the idea in the context of the software verification tool SeaHorn.

1 Introduction

This paper investigates a new approach to relational analysis. Our aim is to develop a method that scales to very large code bases, yet maintains a reasonable degree of precision, also for programs that use non-linear numeric operations.

Abstract interpretation is a well-established theoretical framework for sound reasoning about program properties. It provides means for comparing program analyses, especially with respect to the granularity of information (precision) that analyses allow us to statically extract from programs. On the whole, reducing such questions to questions about *abstract domains*. An abstract domain, essentially, specifies the (limited) language of judgements we are able to use when reasoning statically about a program's runtime behaviour.

A class of abstract domains that has received particular attention are the *numeric* domains—those supporting reasoning about variables of numeric (often integer or rational) type. Numeric domains are important because of the numerous applications in termination and safety analyses, such as overflow detection and out-of-bounds array analysis. The *polyhedral* abstract domain [9] allows us to express linear arithmetic constraints (equalities and inequalities) over program state spaces of arbitrary finite dimension k. But high expressiveness comes at a cost; analysis using the polyhedral domain does not scale well to large code bases. For this reason, a number of abstract domains have been proposed, seeking to strike a better balance between cost and expressiveness.

B. Jobstmann and K.R.M. Leino (Eds.): VMCAI 2016, LNCS 9583, pp. 85–103, 2016.
DOI: 10.1007/978-3-662-49122-5_4

Language Restriction. The primary way of doing this is to limit expressiveness, that is, to restrict the language of allowed judgements. Most commonly this is done by expressing only 1- or 2-dimensional projections of the program's (abstract) state space, often banning all but a limited set of coefficients in linear constraints. Examples of this kind of restriction to polyhedral analysis abound, including zones [19], TVPI [22,23], octagons [20], pentagons [18], and logahedra [14]. These avoid the exponential behaviour of polyhedra, instead offering polynomial (typically quadratic or cubic) decision and normalization procedures. Still, they have been observed to be too expensive in practice for industrial codebases [18,24]. Hence other "restrictive" techniques have been proposed which are sometimes integral to an analysis, sometimes orthogonal.

Dimensionality Restriction. These methods aim to lower the dimension k of the program (abstract) state space, by replacing the full space with several lower-dimension subspaces. Variables are separated into "buckets" or *packs* according to some criterion. Usually the packs are disjoint, and relations can be explored only amongst variables in the same pack (relaxations of this have also been proposed [4]). The criterion for pack membership may be syntactic [8] or determined dynamically [24]. A variant is to only permit relations between sets; in the Gauge domain [25], relations are only maintained between program variables and introduced loop counters, not between sets of program variables.

Closure Restriction. Some methods abandon the systematic transitive closure of relations (and therefore lack a normal form for constraints). Constraints that follow by transitive closure may be discovered lazily, or not at all. Closure restriction was used successfully with the pentagon domain; a tolerable loss of precision was compensated for by a significant cost reduction [18].

All of the work discussed up to this point has, in some sense, started from an ideal (polyhedral) analysis and applied restrictions to the degree of "relationality." A different line of work starts from very basic analyses and adds mechanisms to capture relational information. These approaches do not focus on restrictions, but rather on how to compensate for limited precision using "symbolic" reasoning. Such symbolic methods maintain selected syntactic information about computations and use this to enhance precision. The primary examples are Miné's *linearization* method [21], based on "symbolic constant propagation" and Chang and Leino's congruence closure extension [5].

Polyhedral analysis and its restrictions tend to fall back on overly coarse approximation when faced with non-linear operations such as multiplication, modulus, or bitwise operations. Higher precision is desirable, assuming the associated cost is limited. Consider the example shown in Fig. 1(a). Figure 2(a) shows the possible program states when execution reaches point A. With octagons, the strongest claim that can be made at that point is

$$0 \leq x \leq 10, -10 \leq y \leq 10, y - z \leq 90, z - y \leq 90, x + z \geq -90, z - x \leq 90$$

```
     x = nondet(0,10)           u = nondet(0,10)
     y = nondet(-10,10)         v = nondet(0,10)
     z = x*y                    w = nondet(0,10)
 A:                             if (*)
     if (y < 0) {                   t = u + v   else t = u + w
         z = -z                 if (t < 3)
     }                              u = u + 3   else u = 3
 B:                         C:
```

(a)   (b)

Fig. 1. Two example programs

Fig. 2(b) shows the projection on the y-z plane. Almost all interaction between y and z has been lost and as a result, we fail to detect that z is non-negative at point B. The best possible polyhedral approximation adds

$$z \geq -10x, z \geq 10x + 10y - 100, z \leq 10x, z \leq 100 - 10x + 10y$$

While this expresses more of the relationship between x, y and z, we can still only infer $z \geq -50$ at point B.

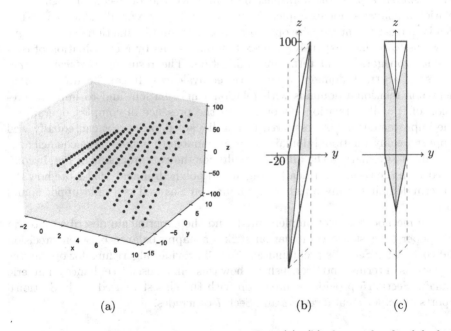

(a)   (b)   (c)

Fig. 2. (a) The reachable states at point A in Fig. 1(a); (b) the result of polyhedral analysis at point A, projected onto the y-z plane, assuming analysis performs case split on the sign of y (the convex hull forming a lozenge);(c) the result of polyhedral analysis at point B. Dashed lines show octagon invariants.

Table 1. States inferred for Fig. 1's programs, points B (left) and C (right)

Octagons	$y - z \leq 90, z - y \leq 90,$	$0 \leq t, 3 \leq u \leq 20, u + t \leq 23$
	$x + z \geq -90, z - x \leq 90$	
Polyhedra	$z \geq -10x, z \geq 10x + 10y - 100,$	$0 \leq t \leq 20, 3 \leq u \leq 5$
	$z \leq 10x, z \leq 100 - 10x + 10y$	
Subterms	$0 \leq z \leq 100$	$0 \leq t \leq 20, 3 \leq u \leq 5$

In practice, weaker results may well be produced. A commonly used octagon library yields $y \in [-10, 10], z \in [-100, 100]$, rather than the dashed projections shown in Fig. 2(b) and (c). For polyhedral analysis, multiplication is often handled by projection and case-splitting. The two grey triangles in Fig. 2(b) show the result, at point A, of case analysis according to the sign of y, as projected onto the y-z plane; the lozenge is the convex hull. This explains how a commonly used library infers $\{z \geq 5y - 50, z \leq 5y + 50\}$ at point A. The pen-nib shaped area in Fig. 2(c) shows the result, at point B, of polyhedral analysis. Note that the triangle below the y axis is in fact infeasible.

Contribution. The proposal presented in this paper differs from all of the above. It combines closure restriction and a novel symbolic approach. We extract and utilise *shared expression* information to improve the precision of cheap non-relational analyses (for example, interval analysis), at a small added cost. The idea is to treat the arithmetic operators as uninterpreted function symbols. This allows us to replace expensive convex hull operations by a combination of constraint propagation and term anti-unification. The resulting *subterm domain* ST is an abstract domain of syntactic equivalences. It can be used to augment non-relational domains with relational information, and to improve precision of (possibly relational) domains in the presence of complex operations. The improvement is not restricted to non-linear operations; it can equally well support weakly relational domains that are unable to handle large coefficients.

Table 1 summarises the analysis results for the two programs in Fig. 1, compared with the results of (ideal) octagon and polyhedral analysis.[1] Note how the subterm domain obtains a tight lower bound on z as well as a tight upper bound on u.

The method has been implemented, and the experiments described later in this paper suggest the combination strikes a happy balance between precision and cost. After Sect. 2's preliminaries, Sect. 3 provides algorithms for operations on systems of terms, and Sect. 4 shows how this can be used to enhance a numeric domain. Section 5 provides comparison with the closest related work. Section 6 reports on experimental results and Sect. 7 concludes.

---

[1] We show transitive reductions and omit trivial bounds for variables. The result obtained by the subterm domain for C, includes, behind the scenes, a *term equation* $t = u + s$ and a bound $0 \leq s \leq 10$ on the freshly introduced variable s.

2 Preliminaries

Abstract Interpretation. In standard abstract interpretation, a concrete domain $C^{\natural}$ and its abstraction $C^{\#}$ are related by a *Galois connection* (α, γ), consisting of an abstraction function $\alpha : C^{\natural} \mapsto C^{\#}$ and concretization function $\gamma : C^{\#} \rightarrow C^{\natural}$. The best approximation of a function $f^{\natural}$ on $C^{\natural}$ is $f^{\#}(\varphi) = \alpha(f^{\natural}(\gamma(\varphi)))$. When analysing imperative programs, $C^{\natural}$ is typically the power-set of program states, and the corresponding lattice operations are $(\subseteq, \cup, \cap)$.

In a non-relational (or *independent attribute*) domain, the abstract state is either the bottom value $\perp_D$ (denoting an infeasible state), or a separate non-$\perp$ abstraction $x^{\#}$ for each variable x in some domain D_V (where each variable admits some feasible value). That is, $D = \{\perp_D\} \cup (D_V \setminus \{\perp_D\})^{|V|}$.

Sometimes *backwards* reasoning is required, to infer the set of states which may/must give rise to some property. The *pre-image* transformer $F_D^{-1}(\llbracket S \rrbracket)(\varphi)$ yields φ_{pre} such that $(F_D(\llbracket S \rrbracket)(\varphi') = \varphi) \Rightarrow (\varphi' \sqsubseteq \varphi_{pre})$. Finding the minimal pre-image of a complex (non-linear) operation can be quite expensive, so pre-image transformers provided by numeric domains are usually coarse approximations.

We shall sometimes need to *rename* abstract values. Given a binary relation $\pi \subseteq V \times V'$ and an element φ of an independent attribute domain over V, the renaming $\pi(\varphi)$ is given by:

$$rename_{\pi}(\varphi) = \{x' \mapsto \prod_{(x,x')\in\pi}^{D} \varphi(x) \mid x' \in image(\varphi)\}$$

The corresponding operation is more involved for relational domains. Assuming $\mathcal{D}$ is closed under existential quantification, $\mathcal{D}$ can maintain systems of equalities and V and V' are disjoint, we have $rename_{\pi}(\varphi) = \exists V. (\varphi \sqcap \{x = x' \mid (x, x') \in \pi\})$.

Term Equations. The set $\mathcal{T}$ of *terms* is defined recursively: every term is either a variable $v \in TVar$ or a construction $F(t_1, \ldots, t_n)$, where $F \in Fun$ has arity $n \geq 0$ and $t_1, \ldots, t_n$ are terms. A *substitution* is an almost-identity mapping $\theta \in TVar \rightarrow \mathcal{T}$, naturally extended to $\mathcal{T} \rightarrow \mathcal{T}$. We use standard notation for substitutions; for example, $\{x \mapsto t\}$ is the substitution θ such that $\theta(x) = t$ and $\theta(v) = v$ for all $v \neq x$. Any term $\theta(t)$ is an *instance* of term t.

If we define $t \sqsubseteq t'$ iff $t = \theta(t')$ for some substitution θ then $\sqsubseteq$ is a preorder. Define $t \equiv t'$ iff $t \sqsubseteq t' \wedge t' \sqsubseteq t$. The set $\mathcal{T}_{/\equiv} \cup \{\perp\}$, that is $\mathcal{T}$ partitioned into equivalence classes by $\equiv$ plus $\{\perp\}$, is known to form a complete lattice, the so-called *term lattice*.[2] A *unifier* of $t, t' \in \mathcal{T}$ is an idempotent substitution θ such that $\theta(t) = \theta(t')$. A unifier θ of t and t' is a *most general unifier* of t and t' iff $\theta' = \theta' \circ \theta$ for every unifier θ' of t and t'.

If we can calculate most general unifiers then we can find meets in the term lattice: if θ is a most general unifier of t and t' then $\theta(t)$ is the most general term that simultaneously is an instance of t and an instance of t', so $\theta(t)$ is the meet of t and t'. Similarly, the join of t and t' is the *most specific generalization*; algorithms are available that calculate most specific generalizations [15].

---

[2] $\sqsubseteq$ is extended to the term lattice by defining $\perp \sqsubseteq t$ for all elements $t \in \mathcal{T}_{/\equiv}$.

Given a set of terms $S \subseteq \mathcal{T}$ and equivalences $E \subseteq (S \times S)$, we can partition S into equivalent terms. Terms t and s are *equivalent* ($t \equiv s$) if they are identical constants, are *deemed* equal, or $t = f(t_1, \ldots, t_m)$ and $s = f(s_1, \ldots, s_m)$ such that for all i, $t_i \equiv s_i$. Finding this partitioning is the well-studied *congruence closure* problem, of complexity $\mathrm{O}(|S| \log |S|)$ [10]. Of relevance is the case $|E| = 1$ (introduction of a single equivalence), which can be handled in $\mathrm{O}(|S|)$ time.

In the following, it will be necessary to distinguish a term as an object from the syntactic expression it represents. We shall use $\mathbf{id}(t)$ to denote the *name* of a term, and $\mathbf{def}(t)$ to denote the expression.

3   The Subterm Domain $\mathcal{ST}$

An element of the subterm domain consists of a mapping $\eta : V \mapsto \mathcal{T}$ of program variables to terms. While the domain structure derives from uninterpreted functions, we must reason about the corresponding concrete computations. We accordingly assume each function symbol F has been given a semantic function $\mathbb{S}(F) : \mathcal{S}^n \to \mathcal{S}$. Given some assignment $\theta : TVar \to \mathcal{S}$ of *term variables* to scalar values, we can then recursively define the evaluation $\mathbb{E}(t, \theta)$ of a term under θ.

$$\mathbb{E}(x, \theta) = \theta(x)$$
$$\mathbb{E}(f(t_1, \ldots, t_n), \theta) = \mathbb{S}(f)(\mathbb{E}(t_1, \theta), \ldots, \mathbb{E}(t_n, \theta))$$

We say a concrete state $\{x_1 \mapsto v_1, \ldots, x_n \mapsto v_n\}$ *satisfies* mapping η iff there is an assignment θ of values to term variables such that for all x_i, $\mathbb{E}(\eta(x_i), \theta) = v_i$. The concretization $\gamma(\eta)$ is the set of concrete states which satisfy η.

However, the syntactic nature of our domain gives us difficulties. While we can safely conclude that two (sub-)terms are equivalent, we have no way to conclude that two terms differ. No Galois connection exists for this domain; multiple sets of definitions could correspond to a given concrete state. Even if states η_1 and η_2 are both valid approximations of the concrete state, the same does not necessarily hold for $\eta_1 \sqcap \eta_2$.

Example 1. Consider two abstract states:

$$\{x \mapsto +(a_1, 7), y \mapsto a_1, z \mapsto a_2\} \quad \{x \mapsto +(3, b_1), y \mapsto b_2, z \mapsto b_1\}$$

These correspond to the sets of states satisfying $x = y + 7$ and $x = 3 + z$ respectively. Many concrete states satisfy both approximations; one is $(x, y, z) = (7, 0, 4)$. However, a naive application of unification would attempt to unify $+(y, 7)$ with $+(3, z)$, which would result in unifying y with 3, and z with 7.

Cousot and Cousot [7] discuss the consequences of a missing best approximation, and propose several approaches for repair: strengthening or weakening the domain, or nominating a best approximation through a widening/narrowing. However, these are of limited value in our application. Strengthening or weakening the domain enough that a best approximation is restored would greatly affect the performance or precision, and explicitly reasoning over the set of equivalent states is impractical. Using a widening/narrowing is sound advice, but offers minimal practical guidance.

3.1   Operations on $\mathcal{ST}$

We must now specify several operations: state transformers for program state-ments, join, meet, and widening. Assignment, join and widening all behave nicely under $\mathcal{ST}$; meet is discussed in Sect. 3.2.

Figure 3 shows assignment and join operations on $\mathcal{ST}$. Calls to generalize are cached, so calls to generalize(s,t) all return the same term variable. In the case of $\mathcal{ST}$, the lattice join is safe: as $\eta_1 \sqsubseteq \eta_2 \Rightarrow \gamma(\eta_1) \sqsubseteq_{C^\natural} \gamma(\eta_2)$ and $\sqcup$ and $\sqcup_{C^\natural}$ are least upper bounds on their respective domains, we have $\gamma(\eta_1) \sqsubseteq \gamma(\eta_1 \sqcup \eta_2)$ and $\gamma(\eta_2) \sqsubseteq \gamma(\eta_1 \sqcup \eta_2)$, so $\gamma(\eta_1) \sqcup_{C^\natural} \gamma(\eta_2) \sqsubseteq_{C^\natural} \gamma(\eta_1 \sqcup \eta_2)$. The worst-case complexity of the join is $O(|\eta_1||\eta_2|)$. But typical behaviour is expected to be closer to linear, as most shared terms are either shared in both (so only considered once) or are trivially distinct (so replaced by a variable). This is borne out in experiments, see Sect. 6. As $\mathcal{ST}$ has no infinite ascending chains, $\sqcup_{\mathcal{ST}}$ also serves as a widening.

$$F_{\mathcal{ST}}[\![x := f(y_1, \ldots, y_n)]\!](\eta) = \eta[x \mapsto f(\eta(y_1), \ldots, \eta(y_n))]$$

$$\eta_1 \sqcup \eta_2 = \{x \mapsto \text{generalize}(\eta_1(x), \eta_2(x)) \mid x \in V\}$$
$$\text{generalize}(c, c) = c$$
$$\text{generalize}(f(t_1, \ldots, t_n), f(s_1, \ldots, s_n)) = f(u_1, \ldots, u_n)$$
$$\textbf{where } u_i = \text{generalize}(t_i, s_i)$$
$$\text{generalize}(X, Y) = \textbf{freshvar}$$

Fig. 3. Definitions of variable assignment and $\sqcup$ in $\mathcal{ST}$.

Every term in $\eta_1 \sqcup \eta_2$ corresponds to some specialization in η_1 and η_2. We shall use $\pi^{\eta_1 \mapsto \eta_1 \sqcup \eta_2}$ to denote the relation that maps terms in η_1 to corresponding terms in $\eta_1 \sqcup \eta_2$.

Example 2. Consider again Fig. 1(b). At the exit of the first if-then-else, we get term-graphs η_1 and η_2 shown in Fig. 4(a) and (b). For $\eta_1 \sqcup \eta_2$, we first compute the generalization of $\eta_1(u) = a_0$ with $\eta_2(u) = b_0$, obtaining a fresh variable c_0. Now, $\eta_1(t)$ and $\eta_2(t)$ are both $(+_2)$ terms, so we recurse on the children; the generalization of (a_0, b_0) has already been computed, so we re-use the existing

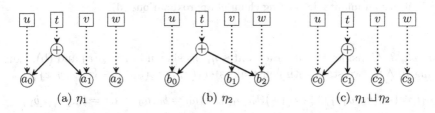

(a) η_1 (b) η_2 (c) $\eta_1 \sqcup \eta_2$

Fig. 4. State at the end of the first (a) *then* and (b) *else* branches in Fig. 1(b), and (c) the join of the two states.

variable; but we must allocate a fresh variable for (a_1, b_2), resulting in t being mapped to $(+)(c_0, c_1)$. We repeat this process for v and w, yielding the state shown in Fig. 4(c). Note that the result captures the fact that in both branches, t is computed by adding some value to u.

3.2   The Quasi-meet $\tilde{\sqcap}$

We require our quasi-meet $\sqcap_{ST}$ to be a sound approximation of the concrete meet, that is, $\gamma(\eta_1) \sqcap_{C^\sharp} \gamma(\eta_2) \sqsubseteq_{C^\sharp} \gamma(\eta_1 \sqcap_{ST} \eta_2)$. Ideally, we would like to preserve several other properties enjoyed by lattice operations:

Minimality: If $\eta_1 \sqsubseteq_{ST} \eta_2$, then $(\eta_1 \sqcap_{ST} \eta_2) = \eta_1$
Monotonicity: If $\eta_1 \sqsubseteq_{ST} \eta_1'$, then $(\eta_1 \sqcap_{ST} \eta_2) \sqsubseteq_{ST} (\eta_1' \sqcap_{ST} \eta_2)$

These are important for precision and termination respectively. However, in the absence of a unique greatest lower bound these properties are mutually exclusive, so the quasi-meet must be handled carefully to avoid non-termination [12].

A simple quasi-meet (denoted by $\tilde{\sqcap}$, as distinct from a 'true' meet $\sqcap$) is to adopt the approach of [21], deterministically selecting the term for each variable from either η_1 or η_2. Minimality can be achieved by selecting the more precise term (according to $\sqsubseteq_{ST}$) when several choices exist. However, this discards a great deal of information present in the conjunction. Of particular concern is the loss of variable equivalences which are implied by $\eta_1 \wedge \eta_2$ (the *logical conjunction* of η_1 and η_2), but not by η_1 and η_2 individually.

We can infer all sub-term (and variable) equivalences of $\eta_1 \wedge \eta_2$ using the congruence closure algorithm. Unfortunately, not only may this yield multiple incompatible definitions for a variable, the resulting definitions may be cyclic.

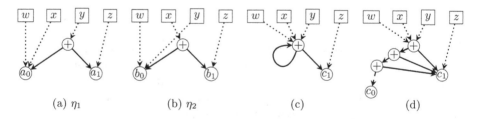

(a) η_1 (b) η_2 (c)   (d)

Fig. 5. Abstract states η_1 and η_2, whose conjunction $\eta_1 \wedge \eta_2$ (c) cannot be represented in ST; it has an infinite descending chain of approximations (d).

Example 3. Consider the abstract states η_1, η_2 shown in Fig. 5(a) and (b). Computing $\eta_1 \wedge \eta_2$, we start with constraints $\{\eta_1(v) = \eta_2(v) \mid v \in \{w, x, y, z\}\}$:

$$\{t = (+)(a_0, a_1)\} \cup \{s = (+)(b_0, b_1)\} \cup \{a_0 = b_0, a_0 = s, t = b_0, a_1 = b_1\}$$

After congruence closure, the terms are split into two equivalence classes:

$$E_1 = \{a_0, b_0, s, t\}, E_2 = \{a_1, b_1\}$$

We then wish to extract an element of $\mathcal{ST}$ which preserves as much of this information as possible. This conjunction, shown in Fig. 5(c), cannot be precisely represented in $\mathcal{ST}$ – Fig. 5(d) gives an infinite descending chain of approximations. Note that we could obtain incomparable elements of $\mathcal{ST}$ by pointing each of $\{w, x, y\}$ at different (+) nodes in Fig. 5(d).

We therefore need a strategy for choosing a finite approximation of $\eta_1 \wedge \eta_2$ in $\mathcal{ST}$. There are two elements to this decision: how a representative for each equivalence class is chosen, and how cycles are broken. We wish to preserve as many equivalences as possible, particularly between variables.

quasi-meet(η_1, η_2)
　% Partition terms into congruence classes
　$Eq :=$ congruence-close$(Defs(\eta_1) \cup Defs(\eta_2) \cup \{\eta_1(x) = \eta_2(x) \mid x \in V\})$
　for each $e \in Eq$
　　$indegree(e) := |\{x \mid \eta_1(x) \in eq\}|$
　$stack := \emptyset,\ repr := \emptyset,\ tvar := \emptyset$
　for each $x \in V$
　　$\eta(x) :=$ build-repr$(Eq(\eta_1(x)))$
　return η

build-repr(eq)
　if $eq \in stack$ % If this is a back-edge, break the cycle
　　if $eq \notin tvar$
　　　$tvar(eq) :=$ freshvar$()$
　　return $tvar(eq)$
　if $eq \in repr$ % If we have already computed the representative, return it
　　return $repr(eq)$
　% The equivalence class has not yet been seen; select best concrete definition
　$stack$.push(eq)
　if $mem(eq) = \emptyset$ % No concrete definition exists
　　$r_{eq} :=$ freshvar
　else
　　$f(s_1, \ldots, s_m) := \mathbf{argmax}_{f(s_1,\ldots,s_m) \in mem(eq)} \sum_i \begin{cases} 0 & \text{if } Eq(s_i) \in stack \\ indegree(Eq(s_i)) & \text{otherwise} \end{cases}$
　　for each $i \in 1, \ldots, m$ % Construct the representative for each subterm
　　　$r_i :=$ build-repr$(Eq(s_i))$
　　$r_{eq} := f(r_1, \ldots, r_m)$
　$repr(eq) := r_{eq}$
　$stack$.pop(eq)
　return r_{eq}

Fig. 6. Algorithm to compute $\tilde{\sqcap}_{\mathcal{ST}}$. Eq, $stack$, $repr$, $tvar$ and $indegree$ are global.

The algorithm for computing $\eta_1 \tilde{\sqcap}_{\mathcal{ST}} \eta_2$ is given in Fig. 6. We first partition the terms in $\eta_1 \cup \eta_2$ into equivalence classes using the congruence closure algorithm, then count the external references to each class. These counts, recorded in *indegree*, give us an indication of how valuable each class is, to discriminate between candidate representatives. $Eq(t)$ returns the equivalence class containing term t, and $mem(eq)$ denotes the set of *non-variable* terms in class eq.

We then progressively construct the resulting system of terms, starting from the mapping of each variable. Each equivalence class eq corresponds to at most two terms in the meet; the main representative $repr(eq)$, and a term variable $tvar(eq)$. Instantiating a term $f(s_1, \ldots, s_m)$, we look-up the corresponding equivalence class $eq_i = Eq(s_i)$, and check whether expanding its definition $repr(eq_i)$ (which may not yet be fully instantiated) would introduce a cycle. We then replace s_i with either the recursively constructed representative of eq_i (if the resulting system is acyclic), or the free variable $tvar(eq)$.

Example 4. Consider the abstract states η_1, η_2 shown in Fig. 5. Congruence closure yields two equivalence classes: $q_1 = \{a_0, (+)(a_0, a_1), b_0, (+)(b_0, b_1)\}$, and $q_2 = \{a_1, b_1\}$. The construction of $\eta_1 \widetilde{\sqcap} \eta_2$ starts with $Eq(w)$. We first mark q_1 as being on the stack to avoid cycles, then choose an appropriate definition to expand. The non-variable members of q_1 are $\{t_1 = (+)(a_0, a_1), t_2 = (+)(b_0, b_1)\}$. Both t_1 and t_2 have a single non-cycle incoming edge ($Eq(a_0) = Eq(b_0) = q_1$, which is already on the stack), so we arbitrarily choose t_1.

We must then expand the sub-terms of t_1. $Eq(a_0)$ is already on the stack, so cannot be expanded; this occurrence of a_0 is replaced with a fresh variable c_0. Now a_1 has no non-variable definitions, so a fresh variable c_1 is introduced. The stack then collapses, yielding $w \mapsto (+)(c_0, c_1)$.

The algorithm next considers x. A representative for q_1 has already been constructed, so x is mapped to $(+)(c_0, c_1)$, as is y. Finally, $Eq(z) = q_2$; this also has an existing representative, so c_1 is returned. The resulting abstract state is shown in Fig. 7. $\qquad\square$

The algorithm given in Fig. 6 runs in $O(n \log n)$ time, where $n = |\eta_1| + |\eta_2|$. The congruence closure step is run once, in $O(n \log n)$ time. The main body of build-repr is run at most once per equivalence class. Computing and scoring the set of candidates is linear in $|eq|$, and happens once per equivalence class. We detect back-edges in constant time, by marking those equivalence classes which remain on the call stack – any edge to a marked class is a back-edge. So the reconstruction of η takes time $O(n)$ in the worst case. Therefore, the overall algorithm takes $O(n \log n)$.

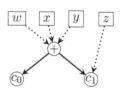

Fig. 7. $\eta_1 \widetilde{\sqcap} \eta_2$

Note that $\eta_1 \widetilde{\sqcap}_{ST} \eta_2$ is sensitive to variable ordering, as this determines which sub-term occurrence is considered a back-edge, and thus not expanded.

As for $\sqcup_{ST}$, each term in $\eta_1 \widetilde{\sqcap}_{ST} \eta_2$ corresponds to some set of terms in η_1 or η_2. As before, $\pi^{\eta_1 \mapsto \eta_1 \widetilde{\sqcap}_{ST} \eta_2}$ denotes the mapping between terms in each operand and the result.

3.3   Logical Assertions

Finally consider assertions $[\![x \bowtie y]\!]$, where $\bowtie \in \{=, \neq, <, \leq\}$. The abstract transformer for $[\![x < y]\!]$ and $[\![x \leq y]\!]$ is the identity function, as ST has no notion of inequalities. ST *can* infer information from a disequality $[\![x \neq y]\!]$, but only where η has already inferred equality between x and y:

$$F[\![x \neq y]\!]\eta = \begin{cases} \bot & \textbf{if } \eta(x) = \eta(y) \\ \eta & \textbf{otherwise} \end{cases}$$

In the case of an equality $[\![x = y]\!]$, we are left in a similar situation as for $\eta_1 \sqcap \eta_2$; we must reconcile the defining terms for x and y, plus any other inferred equivalences. This is done in the same way, by first computing equivalence classes, then extracting an acyclic system of terms. As we introduce only a single additional equivalence, we can use the specialized linear-time algorithm described in Sect. 3.4 of [10], then extract the resulting term system as for the meet.

4 ST as a Functor Domain

Assume we have some abstract domain $\mathcal{D}$ with the usual operations $\sqcap$, $\sqcup$, $F_\mathcal{D}$ and $F_\mathcal{D}^{-1}$ as described in Sect. 2. In the following, we assume $\mathcal{D}$ is not relational, so may only express independent properties of variables.

We would like to use ST to enhance the precision of analysis under $\mathcal{D}$. Essentially, we want a functor domain where ST is the functor instantiated with $\mathcal{D}$. While this is a simple formulation, it provides no path toward an efficient implementation. Where normally we use $\mathcal{D}$ to approximate the values of (or relationships between) variables in V, we can instead approximate the values of *terms* occurring in the program. An element of our lifted domain $ST(\mathcal{D})$ is a pair $\langle \eta, \rho \rangle$ where η is a mapping of program variable to terms, and $\rho \in \mathcal{D}$ approximates the set of satisfying term assignments.

4.1   Operations over $ST(\mathcal{D})$

Evaluating an assignment in the lifted domain may be performed using $F_\mathcal{D}$ and F_{ST}. We construct the updated definition of x in η, then assign the corresponding 'variable' in $\mathcal{D}$ to the result of the computation.

$$F_{ST(\mathcal{D})}[\![x := f(y_1, \ldots, y_n)]\!](\langle \eta, \rho \rangle) = \langle \eta', \rho' \rangle$$
$$\textbf{where } \eta' = F_{ST}[\![x := f(y_1, \ldots, y_n)]\!]\eta$$
$$\rho' = F_\mathcal{D}[\![\text{id}(\eta'(x)) := f(\eta(y_1), \ldots, \eta(y_n))]\!]\rho$$

Formulating $\sqcup_{ST(\mathcal{D})}$, $\nabla_{ST(\mathcal{D})}$ and $\tilde{\sqcap}_{ST(\mathcal{D})}$ is only slightly more involved, assuming the presence of a *renaming* operator over $\mathcal{D}$. We first determine the term structure η' of the result, then map ρ_1 and ρ_2 onto the terms in η' before applying the appropriate operator over $\mathcal{D}$.

$$\langle \eta_1, \rho_1 \rangle \sqcup_{ST(\mathcal{D})} \langle \eta_2, \rho_2 \rangle = \langle \eta', \rho' \rangle$$
$$\textbf{where } \eta' = \eta_1 \sqcup_{ST} \eta_2$$
$$\rho' = \pi^{\eta_1 \mapsto \eta'}(\rho_1) \sqcup_\mathcal{D} \pi^{\eta_2 \mapsto \eta'}(\rho_2)$$

$$\langle \eta_1, \rho_1 \rangle \, \nabla_{\mathcal{ST}(\mathcal{D})} \langle \eta_2, \rho_2 \rangle = \langle \eta', \rho' \rangle$$
where $\eta' = \eta_1 \sqcup_{\mathcal{ST}} \eta_2$
$$\rho' = \pi^{\eta_1 \mapsto \eta'}(\rho_1) \, \nabla_{\mathcal{D}} \, \pi^{\eta_2 \mapsto \eta'}(\rho_2)$$

$$\langle \eta_1, \rho_1 \rangle \, \widetilde{\sqcap}_{\mathcal{ST}(\mathcal{D})} \langle \eta_2, \rho_2 \rangle = \langle \eta', \rho' \rangle$$
where $\eta' = \eta_1 \, \widetilde{\sqcap}_{\mathcal{ST}} \, \eta_2$
$$\rho' = \pi^{\eta_1 \mapsto \eta'}(\rho_1) \sqcap_{\mathcal{D}} \pi^{\eta_2 \mapsto \eta'}(\rho_2)$$

4.2   Inferring Properties from Subterms

While this allows us to maintain approximations of subterms, we cannot use this to directly derive tighter approximations of program variables.

However, upon encountering a branch which restricts x, we can then infer properties on any other terms involving x. For now, we shall restrict ourselves to ancestors of x. If the approximation of x has changed, and p is an immediate parent of x, we can simply *recompute* p from its definition:

$$\rho' = \rho \sqcap F_{\mathcal{ST}} [\![\mathbf{id}(\eta(\mathbf{p})) := \mathbf{def}(\eta(\mathbf{p}))]\!] \rho$$

We can then propagate this information upwards.

We can also infer information about a term from its parents and siblings. Assume the program fragment in Fig. 8 is being analysed using the (term-lifted) domain of intervals. At point D we know only that x is non-negative; this is not enough to infer bounds on z. However, when point E is reached we know $z > 0$. As we already know $x \geq 0$, this can only occur if $y > 0$, $x > 0$.

This requires us to reason about the values from which a given computation could have resulted; this is exactly the pre-image $F_{\mathcal{D}}^{-1}$ discussed in Sect. 2. We

```
x = *; y = *
    assert(x ≥ 0)
D: z = x * y
    assert(z > 0)
E:
```

Fig. 8. If E is reached, y must be positive.

can then augment the algorithm to propagate information in both directions, evaluating $F_{\mathcal{D}}$ and $F_{\mathcal{D}}^{-1}$ on each term until a fixpoint is reached. Unfortunately, attempts to fully reduce an abstract state run into difficulties.

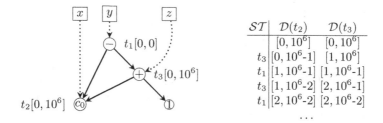

Fig. 9. A system of terms with no solution; encoding $x = x + 1$. Each evaluation of t_1 or t_3 eliminates only two values from the corresponding bounds.

Example 5. Consider the system of terms shown in Fig. 9, augmenting the domain of intervals. Disregarding interval information, it encodes the constraint $y = x - z, z = x + 1$. In the context of $y = 0$ (the interval bounds for y), this is clearly unsatisfiable.

Propagating the consequences of these terms, we first apply the definition $t_3 = t_2 + 1$. Doing so, we trim 0 from the domain of t_3 (or z), and 10^6 from the domain of t_2 (or x). We then evaluate the definition $t_1 = t_2 - t_3$, thus removing 0 and 10^6 from t_1 and t_3 respectively. We can then evaluate the definitions of t_3 and t_1 again, this time eliminating 2 and 10^6-1. This process eventually determines unsatisfiability, but it takes $10^6 + 1$ steps to do so.[3]

This rather undermines our objective of efficiently combining $\mathcal{ST}$ with $\mathcal{D}$. If $\mathcal{D}$ is not finite, the process may not terminate at all. Consider the case where $\mathcal{D}(t_2) = \mathcal{D}(t_3) = [0, \infty]$ – the resulting iterates form an infinite descending chain, where the lower bounds are tightened by one at each iteration step.

The existence of an efficient, general algorithm for normalizing $\langle \eta, \rho \rangle$ seems doubtful. Even for the specific case of finite intervals, computing the fixpoint of such a system of constraints is NP-complete [3] (in the weak sense – the standard Kleene iteration runs in pseudo-polynomial time). Nevertheless, we can apply the system of terms to ρ some bounded number of times in an attempt to improve precision; a naive iterative approach is given in Fig. 10.

tighten($\langle \eta, \rho \rangle$, *iters*):
   while(*iters* > 0)
      ρ' := tighten-step($\langle \eta, \rho \rangle$)
      if ($\rho' = \rho \vee \rho = \bot$)
         return ρ
      ρ := ρ'
      iters := *iters* $- 1$

tighten-step($\langle \eta, \rho \rangle$):
   let $t_1, \dots, t_m$ *be terms in η in*
      order of decreasing height
   for $t \in t_1, \dots, t_m$
      ρ := $\rho \sqcap F_{\mathcal{D}}^{-1} [\![\mathbf{id}(t) = \mathbf{def}(t)]\!] \rho$
   for $t \in t_m, \dots, t_1$
      ρ := $\rho \sqcap F_{\mathcal{D}} [\![\mathbf{id}(t) = \mathbf{def}(t)]\!] \rho$
   return ρ

Fig. 10. Applying a system of terms η to tighten a numeric approximation ρ.

In practice, this iteration is wasteful. In an independent attribute domain, applying $[\![t = \mathbf{f}(c_1, \dots c_k)]\!]$ cannot directly affect terms not in $\{t, c_1, \dots, c_k\}$, and we can easily detect which of these have changed. So we adopt a worklist approach, updating terms with changed abstractions only. The tightening still progresses level by level, to collect the tightest abstraction of each term before re-applying the definitions. The algorithm is outlined in Fig. 11.

tighten-worklist incrementally applies a single pass of tighten-step, where only terms in X have changed. Given the discussion above, the algorithm obviously misses opportunities for propagation; this loss occurs at the point marked †.

---

[3] This behaviour is also a well recognized problem for finite domain constraint solvers (see e.g. [11]).

```
tighten-worklist(X, ⟨η, ρ⟩):
    forall l, Q_l^↓ := Q_l^↑ := ∅
    for(x ∈ X) Q_height(x)^↓ := Q_height(x)^↓ ∪ {x}
    l_min := min_{x∈X} height(x)
    l := l_max := max_{x∈X} height(x)
    while(l ≥ l_min)
        for(t ∈ Q_l^↓)
            enqueue_parents(t)
            ρ' := ρ ⊓ F_D^{-1}([[id(t) = def(t)]])ρ
            for(c ∈ children(t))
                if(changed(c, ρ, ρ')) enqueue_down(c)
            ρ := ρ'
        l := l − 1
    l := l_min
    while(l ≤ l_max)
        for(t ∈ Q_l^↑)
(†)        ρ' := ρ ⊓ F([[id(t) = def(t)]])ρ
            if(changed(t, ρ, ρ')) enqueue_parents(t)
            ρ := ρ'
        l := l + 1
    return ρ
```

```
enqueue_down(t):
    Q_height(t)^↓ := Q_height(t)^↓ ∪ {t}
    l_min := min(l_min, height(t))

enqueue_parents(t):
    for(p in parents(t))
        Q_height(p)^↑ := Q_height(p)^↑ ∪ {p}
        l_max := max(l_max, height(p))
```

Fig. 11. An incremental approach for applying a single iteration of tighten-step.

Given some definition $[[t = f(c_1, c_2)]]$ and new information about c_1, we could potentially tighten the abstraction of *both* t and c_2; however, tighten-worklist only applies this information to t.

It is sound to apply the same algorithm when $\mathcal{D}$ is relational; however, it may miss further potential tightenings, as additional constraints on some term can be reflected in other, apparently unrelated terms.

Care must be taken when combining normalization with widening. As is observed in octagons, closure after widening does not typically preserve termination. A useful exception is the typical widening on intervals which preserves termination when tightening is applied upwards.

5   Other Syntactic Approaches

As mentioned, the closest relatives to the term domain are the symbolic constant domain of Miné [21] and the congruence closure (or *alien expression*) domain of Chang and Leino [5]. Both domains record a mapping between program variables and terms, with the objective of enriching existing numeric domains.

The term domain can be viewed as a generalization of the symbolic constant domain. Both domains arise from the observation that abstract domains, be they relational or otherwise, exhibit coarse handling of expressions outside their *native language* – particularly non-linear expressions. And both store a mapping from variables to defining expressions. The primary difference is in the join.

Faced with non-equal definitions, the symbolic constant domain discards both entirely. The term domain instead attempts to preserve whatever parts of the computation are shared between the abstract states, which it can then use to improve precision in the underlying domain.

The congruence closure domain [5] arises from a different application – coordinating a heterogeneous set of base abstract domains, each supporting only a subset of expressions appearing in the program. Functions which are *alien* to a domain are replaced with a fresh variable; equivalences are inferred from the syntactic terms, and added to the base abstract domains. The congruence closure domain assumes the base domains are relational, maintaining a system of equivalences and supported relations. As a result, it assumes the base domain will take care of maintaining relationships between interpreted expressions and the corresponding subterms. Hence it will not help with the examples from Fig. 1.

While the underlying techniques are similar, the objectives (and thus trade-offs) are quite different. Congruence closure maintains an arbitrary (though finite) system of uninterpreted function equations, allowing multiple – possibly cyclic – definitions for subterms. This potentially preserves more equivalence information than the acyclic system of the subterm domain, but increases the cost and complexity of various operations (notably the join). As far as we know, no experimental evaluation of the congruence-closure domain has been published.

6 Experimental Evaluation

The subterm domain has been implemented in CRAB, a language-agnostic C++ library of abstract domains and fixpoint algorithms. It is available, with the rest of CRAB, at https://github.com/seahorn/crab. One purpose of CRAB is to enhance verification tools by supplying them with inductive invariants that can be expressed in some abstract domain chosen by the client tool. For our experiments we used SEAHORN [13], one of the participants in SV-COMP 2015 [1].

We selected 2304 SV-COMP 2015 programs, in the categories best supported by SEAHORN: ControlFlowInteger, Loops, Sequentialized, DeviceDrivers64, and ProductLines (CFI, Loops, DD64, Seq, PL in Table 3). We first evaluated the performance of the subterm domain by measuring only the time to generate the invariants without running SEAHORN. We compared the subterm domain enhancing intervals $ST(\text{Intv})$ with three other numeric abstract domains: classical intervals Intv [6] (our *baseline* abstract domain since it was the one used by SEAHORN in SV-COMP 2015), the symbolic constant propagation $SC(\text{Intv})$ [21], and an optimized implementation of difference-bound matrices using *variable packing* $VP(\text{DBM})$ [24]. Second, we measured the precision gains using $ST(\text{Intv})$ as an invariant supplier for SEAHORN and compared again with Intv, $SC(\text{Intv})$, and $VP(\text{DBM})$. All experiments were carried out on a AMD Opteron Processor 6172 with 12 cores running at 2.1 GHz Core with 32 GB of memory.

Performance. Table 2(a) shows three scatter plots of analysis times comparing $ST(\text{Intv})$ with Intv (left), with $SC(\text{Intv})$ (middle), and with $VP(\text{DBM})$ (right).

Table 2. Performance of several abstract domains on SV-COMP'15 programs

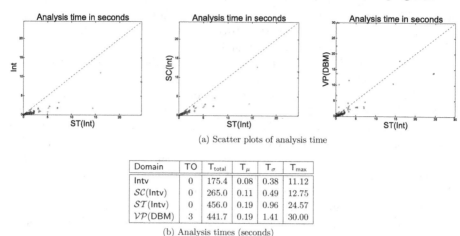

(a) Scatter plots of analysis time

Domain	TO	T_{total}	T_μ	T_σ	T_{max}
Intv	0	175.4	0.08	0.38	11.12
$\mathcal{SC}$(Intv)	0	265.0	0.11	0.49	12.75
$\mathcal{ST}$(Intv)	0	456.0	0.19	0.96	24.57
$\mathcal{VP}$(DBM)	3	441.7	0.19	1.41	30.00

(b) Analysis times (seconds)

Table 2(b) shows additional statistics about the analysis of the 2304 programs. For this experiment, we set a limit of 30 s and 4 GB per program.

CRAB using $\mathcal{ST}$(Intv), Intv, and $\mathcal{SC}$(Intv) inferred invariants successfully for all programs without any timeout (column TO in Table 2(b)). The total time (denoted by T_{total}) indicates that Intv was the fastest with 175 s and $\mathcal{ST}$(Intv) the slowest with 456. The columns T_μ and T_σ denote the time average and standard deviation per program, and the column T_{max} is the time of analyzing the program that took the longest. All domains displayed similar memory usage. Again, Intv was the most efficient with an average memory usage per program of 31 MB and a maximum of 1.34 GB whereas $\mathcal{ST}$(Intv) was the least efficient with an average of 37 MB and maximum of 1.52 GB.

It is not surprising that Intv and $\mathcal{SC}$(Intv) are faster than $\mathcal{ST}$(Intv); interestingly, the evaluation suggests that in practice $\mathcal{ST}$(Intv) incurs only a modest constant-factor overhead of around 2.5. $\mathcal{VP}$(DBM) was faster than $\mathcal{ST}$(Intv) in many cases but was more volatile, reaching the timeout in 3 cases. This is due to the size of variable packs inferred by $\mathcal{VP}$(DBM) [24]. If few interactions are discovered, the packs remain of constant size and the analysis collapses down to Intv. Conversely, if many variables are found to interact, the analysis degenerates into a single DBM with cubic runtime.

Precision. Table 3 shows the results obtained running SEAHORN with CRAB using the four abstract domains. We run SEAHORN on each verification task[4] and count the number of tasks solved (i.e., SEAHORN reports "safe" or "unsafe") shown in columns labelled with #S. In T columns we show the total time in seconds for solving all tasks. The top row gives, in parentheses, the number of programs per category. The row labelled SEA+Intv shows the number of

---

[4] A program with its corresponding safety property also provided by the competition.

Table 3. SEAHORN results on SV-COMP 2015 enhanced with abstract domains

	CFI (48)		Loops (142)		DD64 (1256)		Seq (261)		PL (597)	
	#S	T	#S	T	#S	T	#S	T	#S	T
SEA+Intv	41	1589	115	5432	1215	6283	109	26031	538	20818
SEA+$\mathcal{SC}$(Intv)	41	1613	115	5480	1215	6520	110	25639	539	20741
SEA+$\mathcal{ST}$(Intv)	41	1416	121	4274	1215	6557	110	25469	542	20763
Sea+$\mathcal{VP}$(DBM)	41	1529	117	5071	1214	6854	110	25929	536	20787

tasks solved by SEAHORN using the interval domain (our baseline domain) as invariant supplier, while rows labelled with SEA+$\mathcal{SC}$(Intv), SEA+$\mathcal{ST}$(Intv) and SEA+$\mathcal{VP}$(DBM) are similar but using $\mathcal{SC}$(Intv), $\mathcal{ST}$(Intv) and $\mathcal{VP}$(DBM), respectively. We set resource limits of 200 s and 4GB for each task. In all configurations, we ran SEAHORN with SPACER [16] as back-end solver[5].

The results in Table 3 demonstrate that the subterm domain can produce significant gains in some categories (e.g., Loops and PL) and stay competitive in all. We observe that $\mathcal{SC}$(Intv) rarely improves upon the results of SEA+Intv. Two factors appear to contribute to this: the join operation on $\mathcal{SC}$(Intv) maintains only the definitions that are constant on all code paths; and SEAHORN's frontend (based on LLVM [17]) applies linear constant propagation, subsuming many of the opportunities available to $\mathcal{SC}$(Intv). Our evaluation also shows that the subterm domain helps SEAHORN solve more tasks than $\mathcal{VP}$(DBM) in several categories. One reason could be that $\mathcal{VP}$(DBM) does not perform propagation across different packs and so it is less precise than classical DBMs [19][6] and indeed incomparable with the subterm domain. Another reason might be the more precise modelling of non-linear operations by the subterm domain. Nevertheless, we observed that sometimes $\mathcal{ST}$(Intv) can solve tasks that $\mathcal{VP}$(DBM) cannot, and vice versa. For PL, for example, SEA+$\mathcal{ST}$(Intv) solved 9 tasks for which SEA+$\mathcal{VP}$(DBM) reached a timeout but SEA+$\mathcal{VP}$(DBM) solved 3 tasks that SEA+$\mathcal{ST}$(Intv) missed. This is relevant for tools such as SEAHORN since it motivates the idea of running SEAHORN with a portfolio of abstract domains.

7   Conclusion and Future Work

We have introduced the subterm abstract domain $\mathcal{ST}$, and outlined its application as a functor domain to improve precision of existing analyses. Experiments on software verification benchmarks have demonstrated that $\mathcal{ST}$, when used to enrich an interval analysis, can substantially improve generated invariants while only incurring a modest constant factor performance penalty.

---

[5] We used the command `sea pf --step=large --track=mem` (i.e., large-block encoding [2] of the transition system modelling both pointer offsets and memory contents). For DD64 we add the option `-m64`.

[6] We used an implementation of the classical DBM domain following [19] for the experiment in Table 2 but it took more than three hours to complete.

The performance of $\mathcal{ST}$ is obtained by disregarding algebraic properties of operations. Extending $\mathcal{ST}$ to exploit these properties while preserving performance poses an interesting future challenge.

Acknowledgments. This work has been supported by the Australian Research Council through grant DP140102194. We would like to thank Maxime Arthaud for implementating the abstract domain of difference-bound matrices with variable packing.

References

1. Beyer, D.: Software verification and verifiable witnesses. In: Baier, C., Tinelli, C. (eds.) TACAS 2015. LNCS, vol. 9035, pp. 401–416. Springer, Heidelberg (2015)
2. Beyer, D., Cimatti, A., Griggio, A., Keremoglu, M.E., Sebastiani, R.: Software model checking via large-block encoding. In: Biere, A., Pixley, C., (eds.) Proceedings of the Ninth International Conference on Formal Methods in Computer-Aided Design, pp. 25–32. IEEE Computer Society (2009)
3. Bordeaux, L., Katsirelos, G., Narodytska, N., Vardi, M.Y.: The complexity of integer bound propagation. J. Artif. Intell. Res. (JAIR) **40**, 657–676 (2011)
4. Bouaziz, M.: TreeKs: a functor to make numerical abstract domains scalable. Electron. Notes Theor. Comput. Sci. **287**, 41–52 (2012)
5. Chang, B.-Y.E., M. Leino, K.R.: Abstract interpretation with alien expressions and heap structures. In: Cousot, R. (ed.) VMCAI 2005. LNCS, vol. 3385, pp. 147–163. Springer, Heidelberg (2005)
6. Cousot, P., Cousot, R.: Static determination of dynamic properties of programs. In: Proceedings of the Second International Symposium on Programming, pp. 106–130. Dunod (1976)
7. Cousot, P., Cousot, R.: Abstract interpretation frameworks. J. Logic Comput. **2**(4), 511–547 (1992)
8. Cousot, P., Cousot, R., Feret, J., Mauborgne, L., Miné, A., Rival, X.: Why does Astrée scale up? Formal Meth. Syst. Des. **35**(3), 229–264 (2009)
9. Cousot, P., Halbwachs, N.: Automatic discovery of linear constraints among variables of a program. In: Proceedings of the Fifth ACM Symposium on Principles of Programming Languages, pp. 84–97. ACM Press (1978)
10. Downey, P.J., Sethi, R., Tarjan, R.E.: Variations on the common subexpression problem. J. ACM **27**(4), 758–771 (1980)
11. Feydy, T., Schutt, A., Stuckey, P.: Global difference constraint propagation for finite domain solvers. In: Antoy, S. (ed.) Proceedings of 10th International ACM SIGPLAN Symposium on Principles and Practice of Declarative Programming, pp. 226–235. ACM Press (2008)
12. Gange, G., Navas, J.A., Schachte, P., Søndergaard, H., Stuckey, P.J.: Abstract interpretation over non-lattice abstract domains. In: Logozzo, F., Fähndrich, M. (eds.) Static Analysis. LNCS, vol. 7935, pp. 6–24. Springer, Heidelberg (2013)
13. Gurfinkel, A., Kahsai, T., Komuravelli, A., Navas, J.A.: The seahorn verification framework. In: Kroening, D., Păsăreanu, C.S. (eds.) CAV 2015. LNCS, vol. 9206, pp. 343–361. Springer, Heidelberg (2015)
14. Howe, J.M., King, A.: Logahedra: a new weakly relational domain. In: Liu, Z., Ravn, A.P. (eds.) ATVA 2009. LNCS, vol. 5799, pp. 306–320. Springer, Heidelberg (2009)

15. Huet, G.: Résolution d'Équations dans des Langages d'Ordre 1, 2, ..., ω. Thèse d'État. Université Paris VII (1976)
16. Komuravelli, A., Gurfinkel, A., Chaki, S., Clarke, E.M.: Automatic abstraction in SMT-based unbounded software model checking. In: Sharygina, N., Veith, H. (eds.) CAV 2013. LNCS, vol. 8044, pp. 846–862. Springer, Heidelberg (2013)
17. Lattner, C., Adve, V.: LLVM: a compilation framework for lifelong program analysis and transformation. In: Proceedings of the International Symposium on Code Generation and Optimization, pp. 75–86. IEEE Computer Society (2004)
18. Logozzo, F., Fähndrich, M.: Pentagons: a weakly relational abstract domain for the efficient validation of array accesses. In: Proceedings of the 2008 ACM Symposium on Applied Computing, pp. 184–188. ACM Press (2008)
19. Miné, A.: A new numerical abstract domain based on difference-bound matrices. In: Danvy, O., Filinski, A. (eds.) PADO 2001. LNCS, vol. 2053, pp. 155–172. Springer, Heidelberg (2001)
20. Miné, A.: The octagon abstract domain. High. Ord. Symbolic Comput. **19**(1), 31–100 (2006)
21. Miné, A.: Symbolic methods to enhance the precision of numerical abstract domains. In: Emerson, E.A., Namjoshi, K.S. (eds.) VMCAI 2006. LNCS, vol. 3855, pp. 348–363. Springer, Heidelberg (2006)
22. Simon, A., King, A.: The two variable per inequality abstract domain. High. Ord. Symbolic Comput. **23**(1), 87–143 (2010)
23. Simon, A., King, A., Howe, J.M.: Two variables per linear inequality as an abstract domain. In: Leuschel, M. (ed.) LOPSTR 2002. LNCS, vol. 2664, pp. 71–89. Springer, Heidelberg (2003)
24. Venet, A., Brat, G.: Precise and efficient static array bound checking for large embedded C programs. In: Proceedings of the ACM SIGPLAN 2004 Conference on Programming Language Design and Implementation, pp. 231–242. ACM Press (2004)
25. Venet, A.J.: The gauge domain: scalable analysis of linear inequality invariants. In: Madhusudan, P., Seshia, S.A. (eds.) CAV 2012. LNCS, vol. 7358, pp. 139–154. Springer, Heidelberg (2012)

Property Directed Abstract Interpretation

Noam Rinetzky[1] and Sharon Shoham[2]([⊠])

[1] Tel Aviv University, Tel Aviv, Israel
[2] The Academic College of Tel Aviv Yaffo, Tel Aviv, Israel
sharon.shoham@gmail.com

Abstract. Recently, Bradley proposed the PDR/IC3 model checking algorithm for verifying safety properties, where forward and backward reachability analyses are intertwined, and guide each other. Many variants of Bradley's original algorithm have been developed and successfully applied to both hardware and software verification. However, these algorithms have been presented in an operational manner, in disconnect with the rich literature concerning the theoretical foundation of static analysis formulated by abstract interpretation.

Inspired by PDR, we develop a nonstandard semantics which computes for every $0 \leq N$ an over-approximation of the set of traces of length N leading to a safety violation. The over approximation is *precise*, in the sense that it only includes traces that *do not* start at an initial state, unless the program is unsafe, and in this case the semantics aborts at a special error state. In a way, the semantics computes multiple over-approximations of bounded unsafe program behaviors using a sequence of abstractions whose precision grows automatically with N.

We show that existing PDR algorithms can be described as a specific implementation of our semantics, performing an abstract interpretation of the program, but instead of aiming for a fixpoint, they stop *early* when either the backward analysis finds a counterexample or the states comprising one of the bounded traces provides sufficient evidence that the program is safe. This places PDR within the solid framework of abstract interpretation, and thus provides a unified explanation of the different PDR algorithms as well as a new proof of their soundness.

1 Introduction

Abstract interpretation [6] (*AI*) provides a solid theoretical foundation for static program analysis. *AI* algorithms verify that a program is safe by computing an over-approximation of its concrete semantics: They find a conservative representation of either the set of *reachable traces*, i.e., the traces that the program generates when executing from a given set of *initial states* (forward analysis), or of the set of *evil traces*, i.e., the ones that end in a *bad* state (backward analysis). Using the *AI* framework to develop program analyses is attractive because it elucidates the key semantic properties of the underlying abstraction and ensures, by construction, that the analysis is sound.

Recently, Bradley proposed the *property directed reachability* (PDR/IC3) model checking algorithm for verifying safety properties [3], where forward and

© Springer-Verlag Berlin Heidelberg 2016
B. Jobstmann and K.R.M. Leino (Eds.): VMCAI 2016, LNCS 9583, pp. 104–123, 2016.
DOI: 10.1007/978-3-662-49122-5_5

backward analyses are intertwined, and guide each other. Many variants of Bradley's original algorithm have been developed and successfully applied to both hardware and software verification [1,2,5,7,9,10]. However, these algorithms have been presented in an operational manner, in disconnect with the rich literature concerning abstract interpretation. As a result, it is hard to understand and compare these algorithms without delving into minute, almost implementation-level, details.

In this paper, we provide a fresh view of the emerging family of property directed reachability verification algorithms using abstract interpretation.[1] We begin by developing an abstract trace semantics which conservatively represents the set of evil traces of length N by a sequence ω_N of sets of states, called *cartesian trace*. A cartesian trace abstracts a set of traces T by "forgetting" the fine-grained correlation between consecutive states. Cartesian traces are then further abstracted into sequences $\omega_N^\sharp$ where every set $\omega_N^\sharp(i)$ may include, in addition to the states that lead to a violation in i steps, states which are *not* reachable in $N - i$ or less steps.[2] This form of abstraction ensures that $\omega_N^\sharp$ does not represent counterexamples of length N. Furthermore, if for some N and $i < N$, it holds that $\omega_N^\sharp(i) = \omega_N^\sharp(i + 1)$ then the program is safe.

In a way, our semantics can be seen as an approach to compute a conservative over approximation of the set of states leading to a safety violation, where each sequence $\omega_N^\sharp$ corresponds to a different abstraction whose precision increases automatically as N grows. The semantics considers abstract cartesian traces of every possible length simultaneously. As such, it considers infinitely many abstractions with varying precision.

An important property of our semantics is that it can capture all the *useful* fixpoints of the traditional collecting state semantics, where a fixpoint of a backward semantics is useful if it is disjoint from the set of initial states, and dually, a fixpoint of a forward semantics is useful if it is disjoint from the set of bad states.

We then use our semantics to provide a unified view of existing *PDR* algorithms: We show that they can be formulated as a specific scheduling of the semantics which stops *early* when either a counterexample is found or the program is determined to be safe. Informally, the algorithms combine backward analysis to compute (a conservative over approximation) of ω_N which are then generalized to $\omega_N^\sharp$ using forward analysis. As the formulation in terms of the semantics reveals, these algorithms consider (finitely many) cartesian traces of multiple lengths simultaneously. This places *PDR* within the solid framework of abstract interpretation, and thus presents a unified explanation of the different PDR algorithms and a new proof of their soundness.

---

[1] In this paper, we focus on *linear* property directed reachability, as opposed to, e.g., tree-IC3 [5]. See Sect. 9.

[2] In model checking nomenclature, the abstraction of $\omega_N(i)$ into $\omega_N^\sharp(i)$ is called *generalization*.

2 Preliminaries

Binary Relations. Let $R \subseteq X \times X$ be a *binary relation* over X. We write $x \xrightarrow{R} x'$ to denote that $(x, x') \in R$. We denote the *inverse* relation of R by $\overleftarrow{R}$, i.e., $\overleftarrow{R} = \{(x', x) \mid (x, x') \in R\}$. We denote the sets of elements *preceding* and *following* an element $x \in X$ according to R by $\overleftarrow{R}(x)$ and $R(x)$, respectively, i.e., $\overleftarrow{R}(x) = \{x_0 \in X \mid x_0 \xrightarrow{R} x\}$ and $R(x) = \{x' \in X \mid x \xrightarrow{R} x'\}$.

We lift $R(\cdot)$, and $\overleftarrow{R}(\cdot)$ to sets in a point-wise manner, e.g., $R(X) = \{x_0 \in R(x) \mid x \in X\}$. We write $R^k(\cdot)$, and $\overleftarrow{R}^k(\cdot)$ to denote k applications of $R(\cdot)$, and $\overleftarrow{R}(\cdot)$, respectively. For example, $R^0(X) = X$ and $R^{k+1}(X) = R(R^k(X))$.

Sequences. Given a natural number $N \in \mathbb{N}$, we denote by $[N]$ the set of natural numbers from 0 to N, i.e., $[N] = \{n \in \mathbb{N} \mid 0 \leq n \leq N\}$. A *sequence* s over a set X is a total function from $[N]$, for some $N \in \mathbb{N}$, to X, i.e., $s \in [N] \rightarrow X$. We denote the set of sequences over X (including the empty sequence), by $\text{seq}(X)$. We denote the length of a sequence s by $|s|$ and its i-th element by $s(i)$. For example, $s(0)$ and $s(|s| - 1)$ denote the first and last elements of s, respectively. We denote the *domain* of a sequence s by $\text{dom}(s)$ and its *range* by $\text{range}(s)$, i.e., $\text{dom}(s) = [|s| - 1]$ and $\text{range}(s) = \{s(i) \mid i \in \text{dom}(s)\}$. We denote the concatenation of sequences by juxtaposition. By abuse of notation, we sometimes treat an element $x \in X$ as the sequence $\langle x \rangle$. We denote the set of sequences comprised of single elements of X by $\langle X \rangle$, i.e., $\langle X \rangle = \{\langle x \rangle \mid x \in X\}$. Let R be a binary relation. A sequence s is a *valid sequence* of R if for every $i \in [|s| - 2]$, $s(i) \xrightarrow{R} s(i + 1)$.

Stuttering Simulation. Let X and Y be sets and $R_X \subseteq X \times X$ and $R_Y \subseteq Y \times Y$ be binary relations over X and Y, respectively. A binary relation $sim \subseteq X \times Y$ is a *stuttering simulation relation* with respect to R_X and R_Y if for every $(x, x') \in R_X$ and $(x, y) \in sim$ there exists a valid sequence of R_Y which starts at y and ends in some element $y' \in Y$ such that $(x', y') \in sim$.

States. We assume a given set of *states* Σ, ranged over by the meta-variable σ.

Transition Relations and Traces. We use *transition relations* and *traces* as synonyms for binary relations and sequences, respectively, when semantic elements are involved. We denote the set of transitions over states by $\Delta = \Sigma \times \Sigma$, and the set of traces over states by $\Pi = \text{seq}(\Sigma)$, and range over it using π. We say that a trace is a *valid trace* of a transition relation TR if it is a valid sequence of TR. We denote the set of valid traces of TR by $[\![TR]\!]_\Pi$.

Programs and Properties. We do not commit ourselves to a particular syntax. Instead, given a *program* P, we expect to get its denotation $\text{TR}(P) \subseteq \Delta$ as a transition relation over states. Similarly, we equate properties with their denotation as sets of states.

Verification Problems. A *verification problem* $\mathcal{V}$ is a triple $\mathcal{V} = (Init, P, Bad)$ comprised of a set of *initial states* $Init \subseteq \Sigma$, a *program* P, and a set of *bad states*

$Bad \subseteq \Sigma$ which does not contain initial states, i.e., $Init \cap Bad = \emptyset$. Informally, P is *safe* according to $\mathcal{V}$ if it cannot start executing in an initial state and end up in a bad state.

Conventions. In the rest of the paper, we assume a fixed arbitrary program P whose transition relation is $TR = \mathrm{TR}(P)$ and a fixed arbitrary verification problem $\mathcal{V} = (Init, P, Bad)$. Thus, whenever we say *the program*, an *initial state*, or a *bad state*, we mean P, a state in $Init$, and a state in Bad, respectively.

3   Small Step Collecting Trace Semantics

In this section, we define a small-step operational semantics over *sets* of traces.

Trace Semantics. Our venture point is a rather mundane *trace semantics*, which defines the meaning of a program to be the set of traces it can produce. A trace π is a *forward trace* of P if it is a valid trace of its transition relation, i.e., if $\pi \in [\![\mathrm{TR}(P)]\!]_\Pi$. Similarly, π is a *backward trace* of P if $\pi \in [\![\overleftarrow{\mathrm{TR}(P)}]\!]_\Pi$. We say that a forward trace π of P is *reachable* if it starts in an initial state and that a backward trace π of P is *evil* if it begins in a bad state. We denote P's reachable and evil traces by $[\![P]\!]_\Pi^F$ and $[\![P]\!]_\Pi^B$, respectively:

$$[\![P]\!]_\Pi^F \stackrel{\text{def}}{=} \{\pi \in [\![\mathrm{TR}(P)]\!]_\Pi \mid \pi_0 \in Init\} \text{ , and } [\![P]\!]_\Pi^B \stackrel{\text{def}}{=} \{\pi \in [\![\overleftarrow{\mathrm{TR}(P)}]\!]_\Pi \mid \pi_0 \in Bad\} .$$

Note that evil (backward) traces are read from left-to-right with the leftmost state being a bad state. And thus the backward trace transition relation $\mathrm{TR}_\Pi^B(P)$ used to define $C_\Pi^B(T)$ is in fact adding "pre-states" on the right.

We lift P's transition relation to *forward* and *backward trace transition relations*, denoted by $\mathrm{TR}_\Pi^F(P)$ and $\mathrm{TR}_\Pi^B(P)$, respectively:

$$\mathrm{TR}_\Pi^F(P) \stackrel{\text{def}}{=} \{(\pi\sigma, \pi\sigma\sigma') \mid \sigma \xrightarrow{TR} \sigma'\}, \text{ and } \quad \mathrm{TR}_\Pi^B(P) \stackrel{\text{def}}{=} \{(\pi\sigma, \pi\sigma\sigma') \mid \sigma \xrightarrow{\overleftarrow{TR}} \sigma'\}.$$

A trace π is reachable if there exists a valid sequence of P's forward trace transition relation leading from $\langle\sigma\rangle$ to π, where σ is an initial state. Similarly, π is evil if it is at the end of a valid sequence of the backward trace transitions starting at a trace comprised of a bad state. This allows an characterizing $[\![P]\!]_\Pi^F$ and $[\![P]\!]_\Pi^B$ as least fixpoints:

$$[\![P]\!]_\Pi^F = \mathrm{LFP}\, C_\Pi^F \quad \text{where} \quad C_\Pi^F(T) = \langle Init \rangle \cup \mathrm{TR}_\Pi^F(P)(T), \text{ and}$$
$$[\![P]\!]_\Pi^B = \mathrm{LFP}\, C_\Pi^B \quad \text{where} \quad C_\Pi^B(T) = \langle Bad \rangle \cup \mathrm{TR}_\Pi^B(P)(T).$$

Small Step Collecting Trace Semantics. C_Π^F and C_Π^B, defined above, operate on sets of traces. Such sets are in fact elements of the *collecting trace semantics* of P. The latter interprets P by accumulating the traces generated by its trace semantics. Formally, the *collecting trace domain* $\mathcal{D}_\Pi = (\mathscr{P}(\Pi), \subseteq)$ is a powerset domain over the set of traces, ordered by set inclusion.

A collecting semantics is often used as means to compute fixpoints of an underlying operational semantics. However, it can also be given an operation flavor by defining initial sets of traces and transitions between sets of traces. The initial set of traces is $\langle Init \rangle$ in the forward collecting trace semantics, and $\langle Bad \rangle$ in the backward semantics. The transitions are defined as the pointwise lifting of P's forward and backward trace transition relation to sets of traces, denoted by $\mathrm{TR}^F_{\mathscr{P}(\Pi)}(P)$ and $\mathrm{TR}^B_{\mathscr{P}(\Pi)}(P)$, respectively:

$$\mathrm{TR}^F_{\mathscr{P}(\Pi)}(P) \overset{\mathrm{def}}{=} \{(T, T \cup \{\pi'\}) \mid \exists \pi \in T.\, \pi \xrightarrow{\mathrm{TR}^F_\Pi(P)} \pi'\}, \text{ and}$$
$$\mathrm{TR}^B_{\mathscr{P}(\Pi)}(P) \overset{\mathrm{def}}{=} \{(T, T \cup \{\pi'\}) \mid \exists \pi \in T.\, \pi \xrightarrow{\mathrm{TR}^B_\Pi(P)} \pi'\}.$$

Note that both $\llbracket P \rrbracket^F_\Pi$ and $\llbracket P \rrbracket^B_\Pi$ are elements of $\mathcal{D}_\Pi$. Recall that we consider only finite sequences. Thus, there might not be a valid sequence according to, e.g., $\mathrm{TR}^B_{\mathscr{P}(\Pi)}(P)$ which leads from from $\langle Bad \rangle$ to $\llbracket P \rrbracket^B_\Pi$ because $\llbracket P \rrbracket^B_\Pi \setminus \langle Bad \rangle$ might be an infinite set. However, for every set of traces $T \supseteq \langle Bad \rangle$ and every *finite* set of evil traces T', there is such a valid sequence going from T to T'. Formally:

Lemma 1. *For every trace π, it holds that $\pi \in \llbracket P \rrbracket^F_\Pi$ (respectively, $\pi \in \llbracket P \rrbracket^B_\Pi$) if and only if there is a valid sequence of $\mathrm{TR}^F_{\mathscr{P}(\Pi)}(P)$ (respectively, $\mathrm{TR}^B_{\mathscr{P}(\Pi)}(P)$) going from $\langle Init \rangle$ (respectively, $\langle Bad \rangle$) to T such that $\pi \in T$.*

In Sect. 8, we show that *PDR* can be formalized as an abstract interpretation of a program using (a conservative abstraction of) the collecting trace semantics which develops simultaneously multiple traces. However, instead of trying to compute a fixpoint of the program's collecting trace semantics, *PDR* uses the execution as means to come up with a *useful fixpoint* of its *collecting state semantics* as we explain below.

Collecting State Semantics. It is standard to abstract a set of traces by the set of their states. Formally, the *collecting state semantics* of programs is a powerset domain over the set of states, ordered by set inclusion $\mathcal{D}_\Sigma = (\mathscr{P}(\Sigma), \subseteq)$. We define the expected Galois connection $(\mathcal{D}_\Pi, \alpha_\Sigma, \gamma_\Sigma, \mathcal{D}_\Sigma)$ between sets of traces and sets of states:

$$\gamma_\Sigma : \mathscr{P}(\Sigma) \to \mathscr{P}(\Pi) \quad ::= \quad \gamma_\Sigma(S) = \{\pi \in \Pi \mid \forall i \in \mathrm{dom}(\pi).\, \pi(i) \in S\} \text{ and}$$
$$\alpha_\Sigma : \mathscr{P}(\Pi) \to \mathscr{P}(\Sigma) \quad ::= \quad \alpha_\Sigma(T) = \{\sigma \in \mathrm{range}(\pi) \mid \pi \in T\}.$$

We say that a state is *reachable* if it appears in a reachable trace and *evil* if it appears in an evil one. The sets of reachable and evil states, denoted by $\llbracket P \rrbracket^F_\Sigma$ and $\llbracket P \rrbracket^B_\Sigma$, respectively, are defined using abstraction, and enjoy a least fixpoint characterization:

$$\llbracket P \rrbracket^F_\Sigma \overset{\mathrm{def}}{=} \alpha_\Sigma(\llbracket P \rrbracket^F_\Pi) = \mathrm{LFP}\, C^F_\Sigma \quad \text{where} \quad C^F_\Sigma(S) = Init \cup TR(S), \text{ and}$$
$$\llbracket P \rrbracket^B_\Sigma \overset{\mathrm{def}}{=} \alpha_\Sigma(\llbracket P \rrbracket^B_\Pi) = \mathrm{LFP}\, C^B_\Sigma \quad \text{where} \quad C^B_\Sigma(S) = Bad \cup \overleftarrow{TR}(S).$$

4   Useful and Projected Fixpoints

We refer to an evil trace that leads to an initial state as a *counterexample*. A program P is *safe* if none of its evil traces is a counterexample, and *unsafe* otherwise. In our setting, safety amounts to requiring that $[\![P]\!]_\Sigma^F \cap [\![P]\!]_\Sigma^B = \emptyset$. The goal of *PDR* and of its variants is to compute a superset of the reachable states of P, if P is safe, and report that a counterexample exists, otherwise. This is often done by looking for an inductive fixpoint of the (forward or backward) collecting state semantics.

A set of states S is an *inductive (forward) fixpoint* if $Init \subseteq S$ and $TR(S) \subseteq S$. We say that S is a *useful (forward) fixpoint* if, in addition, $S \cap Bad = \emptyset$. (A useful forward fixpoint is often called a *safe inductive invariant*.) Similarly, S is an *inductive backward fixpoint* if $Bad \subseteq S$ and $\overleftarrow{TR}(S) \subseteq S$. It is *useful* if $S \cap Init = \emptyset$.

A standard technique to find an inductive fixpoint is to iteratively apply the corresponding transformer. For example, to find an inductive fixpoint of the backward collecting state semantics, we would usually repeatedly apply C_Σ^B, while accumulating the discovered states, until no new state is discovered. As C_Σ^B is monotonic, it is ensured by Kleene's Theorem that at the limit we reach its least fixpoint. However, we can find such a fixpoint in a different way via a *projection* of the elements computed by the collecting trace semantics using, what we refer to, as *projected fixpoints*.

Given a set of traces T, we denote by $T|_\Sigma^i = \{\pi(i) \mid \pi \in T \wedge i < |\pi|\}$ the set of states in the i-th index of the traces in T. If there exists an index $i > 0$ such that (i) $Bad \subseteq T|_\Sigma^0$, (ii) for every $0 \leq j \leq i$, $\overleftarrow{TR}(T|_\Sigma^j) \subseteq T|_\Sigma^{j+1}$, and (iii) $T|_\Sigma^i = T|_\Sigma^{i+1}$, then $S = \bigcup_{j=0}^i T|_\Sigma^j$ is an inductive backward fixpoint of the collecting state semantics. We refer to S as a *projected fixpoint* of the collecting trace semantics. Intuitively, every evil trace can go only through states that appear in S. We note that if T has been computed by accumulating the results of some $0 \leq k$ applications of $C_\Pi^B(\cdot)$ starting from $\emptyset$, it suffices to check point (iii) above to determine that T has a projected fixpoint.

5   Small Step Cartesian Trace Semantics

The *cartesian trace semantics* abstracts the (forward and backward) collecting trace semantics using sequences of sets of states, which we refer to as *cartesian traces*. Informally, a cartesian trace ω conservatively represents a set of traces T of length $|\omega|$ or less by abstracting away the correlation between consecutive states. In the following, we focus on abstracting the backward semantics, as it is the one used by *PDR*. The cartesian semantics is suitable for tracking the intermediate results that occur during an iterative conservative fixpoint computation, and thus fits well to describe the sequence of sets of states computed by *PDR*. We refer to the set components of cartesian traces as *anti-frames*, as they correspond to the complements of the sets maintianed by *PDR*, which are often referred to as *frames*. (See Sect. 7.)

5.1   Cartesian Trace Transition Relation

We denote by $\Omega = \text{seq}(\mathscr{P}(\Sigma))$ the set of all sequences of sets of states, ranged over by metavariable ω. Following the intuitive discussion above, we define a function

γ_ω which maps a cartesian trace ω to the set of traces that it represents. The latter is comprised of any trace whose i-th state, for every i, is taken from the corresponding set $\omega(i)$.

$$\gamma_\omega : \Omega \to \mathscr{P}(\Pi) \quad ::= \quad \gamma_\omega(\omega) \stackrel{\text{def}}{=} \{\pi \in \Pi \mid |\pi| \le |\omega| \land \forall i \in \text{dom}(\pi).\, \pi(i) \in \omega(i)\}.$$

Note that if ω represents a trace π, then ω also represents every prefix of π.

Cartesian traces allow to *over-approximate* the (backward) trace semantics of P by lifting P's transition relation to a *backward cartesian trace transition relation*, denoted by $\text{TR}_\Omega^B(P)$:

$$\text{TR}_\Omega^B(P) \stackrel{\text{def}}{=} \{(\omega_1 S_1 S_2 \omega_2,\, \omega_1 S_1 (S_2 \cup S)\omega_2) \mid S \subseteq \overleftarrow{TR}(S_1)\}.$$

Note that while the collecting transition relation $\text{TR}_{\mathscr{P}(\Pi)}^B(P)$ extends traces, the cartesian transition relation relates only traces of the same length. Indeed, it can only add new states to sets that ω already contains. Intuitively, this means that we can only over-approximate at most $|\omega| - 1$ consecutive transitions of P. We do not overcome this limitation, instead we weaken the guarantees we get from abstract interpretation of P according to the cartesian trace semantics, as we shortly explain.

5.2   Cartesian Traces Domain

To define the *cartesian traces domain*, we first introduce the *subsumption* order between cartesian traces. We say that ω_1 *subsumes* ω_2, denoted by $\omega_1 \preceq_\omega \omega_2$, if every entry in ω_2 subsumes the corresponding entry in ω_1. Formally,

$$\omega_1 \preceq_\omega \omega_2 \stackrel{\text{def}}{=} |\omega_1| = |\omega_2| \land \forall i \in \text{dom}(\omega_1).\, \omega_1(i) \subseteq \omega_2(i),$$

The cartesian traces domain $\mathcal{D}_\Omega = (\mathscr{P}(\Omega), \sqsubseteq_\Omega)$ utilizes the powerset of the cartesian traces as its carrier set and it is ordered by a point-wise lifting of subsumption:

$$\mathcal{D}_\Omega = (\mathscr{P}(\Omega), \sqsubseteq_\Omega)\,,\text{ where } O_1 \sqsubseteq_\Omega O_2 \iff \forall \omega_1 \in O_1.\, \exists \omega_2 \in O_2.\, \omega_1 \preceq_\omega \omega_2\,.$$

The Galois connection $(\mathcal{D}_\Pi, \alpha_\Omega, \gamma_\Omega, \mathcal{D}_\Omega)$ between the domain of traces and that of cartesian traces is defined by a pointwise lifting of γ_ω to sets of cartesian traces.

$$\gamma_\Omega : \mathscr{P}(\Omega) \to \mathscr{P}(\Pi) \quad ::= \quad \gamma_\Omega(O) = \{\pi \in \gamma_\omega(\omega) \mid \omega \in O\}\ , \text{ and}$$
$$\alpha_\Omega : \mathscr{P}(\Pi) \to \mathscr{P}(\Omega) \quad ::= \quad \alpha_\Omega(T) = \{\lambda i \in \text{dom}(\pi).\{\pi(i)\} \mid \pi \in T\}.$$

Lemma 2. $(\mathcal{D}_\Pi, \alpha_\Omega, \gamma_\Omega, \mathcal{D}_\Omega)$ *is a Galois connection.*

Lemma 3. *Let π be a trace and ω be a cartesian trace such that $0 < |\pi| < |\omega|$. If $\pi \in \gamma_\omega(\omega)$ then $\text{TR}_\Pi^B(P)(\pi) \subseteq \gamma_\Omega(\text{TR}_\Omega^B(P)(\omega))$.*

Lemma 3 ensures that $\mathrm{TR}_\Omega^B(P)(\cdot)$ is a sound abstract transformer with respect to $\mathrm{TR}_\Pi^B(P)(\cdot)$ when we consider only bounded executions. More specifically, given a cartesian trace ω of length n and a trace π of length m represented by ω, we can over-approximate the set of traces that can be reached by executing $n - m - 1$ trace transitions $\xrightarrow{\mathrm{TR}_\Pi^B(P)}$. In particular, if $\omega(0) = Bad$, we can use $\mathrm{TR}_\Omega^B(P)(\cdot)$ to over-approximate the evil traces of length n or less.

In a sense, the cartesian trace semantics allows to over-approximate bounded under-approximations of the standard collecting trace semantics.

6 Property-Guided Abstraction of the Cartesian Trace Semantics

We abstract the backward cartesian trace semantics in a property-guided manner using two means: Firstly, we go to an *error state* in case we find a counterexample. Secondly, and most importantly, we allow to over-approximate the backward cartesian transition relation in a controlled way which ensures that the abstract trace does not represent spurious counterexamples. This form of abstraction explains the *generalization* operations in *PDR*. (See Sect. 7).

6.1 Property-Guided Cartesian Trace Transition Relation

The property-guided cartesian trace semantics over-approximates the backward cartesian trace transition relation by adding two new kinds transitions: *generalization* transitions, denoted by $\mathrm{TR}_\Omega^{Gen(B)}(P)$, and *error* transitions, denoted by $\mathrm{TR}_\Omega^{Err(B)}(P)$, which lead to a special *error* element $\top$.

$$\mathrm{TR}_\Omega^{Gen(B)}(P) \overset{\mathrm{def}}{=} \{(\omega_1 S_1 S_2 \omega_2, \omega_1 (S_1 \cup Y) S_2 \omega_2) \mid \overleftarrow{TR}(Y) \subseteq S_2 \wedge Y \cap Init = \emptyset\}, \text{ and}$$

$$\mathrm{TR}_\Omega^{Err(B)}(P) \overset{\mathrm{def}}{=} \{(\omega, \top) \mid \omega(|\omega| - 1) \cap Init \neq \emptyset\}.$$

Generalization transitions add a "forward" flavor to the property-guided cartesian trace semantics as they add states at index j based on the states at index $j + 1$. (Recall that these are *backward* traces, hence updates of $j + 1$ based on j correspond to backward steps, while updates of j based on $j + 1$ correspond to forward steps.)

Given a cartesian trace $\omega = \omega_1 S_1 S_2 \omega_2$, a generalization transition allows to add to its j-th anti-frame, where $j = |\omega_1|$, any state σ such that any backward trace of P of length $|\omega| - j$ which starts at σ goes only through states that can be reached by a backward trace starting at one of the states in the $j + 1$ anti-frame. Thus, the states added by the generalization would not open a new route towards an undiscovered state. Specifically, generalization would not lead to over-approximating a counterexample, unless this counterexample is already represented.

An error transition, happens when we find an initial state at the last anti-frame of the trace. Note that this means that we found a counterexample.

It suffices to look for an initial state *only* in the last anti-frame because of our assumption that *Init* and *Bad* are disjoint and the restrictions on the transformers which ensure that if the semantics computes a trace which goes through an initial state, it can also compute a shorter (evil) trace which ends with that state.

We denote the enriched transition relation by $\mathrm{TR}_\Omega^{BGE}(P)$, i.e.,

$$\mathrm{TR}_\Omega^{BGE}(P) = \mathrm{TR}_\Omega^{B}(P) \cup \mathrm{TR}_\Omega^{Gen(B)}(P) \cup \mathrm{TR}_\Omega^{Err(B)}(P).$$

In the following, we refer to the transitions defined in Sect. 5.1 as *pre-transitions*. We say that a pre-transition $(\omega_1 S_1 S_2 \omega_2, \omega_1 S_1 (S_2 \cup S)\omega_2) \in \mathrm{TR}_\Omega^{B}(P)$ *takes place* at index $|\omega_1|$. (Note that we say that although the transition updates the set at index $|\omega_1|+1$). We say that a gen-transition $(\omega_1 S_1 S_2 \omega_2, \omega_1 (S_1 \cup Y) S_2 \omega_2) \in \mathrm{TR}_\Omega^{Gen(B)}(P)$ *takes place* at index $|\omega_1|$ based on the set at index $|\omega_1| + 1$.

6.2   Small Step Collecting Property-Guided Cartesian Trace Semantics

Recall that the cartesian transition relation does not allow to extend the length of a trace ω, nor do the generalization and error transition relations, and hence they are limited to over-approximate bounded executions. To overcome this limitation, we turn to the powerset domain; the underlying domain of the collecting property-guided cartesian trace semantics is the cartesian trace domain, $\mathcal{D}_\Omega$, enriched with the error element, $\top$, which is greater than any other element.

Property-guided Initial Cartesian Traces. We prepare ahead to produce traces of any possible length by starting the interpretation of the program from an unbounded set of cartesian traces: Let $\emptyset^k$ denote a cartesian trace of length $0 \leq k$ whose anti-frames are all empty, i.e., $\emptyset^k = \langle \emptyset, \ldots, \emptyset \rangle$. A cartesian trace ω is *property-guided initial* (*initial* for short) if $\omega = \langle Bad \rangle \emptyset^k \langle \Sigma \setminus Init \rangle$, for some $0 \leq k$, i.e., its first anti-frame is comprised of bad states, its last of the non-initial ones, and all the others are empty. Note that all initial cartesian traces are of length ≥ 2.

We denote the *initial* cartesian trace of length i (for $i \geq 2$) by $\hat{\omega}^i$, i.e., $\hat{\omega}^i = \langle Bad \rangle \emptyset^{i-2} \langle \Sigma \setminus Init \rangle$, and the set of initial cartesian traces by $\hat{\Omega}$. Note that $\hat{\omega}^2$ represents all traces of length 2 that start in a bad state and end in a non-initial state as well as their prefixes, i.e., if the program is safe $\hat{\omega}^2$ represents the largest safe over-approximation (superset) of the evil traces of P of length at most two. All other initial cartesian traces represent $\langle Bad \rangle$, the set of evil traces of length one (which correspond to the prefix of length one since the second element is $\emptyset$). Informally, starting from a given initial cartesian trace $\hat{\omega}^i$, we can simulate evil traces of length i or less.

Property-guided Collecting Cartesian Transition Relation. The *collecting property-guided cartesian trace semantics* is obtained by lifting the enriched transition relation $\mathrm{TR}_\Omega^{BGE}(P)$ to a collecting transition relation $\mathrm{TR}_{\mathscr{P}(\Omega)}^{BGE}(P)$ which works in a pointwise manner on sets of cartesian traces. This is done similarly to the way we obtained the transition relation of the collecting trace semantics $\mathrm{TR}^{B}_{\mathscr{P}(\Pi)}(P)$ out of that of the trace semantics $\mathrm{TR}^{B}_{\Pi}(P)$. (See, Sect. 3.) We also adapt $\mathrm{TR}^{BGE}_{\mathscr{P}(\Omega)}(P)(O)$ to go to $\top$ if there is a cartesian trace in O that leads to $\top$ in one step. The valid sequences of $\mathrm{TR}^{BGE}_{\mathscr{P}(\Omega)}(P)$ from $\hat{\Omega}$ define the property-guided meaning of the program.

Lemma 4 (Soundness and Precision). *A program P is safe if and only if for any $0 \leq k$, it holds that $(\mathrm{TR}^{BGE}_{\mathscr{P}(\Omega)}(P))^{k}(\hat{\Omega}) \neq \top$.*

Lemma 4 ensures that we can use the property-guided cartesian trace semantics to find any evil trace of P. Intuitively, we can compute any evil trace π by first picking an initial cartesian trace of length $|\pi| + 1$ and then executing the sequence of cartesian trace transitions corresponding to the ones which generated π. Furthermore, it ensures that the property-guided semantics does not lose precision when it comes to safety: Thanks to the restrictions on the generalization steps, the semantics never reaches an error state if the program is safe.

We can adapt the notion of projected fixpoints to the cartesian semantics. Given a cartesian trace ω, we say that $\omega(i)$, where $0 < i < |\omega| - 1$, is a *projected fixpoint* if (i) $Bad \subseteq \omega(0)$, (ii) for every $0 \leq j < i$, $\omega(j) \cup \overleftarrow{TR}(\omega(j)) \subseteq \omega(j + 1)$, and (iii) $\omega(i) = \omega(i + 1)$.

Lemma 5 (Projected Fixpoints). *Let ω be a cartesian trace such that $\omega(i)$ is a projected fixpoint. It holds that $\omega(i)$ is an inductive backward fixpoint of the collecting state semantics.*

In fact, given a useful backward fixpoint S, we can use the appropriate generalization transitions starting from $\hat{\Omega}$ to produce a cartesian trace ω which contains S as a projected fixpoint at some index i.

We can now restate the last paragraph of Sect. 3 in a more precise way: In Sect. 8, we show that *PDR* can be formalized as an abstract interpretation of the collecting property-guided cartesian semantics, where every operation of *PDR* can be understood as a sequence of steps taken by the semantics.

The semantics, when looking at it from the viewpoint of *PDR*, interprets the program with two goals in mind. The first goal is to look for a *useful fixpoint* of its *collecting state semantics*. This is done by taking generalization steps. The second goal, which is done in parallel, is to look for a counterexample. This is done using pre-transitions. The two goals affect each other: The states that are discovered using the pre-transitions, are used to compute Y in the generalization transitions by applying an algorithm specific-heuristic. The generalization, on the other hand, might add states that would make future pre-transitions mute as their targets would be detected early. This, could help *PDR* terminate faster than if it had taken only pre-transitions.

The *PDR*-viewpoint helps understand the reason behind placing $\Sigma \setminus Init$ as the last component of the initial cartesian traces: It is apriori known that this set provides (the most coarse) over-approximation of the last state of any evil trace which is not a counterexample. As a result, it provides the greatest opportunity to apply generalization transitions at the penultimate set, and by extension, at the ones preceding it. This flexibility is the reason that the collecting semantics can compute any useful fixpoint.

7   Traditional *PDR*

In this section we describe *PDR* in an operational manner. Traditionally, *PDR* uses a symbolic representation of states and sets of states as formulas in some logic (either propositional or first order logic). In our description of *PDR* we refer to the underlying states or sets of states explicitly.

We start by a high-level description of *PDR* and the data structures used by it. The latter also define its *configurations*. We then describe the different operations performed by the different implementations of *PDR*.

Initially, *PDR* checks if $Init \cap Bad = \emptyset$, and reports a counterexample if this is not the case. For simplicity of the presentation, we consider this check to be done before *PDR* is invoked. We therefore assume that $Init \cap Bad = \emptyset$.

Forward Reachability Sequence. *PDR* computes increasingly longer *forward reachability sequences*. When referring to sequences maintained by *PDR*, we use a subscript notation for the elements of a sequence: F_i instead of $F(i)$. We denote the sequence comprised of the elements $F_0, \ldots, F_N$, for some $0 < N$, by $\langle F_0, \ldots, F_N \rangle$.

Definition 1 (Forward Reachability Sequence). *A forward reachability sequence of length $N + 1$ is a sequence $\varphi_N = \langle F_0, F_1, \ldots, F_N \rangle \in seq(\mathscr{P}(\Sigma))$ which has the following properties:*

1. $F_0 = Init$,
2. $F_i \subseteq F_{i+1}$ for every $0 \leq i < N$,
3. $TR(F_i) \subseteq F_{i+1}$ for every $0 \leq i < N$,
4. $F_i \cap Bad = \emptyset$ for every $0 \leq i \leq N$.

The sets F_i in the sequence φ_N are called frames. N *is called the* iteration counter.

Note that the property $TR(F_i) \subseteq F_{i+1}$ is equivalent to $\overleftarrow{TR}(\Sigma \backslash F_{i+1}) \subseteq \Sigma \backslash F_i$. We use the two interchangeably. The properties of a forward reachability sequence φ_N imply that for every $0 \leq i \leq N$, frame F_i over-approximates the set of states reachable from the initial states in at most i steps. If the sequence includes an index $0 \leq i < N$ such that $F_i = F_{i+1}$ then property 3 simplifies to $TR(F_i) \subseteq F_i$. Hence, together with properties 1 and 4, we conclude that F_i is a useful forward fixpoint (or safe inductive invariant), which implies that P is safe.

PDR computes forward reachability sequences φ_N of increasing lengths, starting from $N = 1$, until either a counterexample is found or a fixpoint is reached.

In the intermediate steps of the computation of the forward reachability sequence φ_N, requirement 3 might not hold (*only*) for $i = N - 1$, in which case we refer to φ_N as an *intermediate forward sequence*. Specifically, for $N = 1$, φ_N is initialized to $\langle Init, \Sigma \setminus Bad \rangle$. For $N > 1$, *PDR* initializes an intermediate forward sequence φ_N by extending the forward reachability sequence φ_{N-1} from the previous iteration with an additional frame $F_N = \Sigma \setminus Bad$. If requirement 3 does not hold due to the addition of F_N, *PDR* tries to strengthen the frames F_i (which over-approximate the reachable states) in order to satisfy requirement 3 for $i = N - 1$ as well. For this purpose, *PDR* iteratively retrieves from F_{N-1} a state for which $TR(\sigma) \subseteq F_N$ does not hold (equivalently, $\sigma \in \overleftarrow{TR}(Bad) \cap F_{N-1}$), and tries to eliminate it by strengthening F_{N-1}. To do so while maintaining the (other) properties of a forward reachability sequence, *PDR* first has to strengthen F_{N-2} to eliminate from it all the predecessors of σ. For the elimination of each predecessor, the same process is needed. This results in a backward traversal of the state space.

Obligations Queue. The states that need to be eliminated from their frames are called *counterexamples to induction* (CTIs), since their removal is needed in order to maintain the induction condition ($TR(F_i) \subseteq F_{i+1}$). A pair (i, σ) consisting of an index i and a CTI σ that needs to be eliminated from F_i is called a *proof obligation* (obligation in short). All obligations have the property that their states lead to a bad state. Technically, *PDR* uses an *obligation queue*, denoted q, to handle the obligations.

If all obligations are handled successfully, φ_N satisfies requirement 3 for $i = N - 1$ as well, and hence it becomes a forward reachability sequence. However, there might be intermediate steps where q is temporarily empty, even though not all obligations have been handled (since not all have been discovered). To distinguish between the former and the latter we use $\perp$ to denote the value of the queue when all obligations are handled, as opposed to $\emptyset$ which denotes an empty queue, possibly temporarily.

PDR *Configurations.* A configuration of *PDR* is a triple $\kappa = (N, \varphi_N, q)$, where

- $N \in \mathbb{N}$,
- $\varphi_N = \langle F_0, F_1, \ldots, F_N \rangle \in (\mathscr{P}(\Sigma))^{N+1}$ is an intermediate forward sequence, and
- $q \in \mathscr{P}([N] \times \Sigma) \cup \{\perp\}$ is an obligations queue, where $[N] = \{0, \ldots, N\}$.

Initial Configuration. Assuming that $Init \cap Bad = \emptyset$, the initial configuration of *PDR* is $\kappa_0 = (1, \langle Init, \Sigma \setminus Bad \rangle, \emptyset)$.

PDR *Operations.* Given a configuration $\kappa = (N, \varphi_N, q)$ as above, *PDR* proceeds by performing one of the following procedures. We denote the resulting configuration by $\kappa' = (N', \varphi', q')$. Each procedure updates a subset of the components of the configuration. We describe only the components that are indeed updated.

Queue Initialization: If $q = \emptyset$, and there is a state $\sigma \in \overleftarrow{TR}(Bad) \cap F_{N-1}$, PDR adds the obligation $(N - 1, \sigma)$ to the queue, resulting in $q' = \{(N - 1, \sigma)\}$. If no such state exist, it sets $q' = \bot$.

Backward Step: Given an obligation $(i, \sigma') \in q$, where $1 \leq i \leq N$ is the minimal frame index in q, such that there is $\sigma \in \overleftarrow{TR}(\sigma') \cap F_{i-1}$, PDR adds $(i - 1, \sigma)$ to q. Namely, $q' = q \cup \{(i - 1, \sigma)\}$.

Obligation Lifting: Once an obligation $(i - 1, \sigma)$ is added to q due to a backward step from $(i, \sigma') \in q$, PDR computes a *lifting* of the obligation, $S = OLift(\sigma, \sigma', F_i)$, and adds the set of obligations $\{i - 1\} \times S$ to the queue, where $OLift(\sigma, \sigma', F_i)$ computes a set of states $S \subseteq \Sigma$ such that $S \subseteq \overleftarrow{TR}(\sigma')$. Namely, $q' = q \cup (\{i - 1\} \times S)$.

Obligation lifting helps accelerating PDR by lifting an obligation discovered by a backward step from some obligation $(i, \sigma') \in q$ to a *set* of obligations, all of which result from a backward step of the same obligation.

Blocking: Given an obligation $(i, \sigma') \in q$, where $1 \leq i \leq N$ is the minimal frame index in q and $\overleftarrow{TR}(\sigma') \cap F_{i-1} = \emptyset$, PDR removes (i, σ') from q, and removes σ' from F_i (if it was not yet removed). Note that since $i \geq 1$, $\sigma' \notin Init$. This results in the configuration $\kappa' = (N, \langle F_0, \ldots, F_{i-1}, F_i \setminus \{\sigma'\}, F_{i+1}, \ldots, F_N \rangle, q \setminus \{(i, \sigma')\})$.

Generalization: Once (i, σ') is blocked, in addition to removing σ' from F_i, PDR computes a *generalization* of the blocked state, $S = Gen(\sigma', F_{i-1})$, and removes S from all F_j such that $j \leq i$, where $Gen(\sigma', F_{i-1})$ computes a set of states $S \subseteq \Sigma$ such that $Init \cap S = \emptyset$ and $TR(F_{i-1}) \cap S = \emptyset$ (i.e., where all states have no predecessor in F_{i-1}). The result is $\varphi' = \langle F_0, F_1 \setminus S, \ldots, F_i \setminus S, F_{i+1}, \ldots, F_N \rangle$.

Inductive Generalization: Once (i, σ') is blocked, in addition to removing σ' from F_i, PDR computes an *inductive generalization* of the blocked state, $S = IGen(\sigma', F_{i-1})$, and removes S from all F_j such that $j \leq i$, where $IGen(\sigma', F_{i-1})$ computes a set of states $S \subseteq \Sigma$ such that $Init \cap S = \emptyset$ and $TR(F_{i-1} \setminus S) \cap S = \emptyset$. The result is $\varphi' = \langle F_0, F_1 \setminus S, \ldots, F_i \setminus S, F_{i+1}, \ldots, F_N \rangle$.

Inductive generalization is an enhancement of generalization which results in a stronger strengthening of frames, as every generalization is also an inductive generalization, but not the other way around. It is based on an attempt to identify sets whose complements are inductive *relatively to the current frame*, and therefore can be used to safely strengthen all frames up to the current one while keeping the properties of an intermediate forward sequence (and in particular, without excluding any reachable state).

Forward Propagation: Once F_i is updated by removing S from it (as a result of generalization, inductive generalization, or forward propagation), i.e. $F_i \cap S = \emptyset$, it is checked whether $TR(F_i) \cap S = \emptyset$, and if so, F_{i+1} is also updated to $F_{i+1} \setminus S$. The result is $\varphi' = \langle F_0, \ldots, F_i, F_{i+1} \setminus S, F_{i+2}, \ldots, F_N \rangle$.

Forward propagation attempts to speculatively strengthen frames before obligations are encountered. Similarly to inductive generalization, it considers sets that are inductive relatively to the current frame (the complement of every set that is removed from a frame corresponds to such a relative inductive set), and checks whether they are also inductive relatively to consecutive frames.

Pushing Obligations Forward: Once an obligation (i, σ') for $1 \leq i \leq N - 1$ is removed from q, an obligation $(i + 1, \sigma')$ is added to q. The result is $q' = q \cup \{(i + 1, \sigma')\}$.

Pushing obligations forward aims at an early discovery of obligations. An obligation (i, σ') consists of a state σ' that reaches a bad state in some $k > 0$ steps. The same holds also when σ' is considered in F_{i+1}, which makes $(i+1, \sigma')$ a legitimate obligation (it will be discovered/handled at the latest when $N = i + 1 + k$). Its early addition can help accelerate the strengthening towards a fixpoint, or enable finding counterexamples that are longer than $N + 1$.

Unfolding: If $q = \bot$ and fixpoint is not obtained, *PDR* initializes F_{N+1} to $\Sigma \setminus Bad$, increases N to $N + 1$, and sets q to an empty queue. This results in the configuration $\kappa' = (N + 1, \langle F_0, F_1, \ldots, F_N, \Sigma \setminus Bad \rangle, \emptyset)$.

Termination. If there is an obligation $(0, \sigma') \in q$, *PDR* terminates and reports a *counterexample*. If $q = \bot$, and there exists $i < N$ such that $F_i = F_{i+1}$, *PDR* terminates with a *fixpoint* and reports safety.

PDR is parametric in the generalization function *Gen*, the inductive generalization function *IGen* (typically only one of them is used), and the lifting function *OLift*.

Remark 1 (Symbolic PDR). PDR is typically implemented as a SAT-based or an SMT-based model checking algorithm. It uses formulas in (propositional or first order) logic over a vocabulary V to describe states and sets of states. In particular, a state is described as a *cube* over V, i.e., a conjunction of literals (predicates or their negations) and a set (e.g., a frame F_i) is described as a CNF formula over V, i.e., conjunction of clauses where each clause consists of a disjunction of literals. The transition relation *TR* is also described by a formula, over a double vocabulary $V \cup V'$, where V represents the current state and $V' = \{v' \mid v \in V\}$ represents the next state.

Checks such as $\overleftarrow{TR}(\sigma') \cap F_{i-1} = \emptyset$ are done by validity checks of the corresponding formulas, e.g. $F_{i-1}(V) \wedge TR(V, V') \Rightarrow \neg\sigma'(V')$, or alternatively, unsatisfiability checks of their negation, i.e., $F_{i-1}(V) \wedge TR(V, V') \wedge \sigma'(V')$. When the formula is satisfiable, a state $\sigma \in \overleftarrow{TR}(\sigma') \cap F_{i-1}$ is retrieved from the satisfying assignment.

In this setting, generalization, inductive generalization and lifting are performed on a cube, representing a state, and a CNF formula, representing a frame. They compute a CNF formula representing a set of states.

For example, a typical implementation of generalization $Gen(\sigma', F_{i-1})$ looks for a sub-clause c of the clause $\neg\sigma'(V)$ such that $Init(V) \Rightarrow c(V)$ and $F_{i-1}(V) \wedge$

$TR(V, V') \Rightarrow c(V')$. If this holds, then $Gen(\sigma', F_{i-1})$ returns $\neg c(V)$ as a formula representing the set of states to be removed from F_j for all $j \leq i$. The removal is performed by conjoining F_j with c. Inductive generalization is performed similarly.

Obligations lifting was performed in the original *PDR* paper [3] statically by considering the k-step cone of influence. [7] performed dynamic lifting using ternary simulation. [4] suggested a SAT-based approach, using unsatisfiability cores, for lifting.

8   PDR as a Property-Guided Abstract Interpretation of the Cartesian Trace Semantics

In this section, we show that the *collecting* property-guided cartesian trace semantics defined in Sect. 6 simulates *PDR*, or in other words, *PDR* is an implementation of the semantics. For this purpose we define a simulation relation mapping *PDR* configurations to elements of the semantics, given by sets of sequences. We show that each step of *PDR* is simulated by a sequence of transitions of the semantics, in the sense that the resulting *PDR* configuration matches the resulting element in the semantics.

The mapping between *PDR* configurations and elements of the semantics is given by a *compatibility relation* defined below. It should be noted that while the sequences of frames used by *PDR* are indexed such that $F_0 = Init$ and increasing indices represent increasing distance (with respect to TR) from the initial states, the sequences used by our semantics are indexed such that $\omega(0) = Bad$ and increasing indices represent increasing distance (with respect to $\overleftarrow{TR}$) from the bad states. In this sense, the two consider opposite directions of the transition relation.

Definition 2 (Compatibility). *Let* $\kappa = (N, \varphi = \langle F_0, F_1, \ldots, F_N \rangle, q)$ *be a* PDR *configuration, and* $\omega \in \Omega$. *The intermediate forward sequence* φ *is proof-compatible* with ω if $|\omega| = |\varphi| = N + 1$ *and for every* $0 \leq i \leq N$, $F_i = \Sigma \setminus \omega(N - i)$. *An obligation* $(i, \sigma) \in q$ *is cex-compatible* with ω if $|\omega| \geq i + 1$ *and* $\sigma \in \omega(|\omega| - 1 - i)$.

We say that κ *is* compatible *with a set of sequences* $O \subseteq \Omega$, *if*

1. *there exists* $\omega_\varphi \in O$ *such that* φ *is proof-compatible with* ω_φ, *and*
2. *either* $q = \bot$ *or for every obligation* $\psi = (i, \sigma) \in q$, *there exists* $\omega_\psi \in O$ *such that* ψ *is cex-compatible with* ω_ψ.

We refer to ω_φ *and* ω_ψ *as the* witnessing sequences *for* φ *and* ψ, *respectively.*

Thus, proof-compatibility requires that that sequences φ and ω are "mirrors" of each other combined with a pointwise complement operation. This also explains the choice of the term "anti-frames" for the sets in a backward cartesian trace. (See Sect. 5.) Cex-compatibility requires that the CTI σ which appears as an obligation in index i with respect to φ, will appear in ω in distance i from the *end* of the sequence.

Lemma 6. *The compatibility relation is a stuttering simulation between reachable PDR configurations and reachable elements of the collecting property-guided cartesian trace semantics.*

Proof. We prove the claim by showing that the initial configurations of *PDR* and the semantics are compatible, and that every step of *PDR* maintains compatibility.

Initial Configuration. Let κ_0 be the initial configuration of *PDR*, and $\hat{\Omega}$ be the initial element of the semantics. Then $\varphi_0 = \langle Init, \Sigma \setminus Bad \rangle$ is proof-compatible with the sequence $\hat{\omega}^2 = \langle Bad, \Sigma \setminus Init \rangle \in \hat{\Omega}$, and q is empty, hence cex-compatibility holds trivially.

Steps of PDR. Let $\kappa = (N, \varphi, q)$ be a configuration of *PDR* (where $N \geq 1$), and let O be an element of the semantics such that κ is compatible with O. For each possible step of *PDR* leading to $\kappa' = (N', \varphi', q')$, we show a corresponding sequence of $\mathrm{TR}^{BGE}_{\mathscr{P}(\Omega)}(P)$ leading from O to O' such that κ' is compatible with O'.

Note that it suffices to show sequences of transitions of $\mathrm{TR}^{BGE}_{\Omega}(P)$ leading to witnesses for φ' and for the obligations in q' separately. Since $\mathrm{TR}^{BGE}_{\mathscr{P}(\Omega)}(P)$ is monotonic and accumulative (i.e., if $\omega \in O$ and O has a transition of $\mathrm{TR}^{BGE}_{\mathscr{P}(\Omega)}(P)$ to O'', then $\omega \in O''$ as well), these sequences of transitions of $\mathrm{TR}^{BGE}_{\Omega}(P)$ can then be lifted to transitions of $\mathrm{TR}^{BGE}_{\mathscr{P}(\Omega)}(P)$, concatenated and applied on O to obtain O'. For the same reason it suffices to show such sequences of transitions only for the components in the *PDR* configuration that have changed in the step from κ to κ': for an unchanged component, the same witness from O, which exists in any subsequent element O'' of O, remains a witness.

Queue Initialization: $\kappa' = (N, \varphi, q')$ where q' is either $\bot$, or a singleton $\{(N-1, \sigma)\}$. Consider first the case where $q' = \bot$. In this case, κ' is compatible with the same O, i.e. no transition of the semantics is needed.

Consider now the case where $q' = \{(N-1, \sigma)\}$, where $\sigma \in \overleftarrow{TR}(Bad) \cap F_{N-1}$. Recall that O is a reachable element of the semantics. Therefore, $\hat{\Omega} \subseteq O$. Starting from $\hat{\omega}^{N+1} \in \hat{\Omega} \subseteq O$ we apply a pre-transition of the semantics in index 0 of $\hat{\omega}^{N+1}$, adding the set $\{\sigma\}$ to $\hat{\omega}^{N+1}(1)$. The transition is applicable since $\sigma \in \overleftarrow{TR}(Bad)$ and $\hat{\omega}^{N+1}(0) = Bad$. The result is ω' of length $N+1$ such that $\sigma \in \omega'(1)$, where $1 = |\omega'| - 1 - (N-1)$. Hence $(N-1, \sigma)$ is cex-compatible with ω'.

Backward Step: $\kappa' = (N, \varphi, q')$, where $q' = q \cup \{(i-1, \sigma)\}$. Let $\omega_{(i,\sigma')}$ be the witnessing sequence for the obligation (i, σ') which is the trigger for this step (where $|\omega_{(i,\sigma')}| \geq i+1$). Similarly to the case of queue initialization, we use a pre-transition of the semantics in index $|\omega_{(i,\sigma')}| - 1 - i$ of $\omega_{(i,\sigma')}$ to add $\{\sigma\}$ to $\omega_{(i,\sigma')}(|\omega_{(i,\sigma')}| - i)$, resulting in $\omega'_{(i,\sigma')}$ of the same length, such that $\sigma \in \omega'_{(i,\sigma')}(|\omega_{(i,\sigma')}| - i)$. Therefore, $\omega'_{(i,\sigma')}$ is a witness for cex-compatibility of the new obligation $(i-1, \sigma)$.

Obligation Lifting: $q' = q \cup (\{i-1\} \times S)$. Similarly to the backward step, let $\omega_{(i,\sigma')}$ be the witnessing sequence for the obligation (i, σ') which is the trigger for the backward step responsible for lifting. A witness is obtained for all $(i-1,\sigma) \in \{i-1\} \times S$, by a pre-transition from $\omega_{(i,\sigma')}$ in index $|\omega_{(i,\sigma')}| - 1 - i$ adding S to $\omega_{(i,\sigma')}(|\omega_{(i,\sigma')}| - i)$. The pre-transition is applicable since $S \subseteq \overleftarrow{TR}(\sigma')$.

Blocking: $q' = q \setminus \{(i,\sigma')\}$, and $\varphi' = \langle F_0, \ldots, F_{i-1}, F_i \setminus \{\sigma'\}, F_{i+1}, \ldots, F_N \rangle$, where $1 \leq i \leq N$. Since q' is a subset of q, the same witnessing sequences for its obligations in O appear in every subsequent element of O. As for φ', let $\omega_\varphi \in O$ be a witnessing sequence for φ. Since $\overleftarrow{TR}(\sigma') \cap F_{i-1} = \emptyset$, we generate a witnessing sequence for φ' by applying a generalization transition on ω_φ at index $N - i$ (i.e., updating index $N - i$ based on $N - i + 1$) using the set $Y = \{\sigma'\}$, similarly to the simulation of a generalization step of *PDR* (see below).

Generalization: In this case, $\varphi' = \langle F_0 \setminus S, \ldots, F_i \setminus S, F_{i+1}, \ldots, F_N \rangle$. Let $\omega_\varphi = \langle \Sigma \setminus F_N, \ldots, \Sigma \setminus F_0 \rangle$ be a witnessing sequence for φ in O. We obtain ω'_φ by a sequence of generalization transitions. For every $j = 1, \ldots, i$ (in increasing order), starting from $\omega^1 = \omega_\varphi$, we apply a generalization transition on $\omega^j = \langle \Sigma \setminus F_N, \ldots, \Sigma \setminus F_j, \Sigma \setminus (F_{j-1} \setminus S), \ldots, \Sigma \setminus (F_1 \setminus S), \Sigma \setminus F_0 \rangle$ in index $N - j$ (i.e., updating index $N - j$ based on $N - j + 1$) using the set $Y = S$, leading to ω^{j+1}. By the requirements of *Gen*, $Init \cap S = \emptyset$ and $TR(F_{i-1}) \cap S = \emptyset$, i.e., $\overleftarrow{TR}(S) \subseteq \Sigma \setminus F_{i-1}$. Since $F_{j-1} \subseteq F_{i-1}$ for every $j \leq i$, we have that $\overleftarrow{TR}(S) \subseteq \Sigma \setminus F_{j-1}$. As such S indeed satisfies the requirements of a generalization transition in index $N - j$ of ω_j. Finally, ω^{i+1} is a witnessing sequence for φ'.

Inductive Generalization: This step is similar to generalization, where now $\overleftarrow{TR}(S) \subseteq \Sigma \setminus F_{j-1}$ does not necessarily hold, but $\overleftarrow{TR}(S) \subseteq \Sigma \setminus (F_{j-1} \setminus S)$ holds (since $TR(F_{i-1} \setminus S) \cap S = \emptyset$). However, since the transitions are performed from $j = 1$ and up, when the generalization transition is performed on $\omega^j = \langle \Sigma \setminus F_N, \ldots, \Sigma \setminus F_j, \Sigma \setminus (F_{j-1} \setminus S), \ldots, \Sigma \setminus (F_1 \setminus S), \Sigma \setminus F_0 \rangle$ in index $N - j$ (i.e., updating index $N - j$ based on $N - j + 1$) using the set $Y = S$, it is already the case that $\omega^j(N - j + i) = \Sigma \setminus (F_{j-1} \setminus S)$. Therefore, $\overleftarrow{TR}(S) \subseteq \omega^j(N - j + i)$ holds.

Forward Propagation: $\varphi' = \langle F_0, \ldots, F_i, F_{i+1} \cup S, F_{i+2}, \ldots, F_N \rangle$. Let ω_φ be a witnessing sequence for φ in O. We obtain ω'_φ by a generalization transition on ω_φ in index $N - i - 1$ (updating index $N - i - 1$ based on $N - i$).

Pushing Obligations Forward: Recall that in this case $\kappa' = (N, \varphi, q \cup \{(i+1, \sigma)\})$. In this case, we show how to obtain a cex-witness ω' for $(i+1, \sigma)$ by a sequence of pre-transitions. By the property of the obligations in *PDR*, there exists k and a sequence $\langle \sigma_k, \sigma_{k-1}, \ldots, \sigma_0 \rangle$ such that $\sigma_k = \sigma$ and $\sigma_0 \in Bad$ (i.e., σ leads to a bad state in k steps). Therefore, starting from $\omega^0 = \hat{\omega}^{i+2+k} \in \hat{\Omega} \subseteq O$ of length $i + 2 + k$, we apply pre-transitions for every $j = 0, \ldots, k - 1$ (in increasing order) in index j of ω^j, adding the singleton $\{\sigma_{j+1}\}$ to the $j + 1$-th index, resulting in ω^{j+1} where $\omega^{j+1}(j+1) = \omega^j(j+1) \cup \{\sigma_{j+1}\}$. The result of the transitions is ω^k of length $i+2+k$ such that $\sigma \in \omega^k(k)$, where $k = |\omega^k| - 1 - (i+1)$. Hence $(i+1, \sigma)$ is cex-compatible with ω^k.

Unfolding: In this case, $\kappa' = (N+1, \langle F_0, F_1, \ldots, F_N, \Sigma \setminus Bad \rangle, \emptyset)$. We show how to obtain a witnessing sequence for $\varphi' = \langle F_0, F_1, \ldots, F_N, \Sigma \setminus Bad \rangle$ by a sequence of generalization transitions. We utilize again the property of reachable elements of the semantics which ensures that $\hat{\omega}^{N+2} = \langle Bad \rangle \emptyset^N \langle \Sigma \setminus Init \rangle \in \hat{\Omega} \subseteq O$. For every $i = 0, \ldots, N-1$ (in increasing order), starting from $\omega^0 = \hat{\omega}^{N+2}$, we apply a generalization transition on $\omega^i = \langle Bad \rangle \emptyset^{N-i} \langle \Sigma \setminus F_i, \ldots, \Sigma \setminus F_1, \Sigma \setminus Init \rangle$ in index $N - i$ (i.e., updating index $N - i$ based on index $N - i + 1$) using the set $Y = \Sigma \setminus F_{i+1}$, leading to $\omega^{i+1} = \langle Bad \rangle \emptyset^{N-i-1} \langle \Sigma \setminus F_{i+1}, \ldots, \Sigma \setminus F_1, \Sigma \setminus Init \rangle$. To be convinced that the transition from ω^i to ω^{i+1} is well defined, we recall the properties of PDR. By the properties of PDR, for every $0 \leq i < N$, $TR(F_i) \subseteq F_{i+1}$, or equivalently, $\overleftarrow{TR}(\Sigma \setminus F_{i+1}) \subseteq \Sigma \setminus F_i$. In addition, $Init \subseteq F_{i+1}$, or equivalently $(\Sigma \setminus F_{i+1}) \cap Init = \emptyset$. As such, $Y = \Sigma \setminus F_{i+1}$ indeed satisfies the requirements of a generalization transition in index $N - i$ of ω^i. Finally, ω^N is a witnessing sequence for φ'. Since $q' = \emptyset$, no witnesses for cex-compatibility are needed. $\qquad\square$

The proof of Lemma 6 shows that different components of the PDR configuration correspond to different sequences in the element of the semantics, O. In this sense, PDR can be thought of as trying to compute multiple sequences of the semantics simultaneously, as it both tries to find counterexamples of different lengths, and at the same time tries to verify safety.

Lemma 6 implies that all reachable configurations of PDR are compatible with reachable configurations of the semantics. This holds in particular for terminal configurations of PDR. We now show that the correctness of the output of PDR in each of the terminal configurations follows from their compatibility with an element of the semantics.

Counterexample: If there is an obligation $(0, \sigma') \in q$, PDR terminates and reports a counterexample. Such an obligation indicates that $\sigma' \in F_0$, i.e. $\sigma' \in Init$. Lemma 6 ensures that there is a reachable element O of the semantics with some $\omega \in O$ such that $\sigma' \in \omega(|\omega| - 1)$. Indeed, since $\sigma' \in Init$, it follows that ω has an *error transition* leading to $\top$ (the error state of the semantics).

Fixpoint: If $q = \bot$, and there exists $i < N$ such that $F_i = F_{i+1}$, PDR terminates and reports safety. PDR has the property that when $q = \bot$, the intermediate forward sequence φ becomes a forward reachability sequence. Lemma 6 ensures that there is a reachable element O of the semantics with some $\omega \in O$ such that φ is proof-compatible with ω. Due to the properties of a forward reachability sequence (that hold for φ), and since $F_i \subseteq F_{i+1}$ and $TR(F_i) \subseteq F_{i+1}$ together imply $(\Sigma \setminus F_{i+1}) \cup \overleftarrow{TR}(\Sigma \setminus F_{i+1}) \subseteq \Sigma \setminus F_i$, it follows that ω has a projected fixpoint at its $N - i - 1$ index.

Remark 2. PDR is sometimes implemented such that F_N is initialized to Σ rather than $\Sigma \setminus Bad$. In this case, in the intermediate forward sequences, requirement 4 of Definition 1 might not hold for $i = N$ (while requirement 3 holds for all frames). States that violate requirement 4 are used as obligations at index N.

Our semantics can simulate such implementations by letting a backward carte-sian trace ω be a witness for an intermediate forward sequence φ if the *suffix* of ω in which the first anti-frame $\omega(0)$ is truncated is compatible with φ.

9 Discussion, Related Work and Conclusions

Implementations of *PDR* use a symbolic representation of states and sets of states, as formulas in logic. In the original description of *PDR* [3,7], addressing finite state systems, propositional formulas over boolean variables are used. In this setting, which is most suitable for hardware designs, a SAT solver is used to preform one step reachability checks. In subsequent works which extended *PDR* to software, formulas in various theories of first order logic are considered, and SMT solvers are used instead of a boolean SAT solver. For example, [5] experi-ments with Linear Rational Arithmetic, [2,9] handle Linear Real Arithmetic, [1] handles Linear Integer Arithmetic, and [10] considers universal formulas in first order logic. In our work, we use an explicit representation for the description of *PDR*, which captures all of these frameworks, in order to provide a view of *PDR* which is not restricted to a certain representation.

Our operational description of *PDR* is inspired by works such as [8,9] which provide an abstract description of *PDR* and its operations in the form of an abstract transition relation (described via formulas). However, we continue and show how this maps to a property-guided abstract interpretation of the program.

We consider linear *PDR*, where the semantics of a program is given via its traces (linear sequences). Some works (e.g. [5,9]) have considered the extension of *PDR* to a non-linear search. [5] defined *tree-IC3* which can be thought of as performing *PDR* on each branch of a program's control flow graph. Handling such algorithms is the subject of future work.

Conclusions. We study, using abstract interpretation [6], the family of linear property directed reachability verification algorithms that has been developed following Bradley's original PDR/IC3 algorithm *PDR* [3]. We show that existing algorithms can be explained and proven sound by relating them to the actions of a non standard semantics which abstracts bounded backward traces. Arguably, the most surprising insight our work provides is that even though *PDR* is typi-cally described as a forward analysis, it is in fact based on an abstraction of the *backward collecting trace* semantics. Besides the conceptual elegance of explain-ing existing algorithms (e.g. [1,2,7,9,10]) using (sequences of) two basic opera-tions, we believe that our work would allow to explain and prove correct future *PDR*-based verification algorithms in a more systematic and abstract way than existing specialized techniques.

Acknowledgments. We thank Mooly Sagiv, Eran Yahav, and the anonymous referees for their helpful comments. This work was supported by the European Research Council under the European Union's Seventh Framework Program (FP7/2007-2013) / ERC grant agreement no. [321174-VSSC], EU FP7 project ADVENT (308830), by Broadcom Foundation and Tel Aviv University Authentication Initiative, and by BSF grant no. 2012259.

References

1. Birgmeier, J., Bradley, A.R., Weissenbacher, G.: Counterexample to induction-guided abstraction-refinement (CTIGAR). In: Biere, A., Bloem, R. (eds.) CAV 2014. LNCS, vol. 8559, pp. 831–848. Springer, Heidelberg (2014)
2. Bjørner, N., Gurfinkel, A.: Property directed polyhedral abstraction. In: D'Souza, D., Lal, A., Larsen, K.G. (eds.) VMCAI 2015. LNCS, vol. 8931, pp. 263–281. Springer, Heidelberg (2015)
3. Bradley, A.: SAT-based model checking without unrolling. In: Jhala, R., Schmidt, D. (eds.) Verification, Model Checking, and Abstract Interpretation. Lecture Notes in Computer Science, vol. 6538, pp. 70–78. Springer, Heidelberg (2011)
4. Chockler, H., Ivrii, A., Matsliah, A., Moran, S., Nevo, Z.: Incremental formal verification of hardware. In: International Conference on Formal Methods in Computer-Aided Design - FMCAD, pp. 135–143 (2011)
5. Cimatti, A., Griggio, A.: Software model checking via IC3. In: Madhusudan, P., Seshia, S.A. (eds.) CAV 2012. LNCS, vol. 7358, pp. 277–293. Springer, Heidelberg (2012)
6. Cousot, P., Cousot, R.: Static determination of dynamic properties of recursive procedures. In: Neuhold, E., (ed.) Formal Descriptions of Programming Concepts, (IFIP WG 2.2, St. Andrews, Canada, August 1977), pp. 237–277. North-Holland (1978)
7. Een, N., Mishchenko, A., Brayton, R.: Efficient implementation of property directed reachability. In: Proceedings of the International Conference on Formal Methods in Computer-Aided Design, FMCAD 2011, pp. 125–134 (2011)
8. Gurfinkel, A.: IC3, PDR and friends. http://arieg.bitbucket.org/pdf/gurfinkel_ssft15.pdf
9. Hoder, K., Bjørner, N.: Generalized property directed reachability. In: Cimatti, A., Sebastiani, R. (eds.) SAT 2012. LNCS, vol. 7317, pp. 157–171. Springer, Heidelberg (2012)
10. Karbyshev, A., Bjørner, N., Itzhaky, S., Rinetzky, N., Shoham, S.: Property-directed inference of universal invariants or proving their absence. In: Kroening, D., Păsăreanu, C.S. (eds.) CAV 2015. LNCS, vol. 9206, pp. 583–602. Springer, Heidelberg (2015)

Abstraction

Program Analysis with Local Policy Iteration

Egor George Karpenkov[1,2]([⊠]), David Monniaux[1,2], and Philipp Wendler[3]

[1] University Grenoble Alpes, VERIMAG, 38000 Grenoble, France
george@metaworld.me
[2] CNRS, VERIMAG, 38000 Grenoble, France
[3] University of Passau, Passau, Germany

Abstract. We present local policy iteration (LPI), a new algorithm for deriving numerical invariants that combines the precision of max-policy iteration with the flexibility and scalability of conventional Kleene iterations. It is defined in the Configurable Program Analysis (CPA) framework, thus allowing inter-analysis communication.

LPI uses adjustable-block encoding in order to traverse loop-free program sections, possibly containing branching, without introducing extra abstraction. Our technique operates over any template linear constraint domain, including the interval and octagon domains; templates can also be derived from the program source.

The implementation is evaluated on a set of benchmarks from the International Competition on Software Verification (SV-COMP). It competes favorably with state-of-the-art analyzers.

1 Introduction

Program analysis by *abstract interpretation* [1] derives facts about the execution of programs that are always true regardless of the inputs. These facts are proved using *inductive invariants*, which satisfy both the initial condition and the transition relation, and thus always hold. Such invariants are found within an *abstract domain*, which specifies what properties of the program can be tracked. Classic abstract domains for numeric properties include [products of] intervals and octagons [2], both of which are instances of *template linear constraint domains* [3].

Consider classic abstract interpretation with intervals over the program int i=0; while (i < 1000000)i ++; After the first instruction, the analyzer has a *candidate invariant* $i \in [0,0]$. Going through the loop body it gets $i \in [0,1]$, thus by least upper bound with the previous state $[0,0]$ the new candidate invariant is $i \in [0,1]$. Subsequent *Kleene iterations* yield $[0,2]$, $[0,3]$ etc. In order to enforce the convergence within a reasonable time, a *widening operator* is used, which extrapolates this sequence to $[0,+\infty)$. Then, a *narrowing iteration* yields $[0,100000]$. In this case, the invariant finally obtained is the best possible, but the

---

The research leading to these results has received funding from the European Research Council under the European Union's Seventh Framework Programme (FP/2007-2013)/ERC Grant Agreement nr. 306595 "STATOR".

B. Jobstmann and K.R.M. Leino (Eds.): VMCAI 2016, LNCS 9583, pp. 127–146, 2016.
DOI: 10.1007/978-3-662-49122-5_6

same approach yields the suboptimal invariant $[0, +\infty)$ if an unrelated nested loop is added to the program: `while (i<100000) {while(unknown()){} i++;}`. This happens because the candidate invariant obtained with widening is its own post-image under the nested loop, hence narrowing cannot shrink the invariant.

In general, widenings and narrowings are brittle: a small program change may result in a different analysis behavior. Their result is *non-monotone*: a locally more precise invariant at one point may result in a less precise one elsewhere.

Max-Policy Iteration. In contrast, max-policy iteration [4] is guaranteed to compute the least *inductive* invariant in the given abstract domain[1]. To compute the bound h of the invariant $i \leq h$ for the initial example above, it considers that h must satisfy $h = \max i'$ s.t. $(i' = 0) \vee (i' = i + 1 \wedge i < 10000000 \wedge i \leq h)$ and computes the least inductive solution of this equation by successively considering separate cases:

(i) $h = (\max i'$ s.t. $i' = 0) = 0$, which is not inductive, since one can iterate from $i = 0$ to $i = 1$.

(ii) $h = \max i'$ s.t. $i' = i + 1 \wedge i < 1000000 \wedge i \leq h$, which has two solutions over $\mathbb{R} \cup \{\infty, -\infty\}$: $h = -\infty$ (representing unreachable state, discarded) and $h = 1000000$, which is finally inductive.

Earlier presentations of policy iteration solve a sequence of global convex optimization problems whose unknowns are the bounds (here h) at every program location. Further refinements [5] allowed restricting abstraction to a cut-set [6] of program locations (a set of program points such that the control-flow graph contains no cycle once these points are removed), through a combination with *satisfiability modulo theory* (SMT) solving. Nevertheless, a global view of the program was needed, hampering scalability and combinations with other analyses.

Contribution. We present the new local-policy-iteration algorithm (LPI) for computing inductive invariants using policy iteration. Our implementation is integrated inside the open-source CPAchecker [7] framework for software verification and uses the maximization-modulo-theory solver νZ [8]. To the best of our knowledge, this is the first policy-iteration implementation that is capable of dealing with C code. We evaluate LPI and show its competitiveness with state-of-the-art analyzers using benchmarks from the International Competition on Software Verification (SV-COMP).

Our solution improves on earlier max-policy approaches:

(i) **Scalability.** LPI constructs optimization queries that are at most of the size of the largest loop in the program. At every step we only solve the optimization problem necessary for deriving the *local* candidate invariant.

(ii) **Ability to Cooperate with Other Analyses.** LPI is defined within the Configurable Program Analysis (CPA) [9] framework, which is designed to allow easy inter-analysis collaboration. Expressing policy iteration as a

---

[1] It does not, however, necessarily output the strongest (potentially non-inductive) invariant in an abstract domain, which in general entails solving the halting problem.

fixpoint-propagation algorithm establishes a common ground with other approaches (lazy abstraction, bounded model checking) and allows communicating with other analyses.

(iii) **Precision.** LPI uses adjustable-block encoding [10], and thus benefits from the precision offered by SMT solvers, effectively checking executions of loop-free program segments without the need for over-approximation. *Path focusing* [5] has the same advantage, but at the cost of pre-processing the control-flow graph, which significantly hinders inter-analysis communication.

Related Work. Policy iteration is not as widely used as classic abstract interpretation and (bounded) model checking. Roux and Garoche [11] addressed a similar problem of embedding the policy-iteration procedure inside an abstract interpreter, however their work has a different focus (finding quadratic invariants on relatively small programs) and the policy-iteration algorithm remains fundamentally un-altered. The tool REAVER [12] also performs policy iteration, but focuses on efficiently dealing with logico-numerical abstract domains; it only operates on Lustre programs. The ability to apply policy iteration on strongly connected components one by one was (briefly) mentioned before [13]. Our paper takes the approach significantly further, as our value-determination problem is more succinct, we apply the principle of locality to the policy-improvement phase, and we formulate policy iteration as a classic fixpoint-iteration algorithm, enabling communication with other analyses. Finally, it is possible to express the search for an inductive invariant as a nonlinear constraint solving problem [14] or as a quantifier elimination problem [15], but both these approaches scale poorly.

2 Background

We represent a program P as a control flow automaton (CFA) (*nodes*, X, *edges*), where *nodes* is a set of control states, and $X = \{x_1, \ldots, x_n\}$ are the variables of P. Each edge $e \in edges$ is a tuple $(A, \tau(X, X'), B)$, where A and B are nodes, and $\tau(X, X')$ is a *transition relation*: a formula defining the semantics of a transition over the set of input variables X and fresh output variables X'. A *concrete state* of the program P is a map $X \to \mathbb{Q}$ from variables to rationals[2]. A set C of concrete states is represented using a first-order formula ϕ with free variables from X, such that for all $c \in C$ we have $c \models \phi$.

Template Linear Constraint Domains. A *template linear constraint* is a linear inequality $t \cdot X \leq b$ where t is a vector of constants (*template*), and b is an unknown. A *template linear constraint domain* [3] (TCD) is an abstract domain defined by a matrix of coefficients a_{ij}, which determines what template linear constraints are expressible within the domain: each row t of the matrix is a template (the word "template" also refers to the symbolic product $t \cdot X$, e.g. $i + 2j$). An abstract state in a TCD is defined by a vector $(d_1, \ldots, d_m)$ and represents the set $\bigwedge_{i=1}^{m} t_i \cdot X \leq d_i$ of concrete states. The d_i's range over extended rationals ($\mathbb{R} \cup \{\infty, -\infty\}$), where positive infinity represents unbounded

---

[2] We support integers as well, as explained in Sect. 4.

```
int i=0;
int j=0;
while (i<10)
    i++;
while (j<10)
    j++;
```

Fig. 1. Running example – C program and the corresponding CFA

templates and negative infinity represents unreachable abstract states. The domain of *products of intervals* is one instance of TCD, where the templates are $\pm x_i \leq c_i$ for program variables x_i. The domain of *octagons* [2] is another, with templates $\pm x_i \pm x_j$ and $\pm x_i$. Any template linear constraint domain is a subset of the domain of convex polyhedra [16].

The strongest abstract postcondition in a TCD is defined by optimization: maximizing all templates subject to the constraints introduced by the semantics of the transition and the previous abstract state. For the edge $e = (A, \tau(X, X'), B)$, previous abstract state $D = (d_1, \ldots, d_m)$, and a set $\{t_1, \ldots, t_m\}$ of templates, the output abstract state is $D' = (d'_1, \ldots, d'_m)$ with

$$d'_i = (\max t_i \cdot X' \text{ s.t. } \bigwedge_i t_i \cdot X \leq d_i \wedge \tau(X, X'))$$

For example, for the abstract state $i \leq 0 \wedge j \leq 0$ under the transition $i' = i + 1 \wedge i \leq 10$ the new abstract state is $i \leq d^i \wedge y \leq d^j$, where $d^i = \max i'$ s.t. $i \leq 0 \wedge j \leq 0 \wedge i' = i + 1 \wedge i < 10 \wedge j' = j$ and d^j is the result of maximizing j' subject to the same constraints. This gets simplified to $i \leq 1 \wedge j \leq 0$.

Kleene iterations in a TCD (known as *value iterations*) may fail to converge in finite time, thus the use of *widenings*, which result in hard-to-control imprecision.

Policy Iteration. Policy iteration addresses the convergence problem of *value-iteration* algorithms by operating on an equation system that an inductive invariant has to satisfy. Consider the running example shown in Fig. 1. Suppose we analyze this program with the templates $\{i, j\}$, and look for the least inductive invariant $D = (d^i_A, d^j_A, d^i_B, d^j_B)$ that satisfies the following for all possible executions of the program (x_N denotes the value of the variable x at the node N):

$$i_A \leq d^i_A \wedge i_B \leq d^i_B \wedge j_A \leq d^j_A \wedge j_B \leq d^j_B$$

To find it, we solve for the smallest D that satisfies the *fixpoint equation [system]* for the running example, stating that the set of abstract states represented by D is equal to its strongest postcondition within the abstract domain:

$$d_A^i = \sup i' \text{ s.t. } (i' = 0 \wedge j' = 0)$$
$$\vee \ (i \leq d_A^i \wedge j \leq d_A^j \wedge i < 10 \wedge i' = i+1 \wedge j' = j) \vee \bot$$
$$d_A^j = \sup j' \text{ s.t. } (i' = 0 \wedge j' = 0)$$
$$\vee \ (i \leq d_A^i \wedge j \leq d_A^j \wedge i < 10 \wedge i' = i+1 \wedge j' = j) \vee \bot$$
$$d_B^i = \sup i' \text{ s.t. } (\neg(i < 10) \wedge i \leq d_A^i \wedge j' \leq d_A^j \wedge i' = i)$$
$$\vee \ (i \leq d_B^i \wedge j \leq d_B^j \wedge j < 10 \wedge j' = j+1 \wedge i' = i) \vee \bot$$
$$d_B^j = \sup j' \text{ s.t. } (\neg(i < 10) \wedge i \leq d_A^i \wedge j' \leq d_A^j \wedge i' = i)$$
$$\vee \ (i \leq d_B^i \wedge j \leq d_B^j \wedge j < 10 \wedge j' = j+1 \wedge i' = i) \vee \bot$$

Note the equation structure: (i) Disjunctions represent non-deterministic choice for a new value. (ii) The argument $\bot$ is added to all disjunctions, representing infeasible choice, corresponding to the bound value $-\infty$. (iii) Supremum is taken because the bound must be higher than all the possible options, and it has to be $-\infty$ if no choice is feasible.

A simplified equation system with each disjunction replaced by one of its arguments is called a *policy*. The least solution of the whole equation system is the least solution of at least one policy (obtained by taking the solution, and picking one argument for each disjunction, such that the solution remains unchanged). Policy iteration finds the least tuple of unknowns (d's) satisfying the fixpoint equation by iterating over possible policies, and finding a solution for each one.

For program semantics consisting of linear assignments and possibly non-deterministic guards it is possible to find a fixpoint of each policy using one linear programming step. This is based on the result that for a monotone and concave function[3] f and x_0 such that $f(x_0) > x_0$, the least fixpoint of f greater than x_0 can be computed in a single step[4].

It is possible to solve the global equation system by solving all (exponentially many) policies one by one. Instead, *policy iteration* [4] computes solutions for a sequence of policies; each solution is guaranteed to be less than the least solution of the original equation system, and the solutions form an ascending sequence. The iteration starts with the policy having least possible value ($\bot$ for each disjunction, the solution is $-\infty$ assignment to all unknowns), and eventually terminates when a solution of the original equation system (an inductive invariant) is found. The termination is guaranteed as there is only a finite number of solutions.

For each policy the algorithm finds a *global value*: the least fixpoint in the template constraints domain of the reduced equation system. For instance, in the running example, for the policy $d_A^i = \sup i'$ s.t. $i' = 0 \wedge j' = 0$ (only one unknown is shown for brevity) the global value is $d_A^i = 0$. This step is called *value determination*. After the global value is computed the algorithm checks whether the policy can be *improved*: that is, whether we can find another policy that

---

[3] Order-concave in the presence of multiple templates, see [4] for detailed discussion.
[4] Over rationals, we discuss the applicability to integers in Sect. 4.

will yield a larger value *than the previously obtained global value*. In the running example we want to test the following policy for the possibility of improvement:

$$d^i_A = \sup i' \text{ s.t. } (i \leq d^i_A \wedge j \leq d^i_A \wedge i < 10 \wedge i' = i+1 \wedge j' = j)$$

We do so by computing the *local value*: substituting the unknown (d^i_A) on the right hand side with the value from the previously obtained global value, and checking whether the result is greater than the previously obtained bound. In our example we get the local value $d^i_A = 1$, which is indeed an improvement over $d^i_A = 0$ (*policy-improvement* step). After the policy is selected, we go back to the value-determination step, obtaining $d^i_A = 10$, and we repeat the process until convergence (reaching a step where no policy can be further improved).

Under the assumption that the operations on the edges can be expressed as conjunctions of linear (in)equalities, it can be shown [4] that: (i) The value-determination step can be performed with linear programming. (ii) The resulting value is an under-approximation of the least inductive invariant. (iii) Each policy is selected at most once and the final fixed point yields the least inductive invariant in the domain.

Example 1 (Policy-Iteration Trace on the Running Example). We solve for the unknowns $(d^i_A, d^j_A, d^i_B, d^j_B)$, defining a (global) abstract value v.

In our example, disjunctions arise from multiple incoming edges to a single node, hence a policy is defined by a choice of an incoming edge per node per template, or $\bot$ if no such choice is feasible. We represent a policy symbolically as a 4-tuple of predecessor nodes (or $\bot$), as there are two nodes, with two policies to be chosen per node. The order corresponds to the order of the tuple of the unknowns. The initial policy s is $(\bot, \bot, \bot, \bot)$. The trace on the example is:

1. Policy improvement: $s = (I, I, \bot, \bot)$,
   obtained with a local value $(0, 0, -\infty, -\infty)$.
2. Value determination: corresponds to the initial condition $v = (0, 0, -\infty, -\infty)$.
3. Policy improvement: $s = (A, I, \bot, \bot)$, selecting the looping edge, local value is $(1, 0, -\infty, -\infty)$.
4. Value determination: accelerates the loop convergence to $v = (10, 0, -\infty, -\infty)$.
5. Policy improvement: $s = (A, I, A, A)$, with a local value $(10, 0, 10, 0)$ finally there is a feasible policy for the templates associated with the node B.
6. Value determination: does not affect the result $v = (10, 0, 10, 0)$.
7. Policy improvement: select the second looping edge: $s = (A, I, A, B)$ obtaining a local value $(10, 0, 10, 1)$.
8. Value determination: accelerate the second loop to $v = (10, 0, 10, 10)$.
9. Finally, the policy cannot be improved any further and we terminate.

On this example we could have obtained the same result by Kleene iteration, but in general the latter might fail to converge within finite time. The usual workaround is to use heuristic widening, with possible and hard-to-control imprecision. Our value-determination step can be seen as a widening that provides an under-approximation to the least fixed point.

Each policy improvement requires at least four (small) linear programming (LP) queries, and each value determination requires one (rather large) LP query.

Path Focusing and Large-Block Encoding. In traditional abstract interpretation and policy iteration, the obtained invariant is expressed as an abstract state at each CFA node. This can lead to a significant loss in precision: for instance, since most abstract domains only express convex properties, it is impossible to express $|x| \geq 1$, which is necessary to prove this assertion: if (abs(x) >= 1) { assert(x != 0); }

This loss can be recovered by reducing the number of "intermediate" abstract states by allowing more expressive formulas associated with edges. Formally, two consecutive edges $(A, \tau_1(X, X'), B)$ and $(B, \tau_2(X, X'), C)$, with no other edges incoming or outgoing to B can be merged into one edge $(A, \tau_1(X, \hat{X}) \wedge \tau_2(\hat{X}, X'), C)$. Similarly, two parallel edges $(A, \tau_1(X, X'), B)$ and $(A, \tau_2(X, X'), B)$, with no other edges incoming to B can be replaced by a new edge $(A, \tau_1(X, X') \vee \tau_2(X, X'), B)$. For a well-structured CFA, repeating this transformation in a fixpoint manner (until no more edges can be merged) will lead to a new CFA where the only remaining nodes are loop heads.

Such a transformation was shown to increase both precision and performance for model checking [17]. Adjustable block encoding [10] gets the same advantages without the need for CFA pre-processing. Independently, the approach was applied with the same result to Kleene iterations [18] and to max-policy iterations [5]. In fact, the CFA in Fig. 1 was already reduced in this manner for the ease of demonstration.

On the reduced CFA the number of possible policies associated with a single edge becomes exponential, and explicitly iterating over them is no longer feasible. Instead, the path focusing approach uses a *satisfiability modulo theory* (SMT) solver to select an improved policy.

Configurable Program Analysis. CPA [9] is a framework for expressing algorithms performing program analysis. It uses a generic fixpoint-computation algorithm, which is *configured* by a given analysis. We formulate LPI as a CPA.

The CPA framework makes no assumptions on the performed analysis, thus many analyses were successfully expressed and implemented within it, such as bounded model checking, abstract interpretation and k-induction (note that an analysis defined within the framework is also referred to as a CPA).

Each CPA configures the fixpoint algorithm by providing an *initial abstract state*, a *transfer relation* (specifying how to produce successors), a *merge operator* (specifying whether and how to merge abstract states), and a *stop operator* (specifying whether a newly produced abstract state is covered). The algorithm keeps a set of reached abstract states and a list of "frontier" abstract states, and at each step produces successor states from the frontier states using the *transfer relation*, and then tries to merge the new states with existing states using the *merge operator*. If a new state is covered by the set of reached states according to the *stop operator*, it is discarded, otherwise it is added to the set of reached states and the list of frontier states. We show the CPA algorithm as Algorithm 1.

Algorithm 1. CPA Algorithm (taken from [9])

1: **Input**: a CPA $(D, \text{transfer-relation}, \text{merge}, \text{stop})$, an initial abstract state $e_0 \in E$
   (let E denote the set of elements of the semi-lattice of D)
2: **Output**: a set of reachable abstract states
3: **Variables**: a set reached of elements of E, a set waitlist of elements of E
4: waitlist $\leftarrow \{e_0\}$
5: reached $\leftarrow \{e_0\}$
6: **while** waitlist $\neq \emptyset$ **do**
7:     Pop e from waitlist
8:     **for all** $e' \in \text{transfer-relation}(e)$ **do**
9:         **for all** $e'' \in$ reached **do**
10:            $\triangleright$ Combine with existing abstract state
11:            $e_{\text{new}} \leftarrow \text{merge}(e', e'')$
12:            **if** $e_{\text{new}} \neq e''$ **then**
13:                waitlist $\leftarrow (\text{waitlist} \cup \{e_{\text{new}}\}) \setminus \{e''\}$
14:                reached $\leftarrow (\text{reached} \cup \{e_{\text{new}}\}) \setminus \{e''\}$
15:        $\triangleright$ Whether e' is already covered by existing states
16:        **if** $\neg\text{stop}(e', \text{reached})$ **then**
17:            waitlist $\leftarrow$ waitlist $\cup \{e'\}$
18:            reached $\leftarrow$ reached $\cup \{e'\}$
19: **return** reached

---

3   Local Policy Iteration (LPI)

The running example presented in the background (Example 1) has four value-determination steps and five policy-improvement steps. Each policy-improvement step corresponds to at most #policies × #templates × #nodes LP queries, and each value-determination step requires solving an LP problem with at least #policies × #templates × #nodes variables. Most of these queries are redundant, as the updates propagate only *locally* through the CFA: there is no need to re-compute the policy if no new information is available.

We develop a new policy-iteration-based algorithm, based on the principle of *locality*, which aims to address the scalability issues and the problem of communicating invariants with other analyses. We call it *local policy iteration* or LPI. To make it scalable, we consider the structure of a CFA being analyzed, and we aim to exploit its *sparsity*.

A large majority of (non-recursive) programs are well-structured: they consist of statements and possibly nested loops. Consider checking a program P against an error property E. If P has no loops, it can be converted into a single formula $\Psi(X')$, and an SMT solver can be queried for the satisfiability of $\Psi(X') \wedge E(X')$, obtaining either a counter-example or a proof of unreachability of E. However, in the presence of loops, representing all concrete states reachable by a program as a formula over concrete states in a decidable first-order logic is impossible, and abstraction is required. For example, bounded model checkers unroll the loop, lazy-abstraction-based approaches partially unroll the loop and use the predicates from Craig interpolants to "cover" future unrollings, and abstract interpretation relies on abstraction within an abstract domain.

In LPI, we use the value-determination step to "close" the loop and compute the fixpoint value for the given policy. Multiple iterations through the loop might be necessary to find the optimal policy and reach the global fixpoint. In the presence of nested loops, the process is repeated in a fixpoint manner: we "close" the inner loop, "close" the outer loop with the new information from the inner loop available, and repeat the process until convergence. Each iteration selects a new policy, thus the number of possible iterations is bounded.

Formally, we state LPI as a Configurable Program Analysis (CPA), which requires defining the lattice of abstract states, the transfer relation, the merge operator, and the stop operator. The CPA for LPI is intended to be used in combination with other CPAs such as a CPA for tracking location information (the program counter), and thus does not need to keep track of this information itself. To avoid losing precision, we do not express the invariant as an abstract state at every node: instead the transfer relation operates on formulas and we only perform over-approximation at certain *abstraction points* (which correspond to loop heads in a well-structured CFA). This approach is inspired by adjustable-block encoding [10], which performs the same operation for predicate abstraction. One difference to path focusing [18] is that we still traverse intermediate nodes, which facilitates inter-analysis communication.

We introduce two lattices: *abstracted states* (not to be confused with *abstract states* in general: both intermediate and abstracted states are *abstract*) for states associated with abstraction points (which can only express abstract states in the template constraints domain) and *intermediate states* for all others (which can express arbitrary concrete state spaces using decidable SMT formulas).

An *abstracted state* is an element of a template constraints domain with meta-information added to record the *policy* being used.

Definition 1 (Abstracted State). An abstracted state is a mapping from the externally given set T of templates to tuples $(d, \text{policy}, \text{backpointer})$, where $d \in \mathbb{R}$ is a bound for the associated template t (the represented property is $t \cdot X \leq d$), policy is a formula representing the policy that was used for deriving d (policy has to be monotone and concave, and in particular contain no disjunctions), and backpointer is an abstracted state that is a starting point for the policy (base case is an empty mapping).

The preorder on abstracted states is defined by component-wise comparison of bounds associated with respective templates (lack of a bound corresponds to an unbounded template). The concretization is given by the conjunction of represented template linear constraints, disregarding policy and backpointer meta-information. For example, an abstracted state $\{x : (10, \_, \_)\}$ (underscores represent meta-information irrelevant to the example) concretizes to $\{c \mid c[x] \leq 10\}$, and the initial abstracted state $\{\}$ concretizes to all concrete states.

Intermediate states represent reachable state-spaces using formulas directly, again with meta-information added to record the "used" policy.

Algorithm 2. LPI Abstraction

1: **Input:** intermediate state (a_0, ϕ), set T of templates
2: **Output:** generated abstracted state *new*
3:   $new \leftarrow$ empty abstracted state
4: **for all** template $t \in T$ **do**
5:     $\hat{\phi} \leftarrow \phi$ with disjunctions annotated using a set of marking variables M
6:     ▷ Maximize subject to the constraints introduced by the formula
7:     ▷ and the starting abstracted state.
8:     $d \leftarrow \max t \cdot X'$ subject to $\hat{\phi}(X, X') \wedge a_0$
9:     $\mathcal{M} \leftarrow$ model at the optimal
10:     ▷ Replace marking variables M in $\hat{\phi}$ with their value from the model $\mathcal{M}$,
11:     ▷ generating a concave formula that represents the policy.
12:     Policy $\psi \leftarrow \hat{\phi}[M/\mathcal{M}]$
13:     $new[t] \leftarrow (d, \psi, a_0)$
14: **return** *new*

Definition 2 (Intermediate State). An *intermediate state* is a tuple (a_0, ϕ), where a_0 is a *starting* abstracted state, and $\phi(X, X')$ is a formula over a set of input variables X and output variables X'.

The preorder on intermediate states is defined by syntactic comparison only: states with identical starting states and identical formulas are deemed equal, and incomparable otherwise. The concretization is given by satisfiable assignments to X' subject to $\phi(X, X')$ and the constraints derived from a_0 applied to input variables X. For example, an intermediate state $(\{x : (10, \_, \_)\}, x' = x + 1)$ concretizes to the set $\{c \mid c[x] \leq 11\}$ of concrete states.

Abstraction (Algorithm 2) is the conversion of an intermediate state (a_0, ϕ) to an abstracted state, by maximizing all templates $t \in T$ subject to constraints introduced by a_0 and ϕ, and obtaining a backpointer and a policy from the produced model $\mathcal{M}$. This amounts to selecting the appropriate disjuncts in each disjunction of ϕ. To do so, we annotate ϕ with *marking variables*: each disjunction $\tau_1 \vee \tau_2$ in ϕ is replaced by $(m \wedge \tau_1) \vee (\neg m \wedge \tau_2)$ where m is a fresh propositional variable. A policy associated to a bound is then identified by the values of the marking variables at the optimum (subject to the constraints introduced by ϕ and a_0), and is obtained by replacing the marking variables in ϕ with their values from $\mathcal{M}$. Thus the abstraction operation effectively performs the *policy-improvement* operation for the given node, as only the policies which are feasible with respect to the current candidate invariant (given by previous abstracted state) are selected.

Example 2 (LPI Propagation and Abstraction) Let us start with an abstracted state $a = \{x : (100, \_, \_)\}$ (which concretizes to $\{c \mid c[x] \leq 100\}$, underscores stand for some policy and some starting abstracted state) and a set $\{x\}$ of templates.

After traversing a section of code if(x <= 10){x += 1;} else {x = 0;} we get an intermediate state (a, ϕ) with $\phi = (x \leq 10 \wedge x' = x + 1 \vee x > 10 \wedge x' = 0)$

Algorithm 3. Local Value Determination

1: **Input:** node n, map *influencing* from nodes to abstracted states, set T of templates
2: **Output:** generated abstracted state *new*
3: $constraints \leftarrow \emptyset$
4: **for all** node $n_i \in influencing$ **do**
5:     state $s \leftarrow influencing[n_i]$
6:     **for all** template $t \in s$ **do**
7:         (bound d, policy ψ, backpointer a_0) $\leftarrow s[t]$
8:         Generate a unique string *namespace*
9:         $\triangleright$ Prefix all variables in ψ.
10:         $\triangleright$ $X'_{namespace}, X_{namespace}$ is a set of namespaced output/input variables for ψ.
11:         $constraints \leftarrow constraints \cup \left\{ \psi[X/X_{namespace}][X'/X'_{namespace}] \right\}$
12:         $d^t_{n_i} \leftarrow$ fresh variable (upper bound on t at n)
13:         $constraints \leftarrow constraints \cup \left\{ d^t_{n_i} = t \cdot X'_{namespace} \right\}$
14:         $n_0 \leftarrow$ location associated with a_0
15:         **for all** $t_0 \in a_0$ **do**
16:             $constraints \leftarrow constraints \cup \left\{ t_0 \cdot X_{namespace} \leq d^{t_0}_{n_0} \right\}$
17: $new \leftarrow$ empty abstracted state
18: **for all** templates $t \in T$ **do**
19:     $(d_0, \psi, a_0) \leftarrow influencing[n]$
20:     $d \leftarrow \max d^t_n$ subject to $constraints$
21:     $new[t] \leftarrow (d, \psi, a_0)$
22: **return** *new*

and a backpointer to the starting *abstracted state* a. Suppose in our example the given C code fragment ends with a loop head. Then we use *abstraction* (Algorithm 2) to convert the intermediate state (a, ϕ) into a new abstracted state.

Firstly, we annotate ϕ with *marking variables*, which are used to identify the selected policy, obtaining $x \leq 10 \wedge x' = x + 1 \wedge m_1 \vee x > 10 \wedge x' = 0 \wedge \neg m_1$. Afterwards, we optimize the obtained formula (together with the constraints from the starting abstracted state a) for the highest values of templates. This amounts to a single OPT-SMT query:

$$\sup x' \text{ s.t. } x \leq 100 \wedge (x \leq 10 \wedge x' = x + 1 \wedge m_1 \vee x > 10 \wedge x' = 0 \wedge \neg m_1)$$

The query is satisfiable with a maximum of 11, and an SMT model $\mathcal{M} : \{x' : 11, m_1 : true, x : 10\}$. Replacing the marking variable m_1 in ϕ with its value in $\mathcal{M}$ gives us a disjunction-free formula $x \leq 10 \wedge x' = x + 1$, which we store as a *policy*. Finally, the newly created abstracted state is $\{x : (11, x \leq 10 \wedge x' = x + 1, a)\}$.

The local *value-determination* step (Algorithm 3) computes the least fixpoint for the chosen policy across the entire strongly connected component where the current node n lies. The algorithm starts with a map *influencing* from nodes to abstracted states, which is generated by transitively following policy backpointers, and converting the resulting set of abstracted states to a map[5]. From this

---

[5] The are no collisions as abstracted states are joined at nodes.

map, we generate a global optimization problem, where the set of fresh variables $d^t_{n_i}$ represents the maximal value a template t can obtain at the node n_i using the policies selected. Variable $d^t_{n_i}$ is made equal to the namespaced[6] *output* value of the policy $\psi(X, X')$ chosen for t at n_i (line 13). For each policy ψ and the associated backpointer a_0, we *constrain* the *input* variables of ψ using a set of variables $d^{t_0}_{n_0}$ representing bounds at the node n_0 associated with a_0 (line 16). This set of "input constraints" for value determination results in a quadratic number of constraints in terms of the number of selected policies. Finally, for each template t we maximize for d^t_n (line 20), which is the maximum possible value for t at node n under the current policy, and we record the bound in the generated abstracted state (line 21), keeping the old policy and backpointer.

The local-value-determination algorithm is almost identical to max-strategy evaluation [5], except for two changes: we only add potentially relevant constraints from the "closed" loop (found by traversing backpointers associated with policies), and we maximize objectives one by one, not for their sum (which avoids special casing infinities, and enables optimizations outlined in Sect. 4). Unlike classic policy iteration, we only run local value determination after merges on loop heads, because in other cases the value obtained by abstraction is the same as the value which could be obtained by value determination.

Formulation as a CPA. The *initial state* is the abstracted state $\{\}$ (empty map), representing $\top$ of the template constraints domain. The *stop operator* checks whether a newly created abstracted state is covered by one of the existing abstracted states using the preorder described above. The *transfer relation* finds the successor state for a given CFA edge. It operates only on intermediate states – an abstracted state a_0 is firstly converted to the intermediate state $(a_0, true)$. Then, the transfer-relation operator runs symbolic execution: the successor of an intermediate state $(a, \phi(X, X'))$ under the edge $(A, \tau(X, X'), B)$ is the intermediate state $(a, \phi'(X, X'))$ with $\phi'(X, X') \equiv \exists \hat{X}.\phi(X, \hat{X}) \wedge \tau(\hat{X}, X')$. If the successor node is a loop head, then *abstraction* (Algorithm 2) is performed on the resulting state.

The *merge operator* has two operation modes, depending on whether we are dealing with abstracted states or with intermediate states.

For two abstracted states, we perform the join: for each template, we pick the largest bound out of the two possible, and we keep the corresponding policy and the backpointer. If the merge "closes" the loop (that is, we merge at the loop head, and one of the updated policies has a backpointer to a state inside the loop), we find the map *influencing* by recursively following the backpointers of the joined state, and run *local value determination* (Algorithm 3). For two intermediate states (a_1, ϕ_1) and (a_2, ϕ_2) with a_1 identical to a_2 the merge operator returns the disjunction $(a_1, \phi_1 \vee \phi_2)$. Otherwise, we keep the states separate.

The local-value-determination problem only contains the constraints resulting from policies of the abstracted states associated with nodes in the current loop. This optimization does not affect the invariant as only the nodes

---

[6] Namespacing means creating fresh copies by attaching a certain *prefix* to variable names.

dominating the loop head can change it. Of those, only the invariants of the nodes reachable from the loop head can be affected by the computation: i.e., the strongly connected component of n.

Properties of LPI

Soundness. LPI, like any configurable program analysis, terminates when no more updates can be performed, and newly produced abstract states are subsumed (in the preorder defined by the lattice) by the already discovered ones. Thus, it is an inductive invariant: the produced abstract states satisfy the initial condition and all successor states are subsumed by the existing invariant. Hence the obtained invariant is sound.

Termination. An infinite sequence of produced *abstract* states must contain infinitely many *abstracted* states, as they are associated with loop heads. However, each subsequent abstraction on the same node must choose a different policy to obtain a successively higher value, but the number of policies is finite. An infinite sequence is thus impossible, hence termination.

Optimality. In the absence of integers, LPI terminates with the same invariant as classical policy iteration with SMT [5]. The outline of the proof is that LPI can be seen as an efficient oracle for selecting the next policy to update (note that policies selected by LPI are always *feasible* with respect to the current invariant candidate). Skipping value-determination steps when they have no effect, and attempting to include only relevant constraints in the value-determination problem do not alter the values of obtained fixed points.

Example 3 (LPI Trace on the Running Example) We revisit the running example (Fig. 1) with LPI:

1. We start with the empty abstracted state $a_0 \equiv \{\}$.
2. Transfer relation under the edge (I, ϕ_1, A) produces the new intermediate state $(a_0, i' = 0 \land j' = 0)$ associated with A. As A is a loop head, we perform an abstraction to obtain the abstracted state $a_1 \equiv \{i : (0, \_, a_0), j : (0, \_, a_0)\}$ (corresponding to $i \leq 0 \land j \leq 0$) [2 linear programming problems].
3. Transfer relation explores the edge (A, ϕ_2, A) and produces the intermediate state $(a_1, i \leq 0 \land j' \leq 0 \land i' = i + 1)$. Again we perform an abstraction, obtaining the abstracted state $a_2 \equiv \{i : (1, \_, a_1), j : (0, \_, a_1)\}$ [2 LP problems].
4. The merge operator on node A merges the new state a_2 with the previous state a_1, yielding the abstracted state $a_3 \equiv \{i : (1, \_, a_1), j : (0, \_, a_0)\}$. Value determination "closes" the loop, producing $a_4 \equiv \{i : (10, \_, a_1), j : (0, \_, a_0)\}$. [1 LP problem].
5. Transfer relation explores the edge (A, ϕ_3, B) and produces the intermediate state $(a_3, i' \leq 10 \land (\neg i' < 10) \land j' \leq 0)$, which is abstracted to $a_5 \equiv \{i : (10, \_, a_4), j : (0, \_, a_4)\}$ [2 LP problems].

6. The edge (B, ϕ_4, B) is explored, resulting in the intermediate state $(a_4, i' \leq 10 \wedge j \leq 0 \wedge j' = j + 1)$, which is abstracted into $a_6 \equiv \{i : (10, \_, a_5), j : (1, \_, a_5)\}$ [2 LP problems].

7. Value determination produces the state $a_7 \equiv \{i : (10, \_, a_4), j : (10, \_, a_5)\}$, and the exploration concludes. [1 LP problem].

Compared to the original algorithm there are two value-determination problems instead of four, both on considerably smaller scale. There are also only ten LP problems, compared to more than twenty in the original version. The improvement in performance is more than a fixed constant: if the number of independent loops in the running example was to increase from 2 to N, the increase in the analysis time of classic policy iteration would be quadratic, while LPI would scale linearly.

4   Extensions and Implementation Aspects

Template Synthesis. The template constraints domain requires templates defined for the given program. In LPI, we can simulate the interval and octagon domains by synthesizing templates of the form $\pm x, \pm x \pm y$ for every numeric variable x, y in the program *alive* at the given program node. Moreover, the templates can be synthesized from error properties: e.g. for `assert(x >= 2 * y)` we could generate the templates $\pm(x - 2y)$.

We show the analysis time of LPI (excluding startup and parsing) in the interval-domain-mode vs. octagon-domain-mode in Fig. 2 (each data point corresponds to an analyzed program). The number of octagon templates is quadratic in terms of the number of interval templates, thus we expect a quadratic rise in analysis time, however in practice we observe a sub-quadratic increase.

This has motivated us to experiment with simulating a more expressive domain. We generate templates $\pm 2x \pm y, \pm x \pm y \pm z$, and even $\pm 2x \pm y \pm z$, for every possible combination of live variables x, y, z at the given program location. Using this new "rich" template generation strategy we achieve a significant precision improvement as shown by the number of verified programs in the legend of Fig. 3a.

Dealing With Integers. Original publications on max-policy iteration in template constraints domain deal exclusively with reals, whereas C programs operate primarily on integers[7]. Excessively naive handling of integers leads to poor results: with an initial condition $x = 0$, $x \in [0, 4]$ is inductive for the transition system $x' = x + 1 \wedge x \neq 4$ in integers, but not in rationals, due to the possibility of the transition $x = 3.5$ to $x = 4.5$. An obvious workaround is to rewrite each strict inequality $a < b$ into $a \leq b - 1$: on this example, the transition becomes $x = x + 1 \wedge (x \leq 3 \vee x \geq 5)$ and $x \in [0, 4]$ becomes inductive on rationals. However, to make use of data produced by an additional *congruence* analysis, we use

---

[7] Previous work [19] deals with finding the exact interval invariants for programs involving integers, but only for a very restricted program semantics.

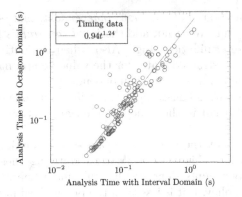

Fig. 2. Octagon vs. interval LPI analysis time (dataset and setup as in Sect. 5)

optimization modulo theory with integer and real variables for abstraction, and mixed integer linear programming for value determination.

Unfortunately, linear relations over the integers are not *concave*, which is a requirement for the least fixpoint property of policy iteration. Thus the encoding described above may still result in an over-approximation. Consider the following program:

```
x=0; x_new=unknown();
while (2 * x_new == x+2) {
    x = x_new; x_new = unknown();
}
```

LPI terminates with a fixpoint $x \leq 2$, yet the least fixpoint is $x \leq 1$.

Congruence. A congruence analysis which tracks whether a variable is even or odd can be run in parallel with LPI (a more general congruence analysis may be used, but we did not find the need for it on our examples). During the LPI abstraction step, the congruence information is conjoined to the formula being maximized, and the bounds from LPI are used for the congruence analysis.

This combination enhances the precision on our dataset (cf. Fig. 3a), and demonstrates the usefulness of expressing policy iteration as a typical fixpoint computation. Furthermore, it provides a strong motivation to use integer formulas for integer variables in programs, and not their rational relaxation.

Optimizations In Sect. 3 we describe the local value-determination algorithm which adds a quadratic number of constraints in terms of policies. In practice this is often prohibitively expensive. The quadratic blow-up results from the "input" constraints to each policy, which determine the bounds on the input variables. We propose multiple optimization heuristics which increase the performance.

As a motivation example, consider a long trace ending with an assignment x = 1. If this trace is feasible and chosen as a policy for the template x, the output bound will be 1, regardless of the input. With that example in mind, consider the abstraction procedure from which we derive the bound d for the template t. Let $(\_, \phi(X, X'))$ be the intermediate state used for the abstraction (Algorithm 2). We check the satisfiability of $\phi(X, X') \wedge t \cdot X' > d$; if the result is unsatisfiable, then the bound of t is *input-independent*, that is, it is always d if the trace is feasible. Thus we do not add the *input constraints* for the associated policy in the value-determination stage. Also, when computing the map *influencing* from nodes to abstracted states for the value-determination problem, we do not follow the backpointers for input-independent policies, potentially drastically shrinking the resulting constraint set. Similarly, if none of the variables of the "input template" occur in the policy, the initial constraint is irrelevant and can be dropped.

Furthermore, we limit the size of the value-determination LP by merging some of the unknowns. This is equivalent to equating these variables, thus strengthening the constraints. The result thus under-approximates the fixed point of the selected policy. If it is less than the policy fixed point (not inductive with respect to the policy), we fall back to the normal value determination.

During *abstraction* on the intermediate state (a_0, ψ), we may skip the optimization query based on a syntactic check: if we are optimizing for the template t, and none of the variables of t occur in ψ, we return the bound associated with $a_0[t]$.

Additionally, during maximization we add a redundant lemma to the set of constraints that specifies that the resultant value has to be strictly larger than the current bound. This significantly speeds up the maximization by shrinking the search space.

Iteration Order. In our experiments, we have found performance to depend on the iteration order. Experimentally, we have determined a good iteration order to be the recursive iteration strategy using the weak topological ordering [20]. This is a strength of LPI: it blends into existing iteration strategies.

Unrolling. We unroll loops up to depth 2, as some invariants can only be expressed in the template constraints domain in the presence of unrollings (e.g., invariants involving a variable whose initial value is set only inside the loop).

Abstraction Refinement for LPI. As a template constraints domain can be configured by the number of templates present, it is a perfect candidate for refinement, as templates can be added to increase the precision of the analysis.

However, a full abstraction-refinement algorithm for LPI would be outside of the scope of this work, and thus to obtain the results we use a naive algorithm that iteratively tries progressively more precise and costly configurations until the program can be verified. The configurations we try are (in that order):

(i)   Intervals
(ii) Octagons
(iii) Previous + Unrolling
(iv) Previous + Rich Templates ($\pm x \pm y \pm z$)
(v)   Previous + Congruence Analysis.

5   Experiments

We have evaluated our tool on the benchmarks from the category "Loops" of the International Competition on Software Verification (SV-COMP'15) [21] consisting of 142 C programs, 93 of which are correct (the error property is unreachable). We have chosen this category for evaluation because its programs contain numerical assertions about variables modified in loops, whereas other categories of SV-COMP mostly involve variables with a small finite set of possible values that can be enumerated effectively. All experiments were performed with the same resources as in SV-COMP'15: an Intel Core i7-4770 quad-core CPU with 3.40 GHz, and limits of 15 GB RAM and 900 s CPU time per program. The tool is integrated inside the open-source verification framework CPAchecker [7], used configuration and detailed experimental results are available at http://lpi.metaworld.me.

We compare LPI (with abstraction refinement) with three tools representing different approaches to program analysis: **BLAST 2.7.3 (SV-COMP'15)** [22], which uses lazy abstraction, **PAGAI (git hash 254c2fc693)** [23], which uses abstract interpretation with path focusing, and **CPAchecker 1.3.10-svcomp15 (SV-COMP'15)** [7], the winner of SV-COMP 2015 category "Overall", which uses an ensemble of different techniques: explicit value, k-induction, and lazy predicate abstraction. For LPI we use CPAchecker in version 1.4.10-lpi-vmcai16.

Because LPI is an incomplete approach, it can only produce safety proofs (no counter-examples). Thus in Table 1 we present the statistics on the number of safety proofs produced by different tools. The first five columns represent *differences* between approaches: the cell corresponding to the row A and a column B (read "A vs. B") displays the number of programs A could verify and B could not. In the column *Unique* we show the number of programs only the given tool could verify (out of the analyzers included in the comparison). The column *Verified* shows the total number of programs a tool could verify. The column *Incorrect* shows false positives: programs that contained a bug, yet were deemed correct by the tool — our current implementation unsoundly ignores integer overflows, as though the program used mathematical integers.[8]

From this table we see that LPI verifies more examples than other tools can, including seven programs that others cannot.

Timing Results. In Sect. 4 we have described the various possible configurations of LPI. As trying all possible combinations of features is exponential, tested configurations represent cumulative stacking of features. We present the timing comparison across those in the quantile plot in Fig. 3a, and in the legend we report the number of programs each configuration could verify. Each data point is an analyzed program, and the series are sorted separately for each configuration.

The quantile plot for timing comparison across different tools is shown in Fig. 3b. We have included two LPI configurations in the comparison: fastest (LPI-Intervals) and the most precise one (LPI-Refinement, switches to a more expensive strategy out of the ones in Fig. 3a if the program cannot be verified). From the plot we can see that LPI performance compares favorably with lazy abstraction, but that it is considerably outperformed by abstract interpretation.

---

[8] It is possible to add sound overflow handling, as done in e.g. Astrée, to our approach, at the expense of extra engineering.

Table 1. Number of verified programs of different tools (LPI in abstraction-refinement mode)

	vs. PAGAI	LPI	BLAST	CPAchecker	Unique	Verified	Incorrect
PAGAI	-	4	13	15	1	52	1
LPI	13	-	20	20	7	61	1
BLAST	6	4	-	8	0	45	1
CPAchecker	21	17	21	-	12	58	2

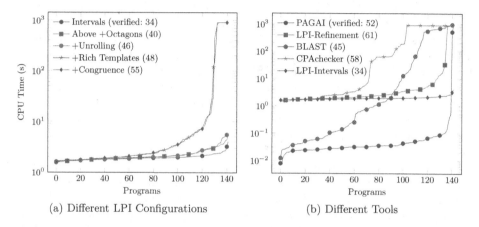

(a) Different LPI Configurations   (b) Different Tools

Fig. 3. Quantile timing plots. Each data point is an analyzed program, timeouts are excluded.

The initial difference in the analysis time between the CPACHECKER-based tools and others is due to JVM start-up time of about 2 s.

6   Conclusion and Future Work

We have demonstrated that LPI is a viable approach to program analysis, which can outperform state-of-the-art competitors either in precision (abstract interpretation), or both in precision and scalability (predicate abstraction). However, much work needs to be done to bring policy-iteration-based approaches to the level of maturity required for analyzing industrial-scale codebases, in particular:

- Sound handling of machine integers and floats, and overflow checking in particular. The only incorrect result given by LPI on the dataset was due to the unsound overflow handling. It is possible to check the obtained invariants for inductiveness using bitvectors or overflow checks.
- Template abstract domains are perfect candidates for *refinement*: dynamically adding templates during the analysis. Using counter-examples and refining the domain using CEGAR [24] approach is a promising research direction.

Acknowledgments. The authors wish to thank Tim King for proof-reading and extremely valuable feedback, Nikolaj Bjørner for improving νZ performance on our difficult cases, and the anonymous reviewers for their helpful suggestions.

References

1. Cousot, P., Cousot, R.: Abstract interpretation: a unified lattice model for static analysis of programs by construction or approximation of fixpoints. In: Graham, R.M., Harrison, M.A., Sethi, R. (eds.) POPL 1977, pp. 238–252. ACM, New York (1977)
2. Miné, A.: The octagon abstract domain. High. Ord. Symbolic Comput. **19**(1), 31–100 (2006)
3. Sankaranarayanan, S., Sipma, H.B., Manna, Z.: Scalable analysis of linear systems using mathematical programming. In: Cousot, R. (ed.) VMCAI 2005. LNCS, vol. 3385, pp. 25–41. Springer, Heidelberg (2005)
4. Gawlitza, T., Seidl, H.: Precise relational invariants through strategy iteration. In: Duparc, J., Henzinger, T.A. (eds.) CSL 2007. LNCS, vol. 4646, pp. 23–40. Springer, Heidelberg (2007)
5. Gawlitza, T.M., Monniaux, D.: Invariant generation through strategy iteration in succinctly represented control flow graphs. Logical Meth. Comput. Sci. vol. 8(3:29) (2012)
6. Shamir, A.: A linear time algorithm for finding minimum cutsets in reducible graphs. SIAM J. Comput. **8**(4), 645–655 (1979)
7. Beyer, D., Keremoglu, M.E.: CPACHECKER: a tool for configurable software verification. In: Gopalakrishnan, G., Qadeer, S. (eds.) CAV 2011. LNCS, vol. 6806, pp. 184–190. Springer, Heidelberg (2011)
8. Bjørner, N., Phan, A.-D., Fleckenstein, L.: νZ - an optimizing SMT solver. In: Baier, C., Tinelli, C. (eds.) TACAS 2015. LNCS, vol. 9035, pp. 194–199. Springer, Heidelberg (2015)
9. Beyer, D., Henzinger, T.A., Théoduloz, G.: Configurable software verification: concretizing the convergence of model checking and program analysis. In: Damm, W., Hermanns, H. (eds.) CAV 2007. LNCS, vol. 4590, pp. 504–518. Springer, Heidelberg (2007)
10. Beyer, D., Keremoglu, M.E., Wendler, P.: Predicate abstraction with adjustable-block encoding. In: Bloem, R., Sharygina, N. (eds.) FMCAD 2010, pp. 189–197. IEEE (2010)
11. Roux, P., Garoche, P.-L.: Integrating policy iterations in abstract interpreters. In: Van Hung, D., Ogawa, M. (eds.) ATVA 2013. LNCS, vol. 8172, pp. 240–254. Springer, Heidelberg (2013)
12. Monniaux, D., Schrammel, P.: Speeding up logico-numerical strategy iteration. In: Müller-Olm, M., Seidl, H. (eds.) Static Analysis. LNCS, vol. 8723, pp. 253–267. Springer, Heidelberg (2014)
13. Gaubert, S., Goubault, É., Taly, A., Zennou, S.: Static analysis by policy iteration on relational domains. In: De Nicola, R. (ed.) ESOP 2007. LNCS, vol. 4421, pp. 237–252. Springer, Heidelberg (2007)
14. Colón, M.A., Sankaranarayanan, S., Sipma, H.B.: Linear invariant generation using non-linear constraint solving. In: Hunt Jr, W.A., Somenzi, F. (eds.) CAV 2003. LNCS, vol. 2725, pp. 420–432. Springer, Heidelberg (2003)
15. Monniaux, D.: Automatic modular abstractions for template numerical constraints. Logical Meth. Comput. Sci. 6(3:4), June 2010

16. Cousot, P., Halbwachs, N.: Automatic discovery of linear restraints among variables of a program. In: Aho, A.V., Zilles, S.N., Szymanski, T.G. (eds.) POPL 1978, pp. 84–96. ACM, New York (1978)
17. Beyer, D., Cimatti, A., Griggio, A., Keremoglu, M.E., Sebastiani, R.: Software model checking via large-block encoding. In: FMCAD 2009, pp. 25–32. IEEE (2009)
18. Monniaux, D., Gonnord, L.: Using bounded model checking to focus fixpoint iterations. In: Yahav, E. (ed.) Static Analysis. LNCS, vol. 6887, pp. 369–385. Springer, Heidelberg (2011)
19. Gawlitza, T., Seidl, H.: Precise fixpoint computation through strategy iteration. In: De Nicola, R. (ed.) ESOP 2007. LNCS, vol. 4421, pp. 300–315. Springer, Heidelberg (2007)
20. Bourdoncle, F.: Efficient chaotic iteration strategies with widenings. In: Broy, M., Pottosin, I.V., Bjørner, D. (eds.) Formal Methods in Programming and Their Applications. LNCS, vol. 735, pp. 128–141. Springer, Heidelberg (1993)
21. Beyer, D.: Software verification and verifiable witnesses. In: Baier, C., Tinelli, C. (eds.) TACAS 2015. LNCS, vol. 9035, pp. 401–416. Springer, Heidelberg (2015)
22. Shved, P., Mandrykin, M., Mutilin, V.: Predicate analysis with BLAST 2.7. In: Flanagan, C., König, B. (eds.) TACAS 2012. LNCS, vol. 7214, pp. 525–527. Springer, Heidelberg (2012)
23. Henry, J., Monniaux, D., Moy, M.: PAGAI: a path sensitive static analyser. Electr. Notes Theor. Comput. Sci. **289**, 15–25 (2012)
24. Clarke, E., Grumberg, O., Jha, S., Lu, Y., Veith, H.: Counterexample-guided abstraction refinement. In: Emerson, EAllen, Sistla, Aravinda Prasad (eds.) CAV 2000. LNCS, vol. 1855. Springer, Heidelberg (2000)

Lazy Constrained Monotonic Abstraction

Zeinab Ganjei[✉], Ahmed Rezine, Petru Eles, and Zebo Peng

Linköping University, Linköping, Sweden
zeinab.ganjei@liu.se

Abstract. We introduce Lazy Constrained Monotonic Abstraction (lazy CMA for short) for lazily and soundly exploring well structured abstractions of infinite state non-monotonic systems. CMA makes use of infinite state and well structured abstractions by forcing monotonicity wrt. refinable orderings. The new orderings can be refined based on obtained false positives in a CEGAR like fashion. This allows for the verification of systems that are not monotonic and are hence inherently beyond the reach of classical analysis based on the theory of well structured systems. In this paper, we consistently improve on the existing approach by localizing refinements and by avoiding to trash the explored state space each time a refinement step is required for the ordering. To this end, we adapt ideas from classical lazy predicate abstraction and explain how we address the fact that the number of control points (i.e., minimal elements to be visited) is a priori unbounded. This is unlike the case of plain lazy abstraction which relies on the fact that the number of control locations is finite. We propose several heuristics and report on our experiments using our open source prototype. We consider both backward and forward explorations on non-monotonic systems automatically derived from concurrent programs. Intuitively, the approach could be regarded as using refinable upward closure operators as localized widening operators for an a priori arbitrary number of control points.

Keywords: Constrained monotonic abstraction · Lazy exploration · Well structured systems · Safety properties · Counter machines reachability

1 Introduction

Well structured transition systems (WSTS:s for short) are maybe everywhere [17], but not all transition systems are well structured [3,18]. Problems such as state reachability (e.g., safety) have been shown to be decidable for WSTS:s [2,17]. This led to the development of algorithms that could check safety for systems ranging from lossy channels and Petri Nets to concurrent programs and broadcast protocols [19,23,25]. Many interesting examples of systems, including list manipulating programs [9], cache protocols [13] and mutex algorithms [1] are "almost" well structured in the sense that they would have been well structured

---

In part supported by the 12.04 CENIIT project.

B. Jobstmann and K.R.M. Leino (Eds.): VMCAI 2016, LNCS 9583, pp. 147–165, 2016.
DOI: 10.1007/978-3-662-49122-5_7

if it was not for a number of transitions that violate the required assumptions. We build on the framework of Constrained Monotonic Abstraction (CMA for short) where we derive well structured abstractions for infinite state systems that are "almost" well structured.

To simplify, a WSTS comes with a well quasi ordering (wqo[1] for short) on the set of configurations. A key property of such systems is *monotonicity*: i.e., if a smaller configuration can fire a transition and get to some configuration c, then any configuration that is larger (wrt. the wqo) can also get to some configuration that is larger than c. In other words, larger configurations simulate smaller ones. Added to some assumptions on the effectivity of natural operations such as computing minimal elements and images of upward closed sets of configurations, it is possible to show the existence of sound and complete algorithms for checking the reachability of upward closed sets of configurations (i.e., coverability).

Systems where only some transitions are non monotonic can be approximated using WSTS:s by adding abstract transitions to restore monotonicity (monotonic abstraction). The resulting abstraction is also infinite state, and reachability of upward closed sets there is decidable. However, the obtained abstractions may fail to enforce invariants that are crucial for establishing unreachability of bad configurations in the original system. For instance, we explain in our recent work [18] how we automatically account for the number of processes synchronizing with (dynamic) barriers when establishing or refuting local (e.g., assertions) and global (e.g., deadlock freedom) properties of programs manipulating arbitrary many processes. Crucial invariants of such systems enforce an inherently non-monotonic behavior (e.g., a barrier transition that is enabled on a configuration is disabled if more processes are considered in a larger configuration).

Checking safety for such non-monotonic systems is not guaranteed to terminate without abstraction. Plain monotonic abstraction [1,20] makes use of sets that are upward closed wrt. natural orderings as a sound symbolic representation. As stated earlier, this ensures termination if the used preorder is a wqo [2]. Of course, this comes at the price of possible false positives. In [3], we adapted existing counter example guided abstraction refinement (CEGAR) ideas to refine the ordering in plain monotonic abstraction. The preorder is strengthened by only relating configurations that happen to be in the same equivalence class, as defined by Craig interpolants obtained from the false positives. The new preorder is also a wqo, and hence, termination is again ensured. As implemented, the predicates are applied on all generated minimal elements to separate upward closed sets and the exploration has to restart from scratch each time a new refinement predicate is encountered.

We address these inefficiencies by adopting a lazy approach. Like in lazy predicate abstraction [21], we strive to localize the application of the refinement predicates and to reuse the explored state space. However, a major difference with plain lazy predicate abstraction is that the number of "control locations"

---

[1] A reflexive and transitive binary relation $\preceq$ over some set A is a preorder. It is said to be a wqo over A if in any infinite sequence $a_1, a_2, \ldots$ of elements of A, there exist $1 \leq i < j$ such that $a_i \preceq a_j$.

(i.e., the locations to which subsets of the refinement predicates are mapped) is a priori unbounded (as opposed to the number of program locations of a non-parameterized system). We propose in this paper three heuristics that can be applied both in backward and in forward (something plain monotonic abstraction is incapable of). All three heuristics adopt a backtracking mechanism to reuse, as much as possible, the state space that has been explored so far. Schematically, the first heuristic (*point-based*) associates refinement predicates to minimal elements. The second heuristic (*order-based*) associates the refinement predicates to preorder related minimal elements. The third heuristic (*descendants-based*) uses for the child the preserved predicates of the parent. We describe in details the different approaches and state the soundness and termination of each refinement step. In addition, we experimentally compare the heuristics against each other and against the eager approach on our open source tool https://gitlab.ida.liu.se/apv/zaama.

Related Work. Coverability of non-monotonic systems is undecidable in general. Tests for zero are one source of non-monotonicy. The work in [8] introduces a methodology for checking coverability by using an extended Karp-Miller acceleration for the case of Vector Addition Systems (VAS:s for short) with at most one test for zero. Our approach is more general and tackles coverability and reachability for counter machines with arbitrary tests.

Verification methods can be lazy in different ways. For instance, Craig interpolants obtained from program runs can be directly used as abstractions [26], or abstraction predicates can be lazily associated to program locations [21]. Such techniques are now well established [5,10,27]. Unlike these approaches, we address lazy exploration for transition systems with "infinite control". Existing WSTS based abstraction approaches do not allow for the possibility to refine the used ordering [23,25], cannot model transfers for the local variables [16], or make use of accelerations without termination guarantees [7]. For example, in [23] the authors leverage on the combination of an exact forward reachability and of an aggressive backward approximation, while in [25], the explicit construction of a Petri Net is avoided.

The work in [24] gives a generalization of the IC3 algorithm and tries to build inductive invariants for well-structured transition systems. It is unclear how to adapt it to the kind of non-monotonic systems that we work with.

We believe the approach proposed here can be combined with such techniques. To the best of our knowledge, there is no previous work that considered making lazy the preorder refinement of a WSTS abstraction.

Outline. We start in Sect. 2 with some preliminaries. We then formalize targeted systems and properties in Sect. 3. We describe the adopted symbolic representation in Sect. 4 and go through a motivating example in Sect. 5. This is followed by a description of the eager and lazy procedures in Sect. 6. We finally report on our experiments in Sect. 7 and conclude in Sect. 8.

2   Preliminaries

We write $\mathbb{N}$ and $\mathbb{Z}$ to respectively mean the sets of natural and integer values. We let $\mathbb{B} = \{\texttt{tt}, \texttt{ff}\}$ be the set of boolean values. Assume in the following a set X of integer variables. We write $\xi(X)$ to mean the set of *arithmetic expressions* over X. An arithmetic expression e in $\xi(X)$ is either an integer constant k, an integer variable x in X, or the sum or difference of two arithmetic expressions. We write $e(X)$ to emphasize that only variables in X are allowed to appear in e. We write $\texttt{atomsOf}(X)$ to mean the set of *atoms* over the variables X. An atom α is either a boolean $\texttt{tt}$ or $\texttt{ff}$ or an inequality $e \sim e'$ of two arithmetic expressions; where $\sim \in \{<, \leq, \geq, >\}$. We write A to mean a set of atoms. Observe that the negation of an atom can be expressed as an atom. We often write ψ to mean a conjunction of atoms, or *conjunct* for short, and use Ψ to mean a set of conjuncts. We use $\Pi(\xi(X))$ to mean arbitrary conjunctions and disjunctions of atoms over X. We can rewrite any presburger predicate over X in negated normal form and replace the negated inequalities with the corresponding atoms to obtain an equivalent predicate π in $\Pi(\xi(X))$. We write $\texttt{atomsOf}(\pi)$ to mean the set of atoms participating in π.

A mapping $\mathfrak{m} : U \to V$ associates an element in V to each element in U. We write $\mathfrak{m} : U \nrightarrow V$ to mean a partial mapping from U to V. We write $\texttt{dom}(\mathfrak{m})$ and $\texttt{img}(\mathfrak{m})$ to respectively mean the domain and the image of $\mathfrak{m}$ and use $\epsilon_U : U \nrightarrow V$ for the mapping with an empty domain. We often write a partial mapping $\mathfrak{m} : U \nrightarrow V$ as the set $\{u \leftarrow \mathfrak{m}(u) |\ u \in \texttt{dom}(\mathfrak{m})\}$ and write $\mathfrak{m} \cup \mathfrak{m}'$ to mean the union of two mappings $\mathfrak{m}$ and $\mathfrak{m}'$ with disjoint domains. Given a partial mapping $\varkappa : X \nrightarrow \xi(X)$, we write $\nu_\varkappa(e)$ to mean the substitution in e of X variables by their respective $\varkappa$ images and the natural evaluation of the result. As usual, $\nu_\varkappa(e)$ is a well defined integer value each time $\varkappa$ is a total mapping to $\mathbb{Z}$. This is generalized to (sets of) atoms, conjuncts and predicates.

We let $\mathbb{X}$ (resp. $\mathbb{X}_{\geq 0}$) be the set of all total mappings $X \to \mathbb{Z}$ (resp. $X \to \mathbb{N}$). We write $\mathbb{0}_X$ for the total mapping $X \to \{0\}$. The denotation of a conjunct ψ over $\mathbb{X}$ (resp. $\mathbb{X}_{\geq 0}$), written $[\![\psi]\!]_{\mathbb{X}}$ (resp. $[\![\psi]\!]_{\mathbb{X}_{\geq 0}}$), is the set of all total mappings $\varkappa$ in $\mathbb{X}$ (resp. in $\mathbb{X}_{\geq 0}$) s.t. $\nu_\varkappa(\psi)$ evaluates to $\texttt{tt}$. We generalize to sets of atoms or conjuncts by taking the union of the individual denotations. Let $\trianglelefteq$ be the preorder over $\mathbb{X}_{\geq 0}$ defined by $\varkappa \trianglelefteq \varkappa'$ iff $\varkappa(x) \leq \varkappa'(x)$ for each $x \in X$. Given a predicate π in $\Pi(\xi(X))$, we say that a set $M \subseteq [\![\psi]\!]_{\mathbb{X}_{\geq 0}}$ is minimal for ψ if: (i) $\varkappa \ntrianglelefteq \varkappa'$ for any pair of different $\varkappa, \varkappa' \in M$, and (ii) for any $\varkappa' \in [\![\psi]\!]_{\mathbb{X}_{\geq 0}}$, there is an $\varkappa \in M$ s.t. $\varkappa \trianglelefteq \varkappa'$. We recall the following facts from Linear Programming and [22].

Lemma 1. *For a finite set of natural variables X, the preorder $\trianglelefteq$ is a partial well quasi ordering. In addition, we can compute a finite and unique minimal set (written $\textbf{min}_\trianglelefteq(\pi)$) for any predicate π in $\Pi(\xi(X))$.*

3   The State Reachability Problem

In this section, we motivate and formally define the reachability problem.

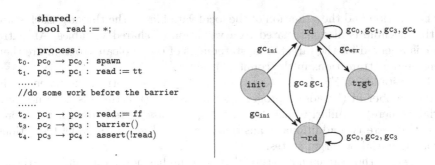

Fig. 1. The counter machine to the right captures the behaviour of the concurrent program to the left. It makes use of one counter per program location. It involves the following guarded commands: $gc_{ini} ::= (c_0, c_1, c_2, c_3, c_4 := 1, 0, 0, 0, 0)$, $gc_0 ::= (c_0 \geq 1 \Rightarrow c_0 := c_0 + 1)$, $gc_1 ::= (c_0 \geq 1 \Rightarrow c_0, c_1 := c_0 - 1, c_1 + 1)$, $gc_2 ::= (c_1 \geq 1 \Rightarrow c_1, c_2 := c_1 - 1, c_2 + 1)$, $gc_3 ::= ((c_2 \geq 1 \wedge c_0 + c_1 = 0) \Rightarrow (c_2, c_3 := c_2 - 1, c_3 + 1))$, $gc_4 ::= (c_3 \geq 1 \Rightarrow c_3, c_4 := c_3 - 1, c_4 + 1)$, and $gc_{err} : (c_3 \geq 1)$. The resulting system is not well structured because of the zero test in gc_3.

An Example. Consider the multi-threaded program to the left of Fig. 1 where only a single thread starts executing the program. A thread can spawn arbitrarily many concurrent threads with t_0. Assume all threads asynchronously run the same program. Each thread can then set the shared flag **read** to **tt**, and perform some reading followed by resetting **read** to **ff**. All threads wait at the barrier. Obviously, **read** should be **ff** after the barrier since all threads that reached pc_3 must have executed t_2. The assertion at pc_3 should therefore hold no matter how many threads are spawned. Capturing the barrier behaviour is crucial for establishing the non-violation of the assertion. The barrier behaviour is inherently non monotonic (adding more threads does not keep the barrier open). Our recent work [18] on combining different abstraction techniques can automatically generate non-monotonic counter machines such as the one to the right of Fig. 1. For this case, the assertion in the concurrent program is violated iff the target state is reachable in the counter machine. We explain briefly in the following how such counter machines are generated.

Our tool PACMAN [18], takes as input multi-threaded programs similar to the one to left of Fig. 1. It automatically performs predicate, counter and monotonic abstractions on them and generates counter machines that overapproximate the behaviour of the original program. It then tries to solve the reachability problem for those machines.

Given a multi-threaded program, PACMAN starts by generating concurrent boolean programs by performing predicate abstraction and incrementally improving it in a CEGAR loop [14]. This results in a boolean multi-threaded program that has the same control flow graph as the original program, but consists of only boolean variables. To the obtained boolean program, PACMAN applies counter abstraction to generate a counter machine. Intuitively, each counter in the machine is associated to each local state valuation of a thread (that consists in the location and the valuation of the local variables of the thread). Each state in the machine is also associated to a valuation of shared variables. An extra state is reserved for the target. The statements of the boolean program are then translated as transitions in the counter machine.

For instance, in Fig. 1, counters c_i, for $i : 0 \leq i \leq 4$, correspond respectively to the number of threads in program locations pc_i (the threads have no local variables here). Similarly, each transition gc_i is associated to each t_i. Moreover, there are two additional transitions gc_{ini} and gc_{err} to model transitions involving initial or target states.

Note that the original multi-threaded program has non-monotonic invariants. For instance, transitions such as barriers, or any transition that tests variables representing the number of threads satisfying some property do not stay enabled if we add more threads. At the same time, the boolean concurrent programs generated above are inherently monotonic. This corresponds to a loss of precision. Thus, proving correctness of those programs whose correctness depends on respecting the non-monotonic behaviour (e.g., the one enforced by a barrier) can become impossible. As a remedy to this fact, PACMAN automatically strengthens counter machine transitions by enforcing barrier invariants or by deriving new invariants (e.g., using an instrumented thread modular analysis) to regain some of the precision. This proved to help in verifying several challenging benchmarks. For example, consider the transition t_3 in the program to the left of Fig. 1. At the moment a thread crosses the barrier first, there should be no thread before location pc_2. This fact holds afterwards and forbids that a thread sets the flag read when some thread is checking the assertion. The transition gc_3 is its corresponding transition in the strengthened counter machine. To ease the presentation of the example, gc_3 is strengthened with the guard ($c_0 + c_1 = 0$). (Observe that this is a simplification to ease the presentation; we can more faithfully capture the barrier by combining the test with a global flag.)

Counter machines. A counter machine is a tuple $(Q, C, A, \Delta, q_{init}, q_{trgt})$ where Q is a finite set of states, C and A are two distinct sets of counters (i.e., variables ranging over $\mathbb{N}$), Δ is a finite set of transitions and q_{init} and q_{trgt} are two states in Q. A transition δ in Δ is of the form $(q, (grd \Rightarrow cmd), q')$ where $src(\delta) = q$ is the source state, $dst(\delta) = q'$ is the destination state and $gc(\delta) = (grd \Rightarrow cmd)$ is the guarded command. A guard grd is a predicate in $\Pi(\xi(A \cup C))$ and a command cmd is a multiple assignment $c_1, \ldots, c_n := e_1, \ldots, e_n$ that involves $e_1, \ldots e_n$ in $\xi(A \cup C)$ and pairwise different $c_1, \ldots c_n$ in C.

Semantics. A *configuration* is a pair $\theta = (q, c)$ with the state $st(\theta) = q$ in Q and the valuation $val(\theta) = c$ in $\mathbb{C}_{\geq 0} : C \to \mathbb{N}$. We let Θ be the set of configurations. We write $\theta \preceq \theta'$ to mean $st(\theta) = st(\theta')$ and $val(\theta) \trianglelefteq val(\theta')$ (see Sect. 2). The relation $\preceq$ is a partial order over Θ. In fact, the pair $(\Theta, \preceq)$ is a partial well quasi ordering [22]. Given two configurations (q, c) and (q', c') and a transition $\delta \in \Delta$ with $q = src(\delta)$, $q' = dst(\delta)$ and $gc(\delta) = (grd \Rightarrow (c_1, \ldots, c_n := e_1, \ldots, e_n))$, we write $(q, c) \xrightarrow{\delta} (q', c')$ to mean that there exists an $a \in A_{\geq 0}$ s.t. $\nu_{c \cup a}(grd)$ evaluates to tt and $c'(c_i) = \nu_{c \cup a}(e_i)$ for each c_i in C. The auxiliary variables allow us to capture transfers (needed by predicate abstraction of concurrent programs). For instance, $(c_0 \geq 1 \wedge c_0 = a_0 \wedge c_1 = a_1 \wedge a_0 + a_1 = a_2 + a_3) \Rightarrow (c_0, c_1, c_2, c_3 := 0, 0, a_2 + c_2, a_3 + c_3)$ captures situations where at least a thread is at pc_0 and all threads at pc_0 and pc_1 move to pc_2 and pc_3. A run ρ is a sequence $\theta_0 \theta_1 \cdots \theta_n$. We say that it *covers* the state $st(\theta_n)$. The run is *feasible* if $st(\theta_0) = q_{init}$ and $\theta_{i-1} \xrightarrow{\delta_i} \theta_i$ for $i : 1 \leq i \leq n$. We write $\rightarrow$ for $\cup_{\delta \in \Delta} \xrightarrow{\delta}$.

Reachability. The reachability problem for a machine $(Q, C, A, \Delta, q_{init}, q_{trgt})$ is to decide whether it has a feasible run that covers q_{trgt}.

4   Symbolic Representation

Assume a machine $(Q, C, A, \Delta, q_{init}, q_{trgt})$. We introduce (operations on) symbolic representations used in our reachability procedures in Sect. 6.

Boxes. A *box* $\mathbb{b}$ over a set A of atoms is a partial mapping from A to booleans $\mathbb{B}$. Intuitively, a box corresponds to a bitvector denoting an equivalence class in classical predicate abstraction. We use it to constrain the upward closure step. The predicate $\psi_\mathbb{b}$ of a box $\mathbb{b}$ is $\wedge_{\alpha \in dom(\mathbb{b})}((\mathbb{b}(\alpha) \wedge \alpha) \vee (\neg \mathbb{b}(\alpha) \wedge \neg \alpha))$ (tt is used for the empty box). Observe that this predicate is indeed a conjunct for any fixed box $\mathbb{b}$ and that $[\![\psi_\mathbb{b}]\!]$ does not need to be finite. We write $\mathbb{b}_{tt}$ for the box of the tt conjunct. We will say that a box $\mathbb{b}$ is weaker than (or is entailed by) a box $\mathbb{b}'$ if $\psi_{\mathbb{b}'} \Rightarrow \psi_\mathbb{b}$ is valid. We abuse notation and write $\mathbb{b} \Leftarrow \mathbb{b}'$. Observe this is equivalent to $[\![\psi_\mathbb{b}]\!] \subseteq [\![\psi_{\mathbb{b}'}]\!]$.

Constraints. A *constraint* over a set A of atoms is a triplet $\phi = (q, \mathbb{c}, \mathbb{b})$ where $st(\phi) \in Q$ is the state of the constraint, $val(\phi) = \mathbb{c}$ is its minimal valuation, and $box(\phi) = \mathbb{b}$ over A is its box. We use Φ to mean a set of constraints. A constraint $(q, \mathbb{c}, \mathbb{b})$ is well formed if $\nu_\mathbb{c}(\psi_\mathbb{b})$ holds. We only consider well formed constraints. We write $clo(\mathbb{c}, \mathbb{b})$ to mean the conjunct $(\wedge_{c \in C}(c \geq \mathbb{c}(c)) \wedge \psi_\mathbb{b})$. Intuitively, $clo(\mathbb{c}, \mathbb{b})$ denotes those valuations that are both "in the box" and in the $\trianglelefteq$-upward closure of $\mathbb{c}$. We let $[\![(q, \mathbb{c}, \mathbb{b})]\!]$ be the set $\{(q, \mathbb{c}') \mid \mathbb{c}' \in [\![clo(\mathbb{c}, \mathbb{b})]\!]\}$. This set contains at least $(q, \mathbb{c})$ by well formedness. Given two constraints $(q, \mathbb{c}, \mathbb{b})$ and $(q', \mathbb{c}', \mathbb{b}')$, we write $(q, \mathbb{c}, \mathbb{b}) \sqsubseteq (q', \mathbb{c}', \mathbb{b}')$ to mean that: (i) $q = q'$, and (ii) $\mathbb{c} \trianglelefteq \mathbb{c}'$, and (iii) $\mathbb{b} \Leftarrow \mathbb{b}'$. Observe that $\phi \sqsubseteq \phi'$ implies $[\![\phi']\!] \subseteq [\![\phi]\!]$. A subset Φ of a set of constraints Φ' is minimal if: (i) $\phi_1 \not\sqsubseteq \phi_2$ for any pair of different constraints $\phi_1, \phi_2 \in \Phi$, and (ii) for any $\phi' \in \Phi'$, there is a $\phi \in \Phi$ s.t. $\phi \sqsubseteq \phi'$.

Lemma 2. *For a finite set of atoms A over C, the ordering $\sqsubseteq$ is a well quasi ordering over the set of well formed constraints over A. In addition, we can compute, for any set Φ of constraints, a finite $\sqsubseteq$-minimal subset $min_\sqsubseteq(\Phi)$.*

Image Computations. Assume a conjunct ψ over C and a guarded command $gc = (grd \Rightarrow cmd)$ for some $\delta \in \Delta$. Recall that grd is in $\Pi(\xi(C \cup A))$ and that cmd is of the form $c_1, \ldots, c_n := e_1, \ldots, e_n$ where, for each $i : 1 \leq i \leq n$, c_i is in C and e_i is also in $\xi(C \cup A)$. We let L' be the set of primed versions of all variables appearing in the left hand side of *cmd*. We write $\mathbf{pre}_{gc}(\psi)$ to mean a set of conjuncts whose disjunction is equivalent to $(\exists A \cup L'.(\wedge_{1 \leq i \leq n}(c_i' = e_i) \wedge grd \wedge \psi[\{c \leftarrow c' \mid c' \in L'\}]))$. We also write $\mathbf{post}_{gc}(\psi)$ to mean a set of conjuncts whose disjunction is equivalent to $(\exists A \cup C.(\wedge_{1 \leq i \leq n}(c_i' = e_i) \wedge grd \wedge \psi))[\{c' \leftarrow c \mid c \in C\}]$. We naturally extend $\mathbf{pre}_{gc}(\psi)$ and $\mathbf{post}_{gc}(\psi)$ to sets of conjuncts.

Lemma 3. *Assume $\delta \in \Delta$ and conjuncts Ψ. We can compute $\mathbf{pre}_{gc(\delta)}(\Psi)$ and $\mathbf{post}_{gc(\delta)}(\Psi)$ s.t. $[\![\mathbf{pre}_{gc(\delta)}(\Psi)]\!]$ (resp. $[\![\mathbf{post}_{gc(\delta)}(\Psi)]\!]$) equals $\{c \mid (src(\delta), c) \xrightarrow{\delta} (dst(\delta), c')$ with $c' \in [\![\Psi]\!]\}$ (resp. $\{c' \mid (src(\delta), c) \xrightarrow{\delta} (dst(\delta), c')$ with $c \in [\![\Psi]\!]\}$).*

Grounded Constraints and Symbolic Sets. A *grounded constraint* is a pair $\gamma = ((q, c, b), \psi)$ that consists of a constraint $\mathtt{cstrOf}(\gamma) = (q, c, b)$ and a conjunct $\mathtt{groundOf}(\gamma) = \psi$. It is well formed if: (q, c, b) is well formed, $\psi \Rightarrow \mathtt{clo}(c, b)$ is valid, and $c \in [\![\psi]\!]$. We only manipulate well formed grounded constraints. Intuitively, the ground ψ in $((q, c, b), \psi)$ represents the "non-approximated" part of the $\trianglelefteq$-upward closure of c. This information will be needed for refining the preorder during the analysis. We abuse notation and write $\mathtt{cstrOf}(\Gamma)$, resp. $\mathtt{groundOf}(\Gamma)$, to mean the set of constraints, resp. grounds, of a set Γ of grounded constraints. A trace σ of length n is a sequence starting with a grounded constraint followed by n transitions and grounded constraints. We say that two traces $(\phi_0, \psi_0) \cdot \delta_1 \cdot (\phi_1, \psi_1) \cdots \delta_n \cdot (\phi_n, \psi_n)$ and $(\phi_0', \psi_0') \cdot \delta_1' \cdot (\phi_1', \psi_1') \cdots \delta_{n'}' \cdot (\phi_{n'}', \psi_{n'}')$ are equivalent if: (i) $n = n'$, and (ii) δ_i is the same as δ_i' for each $i : 1 \leq i \leq n$, and (iii) $\phi_i \sqsubseteq \phi_i'$, $\phi_i' \sqsubseteq \phi_i$ and $\psi_i \Leftrightarrow \psi_i'$ for each $i : 0 \leq i \leq n$. A symbolic set is a set of pairs of grounded constraints and traces. Given a symbolic set T, we also use $\mathtt{cstrOf}(T)$ to mean all constraints ϕ appearing in some $((\phi, \psi), \sigma)$ in T. Recall that we can compute a set $\min_{\sqsubseteq}(\mathtt{cstrOf}(T))$ of $\sqsubseteq$-minimal constraints for $\mathtt{cstrOf}(T)$.

5   An Illustrating Example

We use the example introduced in Sect. 3 to give an intuition of the lazy heuristics described in this paper. A more detailed description follows in Sect. 6.

Plain monotonic abstraction proceeds backwards while systematically closing upwards wrt. the natural ordering $\preceq$ on Θ. The trace depicted in Fig. 2 is a generated false positive. In this description, for $i : 0 \leq i \leq 7$, we write $\gamma_i = (\phi_i, \psi_i)$ to mean the grounded constraint with the grounded constraint ψ_i and the constraint $\phi_i = (q_i, c_i, b_i)$. Intuitively, the grounded constraint represents "exact" valuations while the constraint captures over-approximations that are of the form (q_i, c) where $c_i \trianglelefteq c$ and c satisfies ψ_{b_i}. The computation starts from the grounded constraint $\gamma_7 = ((\mathtt{trgt}, c_7, b_{\mathtt{tt}}), \psi_7)$ where ψ_7 is $\wedge_{c \in C}(c \geq 0)$ (always implicit). For γ_7, the exact and the over-approximated parts coincide.

The trace then computes $\psi_6 = (c_3 \geq 1)$ which captures the valuations of the predecessors of $(\mathtt{trgt}, c_7, b_{\mathtt{tt}})$ wrt. $(\mathtt{rd}, \mathtt{gc}_{\mathtt{err}}, \mathtt{trgt})$. This set happens to be upward closed and there is no need for approximation, hence $\gamma_6 = ((\mathtt{rd}, c_6, b_{\mathtt{tt}}), \psi_6)$. Valuations of the exact predecessors of $(\mathtt{rd}, c_6, b_{\mathtt{tt}})$ wrt.

$(\mathbf{rd}, \mathbf{gc_3}, \mathbf{rd})$ are captured with the conjunct $\psi_5 = (c_0 = c_1 = 0 \wedge c_2 \geq 1)$. These are approximated with the conjunct $(c_0 \geq 0 \wedge c_1 \geq 0 \wedge c_2 \geq 1)$. Continuing to compute the predecessors and closing upwards leads to the constraint ϕ_0 which involves the initial state init. The trace is reported as a possible reachability witness. It is well known [4] that upward closed sets are not preserved by non-monotonic transitions (such as those involving $\mathbf{gc_3}$ in Fig. 1). At the same time, maintaining an exact analysis makes guaranteeing termination impossible.

Following the trace in forward from the left, it turns out that the upward closure that resulted in γ_5 is the one that made the spurious trace possible. Indeed, it is its approximation that allowed the counter c_1 to be non zero. This new value for c_1 is the one that allowed the machine to execute $(\neg\mathbf{rd}, \mathbf{gc_1}, \mathbf{rd})$ in backward from ϕ_5, making reaching the initial state possible. The constraint ϕ_5 is the pivot constraint of the trace. Constrained monotonic abstraction (CMA) proposes to refine the used ordering by strengthening it with a relevant predicate. In this case, $c_1 \leq 0$ is used for strengthening, but in general (the atoms of) any predicate in $\Pi(\xi(C))$ that separates the exact predecessors from the reachable part of the upward closure would do.

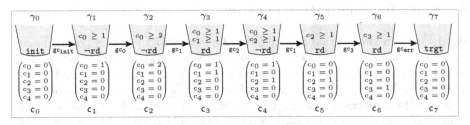

Fig. 2. A spurious trace generated by monotonic abstraction. The γ_5 constraint introduces the first over-approximation that makes the spurious trace possible. The configuration $(\mathbf{rd}, c_5)$ is the pivot configuration of the spurious trace.

Eager CMA. Introduced in [3]. The exploration is restarted from scratch and $(c_1 \leq 0)$ is used to systematically partition all exact predecessors. The upward closure is constrained to not alter the refinement predicate. All generated valuations are therefore approximated with the stronger ordering. Localizing refinement can make possible both reusing a potentially large part of the explored state space and applying the (slower) refinement to a smaller number of sets.

Lazy CMA. When backtracking, we only eliminate those constraints that were obtained as descendants of a constraint that needs to be refined. We refer to this constraint as the pivot constraint, and to its minimal configuration as the pivot configuration. In fact, we identify three localization heuristics:

- *point-based-lazy.* We map the refinement predicates to the pivot configurations. Later in the exploration, when we hit a new pivot configuration, we constrain wrt. those predicates that were already mapped to it.
- *order-based-lazy.* The point-based approach may be too localized as there is an infinite number of pivot configurations. For instance, a similar trace can

continue, after $(\mathbf{rd}, c_2 = 1)$, with $\mathbf{gc}_1$ and get to the minimal configuration sending c_2 to 2. This one is different from the mapped pivot configuration, and hence we need to introduce a new pivot configuration with the same predicate $c_0 \leq 0$. This approach considers the predicates of all larger or smaller pivot configurations. The idea being that, if the predicate was important for the mapped pivot configuration, then it must have been to separate it from a reachable upward closed part, and hence it may be relevant.

- *descendants-based-lazy.* In addition to associating refinement predicates to pivot configurations as in the point-based approach, this heuristic leverages on the fact that predicates may remain relevant for a sequence of transitions. Here we compare the exact predecessors with the predicates used to constrain the upward closure of the parent. If those predicates still hold for the predecessors, then we maintain them when closing upwards. This heuristic bears similarity to forward propagation of clauses in IC3 [24], as in the IC3 algorithm the clauses are propagated in the trace from a preceding formula to the succeeding one if they still hold.

6   State Reachability Checking

We describe in this section four different forward CMA variants (*eager, point-based-lazy, order-based-lazy* and *descendants-based-lazy*). The four procedures can also be applied in backwards (as described in the experiments of Sect. 7). The four variants use grounded constraints as symbolic representations for possibly infinite numbers of machine configurations. The symbolic representation is refined using atoms obtained using a counterexample guided refinement scheme. The difference between the four variants lays in the way discovered predicates (in fact atoms.for simplifying the presentation) are associated to the new symbolic representations and in the way backtracking is carried out. We start by introducing the basic "partition" procedure.

Input: a state q, a conjunct ψ and a finite set of atoms A
Output: a well formed set of grounded constraints
1 $\Gamma := \emptyset$;
2 **foreach** (*total* $\mathbb{b} : A \rightarrow \mathbb{B}$) **do**
3 | **foreach** ($\mathbb{c} \in min_{\unlhd}(\psi \wedge \psi_{\mathbb{b}})$) **do** $\Gamma := \Gamma \cup ((q, \mathbb{c}, \mathbb{b}), \psi \wedge \mathtt{clo}(\mathbb{c}, \mathbb{b}))$;
4 **return** Γ;

Procedure partition(q, ψ, A) is common to all variants.

Partition. "partition(q, ψ, A)" partitions ψ according to all atoms in A. Each obtained conjunct is further decomposed according to its $\unlhd$-minimal valuations. Conjuncts are then used to build a well formed grounded constraint $((q, \mathbb{c}, \mathbb{b}), \psi')$ where $\mathbb{b}$ is a box over A. Observe that the disjunction of the grounds of the obtained grounded constraints is equivalent to ψ. Soundness is stated in Lemma 4.

Lemma 4. *Assume a finite set A of atoms. For any conjunct ψ, it is the case that* $[\![(q, \psi)]\!]$ $=$ $\{(q, \mathbb{c}) | \ \mathbb{c} \in [\![\psi']\!]_{\geq 0}$ *for each* $\psi' \in$ *groundOf*(partition)$(q, \psi, A))\} \subseteq [\![cstrOf(\text{partition})(q, \psi, A))]\!]$.

Input: a machine $M = (Q, C, A, \Delta, q_{init}, q_{trgt})$
Output: A feasible run covering q_{trgt} or the value unreachable
1   **if** $q_{init} = q_{trgt}$ **then return** $(q_{init}, \mathbb{0}_C)$;
2   $\mathsf{S}, \Gamma := \emptyset, \text{partition}(q_{init}, \wedge_{c \in C}(c \geq 0), \emptyset)$;
3   **foreach** $(\gamma \in \Gamma)$ **do** $\mathsf{S} := \mathsf{S} \cup \{(\gamma, \gamma)\}$;
4   **return** $\text{explore}(M, \mathsf{S}, \mathsf{S}, \emptyset, \epsilon_\Theta)$;

Procedure checkReachability(M) is the common entry point for all variants.

Eager CMA, like the other variants, starts by passing a description of the machine to the "checkReachability" procedure. It returns a feasible run covering q_{trgt}, or states that there are no such runs. The procedure returns directly (line 1) if initial and target states coincide. It then calls "partition" to obtain a set of well formed grounded constraints that together capture all initial configurations. These are passed to the "explore" procedure.

Explore. "explore$(M, \mathtt{work}, \mathtt{store}, \mathtt{sleep}, \mathfrak{f})$" results in a working list process that maintains three symbolic sets $\mathtt{work}$, $\mathtt{store}$ and $\mathtt{sleep}$. The last is only relevant for the lazy variants. The partial mapping $\mathfrak{f} : \Theta \nrightarrow \mathtt{atomsOf}(C)$ encapsulates all refinement predicates discovered so far and is therefore empty when the procedure is called from "checkReachability". Intuitively, $\mathfrak{f}(\theta)$ associates to the pivot configuration θ those predicates that helped eliminate a false positive when θ was the minimal configuration of the constraint that made the false positive possible. We will explain how $\mathfrak{f}$ is updated when introducing the procedure "simulate". The symbolic set $\mathtt{work}$ is used for the grounded constraints that are yet to be visited (i.e., for which the successors are still to be computed and approximated). The $\mathtt{store}$ set is used for both those grounded constraints that have been visited and for those in *working*. The $\mathtt{sleep}$ set corresponds to those constraints that might have to be visited but for which there is an $\sqsubseteq$-equivalent representative in $\mathtt{store}$. In case a backtracking eliminates the representative in $\mathtt{store}$, the corresponding grounded constraint in $\mathtt{sleep}$ has to be reconsidered. This is explained in the "backtrack" procedure of the lazy variants.

Input: A machine description $M = (Q, C, A, \Delta, q_{init}, q_{trgt})$, three symbolic sets work, store and sleep, and a partial mapping $\mathfrak{f} : \Theta \nrightarrow \mathtt{atomsOf}(C)$
Output: A feasible run covering q_{trgt} or the value unreachable
1   **while** *there exists* $((\phi, \psi), \sigma)$ *in* work *with* $\phi \in min_\sqsubseteq(\mathtt{cstrOf}(\mathtt{store}))$ **do**
2   remove $((\phi, \psi), \sigma)$ from work;
3      $(q, \mathtt{c}, \mathbb{b}) := \phi$;
4   **if** $q = q_{trgt}$ **then**
5   **return** simulate$(M, \mathtt{work}, \mathtt{store}, \mathtt{sleep}, \mathfrak{f}, \sigma)$;
6   **foreach** $\delta = (q, gc, q')$ *in* Δ **do**
7   **foreach** $\psi_p \in post_{gc}(clo(\mathtt{c}, \mathbb{b}))$ **do**
8   **foreach** (ϕ', ψ') *in* decompose$(q', \psi_p, \mathfrak{f}, \mathbb{b})$ **do**
9                  $\sigma' := \sigma \cdot \delta \cdot (\phi', \psi')$;
10   **if** *there is* $((\phi_e, \psi_e), \sigma_e)$ *in* store *s.t.* ϕ_e *is* $\sqsubseteq$-*equivalent to* ϕ' **then**
11   **if** σ_e *and* σ' *are not equivalent* **then**
12   **add** $((\phi', \psi'), \sigma')$ to sleep;
13   **else add** $((\phi', \psi'), \sigma')$ to both store and work ;
14   **return** unreachable;

Procedure explore$(M, \mathtt{work}, \mathtt{store}, \mathtt{sleep}, \mathfrak{f})$ is common to all variants.

The procedure picks a pair $((\phi, \psi), \sigma)$ from work and $\min_{\sqsubseteq}(\mathtt{cstrOf}(\mathtt{store}))$. If the initial state is reached, it calls procedure "simulate" to check the associated trace and to backtrack if needed (lines 4–5). Otherwise, we start by iterating through all transitions δ in Δ and compute an exact representation of the predecessors of the constraint. The call "$\mathtt{decompose}(q, \psi_p, \mathfrak{f}, \mathfrak{b})$" boils down, for the eager variant, to a call to "$\mathtt{partition}(q, \psi_p, \mathtt{img}(\mathfrak{f}))$". The obtained grounded constraints are used to update the store, work and sleep symbolic sets.

If there was no pair picked at line 1, then we have finished the exploration and return unreachable. In fact, pairs are never removed from store if no target states are encountered at line 4. In addition, two pairs with $\sqsubseteq$-equivalent constraints cannot be added to work (lines 10–13). For this reason, executing the first line an infinite number of times without calling procedure "simulate" would result in an infinite sequence of constraints that would violate Lemma 2.

Input: machine M, symbolic sets work, store and sleep, a mapping $\mathfrak{f} : \Theta \twoheadrightarrow \mathtt{atomsOf}(C)$ and
a trace $\sigma = (\phi_0, \psi_0) \cdot \delta_1 \cdots \delta_n \cdot (\phi_n, \psi_n)$ with $n \geq 1$ and $q_0 = q_{init}$ and $q_n = q_{trgt}$;
Output: A feasible run covering q_{trgt} or the value unreachable

1   $\Psi_n := \{\psi_n\}$;
2   **for** $i \leftarrow (n-1)$ **to** 0 **do**
3   $\quad \Psi_i' := \mathtt{pre}_{\mathtt{gc}(\delta_{i+1})}(\Psi_{i+1})$;
4   $\quad \Psi_i := \{(\psi_i \wedge \psi_i') \mid \psi_i' \in \Psi_i' \text{ and } (\psi_i \wedge \psi_i') \text{ is sat}\}$;
5   $\quad$ **if** Ψ_i *is empty* **then**
6   $\quad\quad \mathfrak{f}((\mathtt{st}(\phi_i), \mathtt{val}(\phi_i))) \cup := \{\alpha \mid \alpha \in \mathtt{atomsOf}(\pi) \text{ with } \pi \in \mathbf{ITP}(\{\psi_i\}, \Psi_i')\}$;
7   $\quad\quad$ **return** $\mathtt{backtrack}(M, \mathtt{work}, \mathtt{store}, \mathtt{sleep}, \mathfrak{f}, \sigma, i)$;
8   **return** a run starting at $(q_{init}, \mathtt{c})$ for some $\mathtt{c} \in \Psi_0$ and following till q_{trgt};

Procedure simulate$(M, \mathtt{work}, \mathtt{store}, \mathtt{sleep}, \mathfrak{f}, \sigma)$ is common to all variants.

Simulate. This procedure checks feasibility of a trace σ from q_{init} to q_{trgt}. The procedure incrementally builds a sequence of sets of conjuncts $\Psi_n, \ldots, \Psi_0$ where each Ψ_i intuitively denotes the valuations that are backwards reachable from q_{trgt} after k steps of σ (starting from $k = 0$), and are still denoted by $\mathtt{clo}(\mathtt{c}_{(n-k)}, \mathfrak{b}_{(n-k)})$. The idea is to systematically intersect (a representation of) the successors of step k with the grounded constraint that gave rise to the constraint at step $k + 1$. If the procedure finds a satisfiable Ψ_0, then a run can be generated by construction. Such a run is then returned at line 8. Otherwise, there must have been a step where the "exact" set of conjuncts does not intersect the conjunct representing the exact part that gave rise to the corresponding constraint. In other words, the trace could be eliminated by strengthening the over-approximation at line 7 of the "explore" procedure. In this case, (at line 6 of the "simulate" procedure), new refinement atoms are identified using an off-the-shelf interpolation procedure for QF_LIA (Quantifier Free Linear Arithmetic). This information will be used differently by the eager and lazy variants when calling their respective "backtrack" procedures.

Input: a machine M, sets work and store and mapping $\mathfrak{f} : \Theta \twoheadrightarrow \mathtt{atomsOf}(C)$;
Output: A feasible run covering q_{trgt} or the value unreachable

1   store, work $:= \emptyset, \emptyset$;
2   $\Gamma := \mathtt{partition}(q_{init}, \wedge_{c \in C}(c \geq 0), \mathtt{img}(\mathfrak{f}))$;
3   **foreach** (ϕ, ψ) *in* Γ **do**
4   $\quad \mathtt{S} := \mathtt{S} \cup \{((\phi, \psi), (\phi, \psi))\}$;
5   **return** explore$(M, \mathtt{S}, \mathtt{S}, \emptyset, \mathfrak{f})$;

Procedure backtrack$(M, \mathtt{work}, \mathtt{store}, \_, \mathfrak{f}, \_, \_)$ this is the eager variant.

Eager backtracking throws away the explored state space (line 1) and restarts the computation from scratch using the new refinement atoms captured in $\mathfrak{f}$.

Lazy Backtracking. Intuitively, all three lazy approaches reuse the part of the explored state space that is not affected by the new refinements. This is done by restarting the exploration from new sets **work** and **store** that are obtained after pruning away the pivot constraint identified by the argument i passed by "simulate" together with all its descendants (identified in lines 1–6). One important aspect is that grounded constraints that have not been added to **store** at line 11 of the "explore" procedure may have been discarded for the wrong reason (i.e., there was an $\sqsubseteq$-equivalent constraint that needs to be pruned away now). This would jeopardize soundness. For this reason we maintain the **sleep** set for tracking the discarded grounded constraints that have to be put back to **work** and **store** if the constraint that blocked them is pruned away (see lines 4–6). The refined pivot is added to the new sets **work** and **store** (lines 10–13). Lines 7–9 are only used by the descendants-based approach which takes into account the box of the parent.

Input: symbolic sets **work**, **store** and **sleep**; a mapping $\mathfrak{f} : \Theta \nrightarrow \mathrm{atomsOf}(C)$, a trace
$\quad \sigma = (\phi_0, \psi_0) \cdot \delta_0 \cdots (\phi_n, \psi_n)$ with $n \geq 1$ and $\mathrm{st}(\phi_0) = q_{init}$ and $\mathrm{st}(\phi_n) = q_{trgt}$, and
$\quad$ a natural $i : 0 \leq i < n$;
Output: A feasible run covering q_{trgt} or the value unreachable
1 **foreach** $((\phi, \psi), \tau) \in$ **store** st. $(\phi_0, \psi_0) \cdot \delta_0 \cdots (\phi_i, \psi_i)$ *is equivalent to a prefix of* τ **do**
2 $\quad$ remove, if present, $((\phi, \psi), \tau)$ from **work**, **store** and **sleep**;
3 $\quad$ **for** $j \leftarrow i$ **to** n **do**
4 $\quad\quad$ **if** *there is still a* $((\phi', \psi'), \tau')$ *in* **sleep** *with* ϕ' *is* $\sqsubseteq$-*equivalent to* ϕ_j **then**
5 $\quad\quad\quad$ remove $((\phi', \psi'), \tau')$ from **sleep**;
6 $\quad\quad\quad$ add $((\phi', \psi'), \tau')$ to both **work** and **store**;
7 **if** $i \geq 1$ **then**
8 $\quad$ $\mathbb{b}_p := \mathbb{b}_{i-1}$
9 **else** $\mathbb{b}_p := \mathbb{b}_{tt}$;
10 **foreach** $(\phi', \psi') \in \mathrm{decompose}(q_i, \psi_i, \mathfrak{f}, \mathbb{b}_p)$ **do**
11 $\quad$ **let** $\sigma' := (\phi_0, \psi_0) \cdot \delta_1 \cdots (\phi_{i-1}, \psi_{i-1}) \cdot \delta_i \cdot (\phi', \psi')$;
12 $\quad$ **if** *there is some* $((\phi_e, \psi_e), \sigma_e)$ *in* **store** *st.* ϕ_e *is* $\sqsubseteq$-*equivalent to* ϕ' **then**
13 $\quad\quad$ **if** σ_e *and* σ' *are not equivalent* **then**
14 $\quad\quad\quad$ add $((\phi', \psi'), \sigma')$ to **sleep**;
15 $\quad$ **else** add $((\phi', \psi'), \sigma')$ to both **store** and **work** ;
16 **return** $\mathrm{explore}(M, \mathbf{work}, \mathbf{store}, \mathbf{sleep}, \mathfrak{f})$;

Procedure $\mathrm{backtrack}(M, \mathbf{work}, \mathbf{store}, \mathbf{sleep}, \mathfrak{f}, \sigma, i)$ common to all lazy variants.

The main difference between the lazy variants is in the way their respective "decompose" procedures associate refinement atoms to "exact" conjuncts.

Point-based. This variant is the one that "localizes" most the refinement. Each time an obtained grounded conjunct is considered for approximation, it checks whether its minimal valuation has already been associated to some refinement atoms. If it is the case, it passes them when calling the "partition" procedure.

Input: a state q, a conjunct ψ and a partial mapping $\mathfrak{f} : \Theta \nrightarrow \mathrm{atomsOf}(C)$
Output: a well formed set of grounded constraints
1 $A := \emptyset$;
2 **foreach** $(\theta \in \mathrm{dom}(\mathfrak{f})$ *with* $\mathrm{val}(\theta) \in \mathrm{min}_{\trianglelefteq}(\psi))$ **do** $A := A \cup \mathfrak{f}(\theta)$;
3 **return** $\mathrm{partition}(q, \psi, A)$.

Procedure $\mathrm{decompose}(q, \psi, \mathfrak{f}, -)$ of the point-based-lazy variant.

Order-based. This variant "localizes" less than the point-based variant. Each time an obtained "exact" conjunct is considered for approximation, it checks whether its minimal valuation is $\trianglelefteq$-related to an already mapped valuation. The union of all corresponding atoms is passed to the "partition" procedure.

Input: a state q, a conjunct ψ and a mapping $\mathbb{f} : \Theta \rightharpoonup \text{atomsOf}(C)$
Output: a well formed set of grounded constraints
1 **let** $A := \emptyset$;
2 **foreach** $(\theta \in dom(\mathbb{f}))$ **do**
3 $\quad$ **foreach** $(\mathbb{c}' \in min_\triangleleft(\psi))$ **do**
4 $\quad\quad$ **if** $((\mathbb{c}' \trianglelefteq val(\theta))$ *or* $(val(\theta) \trianglelefteq \mathbb{c}'))$ **then**
5 $\quad\quad\quad$ $A := A \cup \mathbb{f}(\theta)$;
6 $\quad\quad\quad$ **break** ;
7 **return** partition(q, ψ, A)

Procedure decompose$(q, \psi, \mathbb{f}, \_)$ of the order-based variant.

Descendants-based. This variant "localizes" less than the point-based variant, but is incomparable with the order-based one. The idea is to keep those refinement atoms that were used for the parent constraint, and that are still weaker than the current conjunct that is to be approximated.

Input: a state q, a conjunct ψ, a box $\mathbb{b}$ and a mapping $\mathbb{f} : \Theta \rightarrow \text{atomsOf}(C)$
Output: a well formed set of grounded constraints
1 **let** $A := \emptyset$;
2 **foreach** $(\theta \in dom(\mathbb{f})$ *with* $val(\theta) \in min_\triangleleft(\psi))$ **do** $A := A \cup \mathbb{f}(\theta)$;
3 **foreach** $\alpha \in dom(\mathbb{b})$ **do**
4 $\quad$ **if** $(\mathbb{b}(\alpha) \wedge (\psi \Rightarrow \alpha))$ *or* $(\neg\mathbb{b}(\alpha) \wedge (\psi \Rightarrow \neg\alpha))$ **then**
5 $\quad\quad$ $A := A \cup \{\alpha\}$;
6 **return** partition(q, ψ, A)

Procedure decompose$(q, \psi, \mathbb{f}, \mathbb{b})$ of the descendants-based variant.

Finally, we state the soundness of our four exploration variants. The proof is by observing that store always represents, at the ith iteration of the loop of procedure "explore", an over-approximation of the machine configurations obtained after i steps. Combined with Lemmas 2 and 3 and by well quasi ordering of $\sqsubseteq$ on the set of constraints for a finite number of refinement atoms.

Theorem 1. *All four exploration variants are sound. In addition, each call to procedure "checkReachability" eventually terminates if only a finite number of calls to procedure "simulate" are executed.*

Proof. Sketch. Let work_k, store_k and sleep_k be the sets work, store and sleep obtained at line 1 at the kth iteration of the loop in procedure "explore". We can show the following propositions by induction on k (see the appendix for the details):

(a) $[\![\text{store}_k]\!]$ does not intersect $(q_{trgt}, \mathbb{c})$ for any valuation $\mathbb{c}$
(b) $[\![\text{store}_k]\!]$ intersects $(q_{init}, \mathbb{c})$ for every valuation $\mathbb{c}$
(c) $[\![\text{work}_k \cup \text{sleep}_k]\!]$ is a subset of $[\![\text{store}_k]\!]$
(d) for each element $((\phi, \psi), \sigma)$ of store_k such that $((\phi, \psi), \sigma) \notin \text{work}_k$ and $\phi \in \text{min}_\sqsubseteq(\text{cstrOf}(\text{store}_k))$ and for each transition $\delta = (q, gc, q') \in \Delta$, the configurations in $\{(q', \mathbb{c}')|\ \mathbb{c}' \in [\![\text{post}_{gc}(\text{clo}(val(\phi), \text{box}(\phi)))]\!]\}$ are also in $[\![\text{store}_k]\!]$

Soundness. Suppose the algorithm returns **unreachable**. Then at some iteration, there is no element $((\phi, \psi), \sigma)$ in **work** s.t. $\phi \in \min_{\sqsubseteq}(\texttt{cstrOf(store)})$. Combined with propositions (b), (c) and (d), we have that $[\![\texttt{store}]\!]$ is a fixpoint that is an overapproximation of all reachable configurations. Proposition (a) ensures that no element with state q_{trgt} exists in **store**. If the algorithm returns a trace, then the test at line 4 ensures that $\texttt{st}(\phi_n) = q_{trgt}$ for some $((\phi_n, \psi_n), \sigma)$ and $\sigma = (\phi_0, \psi_0) \cdot \delta_1 \cdots \delta_n \cdot (\phi_n, \psi_n)$ satisfies that $\texttt{st}(\phi_0) = q_{init}$, $\texttt{st}(\phi_n) = q_{trgt}$ and for $0 \leq i < n$, $(\texttt{st}(\phi_i), \texttt{val}(\phi_i)) \xrightarrow{\delta_{i+1}} (\texttt{st}(\phi_{i+1}), \texttt{val}(\phi_{i+1}))$. This because of the form of the added tuple at line 13 of "explore".

Termination. The procedure "checkReachability" terminates if only a finite number of calls to procedure "simulate" are executed. This relies on the fact that the only source of non-termination can be the while loop in "explore" if the set $\texttt{cstrOf(work)} \cap \min_{\sqsubseteq}(\texttt{cstrOf(store)})$ never becomes empty. Suppose there is an infinite sequence of constraints as $\phi_0, \phi_1 \ldots$ obtained in the while loop. First, we show that $i \neq j$ implies ϕ_i is not $\sqsubseteq$-equivalent with ϕ_j for any $i, j \geq 0$. This holds because an element is added to **store** only if there is no $\sqsubseteq$-equivalent element there (line 9 of "explore"). Even if an element is moved from **sleep** to **store** and **work** by "backtrack", then it is done after removing the $\sqsubseteq$-equivalent element in **store** and **work**. Second, we show that for any $0 \leq i < j$, $\phi_i \not\sqsubseteq \phi_j$. This holds because if $\phi_i \sqsubseteq \phi_j$, then ϕ_j could not be in $\min_{\sqsubseteq}(\texttt{cstrOf(store)})$ since ϕ_i (or an $\sqsubseteq$-equivalent constraint) is already there. Finally, since the number of calls to "backtrack" is finite, then the number of predicates being used in the boxes is also finite. Such a sequence would therefore violate Lemma 2. $\square$

7   Experimental Results

We have implemented our techniques in our open source tool ZAAMA. The tool and benchmarks are available online[2]. The tool relies on the Z3 SMT solver [12] for its internal representations and operations.

The input of the prototype are counter machine encodings of boolean multithreaded programs with broadcasts and arbitrary tests (as described in Sect. 3). We have experimented with more than eighty different counter machine reachability problems. These were obtained from our prototype tool PACMAN [18] that checks local (i.e., assertion) or a global (e.g., deadlock freedom) properties in concurrent programs (some inspired from [11,15]).

Given a property to check on a concurrent program, PACMAN proceeds in predicate abstraction iterations. For each set of tracked predicates, it creates a counter machine reachability problem. Combining PACMAN with ZAAMA results in a nested CEGAR loop: an outer loop for generating counter machine reachability problems, and an inner loop for checking the resulting problems. About 45% of the generated counter machines are not monotonic. We tested all those

---

[2] https://gitlab.ida.liu.se/apv/zaama.

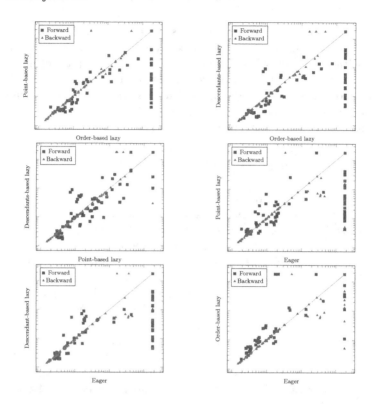

Fig. 3. Comparing eager and lazy variants on a logarithmic scale.

machines separately with ZAAMA in different settings for each benchmark and reported the execution times. Thus, the PACMAN overhead is not included in the reported times. Note that although 55 % of the examples are monotonic, they still need refinement in forward exploration.

We also tested our benchmarks with the tool BREACH introduced in [23]. BREACH cannot take non-monotonic inputs and is inherently incapable of solving reachability problems for such systems which are the main target of this paper. Thus, we could apply it only to the monotonic benchmarks; for which, the runtime of BREACH was less than 5 seconds in each. We consider this to be an encouraging result as we are working on adapting BREACH to non-monotonic systems. The challenge is to have an under-approximation search engine for such systems and we are investigating possibilities to develop our own engine or to use acceleration tools such as FASTer [6].

We have chosen a time-out of 30 min for each of the variants: eager, point-based, order-based and descendants-based, both in forward and in backward. We have conducted our experiments on an Intel Core i7 2.93 GHz processor with 8GB of memory. We report on our results in Fig. 3 where we consider, for each setting, each lazy pair in addition to the pairs consisting in the eager and each lazy.

The forward explorations turned out to be faster than the corresponding backward ones in about 25 % of the examples. We expected the forward exploration to be slower as it needs several refinement steps because it starts from the initial configurations which are typically much more constrained than the target configurations. We considered the forward exploration because it offers more possibilities to test the effect of localizing the refinement in problems that typically require more refinement steps in forward. Indeed, the figures show that the times of the different variants coincide more often in backward than in forward, and overall, there has been many more time-outs in forward than in backward.

Furthermore, the lazy variants were able to conclude on most of the reachability problems, in fact each of the reachability problems has been solved by at least one of the lazy variants (except for one problem in backward), when the eager variant timed out on several of them. This is an encouraging result that confirms the advantages of localizing refinement. There are some cases where the eager variant did better than all lazy ones. These correspond to cases where localization required more refinement efforts to reach a conclusion.

We also observe that the order-based approach times out in about half the forward seraches, while the point-based only times out in two cases. This goes against the initial intuition that larger valuations would profit from the refinement predicates of the smaller ones. One explanation could be that if the larger valuation would require the same predicate as the smaller one, then adding the predicate would result in a redundant representation that should be eliminated. It therefore seems that it does not take long for the point-based to discover this redundancy while still profiting from the localization of the refinement. Instead, the order-based uses predicates even when they are not proven to be needed resulting in finer grained symbolic elements that slow down the exploration.

It is interesting to observe that the descendants-based approach did better in forward than the point-based approach. One explanation could be that, in forward, relevant refinement interpolants sometimes correspond to weak inductive invariants that get propagated by this approach. In backwards it seems, at least for our examples, that the invariants corresponding to the "bad" configurations do not profit from this parent-child transmission.

8   Conclusion

We have introduced and discussed three different ways of localizing constrained monotonic abstraction in systems with infinite control. For this, we have targeted reachability problems for (possibly non-well structured) counter machines obtained as abstractions of concurrent programs. Our new techniques allow us to avoid systematically trashing the state space explored before encountering the false positives that necessitate the introduction of new refinement predicates. This allowed us to consistently improve on the existing eager exploration, both in forward and in backward explorations. Possible future works concern combining forward and backward approximations, using the pivot configuration to make possible the choice of interpolants that are easier to generalize and assessing the feasibility of combination with new partial order techniques.

References

1. Abdulla, P.A., Delzanno, G., Rezine, A.: Parameterized verification of infinite-state processes with global conditions. In: Damm, W., Hermanns, H. (eds.) CAV 2007. LNCS, vol. 4590, pp. 145–157. Springer, Heidelberg (2007)
2. Abdulla, P.A., Čerāns, K., Jonsson, B., Tsay, Y.-K.: General decidability theorems for infinite-state systems. In: Proceedigs of the LICS 1996, 11th IEEE International Symposium on Logic in Computer Science, pp. 313–321 (1996)
3. Abdulla, P.A., Chen, Y.-F., Delzanno, G., Haziza, F., Hong, C.-D., Rezine, A.: Constrained monotonic abstraction: a CEGAR for parameterized verification. In: Gastin, P., Laroussinie, F. (eds.) CONCUR 2010. LNCS, vol. 6269, pp. 86–101. Springer, Heidelberg (2010)
4. Abdulla, P.A., Delzanno, G., Ben Henda, N., Rezine, A.: Regular model checking without transducers (on efficient verification of parameterized systems). In: Grumberg, O., Huth, M. (eds.) TACAS 2007. LNCS, vol. 4424, pp. 721–736. Springer, Heidelberg (2007)
5. Ball, T., Rajamani, S.K.: The SLAM Project: debugging system software via static analysis. In: Proceedings of the 29th ACM SIGPLAN-SIGACT, POPL 2002, pp. 1–3. ACM, New York (2002)
6. Bardin, S., Finkel, A., Leroux, J.: FASTer acceleration of counter automata in practice. In: Jensen, K., Podelski, A. (eds.) TACAS 2004. LNCS, vol. 2988, pp. 576–590. Springer, Heidelberg (2004)
7. Bardin, S., Leroux, J., Point, G.: FAST extended release. In: Ball, T., Jones, R.B. (eds.) CAV 2006. LNCS, vol. 4144, pp. 63–66. Springer, Heidelberg (2006)
8. Bonnet, R., Finkel, A., Leroux, J., Zeitoun, M.: Model checking vector addition systems with one zero-test (2012). arXiv preprint arXiv:1205.4458
9. Bouajjani, A., Bozga, M., Habermehl, P., Iosif, R., Moro, P., Vojnar, T.: Programs with lists are counter automata. In: Ball, T., Jones, R.B. (eds.) CAV 2006. LNCS, vol. 4144, pp. 517–531. Springer, Heidelberg (2006)
10. Clarke, E., Kroening, D., Sharygina, N., Yorav, K.: SATABS: SAT-based predicate abstraction for ANSI-C. In: TACAS, pp. 570–574. Springer (2005)
11. Cogumbreiro, T., Hu, R., Martins, F., Yoshida, N.: Dynamic deadlock verification for general barrier synchronisation. In: Proceeding of the 20th ACM SIGPLAN PPoPP Symposium, pp. 150–160. ACM (2015)
12. de Moura, L., Bjørner, N.S.: Z3: an efficient SMT solver. In: Ramakrishnan, C.R., Rehof, J. (eds.) TACAS 2008. LNCS, vol. 4963, pp. 337–340. Springer, Heidelberg (2008)
13. Delzanno, G.: Automatic verification of parameterized cache coherence protocols. In: Emerson, E.A., Sistla, A.P. (eds.) CAV 2000. LNCS, vol. 1855, pp. 53–68. Springer, Heidelberg (2000)
14. Donaldson, A.F., Kaiser, A., Kroening, D., Tautschnig, M., Wahl, T.: Counterexample-guided abstraction refinement for symmetric concurrent programs. Formal Meth. Syst. Des. $41(1)$, 25–44 (2012)
15. Downey, A.: The Little Book of SEMAPHORES (2nd Edition): The Ins and Outs of Concurrency Control and Common Mistakes. Createspace Ind, Pub (2009). http://www.greenteapress.com/semaphores/
16. Farzan, A., Kincaid, Z., Podelski, A.: Proofs that count. In: Proceedings of the 41st ACM SIGPLAN-SIGACT Symposium on Principles of Programming Languages, POPL 2014, pp. 151–164. ACM, New York (2014)

17. Finkel, A., Schnoebelen, P.: Well-structured transition systems everywhere!. Theor. Comput. Sci. **256**(1–2), 63–92 (2001)
18. Ganjei, Z., Rezine, A., Eles, P., Peng, Z.: Abstracting and counting synchronizing processes. In: D'Souza, D., Lal, A., Larsen, K.G. (eds.) VMCAI 2015. LNCS, vol. 8931, pp. 227–244. Springer, Heidelberg (2015)
19. Geeraerts, G., Raskin, J.-F., Van Begin, L.: Expand, enlarge and check.. made efficient. In: Etessami, K., Rajamani, S.K. (eds.) CAV 2005. LNCS, vol. 3576, pp. 394–407. Springer, Heidelberg (2005)
20. Ghilardi, S., Ranise, S.: MCMT: a model checker modulo theories. In: Giesl, J., Hähnle, R. (eds.) IJCAR 2010. LNCS, vol. 6173, pp. 22–29. Springer, Heidelberg (2010)
21. Henzinger, T.A., Jhala, R., Majumdar, R., Sutre, G.: Lazy abstraction. In: Proceedings of the 29th ACM SIGPLAN-SIGACT, POPL 2002, pp. 58–70. ACM, New York (2002)
22. Higman, G.; Ordering by divisibility in abstract algebras. In: Proceedings of the London Mathematical Society, pp. 326–336 (1952)
23. Kaiser, A., Kroening, D., Wahl, T.: Efficient coverability analysis by proof minimization. In: Koutny, M., Ulidowski, I. (eds.) CONCUR 2012. LNCS, vol. 7454, pp. 500–515. Springer, Heidelberg (2012)
24. Kloos, J., Majumdar, R., Niksic, F., Piskac, R.: Incremental, inductive coverability. In: Sharygina, N., Veith, H. (eds.) CAV 2013. LNCS, vol. 8044, pp. 158–173. Springer, Heidelberg (2013)
25. Liu, P., Wahl, T.: Infinite-state backward exploration of boolean broadcast programs. In: Proceedings of the 14th Conference on Formal Methods in Computer-Aided Design, pp. 155–162. FMCAD Inc (2014)
26. McMillan, K.L.: Lazy abstraction with interpolants. In: Ball, T., Jones, R.B. (eds.) CAV 2006. LNCS, vol. 4144, pp. 123–136. Springer, Heidelberg (2006)
27. Weissenbacher, G., Kroening, D., Malik, S.: WOLVERINE: battling bugs with interpolants. In: Flanagan, C., König, B. (eds.) TACAS 2012. LNCS, vol. 7214, pp. 556–558. Springer, Heidelberg (2012)

Polyhedral Approximation of Multivariate Polynomials Using Handelman's Theorem

Alexandre Maréchal[1]([⊠]), Alexis Fouilhé[1], Tim King[2],
David Monniaux[2], and Michael Périn[1]

[1] Université Grenoble-Alpes, VERIMAG, 38000 Grenoble, France
{alex.marechal,alexis.fouilhe,tim.king,
david.monniaux,michael.perin}@imag.fr
[2] CNRS, VERIMAG, 38000 Grenoble, France

Abstract. Convex polyhedra are commonly used in the static analysis of programs to represent over-approximations of sets of reachable states of numerical program variables. When the analyzed programs contain non-linear instructions, they do not directly map to standard polyhedral operations: some kind of linearization is needed. Convex polyhedra are also used in satisfiability modulo theory solvers which combine a propositional satisfiability solver with a fast emptiness check for polyhedra. Existing decision procedures become expensive when nonlinear constraints are involved: a fast procedure to ensure emptiness of systems of nonlinear constraints is needed. We present a new linearization algorithm based on Handelman's representation of positive polynomials. Given a polyhedron and a polynomial (in)equality, we compute a polyhedron enclosing their intersection as the solution of a parametric linear programming problem. To get a scalable algorithm, we provide several heuristics that guide the construction of the Handelman's representation. To ensure the correctness of our polyhedral approximation, our OCAML implementation generates certificates verified by a checker certified in COQ.

1 Numerical Static Analysis and Satisfiability Testing Using Convex Polyhedra

We present a new method for computing polyhedral approximations of polynomial guards, with applications in both static analysis and satisfiability modulo theory (SMT) solving. It is implemented in the Verimag Verified Polyhedra Library (VPL), a certified library written in OCAML for computing over convex polyhedra [20]. Its operators generate certificates which may optionally be checked by a verifier developed and proved correct in COQ. The VPL is used as an abstract domain within a COQ-certified static analyzer [26].

This work was partially supported by ANR project VERASCO (INS 2011) and the European Research Council under the European Union's Seventh Framework Programme (FP/2007-2013) / ERC Grant Agreement nr. 306595 "STATOR".

© Springer-Verlag Berlin Heidelberg 2016
B. Jobstmann and K.R.M. Leino (Eds.): VMCAI 2016, LNCS 9583, pp. 166–184, 2016.
DOI: 10.1007/978-3-662-49122-5_8

Convex Polyhedra. A convex polyhedron is defined by a conjunction of affine constraints of the form $a_0 + \sum_{i=1}^{n} a_i x_i \geq 0$ where the x_i's are variables, the a_i's and a_0 are constants in $\mathbb{Q}$. We subsequently omit *convex* as we only deal with convex polyhedra. For instance, the polyhedron P defined by

$$P \triangleq \{\, x - 1 \geq 0,\ y + 2 \geq 0,\ x - y \geq 0,\ 5 - x - y \geq 0 \,\} \tag{1}$$

is the set $\{\, (x, y) \mid x \geq 1 \wedge y \geq -2 \wedge x \geq y \wedge x + y \leq 5 \,\}$ represented in Fig. 1. A bounded polyhedron is called a *polytope*.

Polyhedral Static Analysis. Static analyzers are verification tools that aim at proving properties true for all possible executions of a program; desirable properties include for instance the absence of arithmetic overflow. In the abstract interpretation framework, the analyzer attaches to each control point an *invariant* chosen within a given class, called *abstract domain* [11]. Here, we focus on the abstract domain of polyhedra which captures affine relations among program variables [22]. A static analyzer using polyhedra cannot directly infer any information on a variable z assigned with a non-linear expression *e.g.* $z := x*y$. A very rough abstraction is to consider that z is assigned any value in $(-\infty, +\infty)$; the consequence is a dramatic loss of precision which propagates along the analysis, possibly failing to prove a property.

Satisfiability Modulo Theory. The satisfiability of a quantifier-free formula of first-order linear arithmetic over the reals is usually decided by a "DPLL(T)" [21] combination of a propositional solver and a decision procedure for conjunctions of linear inequalities based on the simplex algorithm [17,18]. Nonlinear formulas are more challenging; some solvers implement a variant of cylindrical algebraic decomposition, a very complex and costly approach [27]; some replace the propositional abstraction of DPLL(T) by a direct search for a model [14].

Linearization Techniques. Nonlinear relations between variables, such as $x^2 + y^2 \leq 1$, occur for instance in address computations over matrices, computational geometry, automatic control and in programs that approximate transcendental functions (sin, cos, log...) by polynomials [6,7]. Therefore, *linearization* techniques were developed to preserve precision in the presence of polynomials; they provide an over-approximation of a polynomial on an input polyhedron. Miné proposed two linearization techniques based on variable "intervalization" [34], where some variables of the polynomial are replaced by their interval of variation:

(1) Switching to the abstract domain of polyhedra with interval coefficients [5] to maintain precision, albeit at high algorithmic cost.
(2) Obtaining an affine expression with intervals as coefficients, which is then converted into a polyhedron. This solution was implemented in the APRON polyhedra library [24,34]: intervals are replaced with their center value and the right-hand side constant of the equality is enlarged accordingly. We developed an improved and certified version of this algorithm in the VPL [4]. This linearization technique is efficient but not very precise.

Another well known linearization method consists in representing polynomials in the Bernstein basis. Bernstein coefficients give a bounding polyhedron, made as precise as needed by increasing the degree of the basis [35]. Bernstein's linearization works on systems of generators, either to get the range of each variable, or to refer to variables as barycentric coordinates of the vertices [9]. It would be well-suited for most libraries (APRON [24], PPL [1], POLYLIB [31]), as they maintain a *double representation* of polyhedra: as systems of constraints, and as systems of generators (in the case of polytopes, the generators are the vertices). In contrast, our work aims at adding a precise linearization to the VPL. In order to make certification more convenient, the VPL uses only the constraint representation of polyhedra. Therefore, using Bernstein's method would be hardly appropriate as it would require expensive conversions between representations [32].

Contributions. We present a new algorithm to linearize polynomial guards which only needs constraint representation of polyhedra. Section 2 shows how any other polynomial statement reduces to guards. As explained in Sect. 3, our approach is based on Handelman's theorem [23], which states that a polynomial that is positive on a polytope can always be expressed as a nonnegative linear combination of products of constraints of the polytope. The algorithm consists in computing linear relaxations as solutions of a Parametric Linear Programming Problem (PLOP). Section 4 sketches the principle of PLOP solvers and focuses on an improvement we made to reduce exploration of branches that would yield redundant constraints. The method presented in this paper requires only the constraint representation of the polyhedron, as provided by the VPL or by a DPLL(T) SMT-solver, and returns a polyhedron directly as constraints as well as an emptiness flag. It soundly approximates polynomial operations over convex polyhedra and generates certificates that are checked by a verifier developed and proved in COQ. The precision of the approximation is arbitrary depending on the degree and the number of Handelman products in use; the selection of which is delegated to the heuristics presented in Sect. 5. Precision and efficiency of our algorithm are shown through a comparison with SMT-solvers on Quantifier-Free Nonlinear Real Arithmetic benchmarks in Sect. 6.

This paper elaborates on a preliminary work by the authors [33], which presented the encoding of the linear relaxation problem as a PLOP, focusing on the certification in COQ of the resulting approximation. We reuse the encoding of [33] and we extend the previous work with heuristics, an experimental evaluation and a new application.

2   Focusing on Approximation of Polynomial Guards

The goal of linearization is to approximate nonlinear relations with linear ones. The approximation is sound if it contains the original nonlinear set. In other words, linearization must produce an *over-approximation* of the nonlinear set. In this work, we consider polynomial expressions formed of $(+, -, \times)$, such as

$4 - x \times x - y \times y$. More general algebraic expressions, including divisions and root operators, may be reduced to that format; for instance $y = \sqrt{x^2 + 1}$ is equivalent to $y^2 = x^2 + 1 \wedge y \geq 0$ [36]. The symbol g shall represent a polynomial expression on the variables $x_1, .., x_n$ of a program. We only consider constraints in a positive form $g \geq 0$ or $g > 0$: any other form (including equalities and negation) can be changed into a disjunction of conjunctions of positive constraints, for example $\neg(g_1 = g_2) \equiv (g_1 < g_2 \vee g_1 > g_2) \equiv (g_2 - g_1 > 0 \vee g_1 - g_2 > 0)$.

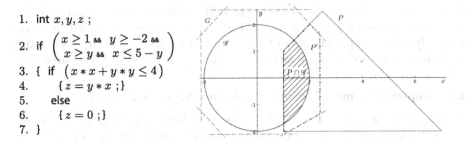

```
1. int x, y, z ;

2. if ( x ≥ 1 && y ≥ -2 &&
        x ≥ y && x ≤ 5 - y )
3. {  if ( x * x + y * y ≤ 4 )
4.       { z = y * x ;}
5.    else
6.       { z = 0 ;}
7. }
```

Fig. 1. *A C program fragment with non-linear expressions $x * x + y * y \leq 4$ and $y * x$. The first guard defines the polyhedron $P \triangleq \{x \geq 1,\ y \geq -2,\ x - y \geq 0,\ x + y \leq 5\}$; the disc $\mathcal{G} \triangleq \{(x, y) \mid x^2 + y^2 \leq 4\}$ corresponds to the second guard; the octagon G is a polyhedral approximation of $\mathcal{G}$; the hashed region is the set $P \cap \mathcal{G}$; the desired approximation of $P \cap \mathcal{G}$ is the polyhedron $P' \triangleq P \wedge G$, drawn with dotted lines.*

We will use the program of Fig. 1 as a running example: our goal is to compute a polyhedral over-approximation of the polynomial guard $x^2 + y^2 \leq 4$ on line 3, which is equivalent to $g \geq 0$ with $g(x, y) \triangleq 4 - x^2 - y^2$, in the context of the polytope $P \triangleq \{x - 1 \geq 0,\ y + 2 \geq 0,\ x - y \geq 0,\ 5 - x - y \geq 0\}$ that corresponds to the condition on line 2.

Note that assignments $x := e$ reduce to guards. Let $\tilde{x}$ denote the value of variable x after the assignment, while x denotes its value before the assignment. Then, the effect of the assignment on a polyhedron P is $((P \wedge \tilde{x} \leq e \wedge \tilde{x} \geq e)_{/x})[\tilde{x}/x]$, where $\cdot_{/x}$ denotes the elimination of x using projection and $[\tilde{x}/x]$ is the renaming of $\tilde{x}$ as x. This works when e is affine. When it is nonlinear, $\tilde{x}$ is approximated by linearizing guards $x' \leq e$ and $x' \geq e$. Therefore, we will exclusively focus on the linearization of polynomial guards.

The effect of a guard $g \geq 0$ on a polyhedron P consists in the intersection of the set of points of P with $\mathcal{G} \triangleq \{(x_1, \ldots, x_n) \mid g(x_1, \ldots, x_n) \geq 0\}$. When the guard is linear, say $x - 2y \geq 0$, $P \cap \mathcal{G}$ is simply the conjunction of P and the constraint $x - 2y \geq 0$; it is already a polyhedron. When the guard is not linear, we approximate $P \cap \mathcal{G}$ by a polyhedron P' such that $P \cap \mathcal{G} \subseteq P'$. Computing, instead, a polyhedral enclosure G of the set $\mathcal{G}$ would not be a practical solution. Indeed, it can be very imprecise: if $\mathcal{G} = \{(x, y) \mid y \leq x^2\}$, then $G = \mathbb{Q}^2$. Moreover, it is superfluous work: only three of the eight constraints of polyhedron G on Fig. 1 are actually useful for the intersection.

3   Linearizing Using Handelman's Representation

Consider an input polyhedron $P \triangleq \{C_1 \geq 0, \ldots, C_p \geq 0\}$ defined on variables $(x_1, \ldots, x_n)$ and a polynomial guard $g \geq 0$. Our goal is to find an affine term $\alpha_0 + \sum_{i=1}^{n} \alpha_i x_i$ denoted by aff such that $P \Rightarrow aff > g$, meaning that aff bounds g on P. By transitivity, we will conclude that $P \wedge g \geq 0 \Rightarrow P \wedge aff > 0$, which can be expressed in terms of sets[1] as $(P \cap g \geq 0) \subseteq (P \sqcap aff > 0)$. Our linearization based on Handelman's theorem provides several affine constraints $aff_1, \ldots, aff_k$ whose conjunction with P forms the approximation of $P \cap g \geq 0$. In static analysis, where P describes the possible values of the program variables $(x_1, \ldots, x_n)$ before a polynomial guard $g \geq 0$, the result $P \sqcap_{i=1}^{i=k} aff_i > 0$ will be a polyhedral approximation of the program state after the guard. When this polyhedron is empty, it means that the original guard $P \wedge g \geq 0$ is unsatisfiable.

3.1   Representation of Positive Polynomials on a Polytope

Notations. Tuples $\boldsymbol{x} = (x_1, \ldots, x_n)$ and multi-indices $\boldsymbol{I} = (i_1, \ldots, i_n) \in \mathbb{N}^n$ are set in boldface. The set of Handelman products associated to a polyhedron $P \triangleq \{C_1 \geq 0, \ldots, C_p \geq 0\}$ is the set $\mathscr{H}_P$ of all products of constraints C_i of P:

$$\mathscr{H}_P = \{C_1^{i_1} \times \cdots \times C_p^{i_p} \mid (i_1, \ldots, i_p) \in \mathbb{N}^p\} \qquad (2)$$

Given a multi-index $\boldsymbol{I} = (i_1, \ldots, i_p)$, $H^{\boldsymbol{I}} \triangleq C_1^{i_1} \times \ldots \times C_p^{i_p}$ denotes an element of $\mathscr{H}_P$. In our running example, $H^{(0,2,0,0)} = (y+2)^2$, $H^{(1,0,1,0)} = (x-1)(x-y)$ and $H^{(1,0,0,3)} = (x-1)(-x-y+5)^3$ all belong to $\mathscr{H}_P$. The $H^{\boldsymbol{I}}$'s are nonnegative polynomials on P as products of nonnegative constraints of P. Handelman's representation of a positive polynomial $g(\boldsymbol{x})$ on P is

$$g(\boldsymbol{x}) = \sum_{\boldsymbol{I} \in \mathbb{N}^p} \underbrace{\lambda_{\boldsymbol{I}}}_{\geq 0} \underbrace{H^{\boldsymbol{I}}}_{\geq 0} \text{ with } \lambda_{\boldsymbol{I}} \in \mathbb{R}^+ \qquad (3)$$

The $\lambda_{\boldsymbol{I}}$'s form a *certificate* that $g(\boldsymbol{x})$ is nonnegative on P. Handelman's theorem states the non-trivial opposite implication: any positive polynomial on P can be expressed in that form [23], [30, Th. 2.24], [37, Th. 5.4.6], [38, Th. 5.5]; a similar result already appeared in Krivine's work on decompositions of positive polynomials on semialgebraic sets [29].

Theorem 1 (Handelman, 1988). *Let $P = \{C_1 \geq 0, \ldots, C_p \geq 0\}$ be a polytope where each C_i is an affine form over $\boldsymbol{x} = (x_1, \ldots, x_n)$. Let $g(\boldsymbol{x})$ be a positive polynomial on P, i.e. $g(\boldsymbol{x}) > 0$ for all $\boldsymbol{x} \in P$. Then there exists a finite subset $\mathcal{I}$ of $\mathbb{N}^p$ and $\lambda_{\boldsymbol{I}} \in \mathbb{R}^+$ for all $\boldsymbol{I} \in \mathcal{I}$, such that $g(\boldsymbol{x}) = \sum_{\boldsymbol{I} \in \mathcal{I}} \lambda_{\boldsymbol{I}} H^{\boldsymbol{I}}$.*

Remark 1. This does not necessarily hold if $g(\boldsymbol{x})$ is only assumed to be nonnegative. Consider the inequalities $x + 1 \geq 0$ and $1 - x \geq 0$ and the nonnegative polynomial x^2. Assume the existence of a decomposition and apply (3) at $x = 0$: $H^{\boldsymbol{I}}(0) > 0$ for any $\boldsymbol{I}$, it follows that $\lambda_{\boldsymbol{I}} = 0$. This null decomposition is absurd.

---

[1] $\cap$ denotes the usual intersection of sets; $\sqcap$ is reserved for the intersection of polyhedra.

Remark 2. One can look for a Handelman representation of a polynomial even on *unbounded polyhedra*: its positivity will then be ensured. The existence of such representation is not guaranteed though.

The common use of Handelman's representation of a polynomial $g(\boldsymbol{x}) - \Delta$ is to determine a lower bound Δ of $g(\boldsymbol{x})$ on P. For instance, Boland et al. use it to compute an upper bound of the polynomial, in $\boldsymbol{x}$ and the error ϵ, which defines the cascading round-off effects of floating-point calculation [3]. Schweighofer's algorithm [38] can iteratively improve such a bound by increasing the degree of the H^I's. We present here another use of Handelman's theorem: we are not interested in just one bound but in a whole set of affine constraints dominating the polynomial $g(\boldsymbol{x})$ on P.

3.2   Linearization as a Parametric Linear Optimization Problem

Recall that we are looking for an affine constraint $\mathit{aff} \triangleq \alpha_0 + \sum_{i=1}^{n} \alpha_i x_i$ that approximates a non-linear guard g, meaning $\mathit{aff} > g$ on P. According to Theorem 1, if P is bounded, $\mathit{aff} - g$ which is positive on the polytope P has a Handelman representation as a nonnegative linear combination of products of the constraints of P, *i.e.*

$$\exists \mathcal{I} \subset \mathbb{N}^p, \ \mathit{aff} - g = \sum_{I \in \mathcal{I}} \lambda_I H^I, \ \lambda_I \in \mathbb{R}^+, \ H^I \in \mathscr{H}_P \qquad (4)$$

Relation (4) ensures that there exists some positive combinations of g and some $H^I \in \mathscr{H}_P$ that remove the monomials of degree >1 and lead to affine forms:

$$\alpha_0 + \alpha_1 x_1 + \ldots + \alpha_n x_n = \mathit{aff} = 1 \cdot g + \sum_{I \in \mathbb{N}^p} \lambda_I H^I$$

Remark 3. This decomposition is not unique in general. Consider $P = \{x \geq 0, \ y \geq 0, \ x - y \geq 0, \ x + y \geq 0\}$. The polynomial $x^2 + 2xy + y^2$ is equal to both $H^{(0,0,0,2)} = (x+y)^2$ and $H^{(2,0,0,0)} + 2H^{(1,1,0,0)} + H^{(0,2,0,0)} = (x^2) + 2(xy) + (y^2)$.

Design of our Linearization Method. The principle of our algorithm is to take advantage of the non-uniqueness of representation to get a precise approximation of the guard: we suppose that a set $\mathcal{I} = \{I_1, \ldots, I_q\}$ of indices is given and we show how to obtain every possible affine form aff_i that can be expressed as $g + \sum_{\ell=1}^{\ell=q} \lambda_\ell H^{I_\ell}$. Each of these aff_i bounds g on P and their conjunction forms a polyhedron that over-approximates the set $P \cap (g \geq 0)$. A major difference between our work and previous work by Schweighofer [38] and Boland [3] is that we are not interested in a constant bound α_0 but an affine bound $\alpha_0 + \alpha_1 x_1 + \ldots + \alpha_n x_n$ which still depends on *parameters* $x_1, \ldots, x_n$. We now show that our problem belongs to the class of *parametric linear problems*; Sect. 5 then describes the heuristics used to determine $\mathcal{I}$.

Example 1. For $g = 4 - x^2 - y^2$, we choose $\mathcal{I}$ that gives these 15 products:

$$H^{I_1} = H^{(0,0,0,0)} = 1 \qquad\qquad H^{I_2} = H^{(1,0,0,0)} = x - 1$$
$$H^{I_3} = H^{(0,1,0,0)} = y + 2 \qquad\quad H^{I_4} = H^{(0,0,1,0)} = x - y$$
$$H^{I_5} = H^{(0,0,0,1)} = -x - y + 5 \quad H^{I_6} = H^{(2,0,0,0)} = (x - 1)^2$$
$$H^{I_7} = H^{(0,2,0,0)} = (y + 2)^2 \qquad H^{I_8} = H^{(0,0,2,0)} = (x - y)^2$$
$$H^{I_9} = H^{(0,0,0,2)} = (-x - y + 5)^2 \quad H^{I_{10}} = H^{(1,1,0,0)} = (x - 1)(y + 2)$$
$$H^{I_{11}} = H^{(1,0,1,0)} = (x - 1)(x - y) \quad H^{I_{12}} = H^{(1,0,0,1)} = (x - 1)(-x - y + 5)$$
$$H^{I_{13}} = H^{(0,1,1,0)} = (y + 2)(x - y) \quad H^{I_{14}} = H^{(0,1,0,1)} = (y + 2)(-x - y + 5)$$
$$H^{I_{15}} = H^{(0,0,1,1)} = (x - y)(-x - y + 5)$$

Considering the products $\{H^{I_1}, \dots, H^{I_q}\}$, finding the Handelman representation of $\mathit{aff} - g$ can be expressed as a linear problem. Relation (4) amounts to finding $\lambda_1, \dots, \lambda_q \geq 0$ such that

$$
\underset{\substack{\| \\ \alpha_0 + \alpha_1 x_1 + \dots + \alpha_n x_n \\ \| \\ \mathcal{M}^\mathsf{T} \cdot (\alpha_0, \dots, \alpha_n, 0, \dots, 0) =}}{\mathit{aff}} = 1 \cdot g + \sum_{\ell=1}^{\ell=q} \lambda_\ell H^{I_\ell} = \underbrace{(\lambda_g, \lambda_1, \dots, \lambda_q)}_{\lambda^\mathsf{T}} \cdot \underbrace{(g, H^{I_1}, \dots, H^{I_q})^\mathsf{T}}_{\mathcal{H}_g^\mathsf{T} \cdot \mathcal{M}}
$$

$$
\underset{\substack{\| \\ \lambda^\mathsf{T} \cdot \mathcal{H}_g^\mathsf{T} \cdot \mathcal{M} \\ \| \\ \mathcal{M}^\mathsf{T} \cdot \mathcal{H}_g \cdot \lambda}}{}
$$

where:

(1) $\mathcal{H}_g$ is the matrix of the coefficients of g and the H^{I_ℓ} organized with respect to $\mathcal{M}$, the sorted list of monomials that appear in the Handelman products generated by $\mathcal{I}$.

(2) the column vector $\lambda = (\lambda_g, \lambda_1, \dots, \lambda_q)^\mathsf{T} = (1, \lambda_1, \dots, \lambda_q)^\mathsf{T}$ characterizes the combination of g and the H^{I_ℓ}. We added a constant coefficient $\lambda_g = 1$ for convenience of notations.

The product $\mathcal{H}_g \cdot \lambda$ is a vector $\alpha \triangleq (\alpha_0, \dots, \alpha_{|\mathcal{M}|-1})^\mathsf{T}$ representing the constraint $\alpha_0 + \alpha_1 x_1 + \dots + \alpha_n x_n + \sum_{i=n+1}^{i=|\mathcal{M}|-1} \alpha_i \cdot (\mathcal{M})_i$ where $(\mathcal{M})_i$ denotes the ith monomial of $\mathcal{M}$. Since we seek an affine constraint aff we are finally interested in finding $\lambda \in \{1\} \times (\mathbb{R}^+)^q$ such that $\mathcal{H}_g \cdot \lambda = (\alpha_0, \dots, \alpha_n, 0, \dots, 0)^\mathsf{T}$. By construction, each λ gives an affine constraint aff that bounds g on P.

Example 2. Here is the matrix $\mathcal{H}_g$ associated to $g \triangleq 4 - x^2 - y^2$ and the Handelman products from Example 1 with respect to $\mathcal{M} = [1, x, y, xy, x^2, y^2]$.

	g	H^{I_1}	H^{I_2}	H^{I_3}	H^{I_4}	H^{I_5}	H^{I_6}	H^{I_7}	H^{I_8}	H^{I_9}	$H^{I_{10}}$	$H^{I_{11}}$	$H^{I_{12}}$	$H^{I_{13}}$	$H^{I_{14}}$	$H^{I_{15}}$
1	4	1	-1	2	0	5	1	4	0	25	-2	0	-5	0	10	0
x	0	0	1	0	1	-1	-2	0	0	-10	2	-1	6	2	-2	5
y	0	0	0	1	-1	-1	0	4	0	-10	-1	1	1	-2	3	-5
xy	0	0	0	0	0	0	0	0	-2	2	1	-1	-1	1	-1	0
x^2	-1	0	0	0	0	0	1	0	1	1	0	1	-1	0	0	-1
y^2	-1	0	0	0	0	0	0	1	1	1	0	0	0	-1	-1	1

The choices $\lambda_g = \lambda_6 = \lambda_7 = 1$ and every other $\lambda_\ell = 0$ are a solution to the problem $\mathcal{H}_g \cdot \lambda = (\alpha_0, \alpha_1, \alpha_2, 0, 0, 0)^\mathsf{T}$. We obtain $\mathcal{H}_g \cdot \lambda = (9, -2, 4, 0, 0, 0)^\mathsf{T}$ that corresponds to $9 - 2x + 4y + 0 \times xy + 0 \times x^2 + 0 \times y^2$. Thus, $\mathit{aff} = 9 - 2x + 4y$ is a constraint that bounds g on P, as shown on Fig. 2.

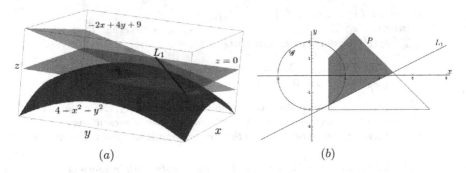

Fig. 2. *(b) is the cut at $z = 0$ of (a) in which we added the polyhedron $P \triangleq \{x - 1 \geq 0,\ y + 2 \geq 0,\ x - y \geq 0,\ -x - y + 5 \geq 0\}$: the circle $\mathscr{G}$ of (b) appears in (a) as the intersection of the surface $z = g(x, y) \triangleq 4 - x^2 - y^2$ with the plane $z = 0$. The polyhedral approximation of g is the inclined plane $z = aff(x, y) \triangleq -2x + 4y + 9$ that dominates g. It cuts the plane $z = 0$ along the line L_1 in (a) which is reported in (b). The line L_1 is the frontier of the affine constraint $-2x + 4y + 9 \geq 0$. The filled area is the polyhedron $P \wedge -2x + 4y + 9 \geq 0$ that over-approximates $P \cap \{(x, y) \mid g(x, y) \geq 0\}$.*

By construction, any solution λ of the problem $\mathcal{H}_g \cdot \lambda = (\alpha_0, \ldots, \alpha_n, 0, \ldots, 0)^\mathsf{T}$ is a polyhedral constraint aff that bounds g on P. Among all these solutions we are only interested in the best approximations. One constraint $aff > g$ is better than another $aff' > g$ at point $(x_1, \ldots, x_n)$ if $aff(x_1, \ldots, x_n) < aff'(x_1, \ldots, x_n)$. It then appears that for a given point $(x_1, \ldots, x_n)$ we are looking for the polyhedral constraint $aff > g$ that minimizes its value on that point. Therefore, we define a linear minimization problem that depends on some parameters: the point $(x_1, \ldots, x_n)$ of evaluation.

Finally, finding the tightest affine forms aff_i that bound g on P with respect to a given set of indices $\mathcal{I}$ can be expressed as the *Parametric Linear Optimization Problem* (PLOP) shown on Fig. 3. Such optimization problems can be solved using the parametric simplex algorithm, which is outlined in Sect. 4. As we shall detail later, the solution of H-PLOP is a function associating an affine form aff_i to the region of the parameter space where aff_i is optimal. The over-approximation of $P \cap (g \geq 0)$ that we return is then $\prod_i \{x \in \mathbb{Q}^n \mid aff_i(x) \geq 0\}$.

Example 3. In our running example, the objective aff, i.e., $g + \sum_{\ell=1}^{\ell=15} \lambda_\ell H^{I_\ell}$, is $4 + \lambda_1 + \lambda_2(x - 1) + \lambda_3(2 + y) + \lambda_4(x - y) + \lambda_5(5 - x - y) + \lambda_6(1 - 2x) + \lambda_7(4 + 4y) + \lambda_9(25 - 10x - 10y) + \lambda_{10}(2x - y - 2) + \lambda_{11}(y - x) + \lambda_{12}(6x + y - 5) + \lambda_{13}(2x - 2y) + \lambda_{14}(10 - 2x + 3y) + \lambda_{15}(5x - 5y)$.

In practice we use this presentation (without α) which exhibits the parametric coefficients in x, y of each variable λ. Nonlinear monomials do not appear since the problem imposes cancelling the non-linear part of $g + \sum_{\ell=1}^{\ell=15} \lambda_\ell H^{I_\ell}$, i.e. $xy(-2\lambda_8 + 2\lambda_9 + \lambda_{10} - \lambda_{11} - \lambda_{12} + \lambda_{13} - \lambda_{14}) + x^2(-1 + \lambda_6 + \lambda_8 + \lambda_9 + \lambda_{11} - \lambda_{12} - \lambda_{15}) + y^2(-1 + \lambda_7 + \lambda_8 + \lambda_9 - \lambda_{13} - \lambda_{14} + \lambda_{15})$. The solutions of the problem are the vectors λ that minimize the objective and cancel the coefficients of xy, x^2 and y^2.

Given a set of indices $\mathcal{I} \triangleq \{\boldsymbol{I}_1, \ldots, \boldsymbol{I}_q\}$,
minimize aff *,i.e.,* $\alpha_0 + \alpha_1 x_1 + \ldots + \alpha_n x_n$, *also equal to* $g +$ $\sum_{\ell=1}^{\ell=q} \lambda_\ell H^{I_\ell}$ **under the constraints**

$$\begin{cases} \mathcal{H}_g \cdot (\lambda_g, \lambda_1, \ldots, \lambda_q)^\mathsf{T} = (\alpha_0, \ldots, \alpha_n, 0, \ldots, 0)^\mathsf{T} \\ \lambda_g = 1, \quad \lambda_\ell \geq 0, \ \ell = 1..q \end{cases} \quad \text{(H-PLOP)}$$

where $\lambda_1, \ldots, \lambda_q$ *are the decision variables of the* PLOP; $x_1, \ldots, x_n$ *are the parameters ; and* $\alpha_0, \ldots, \alpha_n$ *are kept for the sake of presentation ; in practice they are substituted by their expression issued from* $\mathcal{H}_g \cdot \boldsymbol{\lambda}$.

Fig. 3. *Linearization as a parametric linear optimization problem*

4   The Parametric Simplex Algorithm

We use the simplex algorithm for parametric objective functions to find the solutions of the previous H-PLOP problem. This section explains how we obtain the output polyhedron over-approximating $P \cap g \geq 0$ from the solutions of H-PLOP. We assume the reader is familiar with the simplex algorithm (see [8] for an introduction) and we sketch the broad outlines of the parametric simplex algorithm (see [12, 33] for more details).

Principle of the Algorithm. The standard simplex algorithm is used to find the optimal value of an affine function – called the objective – on a space delimited by affine constraints, which is thus a polyhedron. More precisely, it solves linear problems of the form

$$\textit{minimize the objective} \sum_{i=1}^{i=q} \lambda_i \cdot c_i \ \textit{s.t.} \ A \cdot \boldsymbol{\lambda} = \boldsymbol{0}, \ \boldsymbol{\lambda} \geq \boldsymbol{0}$$

where $A \in M_{p,q}(\mathbb{Q})$ is a matrix and the constants $c_i \in \mathbb{Q}$ define the costs associated to each decision variable $(\lambda_1, \ldots, \lambda_q) = \boldsymbol{\lambda}$. To decrease the objective value, recalling that each variable λ_i is nonnegative, a step in the standard simplex algorithm, called a *pivot*, consists in finding a negative coefficient c_i in the objective function and in decreasing the value of the associated variable λ_i as much as the constraints remain satisfied. The pivot operation modifies both the costs of the objective function and the constraints. The optimal value is reached when every c_i is nonnegative, meaning that the objective value cannot be decreased anymore.

The parametric simplex algorithm solves linear problems of the form

$$\textit{minimize the objective} \sum_{i=1}^{i=q} \lambda_i \cdot c_i(x_1, \ldots, x_n) \ \textit{s.t.} \ A \cdot \boldsymbol{\lambda} = \boldsymbol{0}, \ \boldsymbol{\lambda} \geq \boldsymbol{0}$$

where c_i are now affine functions from parameters $(x_1, \ldots, x_n)$ to $\mathbb{Q}$. As in the standard simplex we seek for a pivot to decrease the objective value, *i.e.*

a negative coefficient in the objective function. In general the sign of a parametric coefficient, say c_i, is unknown. The algorithm then explores two branches: one in which c_i is considered as nonnegative and we move to the next coefficient c_{i+1} ; and another branch in which c_i is assumed to be negative and we perform a pivot on the associated variable λ_i exactly as in the standard version. The exploration of a branch stops when the conjunction of the assumptions is unsatisfiable (the branch is then discarded); or when it implies that all the updated parametric coefficients are nonnegative, meaning that an optimum is reached. Both tests of unsatisfiability and implication are polyhedral operations performed by the VPL.

The result of the solver is a decision tree: the values of the decision variables $\boldsymbol{\lambda}$ at leaves give optima of the parametric objective; the conjunction of the assumptions along a branch defines its *region of relevance*, it is a polyhedron in the parameter space. Our solver implements this algorithm in OCAML and works with rationals instead of floating points. It borrows a few optimizations from the PIP algorithm [19] which was developed for the dual case where parameters are in the right-hand side of the constraints, *i.e.* $A \cdot \boldsymbol{\lambda} = \boldsymbol{b}(x_1, \ldots, x_n)$.

Application to Handelman's Linearization. Back to our running example, we obtain the best polyhedral approximations of g by running our parametric simplex on H-PLOP where $(\lambda_\ell)_{\ell=1..q}$ are decision variables, $H^{I_\ell}(x_1, \ldots, x_n)$ are parametric coefficients, x_i are parameters and the matrix A is made of the rows of $\mathcal{H}_g$ corresponding to monomials of degree > 1 (the last three rows of $\mathcal{H}_g$ in Example 2). We obtain a decision tree with 5 optimal solutions $\boldsymbol{\lambda}$ at leaves. Each of them is interpreted as constraint $aff(x_1, \ldots, x_n) \geq 0$ where $aff(\boldsymbol{x}) = g(\boldsymbol{x}) + \sum_{\ell=1}^{\ell=q} \lambda_\ell H^{I_\ell}(\boldsymbol{x})$. These 5 constraints appear on Fig. 4(a) as the lines L_1 to L_5. Their conjunction with P forms the polyhedron P' which over-approximates $P \cap (g \geq 0)$.

Useless Constraint Detection. Figure 4(a) reveals that L_3 and L_4 are useless since they do not intersect P'. This is not due to the parametric simplex: it happens when a constraint aff_j does not cross the plane $z = 0$ on its region of relevance R_j. Figure 4(b) shows the region of relevance of each constraint. This remark leads us to a criterion to detect useless aff_i during exploration. It requires some explanations. Note that the output polyhedron $P' \triangleq P \sqcap (\bigcap_{j=1}^{j=k} aff_j \geq 0)$ is equal to the set $\bigcup_{j=1}^{j=k} (R_j \sqcap aff_j \geq 0)$. That can be proved by reasoning on sets, using (1) distributivity and (2) simplification, exploiting two consequences of the parametric simplex: (1) by construction of the exploration tree, the regions $(R_i)_{i=1}^{i=k}$ form a partition of P; (2) if $i \neq j$, $R_i \sqcap (aff_i \geq 0) \sqcap (aff_j \geq 0) = R_i \sqcap (aff_i \geq 0)$ since $aff_j \geq aff_i$ on R_i. Indeed, we asked the parametric simplex to seek for minimal affine forms.

Now, let us study the equality $P' = \bigcup_{j=1}^{j=k} (R_j \sqcap aff_j \geq 0)$: when the sign of aff_i is negative on its region of relevance R_i, then $(R_i \sqcap aff_i \geq 0) = \emptyset$ and this term vanishes from the union. Therefore, such an aff_i has no impact on P'. We draw upon this remark to design an algorithm that early detects useless exploration. The exploration of a new branch starts with the examination of the

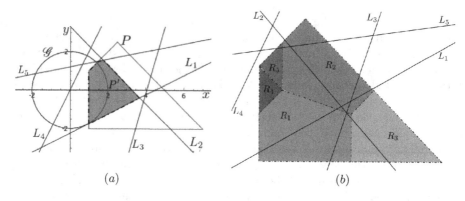

Fig. 4. (a) The polyhedron $P' = P \sqcap \{L_1 \geq 0, \ldots, L_5 \geq 0\}$ is the over-approximation of $P \cap (g \geq 0)$ computed by our linearization without detection of useless constraints. P' is delimited by P and the constraints L_1, L_2, L_5 returned by the parametric simplex; L_3 and L_4 are useless: L_3 is detected by our criterion. The redundancy of L_4 cannot be detected before the intersection with P. (b) Each constraint L_i is the optimum associated to a region R_i of P. Our criterion eliminates L_3 since it is negative on R_3.

possible pivots. For minimization problems, the pivoting operation lowers the objective and the new region is a subpart of the previous one. Therefore, if all pivots give an objective that is negative on the current region, every optimum *aff* generated through this branch will be negative, thus useless; we simply cut this branch. Our experiments are conducted with the parametric simplex algorithm of Sect. 4 improved with this elimination criterion.

5   Heuristics and Certificates

We previously assumed a given set of Handelman products to be considered in H-PLOP; our implementation actually uses Schweighofer products (S^I), which generalize Handelman's ones as shown by Theorem 2 below. We shall now describe the oracle that generates them together with a certificate of nonnegativity, then the heuristics it uses.

Theorem 2 (Schweighofer, 2001). *Let* $P = \{C_1 \geq 0, \ldots, C_p \geq 0\}$ *be a polytope where each* C_i *is an affine polynomial over* $\boldsymbol{x} = (x_1, \ldots, x_n)$. *Let* $g_{p+1}, \ldots, g_q$ *be polynomials. Then* $g(\boldsymbol{x}) > 0$ *on* $P \cap \{g_{p+1} \geq 0, \ldots, g_q \geq 0\}$ *if and only if*

$$g = \lambda_0 + \sum_{I \in \mathbb{N}^q} \lambda_I \cdot S^I, \quad \lambda_0 \in \mathbb{R}^{*+}, \ \lambda_I \in \mathbb{R}^+$$

$$\text{where } S^{(i_1, \ldots, i_q)} = C_1^{i_1} \cdots C_p^{i_p} \cdot g_{p+1}^{i_{p+1}} \cdots g_q^{i_q}.$$

Schweighofer products are products of polyhedral constraints of P and polynomials $(g_i)_{i=p+1}^{i=q}$. They are obviously nonnegative on the set $P \cap \{g_{p+1} \geq 0, \ldots, g_q \geq 0\}$. From a certification viewpoint, the key property of the polynomials resulting from Handelman or Schweighofer products is their nonnegativity on the input polyhedron. Therefore, heuristics must attach to each product a non-negativity certificate as its representation in the OCAML/COQ type nonNegCert given below. The COQ checker contains the proof that this type only yields non-negative polynomials by construction.

type nonNegCert = C of $\mathbb{N}$ with $[\![C(i)]\!] = C_i \geq 0$ of P
 | Square of polynomial $[\![\mathsf{Square}\,(p)]\!] = p^2 \geq 0 \;\; \forall p \in \mathbb{Q}[x]$
 | Power of $\mathbb{N}$ * nonNegCert $[\![\mathsf{Power}\,(n, S)]\!] = S^n \text{ with } S \geq 0$
 | Product of nonNegCert list $[\![\mathsf{Product}\,(L)]\!] = \Pi_{S \in L}\, S \geq 0$

Design of the Oracle. The oracle treats the input polynomial g as the set $\mathcal{M}$ of its monomials and maintains a set $\mathcal{M}_C$ of already-canceled monomials. Each heuristic looks for a monomial m in $\mathcal{M}$ it can apply to, checks that it doesn't belong to $\mathcal{M}_C$ and generates a product S or H for it. Monomial m is then added to $\mathcal{M}_C$ and the monomials of S that are different from m are added to $\mathcal{M}$. The oracle finally returns a list of couples formed of a product H or S and its certificate of nonnegativity. The heuristics are applied according to their priority. The most basic of them consists in taking every Handelman product whose degree is smaller than or equal to that of g. If solving H-PLOP fails with these products, we increase the maximum degree up to which all the products are considered. Theorem 1 ensures eventual success. However, the number of products quickly becomes so large that this heuristic is used as a last resort.

Targeted Heuristics. The following heuristics aim at finding either Handelman products H^I or Schweighofer products S^I which cancel a given nonlinear monomial m. Besides a monomial canceling m, a product may contain non-linear monomials which need to be eliminated. The heuristics guarantee that these monomials are of smaller degree than m when the polyhedron is bounded, thereby ensuring termination. Otherwise, they try to limit the degree of these additional monomials as much as possible, so as to make them easier to cancel. As before, we consider an input polyhedron $\{C_1 \geq 0, \ldots, C_p \geq 0\}$ with $C_i = \sum_{j=1}^{n} a_{ij} x_j + a_{i0}$, where the x_j's are program variables and the a_{ij}'s are constants in $\mathbb{Q}$. We wish to cancel monomial $m \triangleq c_m \times x_1^{e_1} \cdots x_n^{e_n}$, with $c_m \in \mathbb{Q}$.

Extraction of Even Powers. This heuristic builds on squares being always non-negative to apply Schweighofer's theorem in an attempt to simplify the problem. The idea is to rewrite m into $m = m' \times (x_1^{\epsilon_1} \ldots x_n^{\epsilon_n})^2$ where $m' \triangleq c_m \times x_1^{\delta_1} \ldots x_n^{\delta_n}$, with $\delta_j \in \{0, 1\}$. The heuristic recursively calls the oracle in order to find a product S canceling m'. Then, $S \times (x_1^{\epsilon_1} \ldots x_n^{\epsilon_n})^2$ cancels the monomial m. If W_S is the nonnegativity certificate for S, then $\mathsf{Product}\,[W_S; \mathsf{Square}\,(x_1^{\epsilon_1} \ldots x_n^{\epsilon_n})]$ is that of the product.

Simple Products. Consider a monomial $m = c_m \times x_1 \cdots x_n$ where $c_m \in \mathbb{Q}$, as can be produced by the previous heuristic. We aim at finding a Schweighofer product S that cancels m, and such that every other monomial of S has a degree smaller than that of m. We propose an analysis based on intervals, expressing

S as a product of *variable bounds, i.e.* $x_j \in [l_j, u_j]$ where l_j, $u_j \in \mathbb{Q}$. For each variable x_j, we may choose either constraint $x_j + l_j \geq 0$ or $-x_j + u_j \geq 0$, so that the product of the chosen constraints contains $x_1 \cdots x_n$ with the appropriate sign. Moreover, other monomials of this product are ensured to have a degree smaller than that of m. The construction of a product of bounds is guided by the following concerns.

- The sign of the canceling monomial is to be opposite to that of m.
- The bounds that are available in the input constraints are used in priority. It is possible to call the VPL to deduce additional bounds on any variable from the input constraints. However, finding a new bound requires solving a linear problem.
- The selected bounds should exist, which is not necessarily the case if the input polyhedron is not a polytope. If too many bounds don't exist, the heuristic fails.

Thanks to Farkas' lemma [12, Th. 2.14], each implied bound on a variable $(x_j + l_j$ or $-x_j + u_j)$ can be expressed as a nonnegative linear combination of the input constraints, *i.e.* $\sum_{i=1}^{p} \beta_{ij} C_i$ for some $\beta_{ij} \geq 0$ solutions of a linear problem. The combination reduces to C_i if C_i is already a constraint of the input polyhedron P. The resulting product of bounds can then be expressed as follows.

$$\prod_{j \in L} (x_j + l_j) \times \prod_{j \in U} (-x_j + u_j) = \prod_{j \in L \cup U = \{1,\ldots,n\}} \left(\sum_{i=1}^{p} \beta_{ij} \cdot C_i \right), \qquad \beta_{ij} \geq 0$$

The right-hand side expression is then refactorised with the C_i's kept symbolic, so that the Handelman products appear. This case is illustrated in Example 4.

Example 4. We illustrate the behavior of the oracle and the satisfiability test on the polynomial $g = y^2 - x^2 y + xy - 85$ and still the same polytope $P = \{(C_1)\, x - 1 \geq 0, (C_2)\, y + 2 \geq 0, (C_3)\, x - y \geq 0,\ (C_4)\, 5 - x - y \geq 0\}$. The oracle starts with $\mathcal{M} = \{xy, -x^2 y, y^2\}$ and processes the monomials in order.

(xy) For eliminating xy, the simple product heuristic uses constraint $(C_1)\, x - 1 \geq 0$ and the combination $(C_1) + (C_4) = (x - 1) + (-x - y + 5)$ which entails $-y + 4 \geq 0$. Their product $(x - 1)(-y + 4) = -xy + 4x + y - 4$ cancels xy and the development $C_1 \cdot (C_1 + C_4) = C_1^2 + C_1 C_4$ reveals the useful Handelman products: $H_1 \triangleq C_1^2 = x^2 - 2x + 1$ and $H_2 \triangleq C_1 C_4 = -x^2 - xy + 6x + y - 5$. They are returned with their certificates of nonnegativity: Power $(2, C_1)$ and Product $[C_1; C_4]$. Then, xy is added to $\mathcal{M}_C$ as well as the new monomials x^2 and $-x^2$: They are not placed in $\mathcal{M}$ since opposite monomials cancel each other.

$(-x^2 y)$ The heuristic for squares splits the term $-x^2 y$ into $m' \times x^2$ and lets the oracle deal with $m' \triangleq -y$. The simple product heuristic reacts by looking for a constraint with the term $+y$ and as few variables as possible: $(C_2)\, y + 2 \geq 0$ fulfills these criteria. The calling heuristic builds the Schweighofer product $S_3 \triangleq x^2 \cdot C_2 = x^2 y + 2x^2$ that cancels $-x^2 y$, and returns S_3 with its certificate of nonnegativity Product [Square $(x); C_2$]. Then, the oracle removes $x^2 y$ from the working set and places it into the set of cancelled monomials.

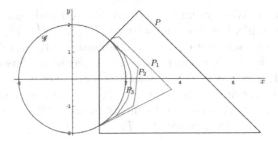

Fig. 5. *The polytopes resulting of 3 iterations of Handelman's linearization:* $P_0 = P$, $P_i = \mathsf{HL}\,(P_{i-1}, 4 - x^2 - y^2 \geq 0)$. P_1, P_2 *and* P_3 *are respectively composed of 5, 9 and 36 constraints.*

(y^2) The heuristic on squares cannot produce $y^2 \times (-1)$ with a certificate of nonnegativity for -1. The last heuristic is then triggered and finds two Handelman's products that generate $(-y^2)$: $H_4 \triangleq C_2 C_3 = (y+2)(x-y) = xy - y^2 + 2x - 2y$ and $H_5 \triangleq C_2 C_4 = (y+2)(5-x-y) = 5y - xy - y^2 + 10 - 2x - 2y$. H_4 is prefered since it does not introduce a new monomial – indeed $xy \in \mathscr{M}_C$ – whereas H_5 would add $-y^2$ to the working set $\mathscr{M}$.

Finally the oracle returns the four polynomials with their certificates. The expanded forms of H_1, H_2, S_3, H_4 are installed in the matrix $\mathcal{H}_g$ and are each associated with a decision variable $\lambda_1, \ldots, \lambda_4$. The parametric simplex computes all the positive, minimal, affine constraints *aff* of the form $1 \cdot g + \lambda_1 \cdot H_1 + \lambda_2 \cdot H_2 + \lambda_3 \cdot S_3 + \lambda_4 \cdot H_4$. With such few products, it returns only one affine constraint $aff = g + 2H_2 + H_3 + H_4 = 13x + y - 95$ from which we build a polyhedral over-approximation of the set $P \cap (g \geq 0)$ as $P \sqcap aff \geq 0$. The VPL reveals that this polyhedron is empty, meaning that $P \wedge (g \geq 0)$ is unsatisfiable.

6   Implementation and Experiments

We implemented our linearization as part of the VPL. The linearization process has two parts: an OCAML oracle, defined in Sect. 5, uses heuristics to select the most promising Handelman-Schweighofer products $S_1, \ldots, S_q$, then it runs the parametric simplex to find coefficients $\lambda_1, \ldots, \lambda_q$ such that $g + \sum \lambda_i S_i$ is affine. The result is fed into a checker implemented and proved correct in COQ. It guarantees in three steps that *aff* is an affine form and dominates g on P: (1) it verifies that *aff* is affine; (2) the proof of $\sum \lambda_i S_i \geq 0$ boils down to "sums and products of nonnegative reals are nonnegative" using the nonnegativity certificates W_i provided by the oracle; (3) it checks that the two polynomials *aff* and $g + \sum \lambda_i S_i$ are equal in expanded form using the internals of the `ring` tactic. We pay some care to efficiency by caching translations of polynomials from certificates to the expanded form to reduce the overhead of certificate checking. The architecture of the checker is detailed in a previous work [33].

Increasing Precision. We show on Fig. 5 the results of Handelman's linearization on the running example. We chose the subset $\{H^{I_1}, \ldots, H^{I_{15}}\}$ from Example 1, meaning that we are faced with a 15-variable linear problem. Precision can be increased without degree elevation by iterating Handelman's linearization (HL): $P_0 = P$, $P_{i+1} = \mathsf{HL}\,(P_i, g \geq 0)$. The linearization operator of the VPL computes this sequence until reaching a fixpoint, *i.e.* $P_{k+1} = P_k$, or a time limit. The sequence is decreasing with respect to inclusion since $\mathsf{HL}\,(P_i, g \geq 0) = P_i \sqcap \bigwedge_i \mathit{aff}_i \geq 0$ is by construction included in P_i.

Showing Emptiness of Nonlinear Sets. A SMT-solver for nonlinear real arithmetic using the DPLL(T) architecture enumerates conjunctions of nonlinear inequalities, each of which having to be tested for satisfiability. We show the unfeasibility of the conjunction of $C_1 \geq 0, \ldots, C_p \geq 0$ and nonlinear ones $g_1 \geq 0, \ldots, g_q \geq 0$ by computing the sequence of approximations: $P_0 = \{C_1 \geq 0, \ldots, C_q \geq 0\}$, $P_{i+1} = \mathsf{HL}\,(P_i, g_i \geq 0)$. The polynomials are added one after the other, meaning that g_{i+1} is linearized with respect to the previous polyhedral approximation P_i. If at some point $P_k = \emptyset$, it means that the conjunction is unsatisfiable, as our approximation is sound. Otherwise, as it is not complete, we cannot conclude. Such a procedure can thus be used to soundly prune branches in DPLL(T) search. Furthermore, the subset of constraints appearing in the products used in the emptiness proof is unsatisfiable, and thus the negation of its conjunction may be used as a learned clause.

Although our contribution applies to both static analysis and SMT solving, we felt that performing our experimental evaluation with SMT-solvers was better suited: the SMT community has a standard set of nonlinear benchmarks from SMT-LIB, which the static analysis community is missing. Therefore, we experimented with conjunctions arising from deciding formulas from the Quantifier-Free Nonlinear Real Arithmetic (QF_NRA) benchmark, from SMT-LIB 2014 [2]. These conjunctions, that we know to be unsatisfiable, are mostly coming from approximations of transcendental functions as polynomial expressions. We added our linearization algorithm as a theory solver for the SMT-solver CVC4 [15]. The calls to our linearization follow a factorization step, where for instance polynomial guards such as $x^2 - y^2 \geq 0$ are split into two cases ($x + y \geq 0 \wedge x - y \geq 0$ and $x + y \leq 0 \wedge x - y \leq 0$), in order to give more constraints to the input polyhedron.

The comparison of our contribution with the state of the art SMT-solvers Z3 [13], Yices2 [16], SMT-RAT [10] and raSat [28] was done on the online infrastructure StarExec [39]. Figure 6 is a cactus plot showing the number of benchmarks proved unsatisfiable depending on time. It illustrates that linearization based on Handelman's representation, implemented as a non-optimized prototype, gives fast answers and that its results are precise enough in many cases. Note that our approach also provides an easy-to-verify certificate, as opposed to the cylindrical algebraic decomposition implemented in Z3 for example. Indeed, if the answer of the VPL is that the final polyhedral approximation is empty, then the nonzero coefficients in the solution $\boldsymbol{\lambda}$ of the parametric problem H-PLOPH-PLOP give a list of sufficient Schweighofer products. Together with the nonlinear guards, the conjunction of the original constraints involved in these

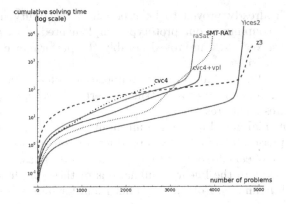

Fig. 6. *Comparison between CVC4+VPL and other* SMT-*solvers on quantifier-free non-linear real arithmetic benchmarks.*

products are actually sufficient for emptiness. As mentioned above, in a SMT-solver the negation of this conjunction may be used as a *learned theory lemma*. However, due to engineering issues we have not been able to fully integrate this procedure into CVC4 by sending back minimized learned lemmas. Over a total of 4898 benchmarks, adding our method (represented in the figure as curve *cvc4+vpl*) allows CVC4 to show the unsatisfiability of 1030 more problems. Failure in showing emptiness may come from strict constraints since up to now, our solver considers each inequality as nonstrict.

7   Conclusions and Future Work

We presented a new approach to the linear approximation of multivariate polynomials, based on Handelman's and Schweighofer's theorems, and implemented it in the Verimag Verified Polyhedra Library (VPL) as an operator of the abstract domain of polyhedra. A verifier implemented and proved correct in COQ can optionally check its results.

The approach is directly usable in static analysis by abstract interpretation: besides linear expressions, the VPL now accepts polynomials as well. Apart from handmade examples [33], we actually did not find programs manipulating integers where the linearization improves the global analysis result: non-linearity is too sparse in such programs. We believe that it could have an impact on the analysis of floating-point computations where polynomials appear more naturally in programs for approximating transcendental functions and in the analysis of the round-off errors [3]. Work in that direction is planned for the very near future but supporting this claim still requires some work on the integration of the VPL into a mature analyzer for floating-point programs, the treatment of round-off errors and some certification effort. The VPL can already deal with strict inequalities over the rationals but the algorithms are not yet certified (the enlargement of any strict inequality $< n$ over the integers to $\leq n-1$, is not valid for polyhedra over the rational field).

Our approach already proved to be useful in satisfiability modulo theory solving. A simple coupling of our prototype, implemented in OCAML, with the competitive SMT-solver CVC4 improved notably the performance of that solver on nonlinear arithmetic.

In contrast to cylindrical algebraic decomposition, which is a complete approach, our method may fail to prove a true property. However, it provides easy-to-check certificates for its results.

From a polynomial guard $g \geq 0$ and an input polyhedron P, our algorithm operates in two phases. The first selects products of constraints of P which are likely to cancel nonlinear monomials from g. The second phase uses parametric programming to explore the linear combinations of these products yielding an affine form which bounds g. Both phases offer room for improvement.

(1) Blindly including all products of degree n is exponential in n and many of them may be useless. This is why we developed an oracle procedure using selection heuristics to obtain good precision at reasonable cost. In a future refinement of this work, an incremental approach could grow the set of products, using feedback from the solver about missing monomials in cancellations.

(2) Our parametric linear solver currently relies on the parametric variant of the simplex algorithm. The latter subdivides regions of relevance, leading to multiple copies of each solution, which makes the exploration more expensive than it should be. We are now working on more efficient exploration algorithms, following previous work by Jones et al. [25].

References

1. Bagnara, R., Hill, P.M., Zaffanella, E.: The Parma Polyhedra Library: Toward a complete set of numerical abstractions for the analysis and verification of hardware and software systems. Sci. Comput. Program. **72**(1–2), 3–21 (2008). Tool available at www.cs.unipr.it/ppl/
2. Barrett, C., Stump, A., Tinelli, C.: The Satisfiability Modulo Theories Library (SMT-LIB) (2010). http://www.SMT-LIB.org
3. Boland, D., Constantinides, G.A.: Bounding variable values and round-off effects using Handelman representations. IEEE Trans. Comput. Aided Des. Integr. Circuits Syst. **30**(11), 1691–1704 (2011)
4. Boulmé, S., Maréchal, A.: Refinement to certify abstract interpretations, illustrated on linearization for polyhedra. In: Urban, C., Zhang, X. (eds.) Interactive Theorem Proving. LNCS, vol. 9236, pp. 100–116. Springer, Heidelberg (2015)
5. Chen, L., Miné, A., Wang, J., Cousot, P.: Interval polyhedra: an abstract domain to infer interval linear relationships. In: Palsberg, J., Su, Z. (eds.) SAS 2009. LNCS, vol. 5673, pp. 309–325. Springer, Heidelberg (2009)
6. Chevillard, S., Joldeş, M., Lauter, C.: Sollya: an environment for the development of numerical codes. In: Fukuda, K., Hoeven, J., Joswig, M., Takayama, N. (eds.) ICMS 2010. LNCS, vol. 6327, pp. 28–31. Springer, Heidelberg (2010)
7. Chevillard, S., Joldeş, M., Lauter, C.: Certified and fast computation of supremum norms of approximation errors. In: Computer Arithmetic (ARITH), pp. 169–176. IEEE Computer Society, June 2009

8. Chvatal, V.: Linear Programming. Series of books in the Mathematical Sciences. W. H., Freeman (1983)
9. Clauss, P., Fernandez, F.J., Gabervetsky, D., Verdoolaege, S.: Symbolic polynomial maximization over convex sets and its application to memory requirement estimation. IEEE Trans. Very Large Scale Integr. (VLSI) Syst. **17**(8), 983–996 (2009)
10. Corzilius, F., Loup, U., Junges, S., Ábrahám, E.: SMT-RAT: an SMT-compliant nonlinear real arithmetic toolbox. In: Cimatti, A., Sebastiani, R. (eds.) SAT 2012. LNCS, vol. 7317, pp. 442–448. Springer, Heidelberg (2012)
11. Cousot, P., Halbwachs, N.: Automatic discovery of linear restraints among variables of a program. In: ACM Principles of Programming Languages (POPL), pp.84–97. ACM Press, January 1978
12. Dantzig, G.B., Thapa, M.N.: Linear Programming 2: Theory and Extensions. Springer, Operations Research (2003)
13. de Moura, L., Bjørner, N.S.: Z3: an efficient SMT solver. In: Ramakrishnan, C.R., Rehof, J. (eds.) TACAS 2008. LNCS, vol. 4963, pp. 337–340. Springer, Heidelberg (2008)
14. de Moura, L., Jovanović, D.: A model-constructing satisfiability calculus. In: Giacobazzi, R., Berdine, J., Mastroeni, I. (eds.) VMCAI 2013. LNCS, vol. 7737, pp. 1–12. Springer, Heidelberg (2013)
15. Deters, M., Reynolds, A., King, T., Barrett, C., Tinelli, C.: A tour of cvc4: How it works, and how to use it. In: Proceedings of the 14th Conference on Formal Methods in Computer-Aided Design, FMCAD 2014, pp. 4:7–4:7, Austin, TX, 2014. FMCAD Inc
16. Dutertre, B.: Yices 2.2. In: Biere, A., Bloem, R. (eds.) CAV 2014. LNCS, vol. 8559, pp. 737–744. Springer, Heidelberg (2014)
17. Dutertre, B., de Moura, L.: A fast linear-arithmetic solver for DPLL(T). In: Ball, T., Jones, R.B. (eds.) CAV 2006. LNCS, vol. 4144, pp. 81–94. Springer, Heidelberg (2006)
18. Dutertre, B., De Moura, L.: Integrating simplex with DPLL(T). Technical Report SRI-CSL-06-01, SRI International, computer science laboratory (2006)
19. Feautrier, P.: Parametric integer programming. RAIRO Rech. Opérationnelle **22**(3), 243–268 (1988)
20. Fouilhe, A., Monniaux, D., Périn, M.: Efficient generation of correctness certificates for the abstract domain of polyhedra. In: Logozzo, F., Fähndrich, M. (eds.) Static Analysis. LNCS, vol. 7935, pp. 345–365. Springer, Heidelberg (2013)
21. Ganzinger, H., Hagen, G., Nieuwenhuis, R., Oliveras, A., Tinelli, C.: DPLL(T): fast decision procedures. In: Alur, R., Peled, D.A. (eds.) CAV 2004. LNCS, vol. 3114, pp. 175–188. Springer, Heidelberg (2004)
22. Halbwachs, N.: Détermination automatique de relations linéaires vérifiées par les variables d'un programme. Université de Grenoble, Thèse de doctorat de troisième cycle, March 1979
23. Handelman, D.: Representing polynomials by positive linear functions on compact convex polyhedra. Pac. J. Math. **132**(1), 35–62 (1988)
24. Jeannet, B., Miné, A.: APRON: a library of numerical abstract domains for static analysis. In: Bouajjani, A., Maler, O. (eds.) CAV 2009. LNCS, vol. 5643, pp. 661–667. Springer, Heidelberg (2009)
25. Jones, C.N., Kerrigan, E.C., Maciejowski, J.M.: Lexicographic perturbation for multiparametric linear programming with applications to control. Automatica (2007)

26. Jourdan, J.-H., Laporte, V., Blazy, S., Leroy, X., Pichardie, D.: A formally-verified C static analyzer. In: ACM Principles of Programming Languages (POPL), pp. 247–259. ACM Press, January 2015
27. Jovanović, D., de Moura, L.: Solving non-linear arithmetic. In: Gramlich, B., Miller, D., Sattler, U. (eds.) IJCAR 2012. LNCS, vol. 7364, pp. 339–354. Springer, Heidelberg (2012)
28. Khanh, T.V., Vu, X., Ogawa, M.: rasat: SMT for polynomial inequality. In: Proceedings of the 12th International Workshop on Satisfiability Modulo Theories, SMT 2014, Vienna, Austria, July 17–18, 2014, p. 67 (2014)
29. Krivine, J.-L.: Anneaux préordonnés. J. d' Anal. Math. **12**, 307–326 (1964)
30. Lasserre, J.B.: Moments, Positive Polynomials and Their Applications. Imperial College Optimization Series, vol. 1. Imperial College Press, London (2010)
31. Loechner, V., Wilde, D.K.: Parameterized polyhedra and their vertices. Int. J. Parallel Program. **2**(6), 525–549 (1997). Tool available at icps.u-strasbg.fr/polylib/
32. Maréchal, A., Périn, M.: Three linearization techniques for multivariate polynomials in static analysis using convex polyhedra. Technical Report 7, Verimag, July 2014
33. Maréchal, A., Périn, M.: A linearization technique for multivariate polynomials using convex polyhedra based on Handelman's theorem. J. Francophones des Langages Applicatifs (JFLA), January 2015
34. Miné, A.: Symbolic methods to enhance the precision of numerical abstract domains. In: Emerson, E.A., Namjoshi, K.S. (eds.) VMCAI 2006. LNCS, vol. 3855, pp. 348–363. Springer, Heidelberg (2006)
35. Muñoz, C., Narkawicz, A.: Formalization of a representation of Bernstein polynomials and applications to global optimization. J. Autom. Reasoning **51**(2), 151–196 (2013)
36. Néron, P.: A Quest for Exactness: Program Transformation for Reliable Real Numbers. Ph.D. thesis, École Polytechnique, Palaiseau, France (2013)
37. Prestel, A., Delzell, C.N.: Positive Polynomials: From Hilbert's 17th Problem to Real Algebra. Springer-Verlag, June 2001
38. Schweighofer, M.: An algorithmic approach to Schmüdgen's Positivstellensatz. J. Pure Appl. Algebra **166**(3), 307–319 (2002)
39. Stump, A., Sutcliffe, G., Tinelli, C.: StarExec: a cross-community infrastructure for logic solving. In: Demri, S., Kapur, D., Weidenbach, C. (eds.) IJCAR 2014. LNCS, vol. 8562, pp. 367–373. Springer, Heidelberg (2014)

D^3: Data-Driven Disjunctive Abstraction

Hila Peleg[1]([✉]), Sharon Shoham[2], and Eran Yahav[1]

[1] Technion, Haifa, Israel
{hilap,yahave}@cs.technion.ac.il
[2] The Academic College of Tel Aviv-Yaffo, Tel Aviv, Israel
sharon.shoham@gmail.com

Abstract. We address the problem of computing an abstraction for a set of examples, which is precise enough to separate them from a set of counterexamples. The challenge is to find an over-approximation of the positive examples that does not represent any negative example. Conjunctive abstractions (e.g., convex numerical domains) and limited disjunctive abstractions, are often insufficient, as even the best such abstraction might include negative examples. One way to improve precision is to consider a general disjunctive abstraction.

We present D^3, a new algorithm for learning general disjunctive abstractions. Our algorithm is inspired by widely used machine-learning algorithms for obtaining a classifier from positive and negative examples. In contrast to these algorithms which cannot generalize from disjunctions, D^3 obtains a disjunctive abstraction that minimizes the number of disjunctions. The result generalizes the positive examples as much as possible without representing any of the negative examples. We demonstrate the value of our algorithm by applying it to the problem of data-driven differential analysis, computing the abstract semantic difference between two programs. Our evaluation shows that D^3 can be used to effectively learn precise differences between programs even when the difference requires a disjunctive representation.

1 Introduction

We address the problem of computing an abstraction for a set of examples, which is precise enough to separate them from a set of counterexamples. Given a set of positive examples C^+ and a set of negative examples C^-, both drawn from some concrete domain $\mathcal{D}$, our goal is to compute an abstraction of C^+ using a *disjunctive* abstract domain, such that the abstraction overapproximates C^+, but does not represent any example from C^-.

The need for such an abstraction arises in many settings [5,13,32], including the problem of differential analysis - computing the abstract semantic difference between two programs [28,29,35]. The abstract semantic difference between two programs often contains ranges of input values for which the programs are known to produce the same outputs, but other ranges for which the output values differ. Computing a safe abstraction of difference/similarity ranges can produce a succinct description of the difference/similarity between programs.

© Springer-Verlag Berlin Heidelberg 2016
B. Jobstmann and K.R.M. Leino (Eds.): VMCAI 2016, LNCS 9583, pp. 185–205, 2016.
DOI: 10.1007/978-3-662-49122-5_9

Unfortunately, computing such an abstraction is tricky due to the delicate interplay between generalization and precision (required to ensure that the abstraction is safe). When there are multiple ranges of equivalence or difference, typical conjunctive abstractions (e.g., convex numerical domains [11,24]) and limited disjunctive abstractions [3,6,15,23,30], are often insufficient, as even the best such abstraction might include negative examples. On the other hand, general (unlimited) disjunctive abstractions are too precise and do not naturally generalize.

We present D^3, a new Data-Driven algorithm for learning general Disjunctive abstractions. D^3 is an active learning algorithm that iteratively accepts an example and its label as positive or negative, and incrementally updates the disjunctive abstraction of all examples seen. D^3 is driven by a new notion of *safe generalization* used to compute the abstraction of the seen examples. Safe generalization *generalizes* a precise disjunctive abstraction of the positive examples into a more abstract one, but does so in a *safe* way that does not represent any negative example.

The exploration of the input space is directed by D^3 by restricting the sampling to advantageous regions of the space derived from the intermediate abstractions.

D^3 is a general algorithm and can be instantiated with different choices for the following: (i) an *oracle* responsible for picking the next sample input from a given region, (ii) an implementation of a *teacher*, used to label each sample, and (iii) the abstract domain over which disjunctive abstractions are computed.

To implement differential analysis, we instantiate D^3 with a code-aware oracle for picking the next input, a teacher that labels an input by executing both programs and comparing outputs, and several abstractions including intervals, congruence intervals, and boolean predicates over arrays.

The main contributions of this paper are:

- A new operation, *safe generalization*, which takes a disjunctive abstraction and generalizes it further while avoiding describing a set of counterexamples.
- A new algorithm D^3 for learning general disjunctive abstractions, which uses safe generalization, as well as a strategy to direct exploration of the input space.
- An implementation of D^3 and its application to the problem of data-driven differential analysis, computing the abstract semantic difference between two programs. Our evaluation shows that D^3 can be used to effectively learn precise differences between programs even when the difference requires a disjunctive representation.

2   Overview

In this section, we provide an informal overview of our approach using a differential analysis example. Figure 1 shows two functions computing the sum of digits in a number.

```
1    def sumOfDigits (x : Int) : Int = {          1    def sumOfDigitsWrong (x : Int) : Int = {
2      @tailrec def sodRec(                        2      var y = Math.abs(x)
3                 sum : Int,                        3      if (y < 10) y
4                 rest : Int) : Int = {             4      else {
5        if (rest == 0) sum                         5        var sum = y % 10
6        else sodRec(sum + rest % 10, rest/10)      6        while (y > 0) {
7      }                                            7          sum += y % 10
8      sodRec(0,Math.abs (x))                       8          y = y / 10
9    }                                              9        }
                                                   10      sum
                                                   11      }
                                                   12    }
```

(a)   (b)

Fig. 1. Two Scala functions for computing the sum of a number's digits. (a) is a correct implementation. (b) has an error in initializing the variable sum and is correct only on numbers that have 0 as the least significant digit, or on single-digit numbers.

Figure 1(a) is a model Scala implementation for summing the digits of an input number. Figure 1(b) is an implementation by a less experienced programmer that uses a loop construct rather than the tail recursive approach. While the second implementation is very similar to a correct implementation, it suffers from an incorrect initialization of the result variable, which is easily missed with poor testing.

The goal of differential analysis is to compute an abstract representation of the difference between programs. For the programs of Fig. 1, the difference can be described as $\bigvee_{i \in \{1..9\}} (x \mod 10 = i) \land (x \leq -11 \lor x \geq 11)$. The similarity between these two programs (inputs for which the programs agree) can be described as $(x \mod 10 = 0) \lor (-9 \leq x \leq 9)$.

We use an *active learning* approach for computing the difference between the programs. In active learning, a *learner* iteratively picks points and asks a *teacher* for the classification of each point. The result of active learning is a *classifier* that generalizes from the observed points and can be used to classify new points.

In our example, the learner is trying to learn the difference between two programs P and P'. We provide a simple teacher that runs the programs and classifies a given input point c as "positive" when both programs produce the same result, i.e. $P(c) = P'(c)$, and "negative" when the results of the two programs differ, i.e. $P(c) \neq P'(c)$.

Our starting point is the *Candidate Elimination* algorithm, presented formally in the next section. Candidate Elimination proceeds iteratively as follows: in each iteration of the algorithm, the learner picks a point to be classified, asks the teacher for a classification, and updates an internal representation that captures the classification that has been learned so far. Based on this internal representation, the learner can pick the next point to be classified. The iterative process is repeated until the generalization of the positive points and the exclusion of the negative points yields the same representation.

Applying the algorithm to our example program yields the following points:

$$(0, pos), (7, pos), (10, pos), (60, pos), (47, neg), (73, neg), (88, neg)$$

The challenge is how to internally represent the set of positive points and the set of negative points. The set of positive points cannot be directly represented using a conjunctive (convex) representation, as the range $[0, 60]$ also includes the negative point 47. On the other hand, the negative range $[47, 88]$ also includes the positive point 60.

Trying to represent the positive points using a precise disjunctive representation yields no generalization in the algorithm (Sect. 3.2), and would yield the formula: $x = 0 \lor x = 7 \lor x = 10 \lor x = 60$. This disjunction would grow as additional positive points are added, does not provide any generalization for points that have not been seen, and cannot represent an unbounded number of points.

The D^3 Algorithm. The main idea of the D^3 algorithm (Algorithm 2) is to incrementally construct a generalized disjunctive representation for the positive and negative examples. Technically, D^3 operates by maintaining two formulas: φ_{pos} that maintains the generalized disjunction representing positive examples, and φ_{neg} that maintains the generalized disjunction representing the negative examples. The algorithm preserves the invariant that φ_{pos} and φ_{neg} both correctly classify all seen points. That is, any seen positive point satisfies φ_{pos}, and any seen negative point satisfies φ_{neg}. When a new point arrives, D^3 uses the generalization of the conjunctive domain as much as possible, but uses disjunctions when needed in order to exclude points of opposite classification.

In the differential analysis setting, φ_{pos} attempts to describe the similarity between programs and φ_{neg} attempts to describe the difference. For the example points above, the algorithm constructs the following φ_{pos}: $(7 \leq x \leq 7 \land x \mod 10 = 7) \lor (0 \leq x \leq 60 \land x \mod 10 = 0)$. Note that this representation correctly generalizes to include the positive points $20, 30, 40, 50$ that were not seen. The resulting φ_{neg} is $(47 \leq x \leq 47 \land x \mod 10 = 7) \lor (73 \leq x \leq 88)$.

The existence of points that satisfy both φ_{neg} and φ_{pos} does not contradict the invariant of the algorithm because both formulas include unseen points due to generalization. In fact, the points in the intersection can be used to *refine* the generalization. Technically, this is done by using the intersection as one of the regions to be sampled.

In addition to φ_{pos} and φ_{neg}, the algorithm maintains φ_S and $\varphi_{\neg G}$, the precise disjunctive representations of the positive and negative examples, respectively. Together, the four formulas determine the regions to be sampled, as depicted in Fig. 2:

- Uncovered: $\neg(\varphi_{pos} \lor \varphi_{neg})$
- Covered disagreement: $\varphi_{pos} \land \varphi_{neg}$
- Positive abstracted disagreement: $\varphi_{pos} \land \neg \varphi_S$
- Negative abstracted disagreement: $\varphi_{neg} \land \neg \varphi_{\neg G}$

The *covered* and *uncovered* are regions where a given point would either satisfy both φ_{pos} and φ_{neg}, or neither. The *positive abstract disagreement* region is where a point would satisfy the generalized disjunctive representation φ_{pos} but not the precise disjunctive representation φ_S (that is, the point is the result of generalization). The *negative abstract disagreement* plays a similar role for φ_{neg} and $\varphi_{\neg G}$.

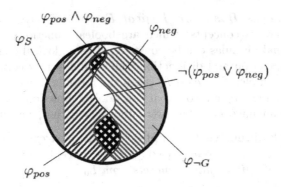

Fig. 2. The regions of the input space as seen by the D^3 algorithm

Sampling from each of these regions ensures the algorithm would progress towards abstracting and refining both positive and negative generalizations. Convergence will occur if φ_{pos} and $\neg\varphi_{neg}$ are equivalent, which means covered disagreement is eliminated, and no region of the space is uncovered.

3   Active Concept Learning

Concept learning is an area of machine learning dedicated to learning a classifier that is an abstraction of a dataset using a predefined language of predicates. This section details the most commonly used concept learning algorithm, Candidate Elimination, and its relation to abstract domains. We further discuss the limitations of Candidate Elimination, which are later addressed by our new algorithm.

Concept Learning. Concept learning aims at learning a concept in a given *concept language*. In our setting, a concept language would be used to describe the space of inputs to a program. From now on, we fix an input space, denoted $\mathcal{D}$ (also called a *domain*).

Definition 1 (Concept Language). *A concept of domain $\mathcal{D}$ is a boolean function a over $\mathcal{D}$. i.e. $a : \mathcal{D} \rightarrow \{true, false\}$. An element $c \in \mathcal{D}$ is described by the concept a if $a(c) = true$. A concept language L is a set of concepts, i.e. $L \subseteq \{true, false\}^{\mathcal{D}}$.*

Each concept describes a subset of $\mathcal{D}$, and a concept language defines the set of possible subsets available to describe the domain. A concept language is usually defined by a set of possible *descriptions* (templates) of boolean functions.

Example 1. The concept language of intervals includes all concepts described as $[l, h] = \lambda x.l \leq x \leq h$ s.t. $l, h \in \mathbb{N}$. $[0, 42]$ is a concept in the intervals concept language, which from a domain of integers describes the subset $\{0, 1, \dots, 42\}$.

Concept Languages Based on Logical Formulas. Given a concept language L_0, we view its concepts (which are boolean functions) as *atoms* over which propositional formulas can be constructed using logical connectives, such as negation, conjunction and disjunction, thus defining new concepts (boolean functions). For example, if $a_1, a_2 \in L_0$, then the formula $\varphi = a_1 \wedge a_2$ represents the function $\lambda x. a_1(x) \wedge a_2(x)$. Note that this boolean function need not be in the original concept language L_0. Thus, we obtain new, richer, concept languages.

Definition 2 (Conjunctive Concepts). *Given a concept language L_0, conjunctive concepts over L_0 (or simply conjunctive concepts) are concepts defined by a conjunction of finitely many concepts from L_0.*

A cartesian product $L_1 \times \ldots \times L_n$ is a special case of a conjunctive concept language over $L_0 = \bigcup_{1 \leq i \leq n} L_i$, where the concepts are tuples comprised of one concept from each L_i, with the meaning of conjunction.

For example, the concept language of rectangles in 2D over a domain consisting of pairs (x, y), is the product of two interval concept languages, one bounding the x axis and the other bounding the y axis, and therefore it is a conjunctive concept language.

Disjunctive concepts are defined similarly to conjunctive concepts. A disjunctive concept language over L_0 corresponds to the powerset domain over L_0 [10]. We therefore denote it $\mathcal{P}(L_0)$.

Concept Lattices. Concept learning algorithms such as Candidate Elimination [25] are based on the fact that every concept language L has an inherent partial order, denoted $\preceq$, based on the implication relation between the individual concepts, defined in [25] as the *more specific than* relation. Formally, $a_1 \preceq a_2$ if and only if for every $c \in \mathcal{D}$, $a_1(c) \Rightarrow a_2(c)$. For example, $c \in [1, 4] \Rightarrow c \in [0, 80]$ which means $[1, 4] \preceq [0, 80]$.

We are particularly interested in cases where this partially ordered set, $(L, \preceq)$, forms a lattice. We assume that all concept languages include $\bot = \lambda x. false$ and $\top = \lambda x. true$, which are the least and greatest concepts w.r.t. $\preceq$, respectively. For instance, in the intervals lattice, $[1, 3] \sqcup [5, 8] = [1, 8]$, and $[1, 3] \sqcap [5, 8] = \bot$.

Concepts as Abstractions. We view a concept language L as an *abstract domain* for $\mathcal{D}$, accompanied by a concretization function $\gamma : L \to 2^{\mathcal{D}}$ that transforms a concept $a \in L$ into all of its described objects, and an abstraction function $\beta : \mathcal{D} \to L$ which transforms an element $c \in \mathcal{D}$ to the *most specific concept representation*.[1] In the intervals concept language, for example, $\beta(c) = [c, c]$ for every $c \in \mathcal{D}$. Note that by definition of the $\preceq$ relation, $a_1 \preceq a_2 \iff \gamma(a_1) \subseteq \gamma(a_2)$.

3.1 Candidate Elimination

Candidate Elimination is a machine learning algorithm aimed at learning a binary classifier from $\mathcal{D}$ to the categories "positive" and "negative". The input

---

[1] A most specific representation need not exist. For simplicity of the presentation, we consider the case where it does, and explain what adaptations are needed when it does not.

to the algorithm is a set of positive examples $C^+ \subseteq \mathcal{D}$ and a set of negative examples $C^- \subseteq \mathcal{D}$. The output is a classifier, given as a concept, also called *hypothesis*, that is consistent with all the examples.

Definition 3 (Consistency). *A hypothesis h is consistent with a set of positive examples C^+ and a set of negative examples C^- if and only if for every $c \in C^+ \cup C^-$, $h(c) = true \iff c \in C^+$.*

The Candidate Elimination algorithm holds a lower bound and an upper bound of possible consistent hypotheses in the lattice, representing all the lattice elements inbetween. Every concept below the upper bound excludes all the concrete points the upper bound excludes, and every concept above the lower bound includes all points that the lower bound includes. The hypotheses represented by the upper and lower bound created by processing a concrete set $C = C^+ \cup C^-$ are called the *version space* of C.

Algorithm 1. The Candidate Elimination algorithm formulated in abstract domain operations

---

```
1 S ← ⊥
2 G ← {⊤}
3 for c ← Samples do
4     if label(c) is positive then  S ← S ⊔ β(c)
5     else G ← {g ⊓ n | g ∈ G, n ∈ comp⁻({c})}
6         G ← {g ∈ G | S ⊑ g}
7     if G = ∅ then
8         return ⊥
9 if S ∈ G then return S
   // Training examples ran out but S and G have not converged
10 return some hypothesis bound between S and G
```

Algorithm 1 describes the full Candidate Elimination algorithm. In the code, we use a function $label(x)$ which for $x \in \mathcal{D}$ returns either "positive" or "negative". In the case of predefined sets of points C^+, C^-, $label$ is a partial function defined for $C^+ \cup C^-$ that will return positive if and only if $x \in C^+$. In the active learning case, it will compute the label for any point in $\mathcal{D}$. In this case it will also be called a *teacher*.

The algorithm starts with a specific (lower) bound, $S = \bot^2$ and a set of generic (upper) bounds $G = \{\top\}$ (every element in G is a possible generic bound). Using concrete examples from the sets C^+ and C^-, the algorithm advances its hypotheses bounds from either direction until the lower and upper

---

[2] If β maps a concrete point to a single concept which best represents it, it is easily shown that it suffices to maintain S as a single element. Candidate Elimination can also handle multiple representations, in which case S will be a *set* of specific bounds, similarly to G.

bound converge. For any positive example c, the algorithm modifies S to include c, and for every negative example c', it modifies *all* the bounds in G to eliminate concepts that include c'. If the concept language used is a lattice, it is easy to describe the Candidate Elimination algorithm in terms of lattice operations. Modifying the bounds to include and exclude examples is done with the join and meet operations, walking through the implication lattice.

The increase of the specific bound uses the abstraction function β. In order to describe the lowering of the generic bound, we define the set which is the underapproximated complementation of a set, $comp^-$.

Definition 4 (Underapproximated Complementation). *Given a set of concrete points* $C \subseteq \mathcal{D}$, $comp^-(C)$ *is the underapproximating complement of* C. $comp^-(C) \subseteq L$ *s.t.*

- **Complementation:** $\forall a \in comp^-(C).\, \gamma(a) \cap C = \emptyset$, *and*
- **Maximal underapproximation:** $\forall a \in L.\, \gamma(a) \cap C = \emptyset \Rightarrow \exists a' \in comp^-(C):$ $a \preceq a'$

For some abstract domains $comp^-$ is an inexpensive operation. For example, in the interval domain its complexity is $O(|C|)$: $comp^-(\{2, 7\}) = \{(-\infty, 1], [3, 6], [8, \infty)\}$, and so on for larger sets. For other domains, however, $comp^-$ will be costly or even not computable. Section 5 discusses several domains, including a boolean predicate domain, where $comp^-$ causes Candidate Elimination to be non-feasible to compute.

Example 2. Using a concept language of intervals, we initialize $S = \bot$ and $G = \{\top\}$ and begin processing examples. The first example is $c = 0$, and $label(0)$ is negative. To handle a negative point, $comp^-(\{c\}) = \{(-\infty, -1], [1, \infty)\}$ is computed, then the new value of $G = \{\top \sqcap (-\infty, -1], \top \sqcap [1, \infty)\} = \{(-\infty, -1], [1, \infty)\}$. All members of G are equal or greater than S (and therefore consistent), so no filtering is required.

A second sample seen is $c' = 2$ and $label(2)$ is positive. To handle a positive sample, the algorithm computes $\beta(c') = [2, 2]$ and then computes the new value of $S = \bot \sqcup [2, 2] = [2, 2]$. We can now see that one of the members of G is no longer consistent with c', since if it were selected it would label c' as negative, which makes it incomparable with S, so it is filtered, yielding $G = \{[1, \infty]\}$.

Candidate Elimination is a general algorithm, which can be used both for active learning and offline learning from a given set of points. It has several active learning variations, including the CAL [8] and A^2 [4] algorithms for active version space concept learning. Since in active learning the algorithm itself selects the next point that will be labeled, these algorithms address the problem of selecting an advantageous next point. For this, they define the *region of disagreement*, as the set of all the points for which some two hypotheses that are currently viable disagree:

Definition 5 (Region of Disagreement). *The* region of disagreement *(sometimes* region of uncertainty*) [8] for a version space* V *is* $R_V = \{c \in \mathcal{D} \mid \exists h_1, h_2 \in V : h_1(c) \neq h_2(c)\}$.

Selecting the next example from this region would guarantee the elimination of at least one hypothesis with every step.

The final result of candidate elimination would be one of the following: a single classifier $S = \bigsqcup_{c \in C+} \beta(c)$, if S and G converge; no classifier, if S and G become inconsistent; or a (possibly infinite) range of classifiers described by the hypotheses bound between S and G, from which one or more can be selected.

3.2   Unbiased Learning

The concepts supported by the Candidate Elimination algorithms are conjunctive (specifically, cartesian concepts), and the need to find the next hypothesis that will be consistent with all examples while using only conjunction is the learner's *bias*. Bias is the way it generalizes about data it has not seen. However, as the following example demonstrates, for the case of programs, conjunctive concepts are not enough:

Example 3. Consider the differential analysis of `f(x)=x` and `g(x)=if (abs(x) < 1000) 0 else x` using the intervals concept language. These programs differ in intervals $[-1000, -1]$ and $[1, 1000]$, and are the same in $[MinInt, -1001]$, $[0, 0]$ and $[1001, MaxInt]$, so describing the difference (or similarity) using intervals requires disjunction. However, the (conjunctive) intervals language only allows to bound a set of points using a single interval. Thus, any concept describing all the positive points (where the programs agree) will also include negative points (where the programs disagree) and vice versa. Specifically, candidate elimination will finish as inconsistent if it sees a single negative sample amidst the positive samples.

Unbiased Learning. When disjunctions are added, more complex concepts can be described despite the limitation of the basic concept language L_0 (this is equatable to the powerset lattice over L_0). However, the added freedom that comes with disjunctions introduces a problem, which is inherent in the join operation of the powerset lattice: $a_1 \sqcup a_2 = a_1 \vee a_2$. If every specific example is generalized to $\beta(c)$ and then joined to the rest, the specific lower bound will never become more abstract than $\varphi_S = \bigvee_{c \in C+} \beta(c)$. Similarly, if allowing arbitrary connectives, the generic upper bound will never become more refined than $\varphi_G = \bigwedge_{c \in C-} \neg\beta(c)$.

This is what Mitchell calls "the futility of the unbiased learner" [25]. Once the ability to abstract is lost, the hypotheses at the bounds of the version space will never be able to answer yes or no about examples they have never seen, and unless the entire space is sampled (if this is at all possible), they will never converge.

3.3   Unbiased Learning by Partitioning the Space

Mitchell's original work on version spaces [26] suggests handling an inconsistency that requires disjunction by working with a pre-partitioned space and performing the candidate elimination algorithm separately in every partition. While this approach is the most efficient, it requires prior knowledge of where the disjunctions are likely to occur, and a more flexible concept language that allows for the partition. Murray's tool HYDRA [27] uses an operation equivalent to $comp^-$ to dynamically partition the domain using the negative samples, creating regions where generalization is allowed. Every division of the space may cause a recalculation of impacted abstract elements, which need to be re-generalized within the newly created regions. In addition to requiring an efficient $comp^-$, HYDRA lacks a simple convergence condition, but rather is intended to run until either samples run out or the teacher is "satisfied" with the resulting description.

4   Learning Disjunctive Abstractions

In this section we describe our algorithm for learning disjunctive concepts. Just as in the Candidate Elimination algorithm, what we seek to find is a boolean function partitioning the input space into the positive and the negative sets, described using the concept language. As in Candidate Elimination, we are dependent on the assumption that this partition is expressible using the concept language. However, unlike Candidate Elimination, we consider a disjunctive concept language, $\mathcal{P}(L)$.

From here on, we interchangeably describe disjunctive concepts in $\mathcal{P}(L)$ as disjunctive formulas, e.g., $a_1 \vee a_2$, and as sets, e.g. $\{a_1, a_2\}$. Further, $\sqcup$ always denotes the join of L, as opposed to the join of $\mathcal{P}(L)$, which is simply disjunction or set union.

Our key idea is to combine the benefits of the generalization obtained by using the join of L, with the expressiveness allowed by disjunctions. We therefore define a *safe generalization* which generalizes a set of concepts (abstract elements) $A \in \mathcal{P}(L)$ in a way that keeps them separate from a concrete set of counterexamples.

Definition 6 (Safe Generalization). *A safe generalization of a set of concepts $A \in \mathcal{P}(L)$ w.r.t. a concrete set of counterexamples $C_{cex} \subseteq \mathcal{D}$ is a set $SG(A, C_{cex}) \in \mathcal{P}(L)$ which satisfies the following requirements:*

1. **Abstraction:** $\forall a \in A. \exists a' \in SG(A, C_{cex}). a \preceq a'$
2. **Separation:** $\forall a \in SG(A, C_{cex}). \gamma(a) \cap C_{cex} = \emptyset$
3. **Precision:** $\forall a \in SG(A, C_{cex}). \exists A' \subseteq A. a = \bigsqcup A'$

We say that $SG(A, C_{cex})$ is maximal if whenever $a \in L$ satisfies the separation and the precision requirements, there exists $a' \in SG(A, C_{cex})$ s.t. $a \preceq a'$.

Note that the separation requirement is the same as the "complementation" requirement of $comp^-$. Unlike the join of L which is restricted to return a concept in L, $SG(A, C_{cex})$ returns a concept in $\mathcal{P}(L)$, and as such it can "refine" the result of join in case $\bigsqcup A$ does not satisfy the separation requirement. The precision requirement is guided by the intuition that each $a \in SG(A, C_{cex})$, which represents a disjunct in the learned disjunctive concept, should generalize in accordance with the generalization of L and not beyond. If any of the conditions cannot be met, then $SG(A, C_{cex})$ is undefined. However, if $\gamma(A)$ and C_{cex} are disjoint, then $SG(A, C_{cex})$ is always defined because it will, at worst, perform no generalization and will return A.

Using safe generalization, we can define the "safe abstractions" of two sets C^+, C^-: $\varphi_{pos} = SG(\{\beta(c) \mid c \in C^+\}, C^-)$, which characterizes the positive examples, or $\varphi_{neg} = SG(\{\beta(c) \mid c \in C^-\}, C^+)$, which characterizes the negative examples (provided that SG is defined for them).

The Ideal Solution. If C^+ and C^- partition the *entire* space and SG computes *maximal* safe generalization, then φ_{pos} and φ_{neg} will be the optimal solutions, in the sense of providing concepts with largest disjuncts which correctly partition $\mathcal{D}$. Note that in the case that the classifier is expressible as a concept in L, the ideal solution is equivalent to the result of Candidate Elimination, which is simply $\bigsqcup\{\beta(c) \mid c \in C^+\}$.

Since this definition, while optimal, is both unfeasible (for an infinite domain) and requires SG, which like $comp^-$ may be very expensive to compute, we propose instead a greedy algorithm to approximate it by directing the sampling of points in C^+ and C^- and by implementing SG with a heuristic approximation of maximality.

Our algorithm, D^3, is presented in Algorithm 2, and described below.

Two Levels of Abstraction. D^3 modifies the version space algorithms to keep four hypotheses, divided into two levels of abstraction.

In the first level of abstraction, $\varphi_S, \varphi_{\neg G} \in \mathcal{P}(L)$ are formula representations of the minimal overapproximation of the points that have actually been seen. φ_S corresponds to Candidate Elimination's S, computed over $\mathcal{P}(L)$, for which join is simply disjunction. In an effort to simplify and only deal with disjunction and not negation, instead of G which underapproximates $\mathcal{D} \setminus C^-$, we use $\varphi_{\neg G}$ that abstracts C^- directly. In the second level of abstraction, $\varphi_{pos}, \varphi_{neg} \in \mathcal{P}(L)$ are added. These are incremental computations of the definition above, which provide safe generalizations of φ_S w.r.t. the current C^-, and of $\varphi_{\neg G}$ w.r.t. the current C^+.

Technically, $\varphi_S = \bigvee_{c \in C^+} \beta(c)$ and $\varphi_{pos} = \bigvee \psi_i$ s.t. $\psi_i = \beta(c_{i_1}) \sqcup \cdots \sqcup \beta(c_{i_k})$ for some $\{c_{i_1}, \ldots, c_{i_k}\} \subseteq C^+$. It can be seen that $C^+ \subseteq \gamma(\varphi_S) \subseteq \gamma(\varphi_{pos})$. Further, both φ_S and φ_{pos} are consistent with all the examples seen (including negative ones). Dually for C^-, $\varphi_{\neg G}$ and φ_{neg}.

D^3 updates the formulas as follows. Every positive sample c that arrives is first added to φ_S, and then if it is not already described by φ_{pos}, φ_{pos} is updated to a safe generalization of $\varphi_{pos} \vee \beta(c)$. If φ_{neg} is inconsistent with c, then any disjunct $\psi_i \in \varphi_{neg}$ for which $\psi_i(c) = true$ is refined by collapsing it into its original set of points, abstracting them using β and re-generalizing while considering the new point. Unlike Candidate Elimination, D^3 is symmetrical for positive and negative samples, hence negative samples are handled dually.

D^3 converges when φ_{pos} and φ_{neg} constitute a partition of $\mathcal{D}$. This means that $\varphi_{pos} \equiv \neg\varphi_{neg}$. This requires that in terms of expressiveness, the partition can be described both positively and negatively.

Algorithm 2. The D^3 algorithm

Input: O oracle, $label$ teacher function

1 $\varphi_{pos} \leftarrow false$; $\varphi_{neg} \leftarrow false$
2 $\varphi_S \leftarrow false$; $\varphi_{\neg G} \leftarrow false$
3 $C^+ \leftarrow \emptyset$; $C^- \leftarrow \emptyset$
4 **while** $((\varphi_{pos} \vee \varphi_{neg} \not\equiv true) \vee (\varphi_{pos} \wedge \varphi_{neg} \not\equiv false)) \wedge \neg timeout$ **do**
    // Check for consistency
5      $c_{pos} \leftarrow O\,|_{\varphi_S}$; $c_{neg} \leftarrow O\,|_{\varphi_{\neg G}}$
6   **if** $label(c_{neg})$ *is positive* $\vee$ $label(c_{pos})$ *is negative* **then**
7   **return** *no classifier*
    // Sample every region of disagreement
8      $c_1 \in O\,|_{\neg\varphi_{pos} \wedge \neg\varphi_{neg}}$
9      $c_2 \in O\,|_{\varphi_{pos} \wedge \varphi_{neg}}$
10     $c_3 \in O\,|_{\varphi_{pos} \wedge \neg\varphi_S}$
11     $c_4 \in O\,|_{\varphi_{neg} \wedge \neg\varphi_{\neg G}}$
12     $C = \{c_1, c_2, c_3, c_4\}$
13   **for** $c \leftarrow C$ **do**
14   **if** $label(c)$ *is positive* **then**
15             $\varphi_S \leftarrow \varphi_S \vee \beta(c)$
16   **if** $\neg\varphi_{pos}(c)$ **then** $\varphi_{pos} \leftarrow \mathrm{SG}(\varphi_{pos} \vee \beta(c), C^-)$;
17   **if** $\varphi_{neg}(c)$ **then** $\varphi_{neg} \leftarrow \mathrm{refine}(\varphi_{neg}, c, C^-, C^+)$;
18             $C^+ \leftarrow C^+ \cup \{c\}$
19   **else** // Symmetrical
20             $\varphi_{\neg G} \leftarrow \varphi_{\neg G} \vee \beta(c)$
21   **if** $\neg\varphi_{neg}(c)$ **then** $\varphi_{neg} \leftarrow \mathrm{SG}(\varphi_{neg} \vee \beta(c), C^+)$;
22   **if** $\varphi_{pos}(c)$ **then** $\varphi_{pos} \leftarrow \mathrm{refine}(\varphi_{pos}, c, C^+, C^-)$;
23             $C^- \leftarrow C^- \cup \{c\}$
24 **return** $\varphi_{pos}, \varphi_{neg}$

Function $\mathrm{SG}(\varphi = \psi_1 \vee \cdots \vee \psi_k, C_{cex})$

---

1 $consistent \leftarrow \{\{\psi_j\} \mapsto \psi_j \mid 1 \leq j \leq k\}$ // $lvl = 1$
2 **for** $lvl \leftarrow 2 \ldots k$ **do**
3      $prevLvl \leftarrow \{S \mid S \in \mathcal{P}(\{\psi_1, \ldots, \psi_k\}), |S| = lvl - 1, S \in dom(consistent)\}$
4      $pairs \leftarrow \{(S, S') \mid S, S' \in prevLvl, |S \cup S'| = lvl\}$
5   **for** $(S, S') \leftarrow pairs$ **do**
        // Can be optimized to not check the same $S \cup S'$ twice
6   **if** $S \cup S' \notin dom(consistent)$ **then**
7              $a \leftarrow consistent[S] \sqcup consistent[S']$
8   **if** $\gamma(a) \cap C_{cex} = \emptyset$ **then**
9                  $consistent \leftarrow consistent \cup \{S \cup S' \mapsto a\}$
10 $seen \leftarrow \emptyset$; $res \leftarrow \emptyset$
11 **while** $seen \neq \{\psi_1, \ldots, \psi_k\}$ **do**
12     $joint \leftarrow \arg\max_x \{cardinality(x) \mid x \in dom(consistent), x \cap seen = \emptyset\}$
13     $seen \leftarrow seen \cup joint$
14     $res \leftarrow res \cup consistent[joint]$
15 **return** $\bigvee res$

Function refine$(\varphi = \psi_1 \vee \cdots \vee \psi_k, c, C_{abstracted}, C_{cex})$

---

1   $contradicting \leftarrow \{\psi_i \mid \psi_i(c), 1 \leq i \leq k\}$
2   $consistent \leftarrow \{\psi_i \mid 1 \leq i \leq k\} \setminus contradicting$
3   **for** $\psi \leftarrow contradicting$ **do**
4      $concrete \leftarrow \{c' \in C_{abstracted} \mid \psi(c')\}$
5      $generalized \leftarrow \text{SG}(\bigvee\{\beta(c') \mid c' \in concrete\}, C_{cex})$
6      $consistent \leftarrow \text{SG}(consistent \cup \{\theta_i \mid generalized = \theta_1 \vee \cdots \vee \theta_j\}, C_{cex})$
7   **return** $\bigvee consistent$

Greedily Computing Safe Generalization. Like $comp^-$, computing SG naively is doubly-exponential. We therefore use a greedy strategy. SG first finds all the subsets of the input whose join is consistent. This is done inductively bottom-up, based on the fact that if $a_1 \sqcup a_2$ is inconsistent with some point c, then $a_1 \sqcup a_2 \sqcup a_3$ will be as well. This means the bottom-up construction can stop generalizing at smaller subsets. From the computed consistent generalized concepts, a coverage of the input is selected greedily using a *cardinality function*: $\mathcal{P}(L) \to \mathbb{N}$ that assigns a value to the desirability of a subset of L to the coverage. A default cardinality function returns the number of concepts in the subset, preferring a generalized element created from the largest subset, but some domains allow for a better one. This greedy selection no longer ensures maximality.

If the domain is assured to be one for which $comp^-$ is efficient to compute, HYDRA's technique (Sect. 3.3) can be used to partition the space so that rejoining after a contradiction has been refined around is linear. While this is not always possible, the greedy computation of SG is improved to an exponential operation. Care is taken to always perform it on the fewest possible elements. With the exception of backtracking (calls to refine that do collapse a disjunct), calls to SG will encounter a set of elements most of which cannot be joined to each other, and the computation will never try computing any larger joins containing them.

Example 4. In sampling inputs for f(x) and g(x) from Example 3, using intervals as our concept language, consider the case where the algorithm has already seen the concrete points: $\{0, 1002, -837\}$ which means it has learned $\varphi_S = [0, 0] \vee [1002, 1002]$ and $\varphi_{\neg G} = [-837, -837]$. (Recall that positive points correspond to program similarity and negative points correspond to a difference.) It has also generalized $\varphi_{pos} = [0, 1002]$, as right now it is a valid hypothesis that is not in contradiction with any data, and since there is nothing to abstract, $\varphi_{neg} = [-837, -837]$.

When the algorithm sees a new concrete point 478, for which $f(478) \neq g(478)$, it expands $\varphi_{\neg G}$ to include the point. It also adds a second clause so $\varphi_{neg} = [-837, -837] \vee [478, 478]$. It then tries to generalize this using the intervals lattice, where $[-837, -837] \sqcup [478, 478] = [-837, 478]$ but this new classifier is consistent with the fact that $f(0) = g(0)$ and $0 \in [-837, 478]$. This means these two points cannot be abstracted together. Likewise, φ_{pos} is tested, and since $478 \in [0, 1002]$ it has become inconsistent, so it is refined into $[0, 0] \vee [1002, 1002]$.

We examine another point, 10004, where $f(10004) = g(10004)$, which is added to φ_S and then to φ_{pos}. φ_{pos} is now comprised of $[0, 0] \vee [1002, 1002] \vee [10004, 10004]$. While $[0, 1002]$ and $[0, 10004]$ are inconsistent with what we know about 478, $[1002, 10004]$ is consistent, so we abstract $\varphi_{pos} = [0, 0] \vee [1002, 10004]$.

It should be noted that while φ_S and $\varphi_{\neg G}$ advance in one direction, φ_{pos} and φ_{neg} travel up and down the lattice in order to stay consistent.

Regions of Disagreement. As shown in Sect. 2, the four formulas maintained by D^3 partition the region of disagreement (Definition 5) into four separate regions, which can be seen in Fig. 2. The *uncovered* and *covered disagreement* regions represent a classification disagreement between the two abstractions, and the *positive* and *negative abstracted disagreement* are a classification disagreement between the bounds and the abstractions. Since all four formulas are consistent with all previously processed points, these will all be unsampled regions of the space.

Sampling the uncovered or covered disagreement regions is guaranteed to advance the algorithm by either abstracting or refining at least one of the formulas. By sampling the region with an *oracle*, advantageous points can be selected. In the case of sampling $\varphi_{pos} \wedge \neg\varphi_S$ or $\varphi_{neg} \wedge \neg\varphi_{\neg G}$ (note that these formulas are not concepts in $\mathcal{P}(L)$, they are just used as an interface to the oracle), it is possible that while the sampled point will be added to φ_S or $\varphi_{\neg G}$, it will make no change in the generalized formulas, and in essence not advance the algorithm toward convergence.

Timeout and Consistency Checks. Like Candidate Elimination, if D^3 recognizes that the concept language is not descriptive enough to allow it to converge, it returns "no classifier". This will happen if the abstraction inherent in β causes inconsistency. To test for this, the algorithm samples specifically for unseen points in φ_S and $\varphi_{\neg G}$ and if they indicate inconsistency, returns "no classifier". If β is precise enough, there will be no such unseen points, and this test will require no action.

Another option is that convergence is unattainable, either because the partition of the space cannot be described by $\mathcal{P}(L)$ from neither the positive nor the negative direction, which will cause a loop of φ_{pos} and φ_{neg} continuously generalizing to intersect each other and refining to create uncovered space, or because the domain is infinite and not advantageously sampled by the oracle. A timeout is introduced to stop the process. Our experiments have shown a timeout of 2000 iterations to be sufficient. In case of timeout, φ_{pos} and φ_{neg} can still be returned (as both are consistent with the seen points).

4.1 D^3 on a Fixed Example Set

If a fixed set of examples C is given to D^3 along with a *label* function defined only over C, which means there is no teacher to query about new samples, the convergence condition no longer applies. D^3 will run until samples are exhausted, and the role of the oracle will no longer be to provide a new sample, but rather to order the samples so that the algorithm will have to do as little backtracking as possible, and will be more efficient than simply computing SG.

For example, for the intervals domain, the oracle would return the samples in ascending order, which would ensure no counterexample dividing an interval disjunct would ever be provided.

5   Prototype Implementation and Evaluation

We have implemented the D^3 algorithm in Scala for several domains, along with several input sampling strategies (oracles). In this section we first describe the sampling strategies and concept languages implemented in our differential analysis experiments. We then describe our experimental results over a small but challenging set of programs.

5.1   Input Sampling Strategy

An ideal oracle would offer points that would lead D^3 to finding every disjunct in the desired φ_{pos} and φ_{neg}, and that would lead to convergence. It would also order the samples so that the number of refinements would always be minimal, and the algorithm would converge on a precise result using the fewest operations (However, note that the result of D^3 is not sensitive to order of the sampled points).

Coming up with an ideal oracle is in general undecidable. Instead, one may choose between different heuristics for discovering interesting input values.

Naively, a requested region is sampled uniformly. However, this often misses singularity points (e.g., due to testing if (x != 0)). A slightly better approach is to use biased sampling with tools such as ScalaCheck [1] that favor "problematic values" such as 0, -1, or Int.MaxValue. Other techniques, typically used to increase test coverage (e.g., concolic testing [33], whitebox fuzzing [16]), can be applied here as well.

Another practical solution is to use a *grey-box* approach. For instance, searching the code for constants and operations, and generating from them a list of special values that should be returned to the algorithm when they match one of the sampled regions. We have implemented a constants-only oracle which has proved sufficient for all implemented numerical domains.

5.2   Intervals and Intervals with Congruence

Intervals. We use a standard intervals lattice [9] with $|\gamma([l, h])|$ as a cardinality measure for an interval $[l, h]$. This measure is easily computed and directs the greedy choice towards the largest intervals.

D^3 with the intervals domain has the property that if some point from a positive or negative region is seen, the algorithm will not converge until the entire region is discovered. This is because $\bigsqcup(\{\beta(c) \mid c \in C\}) = [l, h]$ only if

$l, h \in C$, and since in order for D^3 to converge, the space needs to be covered (i.e. $l - 1$ and $h + 1$ are, themselves, described by φ_{pos} or φ_{neg}), both sides of every boundary between φ_{pos} and φ_{neg} are sampled. This means that the grey-box oracle would be adequate because relevant points are likely to be present as constants in the code.

While intervals are useful for some examples (see Table 1), they cannot handle examples such as that in Fig. 1. Running D^3 with intervals on Fig. 1 and assuming a finite domain of 32-bit integers will only converge by sampling the whole domain. While a full description of similarity ($\{[x, x] \mid x \mod 10 = 0 \wedge -2147483648 \leq x \leq 2147483647\}$ for a 32-bit integer) exists, it consists of 400 million separate disjuncts. And since these disjuncts contain one concrete element each, they are also likely to never be discovered and instead be overapproximated by the description of difference. What the interval concept language lacks is the ability to abstract these into one description.

Intervals with Congruence. We consider a richer domain of intervals with congruences for several divisors. Instead of using the full congruence abstract domain [17], we use its collapsed versions to the divisors 2 through 10 that allow the information on several different congruences to be preserved simultaneously. This allows us to learn the similarity ($x \leq 2147483640 \wedge x \geq -2147483640 \wedge x \mod 2 = 0 \wedge x \mod 5 = 0 \wedge x \mod 10 = 0) \vee (x \leq 9 \wedge x \geq -9)$ for the example of Fig. 1.

Like intervals, the cardinality measure for intervals with congruence counts the number of elements in the interval, accounting for all congruences that are not $\top$. Using the grey-box oracle, the Sum of digits example converges with the expected difference of $\bigvee_{i \in 1...9}(x \leq -1 \wedge x \mod 10 = i) \vee (x \geq 11 \wedge x \mod 10 = i)$.

Larger Arities. Both the intervals and intervals with congruence domains can be applied to functions of different arities by using the product domain for as many arguments to the function as necessary. We have implemented the domain *Intervals × Intervals* for functions that take two **int** parameters.

Using the same grey-box oracle lifted to the product domain for two parameters, and the area of the box as the cardinality function, we tested D^3 on several samples including the **Quadrant** test, in which the exercise is to take a point in the geometric plane (x, y) and return the quadrant it is in. One implementation defines Quadrant I as $x > 0, y > 0$ and the other as $x \geq 0, y \geq 0$, and the same for Quadrant II and IV.

This yields the difference of $x = 0 \vee y = 0$, and similarity of $(x \geq 1 \wedge y \geq 1) \vee (x \geq 1 \wedge y \leq -1) \vee (x \leq -1 \wedge y \geq 1) \vee (x \leq -1 \wedge y \leq -1)$.

5.3   Quantified Boolean Predicates over Arrays

In the domain of quantified boolean predicates over arrays, $comp^-$ causes the number of upper bounds to grow exponentially, which means Candidate Elimination is non feasible to compute, even for simple conjunctive descriptions. D^3 finds these descriptions, as well as disjunctive ones.

Creating Predicates. Since we have no property or assertions from which to draw predicates, we use a template-based abstraction, as in [21,34,36]. For simplicity, we use a fixed set of predicate templates filtered by correctness on the concrete array, similar to those used by the Houdini [14] and Daikon [12] annotation assistants.

The β Function. In our implementation $\beta(c)$ is a conjunction of all the facts the templates discover about it. For very small arrays we can allow a precise beta function that generates specific predicates for $arr(0), arr(1), \ldots$. For larger arrays we keep more compact facts such as: $\forall i.(arr(i) \leq arrMax \wedge arr(i) \geq arrMin)$ for the maximum and minimum values in the array. This is not a precise β, which illustrates the importance of the consistency check in Sect. 4.

Oracle. The grey-box oracle approach, which works for most integer functions, is insufficient for arrays - the simple syntactic analysis of the code is insufficient for inferring meaningful examples. To demonstrate the D^3 algorithm, we provide our experiments with a manual "oracle procedure" specific to the test.

The `Find2` test finds the occurrence of 2 in an array without using array functions. The spec implementation provided is simply `arr.indexOf(2)`, and the tested implementation makes an off-by-one error failing to test `arr(0)`. D^3 learns the difference $arr(0) \geq 2 \wedge arr(0) \leq 2$.

5.4   Experimental Evaluation

Table 1 compares each of the tests to the capabilities of a conjunctive method such as joining all the samples of a large set of positive examples or running an active version of Candidate Elimination. The columns for "conjunctive (difference)" and "conjunctive (similarity)" signify whether the analysis would succeed if performed when treating the different points or the similar points as C^+.

Tests `Example 3`, `Sum of Digits`, `Quadrant` and `Find2` have been discussed in detail previously. `Square` tests the difference between two implementations of squaring a number, one which casts to Long, and another that does not, thus causing an integer overflow, creating a difference in any number that is large enough or small enough so that its square does not fit into an Integer. `StringAtIndex` returns the character at the given index of a string, or null if the index is outside the bounds of the string, where one implementation has an off-by-one error, causing the 0th place in the string to be returned as null and an exception to be thrown at one past the end. `IsOdd` tests a parameter for oddness, where one implementation incorrectly tests negative numbers. `SolveLinEq` returns the solution to a linear equation $ax^2 + b = 0$ where a, b are the arguments of the functions. One implementation is undefined where $a = 0$ and the other only when both a and b are zero. `ArrayAverage` averages the values in an array, where one implementation is undefined (division by zero error) when the array is empty and the other returns zero. `ArrayMaximum` searches for the maximum value in an array, where one implementation has incorrect initialization of the maximum to 0 rather than the first element, thereby returning an incorrect result when $\forall i : arr(i) < 0$.

Table 1. Comparing the D^3 algorithm to the capabilities of conjunctive algorithms

	Test name	Conjunctive (difference)	Conjunctive (similarity)	D^3
Intervals	Example 3	✗	✗	✓
	Square	✗	✓	✓
	StringAtIndex	✗	✗	✓
Intervals with congruence	IsOdd	✗	✓	✓
	Sum of Digits	✗	✗	✓
Boxes	SolveLinEq	✓	✗	✓
	Quadrant	✗	✗	✓
Boolean predicates over arrays	Find2	✗	✗	✓
	ArrayAverage	✗	✗	✓
	ArrayMaximum	✗	✗	✓

As Table 1 shows, while some cases can be solved by attempting a conjunctive technique from both directions separately and taking one if its result has not become inconsistent, this will not work for others. In addition, in domains like predicates on arrays where $comp^-$ is not available, the lowering of the upper bound is not available, so only more primitive techniques such as generating a large number of samples with no guidance and attempting their join remain.

6 Related Work

Disjunctive Abstraction. Since the original work introducing the powerset construction for adding disjunction to a domain [10], there have been attempts to create a more practical abstraction that allows for disjunction but also for the abstraction that is limited by the powerset domain's join operation, as discussed in Sect. 3.2. The easiest limitation which introduces bias is limiting the number of allowed disjuncts [6,23,30]. While this forces an abstraction once the number of disjoint elements is reached, it may still be forced to cover a negative example because the number of elements allowed is insufficient. Another is the *finite powerset domain* [2,3] which keeps only the finite sets in the powerset. However, this still retains the problem of the non-abstracting join.

The Boxes domain [20], based decision diagrams, is compact in representation even for a large number of disjuncted boxes. It is specialized for the *Integer* × *Integer* domain, though the technique might be extendible to other domains. Donut domains [15] allow for "holes" in a single convex set. This does not allow a disjunction of the positive sets, and cannot be used with non-convex domains such as congruence.

Disjunctive Approaches to Candidate Elimination. Several methods have been mentioned in Sect. 3.3. In [22], every step of the algorithm maintains n representations of the specific and general bounds from 1 to n disjuncts, where n is the number of samples seen. Then, the desired option can be selected either by convergence or by other criteria. This method is both wasteful in representation if many samples are required to cover the space, and the criteria for the best disjunction update are complex and require additional learning algorithms. Sebag's [31] approach learns a disjunction of conjunctions of negative examples. This is meant to cope with noisy datasets, which are irrelevant in the case of performing an abstraction, and decides at classification time based on tuning, which means its output is not a description of the space but rather a function capable of labeling individual points.

Abstracting with Learning Algorithms. Thakur et al. [37] use a variation on Candidate Elimination to compute symbolic abstraction. Gupta et al. [19] present an algorithm for actively learning an automaton that separates the language of two models, called the separating automaton. Like D^3, this is an active learning algorithm based on asking a teacher to compute language inclusion. However, this algorithm is relevant only to string languages (models and automata). Counterexample-driven abstraction refinement techniques [5,7,18] for verification behave like a learning algorithm, requesting "classification" of a point or a trace, and eliminating it from the abstract representation, in much the same way as Candidate Elimination and D^3 do.

7   Conclusion

We presented D^3, an active learning algorithm for computing an abstraction of a set of positive examples, separating them from a set of negative examples. A critical component of D^3 is the *safe generalization* operation which transforms an element in a powerset domain into a more general element that does not intersect any negative point. In cases where D^3 can actively query additional points beyond an initial set, it aims at learning a partition of the entire space (and not only abstract the initial samples). We apply D^3 to compute an abstract semantic difference between programs using several abstract domains. We show that D^3 can compute a precise description of difference/similarity for several small but challenging examples.

Acknowledgment. The research leading to these results has received funding from the European Union's - Seventh Framework Programme (FP7) under grant agreement no. 615688 - ERC-COG-PRIME and under ERC grant agreement no. 321174-VSSC, and from the BSF grant no. 2012259.

References

1. Scalacheck: Property-based testing for scala
2. Bagnara, R.: A hierarchy of constraint systems for data-flow analysis of constraint logic-based languages. Sci. Comput. Program. **30**(1), 119–155 (1998)

3. Bagnara, R., Hill, P.M., Zaffanella, E.: Widening operators for powerset domains. STTT **8**(4–5), 449–466 (2006)
4. Balcan, M.-F., Beygelzimer, A., Langford, J.: Agnostic active learning. In: Proceedings of the 23rd International Conference on Machine Learning, pp. 65–72. ACM (2006)
5. Beckman, N.E., Nori, A.V., Rajamani, S.K., Simmons, R.J., Tetali, S.D., Thakur, A.V.: Proofs from tests. IEEE Trans. Softw. Eng. **36**(4), 495–508 (2010)
6. Beyer, D., Henzinger, T.A., Théoduloz, G.: Configurable software verification: concretizing the convergence of model checking and program analysis. In: Damm, W., Hermanns, H. (eds.) CAV 2007. LNCS, vol. 4590, pp. 504–518. Springer, Heidelberg (2007)
7. Clarke, E., Grumberg, O., Jha, S., Lu, Y., Veith, H.: Counterexample-guided abstraction refinement. In: Emerson, E.A., Sistla, A.P. (eds.) CAV 2000. LNCS, vol. 1855. Springer, Heidelberg (2000)
8. Cohn, D., Atlas, L., Ladner, R.: Improving generalization with active learning. Mach. Learn. **15**(2), 201–221 (1994)
9. Cousot, P., Cousot, R.: Static determination of dynamic properties of programs. In: Proceedings of the Second International Symposium on Programming, pp. 106–130, Dunod, Paris, France (1976)
10. Cousot, P., Cousot, R.: Systematic design of program analysis frameworks. In: Proceedings of the 6th ACM SIGACT-SIGPLAN Symposium on Principles of Programming Languages, pp. 269–282. ACM (1979)
11. Cousot, P., Halbwachs, N.: Automatic discovery of linear restraints among variables of a program. In: POPL, pp. 84–96 (1978)
12. Ernst, M.D., Cockrell, J., Griswold, W.G., Notkin, D.: Dynamically discovering likely program invariants to support program evolution. IEEE Trans. Softw. Eng. **27**(2), 99–123 (2001)
13. Ernst, M.D., Perkins, J.H., Guo, P.J., McCamant, S., Pacheco, C., Tschantz, M.S., Xiao, C.: The daikon system for dynamic detection of likely invariants. Sci. Comput. Program. **69**(1), 35–45 (2007)
14. Flanagan, C., Leino, K.R.M.: Houdini, an annotation assistant for ESC/Java. In: Oliveira, J.N., Zave, P. (eds.) FME 2001: Formal Methods for Increasing Software Productivity. LNCS, vol. 2021, pp. 500–517. Springer, Heidelberg (2001)
15. Ghorbal, K., Ivančić, F., Balakrishnan, G., Maeda, N., Gupta, A.: Donut domains: efficient non-convex domains for abstract interpretation. In: Kuncak, V., Rybalchenko, A. (eds.) VMCAI 2012. LNCS, vol. 7148, pp. 235–250. Springer, Heidelberg (2012)
16. Godefroid, P., Levin, M.Y., Molnar, D.: Sage: whitebox fuzzing for security testing. Queue **10**(1), 20 (2012)
17. Granger, P.: Static analysis of arithmetical congruences. International Journal of Computer Mathematics **30**(3–4), 165–190 (1989)
18. Gulavani, B.S., Chakraborty, S., Nori, A.V., Rajamani, S.K.: Automatically Refining Abstract Interpretations. In: Ramakrishnan, C.R., Rehof, J. (eds.) TACAS 2008. LNCS, vol. 4963, pp. 443–458. Springer, Heidelberg (2008)
19. Gupta, A., McMillan, K.L., Fu, Z.: Automated Assumption Generation for Compositional Verification. In: Damm, W., Hermanns, H. (eds.) CAV 2007. LNCS, vol. 4590, pp. 420–432. Springer, Heidelberg (2007)
20. Gurfinkel, A., and Chaki, S. Boxes: A symbolic abstract domain of boxes. In Static Analysis. Springer, 2010, pp. 287–303

21. Lopes, N.P., Monteiro, J.: Weakest Precondition Synthesis for Compiler Optimizations. In: McMillan, K.L., Rival, X. (eds.) VMCAI 2014. LNCS, vol. 8318, pp. 203–221. Springer, Heidelberg (2014)

22. Manago, M., and Blythe, J. Learning disjunctive concepts. In Knowledge representation and organization in machine learning. Springer, 1989, pp. 211–230

23. Mauborgne, L., and Rival, X. Trace partitioning in abstract interpretation based static analyzers. In Programming Languages and Systems. Springer, 2005, pp. 5–20

24. Miné, A.: The octagon abstract domain. Higher-Order and Symbolic Computation **19**(1), 31–100 (2006)

25. Mitchell, T. Machine Learning. McGraw-Hill international editions - computer science series. McGraw-Hill Education, 1997, ch. 2, pp. 20–51

26. Mitchell, T. M. Version spaces: an approach to concept learning. PhD thesis, Stanford University, Dec 1978

27. Murray, K. S. Multiple convergence: An approach to disjunctive concept acquisition. In IJCAI (1987), Citeseer, pp. 297–300

28. Partush, N., Yahav, E.: Abstract Semantic Differencing for Numerical Programs. In: Logozzo, F., Fähndrich, M. (eds.) Static Analysis. LNCS, vol. 7935, pp. 238–258. Springer, Heidelberg (2013)

29. Partush, N., and Yahav, E. Abstract semantic differencing via speculative correlation. In Proceedings of the 2014 ACM International Conference on Object Oriented Programming Systems Languages & #38; Applications (New York, NY, USA, 2014), OOPSLA '14, ACM, pp. 811–828

30. Sankaranarayanan, S., Ivančić, F., Shlyakhter, I., Gupta, A.: Static Analysis in Disjunctive Numerical Domains. In: Yi, K. (ed.) SAS 2006. LNCS, vol. 4134, pp. 3–17. Springer, Heidelberg (2006)

31. Sebag, M. Delaying the choice of bias: A disjunctive version space approach. In ICML (1996), Citeseer, pp. 444–452

32. Seghir, M. N., and Kroening, D. Counterexample-guided precondition inference. In Programming Languages and Systems. Springer, 2013, pp. 451–471

33. Sen, K., Agha, G.: CUTE and jCUTE: Concolic Unit Testing and Explicit Path Model-Checking Tools. In: Ball, T., Jones, R.B. (eds.) CAV 2006. LNCS, vol. 4144, pp. 419–423. Springer, Heidelberg (2006)

34. Sharma, R., Aiken, A.: From Invariant Checking to Invariant Inference Using Randomized Search. In: Biere, A., Bloem, R. (eds.) CAV 2014. LNCS, vol. 8559, pp. 88–105. Springer, Heidelberg (2014)

35. Sharma, R., Schkufza, E., Churchill, B. R., and Aiken, A. Data-driven equivalence checking. In OOPSLA (2013), pp. 391–406

36. Srivastava, S., and Gulwani, S. Program verification using templates over predicate abstraction. In ACM Sigplan Notices (2009), vol. 44, ACM, pp. 223–234

37. Thakur, A., Elder, M., Reps, T.: Bilateral Algorithms for Symbolic Abstraction. In: Miné, A., Schmidt, D. (eds.) SAS 2012. LNCS, vol. 7460, pp. 111–128. Springer, Heidelberg (2012)

Exact Heap Summaries for Symbolic Execution

Benjamin Hillery[1]([✉]), Eric Mercer[1], Neha Rungta[2], and Suzette Person[3]

[1] Brigham Young University, Provo, UT, USA
ben.hillery@byu.edu
[2] NASA Ames, Mountain View, CA, USA
[3] University of Nebraska, Lincoln, NE, USA

Abstract. A recent trend in the analysis of object-oriented programs is the modeling of references as sets of guarded values, enabling multiple heap shapes to be represented in a single state. A fundamental problem with using these guarded value sets is the inability to generate test inputs in a manner similar to symbolic execution based analyses. Although several solutions have been proposed, none have been proven to be sound and complete with respect to the heap properties provable by generalized symbolic execution (GSE). This work presents a method for initializing input references in a symbolic input heap using guarded value sets that exactly preserves GSE semantics. A correctness proof for the initialization scheme is provided with a proof-of-concept implementation. Results from an empirical evaluation on a common set of GSE data structure benchmarks show an increase in the size and number of analyzed heaps over existing GSE representations. The initialization technique can be used to ensure that guarded value set based symbolic execution engines operate in a provably correct manner with regards to symbolic references as well as provide the ability to generate concrete heaps that serve as test inputs to the program.

Keywords: Symbolic execution · Symbolic references · Constraint-based reasoning

1 Introduction

In symbolic execution, the values of program variables are represented as constraints over the program's inputs. During the course of an execution, a program variable may assume a number of possible values under a variety of different conditions. One way to represent this behavior is by pairing each possible value with the constraints under which it is assumed. A set of such value-constraint pairs, called a *guarded value set*[1], represents the state of a program variable.

Guarded value sets are rising in importance in the representation of reference values. First appearing in Verification-Condition Generator (VCG) style techniques [12,35], guarded value sets are a convenient way to represent sets of heap

---

[1] Guarded value sets are variously referred to in the literature as *guarded location sets*, *symbolic value sets*, or *value summaries*. The term guarded value set is sometimes abbreviated in this text as *value set*.

© Springer-Verlag Berlin Heidelberg 2016
B. Jobstmann and K.R.M. Leino (Eds.): VMCAI 2016, LNCS 9583, pp. 206–225, 2016.
DOI: 10.1007/978-3-662-49122-5_10

shapes. More recently, guarded value sets are being used in symbolic execution for the purposes of modularization [36], state merging [30], and for determining invariants [16,32].

A common hurdle to using guarded value sets is the treatment of *symbolic heap inputs*. A symbolic heap input refers to a portion of the heap that is yet unconstrained, meaning that it is able to take on any shape. For many applications, such a symbolic heap input is desirable for modeling sets of heaps in the analysis: the operations on the heap discovered in the analysis further constrain the symbolic heap input structure.

Precisely modeling operations on unconstrained heaps is challenging because it requires formulating logical predicates over an input domain that contains a potentially unbounded number of hidden references [7,27]. Generalized symbolic execution (GSE), and its variants, provide an accurate solution, but they quickly produce an overwhelming number of execution paths for all but the simplest heap shapes [11,21]. Other efforts to create heap inputs for guarded value set-based analysis techniques have yet to produce results provably equivalent to GSE [12,35]. Thus, despite the advantages of using guarded value sets, it remains an open question to how they can be used in symbolic execution to automatically model all possible program behaviors in the case of an arbitrary input heap.

The contribution of this work is *symbolic initialization* for uninitialized references in a fully symbolic heap. Where GSE lazily instantiates uninitialized references to either NULL, a new instance of the correct type, or an alias to a previously initialized object, symbolic initialization creates a guarded value set expressing all of these eventualities in a single symbolic heap. Where GSE branches the search space on each choice, symbolic initialization does not. Symbolic initialization only branches on reference compares; thus it creates equivalence classes over heaps and only partitions those classes at compares to indicate heaps where the references alias and heaps where the references do not.

This paper includes a proof that symbolic initialization is sound and complete with respect to properties provable by GSE. Such a result is important because it means that symbolic initialization can be used to create test inputs for other analyses in a way that is provably correct with regards to GSE: there are no missing GSE heaps and there are no extra GSE heaps.

A proof-of-concept implementation of symbolic initialization is reported in this paper. The implementation is for Java in the Java Pathfinder tool. It demonstrates on a common set of data structure benchmarks for GSE evaluation [3,9,11,16,28] an increase in the number of heaps that can be analyzed when compared to existing GSE methods. Although guarded value sets require extra interaction with an SMT solver, the savings in representing multiple heap shapes in a single structure can overcome the cost of the solver calls. For the tree structures in the standard benchmarks, the comparison shows an exponential increase in the number of heaps that can be analyzed, meaning that other approaches based on GSE fail to complete in the allotted time.

In summary, this paper presents a new initialization technique called symbolic initialization that enables the use of guarded value sets in heap representations

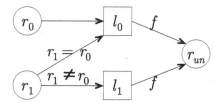

Fig. 1. Example symbolic heap

in a sound and complete manner. Such a result means that guarded value set-based analysis methods [12,16,30,32,35,36] can use symbolic initialization to be assured of precision with regard to GSE semantics. This includes generating concrete heaps for test input generation.

2   A Symbolic Heap

A *symbolic heap*, as defined in this work, is a tuple $(L\ R\ \phi\ \eta)$, indicating a *location map* L, a *reference map* R, a *path condition* ϕ, and an *environment* η. Given a reference r in the heap, $L(r) = \{(\phi\ l)\ ...\}$ is the guarded value set associated with r. The constraint associated with each location is a guard representing the conditions under which the associated reference maps to the given location. By definition, any location appears at most once in any given value set. Unions of value sets containing the same location are resolved by forming a disjunction of the constraints from each set. $R(l, f) = r$ is the reference associated with the given location-field pair in the heap.

The path condition is a predicate of references in the heap. The environment is a partial function so $\eta(x) = r$ is the reference r associated with variable x. The notation $\eta' = \eta[x \mapsto v]$ defines a new partial function η' that is the same as η except that the variable x now maps to v. This notation for update is used with L and R as well.

Conceptually, the symbolic heap may be thought of as a bipartite graph. Figure 1 shows an example symbolic heap graph. References are represented by circles and locations are represented by squares. Arrows leaving references correspond to the guarded value sets returned by the L function, and arrows leaving the squares correspond to the R function. The reference r_1 in the figure has two members in its guarded value set, so the location pointed to by r_1 depends on its aliasing relationship to r_0.

The reference r_{un} is a special reference to indicate something that has yet to be initialized. In general, every symbolic heap contains two special locations, null (l_{null}), and uninitialized (l_{un}), with corresponding references r_{null} and r_{un} where $L(r_{null}) = \{(\textbf{true}\ l_{null})\}$ and $L(r_{un}) = \{(\textbf{true}\ l_{un})\}$.

A *well-formed* symbolic heap is *deterministic* and *type consistent*. Determinism means a reference in $(L\ R\ \phi\ \eta)$ cannot point to multiple locations simultaneously: $\forall r \in L^{\leftarrow}\ (\forall(\phi\ l), (\phi'\ l') \in L(r)\ ((l \neq l' \vee \phi \neq \phi') \Rightarrow (\phi \wedge \phi' = \textbf{false}))$

where $L^{\leftarrow}$ is the pre-image of L. Type consistent means that all locations in a guarded value set from a reference have the same type[2]: $\forall r \in L^{\leftarrow}$ $(\forall(\phi\ l), (\phi'\ l') \in L(r)$ $((\text{Type}(l) = \text{Type}(l'))))$

3   Operational Semantics

This paper defines symbolic initialization using a small-step operational semantics in the context of a syntactic machine with a CESK architecture [15,34]. The surface syntax (input) and machine syntax (state) are shown in Fig. 2. The machine syntax omits the list based syntactic structures for the partial functions in the heap etc. Terminals are in bold face while non-terminals are italicized. Ellipses indicate zero or more repetitions. Tuples omit the commas for compactness. The language only considers objects as values and does not support looping structures to focus the discussion on the symbolic heap representation.

$$
\begin{aligned}
P &::= (\mu\ (C\ m)) \\
\mu &::= (CL\ ...) \\
T &::= \textbf{bool}\ |\ C \\
CL &::= (\textbf{class}\ C\ ([C\ f]\ ...)(M\ ...)) \\
M &::= (T\ m\ [T\ x]\ e) \\
e &::= x\ |\ (\textbf{new}\ C)\ |\ (e\ \$\ f)\ |\ (x\ \$\ f := e)\ |\ (e = e) \\
&\quad |\ (\textbf{if}\ e\ e\ \textbf{else}\ e)\ |\ (\textbf{var}\ T\ x := e\ \textbf{in}\ e)\ |\ (e\ @\ m\ e) \\
&\quad |\ (x := e)\ |\ (\textbf{begin}\ e\ ...)\ |\ v \\
x &::= \textbf{this}\ |\ id \\
f,m,C &::= id \\
v &::= r\ |\ \textbf{null}\ |\ \textbf{true}\ |\ \textbf{false}\ |\ \textbf{error} \\
r &::= \textbf{number}
\end{aligned}
$$

(a)

$$
\begin{aligned}
\phi &::= (\phi)\ |\ \phi \bowtie \phi\ |\ \neg\phi\ |\ \textbf{true}\ |\ \textbf{false}\ |\ r = r\ |\ r \neq r \\
s &::= (\mu\ L\ R\ \phi\ \eta\ e\ k) \\
k &::= \textbf{end}\ |\ (*\ \$\ f \to k)\ |\ (x\ \$\ f := *\ \to k) \\
&\quad |\ (*\ =\ e \to k)\ |\ (v\ =\ *\ \to k)\ |\ (\textbf{if}\ *\ e\ \textbf{else}\ e \to k) \\
&\quad |\ (\textbf{var}\ T\ x := *\ \textbf{in}\ e \to k)\ |\ (x := *\ \to k) \\
&\quad |\ (*\ @\ m\ e \to k)\ |\ (v\ @\ m\ *\ \to k) \\
&\quad |\ (\textbf{begin}\ *\ (e\ ...) \to k)\ |\ (\textbf{pop}\ \eta\ k)
\end{aligned}
$$

(b)

Fig. 2. (a) The surface syntax. (b) The machine syntax.

A program, P, is a registry of classes, μ, with a tuple indicating a class, C, and a method, m, where execution starts. For simplicity in presentation, Booleans are the only primitive type, classes have only non-primitive fields, and methods have a single parameter. Expressions, e, include statements, and they use ':='

---

[2] Although not treated in this presentation, the concept naturally extends to polymorphic languages.

to indicate assignment and '=' to indicate comparison. The dot-operator for field access is replaced by '**\$**', and the dot-operator for method invocation is replaced by '**@**'. There is no explicit return statement; rather, the value of the last expression is used as the return value. A variable is always indicated by x and a value by v. A value can be a reference in the heap, r, or any of the special values shown in Fig. 2(a).

The machine state s includes the program registry μ, the symbolic heap, the current expression (i.e., program), and the continuation k. The registry never changes so it is omitted from the state tuple in the rest of the presentation. The continuation k indicates with the symbol * where the expression e came from, stores temporary computation, and keeps track of the next continuation. For example, the continuation (* **\$** $f \rightarrow k$) indicates that the machine is evaluating the expression for the object reference on which the field f is going to be accessed. Once the field access is complete, the machine continues with k.

The semantics are expressed as rewrites on strings using pattern matching. Consider the rewrite rule for the beginning of a field access instruction:

FIELD ACCESS(EVAL)
$$(L\ R\ \phi\ \eta\ (e\ \textbf{\$}\ f)\ k) \rightarrow_J (L\ R\ \phi\ \eta\ e\ (*\ \textbf{\$}\ f \rightarrow k))$$

If the string representing the current state matches the left side, then it creates the new string on the right. In this example, the new string on the right is now evaluating the expression e in the field access, and it includes the continuation indicating that it still needs to complete the actual field access once the expression is evaluated.

The rewrite relations for the more mundane portions of the language that do not update the symbolic heap are in [20]. Excepting NEW, the rules do not update the heap, and are largely concerned with argument evaluation in an expected way. It is assumed that only type safe programs are input to the machine so there is no type checking. The machine halts if no rewrite is enabled. In the rest of this paper the relation $s \rightarrow_J s'$ indicates that two states are related by these more mundane rules.

4   GSE

This section introduces GSE semantics on which symbolic initialization builds. GSE and its variants have the same non-deterministic choice given a reference to an uninitialized object; that reference can point to null, a new instance of an object with the correct type, or to an object of the same type that has been instantiated previously by GSE [6,10,21,28]. The objects instantiated for new instances are referred to as the *input heap*. Only these objects comprise the potential alias set when GSE encounters references to uninitialized objects. In general, the GSE search space branches at uninitialized objects, and the number of branches depends on the size of the input heap.

The lazy initialization rules for GSE on the symbolic heap are in Fig. 3: NULL, new, and alias. The symbol C represents a type (or class) while *fields*(C) returns the fields in the type. The function $\mathbb{UN}(L, R, r, f) = \{(\phi\ l)\ ...\}$ returns constraint-location pairs where the field f is uninitialized.

$$\mathbb{UN}(L, R, r, f) = \{(\phi\ l) \mid (\phi\ l) \in L(r) \wedge \exists \phi'((\phi'\ l_{un}) \in L(R(l, f)) \wedge \mathbb{S}(\phi \wedge \phi'))\}$$

The function $\mathbb{S}(\phi \wedge \phi')$ returns true if there is a satisfying assignment of references for $\phi \wedge \phi'$; otherwise it returns false.

The rules rely on fresh references and locations that strictly increase so it is possible to minimize over a set to find the first created (i.e., references and locations are ordered). As such, the $\min_l$ function is able to return $(\phi_x\ l_x)$ the earliest created uninitialized location in a set, and similarly, $\min_r$ is able to return the earliest created reference in a set. Further, references are partitioned to support latter proofs: $\mathrm{init}_r()$ for the input heap; $\mathrm{fresh}_r()$ for *auxiliary literals*; and $\mathrm{stack}_r()$ for *stack literals*. In general, as shown in the next section, only input heap references appear in constraints to express potential aliasing, and only stack references appear in environments, expressions, or continuations. Finally, the *isInit* function is true for initialized references from the input heap (i.e., potential aliases).

How the lazy initialization is used is defined in Fig. 4 with the $\rightarrow_g$ relation collecting all the rules into a single relation on states. GSE initialization takes place on the field-access rule in Fig. 4, using the $\rightarrow_I^*$ relation from Fig. 3, to ensure the accessed field is instantiated. Initialization in GSE never happens for more than one object on any use of $\rightarrow_I^*$: the set Λ is either empty or contains exactly one location. This property is an artifact of how GSE case splits when it instantiates: each choice, NULL, new, or an alias, is a new unique heap. This changes in the next section with the new symbolic initialization that collects all the choices into a single heap using guarded value sets. The field-write rule also uses θ to represent a set of constraint-location pairs, which in GSE, again should always be a singleton set for the same reason as previously mentioned.

The rest of the rules in Fig. 4 do not initialize, but they are included to elucidate how symbolic initialization differs from GSE with lazy initialization. In particular, there is no branching in the search space on reference compare for GSE because references point to a single location after initialization. The new symbolic initialization using guarded value sets in this papers changes this behavior.

5   Symbolic Initialization

This work presents a new initialization scheme which avoids the nondeterminism introduced by GSE. Called *symbolic initialization*, this scheme leverages the core idea in generalized symbolic execution with lazy initialization, using on-the-fly reasoning to model a black-box input heap during symbolic execution. Unlike GSE, symbolic initialization constructs a single symbolic heap and polynomially-sized path condition for each control flow path.

There are three sets of rewrite rules specific to the symbolic initialization algorithm: (i) rules to initialize symbolic references, (ii) rules to perform field dereferences and writes, and (iii) rules to check equality and inequality of references. Rules relating to (ii) and (iii) are similar to previously proposed methods

$$\text{INITIALIZE (NULL)}$$

$$\Lambda = \mathbb{UN}(L, R, r, f) \qquad \Lambda \neq \emptyset \qquad (\phi_x \; l_x) = \min_l(\Lambda)$$
$$r' = \text{fresh}_r() \qquad \theta_{null} = \{(\textbf{true} \; l_{null})\}$$

$$\overline{(L \; R \; r \; f \; C) \rightarrow_I (L[r' \mapsto \theta_{null}] \; R[(l_x, f) \mapsto r'] \; r \; f \; C)}$$

$$\text{INITIALIZE (NEW)}$$

$$\Lambda = \mathbb{UN}(L, R, r, f) \qquad \Lambda \neq \emptyset \qquad (\phi_x \; l_x) = \min_l(\Lambda)$$
$$r' = \text{init}_r() \qquad l' = \text{fresh}_l(C)$$
$$\theta_{new} = \{(\textbf{true} \; l')\}$$
$$R' = R[\forall f \in \textit{fields}(C) \; ((l' \; f) \mapsto r_{un})]$$

$$\overline{(L \; R \; r \; f \; C) \rightarrow_I (L[r' \mapsto \theta_{new}] \; R'[(l_x, f) \mapsto r'] \; r \; f \; C)}$$

$$\text{INITIALIZE (ALIAS)}$$

$$\Lambda = \mathbb{UN}(L, R, r, f) \qquad \Lambda \neq \emptyset \qquad (\phi_x \; l_x) = \min_l(\Lambda)$$
$$r' = \text{fresh}_r()$$
$$\rho = \{(r_a \; l_a) \mid \text{isInit}(r_a) \wedge r_a = \min_r(R^{\leftarrow}[l_a]) \wedge \text{type}(l_a) = C\}$$
$$(r_a \; l_a) \in \rho \qquad \theta_{alias} = \{(\textbf{true} \; l_a)\}$$

$$\overline{(L \; R \; r \; f \; C) \rightarrow_I (L[r' \mapsto \theta_{alias}] \; R[(l_x, f) \mapsto r'] \; r \; f \; C)}$$

$$\text{INITIALIZE (END)}$$

$$\Lambda = \mathbb{UN}(L, R, r, f) \qquad \Lambda = \emptyset$$

$$\overline{(L \; R \; r \; f \; C) \rightarrow_I (L \; R \; r \; f \; C)}$$

Fig. 3. Initialization for generalized symbolic execution, $s:: = (L \; R \; r \; fC)$, with $s \rightarrow_I^*$ $s' = s \rightarrow_I \cdots \rightarrow_I s' \rightarrow_I s'$.

utilizing guarded value sets [12,30]. The rules for (i) are novel in how they preserve GSE semantics.

In Fig. 5, similar to before, given the uninitialized set Λ for field f, the $\min_l$ function returns $(\phi_x \; l_x)$ which represents the earliest created uninitialized location in that set. The set ρ contains reference-location pairs that represent potential aliases, where isInit() ensures that the references are initialized. There are four cases encoded in the symbolic heap. The first three correspond to the three types of choices made during lazy initialization: (i) θ_{null} represents the condition where l_{null} is possible, (ii) θ_{new} represents the case where r_f points to a fresh location, (iii) each member of θ_{alias} restricts r_f to a particular alias in ρ, and at the same time, not alias any member of ρ that was initialized earlier than the current choice.

Unlike the first three cases, which correspond directly to GSE initialization rules, θ_{orig}, case (iv), is unique to symbolic initialization. In this case, θ_{orig} implements conditional initialization to preserve the original heap structure. This step is necessary in order to maintain *homomorphism* (i.e., equivalent shapes) between symbolic heaps created using symbolic initialization and the GSE heaps they are intended to represent. The sets from each of the four cases are added into the heap on r_f after the fields for l_f are initialized to r_{un}.

FIELD ACCESS

$$\frac{\{(\phi \ l)\} = L(r) \quad l \neq l_{null} \quad C = \text{type}(l, f)}{(L \ R \ r \ f \ C) \rightarrow_I^* (L' \ R' \ r \ f \ C)}$$
$$\frac{\{(\phi' \ l')\} = L'(R'(l, f)) \quad r' = \text{stack}_r()}{(L \ R \ \phi_g \ \eta \ r \ (* \ \$ \ f \rightarrow k)) \rightarrow_g^A}$$
$$(L'[r' \mapsto (\phi' \ l')] \ R' \ \phi_g \ \eta \ r' \ k)$$

FIELD ACCESS (NULL)

$$\frac{\{(\phi \ l)\} = L(r) \quad l = l_{null}}{(L \ R \ \phi_g \ \eta \ r \ (* \ \$ \ f \rightarrow k)) \rightarrow_g^{A'}}$$
$$(L \ R \ \phi_g \ \eta \ \textbf{error end})$$

FIELD WRITE

$$r_x = \eta(x)$$
$$\frac{\{(\phi \ l)\} = L(r_x) \quad l \neq l_{null}}{\theta = L(r) \quad r' = \text{fresh}_r()}$$
$$\frac{}{(L \ R \ \phi_g \ \eta \ r \ (x \ \$ \ f := * \ \rightarrow \ k)) \rightarrow_g^W}$$
$$(L[r' \mapsto \theta] \ R[(l \ f) \mapsto r'] \ \phi_g \ \eta \ r \ k)$$

FIELD WRITE (NULL)

$$r_x = \eta(x)$$
$$\frac{\{(\phi \ l)\} = L(r_x) \quad l = l_{null}}{(L \ R \ \phi_g \ \eta \ r \ (x \ \$ \ f := * \ \rightarrow \ k)) \rightarrow_g^{W'}}$$
$$(L \ R \ \phi_g \ \eta \ \textbf{error end})$$

EQUALS (REFERENCE-TRUE)

$$\frac{L(r_0) = L(r_1) \quad \phi'_g = (\phi_g \wedge r_0 = r_1)}{(L \ R \ \phi_g \ \eta \ r_0 \ (r_1 = * \ \rightarrow \ k)) \rightarrow_g^E}$$
$$(L \ R \ \phi'_g \ \eta \ \textbf{true} \ k)$$

EQUALS (REFERENCE-FALSE)

$$\frac{L(r_0) \neq L(r_1) \quad \phi'_g = (\phi_g \wedge r_0 \neq r_1)}{(L \ R \ \phi_g \ \eta \ r_0 \ (r_1 = * \ \rightarrow \ k)) \rightarrow_g^{E'}}$$
$$(L \ R \ \phi'_g \ \eta \ \textbf{false} \ k)$$

Fig. 4. Generalized symbolic execution with lazy initialization indicated by $\rightarrow_g = \rightarrow_g^A \cup \rightarrow_g^{A'} \cup \rightarrow_g^W \cup \rightarrow_g^{W'} \cup \rightarrow_g^E \cup \rightarrow_g^{E'} \cup \rightarrow_g^J$.

Figure 6 illustrates the initialization process. The graph in Fig. 6(a) represents the initial heap. The reference superscripts s and i indicate the partition containing the reference: input, auxiliary, or stack. In Fig. 6, r_0^s represents a stack

INITIALIZATION

$$\Lambda = \text{UN}(L, R, r, f)$$
$$\Lambda \neq \emptyset \quad (\phi_x \ l_x) = \min_l(\Lambda) \quad r_f = \text{init}_r() \quad l_f = \text{fresh}_l(C)$$
$$\rho = \{(r_a \ l_a) \mid \text{isInit}(r_a) \wedge r_a = \min_r(R^\leftarrow[l_a]) \wedge \text{type}(l_a) = C\}$$
$$\theta_{null} = \{(\phi \ l_{null}) \mid \phi = (\phi_x \wedge r_f = r_{null})\}$$
$$\theta_{new} = \{(\phi \ l_f) \mid \phi = (\phi_x \wedge r_f \neq r_{null} \wedge (\wedge_{(r'_a \ l'_a) \in \rho} r_f \neq r'_a))\}$$
$$\theta_{alias} = \{(\phi \ l_a) \mid \exists r_a \ ((r_a \ l_a) \in \rho \wedge \phi = (\phi_x \wedge r_f \neq r_{null} \wedge$$
$$r_f = r_a \wedge (\wedge_{(r'_a \ l'_a) \in \rho} (r'_a < r_a) r_f \neq r'_a)))\}$$
$$\theta_{orig} = \{(\phi \ l_{orig}) \mid \exists \phi_{orig}((\phi_{orig} \ l_{orig}) \in L(R(l_x, f)) \wedge \phi = (\neg \phi_x \wedge \phi_{orig})\}$$
$$\theta = \theta_{null} \cup \theta_{new} \cup \theta_{alias} \cup \theta_{orig} \quad R' = R[\forall f \in fields(C) \ ((l_f \ f) \mapsto r_{un})]$$
$$\overline{(L \ R \ r \ f \ C) \rightarrow_S (L[r_f \mapsto \theta] \ R'[(l_x, f) \mapsto r_f] \ r \ f \ C)}$$

Fig. 5. Initializing fields, $s :: = (L \ R \ r \ f \ C)$, with $s \rightarrow_S^* s' = s \rightarrow_S \cdots \rightarrow_S s'$.

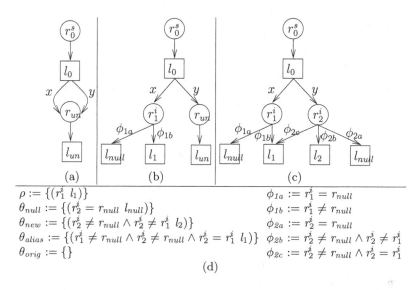

$\rho := \{(r_1^i \; l_1)\}$

$\theta_{null} := \{(r_2^i = r_{null} \; l_{null})\}$

$\theta_{new} := \{(r_2^i \neq r_{null} \land r_2^i \neq r_1^i \; l_2)\}$

$\theta_{alias} := \{(r_1^i \neq r_{null} \land r_2^i \neq r_{null} \land r_2^i = r_1^i \; l_1)\}$

$\theta_{orig} := \{\}$

$\phi_{1a} := r_1^i = r_{null}$

$\phi_{1b} := r_1^i \neq r_{null}$

$\phi_{2a} := r_2^i = r_{null}$

$\phi_{2b} := r_2^i \neq r_{null} \land r_2^i \neq r_1^i$

$\phi_{2c} := r_2^i \neq r_{null} \land r_2^i = r_1^i$

(d)

Fig. 6. An example that initializes (**this \$** x) and (**this \$** y). (a) Initial heap structure. (b) After (**this \$** x) is initialized. (c) After (**this \$** y) is initialized. (d) Sets in the initialization rule and constraints on the edges.

reference for the **this** variable which has two fields x and y of the same type. Note that when no constraint is specified for a location, there is an implicit *true* constraint. For example, r_0^s points to l_0 on the constraint *true*. The fields x and y point to the uninitialized reference r_{un}. The graph in Fig. 6(b) represents the symbolic heap after the initialization of the (**this \$** x) field while the graph in Fig. 6(c) represents the symbolic heap after the initialization of the (**this \$** y) field following the initialization of (**this \$** x). The list in Fig. 6(d) represents the various sets constructed in the initialization for (**this \$** y).

There are two rewrite rules in Fig. 7, one for reading the value of a field (field-access) and the other for writing to a field (field-write). Both rules first check that the operations can be performed on a non-null location. The field-access rewrite rule in Fig. 7 dereferences a field of type C, recall that the heaps are type consistent and programs are type safe, and uses the $\rightarrow_S^*$ relation from Fig. 5, to get a new symbolic heap that is initialized on the field f. The symbolic heap is further modified to include a new stack reference pointing to the guarded value set (possible values of the field) returned during the dereferencing; the new stack reference is the return value from the VS operation.

Definition 1. *The VS function constructs the value set given a heap, reference, and desired field.*

$$VS(L, R, \phi_g, r, f) ::= \{(\phi \land \phi' \; l') \mid \exists l \; ((\phi \; l) \in L(r) \land (\phi' \; l') \in L(R(l, f)) \land S(\phi \land \phi' \land \phi_g))\}$$

For a reference r and field f, the value set function computes the guarded value set of locations and access path constraints that are feasible under the current path condition ϕ_g. The access path constraint is the union of two local constraints: the constraint ϕ from dereferencing r to location l, and the constraint ϕ' from dereferencing the field f of the location l to the actual location of the field, l'. This access path constraint, paired with location l', is a member of the value set only if its union with the path condition is satisfiable, ensuring that the access path is valid and feasible under the path condition.

For field-write in Fig. 7, after the non-null check and strengthening of the global heap constraint, it computes the current references associated with the field in every location in Ψ_x. Note that the reference r_x is the base reference whose field, r_{cur} is being written to, while the reference r is the target reference. The set Ψ_x contains tuples $(\phi\ l\ r_{cur})$ of constraints, locations, and references. These tuples represent access chains leading from r_x to the reference of the field, r_{cur}. The goal is to change the fields to no longer point to r_{cur}, but rather fresh references that have both the original locations before the write and the locations from the write in the value sets (i.e., conditional write). Since the target of the write is r, the rule checks that the constraints of the guarded value set $L(r)$ are satisfiable when accessed through the r_x chain in the strengthening function.

Definition 2. *The function* $\mathbb{ST}(L, r, \phi, \phi_g)$ *strengthens every constraint in* $L(r)$ *with* ϕ *and retains strengthened location-constraint pairs that are satisfiable with the path condition* ϕ_g:

$$\mathbb{ST}(L, r, \phi, \phi_g) ::= \{(\phi \wedge \phi'\ l') \mid (\phi'\ l') \in L(r) \wedge \\ \mathbb{S}(\phi \wedge \phi' \wedge \phi_g)\}$$

Constraints on locations are strengthened with new aliasing conditions and those that are feasible with the current path condition are retained.

Strengthening in the field write creates a value set, X, that contains two types of locations: those for the case where the write is feasible (the first call in X), and those for the case where it is not (the second call in X). In the case that ϕ is true then r_{cur} will point to the guarded value set $L(r)$. Whereas, if ϕ is false then r_{cur} will continue to point to the constraint location pair it currently references. As the references are immutable, the rule creates fresh references for each r_{cur} and points them to the appropriate value sets.

The rewrite rule to compare two references in the symbolic heap is shown in Fig. 8. The equals references-true rewrite rule returns true when two references r_0 and r_1 *can be equal*. Intuitively, Φ_α contains all constraints under which r_0 and r_1 may point to the same location in the symbolic heap. The second set, Φ_0, contains constraints under which the reference r_0 points to corresponding locations such that the reference r_1 *does not* point to those locations under any constraint. Finally, the set, Φ_1, contains constraints under which r_1 points to corresponding locations and r_0 *does not* point to those locations under any constraint. The three sets of constraints are used to create a new path condition ϕ'_g as an update of the current path condition ϕ_g. The update is accomplished by first taking the disjunction of the constraints in Φ_α to indicate that if any of the constraints

FIELD ACCESS

$$\frac{\begin{array}{c}\exists(\phi\ l)\in L(r)\ (l\neq l_{null}\wedge\mathbb{S}(\phi\wedge\phi_g))\\ \theta=\{\phi\mid(\phi\ l_{null})\in L(r)\wedge\mathbb{S}(\phi\wedge\phi_g)\}\\ \phi_g'=\phi_g\wedge(\wedge_{\phi\in\theta}\neg\phi)\\ \{C\}=\{C\mid\exists(\phi\ l)\in L(r)\ (C=\mathrm{type}(l,f))\}\\ (L\ R\ r\ f\ C)\to_{\mathcal{S}}^{*}(L'\ R'\ r\ f\ C)\qquad r'=\mathrm{stack}_r()\end{array}}{(L\ R\ \phi_g\ \eta\ r\ (*\ \$\ f\to k))\to_{\varsigma}^{A}(L'[r'\mapsto\mathbb{VS}(L',R',r,f,\phi_g')]\ R'\ \phi_g'\ \eta\ r'\ k)}$$

FIELD WRITE

$$\frac{\begin{array}{c}r_x=\eta(x)\qquad\exists(\phi\ l)\in L(r_x)\ (l\neq l_{null}\wedge\mathbb{S}(\phi\wedge\phi_g))\\ \theta=\{\phi\mid(\phi\ l_{null})\in L(r_x)\wedge\mathbb{S}(\phi\wedge\phi_g)\}\\ \phi_g'=\phi_g\wedge(\wedge_{\phi\in\theta}\neg\phi)\\ \Psi_x=\{(\phi\ l\ r_{cur})\mid(\phi\ l)\in L(r_x)\wedge r_{cur}=R(l,f)\}\\ X=\{(l\ \theta)\mid\exists\phi\ ((\phi\ l\ r_{cur})\in\Psi_x\wedge\theta=\mathbb{ST}(L,r,\phi,\phi_g')\cup\mathbb{ST}(L,r_{cur},\neg\phi,\phi_g'))\}\\ R'=R[\forall(l\ \theta)\in X\ ((l\ f)\mapsto\mathrm{fresh}_r())]\\ L'=L[\forall(l\ \theta)\in X\ (\exists r_{targ}\ (r_{targ}=R'(l,f)\wedge(r_{targ}\mapsto\theta)))]\end{array}}{(L\ R\ \phi_g\ \eta\ r\ (x\ \$\ f:=*\ \to\ k))\to_{\varsigma}^{W}(L'\ R'\ \phi_g'\ \eta\ r\ k)}$$

Fig. 7. Field read and write relations: Field-access, $\to_\varsigma^A$, and field-write, $\to_\varsigma^W$, rewrite rules for the $\to_\varsigma$ relation.

are satisfiable, then references r_0 and r_1 can be equal. This disjunction is then conjoined with ϕ_g to form ϕ_g'. Furthermore, the conjunctions of negations to the constraints in Φ_0 and Φ_1 is conjoined with ϕ_g'. This indicates for locations that are not common to the references, the negations of their constraints are satisfiable. The rule does not complete (i.e., is not feasible) if the new global constraint is not satisfied on any aliasing assignment. In such a case, the **true** outcome is not possible on any symbolic heap. Before the rewrite rule returns **true**, it verifies the satisfiability of the updated global heap constraint. The reference-false is the logical dual of the rule.

EQUALS (REFERENCES-TRUE)

$$\frac{\begin{array}{c}\Phi_\alpha=\{(\phi_0\wedge\phi_1)\mid\exists l\ ((\phi_0\ l)\in L(r_0)\wedge(\phi_1\ l)\in L(r_1))\}\\ \Phi_0=\{\phi_0\mid\exists l_0\ ((\phi_0\ l_0)\in L(r_0)\wedge\forall(\phi_1\ l_1)\in L(r_1)\ (l_0\neq l_1))\}\\ \Phi_1=\{\phi_1\mid\exists l_1\ ((\phi_1\ l_1)\in L(r_1)\wedge\forall(\phi_0\ l_0)\in L(r_0)\ (l_0\neq l_1))\}\\ \phi'=\phi\wedge(\vee_{\phi_\alpha\in\Phi_\alpha}\phi_\alpha)\wedge(\wedge_{\phi_0\in\Phi_0}\neg\phi_0)\wedge(\wedge_{\phi_1\in\Phi_1}\neg\phi_1)\\ \mathbb{S}(\phi')\end{array}}{(L\ R\ \phi\ \eta\ r_0\ (r_1=*\ \to\ k))\to_{\varsigma}^{E}(L\ R\ \phi'\ \eta\ \mathbf{true}\ k)}$$

Fig. 8. The reference compare rewrite rule for true, $\to_\varsigma^E$ outcomes.

Consider the example in Fig. 6(c). In order to compare r_1^i and r_2^i, the Equals rule gets the guarded value set associated with each of the references:

$$L(r_1^i) = \{(\phi_{1a}\ l_{null})\ (\phi_{1b}\ l_1)\}$$

$$L(r_2^i) = \{(\phi_{2a}\ l_{null})\ (\phi_{2b}\ l_2)\ (\phi_{2c}\ l_1)\}$$

The three constraint sets are:

$$\Phi_\alpha = \{(\phi_{1a} \wedge \phi_{2a})(\phi_{1b} \wedge \phi_{2c})\}\ \Phi_0 = \{\}\ \Phi_1 = \{\phi_{2b}\}$$

Finally the global constraint is

$$\phi' = true \wedge [(\phi_{1a} \wedge \phi_{2a}) \vee (\phi_{1b} \wedge \phi_{2c})] \wedge \neg\phi_{2b}$$

6   Correctness

The theorems in this section establish the soundness and completeness of the symbolic heap approach with respect to GSE. Intuitively, the theorems imply that any properties proven with GSE can also be proven using the symbolic initialization algorithm. What follows is a brief description of the requisite terminology, followed by the theorem statements. The proofs for the theorems, as well as the complete set of semantic rules for GSE and symbolic initialization are in [20].

The theorems assert the existence of a bisimulation between sets of states related by GSE ($p \rightarrow_g p'$) and states related by the symbolic heap and update rules in this paper ($q \rightarrow_s q'$). The relations are on the universe of *well-formed* states S, which have the properties in Sect. 2 with the constraint that the states are *feasible*: successors exist unless at **end**. Let $p \rightarrow_g p'$ be a union over relations for GSE: $\rightarrow_g = \rightarrow_g^A \cup \rightarrow_g^{A'} \cup \rightarrow_g^W \cup \rightarrow_g^{W'} \cup \rightarrow_g^E \cup \rightarrow_g^{E'} \cup \rightarrow_J$, where A is a field access after evaluating the expression for the base reference (*** \$** $f \rightarrow k$), W is a field write after evaluating the expression for the right operand (x **\$** $f := \text{*} \rightarrow k$), E is a reference compare after evaluating the left and right operands ($v = \text{*} \rightarrow k$), the prime symbol indicates a null reference in the operation or a false outcome, and, is everything else in the language. Any state relation, say $\rightarrow_x^Y$, is extended to sets of states as

$$P \hookrightarrow_x^Y P' ::= \forall p \in P\ (\forall p'\ (p \rightarrow_x^Y p' \Leftrightarrow p' \in P'))$$

Let $\hookrightarrow_g$ be the extension of $\rightarrow_g$ to sets of states. From this extension, a new meta transition relation is defined over sets of states as

$$\rightsquigarrow_g ::= \hookrightarrow_g^A \cup \hookrightarrow_g^{A'} \cup \hookrightarrow_g^W \cup \hookrightarrow_g^{W'} \cup \hookrightarrow_g^E \cup \hookrightarrow_g^{E'} \cup \hookrightarrow_J$$

The relation captures the notion of splitting groups of heaps at certain operations. For example, suppose a set P contains a single state p with all references uninitialized. If p is a field access state, it has two potential successors in GSE: a non-null reference and a null reference. Thus, the $\leadsto_g$ relation has two successors and divides P into the two outcomes.

The functional equivalence between heaps in states p and q requires both a mapping to relate the two heaps and a constraint on the feasibility of that mapping in the presence of a path constraint from symbolic execution. Subscripts indicate state tuple members as in $p = (L_p\ R_p\ \phi_p\ \eta_p\ e_p\ k_p)$.

Definition 3. *A **homomorphism**, given the universe of field indices $\mathcal{F}$ and the universe of locations $\mathcal{L}$, is*

$$s_p \rightarrow_h s_q ::= \exists h : \mathcal{L} \mapsto \mathcal{L}\ (\forall l_\alpha\ (\forall l_\beta\ (\forall f \in \mathcal{F}\ (\forall \phi_\alpha\ ($$
$$(\phi_\alpha\ l_\alpha) \in L_p(R_p(l_\beta, f)) \Rightarrow$$
$$\exists \phi_\beta\ ((\phi_\beta\ h(l_\alpha)) \in L_q(R_q(h(l_\beta), f))\ ))))))$$

Definition 4. *The **homomorphism constraint** is*

$$\mathbb{HC}(p \rightarrow_h q) ::= \bigwedge \{\phi_b\ |\exists(\phi_a\ l) \in L_p^{\rightarrow}((\phi_b\ h(l)) \in L_q^{\rightarrow})\}$$

The notation $L_p^{\rightarrow}$ denotes the image of L_p. Functional equivalence asserts a common structure in the two heaps under certain conditions. It is used to relate states in $p \rightarrow_g p'$ to states in $q \rightarrow_\varsigma q'$.

Definition 5. *States $(p\ q)$ are in the **representation relation**, $p \sqsubset q$, if and only if, $\eta_p = \eta_q$, $e_p = e_q$, $k_p = k_q$, and there exists a homomorphism $p \rightarrow_h q$ such that $\mathbb{S}(\phi_q \wedge \mathbb{HC}(s_p \rightarrow_h s_q))$. The represented relation is extended to sets of states P and a single state q as $P \sqsubset q ::= \forall p\ (p \sqsubset q \Leftrightarrow p \in P)$.*

The statement $p \sqsubset q$ ensures that a functionally equivalent heap to the one in p is present, by the homomorphism, and valid, by the heap constraint and path constraint, in q. As the states in P are only differentiated by heaps and those states are only differentiated from q by both the heap and path constraint in q, $P \sqsubset q$ implies that q is representative of all the states in P up to the given point of execution expressed in ϕ_q.

Definition 6. *The **functional associated to bisimulation** applied to $\sqsubset$, denoted as $F_\sim(\sqsubset)$, is the set of all pairs $(P\ q)$ such that*

$$\forall P'\ (P \leadsto_g P' \Rightarrow \exists q'\ (q \rightarrow_\varsigma q' \wedge P' \sqsubset q')) \tag{1}$$

$$\forall q'\ (q \rightarrow_\varsigma q' \Rightarrow \exists P'\ (P \leadsto_g P' \wedge P' \sqsubset q')) \tag{2}$$

If $\sqsubset$ is a bisimulation, then the greatest fixed point of $F_\sim(\sqsubset)$ is the bisimilarity relation denoted by $\sim$.

Other than the use of a meta-relation, $\leadsto_g$, Definition 6 reasons over the typical forward and backward simulation [29].

In the following lemma, S is the universe of well-formed states, and $S_{FA} \subseteq S$ is the set of states at a field access continuation having computed the base reference.

Lemma 1 (FIELD ACCESS Preserves $\sqsubseteq \; \subseteq F_\sim(\sqsubseteq)$). *If $P \in 2^{S_{FA}}$ and $q \in S$ are such that $P \sqsubseteq q$, then $(P\ q)$ is in the functional associated to bisimulation.*

$$\forall P \in 2^{S_{FA}} \; (P \sqsubseteq q \Rightarrow (P\ q) \in F_\sim(\sqsubseteq))$$

Similar lemmas are proven for field write and equals reference. These require additional lemmas on the initialization relation $\rightarrow_S$: that it preserves determinism, the homomorphism, and the satisfiability of the homomorphism constraint.

Theorem 1. *The relation $\sqsubseteq$ is a bisimulation: $\sqsubseteq \; \subseteq \; \sim$*

Corollary 1 ($\rightarrow_\varsigma$ is Complete). *If $P \in 2^{S_A}$ and $q \in S$ are such that $P \sqsubseteq q$ then for any $p \in P \; \forall p' \; (p \xrightarrow{n}_g p' \Rightarrow \exists q' \; (q \xrightarrow{n}_\varsigma q' \wedge p' \sqsubseteq q'))$*

Corollary 2 ($\rightarrow_\varsigma$ is Sound). *If $P \in 2^{S_A}$ and $q \in S$ are such that $P \sqsubseteq q$ then $\forall q' \; (q \xrightarrow{n}_\varsigma q' \Rightarrow \exists p \in P \; (\exists p' \; (p \xrightarrow{n}_g p' \wedge p' \sqsubseteq q')))$*

7 Evaluation

The symbolic initialization algorithm is implemented as an extension to the Symbolic PathFinder (SPF) framework [26]. In addition to the operations presented in this paper, the implementation contains support for operations over integers, calculating per-path preconditions and postconditions, as well as generating test input heaps that exercise all feasible control flow paths. Future work is adding support for floating point operations, arrays, and bit-operations.

The symbolic initialization implementation uses jConstraints with the z3 solver [13,18,22]. The implementation takes advantage of incremental solving and employs caching for performance since only small portions of the heap constraint change during the search.

SPF includes an implementation of GSE with lazy initialization. In recent work, we implemented the Lazier and Lazier# algorithms in SPF [19]; these constitute the state of art approaches to case-splitting based lazy initialization techniques. The goal of our experiment is to evaluate the efficacy of our approach with respect to these other techniques for symbolic execution of programs with unbounded complex data input. The empirical study tries to answer the following research question: How does the cost of the symbolic initialization algorithm compare with that of the GSE and Lazier# algorithms?

The *independent* variable in the study is the k-bound; k-bounding bounds the length of a reference chain from the root of the heap [9]. The study selects three dependent variables and measures: (i) time, (ii) states explored, and (iii) paths generated. The *time* is the total time taken by each algorithm to explore the symbolic execution tree as well as total constraint solving time. The *states explored* represents the number of nodes in the symbolic execution tree, and the *paths generated* represents the number of unique paths in the symbolic execution tree.

The data structures evaluated are a standard set that is commonly used in analyses involving heap-manipulating programs [3,9,11,16,28], including a linked list, binary search tree, and red/black tree. The actual tests use a repOk() method (a class invariant) for data structures in object-oriented code to generate valid inputs for the methods under test via symbolic execution [3,33]. Note that this allows us to have precision in checking properties of the heap that is not possible in static analysis based techniques (i.e., the symbolic execution generated heaps satisfy the repOK() invariant) [12].

Table 1. Comparing symbolic initialization with the GSE and Lazier# algorithms.

Method	k	Time (seconds)			States			Paths		
		GSE	L#	SL	GSE	L#	SL	GSE	L#	SL
LinkedList	3	0.91	1.21	0.69	2465	2844	99	1656	1269	25
	4	2.92	3.35	0.91	25774	29977	155	17485	13550	39
	5	20.78	19.47	1.59	341164	400296	223	232743	181849	56
	6	280.56	299.19	2.36	5447980	6437201	303	3731094	2933027	76
	7	-	-	5.07	-	-	395	-	-	99
	8	-	-	17.49	-	-	499	-	-	125
	9	-	-	63.96	-	-	615	-	-	154
	10	-	-	206.93	-	-	743	-	-	186
BinarySearchTree	1	0.26	0.28	0.36	19	23	29	6	6	6
	2	0.83	1.28	0.93	143	143	145	43	42	33
	3	20.63	25.55	4.03	1953	1703	1485	515	515	328
	4	-	-	410.89	-	-	73635	-	-	15563
TreeMap	1	0.47	0.52	0.77	65	70	215	11	11	11
	2	8.99	9.73	4.72	1009	942	3219	127	122	73
	3	-	-	145.56	-	-	78695	-	-	887

The results of the experiments are presented in Table 1. Each row reports the results for the specified k-bound for each artifact evaluated. The columns show the total time in seconds, states explored, and paths generated for each algorithm. The headings GSE, L#, and SL correspond to the GSE, Lazier#, and symbolic initialization algorithms, respectively. A table entry of '-' indicates the analysis exceeded the allotted time bound of 1 hour.

The number of possible non-isomorphic heap configurations grows exponentially for case-splitting techniques with a monotonic increase in k, resulting in a corresponding exponential increase in analysis times. This is evident in all the examples in Table 1. The GSE and L# algorithms are unable to finish exploration in a time bound of one hour for $k \geq 7$ for the LinkedList, $k \geq 4$ for the BinarySearchTree, and $k \geq 3$ for the TreeMap examples. The improvement in analysis time for the symbolic initialization over the state of the art case splitting techniques range from 4.8x for BinarySearchTree at $k=3$, to 118x for LinkedList at $k=6$. In fact, for some k-bounds, a number of experiments complete exploration using the symbolic initialization algorithm in a few seconds whereas GSE or Lazier# are unable to finish, e.g., BinarySearchTree for $k=4$ and LinkedList for $k=8$.

The number of path explored by the symbolic initialization algorithm are strictly less than or equal to the number of paths explored by GSE for all the evaluated artifacts. This result means it is possible to do more efficient test case generation by using the generated path and corresponding symbolic heap solutions provided by the constraint solver to instantiate a set of concrete heaps. These heaps provide a smaller test suite to achieve control-flow path coverage as compared to GSE and Lazier#. Note that the ability to perform test input generation is another advantage of the symbolic initialization technique over static analysis approaches.

The number of states varies between algorithms, for example, GSE has additional points of nondeterminism during field reads, but in contrast reference compares are completely deterministic. Thus, in example programs with large numbers of reference compares, such as TreeMap, state counts for Lazier# and the symbolic initialization algorithm may exceed those for GSE. Observe that the additional states generated by the summary heap algorithm are unsatisfiable at the point of reference compares; this is why they do not contribute any additional branches in the final symbolic execution tree. More critically, the larger state count and the corresponding satisfiability checks on the constraint solver does not increase the overall runtime of the technique.

In summary, the benefits of avoiding case-splitting based non-determinism outweigh the increased complexity in the constraints over heaps due to the advances made in SMT solvers in these examples. In fact, the symbolic initialization algorithm can analyze certain types of programs with orders of magnitude greater efficiency than that of GSE or Lazier#, while covering exactly the same feasible control flow paths in the program.

8   Related Work

The symbolic heap methods in this work build upon a number of prior program analysis techniques that use guarded value sets to represent program state [12,14,30,32,35]. In particular, the field write and equals reference compare rules are similar to methods appearing in these works. The real contribution of symbolic initialization is the initialization part of the field access rules which preserves the GSE semantics. Guarded value set heap initialization was pioneered in Verification-Condition Generator (VCG) style techniques such as [35], where value sets were used to initialize aliasing-free tree-like heaps. The work in [12] relaxed the aliasing restrictions by using a pre-computed set of symbolic input heaps, but was instead limited to heaps without recursive data structures.

Recently, value sets have been adapted for use in symbolic execution, for the purposes of state merging [30,32] and invariant detection [16]. These methods demonstrate the utility of value sets in combination with symbolic execution. However, none of these techniques address the dereferencing of symbolic input references. Since dereferencing is a fundamental problem treated in this paper, these other works may be considered both orthogonal and complimentary to symbolic initialization.

Symbolic initialization also draws inspiration from lazy initialization, the core idea of GSE [21]. Several projects have used lazy initialization to conduct symbolic execution on programs with more general types, including references and arrays [2, 6, 10, 17]. Improvements to the basic lazy initialization algorithm have been proposed, including delaying aliasing choices [11], or checking initializations against invariants as they occur [4, 28]. However, these GSE techniques branch over multiple copies of the system state during dereferencing operations, exacerbating path explosion.

A number of dynamic symbolic execution (DSE) methods use some form of symbolic heap representation, including PEX [31] and SAGE [14]. These DSE methods have shown a high degree of utility in practical applications with a wide variety of real-world programs. PEX and SAGE use array theories to represent program state instead of guarded value sets. SAGE has been proven complete for programs whose memory allocations are independent of their inputs. This work is complementary to PEX and SAGE and could be leveraged to further improve those tools.

Several separation logic solvers have been proven to be sound and complete for heaps with linked lists [1, 8, 23], trees [25], or data structures satisfying user-supplied invariants [5]. Separation logic solvers can also reason about entailment which is a subject of future work for symbolic initialization. Solutions in separation logic do not lend themselves to test case generation which is a contribution of the new approach in this paper.

9 Conclusion

This paper presents a symbolic initialization algorithm for uninitialized references in a fully symbolic heap. Where GSE lazily instantiates uninitialized references to either NULL, a new instance of the correct type, or an alias to a previously initialized object, the symbolic initialization in this work creates a guarded value set expressing all of these eventualities in the same symbolic heap. The paper includes a proof that the symbolic initialization algorithm is sound and complete with respect to properties provable by GSE.

An initial implementation of the technique has been done within the Java PathFinder framework. The symbolic initialization algorithm outperforms state-of-the-art case-splitting based symbolic execution techniques, and in some cases, the performance gains are considerable in a set of common Java data structure artifacts used to benchmark symbolic representations. The performance gains in symbolic execution may naturally benefit a variety of analyses based on symbolic execution, for example, verification of properties, especially those related to the heap, test case generation, program evolution techniques such as directed incremental symbolic execution [24], and other back-end analyses. Potential future work includes evaluating the impact of analyses that rely on symbolic execution and solving the problem of detecting heap entailment.

References

1. Berdine, J., Calcagno, C., O'hearn, P.W.: A decidable fragment of separation logic. In: Lodaya, K., Mahajan, M. (eds.) FSTTCS 2004. LNCS, vol. 3328, pp. 97–109. Springer, Heidelberg (2004)
2. Blackshear, S., Chang, B.Y.E., Sridharan, M.: Thresher: Precise refutations for heap reachability. In: Proceedings of the 34th ACM SIGPLAN Conference on Programming Language Design and Implementation PLDI 2013, pp. 275–286. ACM, New York (2013)
3. Boyapati, C., Khurshid, S., Marinov, D.: Korat: automated testing based on java predicates. In: ACM SIGSOFT Software Engineering Notes, vol. 27, pp. 123–133. ACM (2002)
4. Braione, P., Denaro, G., Pezzè, M.: Symbolic execution of programs with heap inputs. In: Proceedings of the 2015 10th Joint Meeting on Foundations of Software Engineering, pp. 602–613. ACM (2015)
5. Brotherston, J., Fuhs, C., Pérez, J.A.N., Gorogiannis, N.: A decision procedure for satisfiability in separation logic with inductive predicates. In: Proceedings of the Joint Meeting of the Twenty-Third EACSL Annual Conference on Computer Science Logic (CSL) and the Twenty-Ninth Annual ACM/IEEE Symposium on Logic in Computer Science (LICS), p. 25. ACM (2014)
6. Cadar, C., Dunbar, D., Engler, D.R.: Klee: Unassisted and automatic generation of high-coverage tests for complex systems programs. In: Proceedings of the 8th USENIX Conference on Operating Systems Design and Implementation OSDI 2008, pp. 209–224. USENIX Association, Berkeley (2008)
7. Chen, T., Zhang, X.S., Guo, S.Z., Li, H.Y., Wu, Y.: State of the art: Dynamic symbolic execution for automated test generation. Future Gener. Comput. Syst. **29**(7), 1758–1773 (2013)
8. Cook, B., Haase, C., Ouaknine, J., Parkinson, M., Worrell, J.: Tractable reasoning in a fragment of separation logic. In: Katoen, J.-P., König, B. (eds.) CONCUR 2011. LNCS, vol. 6901, pp. 235–249. Springer, Heidelberg (2011)
9. Deng, X., Lee, J., et al.: Bogor/kiasan: A k-bounded symbolic execution for checking strong heap properties of open systems. In: 21st IEEE/ACM International Conference on Automated Software Engineering ASE 2006, pp. 157–166. IEEE (2006)
10. Deng, X., Robby, Hatcliff, J.: Kiasan/KUnit: Automatic test case generation and analysis feedback for open object-oriented systems. In: TAICPART-MUTATION, pp. 3–12 (2007)
11. Deng, X., Robby, Hatcliff, J.: Towards a case-optimal symbolic execution algorithm for analyzing strong properties of object-oriented programs. In: Fifth IEEE International Conference on Software Engineering and Formal Methods SEFM 2007, pp. 273–282, September 2007
12. Dillig, I., Dillig, T., Aiken, A., Sagiv, M.: Precise and compact modular procedure summaries for heap manipulating programs. In: Proceedings of the 32nd ACM SIGPLAN Conference on Programming Language Design and Implementation PLDI 2011, pp. 567–577. ACM, New York (2011)
13. Dimjašević, M., Giannakopoulou, D., Howar, F., Isberner, M., Rakamarić, Z., Raman, V.: The dart, the psyco, and the doop. In: ACM SIGSOFT Software Engineering Notes, vol. 40, pp. 1–5. ACM (2015)
14. Elkarablieh, B., Godefroid, P., Levin, M.Y.: Precise pointer reasoning for dynamic test generation. In: Proceedings of the Eighteenth International Symposium on Software Testing and Analysis, pp. 129–140. ACM (2009)

15. Felleisen, M., Hieb, R.: The revised report on the syntactic theories of sequential control and state. Theoret. Comput. Sci. **103**(2), 235–271 (1992)
16. Ferrara, P., Müller, P., Novacek, M.: Automatic inference of heap properties exploiting value domains. In: D'Souza, D., Lal, A., Larsen, K.G. (eds.) VMCAI 2015. LNCS, vol. 8931, pp. 393–411. Springer, Heidelberg (2015)
17. Filieri, A., Frias, M.F., Păsăreanu, C.S., Visser, W.: Model counting for complex data structures. In: Fischer, B., Geldenhuys, J. (eds.) SPIN 2015. LNCS, vol. 9232, pp. 222–241. Springer, Heidelberg (2015)
18. Giannakopoulou, D., Howar, F., Isberner, M., Lauderdale, T., Rakamarić, Z., Raman, V.: Taming test inputs for separation assurance. In: Proceedings of the 29th IEEE/ACM International Conference on Automated Software Engineering (ASE), pp. 373–384. ACM (2014)
19. Hillery, B., Mercer, E., Rungta, N., Person, S.: Towards a lazier symbolic pathfinder. SIGSOFT Softw. Eng. Notes **39**(1), 1–5 (2014)
20. Hillery, B., Mercer, E., Rungta, N., Person, S.: Exact heap summaries for symbolic execution. Technical report, Brigham Young University (2015). http://students.cs.byu.edu/egm/papers/SH-long.pdf
21. Khurshid, S., Păsăreanu, C.S., Visser, W.: Generalized symbolic execution for model checking and testing. In: Garavel, H., Hatcliff, J. (eds.) TACAS 2003. LNCS, vol. 2619, pp. 553–568. Springer, Heidelberg (2003)
22. de Moura, L., Bjørner, N.S.: Z3: An efficient SMT solver. In: Ramakrishnan, C.R., Rehof, J. (eds.) TACAS 2008. LNCS, vol. 4963, pp. 337–340. Springer, Heidelberg (2008)
23. Navarro Pérez, J.A., Rybalchenko, A.: Separation logic+ superposition calculus = heap theorem prover. In: ACM SIGPLAN Notices, vol. 46, pp. 556–566. ACM (2011)
24. Person, S., Yang, G., Rungta, N., Khurshid, S.: Directed incremental symbolic execution. In: PLDI, pp. 504–515 (2011)
25. Piskac, R., Wies, T., Zufferey, D.: Automating separation logic with trees and data. In: Biere, A., Bloem, R. (eds.) CAV 2014. LNCS, vol. 8559, pp. 711–728. Springer, Heidelberg (2014)
26. Păsăreanu, C.S., Visser, W., Bushnell, D.H., Geldenhuys, J., Mehlitz, P.C., Rungta, N.: Symbolic PathFinder: integrating symbolic execution with model checking for Java bytecode analysis. Autom. Softw. Eng. **20**(3), 391–425 (2013)
27. Qu, X., Robinson, B.: A case study of concolic testing tools and their limitations. In: 2011 International Symposium on Empirical Software Engineering and Measurement (ESEM), pp. 117–126. IEEE (2011)
28. Rosner, N., Geldenhuys, J., Aguirre, N., Visser, W., Frias, M.: BLISS: Improved symbolic execution by bounded lazy initialization with sat support. Software Engineering, IEEE Transactions on PP(99), 1–1 (2015)
29. Sangiorgi, D.: Introduction to Bisimulation and Coinduction. Cambridge University Press, New York (2011)
30. Sen, K., Necula, G., Gong, L., Choi, P.W.: MultiSE: Multi-path symbolic execution using value summaries. Technical Report UCB/EECS-2014-173, University of California at Berkely Department of Electrical Engineering and Computer Sciences, October 2014
31. Tillmann, Nikolai, de Halleux, Jonathan: Pex–White Box Test Generation for.NET. In: Beckert, Bernhard, Hähnle, Reiner (eds.) TAP 2008. LNCS, vol. 4966, pp. 134–153. Springer, Heidelberg (2008)

32. Torlak, E., Bodik, R.: A lightweight symbolic virtual machine for solver-aided host languages. In: Proceedings of the 35th ACM SIGPLAN Conference on Programming Language Design and Implementation, p. 54. ACM (2014)

33. Visser, W., Păsăreanu, C.S., Khurshid, S.: Test input generation with Java PathFinder. ACM SIGSOFT Softw. Eng. Notes **29**(4), 97–107 (2004)

34. Wesonga, S.O.: Javalite - An Operational Semantics for Modeling Java Programs. Master's thesis, Brigham Young University, Provo UT (2012)

35. Xie, Y., Aiken, A.: Scalable error detection using boolean satisfiability. In: Proceedings of the 32nd ACM SIGPLAN-SIGACT Symposium on Principles of Programming Languages POPL 2005, pp. 351–363. ACM, New York (2005)

36. Yorsh, G., Yahav, E., Chandra, S.: Generating precise and concise procedure summaries. In: ACM SIGPLAN Notices, vol. 43, pp. 221–234. ACM (2008)

Hybrid and Timed Systems

Abstract Interpretation
with Infinitesimals
Towards Scalability in *Nonstandard Static Analysis*

Kengo Kido[1,2]([✉]), Swarat Chaudhuri[3], and Ichiro Hasuo[1]

[1] University of Tokyo, Tokyo, Japan
`k-kido@is.s.u-tokyo.ac.jp`
[2] JSPS Research Fellow, Tokyo, Japan
[3] Rice University, Houston, USA

Abstract. We extend abstract interpretation for the purpose of verifying hybrid systems. Abstraction has been playing an important role
in many verification methodologies for hybrid systems, but some special
care is needed for abstraction of continuous dynamics defined by ODEs.
We apply Cousot and Cousot's framework of abstract interpretation to
hybrid systems, almost *as it is*, by regarding continuous dynamics as an
infinite iteration of *infinitesimal* discrete jumps. This extension follows
the recent line of work by Suenaga, Hasuo and Sekine, where deductive
verification is extended for hybrid systems by (1) introducing a constant
dt for an infinitesimal value; and (2) employing Robinson's *nonstandard
analysis (NSA)* to define mathematically rigorous semantics. Our theoretical results include soundness and termination via *uniform* widening
operators; and our prototype implementation successfully verifies some
benchmark examples.

1 Introduction

Hybrid systems exhibit both discrete *jump* and continuous *flow* dynamics. Quality assurance of such systems are of paramount importance due to the current
ubiquity of *cyber-physical systems (CPS)* like cars, airplanes, and many others. For the formal verification approach to hybrid systems, the challenges are:
(1) to incorporate flow-dynamics; and (2) to do so at the lowest possible cost,
so that the existing discrete framework smoothly transfers to hybrid situations.
A large body of existing work uses *differential equations* explicitly in the syntax;
see the discussion of related work below.

In [34], instead, an alternative approach of *nonstandard static analysis*—
combining *static analysis* and *nonstandard analysis*—is proposed. Its basic idea
is to introduce a constant dt for an *infinitesimal* (i.e. infinitely small) value, and

We thank Kohei Suenaga and the anonymous referees for useful discussions and
comments. This research was supported in part by Grants-in-Aid No. 24680001 &
15KT0012, JSPS; Grant-in-Aid for JSPS Fellows; NSF CAREER award #1156059;
and NSF award #1162076.

B. Jobstmann and K.R.M. Leino (Eds.): VMCAI 2016, LNCS 9583, pp. 229–249, 2016.
DOI: 10.1007/978-3-662-49122-5_11

turn flow into jump. With dt, the continuous operation of integration can be represented by a while-loop, to which existing discrete techniques such as Hoare-style program logics readily apply. For a rigorous mathematical development they employ *nonstandard analysis (NSA)* beautifully formalized by Robinson [33].

Concretely, in [34] they took the common combination of a WHILE-language and a Hoare logic (e.g. in the textbook [36]); and added a constant dt to obtain a modeling and verification framework for hybrid systems. Its components are called WHILE^{dt} and HOARE^{dt}. The soundness of HOARE^{dt} is proved against denotational semantics defined in the language of NSA. Subsequently in the *nonstandard static analysis* program: in [22] they presented a prototype automatic theorem prover for HOARE^{dt}; and in [35] they applied the same idea to stream processing systems, realizing a verification framework for *signal processing* as in Simulink.

Underlying these technical developments is the idea of so-called *sectionwise execution.* Although this paper does not rely explicitly on it, it is still useful for laying out the "operational" intuition of nonstandard static analysis. See the following example.

Example 1.1. Let c_{elapse} be the program on the right. The value of dt is infinitesimal; therefore the while loop will not terminate within finitely many steps. Nevertheless it is somehow intuitive to expect that after an "execution" of this program, the value of t should be infinitesimally close to 1 and larger than it.

$$t := 0 ;$$
$$\mathtt{while}\ t \leq 1\ \mathtt{do}$$
$$t := t + \mathtt{dt}$$

One possible way of thinking is to imagine *sectionwise execution.* For each natural number i we consider the *i-th section* of the program c_{elapse}, denoted by $c_{\mathsf{elapse}}|_i$ and shown on the right. Concretely, $c_{\mathsf{elapse}}|_i$ is obtained by replacing the infinitesimal dt in c_{elapse} with $\frac{1}{i+1}$. Informally $c_{\mathsf{elapse}}|_i$ is the "i-th approximation" of the original c_{elapse}.

$$t := 0 ;$$
$$\mathtt{while}\ t \leq 1\ \mathtt{do}$$
$$t := t + \frac{1}{i+1}$$

A section $c_{\mathsf{elapse}}|_i$ does terminate within finite steps and yields $1 + \frac{1}{i+1}$ as the value of t. Now we collect the outcomes of sectionwise executions and obtain a sequence

$$(1 + 1,\ 1 + \tfrac{1}{2},\ 1 + \tfrac{1}{3},\ \ldots,\ 1 + \tfrac{1}{i},\ \ldots) \tag{1}$$

which is thought of as a progressive approximation of the actual outcome of the original program c_{elapse}. Indeed, in the language of NSA, the sequence (1) represents a *hyperreal number* r that is infinitesimally close to 1.

We note that a program in WHILE^{dt} is *not* intended to be executed: the program c_{elapse} does not terminate. It is however an advantage of *static* approaches to verification and analysis, that programs need not be executed to prove their correctness. Instead well-defined mathematical semantics suffices. This is what we do here as well as in [22,34,35], with the denotational semantics of WHILE^{dt} exemplified in Example 1.1.

Our Contribution. In the previous work [22,34,35] *invariant discovery* has been a big obstacle in scalability of the proposed verification techniques—as is usual in deductive verification. The current work, as a first step towards scalability of the approach, extends *abstract interpretation* [10] with infinitesimals. The abstract interpretation methodology is known for its ample applicability (it is employed in model checking as well as in many deductive verification frameworks) and scalability (the static analyzer Astrée [12] has been successfully used e.g. for Airbus's flight control system).

Our theoretical contribution includes: the theory of *nonstandard abstract interpretation* where (standard) abstract domains are "∗-transformed," in a rigorous NSA sense, to the abstract domains for hyperreals; their soundness in over-approximating semantics of $\mathrm{WHILE}^{\mathrm{dt}}$ programs and hybrid system modeling by them; and introduction of the notion of *uniform* widening operators. With the latter, inductive approximation is guaranteed to terminate within finitely many steps—even after extension to the nonstandard setting. We show that many known widening operators, if not all, are indeed uniform. Although we focus on the domain of convex polyhedra in this paper, it is also possible to extend other abstract domains like ellipsoids [14] in the same way.

These theoretical results form a basis of our prototype implementation,[1] that successfully analyzes: *water-level monitor*, a common example of piecewise-linear hybrid dynamics; and also *thermostat* that is beyond piecewise-linear. The prototype deals with the constant dt as a truly infinitesimal number using computer algebra system.

Related Work. There has been a lot of research work for verification of hybrid systems and it has led to quite a few system verification tools, including HyTech [25], PHAVer [16], SpaceEx [17], HySAT/iSAT [15], Flow* [5] and KeYmaera [32]. All these rely on ODEs (or the explicit solutions of them) for expressing continuous dynamics, much like *hybrid automata* [1] do.

Our nonstandard static analysis approach is completely different from those in the following point: we do not use ODEs at all, and model hybrid systems as an imperative program with an infinitesimal constant. It enables us to apply static methodologies for discrete systems as they are. For example, in HyTech and PHAVer, convex polyhedra is used to over-approximate the reachable sets. They need, however, some special techniques such as linear phase-portrait [24], to reduce the dynamics into piecewise linear one. Our framework does not need such and usual abstract interpretation works as it is.

There are many other works we rely on, such as those on abstract interpretation, nonstandard analysis, etc. These are discussed later when they become relevant.

Organization. In Sect. 2 we start with the water-level monitor example and present how our nonstandard abstract interpretation framework works. Then we go on to its theoretical foundations. In Sect. 3 we review preliminaries on: abstract interpretation; nonstandard analysis; and the modeling language $\mathrm{WHILE}^{\mathrm{dt}}$ from [34]. In Sect. 4 we extend the theory of abstract interpretation with infinitesimals and build the theory of nonstandard abstract interpretation.

---

[1] The prototype [29] is available at http://www-mmm.is.s.u-tokyo.ac.jp/~kkido/.

Its theorems include soundness of approximation, and termination guaranteed by (the *-transform of) a *uniform* widening operator. In Sect. 5 we present our prototype implementation and the experiment results with it.

Appendices of this paper are found in the extended version [28]. Most proofs and some more details of nonstandard analysis are there.

2 Leading Example: Analysis of Water-Level Monitor

We shall start with an example of analysis and let it exemplify how our framework—that extends abstract interpretation with infinitesimals, and handles continuous as well as discrete dynamics—works. We use the common example of the water-level monitor [1]. In the current section, in particular, we will first revisit how the usual abstract interpretation workflow (without extension) would work, using a discretized variant of the problem. We emphasize the fact that our extended framework works just in the same manner: without any explicit ODEs or any additional theoretical infrastructure for ODEs; but only adding a constant dt.

The concrete problem is as follows. See the figure on the right. A water tank has a constant drain (2 cm per second). When the water level x gets lower than 5 cm the switch is turned on, which eventually makes the pump work but only after a time lag of two seconds. While the pump is working, the water level x rises by 1 cm per second. Once x reaches 10 cm the switch is turned off, which will shut down the pump but again after a time lag of two seconds. Our goal is the *reachability analysis* of this hybrid dynamics, that is, to see the water level x remains in a certain "safe" range (we will see that the range is $1 \leq x \leq 12$).

2.1 Analysis by (Standard) Abstract Interpretation, as a Precursor

Let us first revisit the usual workflow in reachability analyses by abstract interpretation. We will use the *discretized* model of the water-level monitor in Fig. 1, where each iteration of its unique loop amounts to the lapse of dt' = 0.2 s. The model in Fig. 1 is an imperative program with while loops, a typical subject of analyses by abstract interpretation.

More specifically: x is the water level, l is the counter for the time lag, p stands for the state of the pump ($p = 0$ if the pump is off, and $p = 1$ if on) and

```
(*Water-Level Monitor*)
l := 0; x := 1; p := 1; s := 0;
dt' := 0.2;
while true do {
    if p = 1 then x := x + dt'
        else x := x - 2 * dt';
    if (x <= 5 && p = 0) then s := 1
        else {if (x >= 10 && p = 1)
                then s := 1
                else s := 0
        };
    if s = 1 then l := l + dt'
        else skip;
    if s = 1 && l >= 2
        then {p := 1 - p; s := 0; l := 0}
        else skip
}
```

Fig. 1. Discretized water-level monitor

s is for "signals," meaning $s = 1$ if the pump has not yet responded to a signal from the switch (such as, when the switch is on but the pump is not on yet).

The first step in the usual abstract interpretation workflow is to fix *concrete* and *abstract domains*. Here in Sect. 2.1 we will use the followings.

- **The Concrete Domain:** $(\mathcal{P}(\mathbb{R}^2))^4$. We have two numerical variables l, x and two Boolean ones p, s in Fig. 1, therefore a canonical concrete domain would be $\mathcal{P}(\mathbb{B}^2 \times \mathbb{R}^2)$. We have the powerset operation $\mathcal{P}$ in it since we are now interested in the *reachable* set of memory states.

  However, for a better fit with our abstract domain (namely convex polyhedra), we shall use the set $(\mathcal{P}(\mathbb{R}^2))^4$ that is isomorphic to the above set $\mathcal{P}(\mathbb{B}^2 \times \mathbb{R}^2)$.

- **The Abstract Domain:** $(\mathbb{CP}_2)^4$. We use the domain of *convex polyhedra* [13], one of the most commonly-used abstract domains. Recall that a convex polyhedron is a subset of a Euclidean space characterized by a finite conjunction of linear inequalities. Specifically, we let $\mathbb{CP}_2$, the set of 2-dimensional convex polyhedra, approximate the set $\mathcal{P}(\mathbb{R}^2)$. Therefore, as an abstract domain for the program in Fig. 1, we take $(\mathbb{CP}_2)^4$ (that approximates $(\mathcal{P}(\mathbb{R}^2))^4$).

The next step in the workflow is to *over-approximate* the set of memory states that are reachable by the program in Fig. 1—this is a subset of the concrete domain $(\mathcal{P}(\mathbb{R}^2))^4$—using the abstract domain $(\mathbb{CP}_2)^4$. Since the desired set can be thought of as a least fixed point, this over-approximation procedure involves: (1) *abstract execution* of the program in $(\mathbb{CP}_2)^4$ (that is straightforward, see e.g. [13]); and (2) acceleration of least fixed-point computation in $(\mathbb{CP}_2)^4$ via suitable use of a *widening operator*. For convex polyhedra several widening operators are well-known. We shall use here ∇_M, so-called the *widening up to M* operator from [20,21]. One big reason for this choice is the *uniformity* of the operator (a notion we introduce later in Sect. 4.3), among others. The set M of linear constraints is a parameter for this widening operator; we fix it as usual, collecting the linear constraints that occur in the program in question. That is, $M = \{x \leq 5, x \geq 5, x \leq 10, x \geq 10, l \leq 2, l \geq 2\}$.

This over-approximation procedure is depicted in the *iteration sequence* in Fig. 3. Let us look at some of its details. The graph 0 represents the initial memory state (before the first iteration), where the pump is on and the water level x is precisely 1. After one iteration the water level will be incremented by $1 \times \mathsf{dt}' = 0.2$ cm; as usual in abstract interpretation, however, at this moment we invoke the widening operator ∇_M, and the next "abstract reachable set" is $x \in [1, 5]$ instead of $x \in [1, 1.2]$. Here the upper bound 5 comes from the constraint $x \leq 5$ that is in the parameter M of the widening operator ∇_M. This results in the graph 1 in Fig. 3.

In the iteration sequence (Fig. 3) the four polyhedra (in four different colors) gradually grow: in the graph 2 the water level x can be 10 cm so in the graph 3 appears a green polyhedron (meaning that a signal is sent from the switch to the pump); after the graphs 3 and 9 we *delay* widening, a heuristic commonly employed in abstract interpretation [9]. In the end, in the graph 12 we have a prefixed point (meaning that the polyhedra do not grow any further). There we can see, from the range of x spanned by the polyhedra, that the water level never reaches beyond $0.6 \leq x \leq 12.2$.

2.2 Analysis by *Nonstandard Abstract Interpretation*

In the above "standard" scenario, we approximated the dynamics of the water level by discretizing the continuous notion of time ($dt' = 0.2$). While this made the usual abstract interpretation workflow go around, there is a price to pay—the analysis result is not *precise*. Specifically, the reachable region thus over-approximated is $0.6 \leq x \leq 12.2$, while the real reachable region is $1 \leq x \leq 12$.[2]

Obviously we can "tighten up" the analysis by making the value dt' smaller. Even better, we can leave the expression dt' in Fig. 1 as a variable, and imagine the "limit" of analysis results when the value of dt' tends to 0. However here is a question: what is that "limit," in mathematically rigorous terms? Taking $dt' = 0$ obviously does not work: do so in Fig. 1 and we have no dynamics whatsoever. The value of dt' must be strictly positive.

```
(*Water-Level Monitor*)
l := 0; x := 1; p := 1; s := 0;
while true do {
    if p = 1 then x := x + dt
    else x := x - 2 * dt;
    if (x <= 5 && p = 0) then s := 1
    else {if (x >= 10 && p = 1)
            then s := 1
            else s := 0
    };
    if s = 1 then l := l + dt
    else skip;
    if s = 1 && l >= 2
    then {p := 1 - p; s := 0; l := 0}
    else skip
}
```

Fig. 2. Water-level monitor in WHILE^{dt}

Our contribution is an extension of abstract interpretation that answers the last question. In our framework, the same (hybrid) dynamics of the water-level monitor is modeled by a program in Fig. 2. Here the expression dt is a new constant that stands for a *positive* and *infinitesimal* (i.e. infinitely small) value. Therefore the modeling is not an approximation by discretization; it is an *exact* modeling.

It is important to notice that the program in Fig. 2 is the same as the one in Fig. 1, except that now dt is some strange constant, while dt' in Fig. 1 stood for a real number (namely 0.2). This difference, however, does not prevent us from applying the *static*, *symbolic* and *syntax-based* analysis by abstract interpretation. We can follow exactly the same path as in Sect. 2.1—taking the abstract domain of convex polyhedra, executing the program in Fig. 2 on it, applying the widening operator ∇_M, and forming an iteration sequence much like in Fig. 3—and this leads to the analysis result $1 - 2dt \leq x \leq 12 + dt$. Since dt is an infinitesimal number, the last result is practically as good as $1 \leq x \leq 12$. We have a prototype implementation that automates this analysis (Sect. 5).

What remains to be answered is the legitimacy of this extended abstract interpretation framework. Is the outcome $1 - 2dt \leq x \leq 12 + dt$ *sound*, in the sense that it indeed over-approximates the true reachable set? Even before that,

---

[2] There are also examples in which discretization even leads to *unsound* analysis results.

what do we mean by the "true reachable set" of the program in Fig. 2, with an exotic infinitesimal constant like dt? Moreover, are iteration sequences via the widening operator ∇_M guaranteed to terminate within finitely many steps, as is the case in the standard framework [20, 21]?

The rest of the paper is mostly devoted to (answering positively to) the last questions. In it we use Robinson's *nonstandard analysis (NSA)* [33] and give infinitesimal numbers—clearly such do not exist in the set of (standard) real numbers—a status as first-class citizens. The program in Fig. 2 is in fact in the programming (or rather *modeling*) language WHILE^{dt} from [22, 34]; and its semantics can be understood in the line of Example 1.1. It turns out that the theory of NSA—in particular its celebrated result of the *transfer principle*— allows us to "transfer" meta results from the standard abstract interpretation to our extension. That is, what is true in the world of standard reals (soundness, termination, etc.) is also true in that of *hyperreals*.

3   Preliminaries

In Sect. 4 we will present our *soundness* and *termination* results as a "metatheory" that justifies the workflow described in Sect. 2.2; in this section we recall some preliminaries that are needed for those theoretical developments. First, the general theory of abstract interpretation is briefly reviewed in Sect. 3.1 and the specific domain of convex polyhedra is presented in Sect. 3.2. Next, some basic notions in nonstandard analysis are explained in Sect. 3.3. Finally, in Sect. 3.4, the modeling language WHILE^{dt} from [34] and its (denotational) collecting semantics based on nonstandard analysis are presented.

3.1   Abstract Interpretation

Abstract interpretation [13] is a well-established technique in static analysis. We make a brief review of its basic theory; it is mostly for the purpose of fixing notations. The goal of abstract interpretation is to over-approximate a *concrete semantics* defined on an *concrete domain* by an *abstract semantics* on an *abstract domain.* We assume that the concrete semantics is defined as a least fixed point on the concrete domain. The following proposition guarantee the over-approximation of the least fixed point in the concrete domain by a prefixed point in the abstract domain. In the proposition, the order $\sqsubseteq$ on the domain L is extended to the order on $L \to L$ pointwisely. And the *least fixed point relative to* $\bot$, denoted by $\mathrm{lfp}_\bot F$, is the least among the fixed points of F above $\bot$; by the cpo structure of L and the continuity of F, it is given by $\bigsqcup_{n \in \mathbb{N}} F^n \bot$. Note that we are using the concretization-based framework described in [11].

Proposition 3.1. *Let* $(L, \sqsubseteq)$ *be a cpo;* $F : L \to L$ *be a continuous function; and* $\bot \in L$ *be such that* $\bot \sqsubseteq F(\bot)$. *Let* $(\overline{L}, \overline{\sqsubseteq})$ *be a preorder;* $\gamma : \overline{L} \to L$ *be a function (it is called* concretization*) such that* $\overline{a} \,\overline{\sqsubseteq}\, \overline{b} \Rightarrow \gamma(\overline{a}) \sqsubseteq \gamma(\overline{b})$ *for all* $\overline{a}, \overline{b} \in \overline{L}$; *and* $\overline{F} : \overline{L} \to \overline{L}$ *be a monotone function such that* $F \circ \gamma \sqsubseteq \gamma \circ \overline{F}$. *Assume further that* $\overline{x} \in \overline{L}$ *is a prefixed point of* $\overline{F}$ *(i.e.* $\overline{F}(\overline{x}) \,\overline{\sqsubseteq}\, \overline{x}$) *such that* $\bot \sqsubseteq \gamma(\overline{x})$.

Then $\overline{x}$ *over-approximates* $\mathrm{lfp}_\bot F$, *that is,* $\mathrm{lfp}_\bot F \sqsubseteq \gamma(\overline{x})$.   □

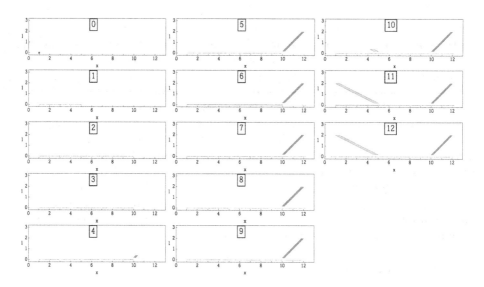

Fig. 3. An iteration sequence for the water-level monitor example.
To save space, here we depict an element of $(\mathbb{CP}_2)^4$—i.e. a quadruple of convex polyhedra—on the same plane $\mathbb{R}^2$. The four convex polyhedra come in different colors: those in blue, green, red and yellow correspond to the values $(p, s) = (1, 0), (1, 1), (0, 0)$ and $(0, 1)$ of the Boolean variables, respectively.

In Sect. 2.1 where we analyzed the discretized water-level monitor, the set $\mathcal{P}(\mathbb{R}^n)$—the set of subsets of memory states—is used as a concrete domain L; and the *domain of convex polyhedra* is used as an abstract domain $\overline{L}$. The interpretations F and $\overline{F}$ on each domains are defined in a standard manner. Towards the goal of obtaining $\overline{x}$ in Proposition 3.1, (i.e. finding a prefixed point in the abstract domain), the following notion of *widening* is used (often together with *narrowing* that we will not be using). Note that in the following definition and proposition, the domain $(L, \sqsubseteq)$ is the abstract domain, corresponding to $(\overline{L}, \sqsubseteq)$ in Proposition 3.1.

Definition 3.2 (widening operator). Let $(L, \sqsubseteq)$ be a preorder. A function $\nabla : L \times L \to L$ is said to be a *widening operator* if the following two conditions hold.

- (*Covering*) For any $x, y \in L$, $x \sqsubseteq x \nabla y$ and $y \sqsubseteq x \nabla y$.
- (*Termination*) For any ascending chain $\langle x_i \rangle \in L^{\mathbb{N}}$, the chain $\langle y_i \rangle \in L^{\mathbb{N}}$ defined by $y_0 = x_0$ and $y_{i+1} = y_i \nabla x_{i+1}$ for each $i \in \mathbb{N}$ is ultimately stationary.

A widening operator on a fixed abstract domain $\overline{L}$ is not at all unique. In this paper we will discuss three widening operators previously introduced for $\mathbb{CP}_n$.

The use of widening is as in the following proposition: the covering condition ensures that the outcome is a prefixed point; and the procedure terminates thanks to the termination condition.

Proposition 3.3 (convergence of iteration sequences). *Let $(L, \sqsubseteq)$ be a preorder; $F : L \to L$ be a monotone function; $\bot \in L$ be such that $\bot \sqsubseteq F(\bot)$; $\nabla : L \times L \to L$ be a widening operator; and $\langle X_i \rangle_{i \in \mathbb{N}} \in L^{\mathbb{N}}$ be the infinite sequence defined by*

$$X_0 = \bot \; ; \quad \text{and, for each } i \in \mathbb{N}, \quad X_{i+1} = \begin{cases} X_i & (\text{if } F(X_i) \sqsubseteq X_i) \\ X_i \nabla F(X_i) & (\text{otherwise}) \end{cases}$$

Then the sequence $\langle X_i \rangle_{i \in \mathbb{N}}$ is increasing and ultimately stationary; moreover its limit $\bigsqcup_{i \in \mathbb{N}} X_n$ is a prefixed point of F such that $\bot \sqsubseteq \bigsqcup_{i \in \mathbb{N}} X_n$. □

3.2   The Domain of Convex Polyhedra

The *domain of convex polyhedra*, introduced in [13], is one of the most commonly used relational numerical abstract domains.

Definition 3.4 (domain of convex polyhedra $\mathbb{CP}_n$). An n-dimensional *convex polyhedron* is the intersection of finitely many (closed) affine half-spaces. We denote the set of convex polyhedra in $\mathbb{R}^n$ by $\mathbb{CP}_n$. Its preorder $\sqsubseteq$ is given by the inclusion order (actually it is a partial order). The concretization function $\gamma_{\mathbb{CP}_n} : \mathbb{CP}_n \to \mathcal{P}(\mathbb{R}^n)$ is defined in an obvious manner.

We study three widening operators on $\mathbb{CP}_n$. They are namely: the *standard widening operator* ∇_S [19];[3] the *widening operator* ∇_M up to M [20,21]; and the *precise widening operator* ∇_N [3]. We briefly describe the former two; the definition of the last is omitted for the lack of space. In the following definitions, the function con maps a set of linear constraints (called a *constraint system*) to the convex polyhedron induced by the conjunction of those linear constraints.

Definition 3.5 (standard widening ∇_S). Let $P_1, P_2 \in \mathbb{CP}_n$; and C_1 and C_2 be constraints system that induce P_1 and P_2, respectively. *The standard widening operator $\nabla_S : \mathbb{CP}_n \times \mathbb{CP}_n \to \mathbb{CP}_n$ is defined by*

$$P_1 \nabla_S P_2 := \begin{cases} P_2 & \text{if } P_1 = \emptyset \\ \text{con}\left(\begin{array}{l} \{\varphi \in C_1 \mid C_2 \text{ implies } \varphi, \text{ i.e.} \varphi \text{ is everywhere true in } P_2\} \\ \cup \{\psi \in C_2 \mid \exists \varphi \in C_1. \, P_1 = \text{con}(C_1[\psi/\varphi])\} \end{array} \right) & \text{otherwise.} \end{cases}$$

Intuitively $P_1 \nabla_S P_2$ is represented by the set of those linear constraints of P_1 which are satisfied by every point of P_2.

The following second widening operator ∇_M refines ∇_S. This is what we use in our implementation. Here M is a parameter.

Definition 3.6 (widening up to M, ∇_M). Let $P_1, P_2 \in \mathbb{CP}_n$, and M be a (given) finite set of linear inequalities. The *widening operator up to M* is defined by

$$P_1 \nabla_M P_2 := (P_1 \nabla_S P_2) \cap \text{con}(\{\varphi \in M \mid P_i \subseteq \text{con}(\{\varphi\}) \text{ for } i = 1, 2\}).$$

The parameter M is usually taken to be the set of linear inequalities that occur in the program under analysis.

---

[3] The name "standard" is confusing with the distinction between *standard* and *nonstandard* entities in NSA. The use of "standard" in the former sense is scarce in this paper.

3.3 Nonstandard Analysis

Here we list a minimal set of necessary definitions and results in nonstandard analysis (NSA) [33]. Some further details can be found in [28, Appendix A]; fully-fledged and accessible expositions of NSA are found e.g. in [18,26].

The following notions will play important roles.

- *Hyperreals* that extends reals by infinitesimals, infinites, etc.;
- The *transfer principle*, a celebrated result in NSA that states that reals and hyperreals share "the same properties";
- The first-order language $\mathscr{L}_X$ that specifies formulas in which syntax, precisely, are preserved by the transfer principle; and finally
- The semantical construct of *superstructure* for interpreting $\mathscr{L}_X$-formulas.

What is of paramount importance is the transfer principle; in order to formulate it in a mathematically rigorous manner, the two last items (the language $\mathscr{L}_X$ on the syntactic side, and superstructures on the semantical side) are used. The first-order language $\mathscr{L}_X$ is essentially that of set theory and has two predicates $=$ and $\in$. The *superstructure* $V(X)$ is then a semantical "universe" for such formulas, constructed from the base set X: concretely $V(X)$ is the union of X, $\mathcal{P}(X)$, $\mathcal{P}(X \cup \mathcal{P}(X))$, and so on. Finally, when we take $X = \mathbb{R}$ then the set $^*X = {^*\mathbb{R}}$ is that of *hyperreals*; and the transfer principle claims that A holds for reals if and only if $^*A$—a formula essentially the same as A—holds for hyperreals. Its precise statement is:

Lemma 3.7 (the transfer principle). *For any closed formula A in $\mathscr{L}_X$, the following are equivalent.*

- *The formula A is valid in the superstructure $V(X)$.*
- *The *-transform $^*A$ of A—this is a formula in the language $\mathscr{L}_{*X}$—is valid in the superstructure $V(^*X)$.*

The transfer principle guarantees that we can employ the same abstract interpretation framework, for reals and hyperreals alike—*literally* the same, in the sense that we express the framework in the language $\mathscr{L}_{\mathbb{R}}$. Concretely, various constructions and meta results (such as soundness and termination) in abstract interpretation will be expressed as $\mathscr{L}_{\mathbb{R}}$-formulas, and since they are valid in $V(\mathbb{R})$, they are valid in the "nonstandard universe" $V(^*\mathbb{R})$ too, by the transfer principle.

Hyperreals We fix an *index set* $I = \mathbb{N}$, and an *ultrafilter* $\mathcal{F} \subseteq \mathcal{P}(I)$ that extends the cofinite filter $\mathcal{F}_c := \{S \subseteq I \mid I \setminus S \text{ is finite}\}$. Its properties to be noted: (1) for any $S \subseteq I$, exactly one of S and $I \setminus S$ belongs to $\mathcal{F}$; (2) if S is *cofinite* (i.e. $I \setminus S$ is finite), then S belongs to $\mathcal{F}$.

Definition 3.8 (hyperreal $r \in {^*\mathbb{R}}$). We define the set $^*\mathbb{R}$ of *hyperreal numbers* (or *hyperreals*) by $^*\mathbb{R} := \mathbb{R}^I / \sim_{\mathcal{F}}$. It is therefore the set of infinite sequences on $\mathbb{R}$ modulo the following equivalence $\sim_{\mathcal{F}}$: we have $(a_0, a_1, \ldots) \sim_{\mathcal{F}} (a'_0, a'_1, \ldots)$ if

$$\{i \in I \mid a_i = a'_i\} \in \mathcal{F}, \quad \text{for which we say "}d_i = d'_i \text{ for almost every } i.\text{"} \quad (2)$$

A *hypernatural* $n \in {^*\mathbb{N}}$ is defined similarly.

It follows that: two sequences $(a_i)_i$ and $(a'_i)_i$ that coincide except for finitely many indices i represent the same hyperreal. The predicates besides $=$ (such as $<$) are defined in the same way. A notable consequence is the existence of infinite numbers in the set of hyperreals and hypernaturals: $\omega := [(1,2,3,\ldots)]$ is a positive infinite since it is larger than any positive real $r = [(r,r,\ldots)]$ ($i > r$ for almost every $i \in \mathbb{N}$). In addition, the set of hyperreals includes infinitesimal numbers: a hyperreal $\omega^{-1} := [(1, \frac{1}{2}, \frac{1}{3}, \ldots)]$ is positive $(0 < \omega^{-1})$ but is smaller than any (standard) positive real r.

Superstructure. A *superstructure* is a "universe," constructed step by step from a certain base set X (whose typical examples are $\mathbb{R}$ and $^*\mathbb{R}$). We assume $\mathbb{N} \subseteq X$.

Definition 3.9 (superstructure). A *superstructure* $V(X)$ over X is defined by $V(X) := \bigcup_{n \in \mathbb{N}} V_n(X)$, where $V_0(X) := X$ and $V_{n+1}(X) := V_n(X) \cup \mathcal{P}(V_n(X))$.

The superstructure $V(X)$ might seem to be a closure of X only under powersets, but it accommodates many set-forming operations. For example, ordered pairs (a,b) and tuples $(a_1, \ldots, a_m)$ are defined in $V(X)$ as is usually done in set theory, e.g. $(a,b) := \{\{a\}, \{a,b\}\}$. The function space $a \to b$ is thought of as a collection of special binary relations (i.e. $a \to b \subseteq \mathcal{P}(a \times b)$), hence is in $V(X)$.

The First-Order Language $\mathscr{L}_X$. We use the following first-order language $\mathscr{L}_X$, defined for each choice of the base set X like $\mathbb{R}$ and $^*\mathbb{R}$.

Definition 3.10 (the language $\mathscr{L}_X$). *Terms* in $\mathscr{L}_X$ consist of: variables $x, y, x_1, x_2, \ldots$; and a constant a for each entity $a \in V(X)$.

Formulas in $\mathscr{L}_X$ are constructed as follows.

- The predicate symbols are $=$ and $\in$; both are binary. The *atomic formulas* are of the form $s = t$ or $s \in t$ (where s and t are terms).
- We allow Boolean combinations of formulas. We use the symbols $\wedge, \vee, \neg$ and $\Rightarrow$.
- Given a formula A, a variable x and a term s, the expressions $\forall x \in s. A$ and $\exists x \in s. A$ are formulas.

Note that quantifiers always come with a bound s. The language $\mathscr{L}_X$ depends on the choice of X (it determines the set of constants). We shall also use the following syntax sugars in $\mathscr{L}_X$, as is common in set theory and NSA.

(s,t) pair $(s_1, \ldots, s_m)$ tuple $s \times t$ direct product
$s \subseteq t$ inclusion, short for $\forall x \in s. x \in t$
$s(t)$ function application; short for x such that $(t,x) \in s$
$s \circ t$ function composition, $(s \circ t)(x) = s(t(x))$
$s \le t$ inequality in $\mathbb{N}$; short for $(s,t) \in \le$ where $\le \subseteq \mathbb{N}^2$

Definition 3.11 (semantics of $\mathscr{L}_X$). We interpret $\mathscr{L}_X$ in the superstructure $V(X)$ in the obvious way. Let A be a closed formula; we say A is *valid* if A is true in $V(X)$.

The ∗-Transform and the Transfer Principle As we mentioned the transfer principle says that a closed formula A in the language $\mathscr{L}_X$ is valid in $V(X)$ if and only if $^*A$ in $\mathscr{L}_{^*X}$ is valid in $V(^*X)$. We shall describe how we syntactically transform A in $\mathscr{L}_X$ into $^*A$ in $\mathscr{L}_{^*X}$.

For that purpose, in particular in translating constants in $\mathscr{L}_X$ (for entities in $V(X)$) to $\mathscr{L}_{^*X}$, we will need the following *semantical* translation. The so-called *ultrapower construction* yields a canonical map

$$^*(\_)\ :\ V(X) \longrightarrow V(^*X), \qquad a \longmapsto {}^*a \tag{3}$$

that is called the *∗-transform*. It is a map from the universe $V(X)$ of standard entities to $V(^*X)$ of nonstandard entities. The details of its construction are in [28, Appendix A] or in [26].

The above map $^*(\_)\colon V(X) \to V(^*X)$ becomes a *monomorphism*, a notion in NSA. Most notably it will satisfy the *transfer principle* (Lemma 3.13).

Definition 3.12 (*-transform of formulas). Let A be a formula in $\mathscr{L}_X$. The *∗-transform* of A, denoted by $^*A$, is a formula in $\mathscr{L}_{^*X}$ obtained by replacing each constant a occurring in A with the constant $^*a$ that designates the element $^*a \in V(^*X)$.

Lemma 3.13 (the transfer principle). *For any closed formula A in $\mathscr{L}_X$, A is valid (in $V(X)$) if and only if $^*A$ is valid (in $V(^*X)$).*   □

For example, the following proposition is proved using the transfer principle (the proof is in [28, Appendix C]). This proposition has a practical implication: our implementation relies on it in simplifying formulas including the infinitesimal constant dt.

Proposition 3.14. *Let A be an $\mathscr{L}_{\mathbb{R}}$-formula with a unique free variable x; to emphasize it we write $A(x)$ for A. Then the validity of the formula*

$$\exists r \in \mathbb{R}.\, (0 < r \wedge \forall x \in \mathbb{R}.\, (0 < x < r \Rightarrow A\,(x)))$$

(in $V(\mathbb{R})$) implies the validity of $^*A(\mathtt{dt})$ in $V(^*\mathbb{R})$.   □

3.4   The Modeling Language While^{dt}

WHILE^{dt}, a modeling language for hybrid systems based on NSA, is introduced in [34]. It is an augmentation of a usual imperative language (such as **IMP** in [36]) with a constant dt that expresses an infinitesimal number.

Definition 3.15. Let **Var** be the set of variables. The syntax of WHILE^{dt} is as follows:

$$\mathbf{AExp} \ni a ::= x \mid r \mid a_1 \ \mathtt{aop} \ a_2 \mid \mathtt{dt}$$
$$\text{where } x \in \mathbf{Var}, r \in \mathbb{R} \ \text{ and } \ \mathtt{aop} \in \{+, -, \cdot, /\}$$
$$\mathbf{BExp} \ni b ::= \mathtt{true} \mid \mathtt{false} \mid b_1 \wedge b_2 \mid \neg b \mid a_1 < a_2$$
$$\mathbf{Cmd} \ni c ::= \mathtt{skip} \mid x := a \mid c_1; c_2 \mid \mathtt{if}\ b\ \mathtt{then}\ c_1\ \mathtt{else}\ c_2 \mid \mathtt{while}\ b\ \mathtt{do}\ c.$$

An expression $a \in \mathbf{AExp}$ is an *arithmetic expression*, $b \in \mathbf{BExp}$ is a *Boolean expression* and $c \in \mathbf{Cmd}$ is a *command*.

As we explained in Sect. 1, the infinitesimal constant dt enables us to model not only discrete dynamics but also continuous dynamics without explicit ODEs. For example, the water-level monitor is modeled as a WHILE^{dt} program shown in Fig. 2. As another example, the thermostat can be modeled as the program on the

```
(*Thermostat*)
x := 22; p := 0;
while true do {
    if p = 0 then x := x - 3 * x * dt
        else x := x + 3 * (30 - x) * dt;
    if x >= 22 then p := 0
        else {if x <= 18 then p := 1
                else skip
        }
}
```

Fig. 4. Thermostat in WHILE^{dt}

right. One can see that the continuous dynamics modeled in this example is beyond piecewise-linear. Even dynamics defined by nonlinear ODEs can be modeled in WHILE^{dt} in the same manner. To go further to accommodate an arbitrary hybrid automaton we must properly deal with *nondeterminism*, a feature currently lacking in WHILE^{dt}. Although we expect that to be not hard, precise comparison between WHILE^{dt} and hybrid automata in expressivity is future work.

In the usual, standard abstract interpretation (without dt), a command c is assigned its *collecting semantics* $\mathcal{P}(\mathbf{Var} \to \mathbb{R}) \to \mathcal{P}(\mathbf{Var} \to \mathbb{R})$ (see e.g. [10]). This is semantics by reachable sets of memory states, as the concrete semantics. Presence of dt in the syntax of WHILE^{dt} calls for an infinitesimal number in the picture. The first thing to try would be to replace $\mathbb{R}$ with $^*\mathbb{R}$, and let WHILE^{dt} commands interpreted as functions of the type $\mathcal{P}(\mathbf{Var} \to {}^*\mathbb{R}) \to \mathcal{P}(\mathbf{Var} \to {}^*\mathbb{R})$. This however is not suited for the purpose of interpreting recursion in presence of dt.[4] We rely instead on our theory of *hyperdomains* that is used in [35] and described in [28, Appendix B] ; see the interpretation of while loops in Table 1. This calls for the interpretation of commands to be of the type $^*\big(\mathcal{P}(\mathbf{Var} \to \mathbb{R}) \to \mathcal{P}(\mathbf{Var} \to \mathbb{R}) \big)$, a subset of $^*\mathcal{P}(\mathbf{Var} \to \mathbb{R}) \to {}^*\mathcal{P}(\mathbf{Var} \to \mathbb{R})$. The last type will be used in the following definition.

Definition 3.16. *Collecting semantics* for WHILE^{dt}, in Table 1, has the following types where $\mathbb{B}$ is $\{\text{tt}, \text{ff}\}$: $[\![a]\!]$: $^*(\mathbf{Var} \to \mathbb{R}) \to {}^*\mathbb{R}$ for $a \in \mathbf{AExp}$; $[\![b]\!]$: $^*(\mathbf{Var} \to \mathbb{R}) \to \mathbb{B}$ for $b \in \mathbf{BExp}$; and $[\![c]\!]$: $^*\mathcal{P}(\mathbf{Var} \to \mathbb{R}) \to {}^*\mathcal{P}(\mathbf{Var} \to \mathbb{R})$ for $c \in \mathbf{Cmd}$.

In [34] and in Sect. 1, the semantics of a while loop is defined using the idea of sectionwise execution, instead of as a least fixed point. This is not suited for employing abstract interpretation—the latter is after all for computing least fixed points. The collecting semantics in Definition 3.16 (Table 1) does use least fixed points; it is based on the alternative WHILE^{dt} semantics introduced in [27] (it will also appear in the forthcoming full version of [22,34]). The equivalence of the two semantics is established in [27].

---

[4] If we interpret commands as functions $\mathcal{P}(\mathbf{Var} \to {}^*\mathbb{R}) \to \mathcal{P}(\mathbf{Var} \to {}^*\mathbb{R})$, the interpretation $[\![\texttt{while } x < 10 \texttt{ do } x := x + \texttt{dt}]\!]\{(x \mapsto 0)\}$ by a least fixed point will be $\{x \mapsto r \mid \exists n \in \mathbb{N}.\ r = n * \texttt{dt}\}$, not $\{x \mapsto r \mid \exists n \in {}^*\mathbb{N}.\ r = n * \texttt{dt} \land r \leq 10\}$ as we expect. The problem is that *internality*—an "well-behavedness" notion in NSA—is not preserved in such a modeling.

In the rest of the paper we assume that the set of variables **Var** is finite. This assumption—a realistic one when we focus on the program to be analyzed—makes our NSA framework much simpler. Therefore $\mathcal{P}(\mathbf{Var} \to \mathbb{R})$ and ${}^*\mathcal{P}(\mathbf{Var} \to \mathbb{R})$ are equal to $\mathcal{P}(\mathbb{R}^n)$ and ${}^*\mathcal{P}(\mathbb{R}^n)$ for some $n \in \mathbb{N}$ respectively; we prefer the latter notations in what follows.

Table 1. WHILE^{dt} collecting semantics

$$[\![x]\!]\sigma := \sigma(x) \text{ for each } x \in \mathbf{Var} \qquad\qquad [\![\mathbf{true}]\!]\sigma := \mathbb{t}$$
$$[\![r]\!]\sigma := r \text{ for each } r \in \mathbb{R} \qquad\qquad\qquad [\![\mathbf{false}]\!]\sigma := \mathrm{ff}$$
$$[\![a_1 \text{ aop } a_2]\!]\sigma := [\![a_1]\!] \text{ aop } [\![a_2]\!] \qquad\qquad [\![b_1 \wedge b_2]\!]\sigma := [\![b_1]\!] \wedge [\![b_2]\!]$$
$$[\![\mathbf{dt}]\!]\sigma := [(1, \tfrac{1}{2}, \tfrac{1}{3}, \cdots)] \qquad\qquad\qquad [\![\neg b]\!]\sigma := \neg([\![b]\!]\sigma)$$

$$[\![\mathbf{skip}]\!]\mathbf{S} := \mathbf{S}$$
$$[\![x := a]\!]\mathbf{S} := \{\sigma[[\![a]\!]\sigma/x] \mid \sigma \in \mathbf{S}\}$$
$$[\![c_1; c_2]\!]\mathbf{S} := [\![c_2]\!]([\![c_1]\!]\mathbf{S})$$
$$[\![\mathbf{if}\ b\ \mathbf{then}\ c_1\ \mathbf{else}\ c_2]\!]\mathbf{S} := \begin{array}{l} \{[\![c_1]\!]\sigma \mid \sigma \in \mathbf{S},\ [\![b]\!]\sigma = \mathbb{t}\} \\ \cup \{[\![c_2]\!]\sigma \mid \sigma \in \mathbf{S},\ [\![b]\!]\sigma = \mathrm{ff}\} \end{array}$$
$$[\![\mathbf{while}\ b\ \mathbf{do}\ c]\!] := \mathrm{lfp}\big({}^*\Phi\,([\![b]\!])\,([\![c]\!])\big)$$

where $\Phi : (\mathbf{St} \to \mathbb{B} \cup \{\bot\}) \to (\mathcal{P}\,(\mathbf{Var} \to \mathbb{R}) \to \mathcal{P}\,(\mathbf{Var} \to \mathbb{R})) \to$
$$\Big((\mathcal{P}\,(\mathbf{Var} \to \mathbb{R}) \to \mathcal{P}\,(\mathbf{Var} \to \mathbb{R})) \to (\mathcal{P}\,(\mathbf{Var} \to \mathbb{R}) \to \mathcal{P}\,(\mathbf{Var} \to \mathbb{R}))\Big)$$

is defined by $\Phi(f)(g) = \lambda\psi.\ \lambda S.\ S \cup \psi\{(g(\sigma)) \mid \sigma \in S,\ f(\sigma) = \mathbb{t}\} \cup \{\sigma \mid \sigma \in S,\ f(\sigma) = \mathrm{ff}\}$.

4   Abstract Interpretation Augmented with Infinitesimals

In the current section are our main theoretical contributions—a metatheory of *nonstandard abstract interpretation* that justifies the workflow in Sect. 2.2.

(Standard) abstract interpretation infrastructure such as Propositions 3.1 and 3.3 is not applicable to WHILE^{dt} programs since ${}^*\mathcal{P}(\mathbb{R}^n)$ is not a cpo.[5] Thus, building on the theoretical foundations in the above, we now extend the abstract interpretation framework for the analysis of WHILE^{dt} programs (and the hybrid systems modeled thereby). We introduce an *abstract hyperdomain* over ${}^*\mathbb{R}$ as the transfer of the (standard, over $\mathbb{R}$) domain of convex polyhedra. We then interpret WHILE^{dt} programs in them, and transfer the three widening operators mentioned in Sect. 3.1 to the nonstandard setting. We classify them into *uniform* ones—for which termination is guaranteed even in the nonstandard setting—and non-uniform ones. The main theorems are Theorems 4.3 and 4.9, for soundness (in place of Proposition 3.1) and termination (in place of Proposition 3.3) respectively.

---

[5] One can see that the ascending chain defined by $X_n := \{k * \mathbf{dt} \mid 0 \le k \le n\}$ does not have the supremum in ${}^*\mathcal{P}(\mathbb{R}^n)$ since $\{k * \mathbf{dt} \mid k \in \mathbb{N}\}$ is not *internal* (see [28, Appendix A]).

4.1 The Domain of Convex Polyhedra over Hyperreals

We extend convex polyhedra to the current nonstandard setting.

Definition 4.1 (convex polyhedra over $^*\mathbb{R}$). A *convex polyhedron* on $(^*\mathbb{R})^n$ is an intersection of finite number of affine half-spaces on $(^*\mathbb{R})^n$, that is, the set of points $\mathbf{x} \in (^*\mathbb{R})^n$ that satisfy a certain finite set of linear inequalities. The set of all convex polyhedra on $(^*\mathbb{R})^n$ is denoted by $\mathbb{CP}_n^{^*\mathbb{R}}$.

Proposition 4.2. *The set $\mathbb{CP}_n^{^*\mathbb{R}}$ of all convex polyhedra over $(^*\mathbb{R})^n$ is a (proper) subset of $^*\mathbb{CP}_n$, the $*$-transform of the (standard) domain of convex polyhedra over $\mathbb{R}^n$.* □

What lies in the difference between the two sets $\mathbb{CP}_n^{^*\mathbb{R}} \subsetneq {^*\mathbb{CP}_n}$ is, for example, a disk as a subset of $\mathbb{R}^2$ (hence of $^*\mathbb{R}^2$). In $^*\mathbb{CP}_2$ one can use a constraint system whose number of linear constraints is a hypernatural number $m \in {^*\mathbb{N}}$; using e.g. $m = \omega = [(0, 1, 2, \ldots)]$ allows us to approximate a disk with progressive precision.

In the following development of nonstandard abstract interpretation, we will use $^*\mathbb{CP}_n$ as an abstract domain since it allows transfer of properties of $\mathbb{CP}_n$. We note, however, that our over-approximation of the interpretation $[\![c]\!]$ of a loop-free WHILE^{dt} program c is always given in $\mathbb{CP}_n^{^*\mathbb{R}}$, i.e. with finitely many linear inequalities.

4.2 Theory of Nonstandard Abstract Interpretation

Our goal is to over-approximate the collecting semantics for WHILE^{dt} programs (Table 1) on convex polyhedra over $^*\mathbb{R}$. As we mentioned at the beginning of this section, however, abstract interpretation infrastructure cannot be applied since $^*\mathcal{P}(\mathbb{R}^n)$ is not a cpo. Fortunately it turns out that we can rely on the $*$-transform (Sect. 3.3) of the theory in Sect. 3.1, where it suffices to impose the cpo structure only on $\mathcal{P}(\mathbb{R})$ and the $*$-continuity—instead of the (standard) continuity—on the function $[\![c]\!]$. This theoretical framework of *nonstandard abstract interpretation*, which we shall describe here, is an extension of the *transferred domain theory* studied in [4,35]. Part of the latter is found also in [28, Appendix B].

Theorem 4.3. *Let $(L, \sqsubseteq)$ be a cpo; $F : {^*L} \to {^*L}$ be a $*$-continuous function; and $\bot \in {^*L}$ be such that $\bot \mathrel{^*\!\sqsubseteq} F(\bot)$. Let $(\overline{L}, \overline{\sqsubseteq})$ be a preorder; $\gamma : \overline{L} \to L$ be a function such that $\overline{a} \mathrel{\overline{\sqsubseteq}} \overline{b} \Rightarrow \gamma(\overline{a}) \sqsubseteq \gamma(\overline{b})$ for all $\overline{a}, \overline{b} \in \overline{L}$; and $\overline{F} : {^*\overline{L}} \to {^*L}$ be a $*$-continuous function that is monotone with respect to $^*\overline{\sqsubseteq}$ and satisfies $F \circ {^*\gamma} \mathrel{^*\!\sqsubseteq} {^*\gamma} \circ \overline{F}$. Note that $(^*\overline{L}, {^*\overline{\sqsubseteq}})$ is also a preorder. Assume further that $\overline{x} \in {^*\overline{L}}$ is a prefixed point of $\overline{F}$ (i.e. $\overline{F}(\overline{x}) \mathrel{^*\overline{\sqsubseteq}} \overline{x}$) such that $\bot \mathrel{^*\!\sqsubseteq} {^*\gamma}(\overline{x})$.*

Then $\overline{x}$ over-approximates $\operatorname{lfp}_\bot F$, that is, $\operatorname{lfp}_\bot F \mathrel{^*\!\sqsubseteq} {^*\gamma}(\overline{x})$. □

Our goal is over-approximation of the semantics of iteration of a loop-free WHILE^{dt} program c, relying on Theorem 4.3. Towards the goal, the next step is to find a suitable $\overline{F} : {^*\overline{L}} \to {^*\overline{L}}$ that "stepwise approximates" $F = [\![c]\!]$, the collecting semantics of c. The next result implies that the $*$-transformation of $[\![\_]\!]_{\text{CP}}$

(defined in a usual manner in standard abstract interpretation, as mentioned in Sect. 3.1) can be used in such $\overline{F}$.

Proposition 4.4. *Let* $(L, \sqsubseteq), (\overline{L}, \overline{\sqsubseteq}), \gamma : \overline{L} \to L$ *satisfy the hypotheses in Theorem 4.3. Assume that a continuous function* $F : L \to L$ *is stepwise approximated by a monotone function* $\overline{F} : \overline{L} \to \overline{L}$, *that is,* $F \circ \gamma \sqsubseteq \gamma \circ \overline{F}$. *Then the* *-continuous function* $^*F : {}^*L \to {}^*L$ *is over-approximated by the monotone and internal function* $^*\overline{F} : {}^*\overline{L} \to {}^*\overline{L}$, *i.e.* $^*F \circ {}^*\gamma \ {}^*\sqsubseteq \ {}^*\gamma \circ {}^*\overline{F}$. □

We summarize what we observed so far on nonstandard abstract interpretation by instantiating the abstract domain to $^*\mathbb{CP}_n$. In the following $[\![c]\!]$ is from Definition 3.16.

Corollary 4.5 (soundness of nonstandard abstract interpretation on $^*\mathbb{CP}_n$). *Let* c *be a loop-free* WHILE^{dt} *command; and let* $\bot \in {}^*(\mathcal{P}(\mathbb{R}^n))$ *and* $\overline{x} \in {}^*\mathbb{CP}_n$ *be such that* $(^*[\![c]\!]_{\mathrm{CP}})(\overline{x}) \ {}^*\sqsubseteq \ \overline{x}$ *and* $\bot \ {}^*\sqsubseteq \ {}^*\gamma_{\mathrm{CP}_n}(\overline{x})$. *Then we have* $\mathrm{lfp}_\bot [\![c]\!] \ {}^*\sqsubseteq \ {}^*\gamma_{\mathrm{CP}_n}(\overline{x})$. □

4.3 Hyperwidening and Uniform Widening Operators

Towards our goal of using Theorem 4.3, the last remaining step is to find a prefixed point $\overline{x}$, i.e. $\overline{F}(\overline{x}) \ {}^*\sqsubseteq \ \overline{x}$. This is where widening operators are standardly used; see Sect. 3.1.

We can try *-transforming a (standard) notion—a strategy that we have used repeatedly in the current section. This yields the following result, that has a problem that is discussed shortly.

Theorem 4.6. *Let* $(L, \sqsubseteq)$ *be a preorder and* $\nabla : L \times L \to L$ *be a widening operator on* L. *Let* $F : {}^*L \to {}^*L$ *be a monotone and internal function; and* $\bot \in {}^*L$ *be such that* $\bot \ {}^*\sqsubseteq \ F(\bot)$. *The iteration* hyper-sequence $\langle X_i \rangle_{i \in {}^*\mathbb{N}}$—*indexed by hypernaturals* $i \in {}^*\mathbb{N}$—*that is defined by*

$$X_0 = \bot, \quad X_{i+1} = \begin{cases} X_i & (\text{if } F(X_i) \ {}^*\sqsubseteq \ X_i) \\ X_i \, {}^*\nabla F(X_i) & (\text{otherwise}) \end{cases} \text{ for all } i \in {}^*\mathbb{N}$$

reaches its limit within some hypernatural number of steps and the limit $\bigsqcup_{i \in \mathbb{N}} X_i$ *is a prefixed point of* F *such that* $\bot \ {}^*\sqsubseteq \ \bigsqcup_{i \in \mathbb{N}} X_i$. □

The problem of Theorem 4.6 is that the *finite-step convergence* of iteration sequences for the original widening operator (described in Proposition 3.3) is now transferred to *hyperfinite-step convergence*. This is not desired. All the entities from NSA that we have used so far are constructs in denotational semantics—whose only role is to ensure soundness of verification methodologies[6] and on which we never actually operate—and therefore their infinite/infinitesimal nature has been not a problem. In contrast, computation of the iteration hypersequence $\langle X_i \rangle_{i \in {}^*\mathbb{N}}$ is what we actually compute to over-approximate program semantics; and therefore its termination guarantee within $i \in {}^*\mathbb{N}$ steps (Theorem 4.6) is of no use.

---

[6] Recall that WHILE^{dt} is a *modeling* language and we do not execute them.

As a remedy we introduce a new notion of *uniformity* of the (standard) widening operators. It strengthens the original termination condition (Definition 3.2) by imposing a uniform bound i for stability of arbitrary chains $\langle x_i \rangle \in L^{\mathbb{N}}$. Logically the change means replacing $\forall\exists$ by $\exists\forall$.

Definition 4.7 (uniform widening). Let $(L, \sqsubseteq)$ be a preorder. A function $\nabla : L \times L \to L$ is said to be a *uniform widening operator* if the following two conditions hold.

– (Covering) For any $x, y \in L$, $x \sqsubseteq x\nabla y$ and $y \sqsubseteq x\nabla y$.
– (Uniform termination) Let $x_0 \in L$. There exists a *uniform bound* $i \in \mathbb{N}$ such that: for any ascending chain $\langle x_k \rangle \in L^{\mathbb{N}}$ starting from x_0, there exists $j \leq i$ at which the chain $\langle y_k \rangle \in L^{\mathbb{N}}$, defined by $y_0 = x_0$ and $y_{k+1} = y_k \nabla x_{k+1}$ for all $k \in \mathbb{N}$, stabilizes (i.e. $y_j = y_{j+1}$).

It is straightforward that uniform termination implies termination.

　　We investigate uniformity of some of the commonly-known widening operators on convex polyhedra.

Theorem 4.8. *Among the three widening operators in Sect. 3.1, ∇_S (Definition 3.5) and ∇_M (Definition 3.6) are uniform, but ∇_N ([3]) is not.* □

For example, the widening operator ∇_S is uniform because if the first element x_0 of an iteration sequence is fixed, the length of the iteration sequence is at most the number of linear inequalities that define the first element x_0. However, ∇_N is not uniform because an iteration sequence can be arbitrarily long even if the first element of it is fixed.

　　The following theorem is a "practical" improvement of Theorem 4.6; its proof relies on instantiating the uniform bound i in a suitable $\mathscr{L}_{\mathbb{R}}$-formula with a Skolem constant, before transfer.

Theorem 4.9. *Let $(L, \sqsubseteq)$ be a preorder and $\nabla \in L \times L \to L$ be a uniform widening operator on L. Let $F : {}^*L \to {}^*L$ be a monotone and internal function; and $\bot \in L$ be such that ${}^*\bot\ {}^*\!\sqsubseteq F({}^*\bot)$. The iteration sequence $\langle X_i \rangle_{i \in \mathbb{N}}$ defined by*

$$X_0 = {}^*\bot, \quad X_{i+1} = \begin{cases} X_i & (\text{if } F(X_i)\ {}^*\!\sqsubseteq X_i) \\ X_i\ {}^*\nabla\ F(X_i) & (\text{otherwise}) \end{cases} \quad \text{for all } i \in \mathbb{N}$$

reaches its limit within some finite number of steps; and the limit $\bigsqcup_{i \in \mathbb{N}} X_i$ is a prefixed point of F such that ${}^*\bot\ {}^*\!\sqsubseteq \bigsqcup_{i \in \mathbb{N}} X_i$. □

Note that uniformity of ∇ is a *sufficient condition* for the termination of nonstandard iteration sequences (by ${}^*\nabla$); Theorem 4.9 does not prohibit other useful widening operators in the nonstandard setting. Furthermore, there can be a useful (nonstandard) widening operator except for the ones ${}^*\nabla$ that arise via standard ones ∇.

　　It is a direct consequence of Theorems 4.8 and 4.9 that the analysis of WHILE^{dt} programs on ${}^*\mathbb{CP}_n$ is terminating with ∇_S or ∇_M.

5   Implementation and Experiments

5.1   Implementation

We implemented a prototype tool for analysis of WHILE^{dt} programs. The tool currently supports: $^*\mathbb{CP}_n$ as an abstract domain; and $^*\nabla_M$, *-transformation of ∇_M in Definition 3.6 as a widening operator. Its input is a WHILE^{dt} program. It outputs a convex polyhedron that over-approximates the set of reachable memory states for each modes (or the values of discrete variables). Our tool consists principally of the following two components: 1) an OCaml frontend for parsing, forming an iteration sequence and making the set M for $^*\nabla_M$; and 2) a Mathematica backend for executing operations on convex polyhedra. The two components are interconnected by a C++ program, via MathLink.

There are some libraries such as Parma Polyhedra Library [2] that are commonly used to execute operations on convex polyhedra. They cannot be used in our implementation because we have to handle the infinitesimal constant dt as an truly infinitesimal value. Instead we implemented Chernikova's algorithm [6–8,30] symbolically, using *computer algebra system (CAS)* on Mathematica. Proposition 3.14 ensures that the transformation from $^*A(\mathtt{dt})$ to $\exists r \in \mathbb{R}. (0 < r \wedge \forall x \in \mathbb{R}. (0 < x < r \Rightarrow A(x)))$ does not violate the soundness of the analysis. Therefore, when we have to evaluate a formula including dt, we instead resolve $\exists r \in \mathbb{R}. (0 < r \wedge \forall x \in \mathbb{R}. (0 < x < r \Rightarrow A(x)))$ using CAS (e.g. quantifier elimination).

5.2   Experiments

We analyzed two WHILE^{dt} programs—the water-level monitor (Fig. 2) and the thermostat (Fig. 4)—with our prototype. The experiments were on Apple MacBook Pro with 2.6 GHz Dual-core Intel Core i5 CPU and 8 GB memory and the execution times are the average of 10 runs.

Water-Level Monitor. This is a piecewise-linear dynamics and a typical example used in hybrid automata literature. Our tool automates the analysis presented in Sect. 2; the execution time was 22.151 s.

Thermostat. The dynamics of this example is beyond piecewise-linear. The nonstandard abstract interpretation successfully analyzes this example without explicit piecewise-linear approximation. We believe this result witnesses a potential of our approach. We skip how it analyzes this example since the procedure is the same as the water-level monitor case. Our tool executes in 2.259 sec. and outputs an approximation from which we obtain an invariant $18 - 54 * \mathtt{dt} \leq x \leq 22 + 24 * \mathtt{dt}$.

6   Conclusions and Future Work

We presented an extended abstract interpretation framework in which hybrid systems are *exactly* modeled as programs with infinitesimals. The logical infrastructure by *nonstandard analysis* (in particular the *transfer principle*) establishes its soundness. Termination is also ensured for *uniform* widening operators. Our prototype analyzer automates the extended abstract interpretation on the domain of convex polyhedra.

Regrettably our current implementation is premature and does not compare—in precision or scalability—with the state-of-art tools for hybrid system reachability such as SpaceEx [17] and Flow* [5]. In fact the two examples in Sect. 5.2 are the only ones that we have so far succeeded to analyze. For other examples—especially nonlinear ones, to which our framework is applicable in principle—the analysis results are too imprecise to be useful. To enhance the precision and scalability there are some possible directions of future work. Firstly, we could utilize trace partitioning [31], narrowing operators (the use of narrowing operators in the domain of convex polyhedra is indicated in [23, Sect. 3.4]) and other techniques that have been introduced for the precision of the analysis. Secondly, we believe abstract domains such as *ellipsoids* [14], or some new ones that are tailored to nonlinear dynamics, can improve our analyzer. Finally, the lack of scalability is mainly due to our current way of eliminating dt (namely via Proposition 3.14): it relies on *quantifier elimination (QE)* that is highly expensive. A faster alternative is desired.

References

1. Alur, R., Courcoubetis, C., Henzinger, T.A., Ho, P.: Hybrid automata: an algorithmic approach to the specification and verification of hybrid systems. In: Grossman, R.L., Ravn, A.P., Rischel, H., Nerode, A. (eds.) HS 1991 and HS 1992. LNCS, vol. 736. Springer, Heidelberg (1993)
2. Bagnara, R., Hill, P.M., Zaffanella, E.: The parma polyhedra library: toward a complete set of numerical abstractions for the analysis and verification of hardware and software systems. Sci. Comput. Program. **72**(1–2), 3–21 (2008)
3. Bagnara, R., Hill, P.M., Ricci, E., Zaffanella, E.: Precise widening operators for convex polyhedra. Sci. Comput. Program. **58**(1–2), 28–56 (2005)
4. Beauxis, R., Mimram, S.: A non-standard semantics for Kahn networks in continuous time. In: CSL, pp. 35–50 (2011)
5. Chen, X., Ábrahám, E., Sankaranarayanan, S.: Flow*: an analyzer for non-linear hybrid systems. In: Sharygina, N., Veith, H. (eds.) CAV 2013. LNCS, vol. 8044, pp. 258–263. Springer, Heidelberg (2013)
6. Chernikova, N.: Algorithm for finding a general formula for the non-negative solutions of a system of linear equations. USSR Comput. Math. Math. Phys. **4**(4), 151–158 (1964)
7. Chernikova, N.: Algorithm for finding a general formula for the non-negative solutions of a system of linear inequalities. USSR Comput. Math. Math. Phys. **5**(2), 228–233 (1965)
8. Chernikova, N.: Algorithm for discovering the set of all the solutions of a linear programming problem. USSR Comput. Math. Math. Phys. **8**(6), 282–293 (1968)
9. Cousot, P.: Semantic foundations of program analysis. In: Muchnick, S., Jones, N. (eds.) Program Flow Analysis: Theory and Applications, chap. 10, pp. 303–342. Prentice-Hall Inc, Englewood Cliffs, New Jersey (1981)

10. Cousot, P., Cousot, R.: Abstract interpretation: A unified lattice model for static analysis of programs by construction or approximation of fixpoints. In: Conference Record of the Fourth ACM Symposium on Principles of Programming Languages, Los Angeles, California, USA, January 1977. pp. 238–252 (1977)

11. Cousot, P., Cousot, R.: Abstract interpretation frameworks. J. Log. Comput. 2(4), 511–547 (1992)

12. Cousot, P., Cousot, R., Feret, J., Mauborgne, L., Miné, A., Monniaux, D., Rival, X.: The ASTREÉ analyzer. In: Sagiv, M. (ed.) ESOP 2005. LNCS, vol. 3444, pp. 21–30. Springer, Heidelberg (2005)

13. Cousot, P., Halbwachs, N.: Automatic discovery of linear restraints among variables of a program. In: Conference Record of the Fifth Annual ACM Symposium on Principles of Programming Languages, Tucson, Arizona, USA, January 1978, pp. 84–96 (1978)

14. Feret, J.: Static analysis of digital filters. In: Schmidt, D. (ed.) ESOP 2004. LNCS, vol. 2986, pp. 33–48. Springer, Heidelberg (2004)

15. Fränzle, M., Herde, C., Teige, T., Ratschan, S., Schubert, T.: Efficient solving of large non-linear arithmetic constraint systems with complex boolean structure. JSAT 1(3–4), 209–236 (2007)

16. Frehse, G.: PHAVer: algorithmic verification of hybrid systems past HyTech. In: Morari, M., Thiele, L. (eds.) HSCC 2005. LNCS, vol. 3414, pp. 258–273. Springer, Heidelberg (2005)

17. Frehse, G., Le Guernic, C., Donzé, A., Cotton, S., Ray, R., Lebeltel, O., Ripado, R., Girard, A., Dang, T., Maler, O.: SpaceEx: scalable verification of hybrid systems. In: Gopalakrishnan, G., Qadeer, S. (eds.) CAV 2011. LNCS, vol. 6806, pp. 379–395. Springer, Heidelberg (2011)

18. Goldblatt, R.: Lectures on the Hyperreals: An Introduction to Nonstandard Analysis. Graduate Texts in Mathematics. Springer, New York (1998)

19. Halbwachs, N.: Determination automatique de relations linaires vrifiespar les variables d'un programme. Thse de 3e cycle, Universit Scientifique et Mdicale de Grenoble (1979)

20. Halbwachs, N.: Delay analysis in synchronous programs. In: Proceedings of 5th International Conference on Computer Aided Verification, CAV 1993, Elounda, Greece, 28 June - 1 July 1993, pp. 333–346 (1993)

21. Halbwachs, N., Proy, Y., Roumanoff, P.: Verification of real-time systems using linear relation analysis. Formal Methods Syst. Des. 11(2), 157–185 (1997)

22. Hasuo, I., Suenaga, K.: Exercises in *Nonstandard Static Analysis* of hybrid systems. In: Madhusudan, P., Seshia, S.A. (eds.) CAV 2012. LNCS, vol. 7358, pp. 462–478. Springer, Heidelberg (2012)

23. Henriksen, K.S., Banda, G., Gallagher, J.P.: Experiments with a convex polyhedral analysis tool for logic programs. CoRR abs/0712.2737 (2007). http://arxiv.org/abs/0712.2737

24. Henzinger, T.A., Ho, P.: Algorithmic analysis of nonlinear hybrid systems. In: Proceedings of 7th International Conference Computer Aided Verification, Liège, Belgium, 3–5 July 1995, pp. 225–238 (1995)

25. Henzinger, T.A., Ho, P., Wong-Toi, H.: HYTECH: A model checker for hybrid systems. STTT 1(1–2), 110–122 (1997)

26. Hurd, A., Loeb, P.: An Introduction to Nonstandard Real Analysis. Pure and Applied Mathematics. Elsevier Science, New York (1985)

27. Kido, K.: An Alternative Denotational Semantics for an Imperative Language with Infinitesimals. Bachelor's thesis, The University of Tokyo: Japan (2013)

28. Kido, K., Chaudhuri, S., Hasuo, I.: Abstract interpretation with infinitesimals–towards scalability in nonstandard static analysis (2015). extended version with appendices http://arxiv.org/
29. Kido, K., Chaudhuri, S., Hasuo, I.: Source code of the prototype nonstandard abstract interpreter (2015). http://www-mmm.is.s.u-tokyo.ac.jp/~kkido/
30. Le Verge, H.: A note on Chernikova's Algorithm. Technical report 635, IRISA, Rennes, France, Febuary 1992
31. Mauborgne, L., Rival, X.: Trace partitioning in abstract interpretation based static analyzers. In: Sagiv, M. (ed.) ESOP 2005. LNCS, vol. 3444, pp. 5–20. Springer, Heidelberg (2005)
32. Platzer, A., Quesel, J.-D.: KeYmaera: a hybrid theorem prover for hybrid systems (system description). In: Armando, A., Baumgartner, P., Dowek, G. (eds.) IJCAR 2008. LNCS (LNAI), vol. 5195, pp. 171–178. Springer, Heidelberg (2008)
33. Robinson, A.: Non-standard Analysis. Studies in logic and the foundations of mathematics. North-Holland Pub. Co., Amsterdam (1966)
34. Suenaga, K., Hasuo, I.: Programming with Infinitesimals: A WHILE-Language for Hybrid System Modeling. In: Aceto, L., Henzinger, M., Sgall, J. (eds.) ICALP 2011, Part II. LNCS, vol. 6756, pp. 392–403. Springer, Heidelberg (2011)
35. Suenaga, K., Sekine, H., Hasuo, I.: Hyperstream processing systems: nonstandard modeling of continuous-time signals. In: The 40th Annual ACM SIGPLAN-SIGACT Symposium on Principles of Programming Languages, POPL 2013, Rome, Italy, 23–25 January 2013, pp. 417–430 (2013)
36. Winskel, G.: The Formal Semantics of Programming Languages: An Introduction. MIT Press, Cambridge (1993)

Lipschitz Robustness of Timed I/O Systems

Thomas A. Henzinger[1], Jan Otop[1,2], and Roopsha Samanta[1(✉)]

[1] IST, Klosterneuburg, Austria
[2] University of Wrocław, Wrocław, Poland
roopsha@utexas.edu

Abstract. We present the first study of robustness of systems that are both timed as well as reactive (I/O). We study the behavior of such timed I/O systems in the presence of *uncertain inputs* and formalize their robustness using the analytic notion of Lipschitz continuity: a timed I/O system is K-(Lipschitz) robust if the perturbation in its output is at most K times the perturbation in its input. We quantify input and output perturbation using *similarity functions* over timed words such as the timed version of the Manhattan distance and the Skorokhod distance. We consider two models of timed I/O systems — timed transducers and asynchronous sequential circuits. We show that K-robustness of timed transducers can be decided in polynomial space under certain conditions. For asynchronous sequential circuits, we reduce K-robustness w.r.t. timed Manhattan distances to K-robustness of discrete letter-to-letter transducers and show PSPACE-completeness of the problem.

1 Introduction

Real-time systems operating in physical environments, i.e., timed I/O systems, are increasingly commonplace today. An inherent problem faced by such computational systems is *input uncertainty* caused by sensor inaccuracies, imprecise environment assumptions etc. This means that the input data may be noisy and/or may have timing errors. In such scenarios, it is not enough for a system to be functionally correct. It is also desirable that the system be *continuous* or *robust*, i.e., the system behavior degrade smoothly in the presence of input disturbances [11]. We illustrate this property with two examples of timed I/O systems.

Example 1. Consider two timed I/O systems which process a sequence of ticks and calibrate the intervals between the ticks (see Fig. 1). In particular, the goal is to track if an interval is greater than some given Δ. The first timed I/O system $\mathcal{T}$ is an *offline* processor: upon arrival of each tick, $\mathcal{T}$ waits till the next tick, and outputs $\top$ if the interval is less than or equal to Δ and $\bot$ otherwise. The second

---

This research was supported in part by the European Research Council (ERC) under grant 267989 (QUAREM), by the Austrian Science Fund (FWF) under grants S11402-N23 (RiSE) and Z211-N23 (Wittgenstein Award), and by the National Science Centre (NCN), Poland under grant 2014/15/D/ST6/04543.

B. Jobstmann and K.R.M. Leino (Eds.): VMCAI 2016, LNCS 9583, pp. 250–267, 2016.
DOI: 10.1007/978-3-662-49122-5_12

timed I/O system $\mathcal{T}'$ is an *online* processor: $\mathcal{T}'$ starts generating $\top$ immediately upon arrival of each tick, and switches its output to $\bot$ after Δ time, until the arrival of the next tick.

Consider two periodic tick sequences: i_1 and i_2 as shown in Fig. 1. The duration between ticks in i_1, i_2 is Δ, $\Delta + \epsilon$, respectively. Hence, i_2 can be viewed as a timing distortion of i_1. While the output o_1 of $\mathcal{T}$ on i_1 is a constant sequence of $\top$, the output o_2 of $\mathcal{T}$ on i_2 consists of $\bot$ entirely. Thus, a small timing perturbation in the input of $\mathcal{T}$ can cause a large perturbation in its output. On the other hand, a small timing perturbation in the input of $\mathcal{T}'$ only causes a proportionally small perturbation in its output. Indeed, while the output o_1' of $\mathcal{T}'$ on i_1 is also a constant sequence of $\top$, the output o_2' of $\mathcal{T}'$ on i_2 is a sequence of $\top$, with periodic $\bot$ intervals of ϵ-duration. Thus, the behaviour of $\mathcal{T}$ is more robust to small input timing distortions than the behaviour of $\mathcal{T}'$.

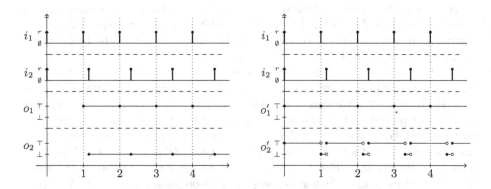

Fig. 1. System behaviour under timing distortion

Example 2. Consider two asynchronous sequential circuits $\mathcal{C}$ and $\mathcal{C}'$ shown in Fig. 2. For each circuit, the input is i, the output is $i \vee y$ and the value of variable y at time t equals the value of variable z at time $t - 1$. In circuit $\mathcal{C}$, variable z equals $i \vee y$ and in circuit $\mathcal{C}'$, variable z equals i. Initially y is set to 0.

Consider inputs i_1 and i_2 such that i_1 is constantly 0, and i_2 is 1 in the interval $[0, \epsilon)$ and 0 otherwise (see Fig. 2). Thus, i_2 can be viewed as representing a transient fault in i_1. The outputs of both $\mathcal{C}$ and $\mathcal{C}'$ for i_1 are constantly 0. For i_2, $\mathcal{C}$ produces a periodic sequence that equals 1 exactly in the intervals $[0, \epsilon), [1, 1 + \epsilon), [2, 2 + \epsilon) \ldots$, whereas $\mathcal{C}'$ produces an output that equals 1 only in the intervals $[0, \epsilon)$ and $[1, 1 + \epsilon]$. Thus, the effect of a small input perturbation propagates forever in the output of $\mathcal{C}$. On the other hand, the effect of a small input perturbation is limited to a bounded time in the output of $\mathcal{C}'$. The behaviour of $\mathcal{C}$ is more robust to transient faults than the behaviour of $\mathcal{C}'$.

We present the first study of robustness of systems that are both timed as well as reactive (I/O). We formalize robustness of timed I/O systems as Lipschitz continuity [12,18,19]. A function is Lipschitz-continuous if its output changes proportionally to every change in the input. Given a constant K and *similarity*

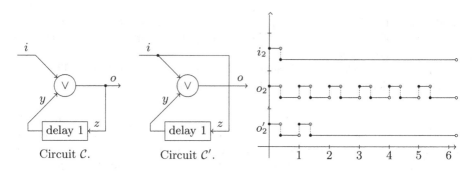

Fig. 2. System behaviour under transient fault

functions d_Σ, d_Γ for computing the input, output perturbation, respectively, a timed I/O system $\mathcal{T}$ is defined to be K-Lipschitz robust (or simply, K-robust) w.r.t. d_Σ, d_Γ if for all timed words w, v in the domain of $\mathcal{T}$ with finite $d_\Sigma(w, v)$, $d_\Gamma(\mathcal{T}(w), \mathcal{T}(v)) \leq K d_\Sigma(w, v)$.

In this work, we focus on K-robustness of two models of timed I/O systems — timed transducers (Example 1) and asynchronous sequential circuits (ASCs) (Example 2). We define a timed transducer as a timed automaton over an alphabet partitioned into an input alphabet d_Σ and an output alphabet d_Γ. A timed transducer defines a transduction over timed words, or a *timed relation*. An ASC is composed of a combinational circuit (CC), *delay elements* and *feedback loops* (see, for instance, Fig. 2). An ASC also defines a timed relation. However, timed transducers and ASCs are expressively incomparable. A simple ASC that delays its inputs by 1 time unit is not expressible by timed transducers — intuitively, the timed transducer at time 1 would need to remember arbitrarily many timed events from the interval $[0, 1)$. Conversely, a simple timed transducer that outputs 1 if the duration between preceding input events is greater than 1, and 0 otherwise cannot be expressed by any ASC.

We show that K-robustness of timed transducers is undecidable is general, and decidable under certain conditions on similarity functions. The key idea behind decidability is a reduction of K-robustness of timed transducers to emptiness of weighted timed automata. In particular, our decidability results include the following:

1. K-robustness w.r.t. timed Manhattan distances is PSPACE-complete,
2. K-robustness w.r.t. accumulated delay distances is PSPACE-complete under practically-viable environment assumptions (e.g., minimum symbol persistence), and,
3. K-robustness is PSPACE-complete if the input perturbation is computed as a Skorokhod distance and the output perturbation is computed as a timed Manhattan distance.

We reduce K-robustness of ASCs w.r.t. timed Manhattan distances to K-robustness of discrete letter-to-letter transducers, and show that K-robustness of ASCs is PSPACE-complete. The reduction consists of two steps. First, we show that on inputs that are *step functions*, ASCs behave like discrete letter-to-letter transducers. Second, we show that if an ASC is not K-robust w.r.t. timed Manhattan distances, there exists a witness consisting of a pair of inputs that are step functions.

The paper is organized as follows. We first recall necessary formalisms (Sect. 2) and present our models of timed I/O systems (Sect. 3). We formalize our notion of robustness for such systems (Sect. 4) and define the similarity functions of interest (Sect. 5). We then present our results on robustness analysis of timed transducers (Sect. 6) and ASCs(Sect. 7) w.r.t. various similarity functions.

Related Work. Robustness of systems has been studied in different contexts such as robust control [13], timed automata [5,10], discrete transducers [12,18,19] and sequential circuits [9]. However, none of these results are directly applicable to robustness of timed I/O systems. There are two main reasons. First, we are interested in robustness w.r.t. *input* perturbation. Second, timed I/O systems exhibit both discrete and continuous behavior. Robust control typically involves reasoning about continuous state-spaces and focuses on designing controllers that function properly in the presence of perturbation in various internal parameters of a system's model. The study of robustness of timed automata focuses on the design of models whose language is robust to infinitesimal timing perturbation (e.g. clock drifts) and does not focus on quantifying the effect of input perturbation on the output. Robustness analysis of finite-state transducers is limited to purely discrete systems and data. In [9], the authors study the robustness of synchronous sequential circuits modeled as discrete Mealy machines. Their notion of robustness bounds the persistence of the effect of a sporadic disturbance and is also limited to discrete data.

In other related work [3,6,16], the authors develop different notions of robustness for discrete reactive systems with ω-regular specifications interacting with uncertain environments. There has also been foundational work on continuity and robustness analysis of software programs manipulating numbers [7,8,17].

2   Preliminaries

2.1   Timed Automata

We briefly present basic notions regarding timed automata. We refer the reader to [2] for a comprehensive survey on timed automata.

Timed Words. Let $\mathbb{R}^+$, $\mathbb{Q}^+$ denote the set of all *nonnegative* real numbers, rational numbers, respectively. A (finite or infinite) *timed word* over an alphabet Σ is a word over $(\Sigma, \mathbb{R}^+)$: $(a_0, t_0)(a_1, t_1) \ldots$ such that $t_0, t_1, \ldots$ is a weakly increasing sequence. A pair (a, t) is referred to as *an event*. We denote by $\mathcal{TL}(\Sigma)$ the set of all timed words over Σ. For a timed word $w = (a_0, t_0)(a_1, t_1) \ldots$, we define untimed$(w) = a_0 a_1 \ldots$ as the projection of w on the Σ component.

Disjoint Union of Timed Words. Let w_1, w_2 be timed words over the alphabet Σ. We define *the disjoint union* of w_1 and w_2, denoted $w_1 \oplus w_2$, as the union of events of w_1 and w_2, annotated with the index of the word (w_1 or w_2) it belongs to. E.g. $\langle a, 0.4 \rangle \langle b, 2.1 \rangle \ \oplus \ \langle b, 0.3 \rangle \langle b, 0.4 \rangle \ = \ \langle (b,2), 0.3 \rangle \langle (a,1), 0.4 \rangle \langle (b,2), 0.4 \rangle \langle (b,1), 2.1 \rangle$. The word $w_1 \oplus w_2$ is a timed word over the alphabet $\Sigma \times \{1,2\}$.

Clocks. Let X be a set of clocks. A *clock constraint* is a conjunction of terms of the form $x \otimes c$, where $x \in X$, $c \in \mathbb{Q}^+$ and $\otimes \in \{<, \leq, =, \geq, >\}$. Let $B(X)$ denote the set of clock constraints. A *clock valuation* ν is a mapping $\nu : X \mapsto \mathbb{R}^+$.

Timed Automata. A *timed automaton* $\mathcal{A}$ is a tuple $(\Sigma, L, l_0, X, \delta, F)$ where Σ is the alphabet of $\mathcal{A}$, L is a set of locations, $l_0 \in L$ is an initial location, X is a set of clocks, $\delta \subseteq L \times \Sigma \times B(X) \times 2^X \times L$ is a switch relation and $F \subseteq L$ is a set of accepting locations.

Semantics of Timed Automata. The semantics of a timed automaton $\mathcal{A}$ is defined using an infinite-state transition system $\mathrm{Pre}_{\mathcal{A}}$ over the alphabet $(\Sigma \cup \{\epsilon\}) \times \mathbb{R}^+$. A *state* q of $\mathrm{Pre}_{\mathcal{A}}$ is a pair (l, ν) consisting of a location $l \in L$ and a clock valuation ν. A state $q = (l, \nu)$ satisfies a clock constraint g, denoted $q \models g$, if the formula obtained from g by substituting clocks from X by their valuations in ν is true. There are two kinds of transitions in $\mathrm{Pre}_{\mathcal{A}}$: (*i*) *elapse of time*: $(l, \nu) \to^\tau (l, \nu')$ iff for every $x \in X$, $\nu'(x) = \nu(x) + \tau$ and (*ii*) *location switch*: $(l, \nu) \to^a (l', \nu')$ iff there is a switch of $\mathcal{A}$, (l, a, g, γ, l'), such that $(l, \nu) \models g$, and for each $x \in X$, $\nu'(x) = 0$ if $x \in \gamma$ and $\nu'(x) = \nu(x)$ otherwise. Consecutive elapses of time can be merged, therefore we assume that an elapse of time is followed by a location switch. The initial state of $\mathrm{Pre}_{\mathcal{A}}$ is the state (l_0, ν) where for each $x \in X$, $\nu(x) = 0$. The accepting states of $\mathrm{Pre}_{\mathcal{A}}$ are all states of the form $\langle l, \nu \rangle$, where $l \in F$. A *run* of $\mathcal{A}$ over a timed word $w = (a_0, t_0)(a_1, t_1) \ldots (a_k, t_k)$ is the sequence: $q_0 \to^{t_0} q_1 \to^{a_0} q_2 \to^{t_1 - t_0} q_3 \to^{a_1} \ldots \to^{a_k} q_{2k+2}$, where q_0 is the initial state of $\mathrm{Pre}_{\mathcal{A}}$. The run is accepting if q_{2k+2} is an accepting state. The set of accepting runs of $\mathcal{A}$ is denoted $[\mathcal{A}]$. We say a timed word w is accepted by $\mathcal{A}$ if there is a run over w in $[\mathcal{A}]$.

The *emptiness* problem for timed automata is as follows: given a timed automaton $\mathcal{A}$, decide whether $[\mathcal{A}]$ is nonempty. The emptiness problem is also referred to as the *reachability* problem as it is equivalent to reachability of an accepting state in $\mathrm{Pre}_{\mathcal{A}}$.

2.2 Weighted Timed Automata

A *weighted timed automaton* (WTA) is a timed automaton augmented by a function $C : L \cup \delta \mapsto \mathbb{Q}$ that associates *weights* with the locations and switches of the timed automaton. The *value* of a run $(l_0, \nu_0) \to^{\tau_0} (l_0, \nu_1) \to^{a_0} \ldots \to^{a_k} (l_k, \nu_{2k+2})$ is given by

$$\sum_{i=0}^{k} C(l_i)\tau_i + \sum_{i=0}^{k} C(e_i)$$

where e_i is the switch taken in the transition $(l_i, \nu_{2i+1}) \to^{a_i} (l_{i+1}, \nu_{2i+2})$. The value of a timed word w assigned by a WTA $\mathcal{A}$, denoted $\mathcal{L}_\mathcal{A}(w)$, is defined as the infimum over values of all accepting runs of $\mathcal{A}$ on w.

The *quantitative emptiness* problem for WTA is as follows: given a WTA $\mathcal{A}$ and $\lambda \in \mathbb{Q}$, decide whether $\mathcal{A}$ has an accepting run with value smaller than λ.

Theorem 3 *[4]. The quantitative emptiness problem for WTA is* PSPACE-*complete.*

A WTA $\mathcal{A}$ is *functional* if for every timed word w, all accepting runs of $\mathcal{A}$ on w have the same value.

2.3   Discrete Transducers

Discrete Transducers. A discrete transducer $\mathcal{T}$ is a tuple $(\Sigma, \Gamma, Q, Q_0, E, F)$ where Σ is the input alphabet, Γ is the output alphabet, Q is a finite nonempty set of states, $Q_0 \subseteq Q$ is a set of initial states, $E \subseteq Q \times \Sigma \times \Gamma^* \times Q$ is a set of transitions, and F is a set of accepting states.

Semantics of Discrete Transducers. A run γ of $\mathcal{T}$ on an input word $s = s[1]s[2] \ldots s[n]$ is defined in terms of the sequence: $(q_0, u_1), (q_1, u_2), \ldots, (q_{n-1}, u_n)$, (q_n, ϕ) where $q_0 \in Q_0$ and for each $i \in \{1, 2, \ldots, n\}$, $(q_{i-1}, s[i], u_i, q_i) \in E$. A run $(q_0, u_1), \ldots (q_{n-1}, u_n), (q_n, \phi)$ is *accepting* if $q_n \in F$. The output of $\mathcal{T}$ along a run is the word $u = u_1 \cdot u_2 \cdot \ldots \cdot u_n$ if the run is accepting, and is undefined otherwise. The *transduction computed* by a discrete transducer $\mathcal{T}$ is the relation $[\![\mathcal{T}]\!] \subseteq \Sigma^\omega \times \Gamma^\omega$ (resp., $[\![\mathcal{T}]\!] \subseteq \Sigma^* \times \Gamma^*$), where $(s, u) \in [\![\mathcal{T}]\!]$ iff there is an accepting run of $\mathcal{T}$ on s with u as the output along that run.

Types of Discrete Transducers. A discrete transducer $\mathcal{T}$ is called *functional* if the relation $[\![\mathcal{T}]\!]$ is a function. In this case, we use $[\![\mathcal{T}]\!](s)$ to denote the unique output word generated along any accepting run of $\mathcal{T}$ on input word s. A discrete transducer is a *letter-to-letter* transducer if in every transition (q, a, u, a') we have $|u| = 1$.

3   Models of Timed I/O Systems

In this section, we present two models of timed I/O systems whose robustness will be studied in the following sections. The reason for studying these models separately is that timed transducers and ASCs are expressively incomparable (as explained in the introduction).

3.1   Timed Transducers

In the following, we define timed transducers, which extend classical discrete transducers.

Definition 4 (Timed Transducer). *A timed transducer T is a timed automaton over an alphabet partitioned into an input alphabet Σ and an output alphabet Γ.*

Semantics of Timed Transducers. Given a timed transducer T, we define a relation $[\![T]\!] \subseteq \mathcal{TL}(\Sigma) \times \mathcal{TL}(\Gamma)$ by $[\![T]\!] = \{(w,v) : w \in \mathcal{TL}(\Sigma), v \in \mathcal{TL}(\Gamma), T$ accepts $w \oplus v\}$. We say that $v \in \mathcal{TL}(\Gamma)$ is an *output* of T on $w \in \mathcal{TL}(\Sigma)$ if $(w,v) \in [\![T]\!]$.

Remark 5. Our model of timed transducers is similar to *timed automata with inputs and outputs* presented in [14]. The main difference is the absence of *deadlines* in our automaton model.

In the following proposition, we relate the discrete part of the relation defined by a timed transducer to the relation defined by a discrete transducer. For a timed relation $R \subseteq \mathcal{TL}(\Sigma) \times \mathcal{TL}(\Gamma)$, let untimed($R$) denote $\{(\text{untimed}(w), \text{untimed}(v)) : (w,v) \in R\}$.

Proposition 6. *(i): For every timed transducer T that has no cycles labeled by Γ, there exists a (nondeterministic) discrete transducer T^d of exponential size in size(T) such that untimed($[\![T]\!]$) and $[\![T^d]\!]$ coincide. (ii): For every discrete transducer T^d, there exists a timed transducer T that has no cycles labeled by Γ such that untimed($[\![T]\!]$) and $[\![T^d]\!]$ coincide.*

Functionality. A transducer is *timed-functional* iff $[\![T]\!]$ is a function, i.e., for all $w \in \mathcal{TL}(\Sigma)$ and $v_1, v_2 \in \mathcal{TL}(\Gamma)$, if both $(w,v_1) \in [\![T]\!]$ and $(w,v_2) \in [\![T]\!]$, then $v_1 = v_2$. For a timed-functional transducer T, we use $[\![T]\!](w)$ to denote the unique output of T on w.

Proposition 7. *Deciding timed functionality of a timed transducer is* PSPACE-*complete.*

Observe that a timed transducer does not have to be timed-functional, even if it is deterministic when viewed as a timed automaton. Indeed, a trivial timed automaton that accepts every word over the alphabet $\Sigma \cup \Gamma$ is deterministic and is a timed transducer. However, it is not functional.

In Proposition 8, we present a sufficient condition for timed-functionality which can be checked in polynomial time. We further identify a class of transducers for which this condition is also necessary. A switch in a timed automaton is *rigid* iff it is guarded by a constraint containing equality. A location l in a timed automaton is unambiguous if for any pair of outgoing switches, their constraints g_1 and g_2 are strongly inconsistent, i.e., for all $x_1, \ldots, x_n, t \in \mathbb{R}^+$, $g_1(x_1, \ldots, x_n) \wedge g_2(x_1 + t, \ldots, x_n + t)$ is false. A transducer is *safe* if every location with outgoing Σ switches is accepting.

Proposition 8. *(1) A deterministic timed transducer in which all switches labeled by Γ are (a) rigid, and (b) all locations with outgoing switches labeled by Γ are unambiguous, is functional. (2) Every function defined by a deterministic safe timed transducer is also defined by a deterministic safe timed transducer satisfying (a) and (b) from (1).*

3.2   Asynchronous Sequential Circuits

The second model of timed I/O systems that we consider is an asynchronous sequential circuit (ASC). A generic ASC is shown in Fig. 3 and some example ASC's are shown in Fig. 2.

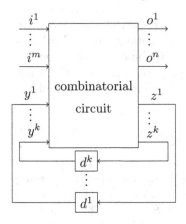

Fig. 3. A generic ASC.

An ASC is an I/O system composed of a combinational circuit (CC) and *memory devices*, or *delay elements*. A CC is simply a Boolean logic circuit that computes Boolean functions of its inputs. A CC is *memoryless*: the values of the circuit's output variables at time instant t are functions of the values of the circuit's input variables at the same time instant t. A delay element is always labeled with some $d > 0$. The output of a d-delay element at time t equals its input at time $t - d$. We consider delays that are natural numbers (see Remark 11). ASC's may contain cycles, or *feedback loops*. Each such cycle is required to contain at least one delay element. Due to the presence of delay elements and feedback loops, an ASC has memory: the outputs of an ASC at time instant t are in general functions of its inputs at time instant t as well as at time instants $t' < t$. The inputs of the delay elements of an ASC are called *excitation variables*. The outputs of the delay elements of an ASC are called *secondary variables*. The relationships between input, output, excitation and secondary variables of an ASC are graphically represented in Fig. 3 and formally defined below.

Definition 9. *Let C be an ASC with input variables $\mathcal{I} = \{i^1, \ldots, i^m\}$, output variables $\mathcal{O} = \{o^1, \ldots, o^n\}$, excitation variables $\mathcal{Z} = \{z^1, \ldots, z^k\}$, secondary variables $\mathcal{Y} = \{y^1, \ldots, y^k\}$ and delay elements $\Delta = \{d^1, \ldots, d^k\}$. Let $i(t)$ and $\mathcal{I}(t)$ denote the values of input i and all inputs $\mathcal{I}$ at time t, respectively. One can similarly define $o(t)$, $\mathcal{Y}(t)$ etc. We have the following:*

$$\forall j \in [1, k] : y^j(t) = \begin{cases} 0 & \text{if } t = [0, d^j) \\ z^j(t - d^j) & \text{if } t \geq d^j \end{cases}$$

$$\forall j \in [1, k] : z^j(t) = f^j(x^1(t), \ldots, x^m(t), y^1(t), \ldots, y^k(t))$$

$$\forall j \in [1, n] : o^j(t) = g^j(x^1(t), \ldots, x^m(t), y^1(t), \ldots, y^k(t)).$$

Here, $f^1, \ldots, f^k$ and $g^1, \ldots, g^n$ are Boolean functions. The input alphabet *of ASC C, denoted Σ, is given by $\{0, 1\}^m$. The* output alphabet *of C, denoted Γ, is given by $\{0, 1\}^n$. The ASC C defines a transduction $[\![C]\!] \subseteq \mathcal{TL}(\Sigma) \times \mathcal{TL}(\Gamma)$ such that $[\![C]\!]$ is a total function. Thus, the domain of C is given by $\mathrm{dom}(C) = \mathcal{TL}(\Sigma)$. We use $[\![C]\!](w)$ to denote the unique output of C on w.*

Remark 10. Our model of ASCs shares some similarities (such as delays) with models of discrete event systems ([20]). The main difference is that, in addition to timing relations, ASCs also express functional relations between inputs and outputs.

Remark 11 (Time stretching for ASCs). Let $s > 0$ and let $\lambda_s : R \mapsto R$ be *time stretching* defined for every $t \in R$ as $\lambda_s(t) = s \cdot t$. Consider an ASC with rational delays $\mathcal{C}$ and an ASC with rational delays $\mathcal{C}_s$ obtained from $\mathcal{C}$ by multiplying all delays by s. Observe that for every input $i(t)$ and the corresponding output $o(t)$ of $\mathcal{C}$, the signal $o(\lambda_s(t))$ is the output of $\mathcal{C}_s$ on input $i(\lambda_s(t))$. Thus, ASCs with rational delays do not introduce any behaviours that are significant for robustness over ASCs with integer delays.

4   Problem Statement

Similarity Functions. In our work, we use similarity functions to measure the similarity between timed words. Let S be a set of timed words and let $\mathbb{R}^\infty$ denote the set $\mathbb{R} \cup \{\infty\}$. A similarity function $d : S \times S \to \mathbb{R}^\infty$ is a function with the properties: $\forall x, y \in S : (1) \ d(x,y) \geq 0$ and $(2) \ d(x,y) = d(y,x)$. A similarity function d is also a distance (function or metric) if it satisfies the additional properties: $\forall x, y, z \in S : (3) \ d(x,y) = 0$ iff $x = y$ and (4) $d(x,z) \leq d(x,y) + d(y,z)$. We emphasize that in our work we do not need to restrict similarity functions to be distances.

In this paper, we are interested in studying the *K-Lipschitz robustness* of timed-functional transducers and ASCs.

Definition 12 (K-Lipschitz Robustness of Timed I/O Systems). *Let $\mathcal{T}$ be a timed-functional transducer or an ASC with $[\![\mathcal{T}]\!] \subseteq \mathcal{TL}(\Sigma) \times \mathcal{TL}(\Gamma)$. Given a constant $K \in \mathbb{Q}$ with $K > 0$ and similarity functions $d_\Sigma : \mathcal{TL}(\Sigma) \times \mathcal{TL}(\Sigma) \to \mathbb{R}^\infty$ and $d_\Gamma : \mathcal{TL}(\Gamma) \times \mathcal{TL}(\Gamma) \to \mathbb{R}^\infty$, the timed I/O system $\mathcal{T}$ is called K-Lipschitz robust w.r.t. d_Σ, d_Γ if:*

$$\forall w, v \in \operatorname{dom}(\mathcal{T}) : \ d_\Sigma(w,v) < \infty \Rightarrow d_\Gamma([\![\mathcal{T}]\!](w), [\![\mathcal{T}]\!](v)) \leq K d_\Sigma(w,v).$$

5   Similarity Functions Between Timed Words

Timed Words as Càdlàg Functions. Consider a timed word $w : (a_0, t_0)(a_1, t_1) \ldots (a_k, t_k)$ over (Σ, I), where $I = [t_0, t_k]$ is an interval in $\mathbb{R}^+$. We define a Càdlàg function $w_C : I \mapsto \Sigma$ corresponding to w as follows: for each $j \in \{0, 1, \ldots, k-1\}$, $w_C(t) = a_j$ if $t \in [t_j, t_{j+1})$, and $w_C(t_k) = a_k$. We define a timed word $\operatorname{timed}(w_C) = (\alpha_0, \delta_0)(\alpha_1, \delta_1) \ldots (\alpha_n, \delta_n)$ corresponding to the Càdlàg function w_C such that: for each $j \in \{0, 1, \ldots, n\}$, $\alpha_j = w_C(\delta_j)$ and $\delta_j \in \{\delta_0, \ldots, \delta_n\}$ iff w_C *changes value* at δ_j. The timed word $\operatorname{timed}(w_C)$ can be interpreted as a *stuttering-free* version of the timed word w. The intervals $[\delta_0, \delta_1), [\delta_1, \delta_2), \ldots, [\delta_{n-1}, \delta_n)$ are called *segments* of w.

Example. Let w be the timed word $(a,0)(b,1.3)(a,2)(a,2.9)(c,3.7)(a,5)$. Then w_C is given by the following Càdlàg function over the interval $[0,5]$.

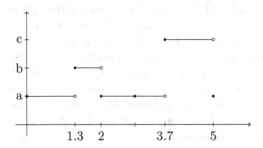

The timed word $\text{timed}(w_C) = (a,0)(b,1.3)(a,2)(c,3.7)(a,5)$.

In what follows, let w, v be timed words over (Σ, I) with $I \subseteq \mathbb{R}^+$. Let w_C, v_C be Càdlàg functions over I, corresponding to w, v, as defined above. We present below several similarity functions between timed words, computed as the similarity function between their corresponding Càdlàg functions. We first present a similarity function between discrete words.

Generalized Manhattan Distance. The *generalized Manhattan distance.* over discrete words s,t is defined as: $d_M(s,t) = \sum_{i=1}^{max(|s|,|t|)} \text{diff}(s[i], t[i])$, where diff is a cost function that assigns costs for substituting letters. When $\text{diff}(a,b)$ is defined to be 1 for all a,b with $a \neq b$, and 0 otherwise, d_M is called the *Manhattan distance.*

Timed Manhattan Distance. The *timed Manhattan distance* d_{TM} extends the generalized Manhattan distance by accumulating the pointwise distance, as defined by diff, between the Càdlàg functions corresponding to timed words. Given diff on Σ:

$$d_{TM}(w,v) = \int_I \text{diff}(w_C(x), v_C(x))dx.$$

Accumulated Delay Distance. The *accumulated delay distance* d_{AD} examines the timed words $\text{timed}(w_C)$ and $\text{timed}(v_C)$. If the projections of these timed words on their Σ components are equal, then the distance $d_{AD}(w,v)$ equals the sum of delays between the corresponding events; otherwise the distance is infinite. Let $\text{timed}(w_C) = (\alpha_0, \delta_0)(\alpha_1, \delta_1) \ldots (\alpha_n, \delta_n)$ and $\text{timed}(v_C) = (\beta_0, \tau_0)(\beta_1, \tau_1) \ldots (\beta_n, \tau_m)$.

$$d_{AD}(w,v) = \begin{cases} \sum_j |\delta_j - \tau_j| & \text{if untimed}(\text{timed}(w_C)) = \text{untimed}(\text{timed}(v_C)) \\ \infty & \text{otherwise.} \end{cases}$$

Skorokhod Distance w.r.t. Timed Manhattan Distance. The *Skorokhod distance* d_S is a popular distance metric for continuous functions. Hence, it is also a natural choice for our Càdlàg functions. The Skorokhod distance permits *wiggling* of the function values as well as the timeline in order to *match up* the functions. The timeline wiggle is executed using continuous bijective functions, denoted λ, over the timeline. The first component of the Skorokhod distance measures the magnitude of the *timing distortion* resulting from a timeline wiggle λ. The second component of the Skorokhod distance measures the magnitude of the *function value mismatch* under λ. The Skorokhod distance is the least value obtained over all such timeline wiggles. The magnitudes of the timing distortion and function value mismatch can be computed and combined in different ways. In our work, the timing distortion is computed as the L_1 norm, the function value mismatch is computed as the timed Manhattan distance and the two are combined using addition. Let Λ be the set of all continuous bijections from the domain I of w_C and v_C onto itself.

$$d_S(w_C, v_C) = \inf_{\lambda \in \Lambda} \left(\|\text{Id} - \lambda\|_1 + d_{TM}(w_C, v_C \circ \lambda) \right),$$

where Id is the identity function over I, $\|.\|_1$ is the L_1-norm over $\mathbb{R}^+$ and $\circ$ is the usual function composition operator.

We now present some helpful connections between the above distances. Let $d_{TM}^{=}$ denote a timed Manhattan distance with diff given by: $\forall a, b \in \Sigma$, $\text{diff}(a, b) = 0$ if $a = b$ and $\text{diff}(a, b) = \infty$ otherwise. Let $D_{TM}^{\leq 1}$ denote a class of timed Manhattan distances, $d_{TM}^{\leq 1}$, with diff satisfying: $\forall a, b \in \Sigma$, $\text{diff}(a, b) \leq 1$.

Proposition 13. *[Relations between distances]. (i) The accumulated delay distance coincides with the Skorokhod distance w.r.t. $d_{TM}^{=}$. (ii) For any $d_{TM}^{\leq 1} \in D_{TM}^{\leq 1}$, the Skorokhod distance w.r.t. $d_{TM}^{\leq 1}$ coincides with $d_{TM}^{\leq 1}$.*

6   Robustness Analysis of Timed Transducers

To investigate K-robustness as a decision problem, one needs to have a finitary encoding of instances of the problem, in particular, of the similarity functions. We use weighted timed automata to represent similarity functions.

Timed-automatic Similarity Function. A timed similarity function d is *computed* by a WTA $\mathcal{A}$ iff for all $w, v \in \mathcal{TL}(\Sigma)$, $d(w, v) = \mathcal{L}_{\mathcal{A}}(w \oplus v)$. A timed similarity function d computed by a WTA is called a *timed-automatic similarity function*.

Unfortunately, checking K-robustness of timed transducers w.r.t. timed-automatic similarity functions is undecidable. The undecidability result follows from a reduction from the universality problem for timed automata, which is undecidable [1].

Theorem 14. *K-robustness of timed transducers w.r.t. timed-automatic similarity functions is undecidable.*

K-robustness can, however, be decided using an automata-based, polynomial-space, sound (but incomplete) procedure: if the procedure certifies a transducer $\mathcal{T}$ to be K-robust, then $\mathcal{T}$ is indeed K-robust. This procedure becomes complete under additional assumptions.

Theorem 15. *(i) There exists a polynomial-space sound procedure that given timed-automatic similarity functions d_Σ, d_Γ and a timed transducer T, decides K-robustness of T w.r.t. d_Σ, d_Γ.*

(ii) There exists a PSPACE-*complete procedure that given timed-automatic similarity functions d_Σ, d_Γ, with d_Γ computed by a functional WTA, and a timed transducer T, decides K-robustness of T w.r.t. d_Σ, d_Γ.*

Proof Sketch. PSPACE-hardness in (ii) follows from a simple reduction from the emptiness problem for timed automata. To show containment in PSPACE, we construct an automaton $\mathcal{A}$ that accepts words that are counterexamples to K-robustness. More precisely, the automaton $\mathcal{A}$ accepts words $w \oplus v \oplus [\![T]\!](w) \oplus [\![T]\!](v)$ with value $K \cdot d_\Sigma(w, v) - d_\Gamma([\![T]\!](w), [\![T]\!](v))$. Therefore, an accepted word with value less than 0 corresponds to timed words w, v that form a counterexample for K-robustness of T w.r.t. d_Σ, d_Γ. The automaton $\mathcal{A}$ is a product automaton that includes a copy of the WTA computing d_Σ, with weights scaled by K, and a copy of the WTA computing d_Γ, with weights scaled by -1. Given words w, v, the value computed by the last WTA is smaller than $-d_\Gamma([\![T]\!](w), [\![T]\!](v))$ in general, and is exactly equal to $-d_\Gamma([\![T]\!](w), [\![T]\!](v))$ if the WTA is functional. It follows that our automata-theoretic procedure for checking K-robustness is sound in general and becomes complete when d_Γ is computed by a functional WTA. □

We now define several timed similarity functions that can be computed by functional and nondeterministic WTA.

Timed Similarity Functions Computed by Functional WTA. We show that the timed Manhattan and accumulated delay distances can be computed by functional WTA.

Lemma 16. *The timed Manhattan distance d_{TM} over timed words is computed by a functional WTA.*

To compute the timed Manhattan distance, the WTA simply tracks the value of `diff` between timed events using its weight function. The semantics of WTA then imply that the value assigned by the automaton to a pair of timed words is precisely the timed Manhattan distance between them.

Lemma 17. *Let D, B be any nonnegative real numbers. The accumulated delay distance d_{AD} over timed words w, v such that:*

1. the duration of any segment in w_C, v_C is greater than D and
2. the delay $|\delta_j - \tau_i|$ between corresponding events in w_C, v_C is less than B, is computed by a functional WTA.

The WTA tracks with its weight function the number of unmatched events. Again, the semantics of WTA imply that the value assigned by the automaton to a pair of timed words is precisely the accumulated delay distance. To make sure that every event is matched to the right event, i.e., the untimed parts are equal, the automaton implements a buffer to store the unmatched events. The assumptions on the minimal duration of events and the maximal delay between the corresponding events imply that the buffer's size is bounded.

Timed Similarity Functions Computed by Nondeterministic WTA. A (restricted) Skorokhod distance can be computed by a nondeterministic WTA. We first prove the following lemma characterizing an essential subset of the set Λ of all timing distortions.

Lemma 18. *[Skorokhod distance is realized by a piecewise linear function]. Let w, v be timed words. Let η be the number of segments in v. For every $\epsilon > 0$, there exists a piecewise linear function λ consisting of η segments such that $|(\|\mathtt{Id} - \lambda\|_1 + d_{TM}(w_C, v_C \circ \lambda)) - d_S(w_C, v_C)| \leq \epsilon$.*

Observe that for piecewise linear functions λ, the value of $\|\mathtt{Id}\|_1 - \lambda$ coincides with the accumulated delay distance between v_C and $v_C \circ \lambda$. This fact, combined with Lemma 18, allows us to compute the Skorokhod distance using a WTA that non-deterministically guesses λ and computes the sum of the accumulated delay between v_C and $v_C \circ \lambda$ and the timed Manhattan distance between w_C and $v_C \circ \lambda$.

Lemma 19. *Let D, B be any nonnegative real numbers. The Skorokhod distance d_S over timed words w, v restricted to timeline wiggles λ such that:*

1. *the duration of any segment in v_C, $v_C \circ \lambda$ is greater than D and*
2. *the delay $|\delta_j - \tau_i|$ between corresponding events in v_C, $v_C \circ \lambda$ is less than B, is computed by a nondeterministic WTA.*

Remark 20. Physical systems typically have a bounded rate at which they can generate/process data. Hence, bounding the minimum possible duration of timed symbols is not a severe restriction from the modeling perspective. Moreover, if an input is delayed arbitrarily, it makes little sense to constraint the system behavior. Hence, for robustness analysis, it is also reasonable to bound the maximum delay between corresponding events.

Summary of Decidability Results. We summarize the decidability results for timed transducers that follow from Theorem 15 and Lemmas 16, 17 and 19.

1. K-robustness is PSPACE-complete for timed Manhattan distances.
2. K-robustness is PSPACE-complete for accumulated delay distances (under environment assumptions from Lemma 17).
3. K-robustness is PSPACE-complete if the input perturbation is computed as a Skorokhod distance (under environment assumptions from Lemma 19) and the output perturbation is computed as a timed Manhattan distance.

7   Robustness Analysis of Asynchronous Sequential Circuits

In this section, we show that robustness of ASCs w.r.t. the timed Manhattan distances is PSPACE-complete. The decision procedure is by reduction to discrete letter-to-letter transducers. Our argument consists of two steps and relies on the use of *step functions* — Càdlàg functions that change values only at integer points. First, we show that on inputs that are step functions, *ASCs* behave like discrete letter-to-letter transducers. Second, we show that if an ASC is not K-robust w.r.t. the timed Manhattan distances, there exists a counterexample consisting of a pair of inputs that are step functions. Therefore, we can reduce K-robustness of ASCs to K-robustness of discrete letter-to-letter transducers, which can be solved employing techniques from [12].

ASCs Transforming Step Functions. There is a natural correspondence between step functions $f : [0, T] \mapsto \{0, 1\}^k$ and words over the alphabet $\{0, 1\}^k$. The function f defines the word $word(f) = f(0)f(1) \ldots f(T-1)$ and, conversely, a word $w \in (\{0, 1\}^k)^*$ defines a step function $func(w)$ such that $word(func(w)) = w$. We aim to show that the behavior of an ASC on a step function f is captured by a discrete transducer on word $word(f)$.

First, observe that an ASC with integer delays transforms step functions into step functions. Indeed, the output at time t depends on the input and secondary variables at time t, which are equal to the values of excitation variables at times $\{t - d^1, \ldots, t - d^k\}$. The excitation variables at times $\{t - d^1, \ldots, t - d^k\}$ depend on inputs and secondary variables at times $\{t - d^1, \ldots, t - d^k\}$. As delays are integers, by unraveling the definition of the output variables (resp., excitation and secondary variables) at time t, we obtain that the variables depend solely on (a subset of) inputs at times $t, t - 1, \ldots, frac(t) + 1, frac(t)$, where $frac(t)$ is the fractional part of t. Therefore, if an input is a step function, then excitation, secondary and output variables are all step functions. Moreover, the value of the step function output in the interval $[j, j + 1)$ with $j \in \mathcal{N}$ can be computed using the input value in the interval $[j, j + 1)$ and the values of excitation variables in the intervals $[j - d^1, j + 1 - d^1), \ldots [j - d^k, j + 1 - d^k)$. Therefore, we can define a discrete letter-to-letter transducer that simulates the given ASC. Such a transducer remembers in its states the values of the excitation variables in the last $\max(d^1, \ldots, d^k)$ intervals.

Lemma 21. *(1) If the input to an ASC is a step function, the output is a step function. (2) Given an ASC C, one can compute in polynomial space a discrete letter-to-letter transducer $\mathcal{T}_C$ such that for every step function f, the output of C on f is $func([\![\mathcal{T}_C(word(f))]\!])$.*

Remark 22. The transducer $\mathcal{T}_C$ in Lemma 21 can be constructed in polynomial space, meaning that its sets of states and accepting states are succinctly representable and we can decide in polynomial time whether a given tuple (q, a, b, q') belongs to the transition relation of $\mathcal{T}_C$.

Counterexamples to K-robustness of ASCs. Consider an ASC with integer delays that is not K-robust w.r.t. d_Σ, d_Γ. Then, there are two input functions f_1, f_2, satisfying $d_\Gamma([\![C]\!](f_1), [\![C]\!](f_2)) > K \cdot d_\Sigma(f_1, f_2)$, that are counterexamples to K-robustness. We show that there exists a pair of step functions g_1, g_2 that are counterexamples to K-robustness as well. Recall that the output of the ASC at time t depends only on inputs at times $t, t - 1, \ldots, frac(t) + 1, frac(t)$. Hence, we argue that if f_1, f_2 are counterexamples to K-robustness, then for some $x \in [0, 1)$, f_1, f_2 restricted to the domains $\Delta_1^x = \{y \in \mathrm{dom}(f_1) \mid frac(y) = x\}$, $\Delta_2^x = \{y \in \mathrm{dom}(f_2) \mid frac(y) = x\}$, respectively, are also counterexamples to K-robustness. Since the sets Δ_1^x, Δ_2^x are discrete, we can define step functions g_1, g_2 based on f_1, f_2 restricted to Δ_1^x, Δ_2^x, respectively..

Lemma 23. *Let $\mathcal{C}$ be an ASC with integer delay elements. If $\mathcal{C}$ is not K-robust w.r.t. timed Manhattan distances d_Σ, d_Γ, then there exists a pair of step functions g_1, g_2 such that $d_\Gamma(\llbracket \mathcal{C} \rrbracket(f_1), \llbracket \mathcal{C} \rrbracket(f_2)) > K \cdot d_\Sigma(f_1, f_2)$.*

K-robustness of Discrete Transducers. We next present a decidability result that follows from [12]. Deciding K-robustness of letter-to-letter transducers w.r.t. generalized Manhattan distances reduces to quantitative non-emptiness of weighted automata with SUM-value function [12]. The latter problem can be solved in nondeterministic logarithmic space, assuming that the weights are represented by numbers of logarithmic length. Hence, we obtain the following result for *short* generalized Manhattan distances, i.e., distances whose `diff` values are represented by numbers of logarithmic length.

Lemma 24. *Deciding K-robustness of letter-to-letter transducers w.r.t. short generalized Manhattan distances is in* NLOGSPACE.

We can now characterize the complexity of checking K-robustness of ASCs.

Theorem 25. *Deciding K-robustness of ASCs with respect to timed Manhattan distances is* PSPACE-*complete.*

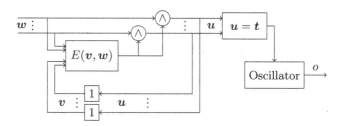

Fig. 4. The diagram of an ASC from the reduction of the reachability in succinctly represented graphs to K-robustness of ASCs.

Proof. Observe that the timed Manhattan distance between step functions f, g equals the generalized Manhattan distance between the words $word(f), word(g)$ corresponding to step functions f, g. This, together with Lemmas 21 and 23, allows us to reduce checking K-robustness of ASCs w.r.t. timed Manhattan distances to checking K-robustness of the corresponding letter-to-letter transducers w.r.t. generalized Manhattan distances. It then follows from Lemma 24 that checking K-robustness of ASCs is in PSPACE. Note that we consider short generalized Manhattan distances whose descriptions are logarithmic in the exponential size of the letter-to-letter transducer.

The PSPACE-hardness of checking K-robustness of ASCs is obtained by a reduction from the reachability problem for *succinctly represented graphs*, which is PSPACE-complete [15]. Succinctly represented graphs are given indirectly by a propositional formula $E(v, w)$, where v, w are vectors of n variables. The vertexes of the graph are binary sequences of length n, and two sequences are connected by an edge iff the formula $E(v, w)$ on these sequences holds. Consider the graph G represented by the formula $E(v, w)$ and its vertex t. We claim that the ASC given in Fig. 4 is K-robust iff the vertex t is not reachable from the zero vector $(0, \ldots, 0)$ in G. Due to Lemma 23 it suffices to focus on inputs that are step functions f, or discrete words $word(f)$. The input is interpreted as a sequence of vertexes of G. The ASC in Fig. 4 consists of (a) a circuit $E(v, w)$ which checks whether there is an edge between v and the input w, (b) a unit that tests whether u equals the target vertex t and, (c) an oscillator (2) which outputs 0 when the input is 0, and once the input is 1, outputs 1 until the end of the input. Initially, v is the zero vector. If there is an edge between v and w, u is set to w, and hence, v equals w in the next step and w is checked for equality with t. If $w = t$, the oscillator is activated. Otherwise, if there is no edge between v and w, u is set to the zero vector, which corresponds to transitioning back to the initial vertex; v equals the zero vector in the next step and the zero vector is checked for equality with t.

If t is not reachable from the zero vector, the output of the ASC is always 0, and hence the ASC is K-robust for every K. Conversely, we claim that if t is reachable from the zero vector, then the ASC is not K-robust for any K. Indeed, consider a shortest path from the zero vector to the target vertex $0, v_1, \ldots, t$ and consider the following two inputs: $i_1 = 0, v_1, \ldots, t, 0^K$, the path leading to activation of the oscillator followed by K inputs that are zero vectors, and, $i_2 = 0, v_1, \ldots, t', 0^K$, which is obtained from i_1 by changing one bit in t. Observe that the oscillator in ASC is not activated on the input i_2, hence the output is 0. Therefore, while the timed Manhattan distance between the inputs is 1, the timed Manhattan distance between the outputs is $K + 1$, for any chosen K. $\square$

Remark 26. Recall that the domain of an ASC $\mathcal{C}$ with input alphabet $\Sigma = \{0, 1\}^m$ is given by $\mathrm{dom}(\mathcal{C}) = \mathcal{TL}(\Sigma)$. For any timed Manhattan distance $d_{TM}^{\leq 1}$ over $\mathrm{dom}(\mathcal{C})$ such that $\forall a, b \in \Sigma$, $\mathrm{diff}^{\leq 1}(a, b) \leq 1$, Proposition 13 states that the Skorohod distance w.r.t. $d_{TM}^{\leq 1}$ coincides with $d_{TM}^{\leq 1}$. Hence, K-robustness w.r.t. such Skorokhod distances is PSPACE-complete as well.

8   Conclusions

In this paper, we investigated the K-Lipschitz robustness problem for timed I/O systems using an automata-theoretic framework. For timed transducers, we showed that K-robustness can be decided in polynomial space for an interesting class of similarity functions. For ASCs, we reduce K-robustness w.r.t. timed Manhattan distances to K-robustness of discrete transducers and show PSPACE-completeness of the problem.

The essence of our framework is the use of weighted timed automata for computing similarity functions. This motivates further study of weighted timed automata; in particular, development of more expressive weighted timed automata (with nice decidability properties) immediately improves our results.

We also plan to study robustness of other models such as probablistic systems and explore specific application domains such as robotics.

References

1. Alur, R., Dill, D.L.: A theory of timed automata. Theoret. Comput. Sci. **126**(2), 183–235 (1994)
2. Alur, R., Madhusudan, P.: Decision problems for timed automata: a survey. In: Bernardo, M., Corradini, F. (eds.) SFM-RT 2004. LNCS, vol. 3185, pp. 1–24. Springer, Heidelberg (2004)
3. Bloem, R., Greimel, K., Henzinger, T., Jobstmann, B.: Synthesizing robust systems. In: Formal Methods in Computer Aided Design (FMCAD), pp. 85–92 (2009)
4. Bouyer, P., Brihaye, T., Bruyère, V., Raskin, J.-F.: On the optimal reachability problem on weighted timed automata. FMSD **31**(2), 135–175 (2007)
5. Bouyer, P., Markey, N., Sankur, O.: Robustness in timed automata. In: Abdulla, P.A., Potapov, I. (eds.) RP 2013. LNCS, vol. 8169, pp. 1–18. Springer, Heidelberg (2013)
6. Černý, P., Henzinger, T.A., Radhakrishna, A.: Simulation distances. In: Gastin, P., Laroussinie, F. (eds.) CONCUR 2010. LNCS, vol. 6269, pp. 253–268. Springer, Heidelberg (2010)
7. Chaudhuri, S., Gulwani, S., Lublinerman, R.: Continuity analysis of programs. In: Principles of Programming Languages (POPL), pp. 57–70 (2010)
8. Chaudhuri, S., Gulwani, S., Lublinerman, R., Navidpour, S.: Proving programs robust. In: Foundations of Software Engineering (FSE), pp. 102–112 (2011)
9. Doyen, L., Henzinger, T.A., Legay, A., Ničković, D.: Robustness of sequential circuits. In: Application of Concurrency to System Design (ACSD), pp. 77–84 (2010)
10. Gupta, V., Henzinger, T.A., Jagadeesan, R.: Robust timed automata. In: Maler, O. (ed.) HART 1997. LNCS, vol. 1201, pp. 331–345. Springer, Heidelberg (1997)
11. Henzinger, T.A.: Two challenges in embedded systems design: predictability and robustness. Philos. Trans. R. Soc. **366**, 3727–3736 (2008)
12. Henzinger, T.A., Otop, J., Samanta, R.: Lipschitz robustness of finite-state transducers. In: FSTTCS 2014, vol. 1, p. 431 (2014)
13. Zhou, K., Doyle, J.C., Glover, K.: Robust and Optimal Control. Prentice Hall, Upper Saddle River (1996)
14. Krichen, M., Tripakis, S.: Conformance testing for real-time systems. Form. Methods Syst. Des. **34**(3), 238–304 (2009)
15. Lozano, A., Balcázar, J.L.: The complexity of graph problems for succinctly represented graphs. Graph-Theoretic Concepts in Computer Science. LNCS, vol. 411, pp. 277–286. Springer, Heidelberg (1990)
16. Majumdar, R., Render, E., Tabuada, P.: A theory of robust omega-regular software synthesis. ACM Trans. Embed. Comput. Syst. **13**, 1–27 (2013)

17. Majumdar, R., Saha, I.: Symbolic robustness analysis. In: IEEE Real-Time Systems Symposium, pp. 355–363 (2009)
18. Samanta, R., Deshmukh, J.V., Chaudhuri, S.: Robustness analysis of networked systems. In: Giacobazzi, R., Berdine, J., Mastroeni, I. (eds.) VMCAI 2013. LNCS, vol. 7737, pp. 229–247. Springer, Heidelberg (2013)
19. Samanta, R., Deshmukh, J.V., Chaudhuri, S.: Robustness analysis of string transducers. In: Van Hung, D., Ogawa, M. (eds.) ATVA 2013. LNCS, vol. 8172, pp. 427–441. Springer, Heidelberg (2013)
20. Stergiou, C., Tripakis, S., Matsikoudis, E., Lee, E.A.: On the verification of timed discrete-event models. In: Braberman, V., Fribourg, L. (eds.) FORMATS 2013. LNCS, vol. 8053, pp. 213–227. Springer, Heidelberg (2013)

A Method for Invariant Generation for Polynomial Continuous Systems

Andrew Sogokon[1]([✉]), Khalil Ghorbal[2], Paul B. Jackson[1], and André Platzer[2]

[1] LFCS, School of Informatics, University of Edinburgh, Edinburgh, Scotland, UK
a.sogokon@sms.ed.ac.uk, pbj@inf.ed.ac.uk
[2] Computer Science Department, Carnegie Mellon University, Pittsburgh, PA, USA
{kghorbal,aplatzer}@cs.cmu.edu

Abstract. This paper presents a method for generating semi-algebraic invariants for systems governed by non-linear polynomial ordinary differential equations under semi-algebraic evolution constraints. Based on the notion of discrete abstraction, our method eliminates unsoundness and unnecessary coarseness found in existing approaches for computing abstractions for non-linear continuous systems and is able to construct invariants with intricate boolean structure, in contrast to invariants typically generated using template-based methods. In order to tackle the state explosion problem associated with discrete abstraction, we present invariant generation algorithms that exploit sound proof rules for safety verification, such as *differential cut* (DC), and a new proof rule that we call *differential divide-and-conquer* (DDC), which splits the verification problem into smaller sub-problems. The resulting invariant generation method is observed to be much more scalable and efficient than the naïve approach, exhibiting orders of magnitude performance improvement on many of the problems.

1 Introduction

Establishing safe operation of embedded systems arising in modern engineering increasingly involves reasoning about the behaviour of hybrid dynamical systems that combine discrete and continuous state evolution. Continuous dynamics is typically specified by ordinary differential equations (ODEs). Non-linear ODEs afford the engineer the means of modelling rich dynamic behaviour that cannot possibly occur in linear systems [12], but are also notoriously difficult to analyse because they rarely possess solutions that can be expressed in closed form.

This paper is concerned with the problem of automating safety verification for continuous systems modelled by non-linear ODEs under evolution constraints, which is a problem of broader interest to automating safety verification for hybrid dynamical systems. To solve the verification problem, one requires a proof that

This material is based upon work supported by the UK Engineering and Physical Sciences Research Council (EPSRC) under grants EP/I010335/1 and EP/J001058/1, the National Science Foundation by NSF CAREER Award CNS-1054246, NSF EXPEDITION CNS-0926181, CNS-0931985 and DARPA FA8750-12-2-0291.

© Springer-Verlag Berlin Heidelberg 2016
B. Jobstmann and K.R.M. Leino (Eds.): VMCAI 2016, LNCS 9583, pp. 268–288, 2016.
DOI: 10.1007/978-3-662-49122-5_13

a given continuous system does not evolve into an unsafe state at any future time from some given initial configuration while obeying its evolution constraint. Additionally, given that solutions are rarely available, it is highly desirable to arrive at such a proof by working with the ODEs directly, i.e. *without solving the initial value problem.*

Traditionally, two popular techniques have been used for proving safety properties without computing solutions or putting a finite bound on the duration of evolution in continuous systems: one based on first *soundly abstracting* the continuous system and performing reachability analysis in the resulting discrete transition system, and a *deductive verification* approach that works by reasoning about appropriate *invariants* in the continuous system.

Deductive verification tools for hybrid systems crucially rely on (**i**) the ability to prove invariance assertions about continuous systems (which was solved for the case of semi-algebraic[1] invariants and polynomial ODEs in [14]) and (**ii**) having the means of *automatically generating* continuous invariants sufficient to prove safety assertions about continuous systems. In practice, this latter point is often the main bottleneck when verifying safety of hybrid systems in which the continuous dynamics are non-linear.

Existing automatic procedures for generating invariants for use in deductive frameworks only make limited use of the boolean structure in invariants. Approaches based on abstraction, in computing reachable sets of discrete systems, (implicitly) create invariants with more intricate boolean structure; their limitations currently stem from the conservative nature of the discrete models, whose transition behaviour is often a very coarse over-approximation of the evolution taking place in the continuous system.

A number of approaches have been proposed for generating invariants for continuous systems [8,11,14,16,24,27,28,38,44], which either put serious restrictions on the form of the invariant or rely on the user pre-defining a *template* and then attempt to find an instantiation of the parameters in the template that yields an invariant. In this paper we pursue an alternative approach that automatically generates semi-algebraic continuous invariants from discrete semi-algebraic abstractions of continuous systems. Our rationale is that recent advances in semi-algebraic invariant checking for polynomial ODEs [14] allow deductive provers to work with arbitrary semi-algebraic invariants, yet few methods for invariant generation are able to synthesize interesting invariants with boolean structure that one might find in reachable sets of discrete abstractions. At the same time, discrete abstraction approaches do not take full advantage of the results on invariant checking in constructing the transition relation for the discrete transition system. We seek to address both of these issues.

Currently available methods for creating semi-algebraic abstractions of non-linear polynomial systems [36,37] result in abstractions that are unsound for certain degenerate cases and unnecessarily coarse even in very simple scenarios. Additionally, discrete abstraction is known to scale poorly owing to (in the worst

---

[1] A semi-algebraic set is a subset of $\mathbb{R}^n$ characterized by a finite boolean combination of sets defined by polynomial equalities and inequalities.

case) an exponential increase in the number of discrete states as the continuous state space is partitioned [37], making it very difficult to refine abstractions. To ameliorate this situation, we give a method for constructing semi-algebraic abstractions that are sound and only as coarse as the partitioning of the continuous state space into discrete regions itself. We then employ ideas from deductive verification to give more scalable and efficient algorithms for generating semi-algebraic invariants for polynomial continuous systems.

Contributions. In Sect. 3 of this paper we (**I**) introduce a method for constructing semi-algebraic abstractions of polynomial continuous systems in which transitions between the discrete states occur *if and only if* a corresponding continuous evolution is possible in the continuous system. In Sect. 4 we give an algorithm for generating semi-algebraic invariants for polynomial continuous systems by efficiently extracting reachable sets from these abstractions. In Sect. 5 we (**II**) introduce a sound proof rule DDC (*differential divide-and-conquer*) which works to split the safety verification problem into smaller sub-problems by exploiting properties of invariant real algebraic sets and (**III**) give more scalable invariant generation algorithms employing sound proof rules *differential weakening* (DW) [19] and *differential cut* (DC) [19,21] together with the new rule DDC to address the discrete state explosion problem associated with computing abstractions. In Sect. 6 we (**IV**) evaluate our techniques on a collection of 100 safety verification problems featuring predominantly non-linear ODEs.

2   Preliminaries

To simplify our presentation, we will use the notation for sets and formulas characterizing those sets interchangeably in this paper, e.g. H will denote both a semi-algebraic set $H \subseteq \mathbb{R}^n$ and a formula H in the first-order theory of real arithmetic with free variables in $x_1, \ldots, x_n$ that characterizes this set. In what follows, we shall restrict our attention to autonomous[2] systems of polynomial ordinary differential equations under semi-algebraic evolution domain constraints[3], i.e. systems of the form:

$$\dot{x}_i = f_i(\boldsymbol{x}), \quad \boldsymbol{x} \in H \subseteq \mathbb{R}^n,$$

where $f_i \in \mathbb{R}[x_1, \ldots, x_n]$ for $1 \leq i \leq n$ and the evolution domain constraint H is semi-algebraic. We will write this concisely using vector notation as $\dot{\boldsymbol{x}} = f(\boldsymbol{x})$ & H.

One may wonder at this stage whether restricting attention to polynomial systems represents a severe limitation; after all, non-linearities involving transcendental functions such as $\sin, \cos, e, \ln$, etc., are not uncommon in systems of practical interest. Fortunately, it is often possible to transform such systems into (larger) polynomial systems by introducing fresh variables and eliminating

---

[2] In the sense of not having an *explicit* dependence on the time variable t.

[3] Evolution constraints are often used to define operating modes in hybrid and cyber-physical systems (so-called *mode*, or *location invariants* in the parlance of hybrid automata [1,13]).

non-polynomial non-linearities in a rather general technique [23], which is known in various scientific communities as *recasting* [17, 30] or *differential axiomatization* [19]. Furthermore, it has been shown that such a transformation can be mechanised for a broad class of non-polynomial systems using a terminating algorithm [15]. Likewise, no generality is lost by only considering autonomous systems because any system with explicit time dependence $\dot{x} = f(x, t)$ & H can be transformed into an autonomous system by introducing a fresh variable to model time evolution, e.g. if we add $\dot{x}_{n+1} = 1$ to the system and replace every instance of t in the system with x_{n+1}.

To state the safety verification problem for continuous systems in full generality we require a set of *initial states* for the system, which we denote by $\psi \subseteq \mathbb{R}^n$, and a set of *safe states* denoted $\phi \subseteq \mathbb{R}^n$. The problem is to prove that starting inside ψ, the system $\dot{x} = f(x)$ & H cannot leave ϕ by evolving inside the evolution domain constraint H. We will only consider semi-algebraic ψ and ϕ in this paper and will state the safety property formally, using notation from differential dynamic logic (d$\mathcal{L}$) [18], as follows:

$$\psi \rightarrow [\dot{x} = f(x) \ \& \ H] \ \phi.$$

The above formula asserts that, starting in any state satisfying the pre-condition (ψ), the system will *necessarily* (box modality [ ]) satisfy the post-condition (ϕ) when following the system $\dot{x} = f(x)$ & H for any amount of time.[4] The semantic definition of the d$\mathcal{L}$ assertion above is given in terms of the solution, which precisely describes how continuous states evolve over time. A solution to the initial value problem for the system $\dot{x} = f(x)$ with initial value $x_0 \in \mathbb{R}^n$ is a differentiable function $\varphi_t(x_0) : (a, b) \rightarrow \mathbb{R}^n$ defined for t in some non-empty *interval of existence* $(a, b) \subseteq \mathbb{R} \cup \{\infty, -\infty\}$ including zero and such that $\frac{d}{dt}\varphi_t(x_0) = f(\varphi_t(x_0))$ for all $t \in (a, b)$. Formally, the d$\mathcal{L}$ continuous safety assertion above is valid if the following is true:

$$\forall \ x_0 \in \psi. \ \forall \ \tau \geq 0. \ (\forall \ t \in [0, \tau] \ .\varphi_t(x_0) \in H) \rightarrow \varphi_\tau(x_0) \in \phi.$$

In practice, solutions to non-linear ODEs are almost never available in closed form (by which we understand a *finite* expression in terms of polynomials and elementary functions); even when they are, the resulting sentences often belong to an undecidable theory [26] due to transcendental functions in the closed form expression. Alternatively, the safety verification problem can sometimes be solved directly in a deductive framework. This involves finding an appropriate set $I \subseteq \mathbb{R}^n$, called a *continuous invariant* [22], that satisfies the three premises (above the bar) of the following rule of inference:

$$(Safety) \ \frac{H \wedge \psi \rightarrow I \quad I \rightarrow [\dot{x} = f(x) \ \& \ H] I \quad I \rightarrow \phi}{\psi \rightarrow [\dot{x} = f(x) \ \& \ H] \phi}$$

---

[4] Considering the continuous system $\dot{x} = f(x)$ & H as a program, the safety assertion $\psi \rightarrow [\dot{x} = f(x) \ \& \ H] \ \phi$ expresses the (continuous) Hoare triple $\{\psi\} \ \dot{x} = f(x) \ \& \ H \ \{\phi\}$.

to conclude (below the bar) that the system is safe. Continuous invariants generalize *positively invariant sets* [6] to systems under evolution constraints.

Definition 1 (Continuous Invariant [22]). *For a continuous system $\dot{x} = f(x) \ \& \ H$, a set $I \subseteq \mathbb{R}^n$ is a continuous invariant if and only if*

$$\forall \ x_0 \in I. \ \forall \ \tau \geq 0. \ (\forall \ t \in [0, \tau]. \ \varphi_t(x_0) \in H) \rightarrow \varphi_t(x_0) \in I.$$

Intuitively, a continuous invariant is any set of states I such that any motion initialized inside I that respects the evolution constraint H is guaranteed to remain inside I.

When H and I are semi-algebraic and f_i are polynomial, a decision procedure for checking whether I is a continuous invariant was reported in [14], enabling us to decide d$\mathcal{L}$ assertions of the form $I \rightarrow [\dot{x} = f(x) \ \& \ H] \ I$. The decision procedure involves computing higher-order Lie derivatives and exploits the ascending chain property of Noetherian rings. The interested reader is invited to consult [14] for a detailed description of the procedure and also [8], where similar ideas were employed. As a direct consequence, every premise of the rule (*Safety*) is known to be decidable, since ψ, ϕ and H are also assumed to be semi-algebraic, the goals $H \wedge \psi \rightarrow I$ and $I \rightarrow \phi$ can be passed to a decision procedure for real arithmetic [35]. The challenge in applying the rule now lies in *finding* an appropriate continuous invariant I.

3   Discrete Abstraction of Continuous Systems

In a certain sense, with discrete abstraction one seeks to approximate continuous systems by finite discrete transition systems. Such a transformation makes it possible to perform reachability analysis and verify safety properties in the simpler discrete model. The approach works by ensuring that the set of behaviours of the discrete (abstract) system *over-approximates* the set of behaviours of the continuous (concrete) system; this is known as *sound abstraction*. If the discrete abstraction is sound, then any violation of the safety property in the continuous system is necessarily reproduced by the abstract discrete transition system. Conversely, an abstraction is *complete* (with respect to the safety property) when any violation of the safety property in the abstraction is reproduced by the concrete continuous system.

Discrete abstraction of continuous systems was previously studied in [2,3] (for linear systems) and [36,37] (for more general non-linear systems), where a simple method for constructing abstractions was proposed but results in discrete systems that may feature transitions between discrete states that are impossible in the continuous system. In this section we describe the process of constructing sound and *exact* abstractions of non-linear continuous systems. That is, the resulting abstraction will feature a discrete transition between two abstract states *if and only if* a corresponding continuous trajectory is possible in the concrete system. The method we use is fundamentally different from [36,37] in computing the discrete transition relation using a *decision procedure* for continuous invariant assertions [14].

3.1   Constructing the Discrete State Space

In this section we describe a way of partitioning the evolution domain constraint H in the continuous system $\dot{x} = f(x)$ & H using a set of polynomial functions.

Definition 2 (Semi-algebraic Decomposition). *A semi-algebraic decomposition of a semi-algebraic set $H \subseteq \mathbb{R}^n$ by a set of m polynomials $A \subset \mathbb{R}[x_1, \dots, x_n]$ is a partition of H into $k \leq 3^m$ regions giving all the* non-empty *intersections of the form $H \cap p_1 \sim_1 0 \cap \cdots \cap p_m \sim_m 0$ where $p_i \in A$ and $\sim_i \in \{<, =, >\}$ for $1 \leq i \leq m$.*

Computing the semi-algebraic decomposition of the evolution domain constraint H for a finite set of polynomials A can be achieved using a simple procedure that we will call *SemiAlgDecomp*. The decomposition defines a partition of H into k non-empty regions, each corresponding to a single *discrete state*, which we denote by s_i, where $1 \leq i \leq k$. We will denote by S the set of all discrete states obtained from the semi-algebraic decomposition, i.e. $S \equiv \{s_i \mid 1 \leq i \leq k\}$.

3.2   Constructing the Transition Relation

We now apply the decision procedure for semi-algebraic continuous invariant assertion checking reported in [14] to exactly determine the transition relation $T \subset S \times S$, enabling us to construct *exact* discrete abstractions, which we denote by the pair (S, T). We will write $s_i \longrightarrow s_j$ for $(s_i, s_j) \in S \times S$, the discrete transition from state s_i to s_j.

We begin with a transition relation $S \times S$ in which every state is reachable from every other state (including itself) in a single discrete transition. First, let us observe that a continuous solution of the differential equation cannot pass from a discrete state where $p > 0$ (for some polynomial $p \in A$) to a state where $p < 0$ without passing through $p = 0$ first, nor vice versa. Using this intuition, we can give a general definition of what it means for two discrete states to be *neighbouring* (or *adjacent* [34]).

Definition 3. *Let S be the set of discrete states constructed from a semi-algebraic decomposition of H by a finite set of polynomials $A \subset \mathbb{R}[x_1, \dots, x_n]$. Two discrete states $s_i, s_j \in S$, where $i \neq j$, are neighbouring if there are* **no** *points $x_1, x_2 \in s_i \cup s_j$ such that $p(x_1) < 0$ and $p(x_2) > 0$ for any p in A.*

We can now construct a *neighbouring transition relation* $T_n \subseteq S \times S$ in which only the neighbouring states are reachable in a single transition (note that a state cannot be its own neighbour using our definition). Intuitively, in the neighbouring transition relation one cannot "jump across" $p = 0$ in a single discrete transition; at the same time, any state is reachable from any other state. An abstraction which results from (S, T_n) is still maximally coarse and therefore not very useful (illustrated in Fig. 1).

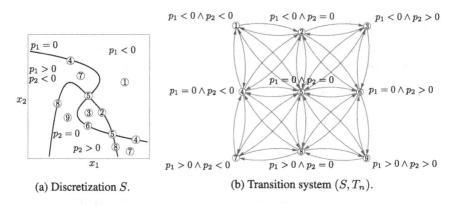

(a) Discretization S.　　　(b) Transition system (S, T_n).

Fig. 1. Semi-algebraic decomposition of $\mathbb{R}^2$ by $A = \{p_1, p_2\}$ resulting in 9 discrete states $S \subset 2^{\mathbb{R}^2}$ and the neighbouring transition relation $T_n \subset S \times S$.

We are only interested in retaining those discrete transitions for which the corresponding continuous transitions are possible in the original continuous system. In order to eliminate impossible discrete transitions we need to *decide* an invariance assertion:

$$\mathbf{s}_i \rightarrow [\dot{\boldsymbol{x}} = f(\boldsymbol{x}) \ \& \ (\mathbf{s}_i \vee \mathbf{s}_j)] \, \mathbf{s}_i,$$

for each pair of neighbouring discrete states $(\mathbf{s}_i, \mathbf{s}_j) \in T_n$; we will proceed to remove transitions $\mathbf{s}_i \longrightarrow \mathbf{s}_j$ from T_n if and only if the decision procedure for continuous invariance assertions returns True. This process can be mechanized in a terminating abstraction algorithm that we call *ExactAbstraction*. The result is a discrete transition system (S, T) with a transition relation $T \subseteq T_n$ that does not feature discrete transitions that are impossible; we will state this property formally.

Proposition 4. *Abstractions (S, T) are **exact** with respect to the discretization, i.e. $\mathbf{s}_i \longrightarrow \mathbf{s}_j$ is in T if and only if*

$$\exists \, \boldsymbol{x}_0 \in \mathbf{s}_i. \, \exists \, \tau > 0. \ \varphi_0(\boldsymbol{x}_0) \in \mathbf{s}_i \ \wedge \ \varphi_\tau(\boldsymbol{x}_0) \in \mathbf{s}_j \quad and \quad \forall \, t \in [0, \tau]. \ \varphi_t(\boldsymbol{x}_0) \in \mathbf{s}_i \cup \mathbf{s}_j,$$

that is, if and only if the system may evolve continuously from state $\mathbf{s}_i$ into a neighbouring state $\mathbf{s}_j$ without leaving their union $\mathbf{s}_i \cup \mathbf{s}_j$. The abstraction is exactly as coarse as the partition of the evolution constraint H into regions corresponding to discrete states.

One can view the process of removing impossible discrete transitions as a sound refinement of the neighbouring transition relation to $T \subseteq T_n$. In the worst case, using a set of m polynomials for the semi-algebraic decomposition of H will result in 3^m discrete states and a neighbouring transition relation T_n with a total of $7^m - 3^m$ discrete transitions that need to be checked. In practice, both the number of discrete states and the number of transitions in T_n will typically be much lower than the pessimistic worst case bound. Furthermore, removing impossible transitions from T_n is a massively parallel problem, allowing one to exploit multi-core parallelism instead of iterating through the transitions sequentially.

3.3   Sound and Exact Abstraction

We will now discuss some important differences between earlier work and our approach. The discrete abstraction method reported in [37] is fundamentally different in the way it constructs the transition relation (let us call it $T_\sim \subseteq S \times S$), which is described in [37, Sect. 3.2.2]. In essence, the method imposes conditions for removing transitions from the neighbouring transition relation T_n in the following way: given two neighbouring states $\mathbf{s}_i$ and $\mathbf{s}_j$, it removes the transition $\mathbf{s}_i \longrightarrow \mathbf{s}_j$ from T_n if *any* of the following conditions are satisfied for any $p \in A$:

1. $\mathbf{s}_i$ has $p < 0$ and $\mathbf{s}_j$ has $p = 0$ and $\mathbf{s}_i \to \frac{dp}{dt} \leq 0$ is true,
2. $\mathbf{s}_i$ has $p > 0$ and $\mathbf{s}_j$ has $p = 0$ and $\mathbf{s}_i \to \frac{dp}{dt} \geq 0$ is true,
3. $\mathbf{s}_i$ has $p = 0$ and $\mathbf{s}_j$ has $p < 0$ and $(\mathbf{s}_i \to \frac{dp}{dt} = 0 \lor \mathbf{s}_i \to \frac{dp}{dt} > 0)$ is true,
4. $\mathbf{s}_i$ has $p = 0$ and $\mathbf{s}_j$ has $p > 0$ and $(\mathbf{s}_i \to \frac{dp}{dt} = 0 \lor \mathbf{s}_i \to \frac{dp}{dt} < 0)$ is true.

Remark 5. The abstraction method in [37] also considers so-called *stuttering* (also *self-looping* [34]) transitions $\mathbf{s}_i \longrightarrow \mathbf{s}_i$, which we disregard here (already in the way we define T_n). This discrepancy makes no practical difference to safety verification as stuttering transitions have no effect on the reachable sets of discrete abstractions.

The approach described in [37] is not (in general) sound when the polynomials in A are allowed to be non-linear. To see this, consider the simple system with constant derivatives $\dot{x}_1 = 1, \dot{x}_2 = 0$ and let $A = \{x_1^2 + x_2, x_2 - x_1^2\}$. The abstraction one obtains (Fig. 2) suggests that the state $x_1^2 + x_2 = 0 \land x_2 - x_1^2 = 0$ (equivalent to $x_1 = 0 \land x_2 = 0$) is invariant under the flow of the system, which is incorrect. The nature of this problem was studied in non-convex analysis; a solution would require reasoning about the *contingent cone* [42], which is not in general computable. A sound and exact abstraction using our approach is shown in Fig. 3.

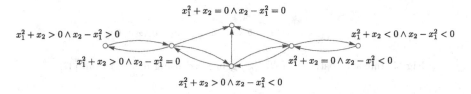

$$x_1^2 + x_2 = 0 \land x_2 - x_1^2 = 0$$

$x_1^2 + x_2 > 0 \land x_2 - x_1^2 > 0$ $x_1^2 + x_2 < 0 \land x_2 - x_1^2 < 0$

$x_1^2 + x_2 > 0 \land x_2 - x_1^2 = 0$ $x_1^2 + x_2 = 0 \land x_2 - x_1^2 < 0$

$$x_1^2 + x_2 > 0 \land x_2 - x_1^2 < 0$$

Fig. 2. Abstraction $(S, T_\sim)$ generated using method from [37].

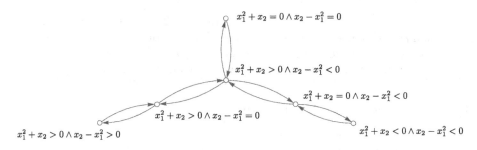

Fig. 3. Sound abstraction (S, T) generated by *ExactAbstraction*.

The abstraction method in [37] additionally suffers from coarseness, because it can introduce discrete transitions that correspond to evolutions that are impossible in the concrete continuous system (the abstraction is therefore *inexact*). For instance, consider a planar system of non-linear ordinary differential equations featuring a stable limit cycle in the form of a unit circle enclosing an equilibrium at the origin:

$$\dot{x}_1 = -x_1^3 - x_2^2 x_1 + x_1 + x_2,$$
$$\dot{x}_2 = -x_2^3 - x_1^2 x_2 + x_2 - x_1.$$

Let the system evolve under no evolution constraints and consider a simple discretization by the axes polynomials, i.e. take $A = \{x_1, x_2\}$. The discrete abstraction $(S, T_\sim)$ generated using the method from [37] is shown in Fig. 4. An exact abstraction (S, T) without impossible transitions generated using our approach is shown in Fig. 5. Abstraction $(S, T_\sim)$ considers the origin reachable, while (S, T) does not.

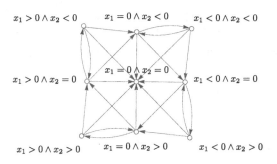

Fig. 4. Inexact abstraction $(S, T_\sim)$ generated using method from [37].

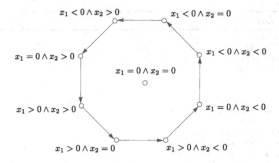

Fig. 5. Exact abstraction (S, T) generated by *ExactAbstraction*.

4 Extracting Continuous Invariants from Discrete Abstractions

If one constructs a (sound) discrete abstraction of some system $\dot{x} = f(x)$ & H using some finite set of polynomials A, one may verify safety properties by showing that they hold in the abstraction. For this, one needs to check whether an unsafe abstract state (i.e. one which contains a state that satisfies the formula $\neg\phi$) is reachable by following the discrete transitions starting from the set of initial abstract states (those defining regions where ψ is satisfiable). If none of the unsafe abstract states are reachable from the initial states in the abstraction, one can conclude that the continuous system is safe.

By computing the forward-reachable set from the set of the initial states ψ in the abstraction, which we denote by $Reach_A^{\rightarrow}(\psi, H) \subseteq H$, one generates a continuous invariant. Provided the abstraction is *exact*, this is the *smallest* continuous invariant with respect to the discretization by the polynomials in A and is furthermore *semi-algebraic*. Formally, we define

$$Reach_A^{\rightarrow}(\psi, H) \equiv \bigvee_{\substack{i \text{ s.t. } \mathbf{s}_i \cap \psi \neq \emptyset, \\ j \text{ s.t. } \mathbf{s}_i \longrightarrow^* \mathbf{s}_j}} \mathbf{s}_j \; ,$$

where $\longrightarrow^*$ represents the reachability relation; that is, $\mathbf{s}_i \longrightarrow^* \mathbf{s}_j$ if state $\mathbf{s}_j$ is reachable from $\mathbf{s}_i$ in zero or more discrete transitions in the exact abstraction (S, T), obtained from the discretization by polynomials in A. Thus, $I \equiv Reach_A^{\rightarrow}(\psi, H)$ is a semi-algebraic set that is (by construction) guaranteed to include the initial set (i.e. $\psi \rightarrow I$) and is a continuous invariant for the system (i.e. $I \rightarrow [\dot{x} = f(x)$ & $H]\, I$). If it is also true that I does not include any unsafe states (i.e. $I \rightarrow \phi$), then I is sufficient to conclude that the system is safe using the proof rule (*Safety*) from Sect. 2.

For invariant generation we are merely interested in extracting a semi-algebraic continuous invariant containing the initial set of states ψ from the abstraction, not the full abstraction (S, T) itself. We now give a simple work-list procedure that we call *LazyReach* (Algorithm 1) for constructing the set

---

Algorithm 1. *LazyReach*

Data: $\psi, \dot{x} = f(x)$ & H, A
Result: $Reach_A^{\rightarrow}(\psi, H)$
1 $S \leftarrow SemiAlgDecomp(\{H\}, A)$;
2 $T_n \leftarrow NeighbourTrans(S)$;
3 $Visited \leftarrow \{s \in S \mid s \cap \psi \neq \emptyset\}$;
4 $Processed \leftarrow \{\}$;
5 **while** $|Processed| < |Visited|$ **do**
6 $\quad$ $Unprocessed \leftarrow Visited \setminus Processed$;
7 $\quad$ $Processed \leftarrow Visited$;
8 $\quad$ **foreach** s_i in $Unprocessed$ **do**
9 $\quad\quad$ $Validate \leftarrow \{(s_i, s_j) \in T_n \mid s_j \notin Visited\}$;
10 $\quad\quad$ **foreach** (s_i, s_j) in $Validate$ **do**
11 $\quad\quad\quad$ **if** $\neg(s_i \rightarrow [\dot{x} = f(x)$ & $(s_i \vee s_j)]\, s_i)$ **then**
12 $\quad\quad\quad\quad$ $Visited \leftarrow Visited \cup \{s_j\}$;

13 **return** $\bigvee_{s \in Visited} s$

$Reach_A^{\rightarrow}(\psi, H)$ *lazily* (on demand), i.e. without eagerly constructing the exact abstraction (S, T) first.

Although the worst-case running time of *LazyReach* is exponential in $m = |A|$, in practice employing Algorithm 1 is often far more efficient than computing the exact abstraction (S, T) in full and then extracting $Reach_A^{\rightarrow}(\psi, H)$.

5   Tackling Discrete State Explosion

Discrete abstractions of continuous systems suffer from the discrete state explosion problem, i.e. the number of discrete states in the abstraction grows exponentially with the number of polynomials $m = |A|$ used for the discretization.

If one is to consider each individual polynomial $p \in A$, it is intuitive that if one can show that

1. for the initial set of states ψ, the polynomial p is sign-invariant, i.e. $p(\psi) \sim 0$ where $\sim \in \{<, =, >\}$, and
2. that this sign condition defines a continuous invariant for the system, i.e.
   $p \sim 0 \rightarrow [\dot{x} = f(x)$ & $H]\, p \sim 0$,

then one can *refine* the evolution constraint to $H \wedge p \sim 0$ and *remove* the polynomial p from A and obtain an abstraction by the polynomials $B \equiv A \setminus \{p\}$ which has the property that

$$Reach_B^{\rightarrow}(\psi, H \wedge p \sim 0) \equiv Reach_A^{\rightarrow}(\psi, H).$$

The number of discrete states generated using B for the semi-algebraic decomposition of $H \wedge p \sim 0$ is at most 3^{m-1} and the process can be repeated for other polynomials that remain in B. This section will explore approaches to tackling the discrete state space explosion based on this observation without making the abstraction unnecessarily coarse. For this purpose we will use sound proof rules *differential cut* and *differential divide-and-conquer.*

5.1   Differential Cut

Platzer and Clarke [22] explored an approach to safety verification based on iteratively refining the evolution constraint H with *differential invariants* (a subset of continuous invariants, see [19]). Such a *sound* refinement of the evolution domain is possible using an inference rule called *differential cut* [21] (henceforth DC). Differential cuts are used repeatedly in a process called *differential saturation* (see [22, Proposition 2]). The DC rule formalizes the idea that it is always sound to restrict the evolution domain H by some continuous invariant F, provided that it includes the initial set ψ, i.e.

$$(DC)\frac{\psi \to [\dot{\boldsymbol{x}} = f(\boldsymbol{x}) \ \& \ H]F \quad \psi \to [\dot{\boldsymbol{x}} = f(\boldsymbol{x}) \ \& \ H \wedge F]\phi}{\psi \to [\dot{\boldsymbol{x}} = f(\boldsymbol{x}) \ \& \ H]\,\phi}$$

the original rationale being that it is easier to prove the safety property in the more restricted system in the right premise.

5.2   Differential Divide-and-Conquer

We now introduce a new proof rule, akin to DC, that goes further and exploits a property of sets that are continuous invariants in both positive and negative time directions to split the continuous system into smaller continuous sub-systems between which there is no continuous evolution.

Proposition 6. *The proof rule DDC given below (with five premises) is sound.*

$$p = 0 \to [\dot{\boldsymbol{x}} = f(\boldsymbol{x}) \ \& \ H]\,p = 0$$
$$p = 0 \to [\dot{\boldsymbol{x}} = -f(\boldsymbol{x}) \ \& \ H]\,p = 0$$

$$(DDC)\frac{\begin{array}{c}\psi \wedge p > 0 \to [\dot{\boldsymbol{x}} = f(\boldsymbol{x}) \ \& \ H \wedge p > 0]\ \phi \\ \psi \wedge p = 0 \to [\dot{\boldsymbol{x}} = f(\boldsymbol{x}) \ \& \ H \wedge p = 0]\ \phi \\ \psi \wedge p < 0 \to [\dot{\boldsymbol{x}} = f(\boldsymbol{x}) \ \& \ H \wedge p < 0]\ \phi\end{array}}{\psi \to [\dot{\boldsymbol{x}} = f(\boldsymbol{x}) \ \& \ H]\ \phi}$$

Proof. For a continuous function p, no continuous trajectory inside H can cross from a region where $p > 0$ to a region where $p < 0$ without first crossing $p = 0$. If the first two premises hold, then $p = 0$ cannot be left inside H in either positive or negative time, i.e. there are no solutions entering or leaving $p = 0$ inside H. The reachable sets of the system initialized in $\psi \wedge p > 0$, $\psi \wedge p = 0$ and $\psi \wedge p < 0$ are thus disjoint and confined to regions of H where $p > 0$, $p = 0$ and $p < 0$ respectively. The union of these sets constitutes the reachable set of the system initialized in ψ and the result follows.   □

Informally, the rule allows one to split the original system into three *dynamically disconnected regions*, that is disjoint regions that are not connected by a continuous flow of the system[5]. Note that unlike DC, the rule DDC does *not* require the

---

[5] All three regions are *invariant sets* in the terminology of dynamical systems [5, Chapter II].

initial set ψ to be wholly contained inside $p > 0$, $p = 0$ or $p < 0$. Instead, DDC splits the initial set of states into three disjoint initial subsets $\psi \wedge p > 0$, $\psi \wedge p = 0$ and $\psi \wedge p < 0$. The rule DDC thus decomposes the original safety assertion into three independent safety assertions about smaller sub-systems, allowing the user to work on these separately. DDC is of practical interest in cases when *two or more* of the sets $\psi \wedge p > 0$, $\psi \wedge p = 0$ and $\psi \wedge p < 0$ are non-empty (otherwise, ψ lies entirely within $p > 0$, $p = 0$ or $p < 0$ and DC may be applied to refine the constraint).

We now turn to applying the rules DC and DDC to tackle the state space explosion problem. In Algorithm 2 we give a procedure for refining the evolution domain constraint and removing polynomials from A, whenever this is possible, using the proof rules DC and DDC. We call this procedure *DWC* as it also exploits the sound reasoning principle of *differential weakening* DW [19], i.e.

$$(\text{DW}) \ \frac{H \rightarrow \phi}{\psi \rightarrow [\dot{\boldsymbol{x}} = f(\boldsymbol{x}) \ \& \ H] \ \phi},$$

which simply requires that the evolution domain be contained within the post-condition to conclude that the system is safe.

Algorithm 2. *DWC*

Data: $\psi, \dot{\boldsymbol{x}} = f(\boldsymbol{x}) \ \& \ H, \phi, A$
Result: Continuous invariant I s.t. $\psi \subseteq I$
1   **if** $H \wedge \psi \rightarrow$ False **then**
2 | **return** False

3   **if** $H \rightarrow \phi$ **then**
4 | **return** H // DW

5   **foreach** $p \in A$ **do**
6 | **if** $(H \wedge \psi \rightarrow p > 0) \wedge (p > 0 \rightarrow [\dot{\boldsymbol{x}} = f(\boldsymbol{x}) \ \& \ H] \ p > 0)$ **then**
7 | | **return** $DWC(\psi, \dot{\boldsymbol{x}} = f(\boldsymbol{x}) \ \& \ H \wedge p > 0, \phi, A \setminus \{p\})$ // DC
8 | **if** $(H \wedge \psi \rightarrow p < 0) \wedge (p < 0 \rightarrow [\dot{\boldsymbol{x}} = f(\boldsymbol{x}) \ \& \ H] \ p < 0)$ **then**
9 | | **return** $DWC(\psi, \dot{\boldsymbol{x}} = f(\boldsymbol{x}) \ \& \ H \wedge p < 0, \phi, A \setminus \{p\})$ // DC
10 | **if** $(H \wedge \psi \rightarrow p = 0) \wedge (p = 0 \rightarrow [\dot{\boldsymbol{x}} = f(\boldsymbol{x}) \ \& \ H] \ p = 0)$ **then**
11 | | **return** $DWC(\psi, \dot{\boldsymbol{x}} = f(\boldsymbol{x}) \ \& \ H \wedge p = 0, \phi, A \setminus \{p\})$ // DC

12   **foreach** $p \in A$ **do**
13 | **if** $(p = 0 \rightarrow [\dot{\boldsymbol{x}} = f(\boldsymbol{x}) \ \& \ H] \ p = 0) \wedge (p = 0 \rightarrow [\dot{\boldsymbol{x}} = -f(\boldsymbol{x}) \ \& \ H] \ p = 0)$ **then**
14 | | $GT \leftarrow DWC(\psi \wedge p > 0, \dot{\boldsymbol{x}} = f(\boldsymbol{x}) \ \& \ H \wedge p > 0, \phi, A \setminus \{p\})$;
15 | | $EQ \leftarrow DWC(\psi \wedge p = 0, \dot{\boldsymbol{x}} = f(\boldsymbol{x}) \ \& \ H \wedge p = 0, \phi, A \setminus \{p\})$;
16 | | $LT \leftarrow DWC(\psi \wedge p < 0, \dot{\boldsymbol{x}} = f(\boldsymbol{x}) \ \& \ H \wedge p < 0, \phi, A \setminus \{p\})$;
17 | | **return** $GT \vee EQ \vee LT$ // DDC

18 **return** H

On lines 3 and 4, *DWC* applies the rule DW as a sufficiency check for termination. On lines 7, 9 and 11 the procedure discards those p for which $p > 0$, $p < 0$ or $p = 0$ describe a continuous invariant containing the initial set ψ (conditionals on lines 6, 8 and 10). This step corresponds to an application of the rule DC with $F \equiv p > 0$, $F \equiv p < 0$ and $F \equiv p = 0$ which, if the rule application is successful, are used to refine the evolution constraint H in the recursive call. If $p = 0$ is an invariant in both positive and negative time and does *not* contain all the initial states ψ, one can use the proof rule DDC to work with 3 smaller sub-systems of the original system whose reachable set may be constructed by *combining the reachable sets of these smaller systems*. This idea is implemented on lines 13-17 of Algorithm 2, where DWC recurses on the 3 smaller sub-systems and removes the polynomial p (used to divide the system) from A. The over-approximations of reachable sets obtained using these 3 recursive calls are then combined into a union (line 17), which gives an over-approximation of the reachable set for the original system. Finally, when no further progress can be made, the procedure returns the evolution constraint H (line 18). Because the procedure only involves applying sound proof rules, one may view DWC as a *proof strategy* that can be implemented in a theorem prover. Indeed, if the procedure returns a result while there are still polynomials remaining in A, one has a proof of safety involving only the proof rules DW, DC and DDC.

Unlike *LazyReach*, the invariant generation procedure DWC will not (in general) always be able to find a sufficiently strong continuous invariant to prove the safety property, even if one exists in the semi-algebraic abstraction by the polynomials A. The invariants DWC is able to generate are thus generally coarser than those generated using *LazyReach*. However, we observe that in the worst case the running-time of DWC is only quadratic in the number of polynomials $m = |A|$, i.e. $T_{DWC}(m) = O(m^2)$, compared the exponential time complexity of *LazyReach*.

We now combine the procedure DWC together with the *LazyReach* algorithm by replacing **return** H on the final line (18) in DWC with

$$\textbf{return } LazyReach(\psi, \dot{\boldsymbol{x}} = f(\boldsymbol{x}) \,\&\, H, A).$$

We call the resulting new invariant generation procedure $DWCL$. Instead of returning H when no further progress can be made with DWC, $DWCL$ falls back to using the more expensive *LazyReach* algorithm with the remaining polynomials. This combined procedure is theoretically as powerful as *LazyReach*, i.e. is capable of extracting the exact reachable set $Reach_A^{\rightarrow}(\psi, H)$ if necessary, but in practice also as fast as DWC, although theoretically the running time of $DWCL$ remains exponential in m.

Example 7 (Invariant generated using DWCL). Consider the non-linear planar system from [7, Ex. 10.7, p. 281] (with $H = \mathbb{R}^2$):

$$\dot{x}_1 = 2x_1 \left(x_1^2 - 3\right)\left(4x_1^2 - 3\right)\left(x_1^2 + 21x_2^2 - 12\right),$$
$$\dot{x}_2 = x_2\big(35x_1^6 + 105x_2^2x_1^4 - 315x_1^4 - 63x_2^4x_1^2 + 378x_1^2 + 27x_2^6 - 189x_2^4 + 378x_2^2 - 216\big),$$

As an initial set, take $\psi \equiv (x_1 - 1)^2 + x_2^2 < \frac{1}{4}$ and let $\phi \equiv x_1^2 + x_2^2 < 8$ be the post-condition. Consider an abstraction of this system using the irreducible polynomial factors of the right-hand side of the system of ODEs and the post-condition, i.e. let

$$A = \{x_1, x_1^2 - 3, 4x_1^2 - 3, x_2, x_1^2 + x_2^2 - 8, x_1^2 + 21x_2^2 - 12,$$
$$35x_1^6 + 105x_2^2x_1^4 - 315x_1^4 - 63x_2^4x_1^2 + 378x_1^2 + 27x_2^6 - 189x_2^4 + 378x_2^2 - 216\}.$$

There are 7 abstraction polynomials in total, which in the worst case could lead to $3^7 = 2187$ discrete states and $7^7 - 3^7 = 821356$ discrete transitions in the neighbouring transition relation T_n. In practice, applying *LazyReach* to generate the reachable set $Reach_A^{\rightarrow}(\psi, H)$ for this problem takes an unreasonable amount of time. The procedure DWC takes significantly less time to run, but is unable to find a suitable invariant using DW, DC and DDC alone. Our implementation of the combined procedure $DWCL$ is able to generate the following continuous invariant $I \subset \phi$ in 104 s:[6]

$$\left(\left(\left(35x_1^6 + 105 \left(x_2^2 - 3 \right) x_1^4 + 27 \left(x_2^6 - 7x_2^4 + 14x_2^2 - 8 \right) < 63x_1^2 \left(x_2^4 - 6 \right) \vee x_2 = 0 \right) \right.$$

$$\wedge\, 4x_1^2 = 3 \wedge x_1 > 0 \right) \vee \left(x_2 = 0 \wedge \left(0 < x_1 < \frac{\sqrt{3}}{2} \vee \frac{\sqrt{3}}{2} < x_1 < \sqrt{3} \right) \right)$$

$$\vee \left(35x_1^6 + 105 \left(x_2^2 - 3 \right) x_1^4 + 27 \left(x_2^6 - 7x_2^4 + 14x_2^2 - 8 \right) < 63x_1^2 \left(x_2^4 - 6 \right) \right.$$

$$\left. \wedge\, x_1^2 + 21x_2^2 < 12 \wedge \left(0 < x_1 < \frac{\sqrt{3}}{2} \vee \left(2x_1 > \sqrt{3} \wedge x_1^2 < 3 \wedge x_2 \neq 0 \right) \right) \right) \right).$$

For this problem, the procedure $DWCL$ makes repeated use of both DC and DDC (each is used 4 times in total) before falling back to *LazyReach*, which in every instance is given 3 polynomials that remain to perform the abstraction (down from 7 in the original list A).

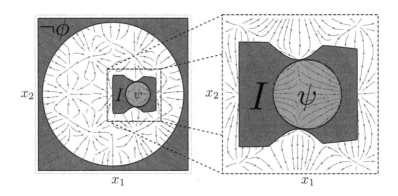

Fig. 6. Phase portrait, unsafe states $\neg\phi$ (**red**), initial set ψ (**green**) and a generated continuous invariant $I \subset \phi$ (**blue**) (Color figure online).

5.3 Sources of Polynomials for Abstraction

Discrete semi-algebraic abstraction relies on the user supplying a set of polynomials A to construct the set of discrete states through semi-algebraic decomposition of the evolution constraint. The verification problem itself is often a good

---

[6] expression simplified in *Mathematica*.

source of polynomials; e.g. they could come from the description of the (semi-algebraic) post-condition ϕ, the pre-condition ψ, or indeed from the right-hand side of the (polynomial) system of ODEs, i.e. the polynomials $f_1, f_2, \ldots, f_n$, their irreducible factors, etc. The use of Lie derivatives as a source of polynomials for abstraction was previously investigated in [37] (see also [39] for related work). In [43] abstraction is explored using *Darboux polynomials* (see [9,10]), whose real roots are invariant under the flow of the system. Recent results on real algebraic invariant checking [8] enable us to consider a more general class of polynomials that share this property but are not necessarily Darboux.

6 Practical Evaluation

In this section we compare the performance of our invariant generation algorithms *LazyReach*, *DWC* and *DWCL* on a set of 100 safety verification problems for continuous systems. The differential equations used in these problems are predominantly non-linear and originate from examples found in texts on dynamical systems [4,5,7,10,33,41], papers on the qualitative theory of ODEs and safety verification of continuous and hybrid systems [11,25,31,32,40].[7]

The running time performance[8] of the algorithms is summarised in Fig. 7. In the graphs, the vertical axis gives the dependent time variable (in seconds on a log scale) and the horizontal axis denotes the number of problems that could be solved in under the time given by the curve for each algorithm. By *solved* we understand that a semi-algebraic continuous invariant has been successfully generated and that it implies the postcondition, i.e. is sufficient to prove the safety assertion.

In our experiments we:

1. use polynomial factors of the right-hand side of the ODEs together with the factors of the polynomials appearing in the postcondition ϕ to create the set of polynomials A for the semi-algebraic decomposition (Fig. 7a),
2. extend the set A generated as in (1.) with Lie derivatives of every polynomial in A (Fig. 7b), and
3. explore the utility of using polynomials whose real roots are invariant real algebraic sets by extending the list of polynomials generated in (1.) and (2.) with polynomials generated using a method presented in [8] (Fig. 7c and d respecitvely).

In our results we observe that the *DWC* algorithm is significantly faster than *LazyReach*, confirming our hopes for gains in efficiency. We observe that, when using polynomial factors of the ODEs and the postcondition to abstract the system, *LazyReach* was able to prove as many problems as *DWC* (43), although the set of problems solved is different. This is not surprising, since a proof strategy involving DW, DC and DDC, while very efficient, cannot in general be used to

---

[7] See http://homepages.inf.ed.ac.uk/s0805753/invgen for the problems.
[8] The comparison was performed on an *i5-3570K* CPU clocked at 3.40 GHz.

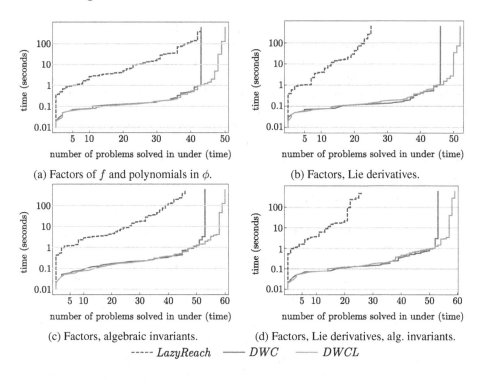

(a) Factors of f and polynomials in ϕ.   (b) Factors, Lie derivatives.

(c) Factors, algebraic invariants.   (d) Factors, Lie derivatives, alg. invariants.

----- *LazyReach*   —— *DWC*   —— *DWCL*

Fig. 7. Safety verification performance.

extract reachable sets of exact abstractions like the more expensive *LazyReach*. The combined method *DWCL* (using DW, DC, and DDC before falling back to *LazyReach*) is seen to be both as practically efficient as *DWC* and able to solve more problems (50) than *LazyReach* under a 600 s timeout; of course, given enough time, *DWCL* and *LazyReach* will both succeed at solving exactly the same problems (with *LazyReach* taking significantly more time).

Adding the first Lie derivatives of the polynomial factors of the ODE and the postcondition effectively doubles the size of the list A which, unsurprisingly, leads to diminished performance of *LazyReach* (only 25 problems solved) because it is heavily affected by the discrete state explosion problem. However, *DWC* is seen to perform slightly better than it did without the Lie derivatives in the list, solving a total of 46 safety verification problems. The *DWCL* algorithm succeeds at proving safety in 52 of the problems.

We observe that adding algebraic invariants to the list of polynomial factors of the ODE and the postcondition resulted in a palpable improvement in the number of problems that could be solved. This is very clearly visible in the case of *DWC*, which is guaranteed to process every algebraic invariant by applying the proof rules DC and DDC. Overall, for this choice of polynomials we see *LazyReach* solving 46, *DWC* solving 52, and *DWCL* solving 60 problems out of 100 (see Fig. 7c). Likewise, by adding algebraic invariants to the list of polynomial factors and their Lie derivatives (as in 2.) we were able to solve 26, 53 and 59 problems using *LazyReach*, *DWC* and *DWCL* respectively (Fig. 7d).

Overall, in every set of benchmarks we observe only one problem for which the algorithm *DWC* times out after 600 s, whereas *LazyReach* times out for many of problems (e.g. in the experiments shown in Fig. 7d *LazyReach* timed out on 59 of the problems and was unable to produce a suitable invariant within the time limit in only 15 instances). The procedure *DWCL* generally times out more often than *DWC*, but significantly less frequently than *LazyReach* (e.g. 25 problems from Fig. 7d resulted in a timeout, and 16 could not be solved using the resulting invariant).

These results are very encouraging as they demonstrate that the discrete state explosion problem can, to a certain extent, be addressed using algorithms such as *DWCL* and that methods for automatic algebraic invariant generation (such as that in [8]) can be used to generate polynomials that will often improve the quality of the resulting abstractions.

It is perhaps surprising to see that many of the atomic predicates featuring irreducible factors of polynomials harvested from the problem define continuous invariants. As such, these polynomials are eminently suitable for processing using our algorithms *DWC* and *DWCL* without incurring the performance penalty associated with building finer abstractions using the conventional approach.

7 Related Work

In [44], the authors apply their earlier results about checking semi-algebraic continuous invariants to address the invariant generation problem using approaches such as pre-defining parametric templates and restricting attention to classes of invariants (such as polyhedra), as well as using qualitative analysis techniques to suggest invariant templates. Our approach is different in that we do not rely on parametric templates and put no restrictions on the form of the semi-algebraic invariant which may be generated. Discrete abstraction of linear systems using *linear polynomials* to discretize the state space was investigated in [2,3]. A method for abstracting non-linear systems using non-linear polynomials was studied in [36,37], but results in abstractions that are inexact; the fundamental differences between this approach and our work is discussed at length in Sect. 3. A powerful technique called *relational abstraction* was introduced in [29]. With relational abstraction one aims to over-approximate the finite time reachability relation between states in a continuous system. Computing relational abstractions requires searching for appropriate invariants in a larger auxiliary continuous system; once a relational abstraction is available, one may use it to extract a continuous invariant containing any given initial state of the system. Computing good relational abstractions for non-linear systems is in practice expensive because it involves searching for invariants in continuous systems with double the original number of state variables.

8 Conclusion

This paper presented a powerful method for automatically discovering continuous invariants that can be used in a formal deductive system to prove safety assertions about continuous systems. We removed some important theoretical limitations (unsoundness and coarseness) in existing methods for constructing discrete abstractions of non-linear continuous systems and presented scalable and efficient algorithms for continuous invariant generation that combine discrete semi-algebraic abstraction with sound proof rules for deductive safety verification. Verification of hybrid systems constructively reduces to proving properties of differential equations [18,20], which provides a wider context for the future development of our work. The results we observe are highly encouraging, but much further work remains before safety verification (in the continuous fragment) of hybrid systems can enjoy a high level of automation. For instance, now that issues associated with inexact abstractions have been removed, the (difficult [39]) problem of finding a good choice of polynomials for constructing the semi-algebraic predicates is the only factor that determines the success of our approach. We observed that polynomials whose real roots themselves define invariants [8] can often be used to improve the quality of abstractions; however the broader problem of choosing the right polynomials leaves many interesting questions for future research.

References

1. Alur, R., Courcoubetis, C., Henzinger, T.A., Ho, P.H.: Hybrid automata: an algorithmic approach to the specification and verification of hybrid systems. In: Grossman, R.L., Ravn, A.P., Rischel, H., Nerode, A. (eds.) HS 1991 and HS 1992. LNCS, vol. 736, pp. 209–229. Springer, Heidelberg (1993)
2. Alur, R., Dang, T., Ivančić, F.: Progress on reachability analysis of hybrid systems using predicate abstraction. In: Maler, O., Pnueli, A. (eds.) HSCC 2003. LNCS, vol. 2623, pp. 4–19. Springer, Heidelberg (2003)
3. Alur, R., Dang, T., Ivančić, F.: Predicate abstraction for reachability analysis of hybrid systems. ACM Trans. Embed. Comput. Syst. 5(1), 152–199 (2006)
4. Arrowsmith, D., Place, C.: Dynamical Systems. Differential Equations, Maps and Chaotic Behaviour. Chapman & Hall, London (1992)
5. Bhatia, N.P., Szegő, G.P.: Stability Theory of Dynamical Systems. Springer, Heidelberg (1970)
6. Blanchini, F.: Set invariance in control. Automatica 35(11), 1747–1767 (1999)
7. Dumortier, F., Llibre, J., Artés, J.C.: Qualitative Theory of Planar Differential Systems. Springer, Berlin (2006)
8. Ghorbal, K., Platzer, A.: Characterizing algebraic invariants by differential radical invariants. In: Ábrahám, E., Havelund, K. (eds.) TACAS 2014 (ETAPS). LNCS, vol. 8413, pp. 279–294. Springer, Heidelberg (2014)
9. Ghorbal, K., Sogokon, A., Platzer, A.: A hierarchy of proof rules for checking differential invariance of algebraic sets. In: D'Souza, D., Lal, A., Larsen, K.G. (eds.) VMCAI 2015. LNCS, vol. 8931, pp. 431–448. Springer, Heidelberg (2015)
10. Goriely, A.: Integrability and Nonintegrability of Dynamical Systems. Advanced series in nonlinear dynamics. World Scientific, Singapore (2001)

11. Gulwani, S., Tiwari, A.: Constraint-based approach for analysis of hybrid systems. In: Gupta, A., Malik, S. (eds.) CAV 2008. LNCS, vol. 5123, pp. 190–203. Springer, Heidelberg (2008)

12. Hale, J.K., LaSalle, J.P.: Differential equations: linearity vs. nonlinearity. SIAM Rev. **5**(3), 249–272 (1963)

13. Henzinger, T.A.: The theory of hybrid automata. In: LICS, pp. 278–292. IEEE Computer Society Press (1996)

14. Liu, J., Zhan, N., Zhao, H.: Computing semi-algebraic invariants for polynomial dynamical systems. In: Chakraborty, S., Jerraya, A., Baruah, S.K., Fischmeister, S. (eds.) EMSOFT, pp. 97–106. ACM (2011)

15. Liu, J., Zhan, N., Zhao, H., Zou, L.: Abstraction of elementary hybrid systems by variable transformation. In: Bjørner, N., Boer, F. (eds.) FM 2015. LNCS, vol. 9109, pp. 360–377. Springer, Heidelberg (2015)

16. Matringe, N., Moura, A.V., Rebiha, R.: Generating invariants for non-linear hybrid systems by linear algebraic methods. In: Cousot, R., Martel, M. (eds.) SAS 2010. LNCS, vol. 6337, pp. 373–389. Springer, Heidelberg (2010)

17. Papachristodoulou, A., Prajna, S.: Analysis of non-polynomial systems using the sum of squares decomposition. In: Henrion, D., Garulli, A. (eds.) Positive Polynomials in Control. Lecture Notes in Control and Information Science, vol. 312, pp. 23–43. Springer, Berlin (2005)

18. Platzer, A.: Differential dynamic logic for hybrid systems. J. Autom. Reason. **41**(2), 143–189 (2008)

19. Platzer, A.: Differential-algebraic dynamic logic for differential-algebraic programs. J. Log. Comput. **20**(1), 309–352 (2010)

20. Platzer, A.: The complete proof theory of hybrid systems. In: LICS, pp. 541–550. IEEE (2012)

21. Platzer, A.: The structure of differential invariants and differential cut elimination. LMCS **8**(4), 1–38 (2012)

22. Platzer, A., Clarke, E.M.: Computing differential invariants of hybrid systems as fixedpoints. In: Gupta, A., Malik, S. (eds.) CAV 2008. LNCS, vol. 5123, pp. 176–189. Springer, Heidelberg (2008)

23. Powers, J.E.: Elimination of special functions from differential equations. Commun. ACM **2**(3), 3–4 (1959)

24. Prajna, S., Jadbabaie, A.: Safety verification of hybrid systems using barrier certificates. In: Alur, R., Pappas, G.J. (eds.) HSCC 2004. LNCS, vol. 2993, pp. 477–492. Springer, Heidelberg (2004)

25. Ratschan, S., She, Z.: Safety verification of hybrid systems by constraint propagation-based abstraction refinement. ACM Trans. Embed. Comput. Syst., vol. 6(1), Febuary 2007

26. Richardson, D.: Some undecidable problems involving elementary functions of a real variable. J. Symb. Log. **33**(4), 514–520 (1968)

27. Sankaranarayanan, S.: Automatic invariant generation for hybrid systems using ideal fixed points. In: HSCC, pp. 221–230 (2010)

28. Sankaranarayanan, S., Sipma, H.B., Manna, Z.: Constructing invariants for hybrid systems. FMSD **32**(1), 25–55 (2008)

29. Sankaranarayanan, S., Tiwari, A.: Relational abstractions for continuous and hybrid systems. In: Gopalakrishnan, G., Qadeer, S. (eds.) CAV 2011. LNCS, vol. 6806, pp. 686–702. Springer, Heidelberg (2011)

30. Savageau, M.A., Voit, E.O.: Recasting nonlinear differential equations as S-systems: a canonical nonlinear form. Math. Biosci. **87**(1), 83–115 (1987)

31. Schlomiuk, D.: Algebraic and geometric aspects of the theory of polynomial vector fields. In: Schlomiuk, D. (ed.) Bifurcations and Periodic Orbits of Vector Fields. NATO ASI Series, vol. 408, pp. 429–467. Springer, Heidelberg (1993)

32. Schlomiuk, D.: Algebraic particular integrals, integrability and the problem of the center. Trans. Am. Math. Soci. **338**(2), 799–841 (1993)

33. Strogatz, S.H.: Nonlinear Dynamics and Chaos. Westview Press, New York (1994)

34. Stursberg, O., Kowalewski, S., Hoffmann, I., Preußig, J.: Comparing timed and hybrid automata as approximations of continuous systems. In: Antsaklis, P.J., Kohn, W., Nerode, A., Sastry, S.S. (eds.) HS 1996. LNCS, vol. 1273. Springer, Heidelberg (1997)

35. Tarski, A.: A decision method for elementary algebra and geometry. Bull. Am. Math. Soci. **59**, 91–93 (1951)

36. Tiwari, A., Khanna, G.: Series of abstractions for hybrid automata. In: Tomlin, C.J., Greenstreet, M.R. (eds.) HSCC 2002. LNCS, vol. 2289, p. 465. Springer, Heidelberg (2002)

37. Tiwari, A.: Abstractions for hybrid systems. FMSD **32**(1), 57–83 (2008)

38. Tiwari, A.: Generating box invariants. In: Egerstedt, M., Mishra, B. (eds.) HSCC 2008. LNCS, vol. 4981, pp. 658–661. Springer, Heidelberg (2008)

39. Tiwari, A., Khanna, G.: Nonlinear systems: approximating reach sets. In: Alur, R., Pappas, G.J. (eds.) HSCC 2004. LNCS, vol. 2993, pp. 600–614. Springer, Heidelberg (2004)

40. Wang, T.C., Lall, S., West, M.: Polynomial level-set method for polynomial system reachable set estimation. IEEE Trans. Autom. Control **58**(10), 2508–2521 (2013)

41. Wiggins, S.: Introduction to Applied Nonlinear Dynamical Systems and Chaos. Texts in Applied Mathematics, 2nd edn. Springer, New York (2003)

42. Wu, Z.: Tangent cone and contingent cone to the intersection of two closed sets. Nonlinear Anal.: Theor., Methods Appl. **73**(5), 1203–1220 (2010)

43. Zaki, M.H., Tahar, S., Bois, G.: A symbolic approach for the safety verification of continuous systems. In: Proceedings of the International Conference on Computational Sciences, pp. 93–100 (2007)

44. Zhao, H., Zhan, N., Kapur, D.: Synthesizing switching controllers for hybrid systems by generating invariants. In: Liu, Z., Woodcock, J., Zhu, H. (eds.) Theories of Programming and Formal Methods. LNCS, vol. 8051, pp. 354–373. Springer, Heidelberg (2013)

Dynamic and Static Verification

Hybrid Analysis for Partial Order Reduction of Programs with Arrays

Pavel Parízek[✉]

Department of Distributed and Dependable Systems,
Faculty of Mathematics and Physics, Charles University in Prague,
Prague, Czech Republic
parizek@d3s.mff.cuni.cz

Abstract. An important component of efficient approaches to software model checking and systematic concurrency testing is partial order reduction, which eliminates redundant non-deterministic thread scheduling choices during the state space traversal. Thread choices have to be created only at the execution of actions that access the global state visible by multiple threads, so the key challenge is to precisely determine the set of such globally-relevant actions. This includes accesses to object fields and array elements, and thread synchronization.

However, some tools completely disable thread choices at actions that access individual array elements in order to avoid state explosion. We show that they can miss concurrency errors in such a case. Then, as the main contribution, we present a new hybrid analysis that identifies globally-relevant actions that access arrays. Our hybrid analysis combines static analysis with dynamic analysis, usage of information from dynamic program states, and symbolic interpretation of program statements. Results of experiments with two popular approaches to partial order reduction show that usage of the hybrid analysis (1) eliminates many additional redundant thread choices and (2) improves the performance of software model checking on programs that use arrays.

1 Introduction

Systematic traversal of the program state space is a popular approach for detecting concurrency-related errors. It is used, for example, in software model checking [22], where the goal is to check the program behavior under all possible thread interleavings.

Each interleaving corresponds to a sequence of thread scheduling decisions and also to a particular sequence of actions performed by the program threads. We divide the actions into two sets: globally-relevant and thread-local. A *globally-relevant* action reads or modifies the global state shared by multiple threads. The set of globally-relevant actions contains accesses to fields of heap objects and array elements, and thread synchronization operations (e.g., acquisition of a lock). Other actions are *thread-local*.

Any non-trivial multithreaded program exhibits a huge number of possible interleavings, but many of them differ only in the order of thread-local actions.

© Springer-Verlag Berlin Heidelberg 2016
B. Jobstmann and K.R.M. Leino (Eds.): VMCAI 2016, LNCS 9583, pp. 291–310, 2016.
DOI: 10.1007/978-3-662-49122-5_14

It is necessary to check just all the possible interleavings of globally-relevant actions, and to explore each of them just once. Techniques based on state space traversal use partial order reduction (POR) [5] to avoid redundant exploration of thread interleavings in order to mitigate state explosion.

The key idea behind POR is to consider non-deterministic thread scheduling choices only at globally-relevant actions, while avoiding redundant choices at thread-local actions. A lot of work has been done on POR in the context of software model checking (e.g., [3,4,6,15]). All the existing approaches to POR have to conservatively over-approximate the set of globally-relevant actions in order to ensure coverage of all distinct thread interleavings. On the other hand, they also strive to be as precise as possible, because the number of thread interleavings explored redundantly during the state space traversal depends on the number of actions that are actually thread-local but were imprecisely identified as globally-relevant. For example, dynamic POR [4] uses dynamic analysis to identify (i) heap objects really accessed by multiple threads and (ii) actions performed upon such objects. Another technique [3] uses escape analysis to identify objects that are reachable from multiple threads. Some work has been done also on the combination of static analysis with dynamic analysis for precise identification of globally-relevant field accesses on shared heap objects [15,16].

An important category of actions that may be globally-relevant are accesses to array objects stored in the heap. However, in the default configuration, POR algorithms in tools like Java Pathfinder [8] do not allow thread scheduling choices at actions that access individual array elements in order to avoid state explosion. For each access to an array element, they make a scheduling choice only at the preceding action that retrieves the array object from the heap (e.g., a field read access).

The problem with this approach to POR is that state space traversal can miss some concurrency errors. Consider the small Java-like program in Fig. 1, where two threads access a shared array (buffer). Each thread retrieves a reference to the array object from the heap through a field read, stores the reference into a local variable buf, and then accesses the first element. The field read actions do not have to be synchronized at all, but there is a race condition that involves the array accesses. A verification tool cannot detect this race condition if it uses a POR algorithm with disabled thread choices at accesses to individual array elements. We found similar race conditions also in some of our benchmark programs — we discuss that in more detail at the end of Sect. 5.

```
1   class Writer extends Thread {        7   class Reader extends Thread {
2     public void run() {                 8     public void run() {
3       int[] buf = SharedData.buffer;     9       int[] buf = SharedData.buffer;
4       buf[0] = x;                       10       v = buf[0];
5     }                                    11     }
6   }                                      12   }
```

Fig. 1. Example: race condition involving an array element

Consequently, the state space traversal procedure with POR has to create thread scheduling choices at array element accesses in order to enable discovery of all such race conditions and other concurrency errors. The basic option for identifying globally-relevant accesses to array elements is to consider heap reachability [3]. When the given array object is not reachable from multiple threads, then every access to elements of the array is a thread-local action and no thread choice is necessary.

We propose a new hybrid analysis that soundly identifies array elements possibly accessed by multiple threads during the program execution. Results of the hybrid analysis can be used by POR to decide more precisely whether a given access to an array element is globally-relevant or thread-local. Then, thread choices at accesses to individual elements can be enabled without a high risk of state explosion. Although the state space size might increase in the worst case, it will stay in reasonable limits because POR avoids many redundant choices at thread-local accesses based on the hybrid analysis.

Our hybrid analysis combines static analysis with dynamic analysis and symbolic interpretation of program statements, and it also uses information from dynamic program states that is available on-the-fly during the state space traversal. We describe key concepts on the examples of multithreaded Java programs, but the analysis is applicable also to programs written in other languages, such as C# and C++. For simplicity of presentation, we consider only arrays with a single dimension in most of the paper and discuss support for multi-dimensional arrays at the end of Sect. 3.

An important feature of the hybrid analysis is compatibility with all memory models that we are aware of, including relaxed memory models such as JMM [10] and TSO [19]. The only requirements are that the underlying tool, which performs state space traversal, has to simulate the given memory model to a full extent and it must provide correct information about the dynamic program state, in particular taking into account delayed propagation of the effects of writes to shared variables among threads.

Experimental results provided in Sect. 5 show that our hybrid analysis helps to avoid many redundant thread choices during the state space traversal. It improves the precision and performance of existing approaches to POR on multithreaded programs that use arrays, and therefore enables more efficient detection of concurrency-related errors that involve array elements by software model checking.

In the next section we provide an overview of the whole approach. Then we discuss situations and code patterns where our hybrid analysis can eliminate a redundant thread choice (Sect. 3), and explain the analysis algorithm in more detail in Sect. 4. The rest of the paper contains evaluation, description of related work, and a brief summary.

2   Overview

Figure 2 shows the basic algorithm for depth-first state space traversal of multithreaded programs with POR. We assume that the program state space is

```
1    visited = {}
2    exploreState(s₀,ch₀)
3
4    procedure exploreState(s,ch)
5      if s ∈ visited then return
6      visited = visited ∪ s
7      for T ∈ getRunnableThreads(ch) do
8        s' = executeTransition(s,T)
9        if isErrorState(s') then terminate
10       ch' = createThreadChoice(s',getRunnableThreads(s'))
11       exploreState(s',ch')
12     end for
13   end proc
14
15   procedure executeTransition(s,T)
16     i = getNextInstruction(T)  // must be globally relevant
17     while i ≠ null do  // while not at the end of the thread
18       s = executeInstruction(s,i)
19       i = getNextInstruction(T)
20       if isGloballyRelevant(s,i,T) then break
21     end while
22     return s
23   end proc
```

Fig. 2. Basic algorithm for state space traversal with POR

constructed on-the-fly during traversal and that statements are interpreted using dynamic concrete execution. In addition, we consider only thread scheduling choices and ignore the data non-determinism in this paper. The symbol s represents a program state, the symbol ch represents a thread choice, and T denotes a thread runnable in a particular state. Exploration starts from the initial state s_0 and the initial choice ch_0, where only the main thread is runnable. An atomic transition between two states corresponds to the execution of a sequence of instructions (program statements) that consists of a globally-relevant action, followed by any number of thread-local actions, and it ends with a thread choice. The POR algorithm creates a new thread choice just before execution of an action that it considers to be globally-relevant. All instructions in a transition are executed by the same thread. Note that many popular tools, including Java Pathfinder [8], use a state space traversal procedure that follows this approach.

In this setting, the POR algorithm itself can use information only from (i) the current dynamic program state, (ii) the current state space path (execution history), and (iii) the already explored part of the state space to decide whether the action to be executed next is globally-relevant or thread-local, because it does not see ahead in program execution. A popular approach is to identify globally-relevant actions based on heap reachability in the current dynamic state [3]. This approach is safe but not very precise — a particular heap object (an array) may be reachable from multiple threads but really accessed only by a single thread during the program execution, or the individual threads may access different elements of a given array. The POR algorithm has to conservatively assume that each thread may in the future access every object reachable in the current state, and therefore many redundant thread choices are created during the state space traversal.

The proposed hybrid analysis determines more precise information about which array elements may be accessed in the future during the rest of program execution from the current state. We used the general principle introduced for field accesses in [15] and adapted it significantly for accesses to array elements. For each program point p in each thread T, the analysis computes the set of array elements (over all array objects that may exist in the heap) possibly accessed by thread T after the point p on any execution path. In other words, the analysis provides over-approximate information about future behavior of T after a specific code location. Array objects are identified by their static allocation sites and individual elements are identified by their symbolic indexes.

Our hybrid analysis has two phases: (1) static analysis that computes partial information, and (2) post-processing on-the-fly during the state space exploration (i.e., at the dynamic analysis time). Full results are generated in the second phase, when data provided by the static analysis are combined with specific information from dynamic program states, including the dynamic call stack of each thread and concrete values of some expressions used as array element indexes. The results are more precise than what would be possible to get with a reasonably expensive static analysis.

Here, in the rest of this section, we describe how the analysis results are used during the state space traversal to avoid redundant thread choices.

When the next action to be executed is an access to some array element, the POR algorithm has to decide whether to make a thread choice or not. Figure 3 captures the procedure at a high level of abstraction. The symbol s represents the current dynamic state, T_c is the currently scheduled thread, and i is the next instruction of T_c.

First, the algorithm checks whether the target array object a is reachable from multiple threads in the state s. If it is, then the procedure retrieves the

```
1   procedure isGloballyRelevant(s,i,Tc)
2       a = getTargetArrayObject(i)
3       if ¬isArrayReachableFromMultipleThreads(s,a) then return false
4       for To ∈ getOtherThreads(s,Tc) do
5           if existsFutureConflictingAccess(To,a) then
6               if possiblyEqualIndexes(s,Tc,To,a) then return true
7           end if
8       end for
9       return false // default
10  end proc
```

Fig. 3. Procedure that identifies globally-relevant accesses to array elements

results of the hybrid analysis for the current point of every thread T_o other than T_c, and inspects the results to find whether some of the other threads may access the array a in a conflicting way (read versus write) on any execution path that starts in s.

For the array accesses that may be performed by some other thread, the hybrid analysis inspects also symbolic indexes of array elements. More specifically, it compares (1) the concrete value of the array element index for the next access in T_c, which can be easily retrieved from the current dynamic state s, and (2) the symbolic index for each of the possible future conflicting accesses to a. Under some conditions, the concrete value of the array element index can be soundly determined also for a possible future access — the respective situations and code patterns are discussed in the next section.

A thread choice has to be created in the state s only when some thread T_o may possibly access the same element of a as T_c, because otherwise the respective action of T_c is thread-local. In particular, if every possible conflicting future access to the array a in some other thread provably uses a different concrete value of an element index, then the POR algorithm does not have to make a thread choice.

3   Array Access Patterns

Here we discuss patterns of concurrent accesses to array elements, for which our hybrid analysis can eliminate a redundant thread choice, and also cases where it cannot eliminate a thread choice due to imprecision. Each code pattern involves two threads:

- the *active thread* whose next action is the array access in question (where a thread choice will be created or not depending on the analysis results), and
- the *conflicting thread*, which may access the same array elements as the active thread in the future on some execution path.

In all the patterns we assume that the array data is reachable from both threads. The various kinds of symbolic expressions that can be used as array element indexes are considered only for the conflicting thread, because for the active thread we can always get the actual concrete index value from the current dynamic program state.

Constants. The most basic pattern is the usage of an integer constant as the array element index. We show on this example how to interpret also the other patterns below.

active thread	conflict thread
data[e] = x	y = data[1]

In the code of the active thread, we use the symbol e to denote the concrete value of the index expression. The symbolic index associated with the possible future access by the conflicting thread (i.e., the constant 1 in the code fragment above) is compared with the value e. If the values are different then a thread choice would be redundant at the array access in the active thread, because each thread accesses different elements.

Local Variables. Another common case is when the symbolic index associated with the future access by the conflicting thread is a local variable v of a method m. In order to decide soundly about making a new choice, the hybrid analysis can use the current value of v (from the dynamic state) only if the following two conditions are satisfied.

1. The conflicting thread is executing the method m in the current dynamic state s.
2. The local variable v is not updated in the rest of the program execution starting from the state s.

We consider all methods on the current dynamic call stack of a given thread as currently executing. The concrete value obviously cannot be retrieved for local variables of methods that are not yet on the dynamic call stack of a respective thread. Note also that the local variable v of m may be updated in the future in two ways — either by assignment in the rest of the current execution of m, or by a future call of m at any time during the program execution.

Consider the following example, where the variable v is not updated after the access to data and the method run is not called again.

active thread	conflict thread
main():	run(args):
...	v = f(args)
data[e] = x	
...	y = data[v]

The hybrid analysis can safely eliminate a thread choice only if the concrete dynamic value of v is different from e.

A typical situation where the variable v may be updated later during the execution of m is shown in the next example. Here, v is also a control variable of the loop.

active thread	conflict thread
main():	run(args):
...	for (v = 0; v < 10; v++)
data[e] = x	y = data[v]

The hybrid analysis cannot determine whether another iteration of the loop might be executed or not, and therefore a future update of v is always possible in this case.

We have to consider also future calls of the method m because every local variable of m has to be initialized (i.e., updated) before it can be used as array index. Although each execution of m has its own instances of local variables, the symbolic name v is common to all of the executions. Therefore, an update of v may occur between the current state and the relevant array access in a future execution of m.

Object Fields. When the symbolic index contains a field access path fp, the analysis can use the current dynamic value of fp only if the following conditions are satisfied.

1. In the case of instance fields, the access path must contain the local variable this associated with one of the currently executing methods of the conflicting thread.
2. No field in the access path fp is updated in the future during the rest of program execution starting from the current dynamic state s.

Then, the dynamic value of fp can be used to compute the concrete value of the array index expression in the conflicting thread. If the result is not equal to the value of the index expression e used by the active thread, then both threads will always access different elements of the shared array at the respective code locations, and thus the POR algorithm does not have to create a new thread choice.

Multi-dimensional Arrays. Our hybrid analysis supports multi-dimensional arrays but only with a limited precision. Element indexes are inspected and compared only for the innermost dimension, using the same approach as for single-dimensional arrays. Index expressions for outer dimensions are completely ignored by the hybrid analysis, which therefore assumes (i) that concurrent threads may use the same index values and (ii) that any two elements of an outer array may be aliased. A possible choice can be safely eliminated only when both threads use provably different values of element indexes for the innermost dimension. This case is illustrated by the following example, where e_1 might be equal to e_2.

active thread	conflict thread
data$[e_1][0] = $ x	y $ = $ data$[e_2][1]$

On the other hand, a choice must be preserved when both threads may use the same index value for the innermost dimension, such as e_1 and e_2 in the example below, even if different values (e.g., 0 and 1) are used at some outer dimension. The expressions data[0] and data[1] may point to the same innermost array because of aliasing.

active thread	conflict thread
data$[0][e_1] = $ x	y $ = $ data$[1][e_2]$

Note also that we have to analyze possible read-write conflicts only for the innermost dimension, because only read-read conflicts may happen at outer dimensions and they do not require thread choices.

4   Hybrid Analysis

The hybrid analysis computes all the information necessary to decide whether a thread choice must be created — in particular, for each of the scenarios described in the previous section. We designed the analysis in a modular way. Each component provides information about one of the following: (1) accesses to array objects, (2) future accesses to specific array elements, (3) symbolic values of element indexes, (4) local variables possibly updated in the future, (5) updated object fields, and (6) future method calls.

First we describe the general principles and then we provide additional details about the individual components. Every component that is an inter-procedural analysis has two phases: static and dynamic. Both phases are designed and executed using an approach that was proposed in [15]. The static analysis runs first, and then follows the state space traversal with dynamic analysis. Results of the static analysis (phase 1) are combined with information taken from the dynamic program state (phase 2) on-the-fly during the state space traversal, i.e. at the dynamic analysis time.

The static phase involves a backward flow-sensitive and context-insensitive analysis that is performed over the full inter-procedural control flow graph (ICFG) of a given thread. For each program point p in the thread T, it provides only information about the behavior of T between the point p and the return from the method m containing p. Note that the result for p in m covers also methods called from m (transitively).

Full results are computed at the dynamic analysis time based on the knowledge of the dynamic call stack of each thread, which is a part of the dynamic program state. The dynamic call stack of a given thread specifies a sequence $p_0, p_1, \ldots, p_N$ of program points, where p_0 is the current program counter of the thread (in the top stack frame), and p_i is the point from which execution of the thread would continue after return from the method associated with the previous stack frame. When the hybrid analysis is queried for data about the current point p of some thread T, it takes the data computed by the static analysis phase for each point $p_i, i = 0, \ldots, N$ on the dynamic call stack of T, where $p = p_0$, and merges them all to get the precise and complete results for p.

The complete results for a program point p in thread T cover the future behavior of T after the point p (until the end of T), and also the behavior of all child threads of T started after p. Here, a child thread of T is another thread created and started by T.

Note also that the complete results of the hybrid analysis are fully context-sensitive for the following two reasons: (1) they reflect the current dynamic calling context of p in T, i.e., the current program counter in each method on the dynamic call stack of T, and (2) they precisely match calls with returns. Only those method call and return edges in the ICFG that can be actually taken during the concrete program execution are considered by the hybrid analysis.

Accesses to Array Objects. This component of the hybrid analysis identifies all arrays possibly accessed in the future by a given thread. More specifically, for each program point p in each thread T, it computes the set of all array objects that may be accessed on some execution path after p. Static allocation sites are used to represent the actual array objects also here. The analysis considers read and write accesses separately in order to enable precise detection of read-write conflicts. It is an inter-procedural analysis, which therefore has two phases — static and dynamic — in our approach.

Instruction	Transfer function
	$\text{after}[\ell] = \bigcup_{\ell' \in \text{succ}(\ell)} \text{before}[\ell']$
ℓ: v = a[i]	$\text{before}[\ell] = \text{after}[\ell] \cup \{r\ a\}$
ℓ: a[i] = v	$\text{before}[\ell] = \text{after}[\ell] \cup \{w\ a\}$
ℓ: return	$\text{before}[\ell] = \emptyset$
ℓ: call M	$\text{before}[\ell] = \text{before}[\text{M.entry}] \cup \text{after}[\ell]$
ℓ: other instr.	$\text{before}[\ell] = \text{after}[\ell]$

Fig. 4. Transfer functions for the static phase of the array objects analysis

Figure 4 shows transfer functions for the static phase. When the analysis encounters a read or write access to an array a, it adds the target array object into the set of data-flow facts. The transfer functions for the call and return statements are defined in this way to ensure that the result of the static phase for a point p in a method m covers only the execution between p and return from m. The merge operator is a set union.

Array Elements. Possible future accesses to individual array elements are identified using an analysis component that works in a very similar way to the one for array objects. This analysis computes, for each program point p in each thread, the set of all possible accesses to array elements that may occur on some execution path after p. It gathers the following information about each access: a target array object (allocation site), method signature, and instruction index (bytecode position). Knowledge of the method signature and bytecode position is used by the next component to associate each particular access with symbolic values of array element indexes.

Symbolic Indexes. This component performs symbolic interpretation of the code in each method to determine symbolic expressions that represent indexes of array elements. A symbolic expression may include local variables, field access paths, nested accesses to array elements, numeric constants, and arithmetic operators.

When processing the code of a method, the analysis maintains a stack of symbolic expressions, which models the concrete dynamic stack containing local variables and operands. The symbolic stack is updated during interpretation to capture the effects of executed program statements. For each statement, all its operands are removed from the stack and then the result is pushed onto it.

The following example illustrates how the symbolic value of an element index is computed for a particular array access. We consider the statement v = a[o.f+2].

instructions	symbolic stack
1: load a	[a]
2: load o	[a, o]
3: getfield f	[a, o.f]
4: const 2	[a, o.f, 2]
5: add	[a, o.f+2]
6: arrayload	[e]
7: store v	[]

The left column contains a sequence of instructions that corresponds to the statement, and the right column shows the content of the symbolic stack after each instruction. At line 5, the top value on the stack represents the symbolic array element index.

Updated Local Variables. The sets of possibly updated local variables are computed by an intra-procedural static analysis of each method. For each point p in method m, the analysis identifies all future write accesses to local variables of m that may occur on some execution path in m. Note that this component of the whole hybrid analysis does not use any information available in the dynamic program state.

Transfer function for the store operation just records the index (name) of the target local variable. For all other statements, the transfer function is identity.

Updated Fields. We use the field access analysis proposed in [15] to find all fields that may be updated on some execution path in thread T after the point p. The analysis is fully inter-procedural and combines the static phase with information taken from the dynamic program state.

However, the field access analysis alone is not sufficient for the following reason: a symbolic value of an array element index may refer to a field of a heap object that does not exist yet in the current dynamic state. It is therefore necessary to consider also possible future allocations of heap objects of the respective class (type). The current dynamic value of a given field may be safely used by the hybrid analysis and POR, as discussed in Sect. 3, only when the following two conditions hold.

1. The field is provably not updated in the future according to the field access analysis.
2. No heap object of the given type may be allocated later during the program execution starting from the current dynamic state.

We use a simple analysis to find allocation sites at which some dynamic heap object may be possibly allocated in the future (on some execution path starting in p).

Although the conditions are quite restrictive, we believe that they will be satisfied in many cases in practice. Based on manual inspection of the source code of our benchmark programs (listed in Sect. 5), we found that array index expressions quite often refer to fields of heap objects that are allocated early during the program execution. The concrete dynamic value of an object field can be safely used in such cases, helping to eliminate many redundant thread choices.

Method Calls. The last component of the hybrid analysis identifies methods that may be called in the future after the current state. It is an inter-procedural analysis that represents methods by their signatures. The transfer function for the call statement adds into the set of facts every method that is a possible target according to the call graph.

5 Evaluation

We implemented the proposed hybrid analysis in Java Pathfinder (JPF) [8], which is a framework for state space traversal of multithreaded Java programs. JPF uses on-the-fly state space construction, depth-first search, and concrete execution of Java bytecode instructions. In order to support decisions about thread choices based on the results of our hybrid analysis, we created a non-standard interpreter of Java bytecode instructions for array access. We used the WALA library [23] for static analysis and JPF API to retrieve information from the dynamic program state. Symbolic interpretation of Java bytecode, which collects symbolic expressions that represent indexes of array elements, is performed by a custom engine that we also built using WALA.

Our prototype implementation, together with the experimental setup and benchmark programs described below, is publicly available at http://d3s.mff. cuni.cz/projects/formal_methods/jpf-static/vmcai16.html.

Benchmarks. We evaluated the hybrid analysis on 11 multithreaded Java programs from widely known benchmark suites (Java Grande Forum [7], CTC [2], pjbench [13]), our previous work, and existing studies by other researchers [20]. Table 1 shows the list of benchmark programs and their quantitative characteristics — the total number of source code lines (Java LoC) and the maximal number of concurrently running threads. All the benchmark programs that we use contain array objects reachable from multiple threads and many accesses to array elements in their source code.

Table 1. Benchmark programs

Benchmark	Java LoC	Threads
CRE Demo	1,300	2
Daisy	800	2
Crypt	300	2
Elevator	300	3
Simple JBB	2700	2
Alarm Clock	200	3
Prod-Cons	130	2
Rep Workers	400	2
SOR	160	2
TSP	420	2
QSort MT	290	2

For selected benchmarks, we provide a more detailed characteristic that is relevant for the discussion of experimental results later in this section. The benchmark program Crypt contains three shared arrays, but each thread accesses different elements of the arrays, and therefore all possible thread choices at the accesses to arrays would be redundant. In the case of CRE Demo and Daisy, each array object used directly in the application source code is reachable only from a single thread, which means that accesses to arrays are thread-local, but the programs involve shared collections (e.g., Vector and HashSet) that use arrays internally.

Experiments. The goal of our experimental evaluation was to find how many redundant thread choices the hybrid analysis really eliminates during the state space traversal, and how much it improves performance and scalability of different approaches to partial order reduction in the context of software model checking. We performed experiments with the hybrid analysis for shared array elements proposed in this paper, the hybrid field access analysis [15], the POR algorithm based on heap reachability, and our implementation of the dynamic POR algorithm described in [4]. For the purpose of our experiments, we have implemented also the dynamic POR algorithm in JPF and combined it with state matching.

Table 2 shows all configurations of POR that we considered in our experiments. For each configuration, it provides a brief description and a short name used in tables with results. Note that we say "array access" instead of "array element access" in some table rows, but with the same intentional meaning, as the table would be too large otherwise.

Table 2. Configurations of POR

Description	Short name
Heap reachability without thread choices at bytecode Instructions for array element access	HR + no array ch
Heap reachability with thread choices enabled at bytecode instructions for array element access	HR + all array ch
Heap reachability with field access analysis and enabled thread choices at array element accesses	HR + fields + all array ch
Heap reachability with field access analysis, thread choices at array accesses, and hybrid analysis	HR + fields + hybrid
Dynamic POR without thread choices at bytecode instructions for array element access	DPOR + no array ch
Dynamic POR with thread choices enabled at bytecode instructions for array access	DPOR + enabled array ch
Dynamic POR with field access analysis and enabled choices at array element accesses	DPOR + fields + enabled array ch
Dynamic POR with field access analysis, enabled choices at array accesses, and hybrid analysis	DPOR + fields + hybrid

For each configuration and benchmark program, i.e. for every experiment, we report the following metrics: (1) the total number of thread choices created by JPF at all kinds of bytecode instructions during the state space traversal, and (2) the total running time of JPF combined with all phases of the hybrid analysis. The number of thread choices shows precision, while the running time indicates performance.

In the first set of experiments, we configured JPF to traverse the whole state space of each benchmark program — we had to disable reporting of errors because otherwise JPF would stop upon reaching an error state. We used the time limit of 8 h and memory limit of 20 GB. The symbol "-", when present in some cell of a table with results, indicates that JPF run out of the limit for a given configuration and benchmark.

Discussion. The results in Tables 3 and 4 show that usage of our hybrid analysis together with POR in general reduces the number of thread choices and improves the running time for both POR algorithms that we considered. In the next few paragraphs, we discuss the results for individual benchmark programs in more detail and highlight important observations.

For many configurations and benchmark programs, the total number of thread choices created during the state space traversal is much higher when choices are enabled at accesses to array elements. This is evident from the values in columns "HR + no array ch" and "HR + all array ch" (Table 3), respectively in the columns "DPOR + no array ch" and "DPOR + enabled array ch" (Table 4). We observed an extreme increase of the number of thread choices in two cases — by the factor of 137 for the Crypt benchmark with POR based on heap reachability, and by the factor of 300 for the SOR benchmark when using the dynamic POR. On the other hand, there is a negligible increase for

Table 3. Experimental results: POR algorithm based on heap reachability

Benchmark	HR + no array ch		HR + all array ch		HR + fields + all array ch		HR + fields + hybrid	
	choices	time	choices	time	choices	time	choices	time
CRE Demo	30942	51 s	103016	174 s	41146	79 s	29737	69 s
Daisy	28436002	17954 s	32347254	18357 s	8453587	5972 s	8453587	6765 s
Crypt	4993	3 s	682273	238 s	674041	237 s	46105	29 s
Elevator	10167560	7656 s	23709139	18339 s	9980240	7426 s	4748393	3872 s
Simple JBB	575519	1779 s	836889	2583 s	515312	1722 s	344428	1269 s
Alarm Clock	531463	432 s	742027	601 s	344791	285 s	344791	289 s
Prod-Cons	6410	4 s	6934	4 s	2792	4 s	2792	6 s
Rep Workers	9810966	6860 s	9983423	7045 s	1714694	1169 s	1714694	1275 s
SOR	222129	123 s	1565386	882 s	772837	451 s	273693	160 s
TSP	35273	572 s	47475	779 s	15386	257 s	13258	221 s

Table 4. Experimental results: dynamic POR

Benchmark	DPOR + no array ch		DPOR + enabled array ch		DPOR + fields + enabled array ch		DPOR + fields + hybrid	
	choices	time	choices	time	choices	time	choices	time
CRE Demo	2015	11 s	2232	20 s	2207	18 s	2197	22 s
Daisy	-	-	-	-	-	-	-	-
Crypt	9	1 s	9	1 s	9	3 s	9	5 s
Elevator	414345	913 s	501732	1371 s	408192	886 s	342817	648 s
Simple JBB	602	30 s	608	36 s	608	36 s	608	38 s
Alarm Clock	102076	147 s	155974	227 s	103964	123 s	103964	125 s
Prod-Cons	429	1 s	444	1 s	407	3 s	407	4 s
Rep Workers	-	-	-	-	-	-	-	-
SOR	135	2 s	40594	208 s	26503	135 s	19819	71 s
TSP	101	67 s	101	94 s	97	66 s	97	58 s

Prod-Cons and Rep Workers, and no increase for the benchmarks Crypt, Simple JBB, and TSP when using the dynamic POR.

Data in Tables 3 and 4 also indicate how many redundant choices were eliminated by the hybrid analysis, and how much it improved the performance and scalability of state space traversal. The result for a particular benchmark and POR based on heap reachability corresponds to the difference between values in the columns "HR + fields + all array ch" and "HR + fields + hybrid" of Table 3. Similarly, in the case of dynamic POR one has to consider values in the columns "DPOR + fields + enabled array ch" and "DPOR + fields + hybrid" of Table 4. We observe that our hybrid analysis eliminates many redundant thread choices at array accesses for 6 out of 10 benchmarks, namely the following: CRE Demo, Crypt, Elevator, Simple JBB, SOR, and TSP. In the case of four benchmark programs — CRE Demo, Crypt, Simple JBB, and TSP — the hybrid analysis significantly reduced the total number of thread choices only when it is combined with the POR based on heap reachability. The factor of reduction in the number of thread choices lies in the range from 1.16 (for TSP and POR based on heap reachability) up to 14.62 (Crypt and again POR based on heap reachability).

Our results for the benchmarks Alarm Clock, Daisy, Prod-Cons, and Rep Workers indicate that all redundant thread choices were eliminated by the field access analysis. For example, by manual inspection of the source code of Prod-Cons we have found that all accesses to array elements are properly synchronized, and therefore no thread choices are created at their execution.

Here we compare dynamic POR with the POR algorithm based on heap reachability. A well-known fact is that dynamic POR is very precise and creates much less thread choices [12,16]. For example, it correctly identifies that all accesses to array elements in the Crypt benchmark are thread-local actions. It analyzes small programs very fast (in few seconds) — see, e.g., the data for Crypt and Prod-Cons in Table 4 — but it has a significantly higher running time and memory consumption for some of the more complex benchmark programs.

Specifically, our implementation of dynamic POR run out of memory for Daisy and Rep Workers. Even though dynamic POR itself avoids many redundant thread choices, usage of our hybrid analysis can still improve precision and also the running time — data for the benchmarks Elevator and TSP highlight this case. We discuss reasons for the observed behavior of dynamic POR in Sect. 6.

The cost of the static phase of the hybrid analysis is negligible, as it runs for few seconds at most. This is apparent especially from the data for benchmarks Crypt and Prod-Cons, where a majority of the total running time is consumed by static analysis. The cost of the dynamic analysis phase, which is performed on-the-fly during the state space traversal, depends heavily on the number of executed actions (program statements) for which JPF queries the hybrid analysis. For every such action, the hybrid analysis must decide whether it is globally-relevant or not. Results for the benchmarks Daisy and Rep Workers in the right-most columns of Table 3 show that the cost of the dynamic analysis phase may be significant if JPF performs many queries — in general, one query for each thread choice created in the configuration "HR + all array ch". Note that for Daisy and Rep Workers, the hybrid analysis for shared array elements does not eliminate any additional thread choices when compared to the configuration "HR + fields + all array ch" that involves just the field access analysis, and therefore hybrid analysis is responsible for the increase of running time. However, despite the relatively high cost, the speedup of JPF achieved due to the elimination of many redundant thread choices makes the proposed hybrid analysis practically useful for many programs.

We also performed experiments with several benchmark programs to find whether our hybrid analysis improves the speed of error detection. For that purpose, we had to manually inject concurrency errors into some of the programs. Table 5 contains results for selected configurations. We have considered both the POR based on heap reachability and the dynamic POR, each with enabled thread choices at accesses to array elements, and then with or without the hybrid analysis.

Usage of the hybrid analysis (i) helped to reduce the number of thread choices created before reaching an error state for all the benchmarks, and (ii) also helped

Table 5. Experimental results: search for concurrency errors

Benchmark	HR + all array ch		HR + fields + hybrid		DPOR + enabled array ch		DPOR + fields + hybrid	
	choices	time	choices	time	choices	time	choices	time
Daisy	253336	143 s	173441	151 s	-	-	-	-
Elevator	31169	14 s	8494	9 s	178748	529 s	80486	165 s
Alarm Clock	428	1 s	161	4 s	179	1 s	71	4 s
Prod-Cons	12073	17 s	3030	8 s	1114	3 s	1101	6 s
Rep Workers	6708	5 s	1545	6 s	4527	6 s	1699	6 s
QSort MT	2635	2 s	1428	4 s	-	-	-	-

to improve performance by a factor greater than 2 for the benchmark Elevator (with dynamic POR) and for the benchmark Prod-Cons (just with POR based on heap reachability). When the error is detected very quickly in the baseline configurations, then the cost of the hybrid analysis is responsible for slight increase of the total running time — see, e.g., the data for Prod-Cons and the dynamic POR. Interestingly, dynamic POR is much slower than JPF with heap reachability for Elevator, and it did not find any error for Daisy and QSort MT.

Regarding the actual errors, JPF reported a race condition involving a particular array element only for the benchmarks Elevator and QSortMT. They could not be detected if threads choices were disabled at array accesses. Other benchmarks contain also race conditions that involve field accesses, and the corresponding error states are discovered by JPF sooner than the possible races at array element accesses.

6 Related Work

We discuss selected approaches to partial order reduction, which are used in software model checking, and also few static analysis-based techniques that can be used to identify shared array elements.

Dwyer et al. [3] proposed to use a heap reachability information that is computed by a static or dynamic escape analysis. If a given heap object is reachable from multiple threads, then all operations upon the object have to be marked as globally-relevant, independently of which threads may really access the object. The dynamic escape analysis is performed on-the-fly during the state space traversal, and therefore it can use knowledge of the dynamic program state to give more precise results than the static escape analysis. An important limitation of this approach is that it works at the granularity of whole objects and arrays. For example, if an array object is reachable from two threads but every element is accessed only by a single thread, then all the accesses are still imprecisely considered as globally-relevant even though they are actually thread-local. Our hybrid analysis is more precise because (i) for each thread T it computes the set of array objects accessed by T and (ii) it can distinguish individual array elements.

The dynamic POR algorithm that was proposed by Flanagan and Godefroid [4] is very precise. It explores each dynamic execution path of the given program separately, and for each path determines the set of array elements that were truly accessed by multiple threads on the path. The main advantage of dynamic POR is that it can distinguish between individual dynamic heap objects, unlike the static pointer analysis whose results we also use in our hybrid analysis. More specifically, dynamic POR can precisely identify every shared memory location, e.g. a dynamic array object with the concrete value of an element index, and creates thread choices retroactively at accesses to such locations. Every added choice corresponds to a new thread interleaving that must be explored later. A limitation of this dynamic POR algorithm performance-wise is that it performs redundant computation because (i) it has to execute each dynamic path until the end state and (ii) it has to track all accesses to object fields and array elements. A given path has to be fully analyzed even if it does not contribute any new thread choices, and this can negatively impact performance in the case of long execution paths. We believe that the redundant computation is the main reason for the surprisingly long running times of the dynamic POR that we reported in Sect. 5. The need to keep track of many accesses to fields and array elements is the main reason for high memory consumption that we observed with our implementation. Our hybrid analysis improves the performance of dynamic POR, when they are combined together, by identifying thread-local accesses to array elements that the dynamic POR does not have to track. In Sect. 5, we also reported that the combination of dynamic POR with hybrid analysis improves precision for some benchmarks. The standalone dynamic POR does not consider reachability of heap objects by individual threads, and therefore it may still create some redundant thread choices. More specifically, when processing two instructions i and j that access the same element on the same array object a, the dynamic POR does not check whether the array a was reachable by thread T_j (which executes j) at the time of the access by instruction i.

Other recent approaches to partial order reduction include, for example, the Cartesian POR [6] and the combination of dynamic POR with state matching [24], which address some limitations of the original approach to dynamic POR. Unnecessary thread choices can be eliminated from the state space also by preemption sealing [1], which allows the user to enable thread scheduler only inside specific program modules.

Many techniques that improve the error detection performance of software model checking are based on bounding the number of explored thread interleavings. See the recent experimental study by Thomson et al. [20] for a comprehensive overview. Techniques from this group are orthogonal to our proposed approach, because they limit the search to a particular region of the state space, while preserving all thread choices.

Another group of related techniques includes static and dynamic analyses that can determine whether a given heap object (field) is stationary according to the definition in [21]. Such objects and fields may be updated only during initialization, while they are reachable only from a single thread. Once the object becomes shared, it can be just read in the rest of the program execution. The analyses for detecting stationary objects [9] and fields [21] could be extended towards array elements, and then used to compute a subset of the information that is produced by our hybrid analysis. No thread choice would have to be created at accesses to a stationary array element during the state space traversal, because there cannot occur any conflicting pair of read-write accesses to such an element from different threads.

Shape analysis together with pointer analysis can be also used to identify heap objects and array elements possibly shared between multiple threads. For example, the analysis proposed by Sagiv et al. [17] determines the set of memory locations that are directly reachable from two or more pointer variables. Client analyses can derive various higher-level sharing properties from this information.

Our hybrid analysis is different especially in that it determines only whether an array element is possibly accessed by multiple threads — it does not compute the heap reachability information and does not perform any kind of shape analysis.

Marron et al. [11] proposed an analysis that determines whether elements of a given array may be aliased. In that case, threads accessing the respective different array elements would in fact access the same object. Our hybrid analysis does not compute aliasing information of such kind — rather it answers the question whether multiple threads can access the same array element (i.e., whether threads can use the same index when accessing the array), independently of possible aliasing between array elements.

7 Conclusion

Our motivation for this work was to optimize the existing popular approaches to partial order reduction in the context of programs that heavily use arrays. We proposed a hybrid static-dynamic analysis that identifies array elements that are possibly accessed by multiple threads during the program execution. Results of experiments that we performed on several benchmark programs show that combination of the hybrid analysis with POR improves performance and scalability of state space traversal. The main benefit of the hybrid analysis is that, in tools like Java Pathfinder, thread choices can be enabled at globally-relevant accesses to individual arrays elements, which is a necessary step for detecting specific race conditions and other kinds of concurrency errors, all that without a high risk of state explosion and at a reasonable cost in terms of the running time.

In the future, we plan to integrate the proposed hybrid analysis for array elements with the may-happen-before analysis [14]. Another possible line of future research work is to design some variant of the dynamic determinacy analysis [18] for multithreaded programs, and use it to improve the precision of our hybrid analyses.

Acknowledgments. This work was partially supported by the Grant Agency of the Czech Republic project 13-12121P.

References

1. Ball, T., Burckhardt, S., Coons, K.E., Musuvathi, M., Qadeer, S.: Preemption sealing for efficient concurrency testing. In: Esparza, J., Majumdar, R. (eds.) TACAS 2010. LNCS, vol. 6015, pp. 420–434. Springer, Heidelberg (2010)
2. Concurrency Tool Comparison repository. https://facwiki.cs.byu.edu/vv-lab/index.php/Concurrency_Tool_Comparison
3. Dwyer, M., Hatcliff, J., Ranganath, V., Robby, : Exploiting object escape and locking information in partial-order reductions for concurrent object-oriented programs. Formal Meth. Syst. Des. **25**, 199–240 (2004)
4. Flanagan, C., Godefroid, P.: Dynamic partial-order reduction for model checking software. In: Proceedings of POPL 2005. ACM (2005)

5. Godefroid, P. (ed.): Partial-Order Methods for the Verification of Concurrent Systems. LNCS, vol. 1032. Springer, Heidelberg (1996)
6. Gueta, G., Flanagan, C., Yahav, E., Sagiv, M.: Cartesian partial-order reduction. In: Bošnački, D., Edelkamp, S. (eds.) SPIN 2007. LNCS, vol. 4595, pp. 95–112. Springer, Heidelberg (2007)
7. The Java Grande Forum Benchmark Suite. https://www2.epcc.ed.ac.uk/computing/research_activities/java_grande/index_1.html
8. Java Pathfinder: a system for verification of Java programs. http://babelfish.arc.nasa.gov/trac/jpf/
9. Li, D., Srisa-an, W., Dwyer, M.B.: SOS: saving time in dynamic race detection with stationary analysis. In: Proceedings of OOPSLA 2011. ACM (2011)
10. Manson, J., Pugh, W., Adve, S.V.: The Java memory model. In: Proceedings of POPL 2005. ACM (2005)
11. Marron, M., Mendez-Lojo, M., Hermenegildo, M., Stefanovic, D., Kapur, D.: Sharing analysis of arrays, collections, and recursive structures. In: Proceedings of PASTE 2008. ACM (2008)
12. Noonan, E., Mercer, E., Rungta, N.: Vector-clock based partial order reduction for JPF. ACM SIGSOFT Softw. Eng. Notes **39**(1), 1–5 (2014)
13. pjbench: Parallel Java Benchmarks. https://bitbucket.org/pag-lab/pjbench
14. Parizek, P., Jancik, P.: Approximating happens-before order: interplay between static analysis and state space traversal. In: Proceedings of SPIN 2014. ACM (2014)
15. Parizek, P., Lhotak, O.: Identifying future field accesses in exhaustive state space traversal. In: Proceedings of ASE 2011. IEEE CS (2011)
16. Parizek, P., Lhotak, O.: Model checking of concurrent programs with static analysis of field accesses. Sci. Comput. Program. **98**, 735–763 (2015)
17. Sagiv, M., Reps, T., Wilhelm, R.: Parametric shape analysis via 3-valued logic. ACM Trans. Program. Lang. Syst. **24**(3), 217–298 (2002)
18. Schaefer, M., Sridharan, M., Dolby, J., Tip, F.: Dynamic determinacy analysis. In: Proceedings of PLDI 2013. ACM (2013)
19. Sewell, P., Sarkar, S., Owens, S., Nardelli, F.Z., Myreen, M.: x86-TSO: a rigorous and usable programmer's model for x86 multiprocessors. Comm. ACM **53**(7), 89–97 (2010)
20. Thomson, P., Donaldson, A., Betts, A.: Concurrency testing using schedule bounding: an empirical study. In: Proceedings of PPoPP 2014. ACM (2014)
21. Unkel, C., Lam, M.S.: Automatic inference of stationary fields: a generalization of Java's final fields. In: Proceedings of POPL 2008. ACM (2008)
22. Visser, W., Havelund, K., Brat, G., Park, S., Lerda, F.: Model checking programs. Autom. Softw. Eng. **10**(2), 203–232 (2003)
23. Wala, T.J.: Watson Libraries for Analysis. http://wala.sourceforge.net/
24. Yang, Y., Chen, X., Gopalakrishnan, G.C., Kirby, R.M.: Efficient stateful dynamic partial order reduction. In: Havelund, K., Majumdar, R. (eds.) SPIN 2008. LNCS, vol. 5156, pp. 288–305. Springer, Heidelberg (2008)

Cloud-Based Verification of Concurrent Software

Gerard J. Holzmann[✉]

NASA Jet Propulsion Laboratory,
California Institute of Technology, Pasadena, CA, USA
gh@jpl.nasa.gov

Abstract. Logic model checkers are unparalleled in their ability to reveal subtle bugs in multi-threaded software systems. The underlying verification procedure is based on a systematic search of potentially faulty system behaviors, which can be computationally expensive for larger problem sizes. In this paper we consider if it is possible to significantly reduce the runtime requirements of a verification with cloud computing techniques. We explore the use of large numbers of CPU-cores, that each perform small, fast, independent, and randomly different searches to achieve the same problem coverage as a much slower stand-alone run on a single CPU. We present empirical results to demonstrate what is achievable.

Keywords: Software verification · Logic model checking · Software testing · Concurrency · Multi-threaded code · Cloud computing · Swarm verification · Massive parallelism

1 Introduction

Although the amount of memory that is available on standard desktop computers continues to increase, clockspeeds have stalled at their current levels for well over a decade. With access to ever larger amounts of RAM memory, logic model checkers could in principle search ever larger problem sizes, but the time required to perform those searches can become substantial. Time, not memory, has become the main bottleneck in formal verification.

As one simple example, consider the CPU-time requirements for the verification of a large problem on a system with 128 GB of main memory. Even if the model checker runs at a fast rate of about 10^5 newly discovered states per second, we can explore only about 9.10^9 states in a 24-hour period.

Using the bitstate storage method [1,6,8], we can record up to 10^{12} unique hash signatures of states in 128 GB, cf. Appendix A. This means that a verification run could take over three months before it fills RAM.

At this point, the search may still be incomplete. Assume it has reached a coverage of $C\%$ of the full search space. There are two things we may want to do:

G.J. Holzmann—This research was carried out at the Jet Propulsion Laboratory, California Institute of Technology, under a contract with the National Aeronautics and Space Administration.

B. Jobstmann and K.R.M. Leino (Eds.): VMCAI 2016, LNCS 9583, pp. 311–327, 2016.
DOI: 10.1007/978-3-662-49122-5_15

increase the coverage until it reaches 100 %, or obtain the same level of coverage faster by performing the search differently, using more machines. We show that both objectives can be realized with the help of a cloud-compute infrastructure and hash-randomization techniques.

To see how this could work, first note that when, in our example, we reduce the size of the hash-arena from 128 GB to 128 MB, we can store 10^3 times fewer states, and as a result the search would also complete up to 10^3 times faster. While it is attractive to see the maximal runtime shrink, we do not like the simultaneous reduction in coverage. But we can fix that.

If we repeat the faster run with a randomly different, statistically independent, hash-function, the new run will take roughly the same amount of time as before, but visit a partly *different* set of states. The two runs together will have greater coverage then either one separately, but they take the same amount of time and since they are independent they can be performed in parallel.

As first noted in [6], we can continue to increase the cumulative coverage of the verification, until it reaches 100 %, by performing more and more independent runs, each time using a different, randomly selected hash-function.

Since each faster run, using 128 MB instead of 128 GB, explores 10^3 fewer states, we may expect that we would need to perform well over 10^3 independent fast runs to make up for the loss of coverage, because inevitably there will be overlap between the state spaces that are explored in the separate runs. The question is how many more parallel runs would we need to bridge the gap. We study that question in this paper.

Earlier work, e.g., [4,9], considered the use of only small numbers of CPUs in multi-core systems or local networks. Here we focus on the potential increase in capability that can result when we make use the massive parallelism that is available today in commercial cloud compute networks.

2   Methodology

We make use of the bitstate storage method [1,6,8] to perform multiple independent partial searches in large state spaces. The method we describe here depends on a capability to generate randomly different hash polynomials to perform the individual searches. The Spin model checker [16], Version 6.4, was extended with an algorithm for generating such polynomials. The algorithm uses an unsigned 32-bit number as a seed for a scan for a usable hash polynomial that completes in a fraction of a second. The use of a 32-bit seed trivially sets an upper-limit to the number of distinct hash polynomials that could be generated to 2^{32}. Not every seed number leads to a usable polynomial in the first round of the scan though, so the true limit is lower.

Figure 1 shows the results of a test of the number of tries that the hash-polynomial generation algorithm makes, starting with random 32-bit numbers. In this tests, the number of tries was between zero and 200, with an average of about 30 tries. This means that an upper limit for the total number of distinct hash polynomials that the algorithm that we use could generate is in the order of 10^8.

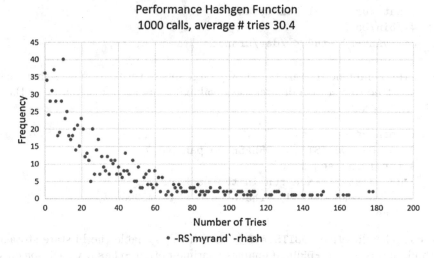

Fig. 1. The number of tries that the hash polynomial generator makes, starting from a randomly chosen unsigned 32-bit number. The average over 1,000 calls was 30.4 tries.

We can increase the diversity of parallel runs further by varying additional search parameters. We can do so, for instance, by randomly changing also the number of hash-polynomials that are used to compute the hash-signature of each state, changing the maximum search depth, changing the search order (considering processes and transitions from left to right in the transition table, right to left, or in random order), and the search discipline itself (e.g., depth-first, breadth-first, or a context-switching bounded search [10]). Randomization and diversification can thus be used to create very large numbers of independent verification engines.

In the measurements we report on in this paper we restrict to just a few of these possible search options. To perform the tests, we used the following runtime flags and parameters that the current version of Spin (Version 6.4.4) provides.

-RSN to seed the random number generator to N
-rhash to randomly generate a bitstate hash polynomial
-wN to set the size of the hash-arena to 2^N bits
-kN to set the number of bits set per state to N
-mN to set the maximum search depth to N

To seed the random number generator we avoid using timestamps or the standard **rand** command from Unix and Linux-based systems. The Unix **rand** command uses a time-based algorithm, which means that it can return the same value if called too quickly in succession. We can avoid this by defining the following command, as a more reliable source for random numbers on Linux and Linux-like systems:

```
$ cat /usr/local/bin/myrand
#!/bin/bash
od -vAn -N4 -tu4 < /dev/urandom | sed 's; *;;'
```

We use this command to start potentially large sets of verification runs that each are guaranteed to receive a different seed value, for instance in a Bourne or Bash shell-script as follows:

```
$ spin -a spec.pml
$ cc -O2 -DBITSTATE -DRHASH -o pan pan.c
$ for i in 'seq 1000'
  do  # start each run in the background
   ./pan -RS'myrand' -rhash -w20 -k1 -m20000 &
  done
```

The compiler directive -DBITSTATE is used here to enable the bitstate storage method, and directive -DRHASH enables runtime option -rhash, which not only triggers the generation of a random hash polynomial but also randomizes the transition selection order to be used as well as the process scheduling orders, to achieve greater diversity.

The argument -w20 sets the hash-arena size to 2^{20} bits (128 Kbytes) for a very fast model checking run. Argument -k1 sets the number of bits set per state to one, and -m20000 sets the maximum search depth to 20,000. The numeric argument to each of these last three arguments can, of course, readily be randomized as well.

3   Measurements

We explore two types of applications of the cloud-based verification approach we discussed above. First we consider the typical case where the purpose of a model checking run is to demonstrate the *presence* of subtle defects in a multi-threaded software application that may be missed in standard testing. A cloud-based verification method could provide an added capability that is both faster and more thorough. Separately, we also consider the potential use of this technique for formally proving the *absence* of defects.

3.1   Defect Discovery

The initial motivation for this study was the verification of the source code for a double-sided queue algorithm using compare-and-swap instructions, referred to as the DCAS algorithm. The implementation described in [2] has a subtle bug, which was discovered when a formal proof of correctness was attempted with the PVS theorem prover [3]. The discovery of the bug took several months of work with the theorem prover.

We are interested here in finding out if the same bug can be discovered faster with a cloud-based verification approach.

We discussed the verification of the DCAS algorithm earlier in [11]. We used Modex [14] to extract a Spin model from the C code, while adding two test drivers, also in C, that would normally be part of a standard test suite. In [11] our objective was to show that we can extract formal models from unmodified C code, while adding only the test code that a tester would normally already provide. The model checking runs can then be automated to significantly increase the accuracy of the tests that are performed.

The verification described in [11] immediately discovered an assertion violation, with just two threads of execution in the DCAS model: a reader and a writer. This was unexpected because the only defect in the algorithm known at that point required at least three threads of execution to complete. Unfortunately, the test drivers we used were faulty, and the assertion violation that was found originated in the test itself, not in the code being tested. A corrected version of the test drivers is given in [12].

With the corrected version of the test drivers, the model checker needs just three seconds of CPU-time to formally prove that with two threads of execution the DCAS algorithm is correct and cannot violate the assertion.

Increasing the number of threads from two to three increases the complexity of verification sufficiently that an exhaustive proof becomes intractable. We aborted a bitstate verification attempt after 138 h of CPU-time, having explored over 10^{11} states, without locating the bug. The question is if a cloud-based swarm of small and randomly different verification tasks can still succeed in locating the bug, and do so quickly and reliably.

As noted, by setting the size of the hash-arena we can control how long the verification tasks can maximally take. Figure 2 illustrates this effect, for the DCAS verification. To check if a fast cloud verification run can identify the flaw in the algorithm we set the size of the bit-state hash-arena to just 128 KB, using runtime parameter -w20. We performed a verification with a swarm of 1,000 small independent verification tasks, differing only in the selection of the hash-function each used. The script below describes the verification steps.

Compared to the earlier examples, we added the compiler directive -DPUTPID to add the process number of each thread of execution to the name of any counter-example traces that are found, to prevent the parallel runs from overwriting each other's output. We also added the directive -DSAFETY, since we're only interested in assertion violations for this example. Note that the verifier is linked to the C source code of the implementation.

```
$ spin -a dcas.pml
$ cc -O2 -DBITSTATE -DSAFETY \
          -DRHASH -DPUTPID -o pan pan.c dcas.c
$ for i in 'seq 1000'
do    ./pan -w20 -RS'myrand' -rhash -k1 &
done
```

Each of the verification runs uses a hash-arena of just 128 KB of memory, and sets one single bit per state visited. Because of the very small hash-arena used,

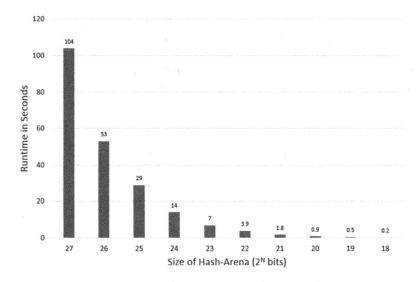

Fig. 2. Correlation between the size of the hash-arena and runtime. A choice of N=20 corresponds to a hash-arena size of 2^{20} bits or 128 KB.

each run completes in a fraction of a second, which means that if all runs are performed in parallel the entire task also completes that quickly.

In this test, two of the 1,000 runs successfully located the assertion violation in the code and generated counter-example traces (Table 1), in a fraction of a second.

If we increase the size of the hash-arena, more runs will be able to locate a counter-example, but the runs will also take longer to complete. If, on the other hand, we decrease the size of the hash-arena, a smaller fraction of the runs can be expected to successfully identify the bug in the algorithm. We can counter that effect by increasing the size of the swarm. To illustrate this, we performed sequential runs of the verifier at a range of different settings of the hash-arena size, stopping each batch as soon as the first counter-example was found (with that hash-arena size), see Fig. 3.

As expected, the number of runs to be performed increases as the size of the hash-arena shrinks. Clearly there is a minimum size of a swarm of parallel tasks before the swarm as a whole can be successful in locating defects. Trivially, if each task has a probability p of locating a defect, we would need to run at least $1/p$ parallel tasks to be successful.

Figure 3 shows the randomness in this process. In these tests it took closer to 5000 runs at a hash-arena size of -w20 to uncover the first counter-example, where in our earlier test fewer than 1,000 runs sufficed. Similarly, for a hash-arena size of -w22 or 512 KB, this test reported a first counter-example after just three attempts, where based on context perhaps a run of 300 would statistically have been more likely. Note that all runs with a hash-arena size smaller than -w26 (16 MB) completed in under a minute of runtime and runs below -w20 in

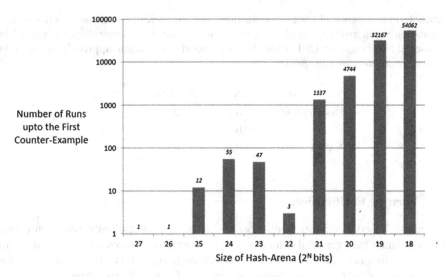

Fig. 3. Correlation between the size of the hash-arena and the number of random runs needed to find a first counter-example. From 16 MB ($2^2 7$ bits) to 32 KB ($2^1 8$ bits).

under a second (cf. Fig. 2). In both cases this is considerably faster than the weeks or months that would be needed for a traditional exhaustive verification attempt.

Other Tests. We performed two other tests of this technique on similarly large models that defy exhaustive verification by traditional means, summarized in Table 1.

The first of these is the Fleet model, which is a pure Promela model of a distributed system architecture designed by Ivan Sutherland [17]. A cloud-based verification attempt using just 100 small parallel bitstate runs, similar to the runs used for the DCAS model, locates multiple variants of the bug (also an assertion violation), again in a fraction of a second. In this case, setting the hash-arena as low as -w13, storing just 2^{13} bits (or 1 Kbyte of memory), sufficed to locate the bug.

In another test we applied the cloud-based verification method to test the C implementation of POSIX routines implementing a non-volatile flash file system (NVFS) designed for use in a spacecraft, cf. [13]. The models were extracted from the C code in this case with the Modex model extractor, [7,11,14]. The resulting models are well beyond the reach of traditional verification techniques. In bug-finding mode we ran 500 parallel tasks with a hash-arena sized to store 2^{17} bits (16 Kbytes) of memory, which sufficed to locate six counter-examples of the correctness properties in under one second of runtime.

Table 1. Performance of Cloud verification runs. In each of the cases considered, the verification tasks are too complex for traditional exhaustive verification to succeed in a reasonable amount of CPU-time, but the cloud verification approach succeeds in locating counter-examples quickly.

Model	Nr. Cores	Run-Time	Defects found
DCAS	1000	0.2s	2
Fleet	100	0.1s	1
NVFS	500	0.5s	6

3.2   Formal Verification

The cloud-based verification approach can be a powerful alternative for bug hunting, since this generally does not require exhaustive coverage of a problem domain. This does not necessarily mean though that it is also be suitable for full formal verification. One important reason for this is that there is no easy way to determine what the cumulative coverage is that is realized by a swarm of small fast verification tasks. On statistical grounds we know that larger swarms provide better coverage than smaller ones, and that swarms using larger hash-arenas similarly provide better coverage than those using smaller hash-arenas.

Measuring the cumulative coverage can be done by instrumenting the code, capturing every state visited by every task, and then post-processing that information to compute the total number of unique states that was explored by all tasks together (i.e., after eliminating the overlap). If we know how many reachable system states there are, we can then compute the cumulative coverage accurately.

If we do not know the total, we can in deduce an approximate coverage by performing two or more swarm runs sequentially, with different hash-arena sizes for each swarm run. Figure 4 illustrates the effect on the number of unique states that is visited when we perform this experiment for a range of different hash-arena sizes.

Note that once 100 % coverage is realized, the number of unique states visited can no longer increase when we increase the size of the hash-arena: the growth ratio will be one. When we are far from complete coverage, on the other hand, the number of unique states visited will double with each doubling of the size of the hash-arena: the growth ratio is now two. If we are somewhere in between these two points, the growth ratio will be somewhere between one and two. The growth ratio measured can thus give us an indication of the problem coverage realized, though not a precise one.

Adding the instrumentation and the processing of the counts will of course lead to the loss of a portion of the speed advantage of a swarm verification search.

For the following tests we performed we chose test examples for which we could measure the cumulative state space size independently with standard verification techniques, so that we could calculate the cumulative coverage of a cloud-based verification run accurately.

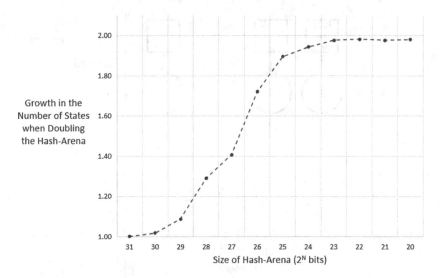

Fig. 4. Growth in the number of unique states visited per run, when the hash-arena size is doubled, for a range of hash-arena sizes. Model from Example 1 in Sect. 3.2, also used in Fig. 6, [5].

We use two medium-sized examples with known state space sizes. The first is an algorithm for concurrent garbage collection [5], with a total of about 192 Million reachable system states. The second is a Spin model of an operating system for small spacecraft [15], with about 22 Million reachable system states.

We setup a test environment for the measurements on a machine with 64 cores and 128 GB of shared memory. We run a single *collector* process on this machine that creates a traditional hash-table, large enough to store all reachable states. The *collector* process creates an array of n buffers (channels) in shared memory, as many as fit, to receive 64-bit state hash signatures from n different *generator* processes that run in parallel.

To test the coverage that is realized by a swarm of N small verification tasks, where generally N is much larger than n, we split up all tasks in n batches of N/n tasks each. The tasks in each batch execute sequentially, and are instrumented to connect to a specific channel to the collector when they start up, to transmit the hash signatures for the states that each of those tasks explore. The *collector* reads the hash signatures from the channels, and adds them to its own state hash-table, while omitting duplicates. At the end of the experiment, the collector can give us a count of the number of unique states that were reported by all tasks cumulatively, so that we can compute the coverage of all N *generator* processes combined. The test setup is illustrated in Fig. 5.

Since each task in the swarm is configured to use a randomly generated hash-polynomial, we have to make sure that the hash signatures that are sent to the *collector* process are computed with a single additional polynomial that is fixed for all verification tasks. To make the measurement possible, the *generator* processes

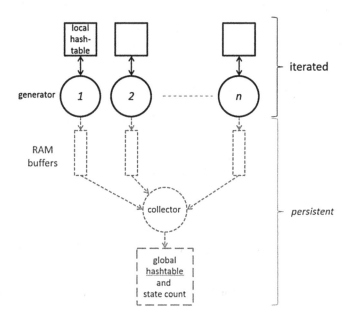

Fig. 5. Test setup for measuring cumulative coverage of cloud-verification

therefore must compute an additional fixed hash-signatures for each state, which slows them down compared to an actual cloud-based verification run.

Example 1. The Spin model we used for this first example was adapted from a formal PVS specification written by Klaus Havelund [5]. As was the case with the DCAS algorithm we discussed earlier, the PVS proof of this concurrent garbage collection algorithm took months of dedicated human time to complete.

In this first example, the search space that must be explored for an exhaustive verification attempt is very deep. A depth-first search attempt, for instance, quickly reaches a depth of 50 Million steps. This feature makes the application of a cloud verification especially interesting, because it may limit the accuracy of each small verification task.

To get an accurate measurement of the full state space size for this model we performed an exhaustive verification with Spin. With compression enabled, the verification requires about 23.2 GByte of memory, and reaches about 192 Million states in 17 min of CPU-time. Note that a cloud based approach is not needed for this model, but we chose it to study the relative performance of this approach.

We tested the coverage for hash-arena sizes that range from a low value of 1 MByte per task (using runtime parameter -w23), or about four orders of magnitude smaller than the 23.2 GByte that is needed for a single exhaustive verification, to 256 MB (-w31), or about two orders of magnitude below the size needed for exhaustive verification. We measured the cumulative coverage for swarms of verification tasks ranging from one single task to 1,048,576 small parallel tasks. Figure 6 summarizes the results.

At the lower end of the scale, a run with parameter -w23 completes in about 20 s of CPU-time, or about 50 times faster than the exhaustive run. A run with parameter -w25 takes four times as long: about 80 s, about 12 times faster than exhaustive.

As expected, the further we shrink the size of the hash-arena, the more cores are needed to make up for the loss of coverage. The increase is exponential. A first set of say 1,000 cores provides most of the problem coverage. Increasing coverage closer and closer to 100 % becomes increasingly expensive for shrinking hash-arena sizes (which is needed to produce faster verification results). For -w28, Table 2 shows how quickly the number of cores needed to reach specific levels of coverage increases.

Table 2. Number of cores needed to reach specific levels of coverage for the verification of the concurrent garbage collection algorithm, using a hash-arena of 32 MB (-w28), which is 0.1 % of the size needed for a single exhaustive verification run.

Nr Cores	Coverage
1	69.7 %
3	90 %
8	99 %
32	99.9 %
64	99.99 %
256	99.999 %
512	99.9999 %
2048	100 %

We can speed up the verification eightfold by shrinking the hash-arena further to -w25, but we will then need 2,048 cores to reach 90 % coverage. To increase coverage to 98.7 % requires 65,536 cores. Substantially more cores would be needed to reach 100 % coverage for this very small hash-arena, but it should still be feasible.

Because all verification tasks are independent, they can be run either in parallel or sequentially, on any available machine. If we have access to a large cloud network, it is advantageous to execute all tasks in parallel for the fastest possible result. If, however, we only have access to a single machine with limited memory that is not large enough to support a single full exhaustive verification run. We can improve the problem coverage by performing a large number of randomized bitstate runs sequentially, although the speed advantage would be lost in that case.

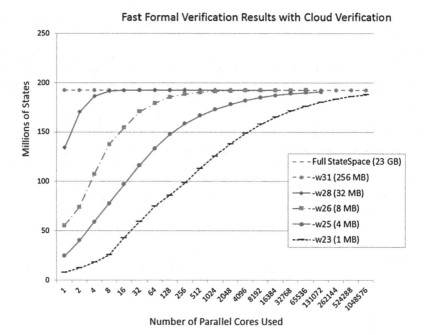

Fig. 6. Number of unique states reached, out of 192 Million known reachable states, for varying hash-arena sizes and varying numbers of cores, for a spin verification model of a concurrent garbage collection algorithm [5]. Storing a compressed version of the full statespace takes 17 min and 23 GB. The same coverage can be realized using a Cloud network in 20 s using four orders of magnitude less storage (1 MB).

Example 2. As a second example we look at a Spin model of the DEOS operating system kernel developed at Honeywell Laboratories, discussed in [15]. The results of a series of experiments are shown in Fig. 7.

Reading the chart in Fig. 7 vertically: when given the same amount of *memory*, the cumulative coverage reached by 100 randomized parallel runs is clearly superior to that of a single run.

Reading the chart horizontally, we can see that the same *coverage* can be realized by a parallel swarm using up to 16 times less memory per task (2^4), and thus also 16 times faster.

4   Comparisons

To understand better what the relative performance of a cloud-based verification approach is relative to standard software testing, we measured the number of unique system states that is reached in a rigorous software test of one module of the flight code for a recent space mission: the NVFS file system code that we saw earlier in Table 1.

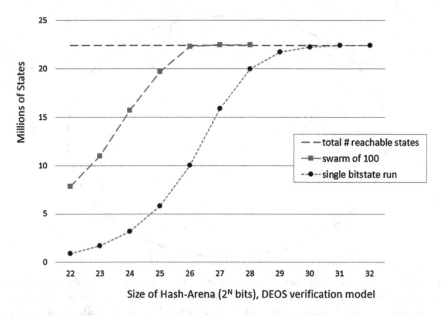

Fig. 7. State coverage of a swarm search for the DEOS verification model. In this experiment we used 100 randomized parallel bitstate runs, and compared the coverage realized with that of a single bitstate run, as a function of the amount of memory used. When sufficient memory is available (right-side of the chart) both methods perform similarly. When less memory is available, though, the swarm approach achieves greater coverage. Every increment (horizontal axis) indicates a doubling of the hash-arena size.

The standard test that was used for this application was designed to realize 98 % MC/DC coverage, which is in line with the prevailing guidance documents DO-178B and DO-178C from the RTCA (Radio Technical Commission for Aeronautics) for safety and mission critical software systems. We independently measured that a total of 35,796 distinct system states were reached in these tests, exploring approximately 100 unique execution paths. These tests and the corresponding execution paths were of course not randomly chosen, but designed to test nominal and moderately off-nominal executions of the code, to make sure they comply with all requirements, cf. Fig. 8.

For comparison, we also performed a full model checking run of the same code, and measured that it reached a total of 745 Million unique system states, while exploring about 50 Million unique execution paths. This means that the standard test provided a coverage four orders of magnitude smaller than the model checking run, or just 0.01 %. In this context it is not surprising that the model checking run was able to uncover a subtle flaw in the code that was missed in the standard software test suite.

This example illustrates what the added value can be in a cloud-based verification approach, even when it falls short of realizing 100 % problem coverage. Consider, for instance, the case where a cloud-based verification achieves only

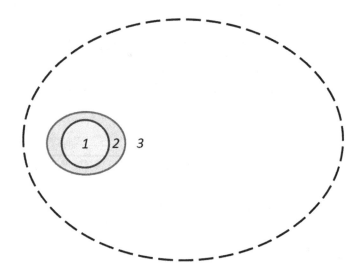

Fig. 8. Set 1 illustrates the set of nominal executions that is normally tested most thoroughly. Set 2 is a small subset of off-nominal executions that are often included in a system test. Set 3 contains all other executions, which is generally dominated by the off-nominal behaviors. In the example of the NVFS file system tests, sets 1 and 2 combined were shown to cover just 0.01 % of all possible behaviors. A randomly chosen execution is most likely to fall in set 3, and is therefore likely to reveal untested erroneous behaviors.

a low level of coverage of just 10 %. Even this low coverage level is still three orders of magnitude better than a typical software test suite.

The two tests are not immediately comparable by their relative levels of problem coverage though. The difference is that the 0.01 % executions form the standard test are carefully chosen to include most nominal and moderately off-nominal executions, while the cloud-based verification samples 10 % of the execution space randomly, independent of how nominal or off-nominal the selected executions are.

The two sets, therefore, do not necessarily overlap, so it would not be valid to say that a cloud-based approach could replace standard software testing.

It is equally invalid, though, to say that unless we can reach exhaustive problem coverage no intermediate step is of value. It should be clear that even the coverage delivered by a cloud-based verification approach near the left-hand side of Fig. 6, with limited problem coverage, can *significantly* increase the chances of finding subtle software bugs that would otherwise escape detection, or failing to do so increase our confidence that such bugs do not exist.

5   Conclusions

We have explored the characteristics of a new method for overcoming the computational complexity of software verification problems, by using *massive parallelism.* This approach is motivated by the expectation that access to large cloud compute networks is quickly becoming routine. Our measurements show that this approach can increase the rigor of software testing in a meaningful way.

Several heuristic strategies are possible to increase the chances of finding software defects in the shortest possible amount of time, given the availability of a fixed maximum number of CPU cores. The simplest strategy would be to pick the desired maximum runtime, and size the hash-array for each verification task the same, so that all complete in roughly the same amount of time. We can, however, also decide to do this only with half of all available CPU cores. On half of the remaining cores we can then give each task only half the size of the hash-array compared to the first set, which makes them complete twice as fast, while providing half the (randomly selected) coverage. We continue that process, each time taking half the number of remaining available cores, and halving the hash-array size. This method trades some coverage for an increased chance to find defects in the shortest amount of time. It is similar to the iterative search refinement strategy that was first described in [7], but with all phases of the search running in parallel, rather than one by one.

With a response time of minutes or less, there is little impediment to perform series of experiments on a cloud network that will either result in defect discovery, or the best available confidence for the absence of defects. In the cases considered here, an investment in this type of cloud-based verification compares favorably with all currently existing alternative techniques, both those that are more rigorous and those that are less so.

A   Appendix: Bitstate Hash Storage

The bitstate hash storage method [6] can most easily be understood as an application of the theory of Bloom filters [1]. The storage method is used in explicit state on-the-fly model checkers, such as Spin [8], for fast approximate searches in statespaces that are too large to be explored exhaustively. The method uses one or more hash functions with uniform random distribution to compute 64-bit signatures of each newly generated reachable state.

A hash-arena of, say, 32 GB (2^{35} bytes) contains 2^{38} addressable bits. If using a single hash-function, we can use the 64 available bits from the hash signature to produce a 35-bit address into the hash-arena. If the bit at this address is at its initial value of *zero*, then we know that the newly generated state was not visited before in the search. We now record the fact that the state has been explored by setting that bit position to a *one*, so that the next time this state shows up in the search we know that we do not have to explore it again.

If the size of a single state descriptor for this example is 2^{10} bytes, we would not be able to store more than $2^{35}/2^{10} = 2^{25}$ unique states in 32 GB (about 33.5 million). The bitstate storage method on the other hand, can in principle store up to 2^{38} or 275 billion unique states, for an increase of almost four orders of magnitude.

In sufficiently many bits are used to index the hash-arena, the probability of hash collisions can be very small. A hash collision would happen if two states that are not equal produce the same 35-bit hash signature. The search truncates in this case, which means that it is no longer guaranteed to be exhaustive. We can reduce the probability of hash collisions effectively by using multiple hash-functions for each state, which then corresponds to checking and setting multiple bit-positions. If h hash-functions are used, for instance, a hash-collision must now occur on all h bit-positions for the state to be affected. The Spin model checker uses three hash-functions per state by default, but the number is user-selectable.

For large state spaces, or large state descriptors, where exhaustive storage of a complete statespace with a traditional method is infeasible, the bitstate storage method is an attractive alternative to increase problem coverage, by a significant margin. Another advantage of the use of a bistate storage method for large problem sizes is that for a given size of the hash-arena, the maximal runtime of the algorithm is fixed and known, independent of the actual statespace size.

References

1. Bloom, B.H.: Space/Time trade-offs in hash coding with allowable errors. Comm. ACM **13**(7), 422–426 (1970)
2. Adsul, B., Flood, C.H., Garthwaite, A.T., Martin, P.A., Shavit, N.N., Steele, Jr., G.L.: Even better DCAS-based concurrent deques. In: Herlihy, M.P. (ed.) DISC 2000. LNCS, vol. 1914, pp. 59–73. Springer, Heidelberg (2000)
3. Doherty, S., Detlefs, D.L., Groves, L., et al.: DCAS is not a silver bullet for non-blocking algorithm design. In: Gibbons, P.B., Adler, M. (eds.) Proceedings of Sixteenth Annual ACM Symposium on Parallel Algorithms, pp. 216–224, Barcelona (2004)
4. Dwyer, M.B., Elbaum, S.G., et al.: Parallel randomized state-space search. In: Proceedings of ICSE 2007, pp. 3–12 (2007)
5. Havelund, K.: Mechanical verification of a garbage collector. In: Proceedings of International Workshop on High-Level Parallel Programming Models and Supportive Environments, pp. 1258–1283, Puerto Rico (1999)
6. Holzmann, G.J.: On limits and possibilities of automated protocol analysis. In: Proceedings of 6th International Conference on Protocol Specification, Testing and Verification INWG IFIP, pp. 339–344 (1987)
7. Holzmann, G.J., Smith, M.H.: Automating software feature verification. Bell Labs Tech. J. **5**(2), 72–87 (2000). Special Issue on Software Complexity
8. Holzmann, G.J.: The Spin Model Checker - Primer and Reference Manual. Addison-Wesley, Reading (2004)
9. Holzmann, G.J., Joshi, R., Groce, A.: Swarm verification techniques. IEEE Trans. Softw. Eng. **37**(6), 845–857 (2011)
10. Holzmann, G.J., Florian, M.: Model checking with bounded context switching. Formal Aspects Comput. **23**(3), 365–389 (2001)
11. Holzmann, G.J.: Mars code. Commun. ACM **57**(2), 64–73 (2014)
12. Erratum to [11]. http://spinroot.com/dcas/
13. Joshi, R., Holzmann, G.J.: A mini challenge: build a verifiable filesystem. In: Proceedings of Verified Software: Theories, Tools, Experiments, Formal Aspects of Computing, vol. 19(2), pp. 269–272 (2007)
14. Modex, a model extractor for C code. http://spinroot.com/modex/

15. Penix, J., Visser, W., Pasareanu, C., et al.: Verifying time partitioning in the DEOS scheduling kernel. Formal Meth. Syst. Des. J. **26**(2), 103–135 (2005)
16. The logic model checker Spin. http://spinroot.com/
17. The Fleet distributed system. https://github.com/coreos/fleet/

Abstraction-driven Concolic Testing

Przemysław Daca[1]([✉]), Ashutosh Gupta[2], and Thomas A. Henzinger[1]

[1] IST Austria, Klosterneuburg, Austria
przemek@ist.ac.at
[2] Tata Institute for Fundamental Research, Mumbai, India

Abstract. Concolic testing is a promising method for generating test suites for large programs. However, it suffers from the path-explosion problem and often fails to find tests that cover difficult-to-reach parts of programs. In contrast, model checkers based on counterexample-guided abstraction refinement explore programs exhaustively, while failing to scale on large programs with precision. In this paper, we present a novel method that iteratively combines concolic testing and model checking to find a test suite for a given coverage criterion. If concolic testing fails to cover some test goals, then the model checker refines its program abstraction to prove more paths infeasible, which reduces the search space for concolic testing. We have implemented our method on top of the concolic-testing tool CREST and the model checker CPACHECKER. We evaluated our tool on a collection of programs and a category of SVCOMP benchmarks. In our experiments, we observed an improvement in branch coverage compared to CREST from 48 % to 63 % in the best case, and from 66 % to 71 % on average.

1 Introduction

Testing has been a corner stone of ensuring software reliability in the industry, and despite the increasing scalability of software verification tools, it still remains the preferred method for debugging large software. A test suite that achieves high code coverage is often required for certification of safety-critical systems, for instance by the DO-178C standard in avionics [2].

Many methods for automated test generation have been proposed [9,10,13, 18,28,32,36,37]. In the recent years, concolic testing has gained popularity as an easy-to-apply method that scales to large programs. Concolic testing [33,35] explores program paths by a combination of concrete and symbolic execution. This method, however, suffers from the path-explosion problem and fails to produce test cases that cover parts of programs that are difficult to reach.

Concolic testing explores program paths using heuristic methods that select the next path depending on the paths explored so far. Several heuristics for path

This research was supported in part by the European Research Council (ERC) under grant 267989 (QUAREM) and by the Austrian Science Fund (FWF) under grants S11402-N23 (RiSE) and Z211-N23 (Wittgenstein Award).

B. Jobstmann and K.R.M. Leino (Eds.): VMCAI 2016, LNCS 9583, pp. 328–347, 2016.
DOI: 10.1007/978-3-662-49122-5_16

exploration have been proposed that try to maximize coverage of concolic testing [11,19,20], e.g., randomly picking program branches to explore, driving exploration toward uncovered branches that are closest to the last explored branch, etc. These heuristics, however, are limited by their "local view" of the program semantics, i.e., they are only aware of the (in)feasibility of the paths seen so far. In contrast to testing, abstraction-based model checkers compute abstract reachability graph of a program [3,26]. The abstract reachability graph represents a "global view" of the program, i.e., the graph contains all feasible paths. Due to abstraction, not all paths contained in the abstract reachability graph are guaranteed to be feasible, therefore abstract model checking is not directly useful for generating test suites.

In this paper, we present a novel method to guide concolic testing by an abstract reachability graph generated by a model checker. The inputs to our method are a program and set of test goals, e.g. program branches or locations to be covered by testing. Our method iteratively runs concolic testing and a counterexample-guided abstraction refinement (CEGAR) based model checker [14]. The concolic tester aims to produce test cases covering as many goals as possible within the given time budget. In case the tester has not covered all the goals, the model checker is called with the original program and the remaining uncovered goals marked as error locations. When the model checker reaches a goal, it either finds a test that covers the goal or it refines the abstraction. We have modified the CEGAR loop in the model checker such that it does not terminate as soon as it finds a test, but instead it removes the goal from the set of error locations and continues building the abstraction. As a consequence, the model checker refines the abstraction with respect to the remaining goals. After the model checker has exhausted its time budget, it returns tests that cover some of the goals, and an abstraction. The abstraction may prove that some of the remaining goals are unreachable, thus they can be omitted by the testing process.

We further use the abstraction computed by the model checker to construct a *monitor*, which encodes the proofs of infeasibility of some paths in the control-flow graph. To this end, we construct a program that is an intersection of the monitor and the program. In the following iterations we run concolic testing on the intersected program. The monitor drives concolic testing away from the infeasible paths and towards paths that still may reach the remaining goals. Due to this new "global-view" information concolic testing has fewer paths to explore and is more likely to find test cases for the remaining uncovered goals. If we are still left with uncovered goals, the model checker is called again to refine the abstraction, which further reduces the search space for concolic testing. Our method iterates until the user-defined time limit is reached.

The proposed method is configured by the ratio of time spent on model checking to the time spent on testing. As we demonstrate in Sect. 2, this ratio has a strong impact on the test coverage achieved by our method.

We implemented our method in a tool called CRABS, which is built on top of a concolic-testing tool CREST [11] and a CEGAR-based model checker CPACHECKER [8]. We applied our tool on three hand-crafted examples, three selected published examples, and on 13 examples from an SVCOMP category.

We compared our implementation with two tools: a concolic tool CREST [11], and a test-case generator FSHELL based on bounded model checking [27]. The test objective was to cover program branches, and we calculate test coverage as the ratio of branches covered by the generated test suite to the number of branches that have not been proved unreachable. For a time limit of one hour, our tool achieved coverage of 63 % compared to 48 % by other tools in the best case, and average coverage of 71 % compared to 66 % on the category examples. In absolute numbers, our experiments may not appear very exciting. However, experience suggests that in automated test generation increasing test coverage by every 1 % becomes harder. The experiments demonstrate that our method can cover branches that are difficult to reach by other tools and, unlike most testing tools, can prove that some testing goals are unreachable.

To summarize, the main contributions of the paper are:

- We present a novel configurable algorithm that iteratively combines concolic testing and model checking, such that concolic testing is guided by a program abstraction and the abstraction is refined for the remaining test goals.
- We also present a modified CEGAR procedure that refines the abstraction with respect to the uncovered goals.
- We provide an open-source tool [1] that implements the presented algorithm.
- An experimental evaluation of our algorithm and comparison with other methods.

The paper is organized as follows. In Sect. 2 we motivate our approach on examples. Section 3 presents background notation and concolic testing. In Sect. 4 we present our modified CEGAR procedure, and in Sect. 5 we describe our main algorithm. Finally, Sect. 6 describes the experimental evaluation.

2   Motivating Example

In this section, we illustrate effectiveness of our method on two examples: a hand-crafted program, and a benchmark for worst-case execution time analysis adapted from [4].

Simple Loop. In Fig. 1 we present a simple program with a single while loop. The program iterates 30 times through the while loop, and in every iteration it reads an input. The test objective is to cover all locations of the program, in particular to cover location 8, where the library function foo() is called. To cover the call site to foo() the inputs in all iterations must equal 10, so only one out of 2^{30} ways to traverse the loop covers foo(). The standard concolic testing easily covers all locations, except for foo() since it blindly explores exponentially many possible ways to traverse the loop. As a consequence, a concolic-testing tool is not able to generate a complete test suite that executes foo() within one hour.

Our algorithm uses a concolic tester and model checker based on predicate abstraction, and runs them in alternation. First, we run concolic tester on the example with a time budget of 1s. As we have observed earlier, the concolic

```
int i=0; bool b = false;

while (i<30){
    int x = input();
    if (x != 10)
        b=true;
    i++;
}

if (b == false)
    foo();
```

(a)

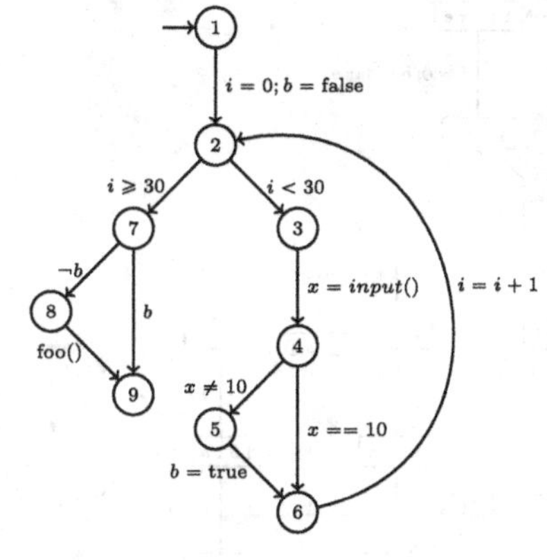

(b)

Fig. 1. (a) A simple while program. (b) The control-flow graph of the program.

tester covers all locations of the program except for foo(). Then, we declare the call site to foo() as an error location and call the model checker on the program for 5s. This time budget is sufficient for the model checker to perform only a few refinements of the abstraction, without finding a feasible path that covers foo(). In particular, it finds an abstract counterexample that goes through locations $1, 2, 3, 4, 5, 6, 2, 7, 8, 9$. This counterexample is spurious, so the refinement procedure finds the predicate "b holds." The abstraction refined with this predicate is showed in Fig. 2(a).

In the second iteration of the algorithm, we convert the refined abstraction into a monitor $\mathcal{M}$ shown in Fig. 2(b). A monitor is a control-flow graph that represents all the paths that are allowed by the abstraction. A monitor is constructed by removing subsumed states from the abstraction. We say that an abstract state s_a is *subsumed* by a state s'_a, if $s_a = s'_a$, or s'_a is more general than s_a. To this end, the monitor includes all the abstract states that are not subsumed and the edges between them. The edges to the subsumed states are redirected to the states that subsume them.

The monitor contains all the feasible paths of the program and is a refinement of the control-flow graph of the original program. Therefore, we may perform our subsequent concolic testing on the monitor interpreted as a program. In our example, the structure of the monitor in Fig. 2(b) encodes the information that foo() can be reached only if b is never set to true. The refined control flow graph makes it easy for concolic testing to cover the call to foo() — it can simply backtrack whenever the search goes to the part of the refined program where foo() is unreachable. Now, if we run CREST on the monitor $\mathcal{M}$ then it finds the test case in less than 1s.

Nsichneu. The "nsichneu" example is a benchmark for worst-case execution time analysis [24] and it simulates a Petri net. This program consists of a large

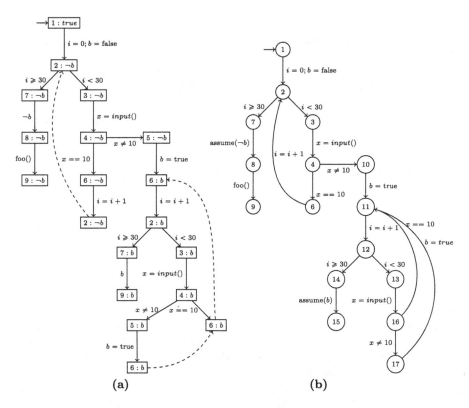

Fig. 2. (a) Abstraction refined with the predicate b. Dashed arrows show subsumption between abstract state. (b) The monitor obtained from the abstraction.

number of if-then-else statements closed in a deterministic loop. The program maintains several integer variables and fixed-sized arrays of integers. These data objects are marked as `volatile` meaning that their value can change at any time. We made their initial values the input to the program.

The structure of this benchmark makes it challenging for many testing techniques. Testing based on bounded model checking (such as FSHELL[27]) unwinds the program up to a given bound and encodes the reachability problem as a constraint-solving problem. However, this method may not find goals that are deep in the program, as the number of constraints grows quickly with the bound. Test generation based on model checking [7] also fails to deliver high coverage on this example. The model checker needs many predicates to find a feasible counterexample, and the abstraction quickly becomes expensive to maintain. In contrast, pure concolic testing quickly covers easy-to-reach parts of the program. However, later it struggles to cover goals that are reachable by fewer paths.

In our method, we run concolic testing and model checking alternatively, each time with a time budget of 100s. Every iteration of model checking gives us a more refined monitor to guide the testing process. Initially, our approach covers goals at similar rate as pure concolic testing. When the easy goals have been reached, our tool covers new goals faster than concolic testing, due to the reachability information encoded in the monitor, which allows the testing process to skip many long paths that would fail to cover new goals. After one hour, our tool covers 63 % of the test goals compared to 48 % by concolic testing.

Furthermore, our method is configurable by the ratio of time spent on model checking and concolic testing. In Fig. 3 we present the effect of changing this ratio on the example. If we run only concolic testing then we obtain only 48 % coverage. As we decrease the time spent on concolic testing, the coverage increases up to 64 % and then starts decreasing. On the other side of the spectrum, we generate tests by model checking (as in [7]) and obtain only 13.9 % coverage. This observation allows one to configure our method for most effective testing depending on the class of examples.

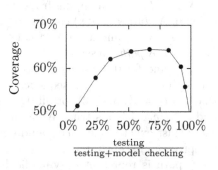

Fig. 3. Test coverage vs. ratio of testing to total time in our method.

3   Preliminaries

In this paper, we consider only sequential programs and, for ease of presentation, we consider programs without procedures. Our method, however, is easily applicable on programs with procedures and our implementation supports them.

Let V be a vector of variables names and V' be the vector of variables obtained by placing prime after each variable in V. Let $F(V)$ be the set of first-order-logic formulas that only contain free variables from V.

Definition 1 (Program). *A program P is a tuple (V, Loc, ℓ^I, E), where V is a vector of variables, Loc is a finite set of locations, $\ell^I \in Loc$ is the initial location, and $E \subseteq Loc \times F(V, V') \times Loc$ is a set of program transitions.*

A *control-flow graph* (CFG) is a graph representation of a program. We define the *product* of two programs $P_{i=1..2} = (V, Loc_i, \ell_i^I, E_i)$ as the program $P_1 \times P_2 = (V, Loc_1 \times Loc_2, (\ell_1^I, \ell_2^I), E)$, where

$$E = \{((\ell_1, \ell_2), e, (\ell_1', \ell_2')) \mid (\ell_1, e, \ell_1') \in E_1 \wedge (\ell_2, e, \ell_2') \in E_2\}.$$

A *guarded command* is a pair of a formula in $F(V)$ and a list of updates to variables in V. For ease of notation, we may write the formula in a program transition as a guarded command over variables in V. For example, let us consider $V = [x, y]$. The formula represented by the guarded command $(x > y, [x := x + 1])$ is $x > y \wedge x' = x + 1 \wedge y' = y$. In our notation if a variable is not updated in the command then the variable remains unchanged. We use a special command *variable := input()* to model inputs to the program, which logically means unconstrained update of the variable. For example, the formula represented by the guarded command $x := input()$ is $y' = y$. For an expression or formula F we write $F[/i]$ to denote a formula that is obtained after adding subscript $i + 1$ to every primed variable and i to every unprimed variable.

A *valuation* is a mapping from the program variables V to values in the data domain. A *state* $s = (l, v)$ consists of a program location l and a valuation v. For a state $s = (l, v)$ and a variable x, let $s(x)$ denote the valuation of x in v and let $loc(s) = l$. A *path* is a sequence $e_0, \ldots, e_{n-1}$ of program transitions such that $e_0 = (\ell^I, \_, \_)$, and for $0 \le i < n$, $e_i = (\ell_i, \_, \ell_{i+1}) \in E$. An *execution* corresponding to the path $e_0, \ldots, e_{n-1}$ is a sequence of states $s_0 = (\ell_0, v_0), \ldots s_n = (\ell_n, v_n)$, such that (1) $\ell_0 = \ell^I$, and (2) for all $0 \le i < n$, if $e_i = (\_, c_i(V, V'), \ell')$ then $\ell_{i+1} = \ell'$ and $c_i(v_i, v_{i+1})$ holds true. We assume that for each execution of the program there exist exactly one corresponding path, i.e., there is no non-determinism in the program except inputs.

A path is represented symbolically by a set of path constraints, which we define as follows. Let $frame(x)$ be the formula $\bigwedge_{y \in V : y \ne x} y' = y$. Let r_k be a variable that symbolically represent the kth input on some path. We assume the program does not contain any variable named r. Let $e_0, \ldots, e_{n-1}$ be a path. If $e_i = (\_, [F, x := exp], \_)$ then let $C_i = (F \wedge x' = exp \wedge frame(x))[/i]$ and if $e_i = (\_, [F, x := input()], \_)$ then let $C_i = (F \wedge frame(x))[/i] \wedge x_{i+1} = r_k$, where r_0 up to r_{k-1} have been used in $C_0, \ldots, C_{i-1}$. The *path constraints* for the path is $C_0, \ldots, C_{n-1}$.

A *test* of the program is a sequence of values. A test $u_1, \ldots, u_k$ *realizes* an execution $s_0, \ldots, s_n$ and its corresponding path $e_0, \ldots, e_{n-1}$ if the following conditions hold true:

- if $n = 0$, then $k = 0$.
- If $n > 0$ and $e_{n-1} = (\_, x := input(), \_)$, $s_n(x) = u_k$ and $u_1, \ldots, u_{k-1}$ realizes $s_0, \ldots, s_{n-1}$.
- Otherwise, $u_1, \ldots, u_k$ realizes $s_0, \ldots, s_{n-1}$.

A path is said to be *feasible* if there exists a test that realizes it. In the above, we assume that the program does not read a variable until its value is initialized within the program or explicitly taken as input earlier. Thus, the initial values are not part of tests.

In the context of test suit generation, we may refer to a transition as a *branch* if the source location of the transition has multiple outgoing transitions. A test t *covers* branch e if the test realizes a path that contains e. Branch e is *reachable* if there exists a test t that covers e. The *test generation problem* is to find a set of tests that covers every reachable branch in the program.

3.1   Concolic Testing

In concolic testing, a test suite is generated using both symbolic and concrete execution. In Algorithm 1 we reproduce the procedure; the presentation is modified such that we may use the procedure in our main algorithm. For simplicity

---

Algorithm 1. CONCOLIC($P = (V, L, \ell^I, E), G, t_b$)

Require: program $P = (V, L, \ell^I, E)$, uncovered branches G, time budget t_b
Ensure: tests suite, uncovered branches
 1: $tst \leftarrow ()$;
 2: $\ell \leftarrow \ell^I$; arbitrary v; $S \leftarrow \lambda x \in V.\bot$ ▷ initial values
 3: $pathC \leftarrow ()$; $suite \leftarrow \emptyset$; $k = 0$;
 4: **while** $ct < t_b$ and $G \neq \emptyset$ **do**   ▷ ct always has the current time
 5:     **if** $\exists e = (\ell, [F, x := exp], \ell') \in E$ such that $v \models F$ **then**   ▷ expand
 6:         $G \leftarrow G - \{e\}$; $\ell \leftarrow \ell'$;
 7:         $pathC.push(F(S))$ ▷ $F(S)$ is substitution
 8:         **if** $exp = input()$ **then**
 9:             **if** $|tst| = k$ **then** $w \leftarrow randVal()$; $tst.push(w)$; **else** $w \leftarrow tst(k)$;
10:             $v \leftarrow v[x \mapsto w]$; $S \leftarrow S[x \mapsto r_k]$; $k = k + 1$
11:         **else**
12:             $v \leftarrow v[x \mapsto exp(v)]$
13:             $S \leftarrow S[x \rightarrow UpdateSymMem(S, exp, v)]$
14:     **else**   ▷ backtrack
15:         $suite \leftarrow suite \cup \{tst\}$
16:         **if** $\exists i < |pathC|$ such that $\phi = \bigwedge_{j<i} pathC(j) \wedge \neg pathC(i)$ is sat **then**
17:             $m = getModel(\phi)$
18:             $l \leftarrow$ number of distinct r_is that occur in ϕ
19:             $tst \leftarrow (m(r_0), \ldots, m(r_{l-1}))$
20:             **goto** 2
21:         **else break;**
22: **return** $(suite, G)$

---

of the presentation, we assume that there are at most two outgoing transitions at any program location and their guards are complementary to each other. This assumption does not restrict the applicability of the method.

The procedure takes a program $P = (V, Loc, \ell^I, E)$, a set of goal branches G, and a time budget t_b as input, and returns a test suite that covers a subset of G within the time budget t_b. The procedure maintains a symbolic memory S, which is a partial function from the program variables V to symbolic expressions. We use the symbol $\bot$ to denote an undefined value in a partial function. In addition, the procedure uses the following data structures: the current location ℓ, current valuation v of variables, list $pathC$ that contains constraints along the current path, test tst that produces the current path, counter k of inputs that have been read on the current path, and a set $suite$ of tests seen so far. We initialize all the collecting data structures to be empty, ℓ is initialized to be the initial location ℓ^I, and the symbolic memory to be empty.

The algorithm proceeds by extending the current path by a transition in each iteration of the while loop at line 4. The loop runs until there are no goals to be covered or the procedure runs out of its time budget. In the loop body, the condition checks if it is possible to extend the current path by a transition $e = (\ell, [F, x := exp], \ell')$. If the guard of e satisfies the current valuation v then e is removed from the set of goals and the current location is updated to ℓ'. In case

e has an input command $x := input()$, then (1) the algorithm updates $v(x)$ to the kth value from tst if it is available, (2) otherwise $v(x)$ is assigned a random value w, and w is appended to tst. In either case, $\mathcal{S}$ is updated by a fresh symbol r_k, assuming r_0 to r_{k-1} have been used so far. If e is not an input command, then both concrete and symbolic values of x are updated in v and $\mathcal{S}$ at line 10.

The symbolic memory is updated by the procedure $UpdateSymMem$. $UpdateSymMem$ first computes $exp(\mathcal{S})$, and if the resulting formula is beyond the capacity of available satisfiability checkers, then it simplifies the formula by substituting the concrete values from v for some symbolic variables to make the formula decidable in the chosen theory. $UpdateSymMem$ is the key heuristics in concolic testing that brings elements of concrete testing and symbolic execution together. For details of this operation see [33,35].

At line 7, $pathC$ is extended by $F(\mathcal{S})$, which is the formula obtained after substituting every variable x occurring in F by $\mathcal{S}(x)$. We assume that variables are always initialized before usage, so $\mathcal{S}$ is always defined for free variables in F.

In case the current path cannot be further extended, at lines 16–19 the procedure tries to find a branch on the path to backtrack. For a chosen branch with index i, a formula is built that contains the path constraints up to $i - 1$ and the negation of the ith constraint. If this formula is satisfiable, then its model is converted to a new test and path exploration restarts. Note that the branch can be chosen non-deterministically, which allows us to choose a wide range of heuristics for choosing the next path. For example, the branch can be chosen at random or in the depth-first manner by picking the largest unexplored branch i. Another important heuristic that is implemented in CREST is to follow a branch that leads to the closest uncovered branch.

4   Coverage-Driven Abstraction Refinement

In this section, we present a modified version of CEGAR-based model checking that we use in our main algorithm. Our modifications are: (1) the procedure continues until all goal branches are covered by tests, proved unreachable or until the procedure reaches the time limit, (2) the procedure always returns an abstract reachability graph that is closed under the abstract post operator.

The classical CEGAR-based model checking executes a program using an abstract semantics, which is defined by an abstraction. Typically, the abstraction is chosen such that the reachability graph generated due to the abstract execution is finite. If the computed reachability graph satisfies the correctness specification, then the input program is correct. Otherwise, the model checker finds an abstract counterexample, i.e., a path in the reachability graph that reaches an error state. The abstract counterexample is spurious if there is no concrete execution that corresponds to the abstract counterexample. If the counterexample is not spurious then a bug has been found and the model checker terminates. In case of a spurious counterexample, the refinement procedure refines the abstract model. This is done by refining the abstraction to remove the spurious counterexample, and the process restarts with the newly refined abstraction. After a number of iterations, the abstract model may have no more counterexamples, which proves the correctness of the input program.

In this paper, we use predicate abstraction for model checking. Let π be a set of predicates, which are formulas over variables V. We assume that π always contains the predicate "false". We define abstraction and concretization functions α and γ between the concrete domain of all formulas over V, and the abstract domain of 2^π:

$$\alpha(\rho) = \{\varphi \in \pi \mid \rho \implies \varphi\} \qquad \gamma(A) = \bigwedge A,$$

where $A \subseteq \pi$, and ρ is a formula over V. An abstract state s_a of our program is an element of $Loc \times 2^\pi$. Given an abstract state (ℓ, A) and a program transition (ℓ, ϕ, ℓ'), the abstract strongest post is defined as:

$$sp_a(A, \phi) = \alpha((\exists V.\ \gamma(A) \wedge \phi(V, V'))[V'/V]).$$

The abstraction is refined by adding predicates to π.

In Algorithm 2, we present the coverage-driven version of the CEGAR procedure. We do not declare error locations or transitions, instead the procedure

---

Algorithm 2. ABSTRACTMC($P = (V, L, \ell^I, E)$, π, G, t_b)

Require: program $P = (V, L, \ell^I, E)$, predicates π, uncovered branches G, time budget t_b

Ensure: tests, remaining branches, branches proved unreachable, new predicates, abstract reachability graph

1:   $worklist \leftarrow \{(\ell^I, \emptyset)\}$; $reach \leftarrow \emptyset$; $subsume \leftarrow \lambda s_a.\bot$; $parent((\ell_0, \emptyset)) \leftarrow \bot$
2:   **while** $worklist \neq \emptyset$ **do**
3:       choose $(\ell, A) \in worklist$
4:       $worklist \leftarrow worklist \setminus \{(\ell, A)\}$
5:       **if** false $\in A$ or $\exists s_a \in parent^*((\ell, A)).\ s_a \in sub$ **then continue**
6:       $reach \leftarrow reach \cup \{(\ell, A)\}$
7:       **if** $\exists(\ell, A') \in reach - sub.\ A \subseteq A'$ **then** $subsume \leftarrow subsume[(\ell, A) \mapsto (\ell, A')]$
8:       **else**
9:          **if** $\exists(\ell, A') \in reach - sub.\ A' \subseteq A$ **then** $subsume \leftarrow subsume[(\ell, A') \mapsto (\ell, A)]$
10:         **for each** $e = (\ell, \rho, \ell') \in E$ **do**
11:           $A' \leftarrow sp_a(A, \rho)$; $worklist \leftarrow worklist \cup \{(\ell', A')\}$
12:           $parent((\ell', A')) = (\ell, A)$; $trans((\ell', A')) = e$
13:           **if** $e \in G$ **then**
14:              **if** $\exists m \models pathCons(\text{path to } (\ell', A'))$ **then**
15:                $G \leftarrow G - \{e\}$
16:                $suite \leftarrow suite \cup \{\text{the sequence of values of } r_k\text{s in } m\}$
17:              **else**
18:                **if** $ct < t_b$ **then** $\triangleright$ ct has current time
19:                  $\pi \leftarrow \pi \cup$ REFINE((ℓ', A')); **goto 1**
20:   $U = G - \{e \mid \exists s_a \in reach.\ trans(s_a) = e\}$ $\triangleright$ Unreachable goals
21:   **return** ($suite$, $G - U$, U, π, ($reach, parent, subsume, trans$))

---

takes goal transitions G as input along with a program $P = (V, Loc, \ell^I, E)$, predicates π, and a time budget t_b. Reachable states are collected in *reach*, while *worklist* contains the frontier abstract states whose children are yet to be computed. The procedure maintains functions *parent* and *trans*, such that if an abstract state s'_a is a child of a state s_a by a transition e, then $parent(s'_a) = s_a$ and $trans(s'_a) = e$. To guarantee termination, one needs to ensure that abstract states are not discovered repeatedly. Therefore, the procedure also maintains the *subsume* function, such that $subsume((\ell, A)) = (\ell', A')$ only if $\ell = \ell'$ and $A \subseteq A'$. We write $sub = \{s \mid subsume(s) \neq \bot\}$ for the set of subsumed states. We denote the reflexive transitive closure of *parent* and *subsume*, by $parent^*$ and $subsume^*$, respectively.

The algorithm proceeds as follows. Initially, all collecting data structures are empty, except *worklist* containing the initial abstract state $(\ell^I, \emptyset)$. The loop at line 2 expands the reachability graph in every iteration. At lines 3–4, it chooses an abstract state (l, A) from *worklist*. If any ancestor of the state is already subsumed or the state is false, the state is discarded and the next state is chosen. Otherwise, (l, A) is added to *reach*. At lines 7–9, the *subsume* function is updated. Afterwords, if (l, A) became subsumed then we proceed to choose another state from *worklist*. Otherwise, we create the children of (l, A) in the loop at line 10 by the abstract post sp_a. At line 12, *parent* and *trans* relations are updated. At line 13, the procedure checks if the abstract reachability has reached any of the goal transitions. If yes, then it checks the feasibility of the reaching path. If the path is found to be feasible, we add the feasible solution as a test to the suite at line 16. Otherwise, we refine and restart the reachability computation to remove the spurious path from the abstract reachability at lines 18–19. In case the algorithm has used its time budget, the refinement is not performed, but the algorithm continues processing the states remaining in *worklist*. As a consequence, the algorithm always returns a complete abstract reachability graph.

We do not discuss details of the REFINE procedure. The interested reader may read a more detailed exposition of CEGAR in [25].

Abstract Reachability Graph (ARG). The relations *parent*, *subsume*, and *trans* together define an *abstract reachability graph (ARG)*, which is produced by ABSTRACTMC. A sequence of transitions $e_0, \ldots, e_{n-1}$ is a *path in an ARG* if there is a sequence of abstract state $s_0, \ldots, s_n \in reach$, such that

1. $s_0 = (\ell^I, \emptyset)$,
2. for $1 < i \leq n$ we have $parent(s_i) \in subsume^*(s_{i-1})$ and $e_{i-1} = trans(s_i)$.

Theorem 1. *Every feasible path of the program P is a path of an ARG. Moreover, every path in the ARG is a path of P.*

ABSTRACTMC returns a set *suite* of tests, set G of uncovered goals, proven unreachable goals U, set π of predicates, and the abstract reachability graph.

Lazy Abstraction. Model checkers often implement various optimizations in the computation of ARGs. One of the key optimization is lazy abstraction [26]. CEGAR may learn many predicates that lead to ARGs that are expensive to compute. In lazy abstraction, one observes that not all applications of sp_a require the same predicates. Let us suppose that the refinement procedure finds a new predicate that *must* be added in specific place along a spurious counterexample to remove this counterexample from future iterations. In other paths, however, this predicate may be omitted. This can be achieved by localizing predicates to parts of an ARG. Support for lazy abstraction can easily be added by additional data structures that record the importance of a predicate in different parts of programs.

5   Abstraction-Driven Concolic Testing

In this section, we present our algorithm that combines concolic testing and model checking. The key idea is to use the ARG generated by a model checker to guide concolic testing to explore more likely feasible parts of programs.

We start by presenting the function MONITORFROMARG that converts an ARG into a monitor program. Let $\mathcal{A} = (reach, parent, subsume, trans)$ be an ARG. The *monitor of* $\mathcal{A}$ is defined as a program $\mathcal{M} = (V, reach - sub, (\ell^I, \emptyset), E_1 \cup E_2)$, where

- $E_1 = \{(s_a, e, s_a') \mid s_a = parent(s_a') \wedge e = trans(s_a') \wedge s_a' \notin sub\}$,
- $E_2 = \{(s_a, e, s_a'') \mid \exists s_a'.\ s_a = parent(s_a') \wedge e = trans(s_a') \wedge \wedge s_a'' \in subsume^+(s_a') \wedge s_a'' \notin sub\}$.

The transitions in E_1 are due to the child-parent relation, when the child abstract state is not subsumed. In case the child state s_a' is subsumed, then E_2 contains a transition from the parent of s_a' to the non-subsumed state s_a'' in $subsume^+(s_a')$, where $subsume^+$ denotes the transitive closure of $subsume$. From the way we built an ARG, it follows that the state s_a'' is uniquely defined and the monitor is always deterministic.

In Algorithm 3 we present our method CRABS. CRABS takes as input a program P, a set G of goal branches to be covered, and time constraints: the total time limit t_b, and time budgets t_c, t_m for a single iteration of concolic testing and model checking, respectively. The algorithm returns a test suite for the covered goals, and a set of goals that are provably unreachable. The algorithm records in G the set of remaining goals. Similarly, U collects the goal branches that are proved unreachable by the model checker. The algorithm maintains a set π of predicates for abstraction, a program $\overline{P}$ for concolic testing, and a set $\overline{G}$ of goals for concolic testing. The program $\overline{P}$ is initialized to the original program P, and in the following iterations becomes refined by the monitors. The algorithm collects in *suite* the tests generated by concolic testing and model checking.

The program $\overline{P}$ is a refinement of the original program P, so a single goal branch in P can map to many branches in the program $\overline{P}$. For this reason, we perform testing for the set $\overline{G}$ of all possible extensions of G to the branches in

---

Algorithm 3. CRABS($P = (V, Loc, \ell^i, E)$, G, t_b, t_c, t_m)

Require: program $P = (V, Loc, \ell^i, E)$, branches $G \subseteq E$ to cover, time budget for concolic testing t_c, time budget for model checking t_m, total time budget t_b,
Ensure: a test suite, set of provably unreachable branches
1: $\pi \leftarrow \{false\}$; $U \leftarrow \emptyset$;   ▷ U is a set of provably unreachable goals
2: $suite \leftarrow \emptyset$ ▷ $suite$ is a set of test
3: $\overline{P} \leftarrow P$; $\overline{G} \leftarrow G$ ▷ program and goals for testing
4:
5: **while** $G \neq \emptyset$ and $ct < t_b$ **do**   ▷ ct always has current time.
6:     $(suite', \_) \leftarrow$ CONCOLICTEST($\overline{P}, \overline{G}, ct + t_c$)
7:     $G \leftarrow G - \{g \in E \mid \exists tst \in suite'.tst$ covers $g\}$
8:     $suite \leftarrow suite \cup suite'$;
9:     **if** $G \neq \emptyset$ **then**
10:        $(suite', G, U', \pi, \mathcal{A}) \leftarrow$ ABSTRACTMC($P, \pi, G, ct + t_m$)
11:        $suite \leftarrow suite \cup suite'$; $U \leftarrow U \cup U'$
12:        $\overline{P} \leftarrow \overline{P} \times$ MONITORFROMARG($\mathcal{A}$)   ▷ see sec. 5 for MonitorFromARG
13:        $\overline{G} = \{((\ell, \_), e, (\ell', \_)) \in E_{\overline{P}} \mid (\ell, e, \ell') \in G\}$
14: **return** $(suite, U)$

$\overline{P}$. For simplicity, in our algorithm concolic testing tries to reach all goals in $\overline{G}$, even if they map to the same goal branch in G. In the implementation, however, once concolic testing reaches a branch in $\overline{G}$, it removes all branches from $\overline{G}$ that have the same projection.

CRABS proceeds in iterations. At line 6, it first runs concolic testing on the program $\overline{P}$ and the goal branches $\overline{G}$ with the time budget t_c. The testing process returns a tests $suite'$ and the set of remaining branches. Afterwords, if some branches remain to be tested, a model checker is called on the program P with predicates π, and a time budget t_m at line 10. As we discussed in the previous section, the model checker builds an abstract reachability graph (ARG), and produces tests if it finds concrete paths to the goal branches. Since the model checker runs for a limited amount of time, it returns an abstract reachability graph that may have abstract paths to the goal branches, but no concrete paths were discovered. Moreover, if the ARG does not reach some goal branch then it is certain that the branch is unreachable. The model checker returns a new set $suite'$ of tests, remaining goals G, and a set U' of newly proved unreachable goals. Furthermore, it also returns a new set π of predicates for the next call to the model checker, and an abstract reachability graph $\mathcal{A}$. At line 12, we construct a monitor from $\mathcal{A}$ by calling MONITORFROMARG. We construct the next program $\overline{P}$ by taking a product of the current $\overline{P}$ with the monitor. We also update $\overline{G}$ to the set of all extensions of the branches in G to the branches in $\overline{P}$. In the next iteration concolic testing is called on $\overline{P}$, which essentially explores the paths of P that are allowed by the monitors generated from the ARG. The algorithm continues until it runs out of time budget t_b or no more goals remain.

The program $\overline{P}$ for testing is refined in every iteration by taking a product with a new monitor. This ensures that $\overline{P}$ always becomes more precise, even if the consecutive abstractions do not strictly refine each other, i.e. the ARG from iteration i allows the set $\mathcal{L}$ of paths, while the ARG from iteration $i + 1$ allows the set $\mathcal{L}'$ such that $\mathcal{L}' \not\subseteq \mathcal{L}$. This phenomenon occurs when the model checker follows the lazy abstraction paradigm, described in Sect. 4. In lazy abstraction, predicates are applied locally and some may be lost due to refinement. As a consequence, program parts that were pruned from an ARG may appear again in some following ARG. Another reason for this phenomenon may be a deliberate decision to remove some predicates when the abstraction becomes too expensive to maintain.

6   Experiments

We implemented our approach in a tool CRABS, built on top of the concolic tester CREST [11] and the model checker CPACHECKER [8]. In our experiments, we observed an improvement in branch coverage compared to CREST from 48 % to 63 % in the best case, and from 66 % to 71 % on average.

Benchmarks. We evaluated our approach on a collection of programs: (1) a set of hand-crafted examples (listed in [1]), (2) example "nsichneu" [24] described in Sect. 2 with varying number of loop iterations, (3) benchmarks "parport" and "cdaudio1" from various categories of SVCOMP [6], (4) all 13 benchmarks from the "ddv-machzwd" SVCOMP category.

Optimizations. Constructing an explicit product of an program and a monitor would be cumbersome, due to complex semantics of the C language, e.g. the type system and scoping rules. To avoid this problem, our tool explores the product on-the-fly, by keeping track of the program and monitor state. We have done minor preprocessing of the examples, such that they can be parsed by both CREST and CPACHECKER. Furthermore, CPACHECKERdoes not deal well with arrays, so in the "nsichneu" example we replaced arrays of fixed size (at most 6) by a collection of variables.

Comparison of Heuristics and Tools. We compare our tool with four other heuristics for guiding concolic search that are implemented in CREST : the depth-first search (DFS), random branch search (RndBr), uniform random search (UnfRnd), and CFG-guided search; for details see [11]. The depth-first search is a classical way of traversing a tree of program paths. In the random branch search, the branch to be flipped is chosen from all the branches on the current execution with equal probability. Similarly, in the uniform random search the branch to be flipped is also picked at random, but the probability decreases with the position of the branch on the execution. In the CFG-guided heuristic the test process is guided by a distance measure between program branches, which is computed statically on the control-flow graph of the program. This heuristic tries to drive exploration in into branches that are closer to the remaining test goals. The concolic component of our tool uses the CFG-guided heuristic to explore the product of a program and a monitor; this way branches closer in the

Table 1. Experimental results for one hour. RndBr stands for "random branch search" and UnfRnd for "uniform random search." TO means that no suite was generated before the time limit.

Example		CRABS-CFG (this paper)	CREST-DFS [33,35]	CREST-CFG [11]	CREST-UnfRnd[11]	CREST-RndBr[11]	FSHELL[27]
name	branches	coverage	coverage	coverage	coverage	coverage	coverage
simple-while	12	12/12 (100%)	11/12 (91.2%)	11/12 (91.2%)	11/12 (91.2%)	11/12 (91.2%)	12/12 (100%)
branches	12	12/12 (100%)	9/12 (75%)	7/12 (58.3%)	12/12 (91.2%)	12/12 (91.2%)	12/12 (100%)
unreach	10	9/9 (100%)	9/10 (90%)	9/10 (90%)	9/10 (90%)	9/10 (90%)	9/9 (100%)
nsichneu(2)	5786	3843/5753 (66.8%)	**5365/5786 (92.7%)**	3098/5786 (53.5%)	2559/5786 (44.2%)	2196/5786 (38.0%)	4520/5786 (78.1%)
nsichneu(9)	5786	3720/5756 (64.6%)	**4224/5786 (73.0%)**	2843/5786 (49.1%)	2493/5786 (43.1%)	2187/5786 (37.8%)	1261/5786 (21.8%)
nsichneu(17)	5786	**3619/5746 (63.0%)**	2086/5786 (36.1%)	2758/5786 (47.7%)	2476/5786 (42.8%)	2161/5786 (37.3%)	TO
parport	920	**215/598 (35.9%)**	215/920 (23.4%)	215/920 (23.4%)	215/920 (23.4%)	215/920 (23.4%)	TO
cdaudio1	340	248/249 (99.6%)	250/340 (73.5%)	250/340 (73.5%)	246/340 (72.3%)	250/340 (73.5%)	**266/266 (100%)**
ddv_outb	206	**137/194 (70.8%)**	78/206 (37.9%)	136/206 (66.2%)	111/206 (54.2%)	135/206 (65.7%)	TO
ddv_pthread	200	**134/189 (71.3%)**	73/200 (36.7%)	131/200 (65.5%)	109/200 (54.8%)	130/200 (65.2%)	TO
ddv_outwp	200	**134/189 (70.8%)**	73/200 (36.7%)	131/200 (65.5%)	107/200 (53.8%)	129/200 (64.7%)	TO
ddv_allfalse	214	**143/199 (72.0%)**	83/214 (38.9%)	141/214 (66.0%)	123/214 (57.6%)	140/214 (65.6%)	TO
ddv_inwp	200	**134/189 (70.7%)**	76/200 (38.2%)	131/200 (65.5%)	108/200 (54.2%)	129/200 (64.8%)	TO
ddv_inbp	200	**133/189 (70.3%)**	73/200 (36.5%)	130/200 (65.3%)	109/200 (54.5%)	130/200 (65.2%)	TO
ddv_outlp	200	**133/189 (70.1%)**	73/200 (36.5%)	130/200 (65.2%)	109/200 (54.7%)	130/200 (65.2%)	TO
ddv_outbp	200	**134/188 (71.2%)**	73/200 (36.5%)	130/200 (65.0%)	106/200 (53.3%)	130/200 (65.0%)	TO
ddv_inl	200	**134/190 (70.7%)**	89/200 (44.8%)	131/200 (65.8%)	109/200 (54.7%)	129/200 (64.8%)	TO
ddv_inlp	200	**134/189 (71.1%)**	75/200 (37.8%)	131/200 (65.5%)	108/200 (54.3%)	129/200 (64.8%)	TO
ddv_inw	206	**139/194 (72.0%)**	80/206 (39.2%)	136/206 (66.3%)	112/206 (54.5%)	135/206 (65.7%)	TO
ddv_inb	200	**133/189 (70.5%)**	73/200 (36.5%)	130/200 (65.3%)	114/200 (57.3%)	130/200 (65.2%)	TO
ddv_outl	200	**133/189 (70.5%)**	73/200 (36.5%)	131/200 (65.5%)	109/200 (54.8%)	131/200 (65.7%)	TO

monitor are explored first. Our additional experiments show that our approach improves coverage for all heuristics implemented in CREST.

We compared our approach with the tool FSHELL [27], which is based on the bounded model checker CBMC. FSHELL unwinds the control-flow graph until it fully explores all loop iterations and checks satisfiability of paths that hit the testing goals. This tool does not return a test suite, unless all loops are fully explored.

Experimental Setup. All the tools were run with branch coverage as the test objective. The coverage of a test suite is measured by the ratio $\frac{c}{r}$, where c is the number of branches covered by a test suite, and r is the number of branches that have not been proved unreachable. For CREST, we set r to be the number of branches that are reachable in the control-flow graph by graph search, which excludes code that is trivially dead. Our tool and CREST have the same number of test goals, while FSHELL counts more test goals on some examples. We run our tool in a configuration, where testing takes approximately 80 % of the time budget. All experiments were performed on a machine with an AMD Opteron 6134 CPU and a memory limit of 12 GB, and were averaged over three runs.

Results. The experimental evaluation for a time budget of one hour is presented in Table 1.

After one hour, our tool achieved the highest coverage on most examples. The best case is "nsichneu(17)," where our tool achieved 63 % coverage compared to 48 % by the best other tool. Our additional experiments show that if we run our tool with the DFS heuristic, we obtain even higher coverage of 69 %. The hand-crafted examples demonstrate that our method, as well as FSHELL, can reach program parts that are difficult to cover for concolic testing. In the benchmark category, our tool obtained average coverage of 71 % compared to 66 % by CREST. In many examples, we obtain higher coverage by both reaching more goals and proving that certain goals are unreachable. FSHELL generated test suites only for three examples, since on other examples it was not able to fully unwind program loops.

7 Related Work

Testing literature is rich, so we only highlight the most prominent approaches. Random testing [9,13,32] can cheaply cover shallow parts of the program, but it may quickly reach a plateau where coverage does not increase. Another testing method is to construct symbolic objects that represent complex input to a program [36,37]. In [10] objects for testing program are systematically constructed up to a given bound. The approach of [18] tests a concurrent program by exploring schedules using partial-order reduction techniques.

Concolic testing suffers from the path-explosion problem, so various search orders testing have been proposed, several of them are discussed in Sect. 6. In [20] multiple input vectors are generated from a single symbolic path by negating constraints on the path one-by-one, which allows the algorithm to exercise paths at different depths of the program. Hybrid concolic testing [30] uses random testing to quickly reach deep program statements and then concolic testing to explore the close neighborhood of that point.

Our work is closest related to SYNERGY [5, 21, 22]. SYNERGY is an approach for verification of safety properties that maintains a program abstraction and a forest of tested paths. Abstract error traces are ordered such that they follow some tested execution until the last intersection with the forest. If an ordered abstract trace is feasible, then a longer concrete path is added to the forest; otherwise, the abstraction is refined. Compared to SYNERGY our method has several key differences. First, in SYNERGY model checking and test generation work as a single process, while in our approach these components are independent and communicate only by a monitor. Second, unlike us, SYNERGY does not pass the complete abstract model of the program to concolic testing, where the testing heuristics guides the search. Finally, in our approach we can configure the ratio of model checking to testing, while in SYNERGY every unsuccessful execution leads to refinement.

Another related work is [12], where concolic testing is guided towards program parts that a static analyzer was not able to verify. In contrast to our approach, the abstraction is not refined. In [17] conditional model checking is used to generate a residual that represents the program part that has been left unverified; the residual is then tested.

The work of [34] applies program analysis to identify control locations in a concurrent program that are relevant for reaching the target state. These locations guide symbolic search toward the target and predicates in failed symbolic executions are analyzed to find new relevant locations. The CHECK'N'CRASH [15] tool uses a constraint solver to reproduce and check errors found by static analysis of a program. In [16] the precision of static analysis was improved by adding a dynamic invariant detection.

The algorithm of [31] presents a testing method, where a program is simplified by replacing function calls by unconstrained input. Spurious counterexample are removed in a CEGAR loop by lazily inserting function bodies. In contrast, our method performs testing on a concrete program and counterexamples are always sound.

A number of papers consider testing program abstraction with bounded model checking (BMC). If the abstraction is sufficiently small, then a program invariant can be established by exhaustively testing the abstraction with BMC. In [29] a Boolean circuit is abstracted, such that it decreases the bound that needs to be explored in an exhaustive BMC search. In [23] BMC is run on an abstract model up to some bound. If the invariant is not violated, then the model is replaced by an unsat core and the bound is incremented. If a spurious counterexample is found, then clauses that appear in the unsat core are added to the abstraction.

8   Conclusion

We presented an algorithm that combines model checking and concolic testing synergistically. Our method iteratively runs concolic testing and model checking, such that concolic testing is guided by a program abstraction, and the abstraction is refined for the remaining test goals. Our experiments demonstrated that the presented method can increase branch coverage compared to both concolic testing, and test generation based on model checking.

We also observed that our method is highly sensitive to optimizations and heuristics available in the model checker. For instance, lazy abstraction allows the model checker to get pass bottlenecks created due to over-precision in some parts of ARGs. However, lazy abstraction may lead to a monitor that is less precise than the monitors of the past iterations, which may lead to stalled progress in covering new goals by our algorithm. In the future work, we will study such complimentary effects of various heuristics in model checkers to find the optimal design of model checkers to assist a concolic-testing tool. We believe that adding this feature will further improve the coverage of our tool.

Acknowledgments. We thank Andrey Kupriyanov for feedback on the manuscript, and Michael Tautschnig for help with preparing the experiments.

References

1. CRABS tool. http://pub.ist.ac.at/~przemek/crabs_tool.html
2. Radio Technical Commission for Aeronautics. www.rtca.org
3. Ball, T., Rajamani, S.K.: The SLAM project: debugging system software via static analysis. In: POPL (2002)
4. Banerjee, A., Chattopadhyay, S., Roychoudhury, A.: Static analysis driven cache performance testing. In: RTSS, pp. 319–329 (2013)
5. Beckman, N.E., Nori, A.V., Rajamani, S.K., Simmons, R.J.: Proofs from tests. In: ISSTA, pp. 3–14 (2008)
6. Beyer, D.: Software verification and verifiable witnesses. In: Baier, C., Tinelli, C. (eds.) TACAS 2015. LNCS, vol. 9035, pp. 401–416. Springer, Heidelberg (2015). (Report on SV-COMP 2015)
7. Beyer, D., Chlipala, A., Henzinger, T.A., Jhala, R., Majumdar, R.: Generating tests from counterexamples. In: Finkelstein, A., Estublier, J., Rosenblum, D.S. (eds.) ICSE, pp. 326–335. IEEE Computer Society (2004)
8. Beyer, D., Keremoglu, M.E.: CPACHECKER: A tool for configurable software verification. In: Gopalakrishnan, G., Qadeer, S. (eds.) CAV 2011. LNCS, vol. 6806, pp. 184–190. Springer, Heidelberg (2011)
9. Bird, D.L., Munoz, C.U.: Automatic generation of random self-checking test cases. IBM Syst. J. **22**(3), 229–245 (1983)
10. Boyapati, C., Khurshid, S., Marinov, D.: Korat: automated testing based on java predicates. In: ISSTA, pp. 123–133 (2002)
11. Burnim, J., Sen, K.: Heuristics for scalable dynamic test generation. In: ASE, pp. 443–446 (2008)

12. Christakis, M., Müller, P., Wüstholz, V.: Guiding dynamic symbolic execution toward unverified program executions. Technical report, ETH Zurich (2015)
13. Ciupa, I., Leitner, A., Oriol, M., Meyer, B.: ARTOO: adaptive random testing for object-oriented software. In: Schäfer, W., Dwyer, M.B., Gruhn, V. (eds.) ICSE, pp. 71–80. ACM (2008)
14. Clarke, E.M., Grumberg, O., Jha, S., Lu, Y., Veith, H.: Counterexample-guided abstraction refinement. In: CAV (2000)
15. Csallner, C., Smaragdakis, Y.: Check 'n' crash: combining static checking and testing. In: ICSE, pp. 422–431 (2005)
16. Csallner, C., Smaragdakis, Y., Xie, T.: DSD-Crasher: A hybrid analysis tool for bug finding. ACM Trans. Softw. Eng. Methodol. **17**(2), 1–37 (2008)
17. Czech, M., Jakobs, M.-C., Wehrheim, H.: Just test what you cannot verify!. In: Egyed, A., Schaefer, I. (eds.) FASE 2015. LNCS, vol. 9033, pp. 100–114. Springer, Heidelberg (2015)
18. Godefroid, P.: Model checking for programming languages using verisoft. In: POPL, pp. 174–186 (1997)
19. Godefroid, P.: Compositional dynamic test generation. In: POPL, pp. 47–54 (2007)
20. Godefroid, P., Levin, M.Y., Molnar, D.A.: Automated whitebox fuzz testing. In: NDSS. The Internet Society (2008)
21. Godefroid, P., Nori, A.V., Rajamani, S.K., Tetali, S.: Compositional may-must program analysis: unleashing the power of alternation. In: POPL, pp. 43–56 (2010)
22. Gulavani, B.S., Henzinger, T.A., Kannan, Y., Nori, A.V., Rajamani, S.K.: Synergy: a new algorithm for property checking. In: SIGSOFT FSE, pp. 117–127 (2006)
23. Gupta, A., Strichman, O.: Abstraction refinement for bounded model checking. In: Etessami, K., Rajamani, S.K. (eds.) CAV 2005. LNCS, vol. 3576, pp. 112–124. Springer, Heidelberg (2005)
24. Gustafsson, J., Betts, A., Ermedahl, A., Lisper, B.: The Mälardalen WCET benchmarks - past, present and future. In: Lisper, B. (ed.) WCET, pp. 137–147. OCG, Brussels (2010)
25. Henzinger, T.A., Jhala, R., Majumdar, R., McMillan, K.L.: Abstractions from proofs. In: POPL (2004)
26. Henzinger, T.A., Jhala, R., Majumdar, R., Sutre, G.: Lazy abstraction. In: POPL (2002)
27. Holzer, A., Schallhart, C., Tautschnig, M., Veith, H.: FSHELL: Systematic test case generation for dynamic analysis and measurement. In: Gupta, A., Malik, S. (eds.) CAV 2008. LNCS, vol. 5123, pp. 209–213. Springer, Heidelberg (2008)
28. Holzer, A., Schallhart, C., Tautschnig, M., Veith, H.: How did you specify your test suite. In: Pecheur, C., Andrews, J., Nitto, E.D. (eds.) ASE, pp. 407–416. ACM (2010)
29. Kroening, D.: Computing over-approximations with bounded model checking. Electr. Notes Theor. Comput. Sci. **144**(1), 79–92 (2006)
30. Majumdar, R., Sen, K.: Hybrid concolic testing. In: ICSE, ICSE 2007, pp. 416–426. IEEE Computer Society, Washington, DC (2007)
31. Majumdar, R., Sen, K.: Latest : Lazy dynamic test input generation. Technical Report UCB/EECS-2007-36, EECS Department, University of California, Berkeley (2007)
32. Pacheco, C., Lahiri, S.K., Ernst, M.D., Ball, T.: Feedback-directed random test generation. In: ICSE, pp. 75–84. IEEE Computer Society (2007)
33. Klarlund, N., Godefroid, P., Sen, K.: DART: directed automated random testing. In: PLDI, pp. 213–223. ACM (2005)

34. Rungta, N., Mercer, E.G., Visser, W.: Efficient testing of concurrent programs with abstraction-guided symbolic execution. In: Păsăreanu, C.S. (ed.) Model Checking Software. LNCS, vol. 5578, pp. 174–191. Springer, Heidelberg (2009)

35. Sen, K., Marinov, D., Agha, G.: CUTE: a concolic unit testing engine for C. In: ESEC/SIGSOFT FSE, pp. 263–272 (2005)

36. Visser, W., Pasareanu, C.S., Khurshid, S.: Test input generation with Java PathFinder. In: Avrunin, G.S., Rothermel, G. (eds.) ISSTA, pp. 97–107. ACM (2004)

37. Xie, T., Marinov, D., Schulte, W., Notkin, D.: Symstra: a framework for generating object-oriented unit tests using symbolic execution. In: Halbwachs, N., Zuck, L.D. (eds.) TACAS 2005. LNCS, vol. 3440, pp. 365–381. Springer, Heidelberg (2005)

Probabilistic Systems

Reward-Bounded Reachability Probability for Uncertain Weighted MDPs

Vahid Hashemi[1,2]($\boxtimes$), Holger Hermanns[2], and Lei Song[3]

[1] Max Planck Institute for Informatics, Saarbrücken, Germany
hashemi@mpi-inf.mpg.de
[2] Department of Computer Science, Saarland University, Saarbrücken, Germany
[3] University of Technology, Sydney, Australia

Abstract. In this paper we present a decision algorithm for computing maximal/minimal reward-bounded reachability probabilities in weighted MDPs with uncertainties. Even though an uncertain weighted MDP (*UwMDP*) represents an equivalent weighted MDP which may be exponentially larger, our algorithm does not cause an exponentially blow-up and will terminate in polynomial time with respect to the size of *UwMDPs*. We also define bisimulation relations for *UwMDPs*, which are compositional and can be decided in polynomial time as well. We develop a prototype tool and apply it to some case studies to show its effectiveness.

1 Introduction

Markov Decision Processes (*MDPs*) are powerful models for systems involving both decision-making and probabilistic dynamics [37]. Prominent applications range from economics to computer networking, verification and artificial intelligence. Model checkers for *MDPs*, such as PRISM [31], Modest [10], and IscasMC [22] have been developed and applied in practice successfully.

A particular practical challenge in modeling probabilistic systems is rooted in the fact that precise models are often hard to obtain, particularly with respect to the probabilities occurring therein. These may be derived from statistical data or repeated experimentation, but the result can still be far from accurate [35]. This makes the consideration of "robust" probabilities important. A viable option in this respect is to resort to using probability intervals instead of single probabilities. This can lead to more robust analysis and verification results in many applications. This motivation is behind several probabilistic models with uncertainties including *interval Markov chains* [26,29], *Interval MDPs* [35,36,40] (*IMDPs*), and abstract probabilistic automata [16].

In this paper we propose to use weighted Markov decision processes to model probabilistic systems with uncertainties. Different from *IMDPs*, each transition in an Uncertain weighted Markov Decision Process (*UwMDP*) is associated with a weight interval such that any integer value in this interval is a feasible weight for that transition[1]. Weights in our models play a similar role as in GSPN [34]

---

[1] We only consider integer weights in this paper. The extension to rational weights is straightforward.

© Springer-Verlag Berlin Heidelberg 2016
B. Jobstmann and K.R.M. Leino (Eds.): VMCAI 2016, LNCS 9583, pp. 351–371, 2016.
DOI: 10.1007/978-3-662-49122-5_17

or EMPA [6], namely, they will be used to induce a distribution over all transitions with the same label. If from a state s, there are transitions leading to s_1 and s_2 with weights 2 and 3, respectively, then this means that s will evolve into s_1 and s_2 with probabilities $\frac{2}{5}$ and $\frac{3}{5}$, respectively. The model of UwMDPs has intervals of weights attached to each transition. One can think of this model as a game between a scheduler and nature. Different from ordinary wMDPs, nature might also be non-deterministic (besides being probabilistic). More precisely, nature selects a realization of weights from a set of feasible weights that is specified in terms of intervals. The selected weights by the nature then induces a probabilistic transition over states.

UwMDPs are more expressive than IMDPs, as in IMDPs there is no information about weights. In case IMDPs were equipped with weights, the two models will have the same expressiveness with respect to properties considered in this paper (cf. Remark 4), as any IMDP can be transformed into an equivalent UwMDP and vice versa. However, such transformations may induce exponential blow-up in both directions. Nevertheless, IMDPs and UwMDPs are distinguished in several aspects. In UwMDPs, weights can be used to denote priorities or preferences, which are quantities used to generate probabilistic behaviors. For instance, a robot may choose to serve its clients stochastically relative to the preferences they expressed. In this respect, UwMDPs offer users more flexibility to model uncertainties. In addition, we will show that UwMDPs are equipped with a compositional theory based on bisimulation. This implies that compositional minimization approaches [8,9,13] can be applied to alleviate state space explosion problems. This has been introduced as a powerful way to abstract from details of systems in the formal verification community; see for instance [3]. More concretely, we define bisimulation relations for UwMDPs and establish compositionality with respect to a parallel operator, which is a conservative extension of the one for probabilistic automata [33]. Furthermore, we point out that bisimulations of UwMDPs can be computed efficiently in polynomial time with respect to sizes of UwMDPs, in contrast to IMDPs [24].

With respect to model analysis, we discuss extreme (maximal/minimal) reward-bounded reachability probabilities [1] of UwMDPs in this paper. Thus each UwMDP is associated with a reward-structure, which assigns to each weighted transition a reward. On the one hand, our work is an extension of the work in [1] enriched with uncertainties, while on the other hand, it can also be seen as an extension of the work in [36] to models with reward-structures. Despite the fact that an UwMDP may represent an equivalent, but exponentially larger, model without uncertainties, we propose an algorithm to compute extreme reward-bounded reachability probabilities in pseudo polynomial time – polynomial with respect to the size of the given UwMDP and quadratic with respect to the reward bound. Along the line of [36], extreme reachability probabilities without reward bounds can be computed efficiently for UwMDPs as well.

Summarizing, the main contributions of this paper are as follows.

– We introduce a novel stochastic model to capture quantities like preferences or priorities in a non-deterministic scenario with uncertainties. The model is very close to the model of *interval MDPs* first introduced by Puggelli et al. [36], but more convenient to model with when non-probability uncertainties like weights, preference, priority, etc. are involved.

- We consider the problem of computing maximal/minimal reward-bounded reachability probabilities on *UwMDPs*, for which we present an efficient algorithm running in pseudo polynomial time. This extends the results in [36] to deal with properties and models with rewards and the work in [1] with non-determinisms and uncertainties.
- We define bisimulation relations on *UwMDPs*, which can be decided efficiently in polynomial time. We also show that bisimulations are compositional, hence they make compositional minimization possible. The proposed compositional minimization approach cannot be performed efficiently for the models considered in [36].
- We show promising results on a variety of case study, obtained by a prototypical implementation of all algorithms.

Related work. Related work falls into two main categories: Verification of PCTL [23] specifications and compositional minimization for uncertain MDPs. Probabilistic modeling formalisms with uncertainties have attracted much attention recently. Interval Markov chains [26,29] or abstract Markov chains [18] extend classical discrete-time Markov chains (MC) with uncertainties; however, they do not reflect non-determinism in transitions. In uncertain MDPs [35,36,40] both non-deterministic and probabilistic choices coexist and more expressive uncertainty sets are allowed to model transition probabilities. Over the last few years, several new verification algorithms for uncertain Markovian models have been proposed in the literature. The problems of computing reachability probabilities and expected total reward were studied for interval Markov chains [14] and Interval MDPs [41]. Model checking of PCTL and LTL has been investigated in [5,14,30] for interval Markov chains and also in [36,40] for *IMDPs*. Strategy synthesis for MDPs with respect to PCTL properties was first studied in [4], which was then extended to parametric MDPs [21] and to MDPs with ellipsoidal uncertainty [35]. Uncertain Markovian models were also extensively studied in the control community [20,35,41], with the aim to maximize expected finite-horizon (un)discounted rewards. We are not aware of any existing result related to reward-bounded reachability for uncertain MDPs. However, our algorithm is inspired by [1], which deals with the model checking of reachability properties on MCs with rewards.

From the point of view of compositional minimization, interval Markov chains [28] and abstract probabilistic automata [15,16] offer extensive specification theories for Markov chains and probabilistic automata. These theories support both satisfaction and various refinement relations [16,17,26]. In [24] probabilistic bisimulation relations were introduced in order to reduce the size of interval MDPs while preserving PCTL properties. Moreover, an algorithm was given to compute the quotients induced by these bisimulations in time polynomial in the size of the model and exponential in the uncertain branching. Notably, we show that for *UwMDPs*, bisimulation quotients can be computed in polynomial time even with respect to the uncertain branching. Furthermore, bisimulation relations are proved to be compositional with respect to a parallel operator. This enables compositional minimization to enhance the model checking of *UwMDPs*.

Structure of the Paper. The rest of the paper is organized as follows. Section 2 gives necessary background on uncertain weighted MDPs and interval MDPs. In Sect. 3, we define the notion of maximal reward-bounded reachability probability for *UwMDPs* and show a least-fixed point characterization. In Sect. 4, we give the definition of bisimulation for *UwMDPs* and show that it is compositional. Then we give a tractable decision algorithm to compute it. In Sect. 5, we demonstrate our approach on some case studies and present promising experimental results. Finally we conclude our paper in Sect. 6.

2   Preliminaries

In this paper, the sets of all integers, positive integers, real numbers and non-negative real numbers are denoted by $\mathbb{Z}$, $\mathbb{N}_0$, $\mathbb{R}$, and $\mathbb{R}^{\geq 0}$, respectively.

For a set X, we denote by $\Delta(X)$ the set of discrete probability distributions over X. The support of $\mu \in \Delta(X)$ is defined by $supp(\mu) = \{x \in X \mid \mu(x) > 0\}$. In case $\mu(x) = 1$ for some $x \in X$, we write μ as δ_x. We often write $\{x : \mu(x) \mid x \in supp(\mu)\}$ alternatively for a distribution μ. For instance, $\{x_1 : 0.4, x_2 : 0.6\}$ denotes a distribution μ such that $\mu(x_1) = 0.4$ and $\mu(x_2) = 0.6$.

2.1   Weighted Markov Decision Processes

Below we introduce the definition of *weighted Markov Decision Processes*, where $w, \ldots$ and $s, t, u, \ldots$ range over $\mathbb{N}_0$ and states, respectively.

Definition 1 (wMDP). *A weighted Markov Decision Process (wMDP) is a tuple* $\mathcal{M}_W = (S_W, \mathcal{A}_W, W_W, \bar{s}_W, AP_W, L_W)$, *where* S_W *is a finite set of states,* $\mathcal{A}_W$ *is a finite set of actions,* $W_W : S_W \times \mathcal{A}_W \times S_W \mapsto \mathbb{N}_0$ *defines a transition relation,* $\bar{s}_W \in S_W$ *is the initial state,* AP_W *is a finite set of atomic propositions,* $L_W : S_W \mapsto 2^{AP_W}$ *is a labelling function.*

We write $s \xrightarrow{a,w} \mu$ iff $w = \sum_{t \in S_W} W_W(s, a, t) > 0$ and $\mu(t) = \frac{W_W(s,a,t)}{w}$. Let $s \xrightarrow{a,w}_c \mu$, called combined transitions [39], iff there exists $\{\mu_i\}_{i \in I}$ and $\{p_i \in [0,1]\}_{i \in I}$ such that $\sum_{i \in I} p_i \cdot \mu_i = \mu$ where $\sum_{i \in I} p_i = 1$ and $s \xrightarrow{a,w} \mu_i$ for each $i \in I$.

In Definition 1, all weights have to be given precisely, which sometimes is not possible, especially when all weights are estimated or based on experiments. On the other hand, uncertain weighted MDPs relax this condition such that it allows weights to vary as long as they are in certain intervals. Formally,

Definition 2 (UwMDP). *An* Uncertain weighted Markov Decision Process *(UwMDP) is a tuple* $\mathcal{M}_\mathcal{U} = (S_\mathcal{U}, \mathcal{A}_\mathcal{U}, W_\mathcal{U}, \bar{s}_\mathcal{U}, AP_\mathcal{U}, L_\mathcal{U})$ *similar as in Definition 1 except that* $W_\mathcal{U} : S_\mathcal{U} \times \mathcal{A}_\mathcal{U} \times S_\mathcal{U} \mapsto [w_l, w_h]$ *defines a transition relation with uncertainties, where* $w_l, w_h \in \mathbb{N}_0$ *with* $w_l \leq w_h$. *Let* $\mathcal{A}_\mathcal{U}(s)$ *denote the set of available actions at state* $s \in S_\mathcal{U}$.

The only difference between Definitions 1 and 2 is that in a wMDP all transitions are labelled by a weight, while in an UwMDP, transitions are labelled by an interval specifying all allowed weights. We denote by w_{st}^a a resolution of uncertainties corresponding to the transition from s to t with label a, i.e.,$\mathrm{w}_{st}^a \in W_\mathcal{U}(s, a, t)$. We write $s \xrightarrow{a,w} \mu$ iff there exists $\mathrm{w}_{st}^a \in W_\mathcal{U}(s, a, t)$ for each $t \in S_\mathcal{U}$ such that $w = \sum_{t \in S_\mathcal{U}} \mathrm{w}_{st}^a > 0$ and $\mu(t) = \frac{\mathrm{w}_{st}^a}{w}$. Similarly, we can define the combined transitions for UwMDPs.

Let us formally state the semantics of an UwMDP $\mathcal{M}_\mathcal{U}$. A transition initialised from state s_i in $\mathcal{M}_\mathcal{U}$ happens in three steps. First, an action $a \in \mathcal{A}_\mathcal{U}(s_i)$ is chosen non-deterministically. Secondly, a resolution $\mathrm{w}_{s_i t}^a \in W_\mathcal{U}(s_i, a, t)$ is chosen for each $t \in S_\mathcal{U}$. The selection of $\mathrm{w}_{s_i t}^a$ models uncertainty in the transition. Lastly, a successor state s_{i+1} is chosen randomly, according to the induced transition probability distribution μ. It is not hard to see that each UwMDP $\mathcal{M}_\mathcal{U}$ corresponds to a wMDP, which may be exponentially larger than $\mathcal{M}_\mathcal{U}$.

A *path* in $\mathcal{M}_\mathcal{U}$ is a finite or infinite sequence of the form $\xi = s_0 \mathrm{w}_{s_0 s_1}^{a_0} s_1 \mathrm{w}_{s_1 s_2}^{a_1} s_2 \cdots$ where $s_i \in S_\mathcal{U}$, $a_i \in \mathcal{A}_\mathcal{U}(s_i)$ and $0 < \mathrm{w}_{s_i s_{i+1}}^{a_i} \in W_\mathcal{U}(s_i, a_i, s_{i+1})$ for any $i \geq 0$. For a finite path ξ, we denote by $\xi \downarrow$ the last state of ξ. The i-th state (action) along a path ξ is denoted by $\xi[i]$ $(\xi(i))$, if it exists. The set of all finite paths and the set of all infinite paths in the given $\mathcal{M}_\mathcal{U}$ are denoted by $Paths_{\mathcal{M}_\mathcal{U}}^{fin}$ and $Paths_{\mathcal{M}_\mathcal{U}}^{inf}$, respectively. Furthermore, let $Paths_{\mathcal{M}_\mathcal{U}}^\xi = \{\xi\xi' \mid \xi' \in Paths_{\mathcal{M}_\mathcal{U}}^{inf}\}$ denote the set of paths with $\xi \in Paths_{\mathcal{M}_\mathcal{U}}^{fin}$ being its finite prefix.

Remark 1. The size of a given $\mathcal{M}_\mathcal{U}$ is determined as follows. Let $|S_\mathcal{U}|$ denote the number of states in $\mathcal{M}_\mathcal{U}$. Then each state has $O(|\mathcal{A}_\mathcal{U}|)$ actions, while each action corresponds to at most $O(|S_\mathcal{U}|^2)$ transitions, each of which is associated with a weight interval. Therefore, the overall size of $\mathcal{M}_\mathcal{U}$ $|\mathcal{M}_\mathcal{U}|$ is in $O(|S_\mathcal{U}|^2 |\mathcal{A}_\mathcal{U}|)$.

Due to the existing of non-determinism, to resolve which, we need to introduce notions of *scheduler* and *nature*.

Definition 3 (Scheduler and Nature in UwMDPs). *Given an UwMDP* $\mathcal{M}_\mathcal{U}$, *a scheduler is a function* $\lambda : Paths_{\mathcal{M}_\mathcal{U}}^{fin} \rightarrow \Delta(\mathcal{A}_\mathcal{U})$ *that to each finite path* ξ *assigns a distribution over the set of actions. A nature is a function* $\gamma : Paths_{\mathcal{M}_\mathcal{U}}^{fin} \times \mathcal{A}_\mathcal{U} \rightarrow \Delta(S_\mathcal{U})$ *that to each finite path* ξ *and action* a *assigns a feasible distribution, i.e.* $\gamma(\xi, a) = \mu$ *if and only if* $\xi \downarrow \xrightarrow{a,w} \mu$ *for some* w. *We denote by* $\Lambda_{\mathcal{M}_\mathcal{U}}$ *the set of all schedulers and by* $\Gamma_{\mathcal{M}_\mathcal{U}}$ *the set of all natures of* $\mathcal{M}_\mathcal{U}$.

For an initial state s, a scheduler λ, and a nature γ, let $\mathrm{Pr}^{\lambda,\gamma}_{\mathcal{M}_{\mathcal{U}},s}$ denote the unique probability measure over $(Paths^{inf}_{\mathcal{M}_{\mathcal{U}}}, \mathcal{B})^2$ such that the probability $\mathrm{Pr}^{\lambda,\gamma}_{\mathcal{M}_{\mathcal{U}},s}[Paths^{s'}_{\mathcal{M}_{\mathcal{U}}}]$ of starting in s' equals 1 if $s = s'$ and 0, otherwise; and the probability $\mathrm{Pr}^{\lambda,\gamma}_{\mathcal{M}_{\mathcal{U}},s}[Paths^{\xi s'}_{\mathcal{M}_{\mathcal{U}}}]$ of traversing a finite path $\xi s'$ equals $\mathrm{Pr}^{\lambda,\gamma}_{\mathcal{M}_{\mathcal{U}},s}[Paths^{\xi}_{\mathcal{M}_{\mathcal{U}}}] \cdot \sum_{a \in \mathcal{A}_{\mathcal{U}}} \lambda(\xi)(a) \cdot \gamma(\xi,a)(s')$.

Observe that a scheduler does not choose an action but a *distribution* over actions. It is well-known [38] that such randomisation brings more power in the context of bisimulations. To the contrary, a nature is not allowed to randomise over the set of feasible distributions. This is in fact not necessary, since the set of feasible distributions is closed under convex combinations. A scheduler λ is said to be *deterministic* if $\lambda(\xi)(a) = 1$ for all finite paths ξ for some action a.

In order to model other quantitative measures of an *UwMDP*, we associate a reward to each weighted transition of a state. This is done by introducing a *reward structure*:

Definition 4. *A* reward structure *for an UwMDP is a function* $\mathbf{r}_{\mathcal{U}}: S_{\mathcal{U}} \times \mathcal{A}_{\mathcal{U}} \times \mathbb{N}_0 \to \mathbb{N}_0$ *that assigns to each state* $s \in S_{\mathcal{U}}$, *action* $a \in \mathcal{A}_{\mathcal{U}}(s)$, *and weight* $w \in \mathbb{N}_0$ *a reward* $\mathbf{r}_{\mathcal{U}}(s,a,w) > 0$.

Note that the definition of reward structure is quite flexible. We could easily define rewards independent of weights of transitions. Below defines the accumulated reward of a path before reaching a set of goal states.

Definition 5. *Given a reward structure* $\mathbf{r}_{\mathcal{U}}$ *and a path* $\xi = s_0 \mathbf{w}^{a_0}_{s_0 s_1} s_1 \mathbf{w}^{a_1}_{s_1 s_2} s_2 \cdots \in Paths^{inf}_{\mathcal{M}_{\mathcal{U}}}$ *and a set* $G_{\mathcal{U}} \subseteq S_{\mathcal{U}}$ *of states, we denote by* $rew(\xi, G_{\mathcal{U}})$ *the accumulated reward along* ξ *until* $G_{\mathcal{U}}$ *is reached; Formally, if* $\xi[t] \in G_{\mathcal{U}}$ *for some* $t \geq 0$ *then* $rew(\xi, G_{\mathcal{U}}) = \sum_{i=0}^{n-1} \mathbf{r}_{\mathcal{U}}(s_i, a_i, \mathbf{w}^{a_i}_{s_i s_{i+1}})$ *where* $n \in \mathbb{N}_0$ *is the smallest integer such that* $\xi[n] \in G_{\mathcal{U}}$; *otherwise* ∞ *if* $\xi[t] \notin G_{\mathcal{U}}$ *for every* $t \geq 0$,

Below presents an example of *UwMDP*.

Example 1. Figure 1 depicts an *UwMDP* containing three states with s being the initial one. Letters in curly braces besides each circle denote the labels of each state. Moreover, $W_{\mathcal{U}}(s,a,t) = [2,3]$, $W_{\mathcal{U}}(s,a,u) = [0,1]$, and $W_{\mathcal{U}}(s,b,u) = [1,2]$. A reward structure for the $\mathcal{M}_{\mathcal{U}}$ can be as follows: $\mathbf{r}_{\mathcal{U}}(s,a,2) = 3, \mathbf{r}_{\mathcal{U}}(s,a,3) = 1,\ \mathbf{r}_{\mathcal{U}}(s,a,4) = 5,\ \mathbf{r}_{\mathcal{U}}(s,b,1) = 4,$ $\mathbf{r}_{\mathcal{U}}(s,b,2) = 3$.

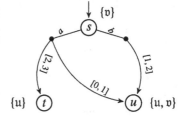

Fig. 1. An example of UwMDP $\mathcal{M}_{\mathcal{U}}$

---

[2] Here, $\mathcal{B}$ is the standard σ-algebra over $Paths^{inf}_{\mathcal{M}_{\mathcal{U}}}$ generated from the set of all cylinder sets $\{Paths^{\xi}_{\mathcal{M}_{\mathcal{U}}} \mid \xi \in Paths^{fin}_{\mathcal{M}_{\mathcal{U}}}\}$. The unique probability measure is obtained by the application of the extension theorem (see, e.g. [7]).

2.2   Interval Markov Decision Processes

In this subsection we shall introduce the notion of *Interval Markov Decision Processes*, which is similar as *UwMDPs* except all uncertainties are represented as probability intervals. Formally,

Definition 6 (*IMDP*). *An* Interval Markov Decision Process *(IMDP) $\mathcal{M}_I$ is a tuple $(S_I, \bar{s}_I, \mathcal{A}_I, AP_I, L_I, I)$, where S_I is a finite set of states, $\bar{s}_I \in S_I$ is the initial state, $\mathcal{A}_I$ is a finite set of actions, AP_I is a finite set of atomic propositions, $L_I \colon S_I \to 2^{AP_I}$ is a labelling function, and $I \colon S_I \times \mathcal{A}_I \times S_I \to \mathbb{I}$ is an interval transition probability function with $\mathbb{I}$ being the set of subintervals of $[0, 1]$. The set of available actions at state $s \in S_I$ is denoted by $\mathcal{A}_I(s)$.*

Furthermore, for each state s and action a, we write $s \xrightarrow{a} \mathfrak{h}_s^a$ if $\mathfrak{h}_s^a \in \Delta(S_I)$ is a *feasible distribution*, i.e. for each state s' we have $\mathfrak{h}_{ss'}^a = \mathfrak{h}_s^a(s') \in I(s, a, s')$. By $\mathcal{H}_s^a$, we denote the set of feasible distributions $\mathfrak{h}_s^a \in \Delta(S_I)$ for state s and action a.

As for *UwMDPs*, we need to define schedulers and natures for *IMDPs* to resolve non-deterministic transitions.

Definition 7 (*Scheduler and Nature in IMDPs*). *Given an IMDP $\mathcal{M}_I$, a* scheduler *is a function $\sigma \colon Paths_{\mathcal{M}_I}^{fin} \to \Delta(\mathcal{A}_I)$ that to each finite path ξ assigns a distribution over the set of actions. A* nature *is a function $\pi \colon Paths_{\mathcal{M}_I}^{fin} \times \mathcal{A}_I \to \Delta(S_I)$ that to each finite path ξ and action a assigns a feasible distribution, i.e. an element of $\mathcal{H}_s^a$ where $s = \xi\downarrow$. We denote by $\Sigma_{\mathcal{M}_I}$ the set of all schedulers and by $\Pi_{\mathcal{M}_I}$ the set of all natures.*

Given a state s_i of an IMDP, a *scheduler* σ, and a *nature* π, we proceed as follows: First, an action $a \in \mathcal{A}_I(s_i)$ is chosen non-deterministically by σ. Then, π resolves the uncertainties and chooses non-deterministically one feasible distribution $\mathfrak{h}_{s_i}^a \in \mathcal{H}_{s_i}^a$. Finally, the next state s_{i+1} is chosen randomly according to the distribution $\mathfrak{h}_{s_i}^a$.

A *path* in $\mathcal{M}_I$ is a finite or infinite sequence of the form $\xi = s_0 \mathfrak{h}_{s_0 s_1}^{a_0} s_1 \mathfrak{h}_{s_1 s_2}^{a_1} \cdots$ where $s_i \in S_I$, $a_i \in \mathcal{A}_I(s_i)$ and $\mathfrak{h}_{s_i s_{i+1}}^{a_i} > 0$ for each $i \geq 0$. For a finite path ξ, we extend notions $\xi\downarrow$, $\xi[i]$, $\xi(i)$ to *IMDPs*. The set of all finite paths and the set of all infinite paths in the given $\mathcal{M}_I$ are denoted by $Paths_{\mathcal{M}_I}^{fin}$ and $Paths_{\mathcal{M}_I}^{inf}$, respectively. Similarly, let $Paths_{\mathcal{M}_I}^{\xi} = \{\xi\xi' \mid \xi' \in Paths_{\mathcal{M}_I}^{inf}\}$ denote the set of paths that have the finite prefix $\xi \in Paths_{\mathcal{M}_I}^{fin}$.

Remark 2. The size of a given $\mathcal{M}_I$ is determined similarly as in Remark 1. Thus, the overall size $|\mathcal{M}_I|$ of an IMDP $\mathcal{M}_I$ is in $O(|S_I|^2 |\mathcal{A}_I|)$.

For an initial state s, a scheduler σ, and a nature π, the unique probability measure $\Pr_{\mathcal{M}_I, s}^{\sigma, \pi}$ can be defined similarly as for *UwMDPs*. A scheduler σ is said to be *deterministic* if $\sigma(\xi)(a) = 1$ for all finite paths ξ for some action a.

As in Definitions 4 and 5, we can also define reward structures for *IMDPs* and accumulated rewards for paths of *IMDPs*. The only difference is that reward structures are defined over states and actions, since transitions of *IMDPs* are not weighted. As we shall see in Sect. 3, this makes no essential difference. Furthermore, for both *IMDP* and *UwMDP* models, it is assumed in Definitions 3 and 7 that the nature is in general history-dependent. However, for the quantitative properties considered in this paper, it is indeed *memoryless*, i.e., the concrete probability values and weights do not depend on the history.

3   Reward-Bounded Reachability Probability

In this section we shall first define maximal reward-bounded reachability probabilities for *UwMDPs* formally, and then show that they can be computed efficiently in pseudo-polynomial time.

Below defines *maximal reward-bounded reachability probabilities for UwMDPs*:

Definition 8. *Let $\lambda \in \Lambda_{\mathcal{M}_\mathcal{U}}$ and $\gamma \in \Gamma_{\mathcal{M}_\mathcal{U}}$ be a scheduler and a nature of a given UwMDP $\mathcal{M}_\mathcal{U}$. Let $G_\mathcal{U}$ be a set of goal states. Define $\mathbf{Pr}^{\lambda,\gamma}_{\mathcal{M}_\mathcal{U},G_\mathcal{U}} : S_\mathcal{U} \times \mathbb{N}_0 \to [0,1]$ by: $\mathbf{Pr}^{\lambda,\gamma}_{\mathcal{M}_\mathcal{U},G_\mathcal{U}}(s,\mathcal{R}) := \mathbf{Pr}^{\lambda,\gamma}_{\mathcal{M}_\mathcal{U},s}(\Omega^\mathcal{R}_{G_\mathcal{U}})$ where $\Omega^\mathcal{R}_{G_\mathcal{U}} := \{\xi \in Paths^s_{\mathcal{M}_\mathcal{U}} \mid rew(\xi, G_\mathcal{U}) \leq \mathcal{R}\}$. Define $\mathbf{Pr}^{max}_{\mathcal{M}_\mathcal{U},G_\mathcal{U}}(s,\mathcal{R}) : S_\mathcal{U} \times \mathbb{N}_0 \to [0,1]$ by:*

$$\mathbf{Pr}^{max}_{\mathcal{M}_\mathcal{U},G_\mathcal{U}}(s,\mathcal{R}) := \sup_{\lambda \in \Lambda_{\mathcal{M}_\mathcal{U}}} \sup_{\gamma \in \Gamma_{\mathcal{M}_\mathcal{U}}} \mathbf{Pr}^{\lambda,\gamma}_{\mathcal{M}_\mathcal{U},G_\mathcal{U}}(s,\mathcal{R}). \tag{1}$$

From the definition, we can see that $\Omega^\mathcal{R}_{G_\mathcal{U}}$ is the set of paths which can reach $G_\mathcal{U}$ within the reward bound $\mathcal{R}$. Therefore, $\mathbf{Pr}^{max}_{\mathcal{M}_\mathcal{U},G_\mathcal{U}}(s,\mathcal{R})$ denotes the maximal probability of reaching states in $G_\mathcal{U}$ from s within $\mathcal{R}$ rewards. It is easy to see that $\Omega^\mathcal{R}_{G_\mathcal{U}}$ is measurable and all functions in Definition 8 are well-defined.

Remark 3. Here we follow the convention of model checking *MDPs* by considering all possible resolutions of non-determinism in an *UwMDP*. Differently, in *UwMDPs*, there are two levels of non-determinism resolved by schedulers and natures, respectively. Therefore, the maximal reachability probability is achieved by maximizing over all possible schedulers and natures as in Eq. (1). We mention that a distinction between schedulers and natures is not necessary. However, such a distinction increases readability of proofs and arguments discussed in the paper, which is also adopted in [36].

In order to compute maximal reward-bounded reachability probabilities, we could have transformed each *UwMDP* to its equivalent *wMDP*, for which existing algorithms [1] can be applied. However, as we mentioned before, the transformation may result in a *wMDP* exponentially larger than the original *UwMDP*, which makes the computation tedious. Instead, we show that each *UwMDP* $\mathcal{M}_\mathcal{U}$ can be alternatively transformed into an *IMDP* $\mathcal{M}_I$, where maximal reward-bounded reachability probabilities are preserved and can be computed efficiently. Notably, the size of the resulting $\mathcal{M}_I$ is in $O(|\mathcal{M}_\mathcal{U}| * W)$, i.e., pseudo polynomial, where

$$W = \max\{w \mid \exists s \xrightarrow{a,w} \mu \land \mathbf{r}_\mathcal{U}(s,a,w) \leq \mathcal{R}\} \tag{2}$$

for a given reward structure $r_\mathcal{U}$ and a reward bound $\mathcal{R}$. Clearly, $W \leq \max\{w \mid \exists s \xrightarrow{a,w} \mu\}$.

Now we describe in details how an *UwMDP* can be transformed into an *IMDP*.

Definition 9. (*Model Transformation*). *Given an UwMDP* $\mathcal{M}_\mathcal{U} = (S_\mathcal{U}, \mathcal{A}_\mathcal{U}, W_\mathcal{U}, \bar{s}_\mathcal{U}, AP_\mathcal{U}, L_\mathcal{U})$, *a given set of goal states* $G_\mathcal{U} \subseteq S_\mathcal{U}$, *a reward structure* $r_\mathcal{U}$, *and a reward bound* $\mathcal{R} \in \mathbb{N}_0$, *the corresponding IMDP* $\mathcal{M}_I = (S_I, \bar{s}_I, \mathcal{A}_I, AP_I, L_I, I)$ *is defined as follows:* $S_I = S_\mathcal{U}$, $\bar{s}_I = \bar{s}_\mathcal{U}$, $AP_I = AP_\mathcal{U}$, $L_I = L_\mathcal{U}$, $\mathcal{A}_I = \{a_w \mid a \in \mathcal{A}_\mathcal{U}, w \in \{1, \cdots, W\}\}$, *where* W *is defined as in Eq. (2). The reward structure* r_I *of* $\mathcal{M}_I$ *is defined by:* $r_I(s, a_w) = r_\mathcal{U}(s, a, w)$ *for each* $s \in S_I$ *and* $a_w \in \mathcal{A}_I(t)$. *Moreover,* $I(s, a_w, t) := (\frac{1}{w} \cdot W_\mathcal{U}(s, a, t)) \cap [0, 1]$ *for each* $s, t \in S_I$ *and* $a_w \in \mathcal{A}_I(s)$, *provided* $I(s, a_w, t) \neq \emptyset$. *Finally, in the resulting IMDP* $\mathcal{M}_I$, *the set of goal states is* $G_I = G_\mathcal{U}$ *and the initial state and the reward bound are the same as the ones in UwMDP* $\mathcal{M}_\mathcal{U}$.

Directly from Definition 9, we can see that the transformation can be done in time polynomial in both the size of the original *UwMDP* and W defined as in Eq. (2). Therefore, the size of the resultant *IMDP* is in $O(|\mathcal{M}_\mathcal{U}| W)$. Without loss of generality, in the sequel we assume $r(s, a, w) = w$, hence $W = \mathcal{R}$.

Example 1 (cont.). Consider the *UwMDP* $\mathcal{M}_\mathcal{U}$ depicted in Fig. 1. Assume the reward bound is $\mathcal{R} = 4$. The value of W is computed as

$$W = \max\{w \mid \exists s \xrightarrow{a,w} \mu \wedge r_\mathcal{U}(s, a, w) \leq 4\} = 3$$

According to the transformation described in Definition 9, we obtain an *IMDP* $\mathcal{M}_I$, which is depicted as in Fig. 2. The bold numbers indicated besides the actions are the reward structure for the generated *IMDP* $\mathcal{M}_I$.

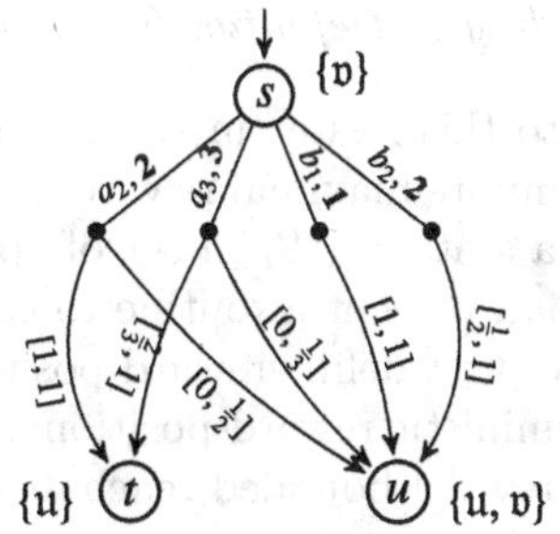

Fig. 2. The resultant *IMDP* $\mathcal{M}_I$ generated from the $\mathcal{M}_\mathcal{U}$ in Fig. 1.

Remark 4. In Definition 9, we show a procedure to transform an *UwMDP* to an *IMDP* preserving all maximal reward-bounded reachability probabilities with reward less than a given value. By setting W to be the largest possible reward associated to transitions in an *UwMDP* in Definition 9, we can obtain an equivalent *IMDP*, where all maximal reward-bounded reachability probabilities coincide with the original *UwMDP*. Indeed, despite that an *UwMDP* represents a discrete set of *wMDPs*, while an *IMDP* corresponds to a continuous set of *MDPs*, *UwMDPs* and *IMDPs* are closely related with respect to properties considered in this paper:

- Any *UwMDP* can be transformed into an *IMDP* by associating its transitions with proper rewards. However, in order to preserve all maximal reward-bounded reachability probabilities, the size of the *IMDP* may blow up, as its size depends on the largest reward in the *UwMDP*, which can be any positive integer in principle.

– Conversely, any *IMDP* essentially corresponds to an *MDP*, whose size may be exponentially larger than the original *IMDP*. It is obvious that any *MDP* can be transformed into a *wMDP*, which in turn can be seen as a special case of *UwMDP*. Thus, the transformation from *IMDPs* to *UwMDPs* may also cause an exponentially blow-up. For the moment, we do not know whether *IMDPs* can be transformed into *UwMDPs* directly without causing exponential blow-up.

Definition 10. *Let $\sigma \in \Sigma_{M_I}$ and $\pi \in \Pi_{M_I}$ be a scheduler and nature of a given IMDP M_I. Define the function $\mathbf{Pr}^{\sigma,\pi}_{M_I,G_I} : S_I \times \mathbb{N}_0 \to [0,1]$ by: $\mathbf{Pr}^{\sigma,\pi}_{M_I,G_I}(s,\mathcal{R}) := \mathbf{Pr}^{\sigma,\pi}_{M_I,s}(\Omega^{\mathcal{R}}_{G_I})$ where $\Omega^{\mathcal{R}}_{G_I} := \{\xi \in Paths^s_{M_I}| \ rew(\xi,G_I) \leq \mathcal{R}\}$. Define $\mathbf{Pr}^{max}_{M_I,G_I}(s,\mathcal{R}) : S_I \times \mathbb{N}_0 \to [0,1]$ by: $\mathbf{Pr}^{max}_{M_I,G_I}(s,\mathcal{R}) := \sup_{\sigma \in \Sigma_{M_I}} \sup_{\pi \in \Pi_{M_I}} \mathbf{Pr}^{\sigma,\pi}_{M_I,G_I}(s,\mathcal{R})$ for each $s \in S_I$ and $\mathcal{R} \in \mathbb{N}_0$.*

In the following proposition, we show that our *model transformation* preserves maximal reward-bounded reachability probabilities. More precisely, our transformation guarantees that all optimal resolutions in the *IMDP* can be projected back to the original given *UwMDP*. Formally,

Proposition 1. *Assume we are given an UwMDP $M_{\mathcal{U}} = (S_{\mathcal{U}}, \mathcal{A}_{\mathcal{U}}, W_{\mathcal{U}}, \bar{s}_{\mathcal{U}}, AP_{\mathcal{U}}, L_{\mathcal{U}})$, a state $s \in S_{\mathcal{U}}$, a set of goal states $G_{\mathcal{U}} \subseteq S_{\mathcal{U}}$, and a reward bound $\mathcal{R} \in \mathbb{N}_0$. Let $M_I = (S_I, \bar{s}_I, \mathcal{A}_I, AP_I, L_I, I)$ be the corresponding IMDP obtained according to Definition 9. Then: $\mathbf{Pr}^{max}_{M_{\mathcal{U}},G_{\mathcal{U}}}(s,\mathcal{R}) = \mathbf{Pr}^{max}_{M_I,G_I}(s,\mathcal{R})$.*

Due to this result, in the rest of this section, we turn our attention to *IMDPs* to compute maximal reward-bounded reachability probabilities. Given an *IMDP* M_I, a state $s \in S_I$, a set of goal states $G_I \subseteq S_I$, and a reward bound $\mathcal{R} \in \mathbb{N}_0$, we shall present a routine to compute $\mathbf{Pr}^{max}_{M_I,G_I}(s,\mathcal{R})$.

We first define reward-positional schedulers and natures and then show that deterministic reward-positional schedulers and natures suffice to obtain the maximal reward-bounded reachability probabilities in an *IMDP*.

Definition 11. *Suppose that $\mathfrak{R}[\xi]$ is total accumulated reward along a finite path ξ. A scheduler σ is reward-positional if and only if $\sigma(\xi) = \sigma(\xi')$ whenever $\xi\!\downarrow = \xi'\!\downarrow$ and $\mathfrak{R}[\xi] = \mathfrak{R}[\xi']$. Similarly, we can define reward-positional natures.*

In an intuitive description, reward-positional schedulers and natures make their decision entirely on the current state and the reward accumulated so far. Below we show that a deterministic reward-positional scheduler and nature suffices to achieve maximal reward-bounded reachability probability in an *IMDP*.

Theorem 1. *Given an IMDP M_I, a set of goal states $G_I \subseteq S_I$, there exist a deterministic reward-positional scheduler σ and nature π such that $\mathbf{Pr}^{max}_{M_I,G_I}(s,\mathcal{R}) = \mathbf{Pr}^{\sigma,\pi}_{M_I,s}(\Omega^{\mathcal{R}}_{G_I})$.*

Because of Theorem 1, we shall assume all schedulers and natures are deterministic reward-positional in the sequel.

Corollary 1. *Given an IMDP $\mathcal{M}_I$ equivalent to some UwMDP $\mathcal{M}_{\mathcal{U}}$, let $\sigma \in \Sigma_{\mathcal{M}_I}$ and $\pi \in \Pi_{\mathcal{M}_I}$ be a scheduler and nature of the given $\mathcal{M}_I$. The function $\mathbf{Pr}^{\sigma,\pi}_{\mathcal{M}_I,G_I}(s,\mathcal{R})$ satisfies the following conditions: 1. If $s \in G_I$, then $\mathbf{Pr}^{\sigma,\pi}_{\mathcal{M}_I,G_I}(s,\mathcal{R}) = 1$; 2. If $s \notin G_I$, then*

$$\mathbf{Pr}^{\sigma,\pi}_{\mathcal{M}_I,G_I}(s,\mathcal{R}) = \sum_{a_w \in \mathcal{A}_I(s) \wedge \mathbf{r}_I(s,a_w) \leq \mathcal{R}} \sigma(s)(a_w) \cdot \left\{ \sum_{s' \in S_I} \mathfrak{h}^{a_w}_{ss'} \cdot \mathbf{Pr}^{\sigma,\pi}_{\mathcal{M}_I,G_I}(s',\mathcal{R}-\mathbf{r}_I(s,a_w)) \right\}$$

where $\mathfrak{h}^{a_w}_{ss'}$ is a feasible transition probability resolved by $\pi(s,a_w)$, i.e., $\mathfrak{h}^{a_w}_{ss'} = \pi(s,a_w)(s')$.

In the following theorem, we present the fixed-point characterization for $\mathbf{Pr}^{max}_{\mathcal{M}_I,G_I}(s,\mathcal{R})$.

Theorem 2. *Given an IMDP $\mathcal{M}_I$ equivalent to some UwMDP $\mathcal{M}_{\mathcal{U}}$, the function $\mathbf{Pr}^{max}_{\mathcal{M}_I,G_I}(\cdot,\cdot)$ is the least fixed-point (w.r.t $\leq$) of the high-order operator $\mathfrak{F}_{G_I}(h) : [S_I \times \mathbb{N}_0 \to [0,1]] \to [S_I \times \mathbb{N}_0 \to [0,1]]$ defined as follows:• $\mathfrak{F}_{G_I}(h)(s,\mathcal{R}) = 1$ for all $s \in G_I$ and $\mathcal{R} \in \mathbb{N}_0$; • For any given $s \notin G_I$,*

$$\mathfrak{F}_{G_I}(h)(s,\mathcal{R}) = \max_{a_w \in \mathcal{A}_I(s) \wedge \mathbf{r}_I(s,a_w) \leq \mathcal{R}} \max_{\mathfrak{h}^{a_w}_s \in \mathcal{H}^{a_w}_s} \sum_{s' \in S_I} \mathfrak{h}^{a_w}_{ss'} \cdot h(s',\mathcal{R}-\mathbf{r}_I(s,a_w))$$

for each $h : S_I \times \mathbb{N}_0 \to [0,1]$.

We show that the problem of computing the maximal reward-bounded reachability probability in an *IMDP* can be reduced to solving a sequence of linear programming problems. The algorithm is shown in Algorithm 1. Intuitively, we let *probs* store all computed reachability probabilities such that $probs[i][r]$ is the maximal probability of reaching G_I from s_i within the reward bound r. We compute *probs* inductively starting from $r = 1$ until $r = \mathcal{R}$. At each step all probabilities $probs[i][r]$ are computed using values $probs[i][r']$ with $r' < r$ which have been computed before. From the moment we fix a bound r. Let x_i denote the probability $probs[i][r]$. Let $y_{i,j,a,w}$ be the probability of going to s_j by choosing the transition with label a_w when at state s_i. Hence the constraint in line 8 has to be satisfied. Line 9 guarantees the probability mass from s_i sums up to 1. Since $y_{i,j,a,w}$ is not arbitrary, but has to be within the given bound, which is guaranteed by line 10.

In the next lemma, we discuss the time complexity of the proposed routine to compute $\mathbf{Pr}^{max}_{\mathcal{M}_I,G_I}(s,\mathcal{R})$. Formally,

Lemma 1. *Algorithm 1 is sound and complete, and it is guaranteed to terminate in time polynomial with respect to the size of IMDP $\mathcal{M}_I$ and the reward bound $\mathcal{R}$.*

As the transformation in Definition 9 is also pseudo polynomial, we obtain the main result of this paper.

Theorem 3. *Maximal reward-bounded reachability probabilities for an UwMDP $\mathcal{M}_{\mathcal{U}}$ can be computed in pseudo polynomial time $O(|\mathcal{M}_{\mathcal{U}}|\mathcal{R}^2)$.*

Algorithm 1. Computing maximal reward-bounded reachability

Input: An *IMDP* M_I, a state s_0, a set of goal states G_I, and a reward bound $\mathcal{R}$.
Output: The maximal probability of reaching G_I from s_0 within the bound $\mathcal{R}$.

1 **begin**
2     $n \leftarrow |S_I|$;
3     $\forall 0 \leq i < n, 0 \leq r \leq \mathcal{R}.probs[i][r] = (1$ if $s_i \in G_I$ else $0)$;
4   **for** $(r = 1$ *to* $\mathcal{R})$ **do**
5        $\forall 0 \leq i < n.probs[i][r] = x_i$, where x_i is determined by the following LP problem;
6        $\min \sum_{0 \leq i < n} x_i$;
7   **for** $(0 \leq i < n$ and $a_w \in \mathcal{A}_I(s_i)$ with $\mathbf{r}_I(s_i, a_w) \leq r)$ **do**
8           $x_i \geq \sum_{0 \leq j < n} probs[j][r - \mathbf{r}_I(s_i, a_w)] \cdot y_{i,j,a,w}$;
9           $\sum_{0 \leq j < n} y_{i,j,a,w} = 1$;
10           $\forall 0 \leq j < n.y_{i,j,a,w} \in I(s_i, a_w, s_j)$;
11   **return** $probs[0][\mathcal{R}]$;

Remark 5. The extension of Algorithm 1 to deal with minimal reward-bounded reachability is straightforward. We note that extreme reachability probabilities without reward bounds in *UwMDPs* can also be computed efficiently using the technique presented in [36]. The only change we need to make is Definition 9, where a reward bound is necessary for the transformation. However, if the reward bound is not available, we can simply let $\mathcal{R}$ be the maximal weight appearing in the given *UwMDP*. After that, the algorithm in [36] can be applied directly. Along the same routine in [1], the algorithm can be extended to deal with full PRCTL. We omit the details in this paper.

4 Compositional Minimization for Uncertain Weighted MDPs

In this section we extend the notion of probabilistic bisimulation [39] to *UwMDPs*. We first show its compositionality with respect to a parallel operator, then give a decision algorithm for it. Finally, we discuss the complexity of the algorithm.

4.1 Probabilistic Bisimulation

Below defines bisimulation relations over states of an *UwMDP*, which is an extension of the definition in [12]. For simplicity, we omit reward structures in this section, which can be integrated easily.

Definition 12. *Let* $M_\mathcal{U} := (S_\mathcal{U}, \mathcal{A}_\mathcal{U}, W_\mathcal{U}, \bar{s}_\mathcal{U}, AP_\mathcal{U}, L_\mathcal{U})$ *be an UwMDP. Let* $R \subseteq S_\mathcal{U} \times S_\mathcal{U}$. *R is a bisimulation iff* $s \ R \ t$ *implies:* • $L_\mathcal{U}(s) = L_\mathcal{U}(t)$; • *whenever* $s \xrightarrow{a,w} \mu$, *there exists* $t \xrightarrow{a,w}_c \nu$ *such that* $\mu \equiv_R \nu$; • *symmetrically* for t. Two states s and t are bisimilar, written as $s \sim t$, iff there exists a bisimulation R such that $s\ R\ t$.

The following proposition is straightforward from Definition 12.

Proposition 2. $\sim$ is an equivalence relation.

4.2 Compositionality

In this subsection we first introduce the notion of parallel operator for UwMDPs, and then we show that bisimulation in Definition 12 is compositional with respect to the parallel operator.

Below introduces the parallel operator for UwMDPs inspired by the one defined in [33] for probabilistic automata.

Definition 13. Let $\mathcal{M}_{\mathcal{U}}^i$ with $i \in \{0,1\}$ be two UwMDPs. Let $A \subseteq \mathcal{A}_{\mathcal{U}}^0 \cap \mathcal{A}_{\mathcal{U}}^1$ be a set of actions. The parallel composition of $\mathcal{M}_{\mathcal{U}}^0$ and $\mathcal{M}_{\mathcal{U}}^1$ by enforcing synchronization on actions in A, denoted $\mathcal{M}_{\mathcal{U}}^0 \parallel_A \mathcal{M}_{\mathcal{U}}^1$, is an UwMDP $\mathcal{M}_{\mathcal{U}}$, where • $S_{\mathcal{U}} = S_{\mathcal{U}}^0 \times S_{\mathcal{U}}^1$; • $\mathcal{A}_{\mathcal{U}} = \mathcal{A}_{\mathcal{U}}^0 \cup \mathcal{A}_{\mathcal{U}}^1$; • whenever $a \in A$ and $\forall i \in \{0,1\}.W_{\mathcal{U}}^i(s^i,a,t^i) = [w_l^i, w_h^i]$, then $W_{\mathcal{U}}(s^0 \parallel_A s^1, a, t^0 \parallel_A t^1) = [w_l, w_h]$, where $w_l = w_l^0 \times w_l^1$ and $w_h = w_h^0 \times w_h^1$; • whenever $a \notin A$ and $\exists i \in \{0,1\}.W_{\mathcal{U}}^i(s^i,a,t^i) = [w_l^i, w_h^i]$, then $W_{\mathcal{U}}(s^0 \parallel_A s^1, a, t^0 \parallel_A t^1) = [w_l^i, w_h^i]$, where $t^{1-i} = s^{1-i}$; • $\bar{s}_{\mathcal{U}} = \bar{s}_{\mathcal{U}}^0 \parallel_A \bar{s}_{\mathcal{U}}^1$; • $L_{\mathcal{U}}(s^0 \parallel_A s^1) = L_{\mathcal{U}}(s^0) \cup L_{\mathcal{U}}(s^1)$.

Definition 13 resembles the definition of parallel operator in [33] in the sense that weights are handled in the same way as probabilities. Since weights in our models play the role of resolving non-deterministic transitions in a probabilistic manner. This explains why weight bounds are multiplied in Definition 13.

Let $\mathcal{M}_{\mathcal{U}}^i$ with $i \in \{0,1\}$ and A be as in Definition 13. We say $\sim$ is compositional with respect to $\parallel_A$ iff for any $s,t \in S_{\mathcal{U}}^0$, whenever $s \sim t$, then $s \parallel_A u \sim t \parallel_A u$ for any $u \in S_{\mathcal{U}}^1$. Below we show that $\sim$ is indeed compositional.

Theorem 4. $\sim$ is compositional.

4.3 Decision Algorithm

In this subsection we show that bisimulations defined in Definition 12 can be decided in polynomial time. Our algorithm follows the classical partition-refinement approach [12,19,25,27].

Before presenting the algorithm we give an alternative definition of bisimulation and show that it is equivalent to Definition 12. Let $W_{\mathcal{U}}^l(s,s') = w_l$ and $W_{\mathcal{U}}^h(s,a,s') = w_h$, where $W_{\mathcal{U}}(s,a,s') = [w_l, w_h]$.

Lemma 2. Let $\mathcal{M}_{\mathcal{U}} := (S_{\mathcal{U}}, \mathcal{A}_{\mathcal{U}}, W_{\mathcal{U}}, \bar{s}_{\mathcal{U}}, AP_{\mathcal{U}}, L_{\mathcal{U}})$ be an UwMDP. Let $R \subseteq S_{\mathcal{U}} \times S_{\mathcal{U}}$ be an equivalence relation. R is a bisimulation iff $s\ R\ t$ implies • $L_{\mathcal{U}}(s) = L_{\mathcal{U}}(t)$; • $W_{\mathcal{U}}^l(s,a,C) = W_{\mathcal{U}}^l(t,a,C)$ and $W_{\mathcal{U}}^h(s,a,C) = W_{\mathcal{U}}^h(t,a,C)$ for each $C \in S_{\mathcal{U}}/R$, where $W_{\mathcal{U}}^l(s,a,C) = \sum_{s' \in C} W_{\mathcal{U}}^l(s,a,s')$ and $W_{\mathcal{U}}^h(s,a,C) = \sum_{s' \in C} W_{\mathcal{U}}^h(s,a,s')$.

Algorithm 2. Deciding bisimulation

Input: An *UwMDP* $\mathcal{M}_\mathcal{U} := (S_\mathcal{U}, \mathcal{A}_\mathcal{U}, W_\mathcal{U}, \bar{s}_\mathcal{U}, \text{AP}_\mathcal{U}, L_\mathcal{U})$, two states $s, t \in S_\mathcal{U}$.
Output: '*true*' if $s \sim t$, or '*false*' otherwise.
1 **begin**
2 | Partition $\leftarrow \{\{S_\mathcal{U}\}\}$;
3 | splitter $\leftarrow$ FINDSPLITTER(Partition);
4 | **while** (splitter $\neq \emptyset$) **do**
5 | | Partition $\leftarrow$ REFINE($\mathcal{M}_\mathcal{U}$, Partition, splitter);
6 | | splitter $\leftarrow$ FINDSPLITTER($\mathcal{M}_\mathcal{U}$, Partition);
7 | **if** *there exists* $C \in$ Partition *such that* $s, t \in C$ **then**
8 | | **return** *true*;
9 | **else**
10 | | **return** *false*;

Algorithm 3. Procedure FINDSPLITTER

Input: An *UwMDP* $\mathcal{M}_\mathcal{U} := (S_\mathcal{U}, \mathcal{A}_\mathcal{U}, W_\mathcal{U}, \bar{s}_\mathcal{U}, \text{AP}_\mathcal{U}, L_\mathcal{U})$ and Partition.
Output: A splitter of Partition with respect to $\sim$.
1 **begin**
2 | **for** ($C \in$ Partition *and* $s, t \in C$) **do**
3 | | **for** ($C' \in$ Partition *and* $a \in \mathcal{A}_\mathcal{U}$) **do**
4 | | | **if** $W_\mathcal{U}^l(s, a, C') \neq W_\mathcal{U}^l(t, a, C')$ *or* $W_\mathcal{U}^h(s, a, C') \neq W_\mathcal{U}^h(t, a, C')$ **then**
5 | | | | **return** (C', a);
6 | **return** $\emptyset$;

Because of Lemma 2, we can now present the algorithm to check whether two states are bisimilar. The key procedure is FINDSPLITTER presented in Algorithm 3, which finds a pair (C', a) of block in the current partition and an action a distinguishing two states in a block. The found splitter (C', a) is then used by Algorithm 2 to further refine the current partition. The algorithm terminates if no splitter can be found and the current partition stays stable.

Even though *UwMDP*s offer a compact manner to encode uncertainties appearing in a weighted MDP, which may be exponentially larger than its corresponding *UwMDP*, we do not need to pay extra costs to compute bisimulation relations on *UwMDP*s. Formally, Algorithm 2 has the same complexity as Algorithm 1 in [12], where n and m are the numbers of states and (uncertain) transitions in an *UwMDP*, respectively.

Theorem 5. *Algorithm 2 terminates in time* $O(n(n^2 + m))$ *in the worst case.*

5   Case Studies

The goal of this experiment is two-fold: (1) quantitatively evaluate the impact of uncertainty on the results of verification of reward-bounded reachability probabilities of *UwMDP*s; (2) assess the impact of compositional minimization, as a pre-processing step, on speeding up the run time of the model checking algorithm. Our prototype is built upon the tool presented in [36], which is able to model check PCTL properties over *IMDP*s. The tool is implemented in Python and relies on MOSEK (http://www.mosek.com) to solve all linear programming problems. All experiments were obtained on a laptop with an Intel i7-4600U 2.1 GHz CPU and 4 GB RAM running Ubuntu.

Our first case study is inspired by "Autonomous Nondeterministic Tour Guides" (ANTG) in [11], which models a complex museum with a variety of collections. Models in [11] are *MDP*s. In our experiment, we will insert some uncertainties in a way that we will describe in details soon. Due to the popularity of the museum, there are many visitors at the same time. Different visitors may have different preferences of arts. We assume the museum divides all collections into different categories so that visitors can choose what they would like to visit and pay tickets according to their preferences. In order to obtain the best experience, a visitor can first assign certain weights to all categories denoting their preferences to the museum, and then design the best strategy for a target. However, the preference of a sort of arts to a visitor may depend on many factors like price, weather, or the length of queue at that moment etc., hence it is hard to assign fixed values to these preferences. In our model we allow uncertainties of preferences such that their values may lie in an interval.

For simplicity we assume all collections are organized in an $n \times n$ square with $n \geq 10$. Let $m = \frac{n-1}{2}$. We assume all collections at (i, j) are assigned with a weight 1 if $|i - m| > \frac{n}{5}$ or $|j - m| > \frac{n}{5}$, with a weight 2 if $|i - m| \in (\frac{n}{10}, \frac{n}{5}]$ or $|j - m| \in (\frac{n}{10}, \frac{n}{5}]$; otherwise they are assigned with a weight interval $[2, 4]$. In other words, we expect collections in the middle will be more popular and subject to more uncertainties than others. Furthermore, we assume that people at each location (i, j) have two non-deterministic choices: either move to the north and west, or to the north and east if $i \geq j$, while if $i \leq j$, they can move either to the south and west, or to the south and east. Therefore, for a model with parameter n, it has n^2 states in total and roughly $2n^2$ transitions, 2% of which are associated with uncertain weights. Notice that a transition with uncertain weights essentially corresponds to several transitions with concrete weights. In each ANTG model, the 2% transitions with uncertain transitions contribute to about 20% of transitions in the resultant *wMDP*.

We define a reward structure denoting the reward one can obtain by visiting each collection. For simplicity, we let the reward be the same as the weight of a collection. Let the point $(0, 0)$ be the entrance and $(n - 1, n - 1)$ the exit. We can ask questions like "Whether it is possible to go through the museum, i.e., from the entrance to the exit, with probability greater than 0.9, while the accumulated reward is not greater than $\mathcal{R}$, i.e., $\mathbf{P}_{\geq 0.9}(\mathsf{F}^{\leq \mathcal{R}} exit)$".

Our experiment results without computing bisimulation quotients are shown in Table 1, which presents the time (in minute) taken to compute $\mathbf{P}_{\geq 0.9}(\mathsf{F}^{\leq \mathcal{R}} exit)$ with corresponding reward bounds and models of different sizes. For each case, we keep increasing the bound until the probability is greater than 0.9. All cells marked with '-' denote cases that we did not reach. We also implemented the

Table 1. Experiment results without bisimulation minimization(in minute)

n \ r	50	100	150	200	250	300	350	400	450	500	550
10	0.08	-	-	-	-	-	-	-	-	-	-
20	0.17	0.42	-	-	-	-	-	-	-	-	-
30	0.32	0.97	1.68	-	-	-	-	-	-	-	-
40	0.56	1.62	3.37	5.04	-	-	-	-	-	-	-
50	1.11	2.85	5.68	8.98	12.33	-	-	-	-	-	-
60	1.85	4.58	8.79	14.47	20.63	26.71	-	-	-	-	-
70	2.95	7.13	12.95	21.63	31.73	42.30	52.69	-	-	-	-
80	5.81	12.59	22.62	37.08	56.42	74.72	94.01	114.19	-	-	-
90	7.52	17.78	31.54	48.99	70.71	97.10	124.47	154.64	182.80	211.43	-
100	11.55	26.94	46.08	69.88	100.78	140.73	182.40	225.46	266.39	308.30	356.15

Table 2. Experiment results without bisimulation minimization(in minute)

n \ r	50	100	150	200	250	300	350	400	450	500	550	BisimMin	Ratio
10	0.05	-	-	-	-	-	-	-	-	-	-	0.00	0.63
20	0.15	0.30	-	-	-	-	-	-	-	-	-	0.0	0.71
30	0.13	0.41	0.72	-	-	-	-	-	-	-	-	0.14	0.43
40	0.60	1.55	2.49	3.45	-	-	-	-	-	-	-	0.48	0.68
50	0.45	1.53	3.95	6.78	9.20	-	-	-	-	-	-	1.03	0.75
60	1.43	4.02	7.41	11.68	16.09	20.21	-	-	-	-	-	2.40	0.76
70	3.81	8.55	14.51	21.06	29.05	37.27	45.16	-	-	-	-	4.21	0.86
80	6.74	13.09	19.39	27.10	36.07	44.88	52.48	60.01	-	-	-	5.27	0.53
90	5.51	13.59	23.39	34.32	47.03	61.20	73.67	86.21	98.89	112.90	-	6.50	0.53
100	11.45	25.04	40.85	57.72	77.02	98.34	120.86	143.89	166.11	184.50	202.85	9.66	0.60

algorithm to compute bisimulation relations. Table 2 presents the experiment results, where bisimulation minimization was conducted before performing verification. In this figure, reported time is sum of the time spent to conduct the minimization and the time spent to check the quotient systems. The column "BisimMin" of Tables 2 denotes the time spent to conduct the minimization, while the column "Ratio" shows ratios between time to compute reachability probabilities with and without bisimulation minimization. All values in column "Ratio" are obtained by comparing time corresponding to the maximal reached reward for each case in Tables 1 and 2. For instance, when $n = 80$, we divide 60.01 by 114.19 ($c = 400$), hence 0.53 is obtained. Similarly, for the case with $n = 100$ and $c = 550$, bisimulation minimization accelerated the verification for more than 40 %. The time of computing reachability probabilities without/with computing bisimulation quotients is visualized in Fig. 3a for $n = 90$ where "BM" denotes "bisimulation minimization". The counterpart for $n = 100$ is depicted in Fig. 3b. We shall see that the larger of the model and the reward bound, the more time we will save by applying bisimulation minimization.

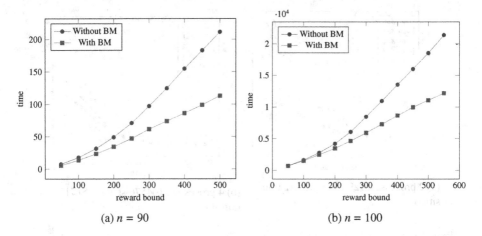

(a) $n = 90$ (b) $n = 100$

Fig. 3. Performance difference with and without bisimulation minimization (in minute)

To the best of our knowledge, there is no algorithm or tool, which can deal with *UwMDPs* directly. However, we can reduce the model checking of *UwMDPs* to checking their equivalent *wMDPs*. For instance if $W_{\mathcal{W}}(s, a, s_1) = [1, 2]$ and $W_{\mathcal{W}}(s, a, s_2) = [2, 3]$, then essentially s has four non-deterministic transitions: $s \xrightarrow{a,3} \{\frac{1}{3} : s_1, \frac{2}{3} : s_2\}$, $s \xrightarrow{a,4} \{\frac{1}{4} : s_1, \frac{3}{4} : s_2\}$, $s \xrightarrow{a,4} \{\frac{1}{2} : s_1, \frac{1}{2} : s_2\}$, and $s \xrightarrow{a,5} \{\frac{2}{5} : s_1, \frac{3}{5} : s_2\}$. After resolving all uncertainties, we can apply the existing algorithm [1] to compute maximal reward-bounded reachability probabilities. Obviously, this step may cause an exponential blow-up. Indeed, our experiment showed that when the proportion of states with uncertain weights in an *UwMDP* is not trivial, such enumeration is very time consuming. For instance when $n = 10$ and $\mathcal{R} = 100$, our algorithm took around 135 seconds, while the naïve approach took more than 10 min, provided that all transitions are associated with a weight interval [1, 6].

In the second case study we consider *randomized consensus protocol* [2,32]. Models are obtained from PRISM benchmarks by adding some uncertainties to the transition probabilities. In order to evaluate how the algorithm scales with respect to weight intervals of different sizes, i.e., their lower and upper bounds and lengths, we performed experiments on models after inserting weight intervals of various sizes. Specifically, instead of using a fair coin, we adopt an unfair coin with uncertainties: After each coin tossing, head and tail will occur with probabilities according to weights in $[6 - \delta, 7 - \delta]$ and $[8 - \delta, 10 - \delta]$, respectively, where δ is an integer in $[0, 5]$. We consider the minimal probability of reaching a set of goal states within a given reward bound, where the goal states are those labeled by atomic propositions "finished" and "all_coins_equal_0". The experiment results are shown in Fig. 4, for which we can see that the amount of uncertainties has an important impact on the verification time, especially when the reward bound is large. This is as expected since the size of the underlying

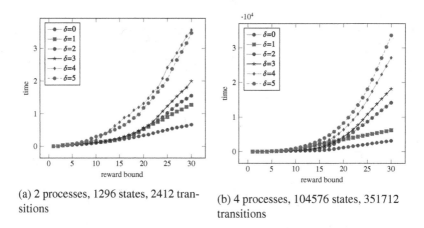

(a) 2 processes, 1296 states, 2412 transitions

(b) 4 processes, 104576 states, 351712 transitions

Fig. 4. Experiment results of randomized consensus protocols (in seconds)

wMDP of an *UwMDP* increases exponentially with respect to the amount of uncertainties in the *UwMDP*.

We have omitted most details of randomized consensus protocol. We refer interested readers to [31] for detailed descriptions.

6   Concluding Remarks

In this paper, we established a fixed-point characterization for maximal reward-bounded reachability probabilities in *UwMDPs* as well as a pseudo polynomial algorithm to compute these probabilities. In this work, we assumed *cooperative* resolution of non-determinisms in which both scheduler and nature are playing *together* to maximize the model performance, i.e., reachability probabilities. We propose a notion of bisimulation relations of *UwMDPs* and show that they are compositional and can be computed efficiently in polynomial time. We demonstrate feasibility of our theory via some case studies. All results proposed in this paper can be extended to model check the Probabilistic Reward Computation Tree Logic (PRCTL) [1] in a standard way [3].

As future work, we aim to address a richer formalism for uncertainties such as likelihood or ellipsoidal uncertainties to capture a less conservative analysis. Optimal control of *UwMDPs* is another interesting direction for future work in which we aim to synthesize a strategy for *UwMDPs* such that the performance of the model becomes optimized under all resolution of uncertainties. Also, we plan to extend our approach to the multi-objective setting, e.g. multi-objective reachability problem under the presence of uncertainties, and to apply the compositional minimization approach to further complicated case studies.

Acknowledgments. This work is supported by the EU 7th Framework Programme under grant agreements 295261 (MEALS) and 318490 (SENSATION), the DFG

Transregional Collaborative Research Centre SFB/TR 14 AVACS, the CAS/SAFEA International Partnership Program for Creative Research Teams, the Australian Research Council under Grant DP130102764, and the National Natural Science Foundation of China under Grant Nos. 61428208, 61472473 and 61361136002.

References

1. Andova, S., Hermanns, H., Katoen, J.-P.: Discrete-time rewards model-checked. In: Larsen, K.G., Niebert, P. (eds.) FORMATS 2003. LNCS, vol. 2791. Springer, Heidelberg (2004)
2. Aspnes, J., Herlihy, M.: Fast randomized consensus using shared memory. J. Algorithms **11**(3), 441–461 (1990)
3. Baier, C., Katoen, J.-P.: Principles of Model Checking. The MIT Press, Cambridge (2008)
4. Baier, C., Größer, M., Leucker, M., Bollig, B., Ciesinski, F.: Controller synthesis for probabilistic systems. In: Proceedings of IFIP TCS 2004. Kluwer (2004)
5. Benedikt, M., Lenhardt, R., Worrell, J.: LTL model checking of interval markov chains. In: Piterman, N., Smolka, S.A. (eds.) TACAS 2013 (ETAPS 2013). LNCS, vol. 7795, pp. 32–46. Springer, Heidelberg (2013)
6. Bernardo, M., Gorrieri, R.: Extended markovian process algebra. In: Sassone, V., Montanari, U. (eds.) CONCUR 1996. LNCS, vol. 1119. Springer, Heidelberg (1996)
7. Billingsley, P.: Probability and Measure. John Wiley and Sons, New York (1979)
8. Böde, E., Herbstritt, M., Hermanns, H., Johr, S., Peikenkamp, T., Pulungan, R., Rakow, J., Wimmer, R., Becker, B.: Compositional dependability evaluation for STATEMATE. ITSE **35**(2), 274–292 (2009)
9. Boudali, H., Crouzen, P., Stoelinga, M.: A rigorous, compositional, and extensible framework for dynamic fault tree analysis. IEEE TDSC **7**(2), 128–143 (2010)
10. Bozga, M., David, A., Hartmanns, A., Hermanns, H., Larsen, K.G., Legay, A., Tretmans, J.: State-of-the-art tools and techniques for quantitative modeling and analysis of embedded systems. In: DATE, pp. 370–375. IEEE, March 2012
11. Cantino, A.S., Roberts, D.L., Isbell, C.L.: Autonomous nondeterministic tour guides: improving quality of experience with TTD-MDPs. In: AAMAS, p. 22. IFAAMAS (2007)
12. Cattani, S., Segala, R.: Decision algorithms for probabilistic bisimulation. In: Brim, L., Jančar, P., Křetínský, M., Kučera, A. (eds.) CONCUR 2002. LNCS, vol. 2421, pp. 371–385. Springer, Heidelberg (2002)
13. Chehaibar, G., Garavel, H., Mounier, L., Tawbi, N., Zulian, F.: Specification and verification of the powerscale bus arbitration protocol: an industrial experiment with LOTOS. In: FORTE, pp. 435–450 (1996)
14. Chen, T., Han, T., Kwiatkowska, M.: On the complexity of model checking interval-valued discrete time Markov chains. Inf. Process. Lett. **113**(7), 210–216 (2013)
15. Delahaye, B., Katoen, J.-P., Larsen, K.G., Legay, A., Pedersen, M.L., Sher, F., Wasowski, A.: New results on abstract probabilistic automata. In: ACSD, pp. 118–127 (2011)
16. Delahaye, B., Katoen, J.-P., Larsen, K.G., Legay, A., Pedersen, M.L., Sher, F., Wąsowski, A.: Abstract probabilistic automata. In: Jhala, R., Schmidt, D. (eds.) VMCAI 2011. LNCS, vol. 6538, pp. 324–339. Springer, Heidelberg (2011)
17. Delahaye, B., Larsen, K.G., Legay, A., Pedersen, M.L., Wąsowski, A.: Decision problems for interval markov chains. In: Dediu, A.-H., Inenaga, S., Martín-Vide, C. (eds.) LATA 2011. LNCS, vol. 6638, pp. 274–285. Springer, Heidelberg (2011)

18. Fecher, H., Leucker, M., Wolf, V.: Don't know in probabilistic systems. In: Valmari, A. (ed.) SPIN. LNCS, vol. 3925, pp. 71–88. Springer, Heidelberg (2006)

19. Gebler, D., Hashemi, V., Turrini, A.: Computing behavioral relations for probabilistic concurrent systems. In: Remke, A., Stoelinga, M. (eds.) Stochastic Model Checking. LNCS, vol. 8453, pp. 117–155. Springer, Heidelberg (2014)

20. Givan, R., Leach, S.M., Dean, T.L.: Bounded-parameter markov decision processes. Artif. Intell. **122**(1–2), 71–109 (2000)

21. Hahn, E.M., Han, T., Zhang, L.: Synthesis for PCTL in parametric markov decision processes. In: Bobaru, M., Havelund, K., Holzmann, G.J., Joshi, R. (eds.) NFM 2011. LNCS, vol. 6617, pp. 146–161. Springer, Heidelberg (2011)

22. Hahn, E.M., Li, Y., Schewe, S., Turrini, A., Zhang, L.: iscasMc: a web-based probabilistic model checker. In: Jones, C., Pihlajasaari, P., Sun, J. (eds.) FM 2014. LNCS, vol. 8442, pp. 312–317. Springer, Heidelberg (2014)

23. Hansson, H., Jonsson, B.: A logic for reasoning about time and reliability. Formal Asp. Comput. **6**(5), 512–535 (1994)

24. Hashemi, V., Hatefi, H., Krčál, J.: Probabilistic bisimulations for PCTL model checking of interval mdps. In: SynCoP, pp. 19–33. EPTCS (2014)

25. Hashemi, V., Hermanss, H., Turrini, A.: On the efficiency of deciding probabilistic automata weak bisimulation. Electron. Commun. EASST, vol. 66 (2013)

26. Jonsson, B., Larsen, K.G.: Specification and refinement of probabilistic processes. In: LICS, pp. 266–277 (1991)

27. Kanellakis, P.C., Smolka, S.A.: CCS expressions, finite state processes, and three problems of equivalence. I&C **86**, 43–68 (1990)

28. Katoen, J.-P., Klink, D., Neuhäußer, M.R.: Compositional abstraction for stochastic systems. In: Ouaknine, J., Vaandrager, F.W. (eds.) FORMATS 2009. LNCS, vol. 5813, pp. 195–211. Springer, Heidelberg (2009)

29. Kozine, I.O., Utkin, L.V.: Interval-valued finite markov chains. Reliable Comput. **8**(2), 97–113 (2011)

30. Chatterjee, K., Sen, K., Henzinger, T.A.: Model-Checking ω-regular properties of interval markov chains. In: Amadio, R.M. (ed.) FOSSACS 2008. LNCS, vol. 4962, pp. 302–317. Springer, Heidelberg (2008)

31. Kwiatkowska, M., Norman, G., Parker, D.: PRISM 4.0: verification of probabilistic real-time systems. In: Gopalakrishnan, G., Qadeer, S. (eds.) CAV 2011. LNCS, vol. 6806, pp. 585–591. Springer, Heidelberg (2011)

32. Kwiatkowska, M., Norman, G., Segala, R.: Automated verification of a randomized distributed consensus protocol using cadence SMV and PRISM. In: Berry, G., Comon, H., Finkel, A. (eds.) CAV 2001. LNCS, vol. 2102, pp. 194–206. Springer, Heidelberg (2001)

33. Lynch, N.A., Segala, R., Vaandrager, F.W.: Compositionality for probabilistic automata. In: Amadio, R.M., Lugiez, D. (eds.) CONCUR 2003. LNCS, vol. 2761, pp. 208–221. Springer, Heidelberg (2003)

34. Marsan, M.A., Conte, G., Balbo, G.: A class of generalized stochastic Petri nets for the performance evaluation of multiprocessor systems. ACM Trans. Comput. Syst. **2**(2), 93–122 (1984)

35. Nilim, A., El Ghaoui, L.: Robust control of Markov decision processes with uncertain transition matrices. Oper. Res. **53**(5), 780–798 (2005)

36. Puggelli, A., Li, W., Sangiovanni-Vincentelli, A.L., Seshia, S.A.: Polynomial-time verification of PCTL properties of MDPs with convex uncertainties. In: Sharygina, N., Veith, H. (eds.) CAV 2013. LNCS, vol. 8044, pp. 527–542. Springer, Heidelberg (2013)

37. Puterman, M.L.: Markov Decision Processes: Discrete Stochastic Dynamic Programming. Probability and Statistics, vol. 594. John Wiley & Sons Inc., New York (2005)
38. Segala, R.: Verification of randomized distributed algorithms. In: Brinksma, E., Hermanns, H., Katoen, J.-P. (eds.) EEF School 2000 and FMPA 2000. LNCS, vol. 2090, pp. 232–260. Springer, Heidelberg (2001)
39. Segala, R., Lynch, N.A.: Probabilistic simulations for probabilistic processes. Nord. J. Comput. **2**(2), 250–273 (1995)
40. Wolff, E.M., Topcu, U., Murray, R.M.: Robust control of uncertain markov decision processes with temporal logic specifications. In: CDC, pp. 3372–3379. IEEE (2012)
41. Wu, D., Koutsoukos, X.D.: Reachability analysis of uncertain systems using boundedparameter markov decision processes. Artif. Intell. **172**(8–9), 945–954 (2008)

Parameter Synthesis for Parametric Interval Markov Chains

Benoît Delahaye[1]([⊠]), Didier Lime[2], and Laure Petrucci[3]

[1] Université de Nantes, LINA, Nantes, France
`benoit.delahaye@univ-nantes.fr`
[2] École Centrale de Nantes, IRCCyN, Nantes, France
[3] LIPN, UMR CNRS 7030, Université Paris 13, Sorbonne Paris Cité, Paris, France

Abstract. Interval Markov Chains (IMCs) are the base of a classic probabilistic specification theory introduced by Larsen and Jonsson in 1991. They are also a popular abstraction for probabilistic systems. In this paper we study parameter synthesis for a parametric extension of Interval Markov Chains in which the endpoints of intervals may be replaced with parameters. In particular, we propose constructions for the synthesis of *all* parameter values ensuring several properties such as consistency and consistent reachability in both the existential and universal settings with respect to implementations. We also discuss how our constructions can be modified in order to synthesise *all* parameter values ensuring other typical properties.

1 Introduction

Interval Markov Chains (IMCs for short) extend Markov Chains by allowing to specify intervals of possible probabilities on transitions instead of precise probabilities. When modelling real-life systems, the exact value of transition probabilities may not be known precisely. Indeed, in most cases, these values are measured from observations or experiments which are subject to imprecision. In this case, using intervals of probabilities that take into account the imprecision of the measures makes more sense than using an arbitrary but precise value.

IMCs have been introduced by Larsen and Jonsson [22] as a *specification* formalism—a basis for a stepwise-refinement-like modelling method, where initial designs are very abstract and underspecified, and then they are made continuously more precise, until they are concrete. Unlike richer specification models such as Constraint Markov Chains [7] or Abstract Probabilistic Automata [13], IMCs are difficult to use for compositional specification due to the lack of basic modelling operators. Nevertheless, IMCs have been intensively used in order to model real-life systems in domains such as systems biology, security or communication protocols [2,6,17,25]. Going further in the abstraction hierarchy, one could then assume that the endpoints of probability intervals are also imprecise.

This work has been partially supported by project PACS ANR-14-CE28-0002 and Pays de la Loire research project AFSEC.

B. Jobstmann and K.R.M. Leino (Eds.): VMCAI 2016, LNCS 9583, pp. 372–390, 2016.
DOI: 10.1007/978-3-662-49122-5_18

As an example, consider that a given component can be built with arbitrary quality by using different, more or less costly, materials. This quality can be related in practice to the maximal error rate of the component, which is reflected in our design by the upper endpoint of the interval associated with a transition leading to an error state. Since this value can be chosen arbitrarily, it can be represented as a parameter. Obviously, if several instances of this component are embedded in our design, the same parameter will be used in several places. In this setting, the designer will be interested in computing the set of acceptable values for this parameter – i.e. ensuring that the overall design satisfies some given properties; or synthesising the best acceptable value for this parameter – i.e. giving the best compromise between some given (quantitative?) property and the production cost.

This new setting thus calls for methods and tools for modelling and analysing IMCs where interval endpoints are not fixed in advance.

Parametric Interval Markov Chains (pIMCs for short) have been introduced in [15] as an extension of IMCs that allows for using parameters instead of numeric values as the lower or upper endpoint of intervals. The goal of using such a model is then to synthesise parameter values ensuring correctness w.r.t. given properties. In this paper, we focus on the first basic property of such models: consistency. Consistency of a parameter valuation in a given pIMC boils down to verifying that the chosen parameter values are not incoherent, i.e. that the resulting IMC can be implemented. While [15] focuses on deciding whether a consistent parameter valuation exists in a given pIMC, we propose in this paper constructions for *synthesising* **all** *consistent parameter valuations of a given pIMC*. In addition, we also consider other objectives such as reachability or avoidability while always guaranteeing consistency. Reachability can be formulated in two flavours: either universal reachability, i.e. ensuring that all implementations reach a given set of states, or existential reachability, i.e. ensuring that there exists at least one implementation that satisfies the property. We therefore propose constructions for solving both problems while still ensuring consistency of the model.

Related work. Our work is a follow-up on [15], which is to the best of our knowledge the only existing work addressing parametric probabilistic specification theories where parameters range over probability values. In [15], we only study the consistency problem in the existential setting and propose an algorithm for deciding whether there exists at least one parameter valuation ensuring consistency for a subclass of pIMCs. In contrast, the results we provide here are fully general, and, more importantly, we attack a slightly different problem that consists in *synthesising all parameter values* ensuring consistency and reachability.

Other classes of systems where parameters give some latitude on probability distributions, such as parametric Markov models [23], have been studied in the literature [19,24]. The activity in this domain has yielded decidability results [21], parametric probabilistic model-checking algorithms [11] and even tools [12,20]. Continuous-time parametric and probabilistic models have also been considered in some very restricted settings [9]. Networks of probabilistic processes where the number of processes is a parameter have also been studied in [4,5], and probabilistic timed automata with parameters in clock constraints and invariants have been studied in [1].

In another setting, the model checking problem for Interval Markov Chains has been addressed in [3,8,10]. In [3,10], the authors propose algorithms and complexity bounds for checking respectively ω-regular and LTL properties on Interval Markov Chains with closed intervals. [3] assumes that parameters can be present in the models and formulae, but these parameters do not range on the probability endpoints of the intervals, as in our work. On the other hand, [8] focuses on Interval Markov Chains with open intervals and proposes algorithms for verifying PCTL properties but does not consider parameters.

Outline. First, Sect. 2 recalls the basic definitions and notations of Interval Markov chains and their parametric extension. Then, Sect. 3 explores the consistency of Parametric Interval Markov Chains and proposes a construction for synthesising *all* the parameter valuations that guarantee consistency. The problem of existential consistent reachability is addressed in Sect. 4, and we show how our constructions can be adapted to solve other problems such as consistent avoidability and universal consistent reachability. Finally, Sect. 5 summarises the paper contributions and gives hints for future work. For space reasons, our proofs are presented in an extended version of this paper [16].

2   Background

Throughout the paper, we use the notion of parameters. A parameter $p \in P$ is a variable ranging through the interval $[0, 1]$. A valuation for P is a function $\psi : P \to [0, 1]$ that associates values with each parameter in P. We write $\texttt{Int}_{[0,1]}(P)$ for the set of all closed parametric intervals of the form $[x, y]$ where x, y can be either reals in the interval $[0, 1]$ or parameters from P. When $P = \emptyset$, we write $\texttt{Int}_{[0,1]} = \texttt{Int}_{[0,1]}(\emptyset)$ to denote closed intervals with real-valued endpoints. Given an interval I of the form $I = [a, b]$, $\texttt{Low}(I)$ and $\texttt{Up}(I)$ respectively denote the lower and upper endpoints of I, i.e. a and b. Given an interval $I = [a, b] \in \texttt{Int}_{[0,1]}$, we say that I is well-formed whenever $a \leq b$. It is worth noting that, for readability reasons, we limit ourselves to closed intervals. Nevertheless, all the results we propose can be extended with minor modifications to open/semi-open intervals whose endpoints contain linear combinations of parameters and constants.

Given a parametric interval $I \in \texttt{Int}_{[0,1]}(P)$ and a parameter valuation $\psi : P \to [0, 1]$, we write $\psi(I)$ for the interval of $\texttt{Int}_{[0,1]}$ obtained by substituting in the endpoints of I each parameter p by the value $\psi(p)$. Constraints on parameter valuations are expressions on parameter variables that restrict their potential values. Given a constraint C over P and a parameter valuation $\psi : P \to [0, 1]$, we write $\psi \Vdash C$ when the parameter valuation satisfies constraint C. In the following, we abuse notations and identify constraints on parameter valuations with the set of parameter valuations that satisfy them. Therefore, given a constraint C over P, we sometimes write $\psi \in C$ instead of $\psi \Vdash C$. We also use intersections (resp. unions) of constraints to represent the set of parameter valuations satisfying their conjunction (resp. disjunction).

Given a finite set S, we denote by $\text{Dist}(S)$ the set of distributions over S, i.e. the set of functions $\rho : S \to [0,1]$ such that $\sum_{s \in S} \rho(s) = 1$. In the rest of the paper, we assume that all the states in our structures are equipped with labels taken from a fixed set of atomic propositions A. A state-labelling function over S is thus a function $V : S \to 2^A$ that assigns to each state a set of labels in A.

2.1 Markov Chains Definitions

We recall the notion of Markov Chains (MCs), that will act as models for (parametric) IMCs. An example of a Markov Chain is given in Fig. 1a.

Definition 1 (Markov Chain). *A Markov Chain is a tuple* $\mathcal{M} = (S, s_0, M, A, V)$, *where S is a finite set of states containing the initial state* s_0, A *is a set of atomic propositions,* $V : S \to 2^A$ *is a labeling function, and* $M : S \times S \to [0,1]$ *is a probabilistic transition function such that* $\forall s \in S, \sum_{t \in S} M(s,t) = 1$.

We now recall the notion of Interval Markov Chains (IMCs), adapted from [14]. IMCs are a specification formalism that allows one to represent an infinite set of MCs. Roughly, IMCs extend MCs by replacing exact probability values on transitions with intervals of allowed probability values. An example of an IMC is given in Fig. 1b.

Definition 2 (Interval Markov Chain [14]). *An Interval Markov Chain (IMC) is a tuple* $\mathcal{I} = (S, s_0, \varphi, A, V)$, *where S, s_0, A and V are as for MCs, and* $\varphi : S \times S \to \text{Int}_{[0,1]}$ *is a transition constraint that associates with each potential transition an interval of probabilities.*

The following definition recalls the notion of satisfaction introduced in [14]. Satisfaction (also called implementation in some cases) allows to characterise the set of MCs represented by a given IMC specification. Crucially, satisfaction abstracts from the syntactic structure of transitions in IMCs: a single transition in the implementation MC can contribute to satisfaction of more than one transition in the specification IMC, by distributing its probability mass against several transitions. Similarly many MC transitions can contribute to the satisfaction of just one specification transition. This crucial notion is embedded in the so-called *correspondence function* δ introduced below. Informally, such a function is given for all pairs of states (t, s) in the satisfaction relation, and associates with each successor state t' of t – in the implementation MC – a distribution over potential successor states s' of s – in the specification IMC – specifying how the transition $t \to t'$ contributes to the transition $s \to s'$.

Definition 3 (Satisfaction Relation [14]). *Let* $\mathcal{I} = (S, s_0, \varphi, A, V^I)$ *be an IMC and* $\mathcal{M} = (T, t_0, M, A, V^M)$ *be a MC. A relation* $\mathcal{R} \subseteq T \times S$ *is a satisfaction relation if whenever* $t\mathcal{R}s$,

1. *the labels of s and t agree:* $V^M(t) = V^I(s)$,
2. *there exists a* correspondence *function* $\delta : T \to (S \to [0,1])$ *such that*
   (a) *for all* $t' \in T$ *such that* $M(t,t') > 0$, $\delta(t')$ *is a distribution on* S,
   (b) *for all* $s' \in S$, *we have* $(\sum_{t' \in T} M(t,t') \cdot \delta(t')(s')) \in \varphi(s,s')$, *and*
   (c) *for all* $t' \in T$ *and* $s' \in S$, *if* $\delta(t')(s') > 0$, *then* $(t', s') \in \mathcal{R}$.
   We say that state $t \in T$ *satisfies state* $s \in S$ *(written* $t \models s$*) iff there exists a (minimal) satisfaction relation containing* (t, s) *and that* $\mathcal{M}$ *satisfies* $\mathcal{I}$ *(written* $\mathcal{M} \models \mathcal{I}$*) iff* $t_0 \models s_0$.

The notion of satisfaction between the MC $\mathcal{M}$ from Fig. 1a and the IMC $\mathcal{I}$ from Fig. 1b is illustrated in Fig. 1c. In this figure, we remark that the transition $1 \to 3$ in the MC $\mathcal{M}$ partly contributes to the satisfaction of transitions $A \to B$ and $A \to C$ in the IMC $\mathcal{I}$. Similarly, transitions $1 \to 2$ and $1 \to 3$ in the MC $\mathcal{M}$ both contribute to the satisfaction of transition $A \to B$ in the IMC $\mathcal{I}$.

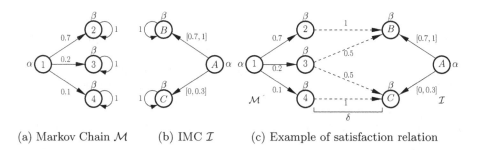

(a) Markov Chain $\mathcal{M}$ (b) IMC $\mathcal{I}$ (c) Example of satisfaction relation

Fig. 1. Markov Chain, Interval Markov Chain and satisfaction relation [14]

The set of MCs satisfying a given IMC $\mathcal{I}$ is written $[\![\mathcal{I}]\!]$. Formally, $[\![\mathcal{I}]\!] = \{\mathcal{M} \mid \mathcal{M} \models \mathcal{I}\}$. We say that an IMC $\mathcal{I}$ is *consistent* iff $[\![\mathcal{I}]\!] \neq \emptyset$. Although the satisfaction relation abstracts from the syntactic structure of transitions, we recall the following result from [15], that states that whenever a given IMC is consistent, it admits at least one implementation that strictly respects its structure.

Theorem 1 ([15]). *An IMC* $\mathcal{I} = (S, s_0, \varphi, A, V)$ *is consistent iff it admits an implementation of the form* $\mathcal{M} = (S, s_0, M, A, V)$ *where, for all reachable states* s *in* $\mathcal{M}$, *it holds that* $M(s, s') \in \varphi(s, s')$ *for all* s'.

In the following, we say that state s is consistent in the IMC $\mathcal{I} = (S, s_0, \varphi, A, V)$ if there exists an implementation $\mathcal{M} = (S, s_0, M, A, V)$ of $\mathcal{I}$ in which state s is reachable with a non-zero probability.

2.2 pIMCs and their Relations to IMCs/MCs

We now recall the notion of Parametric Interval Markov Chain (pIMC), previously introduced in [15]. Intuitively, pIMCs extend IMCs by allowing parameters to be used as interval endpoints.

Definition 4 (Parametric Interval Markov Chain). *A parametric Interval Markov Chain (pIMC) is a tuple $\mathcal{I}^P = (S, s_0, \varphi_P, A, V, P)$, where S, s_0, A and V are as for IMCs, P is a set of variables (parameters) ranging over $[0,1]$ and $\varphi_P : S \times S \to Int_{[0,1]}(P)$ associates with each potential transition a (parametric) interval.*

Given a pIMC $\mathcal{I}^P = (S, s_0, \varphi_P, A, V, P)$ and a parameter valuation $\psi : P \to [0,1]$, we write $\psi(\mathcal{I}^P)$ for the IMC obtained by replacing φ_P by the function $\varphi : S \times S \to Int_{[0,1]}$ defined by $\forall s, s' \in S, \varphi(s, s') = \psi(\varphi_P(s, s'))$. The IMC $\psi(\mathcal{I}^P)$ is called an *instance* of pIMC $\mathcal{I}^P$.

Finally, we say that a MC $\mathcal{M} = (T, t_0, M, A, V^M)$ *implements* pIMC $\mathcal{I}^P$, written $\mathcal{M} \models \mathcal{I}^P$, iff there exists an instance $\mathcal{I}$ of $\mathcal{I}^P$ such that $\mathcal{M} \models \mathcal{I}$. We write $\llbracket \mathcal{I}^P \rrbracket$ for the set of MCs implementing $\mathcal{I}^P$ and say that a pIMC is *consistent* iff its set of implementations is not empty.

In the rest of the paper, and in particular in examples, we sometimes omit atomic propositions in our figures and reasonings as they do not impact any of the problems we solve.

3 Consistency

When considering IMCs, one question of interest is to decide whether it is consistent without computing its set of implementations. This problem has already been addressed in the literature [14,15], yielding polynomial decision algorithms and procedures that produce one implementation when the IMC is consistent. The same question holds for pIMCs, although in a slightly different setting. In [15], we have proposed a polynomial algorithm for deciding whether a given pIMC is consistent, in the sense that it admits at least one parameter valuation for which the resulting IMC is consistent.

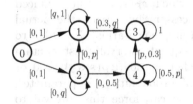

Fig. 2. Consistent pIMC $\mathcal{I}^P$

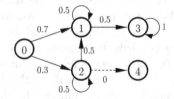

Fig. 3. MC $\mathcal{M}$ implementing $\mathcal{I}^P$

Example 1. Consider pIMC $\mathcal{I}^P$ given in Fig. 2. In this pIMC, parameters p and q appear in the outgoing transitions of several states, therefore the algorithm presented in [15] cannot be used in order to decide if $\mathcal{I}^P$ is consistent. From the outgoing transitions of state 4, we can extract constraints stating that the value of parameter p must be at the same time greater than 0.5 and lower than 0.3. Although state 4 is thus clearly inconsistent, $\mathcal{I}^P$ can still be consistent if there exists implementations avoiding state 4. Hence, the probability to move from state 2 to state 4 must be 0. Such an implementation is given in Fig. 3 for the parameter valuation $p = q = 0.5$.

In this section, we move one step further and introduce a construction that synthesises all parameter valuations ensuring that a given pIMC is consistent. Observe that consistency is a recursive notion: a state is consistent iff there exists a distribution matching its outgoing intervals and such that all states reached through this distribution are themselves consistent. Based on this observation, we propose an inductive notion of n-consistency that follows this reasoning to a given depth n. We then build on this notion to synthesise the set of parameter valuations ensuring that a given pIMC is consistent. The section is organised as follows.

We start by introducing notions and notations that will be used throughout the rest of the paper. We then introduce the notion of n-consistency in the IMC setting, adapt it to the pIMC setting and finally present our main contribution: a construction that synthesises all parameter valuations ensuring that a given pIMC is consistent.

3.1   Notations

Let $\mathcal{I}^P = (S, s_0, \varphi_P, A, V, P)$ be a pIMC and let $s \in S$ be a state of $\mathcal{I}^P$. We say that state s is *consistent* in pIMC $\mathcal{I}^P$ if there exists an implementation $\mathcal{M} = (S, s_0, M, A, V)$ of $\mathcal{I}^P$ in which s is reachable from s_0.

In order to decide whether a given IMC is consistent, we need to address the set of potential successors of a given state s. Obviously, this set of potential successors will depend on the values given to the parameters in $\mathcal{I}^P$. Nevertheless, we can rule out all states s' for which the interval of probabilities going from s to s' in $\mathcal{I}^P$ is $[0, 0]$. We thus write $\mathtt{Succ}(s)$ for the set of states that can be reached from s with a probability interval not reduced to $[0, 0]$. Formally, $\mathtt{Succ}(s) = \{s' \in S \mid \varphi_P(s, s') \neq [0, 0]\}$.

Other states of interest are the states s' for which $\varphi_P(s, s')$ is not reduced to $[0, 0]$, but that can still be avoided as successors by setting the actual probability of going from s to s' to 0 in an implementation. In order to be able to set this probability to 0, the subsequent interval must contain the value 0. As a consequence, s' must be such that $\mathtt{Low}(\varphi_P(s, s')) = 0$ or such that the lower endpoint of the interval of probability is a parameter, i.e. $\mathtt{Low}(\varphi_P(s, s')) \in P$. Indeed, in this case, we can force this interval to contain 0 by setting the value of its lower endpoint to 0. We thus define $LP(s) = \{s' \in \mathtt{Succ}(s) \mid \mathtt{Low}(\varphi_P(s, s')) \in P\}$ and $Z(s) = LP(s) \cup \{s' \in \mathtt{Succ}(s) \mid \mathtt{Low}(\varphi_P(s, s')) = 0\}$. Therefore, states in $Z(s)$ can be avoided as successors of s in some implementations. We now propose a constraint on parameter valuations that ensures that a probability distribution exists that matches the outgoing intervals of s while reaching only states from a given set S'.

$$LC(s, S') = \left[\sum_{s' \in S'} \mathrm{Up}(\varphi_P(s, s')) \geq 1 \right] \cap \left[\sum_{s' \in S'} \mathrm{Low}(\varphi_P(s, s')) \leq 1 \right]$$
$$\cap \left[\bigcap_{s' \in S'} \mathrm{Low}(\varphi_P(s, s')) \leq \mathrm{Up}(\varphi_P(s, s')) \right]$$

Informally, $LC(s, S')$ represents all parameter valuations ensuring that all outgoing intervals of s are well-formed and that the sum of their lower endpoints is lower or equal to 1 while the sum of their upper endpoints is greater or equal to 1.

Example 2. Consider pIMC $\mathcal{I}^P$ from Fig. 2. We illustrate the construction of LC for state 2 of $\mathcal{I}^P$. Let $S' = \{0, 1, 2, 3\}$. From the definition of LC, we obtain $LC(2, \{0, 1, 2, 3\}) = (p + q \geq 1) \cap (0 \leq 1) \cap (p \geq 0) \cap (q \geq 0)$. As a consequence, $\psi \in LC(2, \{0, 1, 2, 3\})$ iff $\psi(p) + \psi(q) \geq 1$.

As a clear consequence of the definition of LC, any parameter valuation ψ is in $LC(s, S')$ iff there exists a distribution in the IMC $\psi(\mathcal{I}^P)$ that avoids all states not in S' and satisfies all the intervals of probability going from s to S'.

Proposition 1. *Given a pIMC $\mathcal{I}^P = (S, s_0, \varphi_P, A, V, P)$, a state $s \in S$ and a set $S' \subseteq \textit{Succ}(s)$, we have that for any parameter valuation ψ,*

$$\psi \in LC(s, S') \iff \exists \rho \in \textit{Dist}(S) \text{ s.t. } \begin{cases} \forall s' \in S \setminus S', \ \rho(s') = 0 \text{ and} \\ \forall s' \in S', \rho(s') \in \psi(\varphi_P(s, s')) \end{cases}$$

We remark that the intervals associated with transitions to states outside of S' are not taken into account in this proposition. Indeed, we only ensure that there exists a distribution ρ such that the intervals of probability going from s to S' are satisfied and $\rho(S \setminus S') = 0$, but we do not ensure that 0 is an admissible probability value for transitions going from s to $S \setminus S'$. Therefore S' has to be well chosen, i.e. such that $(\textit{Succ}(s) \setminus S') \subseteq Z(s)$, and $LC(s, S')$ has to be accompanied with other constraints in order to ensure that 0 is an admissible probability value for transitions going outside of S'.

3.2   The Notion of n-consistency for IMCs

We now introduce the notion of n-consistency in the IMC setting and then adapt this notion to pIMCs. Informally, a state s is n-consistent in IMC $\mathcal{I} = (S, s_0, \varphi, A, V)$ if there exists an unfolding of depth n starting from s for which each node admits a probability distribution satisfying all of its outgoing probability intervals. Intuitively, if one can find a sufficiently deep unfolding satisfying this property from s_0, then the IMC is consistent. Finding the optimal depth for this unfolding is an issue, but we prove later in the section that we do not need to go deeper than $|S|$. In practice, n-consistency is defined by induction over the structure of $\mathcal{I}$. The intuition is that state $s \in S$ is n-consistent iff there exists a distribution ρ matching its outgoing intervals, and if $n > 0$ then $\rho(s') > 0$ implies that s' is $(n-1)$-consistent. Unfortunately, this intuitive definition raises an issue: it may be the case that some state s' appears several times in the unfolding from s and we cannot ensure that the same outgoing distribution is chosen every time s' appears. This is problematic as we want use this unfolding in order to build an implementation respecting the structure of $\mathcal{I}$, and we therefore need to provide a unique distribution for each reachable state in S. We thus propose an alternative definition that first fixes an outgoing distribution for all states via a function $D : S \rightarrow \text{Dist}(S)$ and then enforces this distribution in the induction.

Definition 5 (**n-consistency**). *Let $\mathcal{I} = (S, s_0, \varphi, A, V)$ be an IMC and let $D : S \rightarrow \text{Dist}(S)$ be a function that assigns a distribution on S to each state of $\mathcal{I}$. State $s \in S$ is (n, D)-consistent iff for all $s' \in S$, $D(s)(s') \in \varphi(s, s')$, and, for $n > 0$, $D(s)(s') > 0$ implies s' is $(n-1, D)$-consistent.*

We say that s is n-consistent if there exists $D : S \rightarrow \text{Dist}(S)$ such that s is (n, D)-consistent.

We start with the following intuitive observation: whenever a given state is (n, D)-consistent, then it is also $(n-1, D)$-consistent.

Lemma 1. *Given an IMC $\mathcal{I} = (S, s_0, \varphi, A, V)$, a function $D : S \rightarrow \text{Dist}(S)$ and a state $s \in S$, for all $n > 0$, $s \in S$ is (n, D)-consistent implies $s \in S$ is $(n-1, D)$-consistent.*

Although the definition of n-consistency introduced above requires that a unique distribution is fixed *a priori* for all states in the IMC, we show in the following lemma that this is in fact not necessary and that the function $D : S \rightarrow \text{Dist}(S)$ can be constructed on-the-fly.

Lemma 2. *Given an IMC $\mathcal{I} = (S, s_0, \varphi, A, V)$ and a state $s \in S$, we have that for all $n > 0$, if there exists $\rho \in \text{Dist}(S)$ such that $\rho(s') \in \varphi(s, s')$ for all s' and $\rho(s') > 0$ implies that s' is $(n-1)$-consistent, then there exists a function $D : S \rightarrow \text{Dist}(S)$ such that $D(s) = \rho$ and s is (n, D)-consistent.*

Definition 5 is thus equivalent to the following intuitive inductive definition: a state s is n-consistent iff there exists a distribution ρ satisfying all of its outgoing probability intervals and such that for all $s' \in S$, $\rho(s') > 0$ implies that s' is $(n-1)$-consistent.

Example 3. Consider pIMC $\mathcal{I}^P$ from Fig. 2 and two of its instances $\psi_1(\mathcal{I}^P)$ and $\psi_2(\mathcal{I}^P)$, with $\psi_1(p) = \psi_1(q) = 0.3$ and $\psi_2(p) = \psi_2(q) = 0.5$. In both IMCs, state 4 is not 0-consistent as one cannot find any distribution satisfying its outgoing intervals. On the other hand, State 2 is 0-consistent in both IMCs. State 2 is also 1-consistent in $\psi_2(\mathcal{I}^P)$ as there exists a distribution matching its intervals and avoiding State 4, but not in $\psi_1(\mathcal{I}^P)$ as any distribution satisfying the outgoing intervals of State 2 in $\psi_1(\mathcal{I}^P)$ must assign a positive probability to the transition to State 4, which is not 0-consistent.

As explained above, the intuition is that an IMC $\mathcal{I} = (S, s_0, \varphi, A, V)$ is consistent whenever one can find a sufficiently deep unfolding starting in its initial state and such that every node in this unfolding admits a probability distribution that satisfies its outgoing intervals. We show in the following lemma that the notion of n-consistency admits a fixpoint in the sense that there is a bound N for which being N-consistent is equivalent to being k-consistent for any $k \geq N$. In fact, we show that $|S|$ is an upper bound for the value of N.

Lemma 3. *Given an IMC $\mathcal{I} = (S, s_0, \varphi, A, V)$, a function $D : S \to \text{Dist}(S)$ and a state $s \in S$, for all $n \geq |S|$, s is (n, D)-consistent implies that s is $(n + 1, D)$-consistent.*

As a consequence to Lemmas 1 and 3, we say that state s is D-consistent if it is (n, D)-consistent for some $n \geq |S|$. Similarly, we say that state s is consistent if it is D-consistent for some D.

We now propose two lemmas that link the notion of $(|S|, D)$-consistency of the initial state of a given IMC $\mathcal{I} = (S, s_0, \varphi, A, V)$ to the existence of an implementation $\mathcal{M}$ respecting the structure of $\mathcal{I}$. The intuition of the following lemma is that the transition matrix defined in $\mathcal{M}$ is a candidate function for the $(|S|, D)$-consistency of s_0.

Lemma 4. *Given an IMC $\mathcal{I} = (S, s_0, \varphi, A, V)$, if (S, s_0, M, A, V) is an implementation of $\mathcal{I}$ then s_0 is $(|S|, D)$-consistent, where $D : S \to \text{Dist}(S)$ is defined by $\forall s, s' \in S, D(s)(s') = M(s, s')$.*

Reversely, the next lemma shows that whenever s_0 is $(|S|, D)$-consistent, then D is a candidate transition matrix for an implementation of $\mathcal{I}$ respecting its structure.

Lemma 5. *Given an IMC $\mathcal{I} = (S, s_0, \varphi, A, V)$, if s_0 is $(|S|, D)$-consistent, then the Markov Chain (S, s_0, M, A, V), where M is defined by $\forall s, s' \in S, D(s)(s') = M(s, s')$, is an implementation of $\mathcal{I}$.*

The following theorem follows directly from Theorem 1 and Lemmas 4 and 5 and concludes our section by stating one of our main results: a new characterisation of consistency for IMCs based on the notion of n-consistency.

Theorem 2. *Given an IMC $\mathcal{I} = (S, s_0, \varphi, A, V)$, $\mathcal{I}$ is consistent iff s_0 is $|S|$-consistent.*

3.3 Consistency of pIMCs

We now move to the problem of consistency of pIMCs. As said earlier, our aim in this case is not only to decide whether a given pIMC is consistent, but also to synthesise all parameter valuations that ensure consistency of the resulting IMC. For this purpose, we adapt the notion of n-consistency defined above to pIMCs.

Given a pIMC $\mathcal{I}^P = (S, s_0, \varphi_P, A, V, P)$, we say that $s \in S$ is n-consistent iff there exists an IMC $\mathcal{I} = (S, s_0, \varphi, A, V)$ such that $\mathcal{I}$ is an instance of $\mathcal{I}^P$ and in which s is n-consistent. The set of parameter valuations ensuring that s is n-consistent is $\{\psi \mid s$ is n-consistent in $\psi(\mathcal{I}^P)\}$. We now propose a construction for the set of parameter valuations $\mathrm{Cons}_n(s)$ ensuring that a given state s in $\mathcal{I}^P$ is n-consistent. As in the previous section, this set is defined by induction on n. The intuition is as follows: a given parameter valuation ψ is in $\mathrm{Cons}_n(s)$ iff there exists a distribution ρ that matches the outgoing probability intervals of s in $\psi(\mathcal{I}^P)$ and such that it only leads to $(n-1)$-consistent states. Because of Lemma 2, this ensures that s is indeed n-consistent in $\psi(\mathcal{I}^P)$. The existence of a distribution such as ρ is then conditioned by the set of potential successor states that can be reached from s in $\psi(\mathcal{I}^P)$. We thus start by fixing a set of states X that we want to avoid and then compute the set of valuations $\mathrm{Cons}_n^X(s)$ that ensure n-consistency of s through a distribution ρ that avoids states from X. Formally, we define $\mathrm{Cons}_n^X(s)$ as follows: let $\mathrm{Cons}_0^X(s) = LC(s, \mathrm{Succ}(s) \setminus X) \cap \left[\bigcap_{s' \in X} \mathrm{Low}(\varphi_P(s, s')) = 0\right]$ and for $n \geq 1$,

$$\mathrm{Cons}_n^X(s) = \left[\bigcap_{s' \in \mathrm{Succ}(s) \setminus X} \mathrm{Cons}_{n-1}(s')\right] \cap [LC(s, \mathrm{Succ}(s) \setminus X)]$$

$$\cap \left[\bigcap_{s' \in X} \mathrm{Low}(\varphi_P(s, s')) = 0\right]$$

The set of valuations ensuring n-consistency is then the union, for all potential choices of X, of $\mathrm{Cons}_n^X(s)$. Recall that, because of the definition of LC given at the end of Sect. 3.1, we need to choose X as a subset of $Z(s)$. Therefore, we define $\mathrm{Cons}_n(s) = \bigcup_{X \subseteq Z(s)} \mathrm{Cons}_n^X(s)$. We first observe that the choice of X has no impact on 0-consistency.

Lemma 6. Let $\mathcal{I}^P = (S, s_0, \varphi_P, A, V, P)$ be a pIMC and let $s \in S$. For all $X \subseteq Z(s)$, we have $\mathbf{Cons}_0^X(s) \subseteq \mathbf{Cons}_0^\emptyset(s)$.

As a consequence of Lemma 6 above, we have $\mathrm{Cons}_0(s) = LC(s, \mathrm{Succ}(s))$. We illustrate the construction for Cons_n in the following example.

Example 4. Consider the pIMC $\mathcal{I}^P$ given in Fig. 2. The computation of Cons_n for states $0, 1, 2$ is illustrated in Fig. 4. We start with computing the parameter valuations ensuring 0-consistency of all states: $\mathrm{Cons}_0(0) = \mathrm{Cons}_0(3)$ and both allow all possible parameter valuations, $\mathrm{Cons}_0(4) = (p \leq 0.3) \cap (p \geq 0.5) = \emptyset$, $\mathrm{Cons}_0(2) = (p + q + 0.5 \geq 1)$ and $\mathrm{Cons}_0(1) = (q + 0.3 \leq 1) \cap (q + 1 \geq 1) \cap (q \geq 0.3) = (q \leq 0.7) \cap (q \geq 0.3)$. Observe that for all n, we have $\mathrm{Cons}_n(s) = \mathrm{Cons}_0(s)$ for $s = 1, 3, 4$ since the value of Cons for their successors remains the same. We now reason on 1-consistency for state 2. By construction, its set of possibly avoidable successors is $Z(2) = \{1, 2, 4\}$, and $\mathrm{Cons}_1^X(2) = \emptyset$ when $4 \notin X$ because $\mathrm{Cons}_0(4) = \emptyset$, and also when $X = \{1, 2, 4\}$. For the other values of X, we obtain $\mathrm{Cons}_1^{\{1,4\}}(2) = \mathrm{Cons}_0(2) \cap (q \geq 1) = (p + q + 0.5 \geq 1) \cap (q \geq 1) = (q = 1)$,

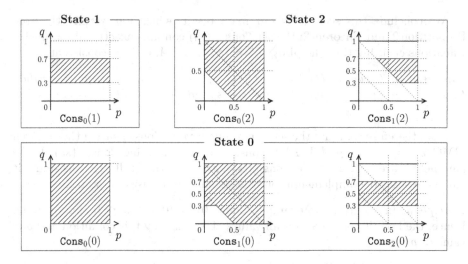

Fig. 4. Illustration of the construction of Cons_n in pIMC $\mathcal{I}^P$ from Fig. 2

$\text{Cons}_1^{\{2,4\}}(2) = \text{Cons}_0(1) \cap (p \geq 1) = (q \leq 0.7) \cap (q \geq 0.3) \cap (p \geq 1)$ and $\text{Cons}_1^{\{4\}}(2) = \text{Cons}_0(1) \cap \text{Cons}_0(2) \cap (p+q \geq 1) = (q \leq 0.7) \cap (q \geq 0.3) \cap (p+q+0.5 \geq 1) \cap (p+q \geq 1) = (q \leq 0.7) \cap (q \geq 0.3) \cap (p+q \geq 1)$. Hence $\text{Cons}_1(2) = \bigcup_{X \subseteq Z(2)} \text{Cons}_1^X(2) = (q = 1) \cup [(q \leq 0.7) \cap (q \geq 0.3) \cap (p \geq 1)] \cup [(q \leq 0.7) \cap (q \geq 0.3) \cap (p+q \geq 1)] = (q = 1) \cup [(q \leq 0.7) \cap (q \geq 0.3) \cap (p+q \geq 1)]$. Furthermore, we can show that $\text{Cons}_n(2) = \text{Cons}_1(2)$ for all $n \geq 1$. Similarly, we can show that $\text{Cons}_1(0) = (p+q \geq 0.5) \cup [(q \leq 0.7) \cap (q \geq 0.3)]$, and $\text{Cons}_n(0) = \text{Cons}_2(0) = [(q \leq 0.7) \cap (q \geq 0.3)] \cup (q = 1)$ for all $n \geq 2$.

Our aim is now to prove that $\text{Cons}_n(s)$ contains exactly all parameter valuations ensuring that s is n-consistent. We first show that $\text{Cons}_n^X(s)$ works as intended, i.e. contains exactly all parameter valuations ψ ensuring that s is n-consistent in $\psi(\mathcal{I}^P)$ while using a distribution that avoids X.

Lemma 7. *Given a pIMC $\mathcal{I}^P = (S, s_0, \varphi_P, A, V, P)$, a state $s \in S$, a set $X \subseteq Z(s)$ and a parameter valuation $\psi : P \rightarrow [0,1]$, we have $\psi \in \text{Cons}_n^X(s)$ iff there exists a function $D : S \rightarrow \text{Dist}(S)$ such that $\forall s, s', s' \in X$ implies $D(s)(s') = 0$ and state s is (n, D)-consistent in the IMC $\psi(\mathcal{I}^P)$.*

A direct consequence of Lemma 7 above is that $\text{Cons}_n(s)$ contains exactly all parameter valuations ensuring that s is n-consistent.

Proposition 2. *Given a pIMC $\mathcal{I}^P = (S, s_0, \varphi_P, A, V, P)$, a state $s \in S$ and a parameter valuation $\psi : P \rightarrow [0,1]$, we have $\psi \in \text{Cons}_n(s)$ iff s is n-consistent in the IMC $\psi(\mathcal{I}^P)$.*

It directly follows from Lemma 1 and Proposition 2 that for all $n \geq 1$ and $s \in S$, $\text{Cons}_n(s) \subseteq \text{Cons}_{n-1}(s)$, i.e. that each computation step restricts the sets of parameter valuations.

We conclude this section by our main result, which follows directly from Proposition 2 and Theorem 2: the set $\mathsf{Cons}_{|S|}(s_0)$ contains exactly all parameter valuations ensuring that the pIMC $\mathcal{I}^P = (S, s_0, \varphi_P, A, V, P)$ is consistent.

Theorem 3. *Given a pIMC $\mathcal{I}^P = (S, s_0, \varphi_P, A, V, P)$ and a parameter valuation $\psi : P \to [0,1]$, we have $\psi \in \mathsf{Cons}_{|S|}(s_0)$ iff the IMC $\psi(\mathcal{I}^P)$ is consistent.*

One can therefore compute the set of parameter valuations ensuring that a given pIMC $\mathcal{I}^P = (S, s_0, \varphi_P, A, V, P)$ is consistent by computing $\mathsf{Cons}_{|S|}(s_0)$. If the parameters are chosen inside $\mathsf{Cons}_{|S|}(s_0)$, the resulting IMC is consistent: it admits at least one implementation that avoids all inconsistent states.

Example 5. In our running example, $\mathsf{Cons}_5(0) = (0.3 \leq q \leq 0.7) \cup (q = 1)$. Hence, the IMC is consistent for all values of q satisfying this condition and any value of p.

Regarding complexity, if, for instance, we represent the sets of parameters by finite unions of systems of linear inequalities, basic set operations like intersection are polynomial in the number of parameters. Then computing $\mathsf{Cons}_0(s)$ for all $s \in S$ is polynomial in the number of parameters, as well as, given some X, n and s, computing $\mathsf{Cons}_n^X(s)$. There are $|S|$ states and here n can also take at most $|S|$ successive values. Set X however is chosen in $Z(s)$ for each s. So there are up to $2^{|Z(S)|}$ possible choices for X. Now, remark that $|Z(s)|$ is typically small compared to $|S|$ but, in the worst case, it can be equal to $|S|$. So the worst case asymptotic complexity of the algorithm is exponential in the number of states of the pIMC.

In the following, we write $\mathsf{Cons}(s)$ (resp. $\mathsf{Cons}^X(s)$) for the sets $\mathsf{Cons}_{|S|}(s)$ (resp. $\mathsf{Cons}_{|S|}^X(s)$).

4   Consistent Reachability

Another interesting problem for IMCs and pIMCs is consistent reachability. This problem can be declined in two flavours: existential and universal. Given an IMC $\mathcal{I} = (S, s_0, \varphi, A, V)$ and a target set of states $G \subseteq S$, existential consistent reachability amounts to deciding whether there exists an implementation $\mathcal{M}$ respecting the structure of $\mathcal{I}$ in which G is reachable from s_0 with a non-zero probability. Dually, universal consistent reachability amounts to deciding whether the set G is reachable from s_0 with a non-zero probability in *all implementations* respecting the structure of $\mathcal{I}$. When moving to pIMCs, as in the previous section, we are interested in synthesising all parameter valuations ensuring that a given set of states is universal/existential consistent reachable in the resulting IMCs. In this section, we first focus on the existential problem and start with providing a construction that allows for deciding the existential consistent reachability problem for IMCs. We then adapt this construction to the pIMC setting and finally discuss how this construction can be adapted in order to solve the universal consistent reachability problem for IMCs/pIMCs.

4.1 Existential Consistent Reachability for IMCs

Given an IMC $\mathcal{I} = (S, S_0, \varphi, A, V)$, we say that a target set $G \subseteq S$ is *existential consistent reachable* in $\mathcal{I}$ iff there exists an implementation $\mathcal{M} = (S, s_0, M, A, V)$ of $\mathcal{I}$ in which the probability of reaching G from s_0 is strictly greater than 0. Formally, there must exist a path $s_0 \rightarrow \cdots \rightarrow s_n$ in $\mathcal{M}$ where $M(s_i, s_{i+1}) > 0$ for all $0 \le i < n$ and $s_n \in G$. We insist on the word *consistent* because it is not only important that there exists a sequence of transitions with positive probability matching the intervals in $\mathcal{I}$ and reaching G, but also that this sequence can be mimicked in an implementation, i.e. that the chosen probability distributions do not violate other intervals or do not impose that inconsistent states are also reached. In the following, when clear from the context, we sometimes omit the words "existential consistent" and only say that G is reachable in $\mathcal{I}$.

Notice that our definition of existential consistent reachability only takes into account implementations that respect the structure of $\mathcal{I}$. Although this looks like a limitation, the following theorem shows that any implementation $\mathcal{M}$ of $\mathcal{I}$ can be turned into an implementation $\tilde{\mathcal{M}}$ that respects the structure of $\mathcal{I}$ and that is equivalent to $\mathcal{M}$ with respect to consistent reachability.

Theorem 4. *Let $\mathcal{I} = (S, s_0, \varphi, A, V)$ be an IMC and $G \subseteq S$ be a target set of states. For all MC $\mathcal{M} = (T, t_0, M, A, V_M) \in [\![\mathcal{I}]\!]$, there exists an MC $\tilde{\mathcal{M}} = (S, s_0, \tilde{M}, A, V) \in [\![\mathcal{I}]\!]$ such that G is reachable in $\tilde{\mathcal{M}}$ iff $\{t \in T \mid \exists s \in G, t \models s\}$ is reachable in $\mathcal{M}$.*

Since the problem of existential consistent reachability mixes the notions of consistency and reachability, we cannot separate these two notions. For consistency of a given state s, one has to show that there exists a distribution matching the outgoing intervals of s and reaching only consistent states. On the other hand, for reachability of G, one has to show that there exists a distribution that reaches a state s' from which G is reachable. The difficulty here is that we have to make sure that the same distribution is chosen for both problems, not only in state s but also in all the states that are reached both through the unfolding inherent to consistency and through the path inherent to reachability. As for consistency, we thus propose to start by fixing a unique outgoing distribution for all states in S with a function $D : S \rightarrow \texttt{Dist}(S)$ and enforce that these distributions have to be chosen in our inductive definition of consistent existential reachability.

Formally, we say that $G \subseteq S$ is $(0, D)$-reachable from $s \in S$ iff s is D-consistent and $s \in G$. For $n > 0$, G is (n, D)-reachable from s iff s is D-consistent and either $s \in G$ or there exists s' such that $D(s)(s') > 0$ and G is $(n - 1, D)$-reachable from s'. The intuition is that G is (n, D)-reachable from s if s is consistent and G can be reached in at most n steps from s using distributions from D. We then say that G is n-reachable from s if there exists a function $D : S \rightarrow \texttt{Dist}(S)$ such that G is (n, D)-reachable from s.

As for consistency, we can also provide another equivalent definition for n-reachability in which the function $D : S \rightarrow \texttt{Dist}(S)$ is constructed on the fly: $G \subseteq S$ is n-reachable from $s \in S$ iff either $s \in G$ and s is consistent, or there exists a distribution matching the outgoing intervals of s, reaching only consistent states and at least one state s' from which G is $(n - 1)$-reachable.

We start with the following intuitive observation: whenever G can be reached in at most n steps from s through D, it can also be reached in at most k steps for any $k \geq n$. This is formalised in the following lemma.

Lemma 8. *Let* $\mathcal{I} = (S, s_0, \varphi, A, V)$ *be an IMC,* $G \subseteq S$ *a target set of states and* $D : S \rightarrow \text{Dist}(S)$ *a function that associates a distribution on* S *with all states. We have that for all* $n \geq 0$ *and* $s \in S$, *if* G *is* (n, D)-*reachable from* s *then* G *is* $(n + 1, D)$-*reachable from* s.

From our definitions, we can say that G is reachable in $\mathcal{I}$ iff there exists N such that G is N-reachable from the initial state s_0. Intuitively, we expect that $N \leq |S|$, i.e. that if a path of length at most $|S|$ leading to G cannot be found, then there is no hope of finding a longer path leading to G. This result is formalised in the following lemma.

Lemma 9. *Given an IMC* $\mathcal{I} = (S, s_0, \varphi, A, V)$ *and a target set* $G \subseteq S$, G *is existential consistent reachable in* $\mathcal{I}$ *iff* G *is* $|S|$-*reachable from* s_0.

We thus conclude that our construction for n-reachability allows deciding in a linear number of iterations whether a given set G is reachable in the IMC $\mathcal{I}$.

4.2 Existential Consistent Reachability for pIMCs

We now move to the pIMC setting. As said previously, given a pIMC $\mathcal{I}^P = (S, s_0, \varphi_P, A, V, P)$ and a target set of states $G \subseteq S$, our aim is to compute the set of parameter valuations ψ ensuring that there exists an implementation of IMC $\psi(\mathcal{I}^P)$ in which G is reachable. We proceed as for the consistency problem presented in the previous section: we propose a construction based on the notion of n-reachability for IMCs that, for each state $s \in S$, inductively constructs a set of parameter valuations $\text{Reach}_n^G(s)$ that eventually converges to the desired set. The intuition is similar to the construction for $\text{Cons}_n(s)$: we first select a set $X \subseteq Z(s)$ of states that we want to avoid and define the set of valuations $\text{Reach}_n^{G,X}(s)$ that ensure that G can be reached from s in at most n steps with a distribution that avoids X while preserving consistency. In the rest of the section, we use the constraint on parameters $(s \in G)$ with the following meaning: $(s \in G)$ is empty if $s \notin G$ and universal otherwise. We formally define $\text{Reach}_n^{G,X}(s)$ for all $s \in S$, $n \geq 0$ and $X \subseteq Z(s)$ inductively as follows: $\text{Reach}_0^{G,X}(s) = \text{Cons}^X(s) \cap (s \in G)$, and for $n > 0$

$$\text{Reach}_n^{G,X}(s) = \text{Cons}^X(s) \cap$$

$$\left[(s \in G) \cup \bigcup_{s' \in \text{Succ}(s) \setminus X} \text{Reach}_{n-1}^G(s') \cap \text{Up}(\varphi_P(s, s')) > 0 \cap \sum_{s'' \neq s'} \text{Low}(\varphi_P(s, s'')) < 1 \right]$$

Informally, $\text{Reach}_0^{G,X}(s)$ is empty if $s \notin G$ and contains exactly all parameter valuations ensuring that s is consistent while avoiding X otherwise. For $n > 0$, $\text{Reach}_n^{G,X}(s)$ either contains exactly all parameter valuations ensuring that s is consistent while avoiding X if $s \in G$ or all parameter valuations ensuring that s is consistent while avoiding X and that G is reachable in at most $n-1$ steps from at least one potential successor s' of s not in X that can be reached in one step from s with a strictly positive probability. In some sense, choosing a given set X constrains the structure of the implementations we are looking for. Since we are attacking the problem of *existential* consistent reachability, we therefore need to explore every possible choice for X, and return all parameter valuations ensuring the property for at least one set X. We thus define $\text{Reach}_n^G(s)$ as the union, for all potential choices of X, of $\text{Reach}_n^{G,X}(s)$: $\text{Reach}_n^G(s) = \bigcup_{X \subseteq Z(s)} \text{Reach}_n^{G,X}(s)$. Remark that, for $n = 0$, we obviously have $\text{Reach}_0^G(s) = \text{Cons}(s) \cap (s \in G)$.

We show in the following lemma that the definition of $\text{Reach}_n^{G,X}(s)$ is faithful to our intuition and contains exactly all parameter valuations ψ ensuring that G is n-reachable from s while avoiding X in the IMC $\psi(\mathcal{I}^P)$.

Lemma 10. *Given a pIMC $\mathcal{I}^P = (S, s_0, \varphi_P, A, V, P)$, a state $s \in S$, a target set of states $G \subseteq S$, $X \subseteq Z(s)$ and $n \geq 0$, $\psi \in \text{Reach}_n^{G,X}(s)$ iff there exists a function $D : S \to \text{Dist}(S)$ such that $D(s)(s') = 0$ for all $s' \in X$ and G is (n, D)-reachable from s in the IMC $\psi(\mathcal{I}^P)$.*

A direct consequence of Lemma 10 is the following proposition, stating that $\text{Reach}_n^G(s)$ contains exactly all the parameter valuations ψ ensuring that G is n-reachable from s in the IMC $\psi(\mathcal{I}^P)$.

Proposition 3. *Given a pIMC $\mathcal{I}^P = (S, s_0, \varphi_P, A, V, P)$, a state $s \in S$, a target set of states $G \subseteq S$ and $n \geq 0$, $\psi \in \text{Reach}_n^G(s)$ iff G is n-reachable from state s in the IMC $\psi(\mathcal{I}^P)$.*

Based on Proposition 3 and Lemma 9, we conclude with the following theorem that shows that the set of parameter valuations ensuring existential consistent reachability can be computed in a linear number of iterations using our construction.

Theorem 5. *Given a pIMC $\mathcal{I}^P = (S, s_0, \varphi_P, A, V, P)$ and a target set $G \subseteq S$, $\text{Reach}_{|S|}^G(s_0)$ is the exact set of parameter values such that G is reachable in $\mathcal{I}^P$.*

4.3 Consistent Avoidability and Universal Consistent Reachability

We now briefly show how the results presented in this paper can be adapted to universal consistent reachability, i.e. the problem of synthesising all parameter valuations ensuring that a set G is reachable in *all implementations* of the corresponding instances of a given pIMC $\mathcal{I}^P$. We first start with a related problem, consistent avoidability, and then build a solution to the universal consistent reachability problem from the proposed solution.

Consistent Avoidability. Given an IMC $\mathcal{I} = (S, s_0, \varphi, A, V)$, we say that a set $G \subseteq S$ is consistent avoidable in $\mathcal{I}$ iff $\mathcal{I}$ is consistent and there exists an implementation $\mathcal{M}$ respecting the structure of $\mathcal{I}$ in which G is not reachable from s_0.

Given a pIMC $\mathcal{I}^P = (S, s_0, \varphi_P, A, V, P)$, we want to synthesise all parameter valuations ψ such that $G \subseteq S$ is consistent avoidable in $\psi(\mathcal{I}^P)$. The construction for consistent avoidability resembles the construction for consistency presented in Sect. 3. Intuitively, consistency is an avoidability property, in which we want to avoid the locally inconsistent states. We therefore need only to update our notion of local consistency: formally, we say that G is 0-avoidable from s if $s \notin G$ and s is 0-consistent. For $n > 0$, we say that G is n-avoidable from s if $s \notin G$ and there exists a distribution ρ satisfying the outgoing intervals of s and reaching only states from which G is $(n-1)$-avoidable. Following the same reasoning as in Sect. 3, we can show that, given an IMC $\mathcal{I} = (S, s_0, \varphi, A, V)$ and a set $G \subseteq S$, G is avoidable in $\mathcal{I}$ iff G is $|S|$-avoidable from s_0.

In the pIMC setting, we proceed similarly: we directly use the formula for $\mathtt{Cons}_n(s)$ replacing all occurrences of $LC(s, S')$, for any s ans S', with $LC(s, S') \cap (s \notin G)$. We thus define the new operator $\mathtt{Avoid}_n^G(s)$, for all $n \geq 0$ and all states s of the pIMC. It is then easy to show that the set $\mathtt{Avoid}_{|S|}^G(s_0)$, hereafter written just $\mathtt{Avoid}^G(s_0)$, represents the desired set of parameter valuations, i.e. exactly all parameter valuations ψ ensuring that G is consistent avoidable in $\psi(\mathcal{I}^P)$.

Universal Consistent Reachability. Given an IMC $\mathcal{I} = (S, s_0, \varphi, A, V)$ and a target set of states $G \subseteq S$, we say that G is *universal consistent reachable* in $\mathcal{I}$ iff G is reachable from s_0 in *all implementations* respecting the structure of $\mathcal{I}$. In the pIMC setting, our aim is to synthesise all parameter valuations ensuring that a given target set of states G is universal consistent reachable in the resulting IMCs. This set can be directly derived from the constructions proposed in the previous sections. Indeed, the complement set of $\mathtt{Avoid}^G$ as presented above represents all the parameter valuations ensuring either that the resulting IMC is inconsistent or that the set G is reachable in all implementations of the resulting IMC. Therefore, given a pIMC $\mathcal{I}^P = (S, s_0, \varphi_P, A, V, P)$ and a target set of states $G \subseteq S$, we can define $\mathtt{uReach}^G(s_0) = \mathtt{Cons}(s_0) \cap \overline{\mathtt{Avoid}^G(s_0)}$ and show that $\mathtt{uReach}^G(s_0)$ contains exactly all parameter valuations ψ ensuring that G is universal consistent reachable in $\psi(\mathcal{I}^P)$.

5   Conclusion and Future Work

In this paper, we have explored the problem of consistency of pIMCs, an extension of Interval Markov Chains that allows parameters as endpoints of the intervals. Indeed, parameter valuations must satisfy constraints so that all the outgoing intervals of reachable states are well-formed and the sum of their endpoints surround 1. We show that such consistency constraints can be iteratively explored, solved and combined, thus synthesising all parameter values ensuring consistency. A similar approach also applies to consistent reachability and avoidability problems.

The properties in this paper give a good view of how to proceed to synthesise parameters in order to guarantee consistency and reachability. Future work will aim at providing efficient algorithms and heuristics for pIMCs exploration.

References

1. André, É., Fribourg, L., Sproston, J.: An extension of the inverse method to probabilistic timed automata. Formal Meth. Syst. Des. **42**(2), 119–145 (2013)
2. Barbuti, R., Levi, F., Milazzo, P., Scatena, G.: Probabilistic model checking of biological systems with uncertain kinetic rates. Theor. Comput. Sci. **419**, 2–16 (2012)
3. Benedikt, M., Lenhardt, R., Worrell, J.: LTL model checking of interval markov chains. In: Piterman, N., Smolka, S.A. (eds.) TACAS 2013 (ETAPS 2013). LNCS, vol. 7795, pp. 32–46. Springer, Heidelberg (2013)
4. Bertrand, N., Fournier, P.: Parameterized verification of many identical probabilistic timed processes. FSTTCS. LIPIcs **24**, 501–513 (2013)
5. Bertrand, N., Fournier, P., Sangnier, A.: Playing with probabilities in reconfigurable broadcast networks. In: Muscholl, A. (ed.) FOSSACS 2014 (ETAPS). LNCS, vol. 8412, pp. 134–148. Springer, Heidelberg (2014)
6. Biondi, F., Legay, A., Nielsen, B.F., Wąsowski, A.: Maximizing entropy over markov processes. In: Dediu, A.-H., Martín-Vide, C., Truthe, B. (eds.) LATA 2013. LNCS, vol. 7810, pp. 128–140. Springer, Heidelberg (2013)
7. Caillaud, B., Delahaye, B., Larsen, K., Legay, A., Pedersen, M., Wasowski, A.: Constraint markov chains. Theor. Comput. Sci. **412**(34), 4373–4404 (2011)
8. Chakraborty, S., Katoen, J.-P.: Model checking of open interval markov chains. In: Remke, A., Manini, D., Gribaudo, M. (eds.) ASMTA 2015. LNCS, vol. 9081, pp. 30–42. Springer, Heidelberg (2015)
9. Chamseddine, N., Duflot, M., Fribourg, L., Picaronny, C., Sproston, J.: Computing expected absorption times for parametric determinate probabilistic timed automata. In: QEST, pp. 254–263. IEEE Computer Society (2008)
10. Chatterjee, K., Sen, K., Henzinger, T.A.: Model-checking ω-regular properties of interval markov chains. In: Amadio, R.M. (ed.) FOSSACS 2008. LNCS, vol. 4962, pp. 302–317. Springer, Heidelberg (2008)
11. Daws, C.: Symbolic and parametric model checking of discrete-time markov chains. In: Liu, Z., Araki, K. (eds.) ICTAC 2004. LNCS, vol. 3407, pp. 280–294. Springer, Heidelberg (2005)
12. Dehnert, C., Junges, S., Jansen, N., Corzilius, F., Volk, M., Bruintjes, H., Katoen, J.-P., Ábrahám, E.: PROPhESY: a probabilistic parameter synthesis tool. In: Kroening, D., Păsăreanu, C.S. (eds.) CAV 2015. LNCS, vol. 9206, pp. 214–231. Springer, Heidelberg (2015)
13. Delahaye, B., Katoen, J., Larsen, K., Legay, A., Pedersen, M., Sher, F., Wasowski, A.: Abstract probabilistic automata. Inf. Comput. **232**, 66–116 (2013)
14. Delahaye, B., Larsen, K., Legay, A., Pedersen, M., Wasowski, A.: Consistency and refinement for interval Markov chains. J. Log. Algebr. Program. **81**(3), 209–226 (2012)
15. Delahaye, B.: Consistency for parametric interval Markov chains. In: SynCoP, OASIcs, Schloss Dagstuhl (2015)
16. Delahaye, B., Lime, D., Petrucci, L.: Parameter Synthesis for Parametric Interval Markov Chains. HAL research report hal-01219823 (2015)
17. Ferrer Fioriti, L.M., Hahn, E.M., Hermanns, H., Wachter, B.: Variable probabilistic abstraction refinement. In: Chakraborty, S., Mukund, M. (eds.) ATVA 2012. LNCS, vol. 7561, pp. 300–316. Springer, Heidelberg (2012)
18. Gori, R., Levi, F.: An analysis for proving probabilistic termination of biological systems. Theor. Comput. Sci. **471**, 27–73 (2013)

19. Hahn, E.M., Han, T., Zhang, L.: Synthesis for PCTL in parametric markov decision processes. In: Bobaru, M., Havelund, K., Holzmann, G.J., Joshi, R. (eds.) NFM 2011. LNCS, vol. 6617, pp. 146–161. Springer, Heidelberg (2011)

20. Hahn, E.M., Hermanns, H., Wachter, B., Zhang, L.: PARAM: a model checker for parametric markov models. In: Touili, T., Cook, B., Jackson, P. (eds.) CAV 2010. LNCS, vol. 6174, pp. 660–664. Springer, Heidelberg (2010)

21. Hahn, E., Hermanns, H., Zhang, L.: Probabilistic reachability for parametric Markov models. Software Tools for Technology Transfer **13**(1), 3–19 (2011)

22. Jonsson, B., Larsen, K.: Specification and refinement of probabilistic processes. In: LICS, pp. 266–277. IEEE Computer (1991)

23. Lanotte, R., Maggiolo-Schettini, A., Troina, A.: Decidability results for parametric probabilistic transition systems with an application to security. In: SEFM, pp. 114–121. IEEE Computer Society (2004)

24. Lanotte, R., Maggiolo-Schettini, A., Troina, A.: Parametric probabilistic transition systems for system design and analysis. Formal Aspects Comput. **19**(1), 93–109 (2007)

25. Sen, K., Viswanathan, M., Agha, G.: Model-checking markov chains in the presence of uncertainties. In: Hermanns, H., Palsberg, J. (eds.) TACAS 2006. LNCS, vol. 3920, pp. 394–410. Springer, Heidelberg (2006)

Concurrent Programs

Pointer Race Freedom

Frédéric Haziza[1], Lukáš Holík[2], Roland Meyer[3]([✉]), and Sebastian Wolff[3]

[1] Uppsala University, Uppsala, Sweden
[2] Brno University of Technology, Brno, Czech Republic
[3] University of Kaiserslautern, Kaiserslautern, Germany
meyer@cs.uni-kl.de

Abstract. We propose a novel notion of pointer race for concurrent programs manipulating a shared heap. A pointer race is an access to a memory address which was freed, and it is out of the accessor's control whether or not the cell has been re-allocated. We establish two results. (1) Under the assumption of pointer race freedom, it is sound to verify a program running under explicit memory management as if it was running with garbage collection. (2) Even the requirement of pointer race freedom itself can be verified under the garbage-collected semantics. We then prove analogues of the theorems for a stronger notion of pointer race needed to cope with performance-critical code purposely using racy comparisons and even racy dereferences of pointers. As a practical contribution, we apply our results to optimize a thread-modular analysis under explicit memory management. Our experiments confirm a speed-up of up to two orders of magnitude.

1 Introduction

Today, one of the main challenges in verification is the analysis of concurrent programs that manipulate a shared heap. The numerous interleavings among the threads make it hard to predict the dynamic evolution of the heap. This is even more true if explicit memory management has to be taken into account. With garbage collection as in Java, an allocation request results in a fresh address that was not being pointed to. The address is hence known to be owned by the allocating thread. With explicit memory management as in C, this ownership guarantee does not hold. An address may be re-allocated as soon as it has been freed, even if there are still pointers to it. This missing ownership significantly complicates reasoning against the memory-managed semantics.

In the present paper[1], we carefully investigate the relationship between the memory-managed semantics and the garbage-collected semantics. We show that the difference only becomes apparent if there are programming errors of a particular form that we refer to as pointer races. A pointer race is a situation

---

This work was supported by the Czech Science Foundation, project 13-37876P, and by the German Science Foundation (DFG), project R2M2.

[1] The full version is available as technical report [9].

© Springer-Verlag Berlin Heidelberg 2016
B. Jobstmann and K.R.M. Leino (Eds.): VMCAI 2016, LNCS 9583, pp. 393–412, 2016.
DOI: 10.1007/978-3-662-49122-5_19

where a thread uses a pointer that has been freed before. We establish two theorems. First, if the memory-managed semantics is free from pointer races, then it coincides with the garbage-collected semantics. Second, whether or not the memory-managed semantics contains a pointer race can be checked with the garbage-collected semantics.

The developed semantic understanding helps to optimize program analyses. We show that the more complicated verification of the memory-managed semantics can often be reduced to an analysis of the simpler garbage-collected semantics — by applying the following policy: check under garbage collection whether the program is pointer race free. If there are pointer races, tell the programmer about these potential bugs. If there are no pointer races, rely on the garbage-collected semantics in all further analyses. In thread-modular reasoning, one of the motivations for our work, restricting to the garbage-collected semantics allows us to use a smaller abstract domain and an optimized fixed point computation. Particularly, it removes the need to correlate the local states of threads, and it restricts the possibilities of how threads can influence one another.

Example 1. We illustrate the idea of pointer race freedom on Treiber's stack [14], a lock-free implementation of a concurrent stack that provides the following methods:

```
// global variables: pTop            bool : pop(&v)
void : push(v)                       (7)   repeat
(1)  pnode := malloc;                (8)     ptop := pTop;
(2)  pnode.data := v;                (9)     if (ptop = null) return false;
(3)  repeat                          (10)    pnode := ptop.next;
(4)    ptop := pTop;                 (11)  until cas(pTop, ptop, pnode);
(5)    pnode.next := ptop;           (12)  v := ptop.data;
(6)  until cas(pTop, ptop, pnode);   (13)  ptop := free; return true;
```

This code is correct (i.e. linearizable and pops return the latest value pushed) in the presence of garbage collection, but it is incorrect under explicit memory management. The memory-managed semantics suffers from a problem known as ABA, which indeed is related to a pointer race. The problem arises as follows. Some thread t executing pop sets its local variable $ptop$ to the global top of the stack $pTop$, say address a. The variable $pnode$ is assigned the second topmost address b. While t executes pop, another thread frees address a with a pop. Since it has been freed, address a can be re-allocated and pushed, becoming the top of the stack again. However, the stack might have grown in between the free and the re-allocation. As a consequence, b is no longer the second node from the top. Thread t now executes the cas (atomic compare-and-swap). The command first tests $pTop = ptop$ (to check for consistency of the program state: has the top of the stack moved?). The test passes since $pTop$ has come back to a due to the re-allocation. Thread t then redirects $pTop$ to $pnode$. This is a pointer race: t relies on the variable $ptop$ where the address was freed, and the re-allocation was not under t's control. At the same time, this causes an error. If *pnode* no longer points to the second address from the top, moving *pTop* loses stack content. □

Performance-critical implementations often intentionally make use of pointer races and employ other mechanisms to protect themselves from harmful effects due to accidental re-allocations. The corrected version of Treiber's stack [10] for example equips every pointer with a version counter logging the updates. Pointer assignments then assign the address together with the value of the associated version counter, and the counters are taken into account in the comparisons within cas. That is, the cas($pTop, ptop, pnode$) command atomically executes the following code:

> if $(pTop = ptop \; \wedge \; pTop.\mathsf{version} = ptop.\mathsf{version})$ {
>
> $\quad pTop := pnode; \; pTop.\mathsf{version} := ptop.\mathsf{version} + 1$; return *true*;
>
> } *else* { return *false*; }

This makes the cas from Example 1 fail and prevents stack corruption. Another pointer race occurs when the pop in Line (10) dereferences a freed pointer. With version counters, this is harmless. Our basic theory, however, would consider the comparison as well as the dereference pointer races, deeming the corrected version of Treiber's stack buggy.

To cope with performance-critical applications that implement version counters or techniques such as hazard pointers [11], reference counting [6], or grace periods [8], we strengthen the notion of pointer race. We let it tolerate assertions on freed pointers and dereferences of freed pointers where the value obtained by the dereference does not visibly influence the computation (e.g., it is assigned to a dead variable). To analyse programs that are only free from strong pointer races, the garbage-collected semantics is no longer sufficient. We define a more general ownership-respecting semantics by imposing an ownership discipline on top of the memory-managed semantics. With this semantics, we are able to show the following analogues of the above results. First, if the program is free from strong pointer races (SPRF) under the memory-managed semantics, then the memory-managed semantics coincides with the ownership-respecting semantics. Second, the memory-managed semantics is SPRF if and only if the ownership-respecting semantics is SPRF.

As a last contribution, we show how to apply our theory to optimize thread-modular reasoning. The idea of thread-modular analysis is to buy efficiency by abstracting from the relationship between the local states of individual threads. The loss of precision, however, is often too severe. For instance, any inductive invariant strong enough to show memory safety of Treiber's stack must correlate the local states of threads. Thread-modular analyses must compensate this loss of precision. Under garbage collection, an efficient way used e.g. in [7,17] is keeping as a part of the local state of each thread information about the ownership of memory addresses. A thread owns an allocated address. No other thread can access it until it enters the shared part of the heap. Unfortunately, this exclusivity cannot be guaranteed under the memory-managed semantics. Addresses can be re-allocated with pointers of other threads still pointing to them. Works such as

[1,15] therefore correlate the local states of threads by more expensive means (cf. Sect. 5), for which they pay by severely decreased scalability.

We apply our theory to put back ownership information into thread-modular reasoning under explicit memory management. We measure the impact of our technique on the method of [1] when used to prove linearizability of programs such as Treiber's stack or Michael & Scott's lock-free queue under explicit memory management. We report on resource savings of about two orders of magnitude.

Contributions. We claim the following contributions, where $[\![P]\!]_{mm}$ denotes the memory-managed semantics, $[\![P]\!]_{own}$ the ownership-respecting semantics, and $[\![P]\!]_{gc}$ the garbage-collected semantics of program P.

(1) We define a notion of pointer race freedom (PRF) and an equivalence $\approx$ among computations such that the following two results hold.
  (1.1) If $[\![P]\!]_{mm}$ is PRF, then $[\![P]\!]_{mm} \approx [\![P]\!]_{gc}$.
  (1.2) $[\![P]\!]_{mm}$ is PRF if and only if $[\![P]\!]_{gc}$ is PRF.
(2) We define a notion of strong pointer race freedom (SPRF) and an ownership-respecting semantics $[\![P]\!]_{own}$ such that the following two results hold.
  (2.1) If $[\![P]\!]_{mm}$ is SPRF, then $[\![P]\!]_{mm} = [\![P]\!]_{own}$.
  (2.2) $[\![P]\!]_{mm}$ is SPRF if and only if $[\![P]\!]_{own}$ is SPRF.
(3) Using the Results (2.1) and (2.2), we optimize the recent thread-modular analysis [1] by a use of ownership and report on an experimental evaluation.

The Results (2.1) and (2.2) give less guarantees than (1.1) and (1.2) and hence allow for less simplifications of program analyses. On the other hand, the stronger notion of pointer race makes (2.1) and (2.2) applicable to a wider class of programs which would be racy in the original sense (which is the case for our most challenging benchmarks).

Finally, we note that our results are not only relevant for concurrent programs but apply to sequential programs as well. The point in the definition of pointer race freedom is to guarantee the following: the execution does not depend on whether a malloc has re-allocated an address, possibly with other pointers still pointing to it, or it has allocated a fresh address. However, it is mainly reasoning about concurrent programs where we see a motivation to strive for such guarantees.

Related Work. Our work was inspired by the data race freedom (DRF) guarantee [2]. The DRF guarantee can be understood as a contract between hardware architects and programming language designers. If the program is DRF under sequential consistency (SC), then the semantics on the actual architecture will coincide with SC. We split the analogue of the statement into two, coincidence ($[\![P]\!]_{mm}$ PRF implies $[\![P]\!]_{mm} \approx [\![P]\!]_{gc}$) and means of checking ($[\![P]\!]_{mm}$ PRF iff $[\![P]\!]_{gc}$ PRF). There are works that weaken the DRF requirement while still admitting efficient analyses [3,4,13]. Our notion of strong pointer races is along this line.

The closest related work is [8]. Gotsman et al. study re-allocation under explicit memory management. The authors focus on lock-free data structures implemented with hazard pointers, read-copy-update, or epoch-based reclamation. The key observation is that all three techniques rely on a common synchronization pattern called grace periods. Within a grace period of a cell a and a thread t, the thread can safely access the cell without having to fear a free command. The authors give thread-modular reasoning principles for grace periods and show that they lead to elegant and scalable proofs.

The relationship with our work is as follows. If grace periods are respected, then the program is guaranteed to be SPRF (there are equality checks on freed addresses). Hence, using Theorem 3 in this work, it is sufficient to verify lock-free algorithms under the ownership-respecting semantics. Interestingly, Gotsman et al. had an intuitive idea of pointer races without making the notion precise (quote: ...*potentially harmful race between threads accessing nodes and those trying to reclaim them is avoided* [8]). Moreover, they did not study the implications of race freedom on the semantics, which is the main interest of this paper. We stress that our approach does not make assumptions about the synchronization strategy. Finally, Gotsman et al. do not consider the problem of checking the synchronization scheme required by grace periods. We show that PRF and SPRF can actually be checked on simpler semantics.

Data refinement in the presence of low-level memory operation is studied in [12]. The work defines a notion of substitutability that only requires a refinement of *error-free computations*. In particular, there is no need to refine computations that dereference dangling pointers. In our terms, these dereferences yield pointer races. We consider [12] as supporting our requirement for (S)PRF.

The practical motivation of our work, thread-modular analysis [5], has already been discussed. We note the adaptation to heap-manipulating programs [7]. Interesting is also the combination with separation logic from [16,17] (which uses ownership to improve precision). There are other works studying shape analysis and thread-modular analysis. As these fields are only a part of the motivation, we do not provide a full overview.

2   Heap-Manipulating Programs

Syntax We consider **concurrent heap-manipulating programs**, defined to be sets of threads $P = \{t_1, t_2, \ldots\}$ from a set *Thrd*. We do not assume finiteness of programs. This ensures our results carry over to programs with a parametric number of threads. Threads t are ordinary while-programs operating on data and pointer variables. Data variables are denoted by $x, y \in DVar$. For pointer variables, we use $p, q \in PVar$. We assume $DVar \cap PVar = \emptyset$ and obey this typing. Pointer variables come with selectors $p.\text{next}_1, \ldots, p.\text{next}_n$ and $p.\text{data}$ for finitely many pointer fields and one data field (for simplicity; the generalization to arbitrary data fields is straightforward). We use pt to refer to pointers p and $p.\text{next}$. Similarly, by dt we mean data variables x and the corresponding selectors $p.\text{data}$. Pointer and data variables are either *local* to a thread, indicated by $p, x \in local_t$, or they are *shared* among the threads in the program. We use *shared* for the set of all shared variables.

The **commands** $com \in Com$ employed in our while-language are

$$
\begin{aligned}
cond ::=\ & p = q \mid x = y \mid \neg cond \\
com ::=\ & \texttt{assert}\ cond \mid p := \texttt{malloc} \mid p := \texttt{free} \\
& \mid q := p.\texttt{next} \mid p.\texttt{next} := q \mid p := q \\
& \mid x := p.\texttt{data} \mid p.\texttt{data} := x \mid x := \texttt{op}(x_1, \ldots, x_n) \ .
\end{aligned}
$$

Pointer variables are allocated with $p := \texttt{malloc}$ and freed via $p := \texttt{free}$. Pointers and data variables can be used in assignments. These assignments are subject to typing: we only assign pointers to pointers and data to data. Moreover, a thread only uses shared variables and its own local variables. To compute on data variables, we support operations op that are not specified further. We only assume that the program comes with a data domain (Dom, Op) so that its operations op stem from Op. We support assertions that depend on equalities and inequalities among pointers and data variables. Like in if and while commands, we require assertions to have complements: if a control location has a command $\texttt{assert}\ cond$, then it also has a command $\texttt{assert}\ \neg cond$. We use as a running example the program in Example 1, Treiber's stack [14].

Semantics. A heap is defined over a set of addresses Adr that contains the distinguished element $\texttt{seg}$. Value $\texttt{seg}$ indicates that a pointer has not yet been assigned a cell and thus its data and next selectors cannot be accessed. Such an access would result in a segfault. A heap gives the valuation of pointer variables $PVar \nrightarrow Adr$, the valuation of the next selector functions $Adr \nrightarrow Adr$, the valuation of the data variables $DVar \nrightarrow Dom$, and the valuation of the data selector fields $Adr \nrightarrow Dom$. In Sect. 3, we will restrict heaps to a subset of so-called valid pointers. To handle such restrictions, it is convenient to let heaps evaluate expressions $a.\texttt{next}$ rather than next functions. Moreover, with the use of restrictions valuation functions will typically be partial.

Let $PExp := PVar \uplus \{a.\texttt{next} \mid a \in Adr \setminus \{\texttt{seg}\}$ and $\texttt{next}$ a selector$\}$ be the set of pointer expressions and $DExp := DVar \uplus \{a.\texttt{data} \mid a \in Adr \setminus \{\texttt{seg}\}\}$ be the set of data expressions. A **heap** is a pair $h = (pval, dval)$ with $pval : PExp \nrightarrow Adr$ the valuation of the pointer expressions and $dval : DExp \nrightarrow Dom$ the valuation of the data expressions. We use $pexp$ and $dexp$ for a pointer and a data expression, and also write $h(pexp)$ or $h(dexp)$. The valuation functions are clear from the expression. The addresses inside the heap that are actually in use are

$$
adr(h) := (dom(pval) \cup range(pval) \cup dom(dval)) \cap Adr.
$$

Here, we use $\{a.\texttt{next}\} \cap Adr := \{a\}$ and similar for data selectors.

We model heap modifications with **updates** $[pexp \mapsto a]$ and $[dexp \mapsto d]$ from the set Upd. Update $[pexp \mapsto a]$ turns the partial function $pval$ into the new partial function $pval[pexp \mapsto a]$ with $dom(pval[pexp \mapsto a]) := dom(pval) \cup \{pexp\}$. It is defined by $pval[pexp \mapsto a](qexp) := pval(qexp)$ if $qexp \neq pexp$, and $pval[pexp \mapsto a](pexp) := a$. We also write $h[pexp \mapsto a]$ since the valuation that is altered is clear from the update.

We define three semantics for concurrent heap-manipulating programs. All three are in terms of computations, sequences of actions from $Act := Thrd \times Com \times Upd$. An action $act = (t, com, up)$ consist of a thread t, a command com executed in the thread, and an update up. By $thrd(act) := t$, $com(act) := com$, and $upd(act) := up$ we access the thread, the command, and the update in act. To make the heap resulting from a computation $\tau \in Act^*$ explicit, we define $h_\varepsilon := (\emptyset, \emptyset)$ and $h_{\tau.act} := h_\tau[upd(act)]$. So we modify the current heap with the update required by the last action.

The garbage-collected semantics and the memory-managed semantics only differ on allocations. We define a strict form of garbage collection that never re-allocates a cell. With this, we do not have to define unreachable parts of the heap that should be garbage collected. We only model computations that are free from segfaults. This means a transition accessing next and data selectors is enabled only if the corresponding pointer is assigned a cell.

Formally, the **garbage-collected semantics** of a program P, denoted by $[\![P]\!]_{gc}$, is a set of computations in Act^*. The definition is inductive. In the base case, we have single actions $(\bot, \bot, [pval, dval]) \in [\![P]\!]_{gc}$ with $pval : PVar \to \{\mathtt{seg}\}$ and $dval : DVar \to Dom$ arbitrary. No pointer variable is mapped to a cell and the data variables contain arbitrary values. In the induction step, consider $\tau \in [\![P]\!]_{gc}$ where thread t is ready to execute command com. Then $\tau.(t, com, up) \in [\![P]\!]_{gc}$, provided one of the following rules holds.

(Asgn). Let com be $p.\mathtt{next} := q$, $h_\tau(p) = a \neq \mathtt{seg}$, $h_\tau(q) = b$. We set $up = [a.\mathtt{next} \mapsto b]$. The remaining assignments are similar.

(Asrt). Let com be $\mathtt{assert}\ p = q$. The precondition is $h_\tau(p) = h_\tau(q)$. There are no updates, $up = \emptyset$. The assertion with a negated condition is defined analogously. A special case occurs if $h_\tau(p)$ or $h_\tau(q)$ is $\mathtt{seg}$. Then the assert and its negation will pass. Intuitively, undefined pointers hold arbitrary values. Our development does not depend on this modeling choice.

(Free). If com is $p := \mathtt{free}$, there are no constraints and no updates.

(Malloc1). Let com be $p := \mathtt{malloc}$, $a \notin adr(h_\tau)$, and $d \in Dom$. Then we define $up = [p \mapsto a, a.\mathtt{data} \mapsto d, \{a.\mathtt{next} \mapsto \mathtt{seg}\ |\ \text{for every selector}\ \mathtt{next}\}]$. The rule only allocates cells that have not been used in the computation. Such a cell holds an arbitrary data value and the next selectors have not yet been allocated.

With explicit memory management, we can re-allocate a cell as soon as it has been freed. Formally, the **memory-managed semantics** $[\![P]\!]_{mm} \subseteq Act^*$ is defined like $[\![P]\!]_{gc}$ but has a second allocation rule:

(Malloc2). Let com be $p := \mathtt{malloc}$ and $a \in freed_\tau$. Then $up = [p \mapsto a]$.

Note that (Malloc2) does not alter the selectors of address a. The set $freed_\tau$ contains the addresses that have been allocated in τ and freed afterwards. The definition is by induction. In the base case, we have $freed_\varepsilon := \emptyset$. The step case is

$$
\begin{aligned}
freed_{\tau.(t,p:=\texttt{free},up)} &:= freed_\tau \cup \{a\}, & \text{if } h_\tau(p) = a \neq \texttt{seg} \\
freed_{\tau.(t,p:=\texttt{malloc},up)} &:= freed_\tau \setminus \{a\}, & \text{if } \texttt{malloc} \text{ returns } a \\
freed_{\tau.(t,act,up)} &:= freed_\tau, & \text{otherwise.}
\end{aligned}
$$

3 Pointer Race Freedom

We show that for well-behaved programs the garbage-collected semantics coincides with the memory-managed semantics. Well-behaved means there is no computation where one pointer frees a cell and later a dangling pointer accesses this cell. We call such a situation a **pointer race**, referring to the fact that the free command and the access are not synchronized, for otherwise the access should have been avoided. To apply this equivalence, we continue to show how to reduce the check for pointer race freedom itself to the garbage-collected semantics.

3.1 PRF Guarantee

The definition of pointer races relies on a notion of validity for pointer expressions. To capture the situation sketched above, a pointer is invalidated if the cell it points to is freed. A pointer race is now an access to an invalid pointer. The definition of validity requires care when we pass pointers. Consider an assignment $p := q.\texttt{next}$ where q points to a and $a.\texttt{next}$ points to b. Then p becomes a valid pointer to b only if both q and $a.\texttt{next}$ were valid. In Definition 1, we use $pexp$ to uniformly refer to p and $a.\texttt{next}$ on the left-hand side of assignments. In particular, we evaluate pointer variables p to $h_\tau(p) = a$ and write $a.\texttt{next} := q$ for the assignment $p.\texttt{next} := q$.

Definition 1. *The **valid** pointer expressions in a computation* $\tau \in [\![P]\!]_{mm}$, *denoted by* $valid_\tau \subseteq PExp$, *are defined inductively by* $valid_\varepsilon := PExp$ *and*

$$
\begin{aligned}
valid_{\tau.(t,p:=q.\texttt{next},up)} &:= valid_\tau \cup \{p\}, & \text{if } q \in valid_\tau \wedge h_\tau(q).\texttt{next} \in valid_\tau \\
valid_{\tau.(t,p:=q.\texttt{next},up)} &:= valid_\tau \setminus \{p\}, & \text{if } q \notin valid_\tau \vee h_\tau(q).\texttt{next} \notin valid_\tau \\
valid_{\tau.(t,pexp:=q,up)} &:= valid_\tau \cup \{pexp\}, & \text{if } q \in valid_\tau \\
valid_{\tau.(t,pexp:=q,up)} &:= valid_\tau \setminus \{pexp\}, & \text{if } q \notin valid_\tau \\
valid_{\tau.(t,p:=\texttt{free},up)} &:= valid_\tau \setminus invalid_a, & \text{if } a = h_\tau(p) \\
valid_{\tau.(t,p:=\texttt{malloc},up)} &:= valid_\tau \cup \{p\}, & \\
valid_{\tau.(t,act,up)} &:= valid_\tau, & \text{otherwise.}
\end{aligned}
$$

If $a \neq \texttt{seg}$, *then* $invalid_a := \{pexp \mid h_\tau(pexp) = a\} \cup \{a.\texttt{next}_1, \ldots, a.\texttt{next}_n\}$. *If* $a = \texttt{seg}$, *then* $invalid_a := \emptyset$.

When we pass a valid pointer, this validates the receiver (adds it to $valid_\tau$). When we pass an invalid pointer, this invalidates the receiver. As a result, only some selectors of an address may be valid. When we free an address $a \neq \texttt{seg}$, all expressions that point to a as well as all next selectors of a become invalid. This has the effect of isolating a so that the address behaves like a fresh one for valid pointers. A malloc validates the respective pointer but does not validate the next selectors of the allocated address.

Definition 2 (Pointer Race). *A computation* $\tau.(t, com, up) \in [\![P]\!]_{mm}$ *is called a **pointer race (PR)**, if com is*

(i) a command containing $p.\mathsf{data}$ *or* $p.\mathsf{next}$ *or* $p := \mathsf{free}$ *with* $p \notin valid_\tau$, *or*
(ii) an assertion containing $p \notin valid_\tau$.

The last action of a PR is said to **raise a PR**. A set of computations is **pointer race free (PRF)** if it does not contain a PR. In Example 1, the discussed comparison $pTop = ptop$ within cas raises a PR since $ptop$ is invalid. It is worth noting that we can still pass around freed addresses without raising a PR. This means the memory-managed and the garbage-collected semantics will not yield isomorphic heaps, but only yield isomorphic heaps on the valid pointers. We now define the notion of isomorphism among heaps h.

A function $f_{adr} : adr(h) \rightarrow Adr$ is an address mapping, if $f_{adr}(a) = \mathsf{seg}$ if and only if $a = \mathsf{seg}$. Every address mapping induces a function $f_{exp} : dom(h) \rightarrow PExp \cup DExp$ on the pointer and data expressions inside the heap by

$$f_{exp}(p) := p \qquad\qquad f_{exp}(x) := x$$
$$f_{exp}(a.\mathsf{next}) := f_{adr}(a).\mathsf{next} \qquad\qquad f_{exp}(a.\mathsf{data}) := f_{adr}(a).\mathsf{data}.$$

Pointer and data variables are mapped identically. Pointers on the heap $a.\mathsf{next}$ are mapped to $f_{adr}(a).\mathsf{next}$ as defined by the address mapping, and similar for the data.

Definition 3. *Two heaps* h_1 *and* h_2 *with* $h_i = (pval_i, dval_i)$ *are* **isomorphic**, *denoted by* $h_1 \equiv h_2$, *if there is a bijective address mapping* $iso_{adr} : adr(h_1) \rightarrow adr(h_2)$ *where the induced* $iso_{exp} : dom(h_1) \rightarrow dom(h_2)$ *is again bijective and satisfies*

$$iso_{adr}(pval_1(pexp)) = pval_2(iso_{exp}(pexp)) \quad dval_1(dexp) = dval_2(iso_{exp}(dexp)).$$

To prove a correspondence between the two semantics, we restrict heaps to the valid pointers. The restriction operation keeps the data selectors for all addresses that remain. To be more precise, let $h = (pval, dval)$ and $P \subseteq PExp$. The **restriction of** h **to** P is the new heap $h|_P := (pval|_P, dval|_D)$ with

$$D := DVar \cup \{a.\mathsf{data} \mid \exists pexp \in dom(pval) \cap P : pval(pexp) = a\}.$$

Restriction and update enjoy a pleasant interplay with isomorphism.

Lemma 1. *Let* $h_1 \equiv h_2$ *via* iso_{adr} *and let* $P \subseteq PExp$. *Then*

$$h_1|_P \equiv h_2|_{iso_{exp}(P)} \tag{14}$$
$$h_1[a.\mathsf{next} \mapsto b] \equiv h_2[a'.\mathsf{next} \mapsto b'] \tag{15}$$
$$h_1[a.\mathsf{data} \mapsto d] \equiv h_2[a'.\mathsf{data} \mapsto d]. \tag{16}$$

Isomorphisms (15) and (16) have a side condition. If $a \in adr(h_1)$ then $a' = iso_{adr}(a)$. If $a \notin adr(h_1)$ then $a' \notin adr(h_2)$, and similar for b.

Two computations are heap equivalent, if their sequences of actions coincide when projected to the threads and commands, and if the resulting heaps are isomorphic on the valid part. We use $\downarrow$ for projection.

Definition 4. *Computations $\tau, \sigma \in [\![P]\!]_{mm}$ are* **heap-equivalent**, $\tau \approx \sigma$, *if*

$$\tau \downarrow_{Thrd \times Com} = \sigma \downarrow_{Thrd \times Com} \qquad and \qquad h_\tau|_{valid_\tau} \equiv h_\sigma|_{valid_\sigma} .$$

We also write $[\![P]\!]_{mm} \approx [\![P]\!]_{gc}$ to state that for every computation $\tau \in [\![P]\!]_{mm}$, there is a computation $\sigma \in [\![P]\!]_{gc}$ with $\tau \approx \sigma$, and vice versa.

We are now ready to state the PRF guarantee. The idea is to consider pointer races programming errors. If a program has pointer races, the programmer should be warned. If the program is PRF, further analyses can rely on the garbage-collected semantics:

Theorem 1 (PRF Guarantee). *If $[\![P]\!]_{mm}$ is PRF, then $[\![P]\!]_{mm} \approx [\![P]\!]_{gc}$.*

The memory-managed semantics of Treiber's stack suffers from the ABA-problem while the garbage-collected semantics does not. The two are not heap-equivalent. By Theorem 1, the difference is due to a PR. One such race is discussed in Example 1.

In the proof of Theorem 1, the inclusion from right to left always holds. The reverse direction needs information about the freed addresses: if an address has been freed, it no longer occurs in the valid part of the heap — provided the computation is PRF.

Lemma 2. *Assume $\tau \in [\![P]\!]_{mm}$ is PRF. Then $freed_\tau \cap adr(h_\tau|_{valid_\tau}) = \emptyset$.*

Lemmas 1 and 2 allow us to prove Proposition 1. The result implies the missing direction of Theorem 1 and will also be helpful later on.

Proposition 1. *Consider $\tau \in [\![P]\!]_{mm}$ PRF. Then there is $\sigma \in [\![P]\!]_{gc}$ with $\sigma \approx \tau$.*

To apply Theorem 1, one has to prove $[\![P]\!]_{mm}$ PRF. We develop a technique for this.

3.2   Checking PRF

We show that checking pointer race freedom for the memory-managed semantics can be reduced to checking pointer race freedom for the garbage-collected semantics. The key argument is that the earliest possible PR always lie in the garbage-collected semantics. Technically, we consider a shortest PR in the memory-managed semantics and from this construct a PR in the garbage-collected semantics.

Theorem 2 (Checking PRF). *$[\![P]\!]_{mm}$ is PRF if and only if $[\![P]\!]_{gc}$ is PRF.*

To illustrate the result, the pointer race in Example 1 belongs to the memory-managed semantics. Under garbage collection, there is a similar computation which does not re-allocate a. Freeing a still renders *ptop* invalid and, as before, leads to a PR in cas. The proof of Theorem 2 applies Proposition 1 to mimic the shortest racy computation up to the last action. To mimic the action that raises the PR, we need the fact that an invalid pointer variable does not hold seg, as stated in the following lemma.

Lemma 3. *Consider a PRF computation* $\sigma \in [\![P]\!]_{gc}$. *(i) If* $p \notin valid_\sigma$, *then* $h_\sigma(p) \neq$ seg. *(ii) If* $pexp \in valid_\sigma$, $h_\sigma(pexp) = a \neq$ seg, *and* a.next $\notin valid_\sigma$, *then* $h_\sigma(a.\text{next}) \neq$ seg.

While the completeness proof of Theorem 2 is non-trivial, checking PRF for $[\![P]\!]_{gc}$ is an easy task. One instruments the given program P to a new program P' as follows: P' tags every address that is freed and checks whether a tagged address is dereferenced, freed, or used in an assertion. In this case, P' enters a distinguished goal state.

Proposition 2. $[\![P]\!]_{gc}$ *is PRF if and only if* $[\![P']\!]_{gc}$ *cannot reach the goal state.*

For the correctness proof, we only need to observe that under garbage collection the invalid pointers are precisely the pointers to the freed cells.

Lemma 4. *Let* $\sigma \in [\![P]\!]_{gc}$ *and* $h_\sigma(pexp) = a \neq$ seg. *Then* $pexp \notin valid_\sigma$ *iff* $a \in freed_\sigma$.

The lemma does not hold for the memory-managed semantics. Moreover, the statement turns Lemma 2, which can be read as an implication, into an equivalence. Namely, Lemma 2 says that if a pointer has been freed, then it cannot be valid. Under the assumptions of Lemma 4, it also holds that if a pointer is not valid, then it has been freed.

4   Strong Pointer Race Freedom

The programing style in which a correct program should be pointer race free counts on the following policy: a memory address is freed only if it is not meant to be touched until its re-allocation, by any means possible.

This simplified treatment of dynamic memory is practical in common programing tasks, but the authors of performance-critical applications are often forced to employ subtler techniques. For example, the version of Treiber's stack equipped with version counters to prevent ABA under explicit memory management contains two violations of the simple policy, both of which are pointer races. (1) The cas may compare invalid pointers. This could potentially lead to ABA, but the programmer prevents the harmful effect of re-allocation using version counters, which make the cas fail. (2) The command *pnode* := *ptop*.next in Line 10 of pop may dereference the next field of a freed (and therefore invalid) pointer. This is actually correct only under the assumption that neither the environment nor any thread of the program itself may redirect a once valid pointer outside the accessible memory (otherwise the dereference could lead to a segfault). The value obtained by the dereference may again be influenced by that the address was re-allocated. The reason for why this is fine is that the subsequent `cas` is bound to fail, which makes *pnode* a dead variable — its value does not matter.

In both cases, the programmer only prevents side effects of an accidental re-allocation. He uses a subtler policy and frees an address only if its *content* is not meant to be of any relevance any more. Invalid addresses can still be compared, and their pointer fields can even be dereferenced unless the obtained value influences the control.

4.1   SPRF Guarantee

We introduce a stronger notion of pointer race that expresses the above subtler policy. In the definition, we will call strongly invalid the pointer expressions that have obtained their value from dereferencing an invalid/freed pointer.

Definition 5 (Strong Invalidity). *The set of* **strongly invalid** *expressions in $\tau \in \llbracket P \rrbracket_{mm}$, denoted by $sinvalid_\tau \subseteq PExp \cup DExp$, is defined inductively by $sinvalid_\varepsilon := \emptyset$ and*

$$
\begin{aligned}
sinvalid_{\tau.(t,p:=q.\texttt{next},up)} &:= sinvalid_\tau \cup \{p\}, && if\ q \notin valid_\tau \\
sinvalid_{\tau.(t,pexp:=q,up)} &:= sinvalid_\tau \cup \{pexp\}, && if\ q \in sinvalid_\tau \\
sinvalid_{\tau.(t,x:=q.\texttt{data},up)} &:= sinvalid_\tau \cup \{x\}, && if\ q \notin valid_\tau \\
sinvalid_{\tau.(t,dexp:=x,up)} &:= sinvalid_\tau \cup \{dexp\}, && if\ x \in sinvalid_\tau \\
sinvalid_{\tau.act} &:= sinvalid_\tau \setminus valid_{\tau.act}, && in\ all\ other\ cases.
\end{aligned}
$$

The value obtained by dereferencing a freed pointer may depend on actions of other threads that point to the cell due to re-allocation. However, by assuming that a once valid pointer can never be set to `seg`, we obtain a guarantee that the actions of other threads cannot prevent the dereference itself from being executed (they cannot make it segfault). Assigning the uncontrolled value to a local variable is therefore not harmful. We only wish to prevent a correct computation from being influenced by that value. We thus define incorrect/racy any attempt to compare or dereference the value. Then, besides allowing for the creation of strongly invalid pointers, the notion of strong pointer race strengthens PR by tolerating comparisons of invalid pointers.

Definition 6 (Strong Pointer Race). *A computation $\tau.(t, com, up) \in \llbracket P \rrbracket_{mm}$ is a* **strong pointer race (SPR)***, if the command com is one of the following:*

(i) p.next := q or p.data := x or p := free with $p \notin valid_\tau$
(ii) an assertion containing p or x in $sinvalid_\tau$
(iii) a command containing p.next or p.data where $p \in sinvalid_\tau$.

The last action of an SPR **raises an SPR.** A set of computations is **strong pointer race free (SPRF)** if it does not contain an SPR. An SPR can be seen in Example 1 as a continuation of the race ending at `cas`. The subsequent

$ptop := \mathtt{free}$ raises an SPR as $ptop$ is invalid. The implementation corrected with version counters is SPRF.

Theorems 1 and 2 no longer hold for strong pointer race freedom. It is not possible to verify $[\![P]\!]_{mm}$ modulo SPRF by analysing $[\![P]\!]_{gc}$. The reason is that the garbage-collected semantics does not cover SPRF computations that compare or dereference invalid pointers. To formulate a sound analogy of the theorems, we have to replace $[\![.]\!]_{gc}$ by a more powerful semantics. This, however, comes with a trade-off. The new semantics should still be amenable to efficient thread-modular reasoning.

The idea of our new semantics $[\![P]\!]_{own}$ is to introduce the concept of ownership to the memory-managed semantics, and show that SPRF computations stick to it. Unlike with garbage collection, we cannot use a naive notion of ownership that guarantees the owner exclusive access to an address. This is too strong a guarantee. In $[\![P]\!]_{mm}$, other threads may still have access to an owned address via invalid pointers. Instead, we design ownership such that dangling pointers are not allowed to influence the owner. The computation will thus proceed as if the owner had allocated a fresh address.

To this end, we let a thread own an allocated address until one of the two events happen: either (1) the address is *published*, that is, it enters the shared part of the heap (which consists of addresses reached from shared variables by following valid pointers and of freed addresses), or (2) the address is *compromised*, that is, the owner finds out that the cell is not fresh by comparing it with an invalid pointer. Taking away ownership in this situation is needed since the owner can now change its behavior based on the re-allocation. The owner may also spread the information about the re-allocation among the other threads and change their behavior, too. It can thus no longer be guaranteed that the computation will continue as if a fresh address had been allocated.

Definition 7 (Owned Addresses). *For* $\tau \in [\![P]\!]_{mm}$ *and a thread* t, *we define the set of addresses* **owned by** t, *denoted by* $own_\tau(t)$, *as* $own_\varepsilon(t) := \emptyset$ *and*

$$
\begin{aligned}
own_{\tau.(t,p:=\mathtt{malloc},up)}(t) &:= own_\tau(t) \cup \{a\}, &&\text{if } p \in local_t \text{ and } \mathtt{malloc} \text{ returns } a \\
own_{\tau.(t,p:=\mathtt{free},\emptyset)}(t) &:= own_\tau(t) \setminus \{h_\tau(p)\}, &&\text{if } p \in valid_\tau \\
own_{\tau.(t,p:=q,[p\mapsto a])}(t) &:= own_\tau(t) \setminus \{a\}, &&\text{if } p \in shared \wedge q \in valid_\tau \\
own_{\tau.(t,p:=q.\mathtt{next},[p\mapsto a])}(t) &:= own_\tau(t) \setminus \{a\}, &&\text{if } p \in shared \wedge q, h_\tau(q).\mathtt{next} \in valid_\tau \\
own_{\tau.(\cdot,p:=q.\mathtt{next},[p\mapsto a])}(t) &:= own_\tau(t) \setminus \{a\}, &&\text{if } h_\tau(q) \notin own_\tau(t) \wedge q, h_\tau(q).\mathtt{next} \in valid_\tau \\
own_{\tau.(t,\mathtt{assert}\ p=q,\emptyset)}(t) &:= own_\tau(t) \setminus \{h_\tau(p)\}, &&\text{if } p \notin valid_\tau \vee q \notin valid_\tau \\
own_{\tau.act}(t) &:= own_\tau(t), &&\text{in all other cases.}
\end{aligned}
$$

The first four cases of losing ownership are due to publishing, the last case is due to the address being compromised by comparing with an invalid pointer.

The following lemma states the intuitive fact that an owned address cannot be pointed to by a valid shared variable or by a valid local variable of another thread, since such a configuration can be achieved only by publishing the address.

Lemma 5. *Let* $\tau \in [\![P]\!]_{mm}$ *and* $p \in valid_\tau$ *with* $h_\tau(p) \in own_\tau(t)$. *Then* $p \in local_t$.

We now define ownership violations as precisely those situations in which the fact that an owned address was re-allocated while an invalid pointer was still pointing to it influences the computation. Technically, the address is freed or its content is altered due to an access via a pointer of another thread or a shared pointer.

Definition 8 (Ownership Violation). *A computation* $\tau.(t, com, up) \in [\![P]\!]_{mm}$ **violates ownership,** *if com is one of the following*

$$q.\texttt{next} := p, \quad q.\texttt{data} := x, \quad or \quad q := \texttt{free},$$

where $h_\tau(q) \in own_\tau(t')$ *and* $(t' \neq t$ *or* $q \in shared)$.

The last action of a computation violating ownership is called an **ownership violation** and a computation which does not violate ownership **respects ownership.** We define the **ownership-respecting semantics** $[\![P]\!]_{own}$ as those computations of $[\![P]\!]_{mm}$ that respect ownership. The following lemma shows that SPRF computations respect ownership.

Lemma 6. *If* $\tau.(t, com, act) \in [\![P]\!]_{mm}$ *violates ownership, then it is an SPR.*

The proof of Lemma 6 is immediate from Lemma 5 and the definitions of ownership violation and strong pointer race. The lemma implies the main result of this section: the memory-managed semantics coincides with the ownership-respecting semantics modulo SPRF.

Theorem 3 (SPRF Guarantee). *If* $[\![P]\!]_{mm}$ *is SPRF, then* $[\![P]\!]_{mm} = [\![P]\!]_{own}$.

4.2   Checking SPRF

This section establishes that checking SPRF may be done in the ownership-respecting semantics. In other words, if $[\![P]\!]_{mm}$ has an SPR, then there is also one in $[\![P]\!]_{own}$. This result, perhaps much less intuitively expected than the symmetrical result of Sect. 3.2, is particularly useful for optimizing thread-modular analysis of lock-free programs (cf. Section 5). Its proof depends on a subtle interplay of ownership and validity.

Let $ownpntrs_\tau$ be the *owning pointers*, pointers in h_τ to addresses that are owned by threads and the next fields of addresses owned by threads. To be included in $ownpntrs_\tau$, the pointers have to be valid. A set of pointers $O \subseteq ownpntrs_\tau$ is *coherent* if for all $pexp, qexp \in ownpntrs_\tau$ with the same target or source address (in case of $a.\texttt{next}$ or $a.\texttt{data}$) we have $pexp \in O$ if and only if $qexp \in O$.

Lemma 7 below establishes the following fact. For every computation that respects ownership, there is another one that coincides with it but assigns fresh cells to some of the owning pointers. To be more precise, given a computation $\tau \in [\![P]\!]_{own}$ and a coherent set of owning pointers $O \subseteq ownpntrs_\tau$, we can find another computation $\tau' \in [\![P]\!]_{own}$ where the resulting heap coincides with h_τ except for O. These pointers are assigned fresh addresses. The proof of Lemma 7 is nontrivial and can be found in [9].

Lemma 7. *Consider* $\tau \in [\![P]\!]_{own}$ *SPRF and* $O \subseteq ownpntrs_\tau$ *a coherent set. There is* $\tau' \in [\![P]\!]_{own}$ *and an address mapping* $f_{adr} : adr(O) \to Adr$ *that satisfy the following:*

(1)	$\tau \downarrow_{Thrd \times Com} = \tau' \downarrow_{Thrd \times Com}$	$freed_\tau \subseteq freed_{\tau'}$	(4)
(2)	$h_\tau|_{PExp \setminus O} = h_{\tau'}|_{PExp \setminus f_{exp}(O)}$	$ownpntrs_{\tau'} = (ownpntrs_\tau \setminus O) \cup f_{exp}(O)$	(5)
(3)	$h_\tau|_{valid_\tau} \equiv h_{\tau'}|_{valid_{\tau'}}$ by $f_{adr} \cup id$	$adr(h_\tau) \cap h_{\tau'}(f_{exp}(O)) = \emptyset.$	(6)

In this lemma, function f_{adr} specifies the new addresses that τ' assigns to the owning expressions in O. These new addresses are fresh by Point (6). Point (1) says that τ and τ' are the same up to the particular addresses they manipulate, and Point (2) says that the reached states h_τ and $h_{\tau'}$ are the same up to the pointers touched by f_{adr}. Point (3) states that the valid pointers of h_τ stay valid or become valid f_{exp}-images of the originals. Point (5) says that also the owned pointers of h_τ remain the same or become f_{exp}-images of the originals. Finally, Point (4) says that $h_{\tau'}$ re-allocates less cells.

Lemma 7 is a cornerstone in the proof of the main result in this section, namely that SPRF is equivalent for the memory-managed and the ownership-respecting semantics.

Theorem 4 (Checking SPRF). $[\![P]\!]_{mm}$ *is SPRF if and only if* $[\![P]\!]_{own}$ *is SPRF.*

Proof. If $[\![P]\!]_{mm}$ is SPRF, by $[\![P]\!]_{own} \subseteq [\![P]\!]_{mm}$ this carries over to the ownership-respecting semantics. For the reverse direction, assume $[\![P]\!]_{mm}$ has an SPR. In this case, there is a shortest computation $\tau.act \in [\![P]\!]_{mm}$ where act raises an SPR. In case $\tau.act \in [\![P]\!]_{own}$, we obtain the same SPR in the ownership-respecting semantics.

Assume $\tau.act \notin [\![P]\!]_{own}$. We first argue that act violates ownership. By prefix closure, $\tau \in [\![P]\!]_{mm}$. By minimality, τ is SPRF. Since ownership violations are SPR by Lemma 6, τ does not contain any, $\tau \in [\![P]\!]_{own}$. Hence, if act respected ownership we could extend τ to the computation $\tau.act \in [\![P]\!]_{own}$ — a contradiction to our assumption.

We turn this ownership violation in the memory-managed semantics into an SPR in the ownership-respecting semantics. To this end, we construct a new computation $\tau'.act' \in [\![P]\!]_{own}$ that mimics $\tau.act$, respects ownership, but suffers from SPR. Since $\tau.act$ is an ownership violation, act takes the form (t, com, up) with com being

$$q.\textbf{next} := p, \quad q.\textbf{data} := x, \quad \text{or} \quad q := \textbf{free}.$$

Here, $h_\tau(q) \in own_\tau(t')$ and $(t' \neq t$ or $q \in shared)$. Since the address is owned, Lemma 5 implies $q \notin valid_\tau$.

As a first step towards the new computation, we construct τ'. Let $O := ownpntrs_\tau$ be the (coherent) set of all owning pointers in all threads (with $q \notin O$). With this choice of O, we apply Lemma 7. It returns $\tau' \in [\![P]\!]_{own}$ with $\tau' \downarrow_{Thrd \times Com} = \tau \downarrow_{Thrd \times Com}$ and

$$h_{\tau'}|_{PExp \setminus f_{exp}(O)} = h_\tau|_{PExp \setminus O} \quad \text{and} \quad h_{\tau'}|_{valid_{\tau'}} \equiv h_\tau|_{valid_\tau}.$$

Address $h_{\tau'}(q)$ is not owned by any thread. This follows from

$$ownpntrs_{\tau'} = (ownpntrs_\tau \setminus O) \cup f_{exp}(O) = f_{exp}(O)$$

and $q \notin f_{exp}(O)$. Finally, $q \notin valid_{\tau'}$ by the isomorphism $h_{\tau'}|_{valid_{\tau'}} \equiv h_\tau|_{valid_\tau}$.

As a last step, we mimic $act = (t, com, up)$ by an action $act' = (t, com, up')$. If com is $q :=$ free, then we free the invalid pointer $q \notin valid_{\tau'}$ and obtain an SPR in $[\![P]\!]_{own}$. Assume com is an assignment $q.\text{next} := p$ (the case of $q.\text{data} := x$ is similar). Since act is enabled after τ and $h_{\tau'}(q) = h_\tau(q)$, we have $h_{\tau'}(q) \neq$ seg. Hence, the command is also enabled after τ'. Since $q \notin valid_{\tau'}$, the assignment is again to an invalid pointer. It is thus an SPR according by Definition 6.(i). $\square$

5   Improving Thread-Modular Analyses

We now describe how the theory developed so far can be used to increase the efficiency of thread-modular analyses of pointer programs under explicit memory management.

Thread-modular reasoning abstracts a program state into a set of states of individual threads. A thread's state consists of the local state, the part of the heap reachable from the local variables, and the shared state, the heap reachable from the shared variables.

The analysis saturates the set of reachable thread states by a fixpoint computation. Every step in this computation creates new thread states out of the existing ones by applying the following two rules. (1) Sequential step: a thread's state is modified by an action of this thread. (2) Interference: a state of a victim thread is changed by an action of another, interfering thread. This is accounted for by creating combined two-threads states from existing pairs of states of the victim and the interferer thread. The states that are combined have to agree on the shared part. The combined state is constructed by deciding which addresses in the two local states coincide. It is then observed how an action of the interferer changes the state of the victim within the combined state.

Pure thread-modular reasoning does not keep any information about what thread states can appear simultaneously during a computation and what identities can possibly hold between addresses of local states of threads. This brings efficiency, but also easily leads to false positives. To see this, consider in Treiber's stack a state s of a thread that is just about to perform the cas in push. Variable $pnode$ points to an address a allocated in the first line of push, $pTop$, $ptop$, and $pnode.\text{next}$ are at the top of the stack. Consider an interference step where the states s_v of the victim and s_i of the interferer are isomorphic to s, with $pnode$ pointing to the newly allocated addresses a_v and a_i, respectively. Since the shared states coincide, the interference is triggered. The combination must account for all possible equalities among the local variables. Hence, there is a combined state with $a_v = a_i$, which does not occur in reality. This is a crucial imprecision, which leads to false positives. Namely, the interferer's cas succeeds, resulting in the new victim's state s'_v with $pTop$ on a_i (which is equal to a_v). The victim's `cas` then fails, and the thread continues with the commands $ptop := pTop; pnode.\texttt{next} := ptop$. This results in $a_v.\texttt{next}$ pointing back to a_v, and a loss of the stack content.

Methods based on thread-modular reasoning must prevent such false positives by maintaining the necessary information about correlations of local states. An efficient technique commonly used under garbage collection is based on ownership: a thread's state records that a has just been allocated and hence no other thread can access the address, until it enters the shared state. This is enough to prevent false positives such as the one described above. Namely, the addresses a_i and a_v are owned by the respective threads and therefore they cannot be equal. Interference may then safely ignore the problematic case when $a_v = a_i$. Moreover, besides the increased precision, the ability to avoid interference steps due to ownership significantly improves the overall efficiency. This technique was used for instance to prove safety (and linearizability) of Treiber's stack and other subtle lock-free algorithms in [17].

Under explicit memory management, ownership of this form cannot be guaranteed. Addresses can be freed and re-allocated while still being pointed to. Other techniques must be used to correlate the local states of threads. The solution chosen in [1,15] is to replace the states of individual threads by states of pairs of threads. Precision is thus restored at the cost of an almost quadratic blow-up of the abstract domain that in turn manifests itself in a severe decrease of scalability.

5.1   Pointer Race Freedom Saves Ownership

Using the results from Sects. 3 and 4, we show how to apply the ownership-based optimization of thread-modular reasoning to the memory-managed semantics. To this end, we split the verification effort into two phases. Depending on the notion of pointer race freedom, we first check whether the program under scrutiny is (S)PRF. If the check fails, we report pointer races as potential errors to the developer. If the check succeeds, the second phase verifies the property of interest (here, linearizability) assuming (S)PRF.

When the notion of PRF from Sect. 3 is used, the second verification phase can be performed in the garbage-collected semantics due to Theorem 1. This allows us to apply the ownership-based optimization discussed above. Moreover, Theorem 2 says that the first PR has to appear in the garbage-collected semantics. Hence, even the first phase, checking PRF, can rely on garbage collection and ownership. The PRF check itself is simple. Validity of pointers is kept as a part of the individual thread states and updated at every sequential and interference step. Based on this, every computation step is checked for raising a PR according to Definition 2. Our experiments suggest that the overhead caused by the recorded validity information is low.

For SPRF, we proceed analogously. Due to the Theorems 3 and 4, checking SPRF in the first phase and property verification in the second phase can both be done in the ownership-respecting semantics. The SPRF check is similar to the PRF check. Validity of pointers together with an information about strong invalidity is kept as a part of a thread's state, and every step is checked for raising an SPR according to Definition 6.

The surprising good news is that both phases can again use the ownership-based optimization. That is, also in the ownership-respecting semantics, interferences on the owned memory addresses can be skipped. We argue that this is sound. Due to Lemma 5, if a thread t owns an address a, other threads may access a only via invalid pointers. Therefore, (1) modifications of a by t need not be considered as an interference step for other threads. Indeed, if a thread $t' \neq t$ was influenced by such a modification (t' reads a next or the data field of a), then the corresponding variable of t' would become strongly invalid, Definition 5. Hence, either this variable is never used in an assertion or in a dereference again (it is effectively dead), or the first use raises an SPR, Cases (ii) and (iii) in Definition 6. (2) In turn, in the ownership-respecting semantics, another thread t' cannot make changes to a, by Definition 8 of ownership violations. This means we can also avoid the step where t' interferes with the victim t.

5.2 Experimental Results

To substantiate our claim for a more efficient analysis with practical experiments, we implemented the thread-modular analysis from [1] in a prototype tool. This analysis is challenging for three reasons: it checks linearizability as a non-trivial requirement, it handles an unbounded number of threads, and it supports an unbounded heap. Our tool covers the garbage-collected semantics, the new ownership-respecting semantics of Sect. 4, and the memory-managed semantics. For the former two, we use the abstract domain where local states refer to single threads. Moreover, we support the ownership-based pruning of interference steps from Sect. 5.1. For the memory-managed semantics, to restore precision as discussed above, the abstract domain needs local states with pairs of threads. Rather than running two phases, our tool combines the PRF check and the actual analysis. We tested our implementation on lock-free data structures from the literature and verified linearizability following the approach in [1].

The experimental results are listed in Table 1. The experiments were conducted on an Intel Xeon E5-2650 v3 running at 2.3 GHz. The table includes the following: (1) runtime taken to establish correctness, (2) number of explored thread states (i.e. size of the search space), (3) number of sequential steps, (4) number of interference steps, (5) number of interference steps that have been pruned by the ownership-based optimization, and (6) the result of the analysis, i.e. whether or not correctness could be established. For a comparison, we also include the results with the ownership-based optimization turned off (suffix $^-$). Recall that the optimization does not apply to the memory-managed semantics. We elaborate on our findings.

Table 1. Experimental results for thread-modular reasoning using different memory semantics.

Program		Time in seconds	Explored state count	Sequential step count	Interference step count	Pruned interferences	Correctness established
Single lock stack	GC	0.053	328	941	3276	10160	yes
	OWN	0.21	703	1913	6983	22678	yes
	GC⁻	0.20	507	1243	19321	–	yes
	OWN⁻	0.60	950	2474	38117	–	yes
	MM⁻	5.34	16117	25472	183388	–	yes
Single lock queue	GC	0.034	199	588	738	5718	yes
	OWN	0.56	520	1336	734	31200	yes
	GC⁻	0.19	331	778	9539	–	yes
	OWN⁻	2.52	790	1963	65025	–	yes
	MM⁻	31.7	27499	60263	442306	–	yes
Treiber's lock	GC	0.052	269	779	3516	15379	yes
free stack	OWN	2.36	744	2637	43261	95398	yes
(with version	GC⁻	0.16	296	837	11530	–	yes
counters) [10]	OWN⁻	4.21	746	2158	73478	–	yes
	MM⁻	602	116776	322057	7920186	–	yes
Michael & Scott's	GC	2.52	3134	6607	46838	1237012	yes
lock free queue	OWN	10564	19553	43305	6678240	20747559	yes
[10] (with hints)	GC⁻	9.08	3309	7753	187349	–	yes
	OWN⁻	51046	31329	64234	35477171	–	yes
	MM⁻	aborted	≥ 69000	≥ 90000		–	false positive

Our experiments confirm the usefulness of pointer race freedom. When equipped with pruning (OWN), the ownership-respecting semantics provides a speed-up of two orders of magnitude for Treiber's stack and the single lock data structures compared to the memory-managed semantics (MM⁻). The size of the explored state space is close to the one for the garbage-collected semantics (GC) and up to two orders of magnitude smaller than the one for explicit memory management. We also stress tested our tool by purposely inserting pointer races, for example, by discarding the version counters. In all cases, the tool was able to detect those races.

For Michael & Scott's queue we had to provide hints in order to eliminate certain patterns of false positives. This is due to an imprecision that results from joins over a large number of states (we are using the joined representation of states from [1] based on Cartesian abstraction). Those hints are sufficient for the analysis relying on the ownership-respecting semantics to establish correctness. The memory-manged semantics produces more false positives, the elimination of which would require more hinting, as also witnessed by the implementation of [1]. Regarding the stress tests from above, note that we ran those tests with the same hints and were still able to find the purposely inserted bugs.

References

1. Abdulla, P.A., Haziza, F., Holík, L., Jonsson, B., Rezine, A.: An integrated specification and verification technique for highly concurrent data structures. In: Piterman, N., Smolka, S.A. (eds.) TACAS 2013 (ETAPS 2013). LNCS, vol. 7795, pp. 324–338. Springer, Heidelberg (2013)
2. Adve, S.V., Hill, M.D.: A unified formalization of four shared-memory models. IEEE Trans. Parallel Distrib. Syst. 4(6), 613–624 (1993)
3. Alglave, J., Maranget, L.: Stability in weak memory models. In: Gopalakrishnan, G., Qadeer, S. (eds.) CAV 2011. LNCS, vol. 6806, pp. 50–66. Springer, Heidelberg (2011)
4. Bouajjani, A., Meyer, R., Möhlmann, E.: Deciding robustness against total store ordering. In: Aceto, L., Henzinger, M., Sgall, J. (eds.) ICALP 2011, Part II. LNCS, vol. 6756, pp. 428–440. Springer, Heidelberg (2011)
5. Flanagan, C., Qadeer, S.: Thread-modular model checking. In: Ball, T., Rajamani, S.K. (eds.) SPIN 2003. LNCS, vol. 2648, pp. 213–224. Springer, Heidelberg (2003)
6. Detlefs, D.L., Martin, P.A., Moir, M., Steele, G.L.: Lock-free reference counting. Distrib. Comput. 15(4), 255–271 (2002)
7. Gotsman, A., Berdine, J., Cook, B., Sagiv, M.: Thread-modular shape analysis. In: PLDI, pp. 266–277. ACM (2007)
8. Gotsman, A., Rinetzky, N., Yang, H.: Verifying concurrent memory reclamation algorithms with grace. In: Felleisen, M., Gardner, P. (eds.) ESOP 2013. LNCS, vol. 7792, pp. 249–269. Springer, Heidelberg (2013)
9. Haziza, F., Holík, L., Meyer, R., Wolff, S.: Pointer race freedom. Technical Report FIT-TR-2015-05, Brno University of Technology, FIT (2015)
10. Michael, M., Scott, M.: Nonblocking algorithms and preemption-safe locking on multiprogrammed shared memory multiprocessors. J. Parallel Dist. Comp. 51(1), 1–26 (1998)
11. Michael, M.M.: Hazard pointers: Safe memory reclamation for lock-free objects. IEEE Trans. Parallel Distrib. Syst. 15(6), 491–504 (2004)
12. Mijajlović, I., Yang, H.: Data refinement with low-level pointer operations. In: Yi, K. (ed.) APLAS 2005. LNCS, vol. 3780, pp. 19–36. Springer, Heidelberg (2005)
13. Owens, S.: Reasoning about the implementation of concurrency abstractions on x86-TSO. In: D'Hondt, T. (ed.) ECOOP 2010. LNCS, vol. 6183, pp. 478–503. Springer, Heidelberg (2010)
14. Treiber, R.K.: Systems programming: coping with parallelism. In: RJ5118 (1986)
15. Segalov, M., Lev-Ami, T., Manevich, R., Ganesan, R., Sagiv, M.: Abstract transformers for thread correlation analysis. In: Hu, Z. (ed.) APLAS 2009. LNCS, vol. 5904, pp. 30–46. Springer, Heidelberg (2009)
16. Vafeiadis, V.: Shape-value abstraction for verifying linearizability. In: Jones, N.D., Müller-Olm, M. (eds.) VMCAI 2009. LNCS, vol. 5403, pp. 335–348. Springer, Heidelberg (2009)
17. Vafeiadis, V.: RGSep action inference. In: Barthe, G., Hermenegildo, M. (eds.) VMCAI 2010. LNCS, vol. 5944, pp. 345–361. Springer, Heidelberg (2010)

A Program Logic for C11 Memory Fences

Marko Doko$^{(\boxtimes)}$ and Viktor Vafeiadis

Max Planck Institute for Software Systems (MPI-SWS), Kaiserslautern, Germany
mdoko@mpi-sws.org

Abstract. We describe a simple, but powerful, program logic for reasoning about C11 relaxed accesses used in conjunction with release and acquire memory fences. Our logic, called fenced separation logic (FSL), extends relaxed separation logic with special modalities for describing state that has to be protected by memory fences. Like its precursor, FSL allows ownership transfer over synchronizations and can be used to verify the message-passing idiom and other similar programs. The soundness of FSL has been established in Coq.

1 Introduction

In order to achieve good performance, modern hardware provides rather weak guarantees on the semantics of concurrent memory accesses. Similarly, to enable as many compiler optimizations as possible, modern "low-level" programming languages (such as C or C++) provide very weak memory models. In this paper we will focus on the memory model defined in the C and C++ standards from 2011 [6,7] (henceforth, *the C11 memory model*).

The C11 memory model successfully provides a concise abstraction over the various existing hardware implementations, encompassing all the behaviors of widely used hardware platforms. In order not to restrict the set of behaviors exhibited by hardware, the C11 model had to be weaker than any of the hardware models, which makes the guarantees it provides very weak. This pronounced lack of guarantees provided by the C11 model makes it difficult to reason about the model, but those difficulties can be overcome, as evidenced by *Relaxed Separation Logic (RSL)* [16] and *GPS* [14].

Both of these program logics provide a framework for reasoning about the main novel synchronization mechanism provided by the C11 model, namely release and acquire atomic accesses. However, release and acquire accesses are not the only synchronization mechanism that C11 provides. A more advanced mechanism are memory fences, which are not supported by any existing program logics.

In this paper, our goal is to provide simple proof rules for memory fences that can give users of the logic insight and intuition about the behavior of memory fences within the C11 memory model. In order to achieve this goal, we are going to design *Fenced Separation Logic (FSL)* as an extension of RSL. We are choosing to build on top of RSL, because we want our rules for fences to be in the spirit of the RSL rules – clean, simple and intuitive.

© Springer-Verlag Berlin Heidelberg 2016
B. Jobstmann and K.R.M. Leino (Eds.): VMCAI 2016, LNCS 9583, pp. 413–430, 2016.
DOI: 10.1007/978-3-662-49122-5_20

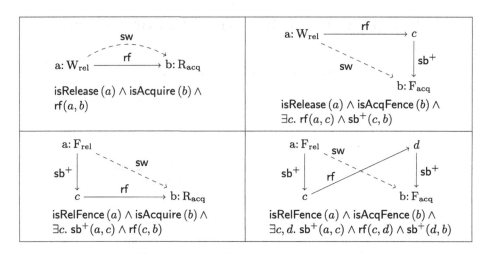

Fig. 1. Definition of the synchronizes-with relation. For all actions a and b, a synchronizes with b, written $\mathsf{sw}(a, b)$, if one of the cases above holds.

We will show that in spite of memory fences having a very global effect on the semantics of C11 programs, we can specify them cleanly by local rules in the style of separation logic.

The remainder of the paper recalls the C11 memory model and RSL (Sect. 2), presents the rules of our logic (Sect. 3), applies them to a few illustrative examples (Sect. 4), and outlines its semantics (Sect. 5) and the proof of soundness (Sect. 6). The full soundness proof was mechanized in Coq and can be found at http://plv.mpi-sws.org/fsl/.

2 Background

2.1 The C11 Memory Model

For the purposes of this paper, we will consider the relevant subset of the C11 memory model. Fuller formalizations of C11 can be found in [3,15,16].

The C11 memory model defines the semantics of a program as a set of executions consistent with a certain set of axioms. A program execution is a directed graph whose nodes represent actions (such as memory accesses or fences) and whose edges represent various relations between the actions.

The types of edges that will be of interest in order to prove soundness of FSL are *sequenced-before* and *reads-from* edges.

- *Sequenced-before* (sb) edges describe the program flow. We have an sb edge from a to b if a immediately precedes b in the thread's control flow. Fork actions are considered to immediately precede all of the initial actions of the forked threads, while join actions are considered to be immediate successors of all the joined threads' last actions.
- There is a *reads-from* (rf) edge from a to b if a is the write action that wrote the value read by the read action b.

In the restricted model we are considering, each memory access can be either *non-atomic* or *atomic*, where atomic accesses are further subdivided into *relaxed*, *release*, and *acquire* access types.

Non-atomic accesses should be used as regular accesses throughout the program, whenever we are not implementing a synchronization mechanism. The C11 memory model does not allow data races on non-atomic accesses, and programs with such data races are considered to have undefined semantics.

The intended use of the atomic accesses is to implement synchronization mechanisms. As can be seen from Fig. 1, release writes synchronize with acquire reads, whereas in order to achieve synchronization with relaxed accesses, we need some help from acquire and release fences.

Two additional relations between events are derived from the two relations mentioned above: *synchronizes-with* and *happens-before*.

- *Synchronizes-with* (sw) relates a release event with an acquire event, according to the rules summarized in Fig. 1. Intuitively, synchronization happens when an acquire event can "see" a release event through an rf edge.
- *Happens-before* (hb) is a partial order representing the intuitive notion that one action completed before the other one started. For the subset of the model we are considering, $\mathsf{hb} = (\mathsf{sb} \cup \mathsf{sw})^+$.

2.2   Relaxed Separation Logic

Relaxed Separation Logic (RSL) allows reasoning about the release-acquire fragment of the C11 model. More precisely, using RSL we can reason about ownership transfer that happens when an acquire read reads from a release write. The two most important inference rules in RSL that enable this kind of reasoning are the release write rule (RSL-W-REL) and the acquire read rule (RSL-R-ACQ).

Besides having rules for read and write accesses, RSL also deals with compare-and-swap (CAS) accesses. In this paper, we want to concentrate on dealing with memory fences; so, for the sake of simplicity, we will not model CAS accesses.

Before explaining (RSL-W-REL) and (RSL-R-ACQ), we need to talk about RSL's view of memory locations. Since the C11 model provides us with two classes of accesses (atomic and non-atomic), RSL classifies each location as either atomic or non-atomic, depending on the access mode that will be used throughout the program. For this reason, RSL provides two allocation rules. Rule (A-NA) gives us an uninitialized non-atomic location, while (A-AT) allocates an atomic location by providing us with corresponding release and acquire permissions.

$$\{\mathsf{emp}\} \ \mathbf{alloc}() \ \{\ell. \ \mathsf{Uninit}(\ell)\} \qquad\qquad (\text{A-NA})$$

$$\{\mathsf{emp}\} \ \mathbf{alloc}() \ \{\ell. \ \mathsf{Rel}(\ell, \mathcal{Q}) * \mathsf{Acq}(\ell, \mathcal{Q})\} \qquad (\text{A-AT})$$

The assertions $\mathsf{Rel}(\ell, \mathcal{Q})$ and $\mathsf{Acq}(\ell, \mathcal{Q})$ "attach" a mapping $\mathcal{Q}$ from values to assertions to location ℓ. This mapping should be used to describe the manner in which we intend to use the location ℓ. We can roughly consider $\mathcal{Q}$ to be an invariant stating: "if location ℓ holds value v, then the assertion $\mathcal{Q}(v)$ is true."

We can now proceed with presenting RSL's rules for atomic accesses in which we will further clarify how release and acquire permissions are used. For non-atomic accesses, RSL imports the standard separation logic rules.

Release Write. RSL's release write rule

$$\left\{ \mathsf{Rel}(\ell, \mathcal{Q}) * \mathcal{Q}(v) \right\} [\ell]_{\mathrm{rel}} := v \left\{ \mathsf{Rel}(\ell, \mathcal{Q}) * \mathsf{Init}(\ell) \right\} \qquad \text{(RSL-W-REL)}$$

says that in order to do a release write of value v to location ℓ, we need to have a permission to do so, $\mathsf{Rel}(\ell, \mathcal{Q})$, and we have to satisfy the invariant specified by that permission, namely $\mathcal{Q}(v)$. After the write is done, we no longer own the resources specified by the invariant (so that readers can obtain them), and we gain the knowledge that the location ℓ has been initialized.

Acquire Read. The acquire read rule

$$\frac{\forall x.\ \mathsf{precise}(\mathcal{Q}(x))}{\left\{ \mathsf{Init}(\ell) * \mathsf{Acq}(\ell, \mathcal{Q}) \right\} [\ell]_{\mathrm{acq}} \left\{ v.\ \mathsf{Acq}(\ell, \mathcal{Q}[v{:=}\mathsf{emp}]) * \mathcal{Q}(v) \right\}} \qquad \text{(RSL-R-ACQ)}$$

complements the release write rule. Here we are able to execute an acquire read of location ℓ if we know that it is initialized, and we have an acquire permission for ℓ. Just as in a release permission, an acquire permission carries a mapping $\mathcal{Q}$ from values to assertions. In case of an acquire permission this mapping describes what resource will be acquired by reading a certain value, so if the value v is read, resource $\mathcal{Q}(v)$ is acquired.

This rule is slightly complicated by two technical details. First, we have to lose the permission to acquire the same ownership by reading v again. Hence, the acquire permission becomes $\mathcal{Q}[v{:=}\mathsf{emp}] \stackrel{\text{def}}{=} \lambda y.\ \textbf{if } y{=}v \textbf{ then } \mathsf{emp} \textbf{ else } \mathcal{Q}(y)$ in the postcondition. Second, we require all the assertions $\mathcal{Q}(x)$ to be precise [10]. This technical detail arises from the nature of the semantics of RSL triples. For details, see [16].

With these two rules, various message passing idioms can be proven correct, as long as we refrain from using relaxed atomic accesses.

Relaxed Atomic Accesses. RSL also provides simple and intuitive rules for dealing with relaxed atomic reads and writes. Since relaxed accesses do not synchronize, we are going to allow relaxed writes only when our permission states that we are releasing an empty resource. Similarly when doing an acquire read, we have to know that the location is initialized, but we will not be acquiring any ownership. The only thing we assert about the value read is that it is one of those that, given the permission structure, could have been written.

$$\frac{\mathcal{Q}(v) = \mathsf{emp}}{\left\{ \mathsf{Rel}(\ell, \mathcal{Q}) \right\} [\ell]_{\mathrm{rlx}} := v \left\{ \mathsf{Init}(\ell) \right\}} \qquad \text{(RSL-W-RLX)}$$

$$\left\{ \mathsf{Init}(\ell) * \mathsf{Acq}(\ell, \mathcal{Q}) \right\} [\ell]_{\mathrm{rlx}} \left\{ v.\ \mathsf{Acq}(\ell, \mathcal{Q}) \wedge (\mathcal{Q}(v) \neq \mathsf{false}) \right\} \qquad \text{(RSL-R-RLX)}$$

Unfortunately, no matter how reasonable the rules seem, both (RSL-W-RLX) and (RSL-R-RLX) are unsound under the standard C11 model, due to the well known problem of the so called thin-air reads [2,16]. Since this behavior makes the standard C11 relaxed atomics unusable, when dealing with relaxed accesses RSL assumes a certain strengthening of the C11 model. Namely, we consider the union of the happens-before and reads-from relations to be acyclic. Since this strengthening was necessary even for the simple rules above, we consider it justifiable to work under the same strengthened model when developing a logic that will enable us to do ownership transfer using relaxed accesses together with memory fences.

3   Fenced Separation Logic (FSL)

Our goal is to enhance the rules from the previous section to allow ownership transfer through relaxed accesses. Ideally, we would like the rules for release writes and acquire reads to remain unchanged, so that all valid RSL proofs remain valid FSL proofs. We will therefore need to change the rules for dealing with relaxed accesses, and we will need to come up with rules for memory fences.

Looking back at Fig. 1, we can see how the rules (RSL-W-REL) and (RSL-R-ACQ) describe the simple situation in the top left corner. Imagine how the resource released by the read travels along the rf-edge in order to appear as acquired resource after the acquire read has been done.

Note also how the other three situations look like decompositions of the simplest one. The release write has been split into a release fence after which comes a relaxed write, and the acquire read has been split into a relaxed read after which comes an acquire fence. This is more than just a good intuition: release writes and acquire reads can, in fact, be implemented in this fashion.

Now, the question is, can we extend our mental image of a released resource "traveling" over the rf-edge to the point of it being acquired? Well, in the simple case, we were lucky, since the rf-edge coincided with the synchronization arrow, but in other cases the situation is a bit more complicated. We would like for the resource to disappear from the release point, and reappear at the acquire point, but the problem arises from the fact that the only point of transfer possible is the rf-edge.

A solution to the above mentioned conundrum is, in the presence of fences and relaxed accesses, to think of resource transfer in the following way. If we are releasing a resource by a combination of a release fence and a relaxed write, at the fence we should decide what is going to be released, and not touch that resource until we finally send it away by doing the write. Conversely, when acquiring a resource using a pair of a relaxed read and an acquire fence, once we do the read, we know which resources we are going to get, but we will not be able to use those resources until we reach a synchronization point marked by the acquire fence.

In order to formally represent our intuition, we will introduce two modalities into RSL's language of assertions. We will mark the resources that have been prepared to be released by $\triangle$, while $\triangledown$ will mark resources that are waiting for synchronization. Therefore, we define FSL assertions by the following grammar:

$$P, Q :: = \text{false} \mid P \to Q \mid P * Q \mid \forall x.\ P \mid \text{emp} \mid e \mapsto e' \mid \text{Uninit}(e)$$
$$\mid \text{Rel}(e, \mathcal{Q}) \mid \text{Acq}(e, \mathcal{Q}) \mid \text{Init}(e) \mid \triangle P \mid \triangledown P.$$

FSL judgments follow the form of RSL judgments $\{P\}\ E\ \{y.Q\}$, where y binds the return value of the expression E.

FSL supports all the standard rules of Hoare and separation logic, just as RSL does. Non-atomics and allocation are also treated exactly as in RSL. Furthermore, FSL support RSL's program relaxation rule. Namely, if we define relaxation of a program E to be a program E' identical to E except that E' can have weaker atomic accesses according to the following partial order: $\text{rlx} \sqsubseteq \text{rel} \sqsubseteq \text{sc}, \text{rlx} \sqsubseteq \text{acq} \sqsubseteq \text{sc}$; the following rule is sound:

$$\frac{\{P\}\ E'\ \{y.\ Q\} \qquad E' \sqsubseteq E}{\{P\}\ E\ \{y.\ Q\}} . \tag{RELAX}$$

Which RSL rules saw changes happen to them? As expected, rules for atomic accesses.

Atomic Writes. First we take a look at the rule for release writes. It got a small cosmetic change:

$$\frac{\text{normalizable}(\mathcal{Q}(v))}{\left\{\text{Rel}(\ell, \mathcal{Q}) * \mathcal{Q}(v)\right\}\ [\ell]_{\text{rel}} := v\ \left\{\text{Rel}(\ell, \mathcal{Q}) * \text{Init}(\ell)\right\}} . \tag{W-REL}$$

We will define the notion of normalizability in Sect. 5.1. For now, the important thing to note is that any RSL assertion (i.e., any FSL formula in which modalities $\triangle$ and $\triangledown$ do not appear) is normalizable. For this reason, our stated goal to keep RSL proofs to be valid FSL proofs has not been compromised.

The rule for relaxed writes is almost exactly the same as (W-REL).

$$\left\{\text{Rel}(\ell, \mathcal{Q}) * \triangle\mathcal{Q}(v)\right\}\ [\ell]_{\text{rlx}} := v\ \left\{\text{Rel}(\ell, \mathcal{Q}) * \text{Init}(\ell)\right\} \tag{W-RLX}$$

All the main ingredients are the same: we have to have a release permission, and we have to own the resource specified by the permission. The only additional requirement is that the resource has to be under the modality stating that it can be released by a relaxed write. As we will later see this ensures that our write is placed after a release fence.

Atomic Reads. The acquire read rule got changed in the same vein as the release write rule, by adding a normalizability requirement:

$$\frac{\forall x.\ \text{precise}(\mathcal{Q}(x)) \wedge \text{normalizable}(\mathcal{Q}(x))}{\left\{\text{Init}(\ell) * \text{Acq}(\ell, \mathcal{Q})\right\}\ [\ell]_{\text{acq}}\ \left\{v.\ \text{Acq}(\ell, \mathcal{Q}[v:=\text{emp}]) * \mathcal{Q}(v)\right\}} . \tag{R-ACQ}$$

Just as it was the case for writes, the rule for relaxed reads differs only in a single modality appearance:

$$\frac{\forall x.\ \text{precise}(\mathcal{Q}(x)) \wedge \text{normalizable}(\mathcal{Q}(x))}{\left\{\text{Init}(\ell) * \text{Acq}(\ell, \mathcal{Q})\right\}\ [\ell]_{\text{rlx}}\ \left\{v.\ \text{Acq}(\ell, \mathcal{Q}[v:=\text{emp}]) * \triangledown\mathcal{Q}(v)\right\}} . \tag{R-RLX}$$

In order to do an atomic read, we have to have an acquire permission, and to know that the location has been initialized. After an acquire read, we gain ownership of the resource described by the permission. In the case of a relaxed read, we get the same resource, but under the ∇ modality. This, as we will see below, makes the resource unusable before we reach an acquire fence.

Fences. Finally, let us turn our attention to the two rules describing the actions of memory fences. These are by far the simplest rules, as the only job of fences is to manage the two modalities. This is achieved by the following two rules:

$$\frac{\text{normalizable}(P)}{\{P\}\,\text{FENCE}_{\text{rel}}\,\{\triangle P\}}\quad\text{(F-REL)}\qquad\qquad\{\nabla P\}\,\text{FENCE}_{\text{acq}}\,\{P\}\quad\text{(F-ACQ)}$$

Release fences protect resources that are to be released by putting them under the $\triangle$ modality, while acquire fences clear the ∇ modality making resources under it usable.

A Note About Normalizability. Even though the normalizability requirement that appears in several places in atomic accesses and fence rules looks pretty cumbersome, we can easily see that is not the case. The requirement is formally necessary, but a user of the logic, when doing proofs, will never even notice it. In practice, the only resources we want to transfer are the ones described by formulas containing no modalities, which are always normalizable. Because of this, the only situation where we are forced to think of normalizability is when proving the inference rules sound, and not when proving programs correct.

4   Examples

Let us first take a look at the message passing example in Fig. 2. In this example, the middle thread initializes two non-atomic variables (a and b), and then uses two atomic variables (x and y) to signal to consumer threads that the resources are ready. The consumer threads then proceed to increment the variables a and b.

The middle thread uses only one release fence in order to transfer ownership using two different relaxed writes. In order to be able to verify such idioms, it is necessary for our modalities to distribute over separating conjunction (see Sect. 5.1).

The most interesting part of the proof in the consumer threads is the waiting loop. Let us have a more detailed look at how we derive the triple

$$\{\text{Acq}(x,\mathcal{P})*\text{Init}(x)\}\,\textbf{while}([x]_{\text{rlx}} == 0);\,\{\text{true}*\nabla a \mapsto 42\}\ .$$

We first use the equivalence $\text{Init}(x) \iff \text{Init}(x)*\text{Init}(x)$, and apply (R-RLX) (together with the frame rule) inside the loop:

$$\{\text{Acq}(x,\mathcal{P})*\text{Init}(x)*\text{Init}(x)\}\,[x]_{\text{rlx}}\,\{v.\ \text{Acq}(x,\mathcal{P}[v:=\text{emp}])*\nabla\mathcal{P}(v)*\text{Init}(x)\}\ .$$

Let $\mathcal{P} \overset{\text{def}}{=} \lambda v.$ **if** $v = 0$ **then** emp **else** $a \mapsto 42$,

and $\mathcal{Q} \overset{\text{def}}{=} \lambda v.$ **if** $v = 0$ **then** emp **else** $b \mapsto 7$.

$$\{\mathsf{emp}\}$$
$$a := \mathbf{alloc}(); b := \mathbf{alloc}();$$
$$\{\mathsf{Uninit}(a) * \mathsf{Uninit}(b)\}$$
$$x := \mathbf{alloc}(); y := \mathbf{alloc}();$$
$$\{\mathsf{Uninit}(a) * \mathsf{Uninit}(b) * \mathsf{Rel}(x, \mathcal{P}) * \mathsf{Acq}(x, \mathcal{P}) * \mathsf{Rel}(y, \mathcal{Q}) * \mathsf{Acq}(y, \mathcal{Q})\}$$
$$[x]_{\mathrm{rlx}} := 0; [x]_{\mathrm{rlx}} := 0$$
$$\{\mathsf{Uninit}(a) * \mathsf{Uninit}(b) * \mathsf{Rel}(x, \mathcal{P}) * \mathsf{Acq}(x, \mathcal{P}) * \mathsf{Rel}(y, \mathcal{Q}) * \mathsf{Acq}(y, \mathcal{Q}) * \mathsf{Init}(x) * \mathsf{Init}(y)\}$$

$\{\mathsf{Acq}(x, \mathcal{P}) * \mathsf{Init}(x)\}$	$\{\mathsf{Uninit}(a) * \mathsf{Uninit}(b) * \mathsf{Rel}(x, \mathcal{P}) * \mathsf{Rel}(y, \mathcal{Q})\}$	$\{\mathsf{Acq}(y, \mathcal{Q}) * \mathsf{Init}(y)\}$
while$([x]_{\mathrm{rlx}} == 0);$	$[a]_{\mathrm{na}} := 42; [b]_{\mathrm{na}} := 7;$	**while**$([y]_{\mathrm{rlx}} == 0);$
$\{\mathsf{true} * \nabla a \mapsto 42\}$	$\{a \mapsto 42 * b \mapsto 7 * \mathsf{Rel}(x, \mathcal{P}) * \mathsf{Rel}(y, \mathcal{Q})\}$	$\{\mathsf{true} * \nabla b \mapsto 7\}$
$\mathbf{FENCE}_{\mathrm{acq}};$	$\mathbf{FENCE}_{\mathrm{rel}};$	$\mathbf{FENCE}_{\mathrm{acq}};$
$\{\mathsf{true} * a \mapsto 42\}$	$\{\triangle(a \mapsto 42 * b \mapsto 7) * \mathsf{Rel}(x, \mathcal{P}) * \mathsf{Rel}(y, \mathcal{Q})\}$	$\{\mathsf{true} * b \mapsto 7\}$
$[a]_{\mathrm{na}} := [a]_{\mathrm{na}} + 1;$	$\{\triangle a \mapsto 42 * \triangle b \mapsto 7 * \mathsf{Rel}(x, \mathcal{P}) * \mathsf{Rel}(y, \mathcal{Q})\}$	$[b]_{\mathrm{na}} := [b]_{\mathrm{na}} + 1;$
$\{\mathsf{true} * a \mapsto 43\}$	$[x]_{\mathrm{rlx}} := 1;$	$\{\mathsf{true} * b \mapsto 8\}$
	$\{\mathsf{Init}(x) * \triangle b \mapsto 7 * \mathsf{Rel}(y, \mathcal{Q})\}$	
	$[y]_{\mathrm{rlx}} := 1;$	
	$\{\mathsf{Init}(x) * \mathsf{Init}(y)\}$	

$$\{a \mapsto 43 * b \mapsto 8 * true\}$$

Fig. 2. Double message passing example.

It is important to note that $\mathcal{P}(0) = \mathsf{emp}$, and consequently $\mathcal{P}[0:=\mathsf{emp}] = \mathcal{P}$. Therefore, as long as we stay in the loop (i.e., the value being read is 0), our postcondition reads $\{\mathsf{Acq}(x, \mathcal{P}) * \nabla\mathsf{emp} * \mathsf{Init}(x)\}$. Since we have $\nabla\mathsf{emp} \iff \mathsf{emp}$, this is equivalent to $\{\mathsf{Acq}(x, \mathcal{P}) * \mathsf{Init}(x) * \mathsf{Init}(x)\}$. With this, the loop invariant has been established.

Once we are out of the loop, we know that the value we read from x is not 0. Therefore, we have

$$\{\mathsf{Acq}(x, \mathcal{P}) * \mathsf{Init}(x)\}$$
$$\mathbf{while}([x]_{\mathrm{rlx}} == 0);$$
$$\{v.\ v \neq 0 \wedge \mathsf{Acq}(x, \mathcal{P}[v:=\mathsf{emp}]) * \nabla\mathcal{P}(v) * \mathsf{Init}(x)\}.$$

We can transform the postcondition into $\{v.\ v \neq 0 \wedge \mathsf{true} * \nabla\mathcal{P}(v)\}$, using the consequence rule. Expanding the definition of $\mathcal{P}$, and using the fact that $v \neq 0$, the postcondition becomes

$$\{v.\ v \neq 0 \wedge \mathsf{true} * \nabla a \mapsto 42\}.$$

We can now use the consequence rule to transform the loop postcondition into

$$\{\mathsf{true} * \nabla a \mapsto 42\}.$$

Note how the consumer threads encounter a fence only once, when the resource they have been waiting for has been made ready. On architectures such as PowerPC and ARM, this way of implementing waiting loops gives us performance benefit over doing an acquire read in the loop. The difference comes from

Let $Q \overset{\text{def}}{=} \lambda v.$ if $v = 0$ then emp else $a \mapsto 42$.

$$\{a \mapsto 0 * \mathsf{Rel}(x, Q)\}$$
$$[a]_{\text{na}} := 42;$$
$$\{a \mapsto 42 * \mathsf{Rel}(x, Q)\}$$
$$\text{FENCE}_{\text{rel}};$$
$$\{\Diamond a \mapsto 42 * \mathsf{Rel}(x, Q)\}$$
$$[x]_{\text{rlx}} := 1;$$
$$\{\text{true}\}$$

$$\{\mathsf{Acq}(x, Q) * \mathsf{Init}(x)\}$$
$$\textbf{while}([x]_{\text{rlx}} == 0);$$
$$\{\Diamond a \mapsto 42 * \text{true}\}$$
$$[y]_{\text{rlx}} := 1;$$
$$\{\text{true}\}$$

$$\{\mathsf{Acq}(y, Q) * \mathsf{Init}(y)\}$$
$$\textbf{while}([y]_{\text{rlx}} == 0);$$
$$\{\Diamond a \mapsto 42 * \text{true}\}$$
$$\text{FENCE}_{\text{acq}};$$
$$\{a \mapsto 42 * \text{true}\}$$
$$[a]_{\text{na}} := [a]_{\text{na}} + 1;$$
$$\{a \mapsto 43 * \text{true}\}$$

Fig. 3. Example showing that merging the two modalities into one is unsound.

the fact that those architectures require placing a hardware fence instruction in order to implement acquire reads, while relaxed reads can be implemented by plain read instructions. This shows that the ability to reason about memory fences enables verification of an important class of programs.

Our next example, given in Fig. 3, shows that we could not have designed our logic to have only one modality. In the example, we assume that all our inference rules use only one modality $\Diamond$ in all the places where $\triangle$ or $\triangledown$ are used. Before the fork, x and y have been allocated as atomic variables, and a has been allocated as non-atomic. All variables have been initialized to 0. As we can see, using the rules with only one modality, we can verify the ownership transfer from the left thread to the right thread via the middle thread.

The problem here is that, since there is no rf communication between the threads on the left and right, no synchronization can happen between them, which means that the two accesses of the non-atomic location a are racing. According to the C11 model, this program has undefined semantics, and we should not have been able to verify it.

The problem lies in the middle thread. After we use the (R-RLX) rule to get the protected resource $\Diamond a \mapsto 42$, we can now immediately use the (W-RLX) rule to send that resource away to be acquired in the right thread, and subsequently used in a racy manner. In order to avoid this behavior, we have to make resources produced by the (R-RLX) rule unusable by the (W-RLX) rule, and that is exactly what has been done by introducing two different modalities.

5 Semantics

5.1 Semantics of Assertions

We first briefly describe the interpretation of the Rel and Acq assertions. In order to model release and acquire permissions, we store equivalence classes of assertions (Assn), modulo an equivalence relation $\sim$ (e.g., treating conjunctions up to commutativity and associativity). For our purposes, we can take the relation used in RSL, extending it with the requirement that for any two assertions P and Q, if $P \sim Q$ holds, then $\triangle P \sim \triangle Q$ and $\triangledown P \sim \triangledown Q$ also have to hold.

The greatest challenge in defining the semantics of FSL assertions is interpreting the modalities, especially when applied to the Acq and Rel assertions.

The obvious idea is to add a single label to each location, and use that label to track its "protection status" (is it under a modality and which one). This solution works perfectly for dealing with locations that are being accessed non-atomically. For atomic locations, the situation is more complicated because of the three splitting rules inherited from RSL, which we also have to support in FSL.

$$\mathsf{Init}(\ell) \iff \mathsf{Init}(\ell) * \mathsf{Init}(\ell) \tag{INIT-SPLIT}$$

$$\mathsf{Rel}(\ell, \mathcal{Q}_1) * \mathsf{Rel}(\ell, \mathcal{Q}_2) \iff \mathsf{Rel}(\ell, \lambda v.\ \mathcal{Q}_1(v) \vee \mathcal{Q}_2(v)) \tag{REL-SPLIT}$$

$$\mathsf{Acq}(\ell, \mathcal{Q}_1) * \mathsf{Acq}(\ell, \mathcal{Q}_2) \iff \mathsf{Acq}(\ell, \lambda v.\ \mathcal{Q}_1(v) * \mathcal{Q}_2(v)) \tag{ACQ-SPLIT}$$

When thinking of modalities, we are thinking about them protecting locations from being tampered with after being prepared for being released by a release fence, or from being prematurely accessed while waiting on a synchronizing acquire fence. We can think of release permissions as giving us the right to write to a location and initializations as giving us the right to read the location. Therefore, for each atomic location we should keep separate labels for release permissions and initialization. Keeping labels for acquire permissions is not necessary, because acquire permissions are always used in conjunction with initializations.

The model of heaps is as follows:

$$\mathsf{Lab} \overset{\text{def}}{=} \{\circ, \triangle, \triangledown\},$$

$$\mathcal{M} \overset{\text{def}}{=} \mathsf{Val} \to \mathsf{Assn}/\!\sim,$$

$$\mathsf{Heap}_{\mathrm{spec}} \overset{\text{def}}{=} \mathsf{Loc} \rightharpoonup \mathsf{NA}[(\mathbb{U} + \mathsf{Val}) \times \mathsf{Lab}] + \mathsf{Atom}[\mathcal{M} \times \mathcal{M} \times \mathbb{P}(\mathsf{Lab}) \times \mathbb{P}(\mathsf{Lab})].$$

Locations can be either non-atomic or atomic. Non-atomic locations have a label and are either uninitialized (denoted by the symbol $\mathbb{U}$) or contain a value. Atomic locations contain two permission mappings, representing the release and acquire permissions, and two sets of labels, for keeping track of protection status of the release permission and of the location's initialization. We need to keep sets of labels in order to give meaning to assertions such as $\mathsf{Init}(\ell) * \triangle\mathsf{Init}(\ell)$. Heap composition $\oplus$ is defined as follows:

$$h_1 \oplus' h_2 \overset{\text{def}}{=} \lambda\ell. \begin{cases} h_1(\ell) & \text{if } \ell \in \mathsf{dom}(h_1) \setminus \mathsf{dom}(h_2) \\ h_2(\ell) & \text{if } \ell \in \mathsf{dom}(h_2) \setminus \mathsf{dom}(h_1) \\ \mathsf{Atom}[\lambda v.\ \mathcal{P}_1(v) \vee \mathcal{P}_2(v), \\ \quad \lambda v.\ \mathcal{Q}_1(v) * \mathcal{Q}_2(v), \Lambda_1 \cup \Lambda_2, \Gamma_1 \cup \Gamma_2] & \text{if } h_i(\ell) = \mathsf{Atom}[\mathcal{P}_i, \mathcal{Q}_i, \Lambda_i, \Gamma_i] \\ & \quad \text{for } i = 1, 2 \\ \mathsf{undef} & \text{otherwise} \end{cases}$$

$$h_1 \oplus h_2 \overset{\text{def}}{=} \begin{cases} h_1 \oplus' h_2 & \text{if } \mathsf{dom}(h_1 \oplus' h_2) = \mathsf{dom}(h_1) \cup \mathsf{dom}(h_2) \\ \mathsf{undef} & \text{otherwise} \end{cases}$$

In order to define the semantics of assertions, we need to define two more notions.

Definition 1 (Heap Similarity). *Heaps h_1 and h_2 are similar ($h_1 \approx h_2$) if* $\mathsf{dom}(h_1) = \mathsf{dom}(h_2)$ *and for all locations ℓ, $h_1(\ell) \simeq h_2(\ell)$, where $\simeq$ is defined as follows:*

$$\mathsf{NA}[x, \lambda] \simeq \mathsf{NA}[x', \lambda'] \stackrel{\text{def}}{\Longleftrightarrow} x = x',$$

$$\mathsf{Atom}[\mathcal{P}, \mathcal{Q}, \Lambda, \Gamma] \simeq \mathsf{Atom}[\mathcal{P}', \mathcal{Q}', \Lambda', \Gamma'] \stackrel{\text{def}}{\Longleftrightarrow} \begin{array}{l} \mathcal{P} = \mathcal{P}' \wedge \mathcal{Q} = \mathcal{Q}' \wedge \\ (\Lambda = \emptyset \Longleftrightarrow \Lambda' = \emptyset) \\ (\Gamma = \emptyset \Longleftrightarrow \Gamma' = \emptyset). \end{array}$$

Definition 2 (Exact Label). *Heap h is exactly labeled by $\lambda \in \mathsf{Lab}$ (notation:* $\mathsf{labeled}(h, \lambda)$*) if, for all locations ℓ, $h(\ell) = \mathsf{NA}[x, \gamma] \Rightarrow \gamma = \lambda$, and $h(\ell) = \mathsf{Atom}[\mathcal{P}, \mathcal{Q}, \Lambda, \Gamma] \Rightarrow \Lambda \setminus \{\lambda\} = \Gamma \setminus \{\lambda\} = \emptyset$.*

In short, two heaps are similar when they only differ in labels which appear in the heap, and a heap is exactly labeled by a label if that's the only label appearing in the heap.

We are now ready to define semantics of FSL assertions.

Definition 3 (Assertion Semantics). *Let $\llbracket - \rrbracket : \mathsf{Assn} \to \mathbb{P}(\mathsf{Heap}_{\mathrm{spec}})$ be:*

$$\llbracket \mathsf{false} \rrbracket \stackrel{\text{def}}{=} \emptyset \qquad\qquad \llbracket P * Q \rrbracket \stackrel{\text{def}}{=} \{h_1 \oplus h_2 \mid h_1 \in \llbracket P \rrbracket \wedge h_2 \in \llbracket Q \rrbracket\}$$

$$\llbracket \mathsf{emp} \rrbracket \stackrel{\text{def}}{=} \{\emptyset\} \qquad\qquad \llbracket P \to Q \rrbracket \stackrel{\text{def}}{=} \{h \mid h \in \llbracket P \rrbracket \Longrightarrow h \in \llbracket Q \rrbracket\}$$

$$\llbracket \forall x.\ P \rrbracket \stackrel{\text{def}}{=} \{h \mid \forall v.\ h \in \llbracket P[v/x] \rrbracket\} \qquad \llbracket \mathsf{Init}(\ell) \rrbracket \stackrel{\text{def}}{=} \{\{\ell \mapsto \mathsf{Atom}[\mathsf{False}, \mathsf{Emp}, \emptyset, \{\circ\}]\}\}$$

$$\llbracket \mathsf{Uninit}(\ell) \rrbracket \stackrel{\text{def}}{=} \{\{\ell \mapsto \mathsf{NA}[\mathsf{U}, \circ]\}\} \qquad \llbracket \mathsf{Rel}(\ell, \mathcal{Q}) \rrbracket \stackrel{\text{def}}{=} \{\{\ell \mapsto \mathsf{Atom}[\mathcal{Q}, \mathsf{Emp}, \{\circ\}, \emptyset]\}\}$$

$$\llbracket \ell \mapsto v \rrbracket \stackrel{\text{def}}{=} \{\{\ell \mapsto \mathsf{NA}[v, \circ]\}\} \qquad\quad \llbracket \mathsf{Acq}(\ell, \mathcal{Q}) \rrbracket \stackrel{\text{def}}{=} \{\{\ell \mapsto \mathsf{Atom}[\mathsf{False}, \mathcal{Q}, \emptyset, \emptyset]\}\}$$

$$\llbracket \triangle P \rrbracket \stackrel{\text{def}}{=} \{h \mid \mathsf{labeled}(h, \triangle) \wedge \exists h' \in \llbracket P \rrbracket.\ h \approx h' \wedge \mathsf{labeled}(h', \circ)\}$$

$$\llbracket \triangledown P \rrbracket \stackrel{\text{def}}{=} \{h \mid \mathsf{labeled}(h, \triangledown) \wedge \exists h' \in \llbracket P \rrbracket.\ h \approx h' \wedge \mathsf{labeled}(h', \circ)\}$$

With this definition, we can prove the splitting rules sound and that the modalities distribute over conjunction, disjunction, and separating conjunction.

Lemma 1. *The properties* (INIT-SPLIT), (REL-SPLIT), (ACQ-SPLIT) *hold universally, as well as the following equivalences:*

$$\triangle(P \wedge Q) \Longleftrightarrow \triangle P \wedge \triangle Q \qquad \triangledown(P \wedge Q) \Longleftrightarrow \triangledown P \wedge \triangledown Q$$

$$\triangle(P \vee Q) \Longleftrightarrow \triangle P \vee \triangle Q \qquad \triangledown(P \vee Q) \Longleftrightarrow \triangledown P \vee \triangledown Q$$

$$\triangle(P * Q) \Longleftrightarrow \triangle P * \triangle Q \qquad \triangledown(P * Q) \Longleftrightarrow \triangledown P * \triangledown Q$$

As conditions in several inference rules presented in Sect. 3, we encountered precision and normalizability. The definition of precision is standard [10], and normalizability means that if an assertion is satisfied by some heap, then it is also satisfied by some subheap exactly labeled by $\circ$.

Definition 4 (Normalizability). *An assertion P is normalizable if for all $h \in \llbracket P \rrbracket$, there exist $h_\circ$ and h' such that $h = h_\circ \oplus h'$, $h_\circ \in \llbracket P \rrbracket$, and $\mathsf{labeled}(h_\circ, \circ)$.*

5.2   The Semantics of Triples

The semantics of FSL triples closely follows that of RSL triples. To define the semantics of a triple $\{P\}\,E\,\{y.Q\}$, we annotate edges of executions of E, put into an arbitrary context, with the restriction that each execution of E should have a unique incoming sb-edge and a unique outgoing sb-edge from/to its context. These edges will be responsible for carrying heaps satisfying precondition P and postcondition Q.

Triple semantics is defined in terms of *annotation validity*. In short, validity states that the sum of heaps on all incoming edges of a node is equal to the sum of heaps on all outgoing edges, modulo the effect of the node's action (e.g., allocation will produce a new heap cell).

Figure 4 showcases the most important parts of FSL's validity definition, namely the conditions for nodes corresponding to atomic accesses and fences. In the figure, *hmap* is the function that annotates edges of the execution with heaps, and $\mathsf{SB_{in}}(a)$, $\mathsf{SB_{out}}(a)$, $\mathsf{RF_{in}}(a)$, and $\mathsf{RF_{out}}(a)$ denote sets of incoming sb-edges, outgoing sb-edges, incoming rf-edges, and outgoing rf-edges of node a, respectively. We also extend each execution by adding a special *sink node*. Each node a of the execution is connected to the sink node by an edge which we denote by $\mathsf{Sink}(a)$.

The main idea of the validity conditions is to have heaps satisfying pre-conditions of inference rules on the incoming sb-edges, while heaps satisfying postconditions go on the outgoing sb-edges. If there is some ownership transfer, we will put the resources being transferred on rf-edges.

Let us now take a closer look at the validity conditions presented in Fig. 4.

The first line of the validity condition for the $W_Z(\ell, v)$ action establishes that the outgoing sb-edge contains everything there was on the incoming edge, except h_r, the resources released by the write. In addition, the outgoing sb-edge can contain the knowledge that the location ℓ has been initialized. The second line says that the outgoing sb-edge (and by the first line, also the incoming sb-edge) contains release permission $\mathsf{Rel}(\ell, \mathcal{Q})$. Note that the release permission label contains ∘. We need this to ensure that only resources labeled by ∘ are being accessed. We often refer to resources labeled by ∘ as *normal resources*. For the same reason, we force the initialization label on the outgoing sb-edge to contain ∘.

The next two lines ensure that the resource being released (h_r) is, in fact, described by $\mathcal{Q}(v)$, as stated by the release permission. The idea is for the resources that have been acquired by some read to go on the corresponding rf-edges, and those that have been released, but not (yet) acquired to be annotated on the sink edge. Note how we require resources that have been released to be labeled only by $\triangledown$. This is to mark them as unusable until a synchronization point is reached. The last line states that only release writes can release normal resources. Relaxed writes can only release resources marked by $\triangle$, which means that those resources have been protected by a release fence.

The first line of the validity condition for $R_Z(\ell, v)$ states that the incoming sb edge has to contain initialization information for ℓ (labeled with ∘), together

- If $a = W_Z(\ell, v)$ and $Z \neq$ na, then there exist h_r, h_F, $\mathcal{Q}$ such that

$hmap(\mathsf{SB_{in}}(a)) \oplus \{\ell \mapsto \mathsf{Atom}[\mathsf{False}, \mathsf{Emp}, \emptyset, \{\circ\}]\} = hmap(\mathsf{SB_{out}}(a)) \oplus h_r \wedge$
$hmap(\mathsf{SB_{out}}(a)) = \{\ell \mapsto \mathsf{Atom}[\mathcal{Q}, \mathsf{Emp}, \{\circ\}, \{\circ\}]\} \oplus h_F \wedge$
$h_r \approx hmap(\mathsf{RF_{out}}(a)) \oplus hmap(\mathsf{Sink}(a)) \wedge$
$hmap(\mathsf{RF_{out}}(a)) \oplus hmap(\mathsf{Sink}(a)) \in [\![\nabla \mathcal{Q}(v)]\!] \wedge$
$(\mathsf{labeled}(h_r, \triangle) \vee (Z \neq \mathsf{rlx} \wedge \mathsf{labeled}(h_r, \circ)))$,

- If $a = R_Z(\ell, v)$ and $Z \neq$ na, then there exist h_r, h_F, $\mathcal{Q}$ such that

$hmap(\mathsf{SB_{in}}(a)) = \{\ell \mapsto \mathsf{Atom}[\mathsf{False}, \mathcal{Q}, \emptyset, \{\circ\}]\} \oplus h_F \wedge$
$hmap(\mathsf{Sink}(a)) = \{\ell \mapsto \mathsf{Atom}[\mathsf{False}, \mathsf{Emp}[v := \mathcal{Q}(v)], \emptyset, \emptyset]\} \wedge$
$hmap(\mathsf{RF_{in}}(a)) \in [\![\nabla \mathcal{Q}(v)]\!] \wedge h_r \approx hmap(\mathsf{RF_{in}}(a)) \in [\![\nabla \mathcal{Q}(v)]\!] \wedge$
$hmap(\mathsf{SB_{out}}(a)) = \{\ell \mapsto \mathsf{Atom}[\mathsf{False}, \mathcal{Q}[v := \mathsf{emp}], \emptyset, \{\circ\}]\} \oplus h_r \oplus h_F \wedge$
$\mathsf{precise}(\mathcal{Q}(v)) \wedge \mathsf{normalizable}(\mathcal{Q}(v)) \wedge$
$(\mathsf{labeled}(h_r, \nabla) \vee (Z \neq \mathsf{rlx} \wedge \mathsf{labeled}(h_r, \circ)))$

- If $a = \textsc{Fence}_Z$, then there exist h_{rel}, h'_{rel}, h_{acq}, h'_{acq}, h_F, such that

$hmap(\mathsf{SB_{in}}(a) = h_{\mathsf{rel}} \oplus h_{\mathsf{acq}} \oplus h_F \wedge hmap(\mathsf{SB_{out}}(a) = h'_{\mathsf{rel}} \oplus h'_{\mathsf{acq}} \oplus h_F \wedge$
$h_{\mathsf{rel}} \approx h'_{\mathsf{rel}} \wedge \mathsf{labeled}(h_{\mathsf{rel}}, \circ) \wedge \mathsf{labeled}(h'_{\mathsf{rel}}, \triangle) \wedge$
$h_{\mathsf{acq}} \approx h'_{\mathsf{acq}} \wedge \mathsf{labeled}(h_{\mathsf{acq}}, \nabla) \wedge \mathsf{labeled}(h'_{\mathsf{acq}}, \circ) \wedge$
$Z = \mathsf{rel} \rightarrow h_{\mathsf{acq}} = \emptyset \wedge Z = \mathsf{acq} \rightarrow h_{\mathsf{rel}} = \emptyset$.

where $\mathsf{False} \stackrel{\text{def}}{=} \lambda v.\, \mathsf{false}$, $\mathsf{Emp} \stackrel{\text{def}}{=} \lambda v.\, \mathsf{emp}$,
and $f[s := t] \stackrel{\text{def}}{=} \lambda x.\, \mathsf{if}\ x = s\ \mathsf{then}\ t\ \mathsf{else}\ f(x)$.

Fig. 4. Validity conditions for atomic accesses and fences.

with the acquire permission $\mathsf{Acq}(\ell, \mathcal{Q})$. We lose the permission to acquire more ownership by reading the same value, and that lost permission gets placed on the sink edge (line 2). Line 3 states that the resources acquired via the rf-edge are exactly those described by the acquire permission. The contents of the incoming sb-edge (without the lost permission), together with the resources acquired via the rf-edge, are to be placed on the sb-edge (line 4). Line 5 states the technical requirements of precision and normalizability.

The last line serves a purpose analogous to the last line in the validity of writes. Only acquire reads can make acquired resources immediately usable (by changing their label from ∇ to $\circ$). Acquire reads can do this because they serve as synchronization points. Relaxed reads have to leave the ∇ label on the acquired resources, which will force us to wait for a synchronization point provided by an acquire fence before we will be able to use those resources.

Note 1 (Sink Edges). Using sink edges to keep track of lost permissions and resources that have been released but that nobody has acquired may seem like an unnecessary complication. Why do we not just forget about them? The reason for introducing sink edges is pragmatism. Keeping track of those "lost" annotations greatly simplifies the soundness proofs of (R-ACQ) and (R-RLX) rules because it makes Lemma 2 in Sect. 6 more widely applicable.

The validity conditions for fences are fairly straightforward. Release fences take some normal resource and protect it by setting its labels to $\triangle$, while acquire fences make resources usable by changing labels from $\triangledown$ to $\circ$.

Now that we have defined annotation validity, we can proceed to discuss the semantics of triples.

Somewhat simplified, in RSL the triple $\{P\}\,E\,\{y.Q\}$ holds if all executions of E satisfying the precondition P (i.e. the unique incoming sb-edge to the execution of E is annotated by a heap satisfying $P * R$, where R is some frame) can be validly annotated such that the annotation of the unique outgoing sb-edge from the execution of E satisfies $Q * R$.

In FSL, the triple semantics differs from the one in RSL in one minor detail. Whereas in RSL the heap annotating the outgoing sb-edge should satisfy $Q * R$, here we allow it to be bigger: it suffices that the heap can be split into the sum of two heaps $h \oplus h'$ such that $h \in [\![Q * R]\!]$, while h' can be arbitrary. The reason for this change will be discussed in the next section.

6 Soundness

In this section, we illustrate some key points in the soundness proof of FSL. Of particular interest are the places where the proof structure deviates from that of RSL. The full soundess proof can be found at http://plv.mpi-sws.org/fsl/.

When talking about the soundness of a program logic like FSL, it is, of course, necessary to prove the inference rules valid according to the semantics of triples, but we also want to say that if $\{P\}\,E\,\{Q\}$ holds, then the program E satisfies some useful properties. The properties of interest here are race-freedom, memory safety and absence of reads of uninitialized locations. In the definitions below, we list formal statements of these three properties.

Definition 5 (Conflicting Accesses). *Two actions are* conflicting *if both of them are accesses (i.e. reads or writes) of the same location, at least one of them is a write, and at least one of them is non-atomic.*

Definition 6 (Race-Freedom). *Execution $\mathcal{X}$ is* race-free *if for every two conflicting actions a and b in $\mathcal{X}$, we have* $\mathsf{hb}(a, b)$ *or* $\mathsf{hb}(b, a)$.

Definition 7 (Memory Safety). *Execution $\mathcal{X}$ is* memory safe *if for every access action b in $\mathcal{X}$ there is an allocation action a in $\mathcal{X}$ such that a allocates the location accessed by b, and* $\mathsf{hb}(a, b)$.

Definition 8 (Initialized Reads). *We say that in execution $\mathcal{X}$ all reads are* initialized *if for every read action r in $\mathcal{X}$ there is a write action w in $\mathcal{X}$ accessing the same location such that* $\mathsf{hb}(w, r)$.

Recall that for $\{P\}\,E\,\{Q\}$ to hold, there has to be a way to validly annotate every execution of E. Therefore, to establish the properties we are interested in, it suffices to prove the following theorem.

Theorem 1. *If $\mathcal{X}$ is a validly annotated execution, then $\mathcal{X}$ is memory safe and race-free, and all reads in $\mathcal{X}$ are initialized.*

Let us first concentrate on proving race-freedom for a validly annotated execution, $\mathcal{X}$. We start with two conflicting accesses a and b, and we first want to show is that there is a path in $\mathcal{X}$ connecting a and b. For this, we need the *heap compatibility* lemma.

Definition 9 (Independent Edges). *In an execution, $\mathcal{X}$, a set of edges, $\mathcal{T}$, is pairwise independent if for all $(a, a'), (b, b') \in \mathcal{T}$, we have $\neg(\mathsf{sb} \cup \mathsf{rf})^*(a', b)$.*

Lemma 2 (Independent Heap Compatibility). *For every consistent execution $\mathcal{X}$, validly annotated by hmap, and pairwise independent set of edges $\mathcal{T}$, $\bigoplus_{e \in \mathcal{T}} hmap(e)$ is defined.*

Since this is exactly the same lemma that appears in the soundness proof of RSL, details of its proof can be found in [16].

Now, since our accesses a and b access the same location, and at least one of them is non-atomic, validity conditions guarantee that $hmap(\mathsf{SB}_{\mathsf{in}}(a)) \oplus hmap(\mathsf{SB}_{\mathsf{in}}(b))$ is undefined. Therefore, according to independent heap compatibility, execution $\mathcal{X}$ has to contain a path between a and b. Without loss of generality we can assume that the path goes from a to b.

Here we hit the main difference between RSL and FSL. In RSL existence of a path from a to b immediately implies $\mathsf{hb}(a, b)$, but in FSL we need to do some more work before getting there.

What we are going to do is take a closer look at the location ℓ that is being accessed by a and b. Denote the immediate sb predecessor of b by b'. We want to obtain a path π from a to b' such that for any edge $e \in \pi$, $\ell \in \mathsf{dom}(hmap(e))$. The building blocks for showing the existence of path π are the validity conditions and the independent heap compatibility lemma. Using these two, we can start at $\mathsf{SB}_{\mathsf{in}}(a)$ and inductively build our path π, eventually reaching the node b'.

If we can show that the endpoints of π are related by hb, our work is done. In order to do that, let us look at the labels assigned to location ℓ by the edges along the path $\mathsf{SB}_{\mathsf{in}}(a); \pi; \mathsf{SB}_{\mathsf{in}}(b)$. (If $hmap(e)(\ell) = \mathsf{NA}[\_, \lambda]$, we say that edge e assigns label λ to location ℓ.) If we write out these labels, we get a string described by the regular expression $(\circ^+ \triangle^* \triangledown^+ \circ^+)^+$.

Sequences of "normal labels" $\circ$ are of no concern, since validity conditions mandate that $\circ$ appears only on sb-edges, which are part of hb relation. Therefore we turn our attention to the parts of the path where labeling of location ℓ is described by $\circ \triangle^* \triangledown^+ \circ$. Luckily, our validity conditions are designed in such a way as to reflect the definition sw relation (Fig. 1), which means that the node at which the $\circ$ label disappears is always sw-related with the node at which the $\circ$ label reappears.

This concludes the race-freedom part of the proof.

Next, we turn our attention to memory safety. If a is an action that accesses location ℓ, we follow the location ℓ starting from the $\mathsf{SB_{in}}(a)$ edge backwards in the execution until we reach the node that allocates ℓ. Along the way we make note of the labels appearing alongside ℓ, and similarly to the race-freedom proof, use the validity conditions to establish happens-before relation between the allocation and the access of ℓ.

The analysis here is a bit more complicated since now we have to also deal with atomic locations, which have a more complicated labeling structure, while in the case of race-freedom it sufficed to consider only non-atomic locations.

Finally, the fact that all reads are initialized is proven analogously to memory safety. We start at the read and in case the location that has been read is non-atomic, we follow it backwards until we reach a write to that location that happened before the read. When dealing with an atomic location, we have to be more careful. For atomic locations, we follow its initialization label until we find a write that happened before our read.

The only thing left to do is to prove all the inference rules valid according to the semantics of triples. Since all the proofs are analogous to the validity proofs of RSL's rules, we will concentrate on explaining the normalizability condition and the reason for the change in the definition of the triple semantics (see Sect. 5.2). We will do this by taking a look at the two rules that are new to FSL, (F-REL) and (F-ACQ).

Let us first turn our attention to the one that does not use the normalizability condition, namely (F-ACQ). To prove the rule valid, we need to validly annotate a very simple execution. It consists of a single node a, representing the acquire fence, one incoming and one outgoing sb-edge. Incoming edge ($\mathsf{SB_{in}}(a)$), is annotated by a heap satisfying precondition $\triangledown P$, plus some heap satisfying the frame R. In short, $hmap(\mathsf{SB_{in}}(a)) = h_P \oplus h_R$, where $h_P \in [\![\triangledown P]\!]$ and $h_R \in [\![R]\!]$. Our job is to annotate outgoing edge ($\mathsf{SB_{out}}(a)$) satisfying both the validity condition and triple semantics.

Since $h_P \in [\![\triangledown P]\!]$, from the assertion semantics we know that labeled $h_P \triangledown$ holds, and that there is a heap $h_{\circ P} \in [\![P]\!]$ such that $h_P \approx h_{\circ P}$ and labeled $h_{\circ P} \circ$. We set $hmap(\mathsf{SB_{out}}(a)) = h_{\circ P} \oplus h_R$. This satisfies the triple semantics, because $h_{\circ P} \oplus h_R \in [\![P * R]\!]$. The validity conditions are also satisfied by selecting $h_{rel} = h'_{rel} = \emptyset$, $h_{acq} = h_P$, $h'_{acq} = h_{\circ P}$, and $h_F = h_R$.

Let us now see what happens in the proof of validity of the (F-REL) rule. Here we start in a very similar situation with node a representing the release fence, one incoming and one outgoing sb-edge. The initial annotation is $hmap(\mathsf{SB_{in}}(a)) = h_P \oplus h_R$, where $h_R \in [\![R]\!]$, $h_P \in [\![P]\!]$, and $\mathsf{normalizable}(P)$. Before even trying to select a proper annotation for $\mathsf{SB_{out}}(a)$, we can see that there is a problem when trying to satisfy the validity condition. Namely, what should we choose for h_{rel}? There is no obvious heap labeled exactly by $\circ$, and validity requires labeled($h_{rel}, \circ$). This is where normalizability saves the day.

Normalizability of P gives us a decomposition $h_P = h_{\circ P} \oplus h'$, where $h_{\circ P} \in [\![P]\!]$, and labeled($h_{\circ P}, \circ$). We can now set $hmap(\mathsf{SB_{out}}(a)) = h_{\triangle P} \oplus h' \oplus h_R$, where

$h_{\triangle P}$ is obtained from $h_{\circ P}$ by replacing all the labels appearing in $h_{\circ P}$ with $\triangle$. Validity is now satisfied by selecting $h_{\text{rel}} = h_{\circ P}$, $h'_{\text{rel}} = h_{\triangle P}$, $h_{\text{acq}} = h'_{\text{acq}} = \emptyset$, and $h_F = h' \oplus h_R$.

The RSL-style triple semantics is not satisfied by setting $hmap(\mathsf{SB}_{\text{out}}(a)) = h_{\triangle P} \oplus h' \oplus h_R$, since we cannot guarantee $h_{\triangle P} \oplus h' \oplus h_R \in [\![\triangle P * R]\!]$, but FSL allows us to "forget" about h', and since $h_{\triangle P} \oplus h_R \in [\![\triangle P * R]\!]$, we satisfied our new triple semantics.

7   Related Work and Conclusion

We have presented FSL, an extension of RSL [16] for handling C11 memory fences. FSL is the first program logic that can handle C11 fences, as both existing program logics for C11, namely RSL [16] and GPS [14], do not support reasoning about these programming language features.

In this paper, our focus was on exploring modalities we introduced in order to specify the behavior of memory fences within the C11 model. We therefore chose to base our logic on the simpler logic (RSL) instead of the more powerful one, GPS. The simpler structure of RSL enabled us to give very simple specifications to fences, and retain simple rules for atomic accesses.

GPS is a noticeably more powerful logic than RSL. Its strength stems from the more flexible way in which GPS handles ownership transfer. Instead of relying on release and acquire permissions, GPS offers protocols, ghost resources and escrows, with which it is possible to verify a wider range of programs, such as an implementation of the RCU synchronization mechanism [13].

The soundness proof of GPS closely follows the structure of the soundness proof of RSL. Because of this, we feel confident that lessons learned in building FSL on top of RSL can be used in order to enrich GPS with FSL-style modalities, giving rise to a much more useful logic for reasoning about memory fences.

There have been other logics dealing with weak memory, mainly focusing on the TSO memory model. Notable examples include a rely-guarantee logic for x86-TSO by Ridge [11], and iCAP-TSO [12] which embeds separation logic inside a logic that deals with TSO concurrency. For the release-acquire model, there is also a recent Owicki-Gries logic called OGRA [8]. All of these logics assume stronger memory models than we have done in this paper.

Aside from program logics, there are model checking tools for C11 programs. Worth noting is CDSCHECKER [9] which includes support for memory fences.

An alternative approach to reasoning about weak memory behaviors is to restore sequential consistency. This can be done by placing fences in order to eliminate weak behavior [1], or by proving robustness theorems [4,5] stating conditions under which programs have no observable weak behaviors. So far, none of these techniques have been used to specifically target the C11 memory model.

Acknowledgments. We would like to thank Rayna Dimitrova, Ori Lahav, and the anonymous VMCAI'16 reviewers for their feedback. This work was supported by EC FET project ADVENT (308830).

References

1. Alglave, J., Kroening, D., Nimal, V., Poetzl, D.: Don't sit on the fence. In: Biere, A., Bloem, R. (eds.) CAV 2014. LNCS, vol. 8559, pp. 508–524. Springer, Heidelberg (2014)
2. Batty, M., Memarian, K., Nienhuis, K., Pichon-Pharabod, J., Sewell, P.: The problem of programming language concurrency semantics. In: Vitek, J. (ed.) ESOP 2015. LNCS, vol. 9032, pp. 283–307. Springer, Heidelberg (2015)
3. Batty, M., Owens, S., Sarkar, S., Sewell, P., Weber, T.: Mathematizing C++ concurrency. In: POPL 2011, pp. 55–66. ACM (2011)
4. Bouajjani, A., Meyer, R., Möhlmann, E.: Deciding robustness against total store ordering. In: Aceto, L., Henzinger, M., Sgall, J. (eds.) ICALP 2011, Part II. LNCS, vol. 6756, pp. 428–440. Springer, Heidelberg (2011)
5. Derevenetc, E., Meyer, R.: Robustness against power is pspace-complete. In: Esparza, J., Fraigniaud, P., Husfeldt, T., Koutsoupias, E. (eds.) ICALP 2014, Part II. LNCS, vol. 8573, pp. 158–170. Springer, Heidelberg (2014)
6. ISO/IEC 14882:2011: Programming language C++ (2011)
7. ISO/IEC 9899:2011: Programming language C (2011)
8. Lahav, O., Vafeiadis, V.: Owicki-gries reasoning for weak memory models. In: Halldórsson, M.M., Iwama, K., Kobayashi, N., Speckmann, B. (eds.) ICALP 2015. LNCS, vol. 9135, pp. 311–323. Springer, Heidelberg (2015)
9. Norris, B., Demsky, B.: CDSChecker: Checking concurrent data structures written with C/C++ atomics. In: Hosking, A.L., Eugster, P.T., Lopes, C.V. (eds.) OOPSLA 2013, pp. 131–150. ACM (2013)
10. O'hearn, P.W., Yang, H., Reynolds, J.C.: Separation and information hiding. ACM Trans. Program. Lang. Syst. **31**(3), 1–50 (2009)
11. Ridge, T.: A rely-guarantee proof system for x86-TSO. In: Leavens, G.T., O'hearn, P., Rajamani, S.K. (eds.) VSTTE 2010. LNCS, vol. 6217, pp. 55–70. Springer, Heidelberg (2010)
12. Sieczkowski, F., Svendsen, K., Birkedal, L., Pichon-Pharabod, J.: A separation logic for fictional sequential consistency. In: Vitek, J. (ed.) ESOP 2015. LNCS, vol. 9032, pp. 736–761. Springer, Heidelberg (2015)
13. Tassarotti, J., Dreyer, D., Vafeiadis, V.: Verifying read-copy-update in a logic for weak memory. In: Grove, D., Blackburn, S. (eds.) PLDI 2015, pp. 110–120. ACM (2015)
14. Turon, A., Vafeiadis, V., Dreyer, D.: GPS: Navigating weak-memory with ghosts, protocols, and separation. In: Black, A.P., Millstein, T.D. (eds.) OOPSLA 2014, pp. 691–707. ACM (2014)
15. Vafeiadis, V., Balabonski, T., Chakraborty, S., Morisset, R., Zappa Nardelli, F.: Common compiler optimisations are invalid in the C11 memory model and what we can do about it. In: Rajamani, S.K., Walker, D. (eds.) POPL 2015, pp. 209–220. ACM (2015)
16. Vafeiadis, V., Narayan, C.: Relaxed separation logic: A program logic for C11 concurrency. In: Hosking, A.L., Eugster, P.T., Lopes, C.V. (eds.) OOPSLA 2013, pp. 867–884. ACM (2013)

From Low-Level Pointers to High-Level Containers

Kamil Dudka[1], Lukáš Holík[1], Petr Peringer[1],
Marek Trtík[2], and Tomáš Vojnar[1(✉)]

[1] FIT, Brno University of Technology, Brno, Czech Republic
vojnar@fit.vutbr.cz
[2] FI, Masaryk University, Brno, Czech Republic

Abstract. We propose a method that transforms a C program manipulating containers using low-level pointer statements into an equivalent program where the containers are manipulated via calls of standard high-level container operations like `push_back` or `pop_front`. The input of our method is a C program annotated by a special form of shape invariants which can be obtained from current automatic shape analysers after a slight modification. The resulting program where the low-level pointer statements are summarized into high-level container operations is more understandable and (among other possible benefits) better suitable for program analysis. We have implemented our approach and successfully tested it through a number of experiments with list-based containers, including experiments with simplification of program analysis by separating shape analysis from analysing data-related properties.

1 Introduction

We present a novel method that recognizes low-level pointer implementations of operations over containers in C programs and transforms them to calls of standard high-level container operations, such as `push_back`, `insert`, or `is_empty`. Unlike the related works that we discuss below, our method is fully automated and yet it guarantees preservation of the original semantics. Transforming a program by our method—or even just the recognition of pointer code implementing container operations that is a part of our method—can be useful in many different ways, including simplification of program analysis by separating shape and data-related analyses (as we show later on in the paper), automatic parallelization [11], optimization of garbage collection [21], debugging and automatic bug finding [2], profiling and optimizations [18], general understanding of the code, improvement of various software engineering tasks [6], detection of abnormal data structure behaviour [12], or construction of program signatures [4].

We formalize the main concepts of our method instantiated for NULL-terminated doubly-linked lists (DLLs). However, the concepts that we introduce can be generalized (as we discuss towards the end of the paper) and used to handle code implementing other kinds of containers, such as singly-linked lists, circular lists, or trees, as well.

© Springer-Verlag Berlin Heidelberg 2016
B. Jobstmann and K.R.M. Leino (Eds.): VMCAI 2016, LNCS 9583, pp. 431–452, 2016.
DOI: 10.1007/978-3-662-49122-5_21

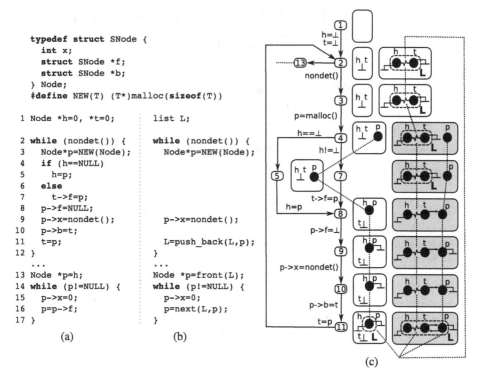

```
typedef struct SNode {
    int x;
    struct SNode *f;
    struct SNode *b;
} Node;
#define NEW(T) (T*)malloc(sizeof(T))
```

```
 1  Node *h=0, *t=0;          list L;

 2  while (nondet()) {        while (nondet()) {
 3    Node*p=NEW(Node);          Node*p=NEW(Node);
 4    if (h==NULL)
 5      h=p;
 6    else
 7      t->f=p;
 8    p->f=NULL;
 9    p->x=nondet();            p->x=nondet();
10    p->b=t;
11    t=p;                      L=push_back(L,p);
12  }                         }
        ...                       ...
13  Node *p=h;                Node *p=front(L);
14  while (p!=NULL) {         while (p!=NULL) {
15    p->x=0;                   p->x=0;
16    p=p->f;                   p=next(L,p);
17  }                         }
          (a)                       (b)
```

Fig. 1. A running example. (a) A C code using low-level pointer manipulations. (b) The transformed *pseudo*-C++ code using container operations. (c) A part of the CFG of the low-level code from Part (a) corresponding to lines 1–12, annotated by shape invariants.

We have implemented our method and successfully tested it through a number of experiments with programs using challenging pointer operations. Our benchmarks cover a large variety of program constructions implementing containers based on NULL-terminated DLLs. We have also conducted experiments showing that our method can be instantiated to other kinds of containers, namely circular DLLs as well as DLLs with head/tail pointers (our implementation is limited to various kinds of lists due to limitations of the shape analyser used). We further demonstrate that our method can simplify verification of pointer programs by separating the issue of shape analysis from that of verification of data-related properties. Namely, we first obtain shape invariants from a specialised shape analyser (Predator [8] in our case), use it within our method to transform the given pointer program into a container program, and then use a tool that specialises in verification of data-related properties of container programs (for which we use the J2BP tool [15,16]).

Overview of the Proposed Method. We demonstrate our method on a running example given in Fig. 1(a). It shows a C program that creates a DLL of non-deterministically chosen length on lines 2–12 and then iterates through all its elements on lines 13–17. Figure 1(b) shows the code transformed by our method. It is an equivalent C++-like program where the low-level pointer operations are replaced by calls of container operations which they implement. Lines 4–8, 10, and 11 are identified as push_back (i.e., insertion of an element at the end of the list), line 13 as setting an iterator to the first element of a list, and line 16 as a shift of the iterator.

The core of our approach is recognition of low-level pointer implementations of *destructive container operations*, i.e., those that change the shape of the memory, such as push_back in our example. In particular, we search for control paths along which pieces of the memory evolve in a way corresponding to the effect of some destructive container operations. This requires (1) a control-flow graph with edges annotated by an (over)approximation of the effect of program statements on the memory (i.e., their semantics restricted to the reachable program configurations) and (2) a specification of the operational semantics of the container operations that are to be searched for.

We obtain an approximation of the effect of program statements by extending current methods of shape analysis. These analyses are capable of inferring a shape invariant for every node of the control-flow graph (CFG). The shape invariants are based on using various abstract objects to represent concrete or summarized parts of memory. For instance, tools based on separation logic [14] use points-to and inductive predicates; TVLA [20] uses concrete and summary nodes; the graph-based formalism of [8] uses regions and list-segments; and sub-automata represent list-like or tree-like structures in [9]. In all these cases, it is easy to search for configurations of abstract objects that may be seen as having a *shape of a container* (i.e., a list-like container, a tree-like container, etc.) within every possible computation. This indicates that the appropriate part of memory may be used by the programmer to implement a container.

To confirm this hypothesis, one needs to check that this part of memory is actually *manipulated as a container* of the appropriate type across all statements that work with it. Additional information about the dynamics of memory changes is needed. In particular, we need to be able to track the lifecycle of each part of the memory through the whole computation, to identify its abstract encodings in successive abstract configurations, and by comparing them, to infer how the piece of the memory is changing. We therefore need the shape analyser to explicitly tell us which abstract objects of a successor configuration are created from which abstract objects of a predecessor configuration or, in other words, which abstract objects in the predecessor configuration denote parts of the memory intersecting with the denotation of an object in the successor configuration. We say that the former objects are *transformed* into the latter ones, and we call the relationship a *transformation relation*. A transformation relation is normally not output by shape analysers, however, tools such as Predator [8] (based on SMGs), Slayer [1] (based on separation logic), or Forester [9] (based on automata) actually work with it at least implicitly when applying abstract transformers. We only need them to output it.

The above concepts are illustrated in Fig. 1(c). It shows a part of the CFG of the program from Fig. 1(a) with lines annotated by the shape invariant in the round boxes on their right. The invariant is expressed in the form of so-called symbolic memory graphs (SMGs), the abstract domain of the shape analyser Predator [8], simplified to a bare minimum sufficient for exposing main concepts of our method. The basic abstract objects of SMGs are shown as the black circles in the figure. They represent continuous memory regions allocated by a single allocation command. Every region has a **next** selector, shown as the line on its right-top leading into its target region on the right, and **prev** selector, shown as a line on its left-bottom leading to the target region on the left. The $\bot$ stands for the value NULL. Pairs of regions connected by the ⌄ represent the second type of abstract object, so called doubly-linked segments (DLS). They represent doubly-linked lists of an arbitrary length connecting the two regions. The dashed envelope ⌇ indicates a memory that has the shape of a container, namely of a NULL-terminated doubly-linked list. The transformation relation between objects of successive configurations is indicated by the dashed lines. Making the tool Predator [8] output it was easy, and we believe that it would be easy for other tools as well.

Further, we propose a specification of operational semantics of the container operations which has the same form as the discussed approximation of operational semantics of the program. It consists of input and output symbolic configuration, with abstract objects related by a transformation relation. For example, Fig. 2 shows a specification of **push_back** as an operation which appends a region pointed by a variable y to a doubly-linked list pointed by x. The left pair specifies the case when the input DLL is empty, the right pair the case when it is not.

To find an implementation of thus specified **push_back**, semantic annotations of the CFG are searched for chains of the transformation relation matching the specification. That is, they start and end by configurations that include the input and the output of the **push_back** specification, resp., and the composition of the transformation relation between these configurations matches the transformation relation specified.

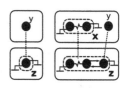

Fig. 2. Specification of $z = push\_back(x, y)$.

In Fig. 1(c), one of the chains implementing **push_back** is shown as the sequence of greyed configurations. It matches the case of the non-empty input DLL on the right of Fig. 2. Destructive program statements within the chain implementing the found operation are candidates for replacement by a call of the container operation. In the figure, lines 7, 8, 10 are candidates for replacement by L=push_back(L,p). However, the replacement can be done only if a set of chains is found that together gives a consistent image about a use of containers in the whole program. In our example, it is important that on the left of the greyed chain, there is another chain implementing the case of push_back for empty DLLs (matching the left part of the specification in Fig. 2).

After identifying containers and destructive container operations as discussed above, we search for implementations of non-destructive operations (like iterators or emptiness tests). This leads to replacement of lines 13 and 16 in Fig. 1(a) by the initialization and shift of the iterator shown on the same lines in Fig. 1(b). This step is much simpler, and we will only sketch it in the paper. We then simplify the code using standard static analysis. In the example, the fact that h and t become a dead variable until line 13 leads to removing lines 4, 5, 6, and 11.

Our method copes even with cases when the implementation of a container operation is interleaved with other program statements provided that they do not interfere with the operation (which may happen, e.g., when a manipulation of several containers is interleaved). Moreover, apart from the container operations, arbitrary low-level operations can be used over the memory structures linked in the containers provided they do not touch the container linking fields.

Related Work. There have been proposed many dynamic analyses for recognition of heap data structures, such as, e.g., [4,10,13,17,18,23]. These approaches are typically based on observing program executions and matching observed heap structures against a knowledge base of predefined structures. Various kinds of data structures can be recognised, including various kinds of lists, red-black trees, B-trees, etc. The main purposes of the recognition include reverse engineering, program understanding, and profiling. Nevertheless, these approaches do not strive for being so precise that the inferred information could be used for safe, fully automatic code replacement.

There exist static analyses with similar targets as the dynamic analyses above. Out of them, the closest to us is probably the work [5]. Its authors do also target transformation of a program with low-level operations into high-level ones. However, their aim is program understanding (design recovery), not generation of an equivalent "executable" program. Indeed, the result does not even have to be a program, it can be a natural language description. Heap operations are recognised on a purely syntactical level, using a graph representation of the program on which predefined rewriting rules are applied.

Our work is also related to the entire field of shape analysis, which provides the input for our method. Due to a lack of space, we cannot give a comprehensive overview here (see, e.g., [1,8,9] for references). Nevertheless, let us note that there is a line of works using separation-logic-based shape analysis for recognition of concurrently executable actions (e.g., [19,22]). However, recognizing such actions is a different task than recognizing low-level implementation of high-level container usage.

In summary, to the best of our knowledge, our work is the first one which targets automatic replacement of a low-level, pointer-manipulating code by a high-level one, with guarantees of preserving the semantics.

2   Symbolic Memory Graphs with Containers

We now present an abstract domain of *symbolic memory graphs* (SMGs), orig-
inally introduced in [8], which we use for describing shape invariants of the
programs being processed. SMGs are a graph-based formalism corresponding to
a fragment of separation logic capable of describing classes of heaps with linked
lists. We present their simplified version restricted to dealing with doubly-linked
lists, sufficient for formalising the main concepts of our method. Hence, nodes of
our SMGs represent either concrete memory *regions* allocated by a single allocation statement or *doubly-linked list segments* (DLSs). DLSs arise by abstraction
and represent sets of doubly-linked sequences of regions of an arbitrary length.
Edges of SMGs represent pointer links.

In [8], SMGs are used to implement a *shape analysis* within the generic framework of *abstract interpretation* [3]. We use the output of this shape analysis,
extended with a *transformation relation*, which provides us with precise information about the dynamics of the memory changes, as a part of the input of our
method (cf. Sect. 4). Further, in Sect. 3, we propose a way how SMGs together
with a transformation relation can be used to specify the container operations
to be recognized.

Before proceeding, we recall that our use of SMGs can be changed for other
domains common in the area of shape analysis (as mentioned already in the
introduction and further discussed in Sect. 7).

Symbolic Memory Graphs. We use $\top$ to explicitly denote undefined values of
functions. We call a *region* any block of memory allocated as a whole (e.g., using a
single `malloc()` statement), and we denote by $\bot$ the special *null region*. For a set
A, we use $A_\bot$, $A_\top$, and $A_{\bot,\top}$ to denote the sets $A\cup\{\bot\}$, $A\cup\{\top\}$, and $A\cup\{\bot,\top\}$,
respectively. Values stored in regions can be accessed through *selectors* (such as
next or *prev*). To simplify the presentation, we assume dealing with *pointer* and
integer values only.

For the rest of the paper, we fix sets of pointer selectors $\mathbb{S}_p$, data selectors $\mathbb{S}_d$,
regions $\mathbb{R}$, pointer variables $\mathbb{V}_p$, and container variables $\mathbb{V}_c$ (container variables
do not appear in the input programs, they get introduced by our transformation
procedure to denote parts of memory which the program treats as containers).
We assume all these sets to be pairwise disjoint and disjoint with $\mathbb{Z}_{\bot,\top}$. We use
$\mathbb{V}$ to denote the set $\mathbb{V}_p \cup \mathbb{V}_c$ of all variables, and $\mathbb{S}$ to denote the set $\mathbb{S}_p \cup \mathbb{S}_d$ of
all selectors.

A *doubly-linked list segment* (DLS) is a pair $(r, r') \in \mathbb{R} \times \mathbb{R}$ of regions that
abstracts a doubly-linked sequence of regions of an arbitrary length that is unin-
terrupted by any external pointer pointing into the middle of the sequence and
interconnects the front region represented by r with the back region r'. We use
$\mathbb{D}$ to denote the set of all DLSs and assume that $\mathbb{R} \cap \mathbb{D} = \emptyset$. Both regions and
DLSs will be called *objects*.

To illustrate the above, the top-left part of Fig. 3 shows a memory layout
with five regions (black circles), four of which form a NULL-terminated DLL.
The bottom-left part of Fig. 3 shows a sequence of three doubly-linked regions

abstracted into a DLS (depicted as a pair of regions linked via the "spring" $\rightsquigarrow$).
Note that we could also abstract all four doubly-linked regions into a single DLS.

We can now define a *symbolic memory graph* (SMG) formally. It is a triple $G = (R, D, \mathsf{val})$ consisting of a set $R \subseteq \mathbb{R}$ of regions, a set $D \subseteq R \times R \subseteq \mathbb{D}$ of DLSs, and a map val defining the pointer and data fields of regions in R. It assigns to every pointer selector $sel_p \in \mathbb{S}_p$ a function $\mathsf{val}(sel_p) : R \rightarrow R_{\perp,\top}$ that defines the

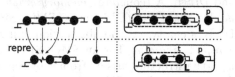

Fig. 3. A DLL and an SDLL, a PC and an SPC.

successors of every region $r \in R$. Further, it assigns to every data selector $sel_d \in \mathbb{S}_d$ a function $\mathsf{val}(sel_d) : R \rightarrow \mathbb{Z}_\top$ that defines the data values of every region $r \in R$. We will sometimes abuse the notation and write simply $sel(r)$ to denote $\mathsf{val}(sel)(r)$. An SMG $G' = (R', D', \mathsf{val}')$ is a *sub-SMG* of G, denoted $G' \preceq G$, if $R' \subseteq R$, $D' \subseteq D$, and $\mathsf{val}'(sel) \subseteq \mathsf{val}(sel)$ for all $sel \in \mathbb{S}$.

Container Shapes. We now proceed to defining a notion of container shapes that we will be looking for in shape invariants produced by shape analysis and whose manipulation through given container operations we will be trying to recognise. For simplicity, we restrict ourselves to NULL-terminated DLLs. However, in our experimental section, we present results for some other kinds of list-shaped containers too. Moreover, at the end of the paper, we argue that a further generalization of our approach is possible. Namely, we argue that the approach can work with other types of container shapes as well as on top of other shape domains.

A *symbolic doubly-linked list (SDLL)* with a *front region* r and a *back region* r' is an SMG in the form of a sequence of regions possibly interleaved with DLSs, interconnected so that it represents a DLL. Formally, it is an SMG $G = (R, D, \mathsf{val})$ where $R = \{r_1, \ldots, r_n\}$, $n \geq 1$, $r_1 = r$, $r_n = r'$, and for each $1 \leq i < n$, either $next(r_i) = r_{i+1}$ and $prev(r_{i+1}) = r_i$, or $(r_i, r_{i+1}) \in D$ and $next(r_i) = prev(r_{i+1}) = \top$. An SDLL which is NULL-terminated, i.e., with $prev(r) = \perp$ and $next(r') = \perp$, is called a *container shape* (CS). We write $csh(G)$ to denote the set of all CSs G' that are sub-SMGs of an SMG G. The bottom-right part of Fig. 3 contains an SDLL connecting a DLS and a region. It is NULL-terminated, hence a CS, which is indicated by the dashed envelope $\vdots$.

Symbolic Program Configurations. A *symbolic program configuration* (SPC) is a pair (G, σ) where $G = (R, D, \mathsf{val})$ is an SMG and $\sigma : (\mathbb{V}_p \rightarrow R_{\perp,\top}) \cup (\mathbb{V}_c \rightarrow csh(G)_\top)$ is a *valuation* of the variables. An SPC $C' = (G', \sigma')$ is a *sub-SPC* of an SPC $C = (G, \sigma)$, denoted $C' \preceq C$, if $G' \preceq G$ and $\sigma \subseteq \sigma'$. The bottom-right part of Fig. 3 depicts an SPC with pointer variables h and t positioned next to the regions $\sigma(\mathtt{h})$ and $\sigma(\mathtt{t})$ they evaluate to. The figure further shows a variable L positioned next to the CS $\sigma(\mathtt{L})$ it evaluates to. The top-right part of Fig. 3 is a PC as it has no DLSs. Examples of other SPCs are shown in the annotations of program locations in Fig. 1(c)—for some more, see [7].

Additional Notation. For an SMG or an SPC X, we write $reg(X)$ to denote the set of its regions, and $obj(X)$ to denote the set of all its objects (regions and DLSs). A (concrete) *memory graph (MG)*, *program configuration (PC)*, or *doubly-linked list (DLL)* is an SMG, SPC, or DLL, respectively, whose set of DLSs is empty, i.e., no abstraction is involved. A bijection $\pi : \mathbb{R} \to \mathbb{R}$ is called a *region renaming*. For an SMG, SPC, or a variable valuation x, we denote by $\pi(x)$ the structure arising from x by replacing each occurrence of $r \in \mathbb{R}$ by $\pi(r)$. A bijection $\lambda : \mathbb{V} \to \mathbb{V}$ is called a *variable renaming*, and we define $\lambda(x)$ analogous to $\pi(x)$.

Abstraction and Concretization. We now formalize the standard pair of abstraction and concretization functions used in abstract interpretation for our domains of MGs and SMGs. An SMG G is an *abstraction* of an MG g iff it can be obtained via the following three steps: (i) Renaming regions of g by some region renaming π (making the semantics of an SMG closed under renaming). (ii) Removing some regions (which effectively removes some constraint on a part of the memory, thus making its representation more abstract). (iii) Folding some DLLs into DLSs (abstracting away some details of the internal structure of the DLLs). In particular, a DLL l with a front region r and a back region r' may be *folded* into a DLS $d_l = (r, r')$ by removing the inner regions of l (we say that these regions get folded into d_l), removing the *next*-value of r and the *prev*-value of r' (unless $r = r'$), and adding d_l into the set D_G of DLSs of G.

Now, let g be a component of a PC (g, σ). The PC may be abstracted into an SPC (G, σ') by (a) forgetting values of some variables $x \in \mathsf{dom}(\sigma)$, i.e., setting $\sigma'(x)$ to $\top$, and (b) abstracting g into G by Steps (i–iii) above. Here, Step (i) is augmented by redirecting every $\sigma'(x)$ to $\pi(\sigma(x))$, Step (ii) is allowed to remove only regions that are neither in $\mathsf{dom}(\sigma')$ nor in any CS that is in $\mathsf{dom}(\sigma')$, and Step (iii) may fold a DLL into a DLS only if none of its inner regions is in $\mathsf{dom}(\sigma')$, redirecting values of container variables from the original CSs to the ones that arise from it by folding.

The *concretization* of an SPC (SMG) X is then the set $[\![X]\!]$ of all PCs (MGs, resp.) that can be abstracted to X. When $\mathbb{X}$ is a set of SPCs (SMGs), then $[\![\mathbb{X}]\!] = \bigcup_{X \in \mathbb{X}} [\![X]\!]$.

The left part of Fig. 3 shows an abstraction of an MG (top) into an SMG (bottom). Step (i) renames all regions in the MG into the regions of the SMG, Step (ii) is not applied, and Step (iii) folds three left-most regions of the DLL into a DLS. The *repre* arrows show the so-called assignment of representing objects defined below.

3   Operations and Their Specification

In this section, we introduce a notion of *operations* and propose their finite encoding in the form of the so-called *symbolic operations*. Symbolic operations play a crucial role in our approach since they are used to describe both of the two inputs of our algorithm for recognition of high-level container operations in low-level code. In particular, on one hand, we assume a (slightly extended) shape analyser to provide us with a CFG of the program being processed annotated by symbolic operations characterizing the effect of the low-level pointer statements used in the program (as discussed in Sect. 4). On the other hand, we assume the high-level container operations whose effect—implemented by sequences of low-level pointer statements—is to be sought along the annotated CFG to be also described as symbolic operations. This can either be done by the users of the approach (as discussed at the end of this section), or a library of typical high-level container operations can be pre-prepared.

Below, we, in particular, concentrate on destructive container operations, i.e., those container operations which change the shape of the heap. Non-destructive container operations are much easier to handle, and we discuss them at the end of Sect. 5.

Operations and Symbolic Operations. We define an *operation* as a binary relation δ on PCs capturing which input configurations are changed to which output configurations by executing the operation. The individual pairs $u = (c, c') \in \delta$ relating one input and one output configuration are called *updates*. Operations corresponding to pointer statements or container operations relate infinitely many different input and output configurations, hence they must be represented symbolically. We therefore define a *symbolic update* as a triple $U = (C, \rightsquigarrow, C')$ where $C = (G, \sigma)$, $C' = (G', \sigma')$ are SPCs, and $\rightsquigarrow$ is a binary relation over objects (regions and DLSs) called *transformation relation*. A *symbolic operation* is then simply a (finite) set Δ of symbolic updates.

Symbolic updates will be used to search for implementation of destructive container operations based on changes of the SMGs labelling the given CFG. To be able to do this with enough precision, symbolic updates must describe the "destructive" effect that the operation has on the shape of the memory (addition/removal of a region or a change of a selector value). For this, we require the semantics of a symbolic update to be *transparent*, meaning that every destructive change caused by the operation is *explicitly* and *unambiguously* visible in the specification of the operation (i.e., it cannot, e.g., happen in an invisible way somewhere inside a DLS). On the other hand, we are not interested in how the code modifies data values of regions. The semantics of a symbolic update thus admits their arbitrary changes.

Semantics of Symbolic Updates. To define semantics of symbolic operations, we need to distinguish abstract object (region or DLS) of an SPC $C = (G, \sigma)$ representing a region r of a PC $c = (g, \sigma') \in [\![C]\!]$. Recall that G arises by abstracting g by Steps (i–iii). Let π be the region renaming used in Step (i). We define the *representing object repre(r)* of r in C as (1) the region $\pi(r)$ if $\pi(r) \in reg(G)$, (2) $\top$ if $\pi(r)$ is removed in G by Step (ii), and (3) the DLS d if $\pi(r)$ is folded into $d \in obj(G)$ in Step (iii). We use $c \in_{repre} [\![C]\!]$ to denote that the function *repre* is an *assignment of representing objects* of C to regions of c. The inverse $repre^{-1}(o)$ gives the set of all regions of c that are represented by the object $o \in obj(C)$. Notice that the way of how g is abstracted to G by Steps (i–iii) is not necessarily unique, hence the assignment *repre* is not unique either. The right part of Fig. 3 shows an example of abstraction of a PC c (top) to an SPC C (bottom), with the assignment of representing objects *repre* shown via the top-down arrows.

Using this notation, the semantics of a symbolic update $U = (C, \rightsquigarrow, C')$ can be defined as the operation $[\![U]\!]$ which contains all updates $u = (c, c')$ such that:

1. $c \in_{repre} [\![C]\!]$ and $c' \in_{repre'} [\![C']\!]$.
2. An object $o \in obj(C)$ transforms into an object $o' \in obj(C')$, i.e., $o \rightsquigarrow o'$, iff the denotations $repre^{-1}(o)$ and $(repre')^{-1}(o)$ share some concrete region, i.e., $\exists r \in reg(c) \cap reg(c') : repre(r) = o \wedge repre'(r) = o'$.
3. The semantics is transparent: (i) each selector change is explicit, i.e., if $sel(r)$ in c differs from $sel(r)$ in c' for a region $r \in reg(c) \cap reg(c')$, then $repre(r) \in reg(C)$ and $repre'(r) \in reg(C')$ are regions such that $sel(repre(r))$ in C differs from $sel(repre'(r))$ in C'; (ii) every deallocation is explicit meaning that if a region r of c is removed (i.e., it is not a region of c'), then $repre(r)$ is a region (not a DLS) of C; (iii) every allocation is explicit meaning that if a region r of c' is added (i.e., it is not a region of c), then $repre'(r)$ is a region of C'.

The semantics of a symbolic operation Δ is naturally defined as $xs[\![\Delta]\!] = \bigcup_{U \in \Delta} [\![U]\!]$.

An example of a symbolic update is shown e.g. in Fig. 1(c), on the right of the program edge between locations 3 and 4. It consists of the right-most SPCs attached to these locations (denote them as $C = (G, \sigma)$ and $C' = (G', \sigma')$, and their DLSs as d and d', respectively) and the transformation relation between their objects denoted by the dotted vertical lines. The allocation done between the considered locations does not touch the DLSs, it only adds a new region pointed to by p. This is precisely expressed by the symbolic update $U = (C, \rightsquigarrow, C')$ where $\rightsquigarrow = \{(\sigma(L), \sigma'(L))\}$. The relation $\rightsquigarrow$ (the dotted line between objects $\sigma(L)$ and $\sigma'(L)$) says that, for every update from $[\![U]\!]$, denotations of the two DLSs d and d' share regions (by Point 2 above). By Point 3, there are no differences in pointer links between the DLLs encoded by the two DLSs; the DLLs encoded by d and the ones encoded by d' must be identical up to values of data fields. The only destructive change that appears in the update is the addition of the freshly allocated region $\sigma'(p)$ that does not have a $\rightsquigarrow$-predecessor (due to Point 3 (iii) above).

User Specification of Destructive Container Operations. As stated already above, we first concentrate on searching for implementations of user-specified destructive container operations in low-level code. In particular, we consider *non-iterative* container operations, i.e., those that can be implemented as non-looping sequences of destructive pointer updates, region allocations, and/or de-allocations.[1]

---

[1] Hence, e.g., an implementation of a procedure inserting an element into a sorted list, which includes the search for the element, will not be understood as a single destructive container operation, but rather as a procedure that calls a container iterator in a loop until the right place for the inserted element is found, and then calls a destructive container operation that inserts the given region at a position passed to it as a parameter.

We require the considered destructive container operations to be operations $\delta_{\overline{y}=op(\overline{x})}$ that satisfy the following requirements: (1) Each $\delta_{\overline{y}=op(\overline{x})}$ is deterministic, i.e., it is a function. (2) The sets $\overline{x} = x_1, ..., x_n \in \mathbb{V}^n$ and $\overline{y} = y_1, ..., y_m \in \mathbb{V}^m$, $n, m \geq 0$, are the input and output parameters of the operation so that for every update $((g, \sigma), (g', \sigma')) \in \delta_{\overline{y}=op(\overline{x})}$, the input PC has $\mathsf{dom}(\sigma) = \{x_1, ..., x_n\}$ and the output PC has $\mathsf{dom}(\sigma') = \{y_1, ..., y_m\}$. (3) Since we concentrate on destructive operations only, the operation does not modify data values, i.e., $\delta_{\overline{y}=op(\overline{x})} \subseteq \delta_{const}$ where δ_{const} contains all updates that do not change data values except for creating an unconstrained data value or destroying a data value when creating or destroying some region, respectively.

Container operations $\delta_{\overline{y}=op(\overline{x})}$ of the above form can be specified by a user as symbolic operations, i.e., sets of symbolic updates, $\Delta_{\overline{y}=op(\overline{x})}$ such that $\delta_{\overline{y}=op(\overline{x})} = [\![\Delta_{\overline{y}=op(\overline{x})}]\!] \cap \delta_{const}$. Once constructed, such symbolic operations can form a reusable library.

For instance, the operation $\delta_{\texttt{z=push\_back(x,y)}}$ can be specified as a symbolic operation $\Delta_{\texttt{z=push\_back(x,y)}}$ which inputs a CS referred to by variable x and a region pointed to by y and outputs a CS referred by z. This symbolic operation is depicted in Fig. 2. It consists of two symbolic updates in which the user relates possible initial and final states of the memory. The left one specifies the case when the input container is empty, the right one the case when it is nonempty.

4   Annotated Control Flow Graphs

In this section, we describe the semantic annotations of a control-flow graph that our procedure for recognizing implementation of high-level container operations in low-level code operates on.

Control-Flow Graph. A *control flow graph* (CFG) is a tuple $cfg = (L, E, \ell_I, \ell_F)$ where L is a finite set of (control) locations, $E \subseteq L \times \mathsf{Stmts} \times L$ is a set of *edges* labelled by *statements* from the set Stmts defined below, ℓ_I is the *initial location*, and ℓ_F the *final location*. For simplicity, we assume that any two locations ℓ, ℓ' are connected by at most one edge $\langle \ell, stmt, \ell' \rangle$.

The set of statements consists of pointer statements $stmt_p \in \mathsf{Stmts}_p$, integer data statements $stmt_d \in \mathsf{Stmts}_d$, container statements $stmt_c \in \mathsf{Stmts}_c$, and the skip statement $\texttt{skip}$, i.e., $\mathsf{Stmts} = \mathsf{Stmts}_p \cup \mathsf{Stmts}_d \cup \mathsf{Stmts}_c \cup \{\texttt{skip}\}$. The container statements and the skip statement do not appear in the input programs, they are generated by our transformation procedure. The statements from Stmts are generated by the following grammar (we present a simplified minimalistic form to ease the presentation):

$$stmt_p ::= p = (p \mid p{\rightarrow}s \mid \texttt{malloc()} \mid \bot) \mid p{\rightarrow}s = p \mid \texttt{free}(p) \mid p\texttt{==}(p \mid \bot) \mid p\texttt{!=}(p \mid \bot)$$
$$stmt_d ::= p{\rightarrow}d = (n \mid p{\rightarrow}d) \mid p{\rightarrow}d \texttt{==} p{\rightarrow}d \mid p{\rightarrow}d \texttt{ != } p{\rightarrow}d \qquad stmt_c ::= \overline{y} = op(\overline{x})$$

Above, $p \in \mathbb{V}_p$, $s \in \mathbb{S}_p$, $d \in \mathbb{S}_d$, $n \in \mathbb{Z}$, and $\overline{x}, \overline{y} \in \mathbb{V}^*$.

For each $stmt \in \mathsf{Stmts}_p \cup \mathsf{Stmts}_d$, let δ_{stmt} be the operation encoding its standard C semantics. For example, the operation $\delta_{\texttt{x=y->next}}$ contains all updates (c, c') where $c = (g, \sigma)$ is a PC s.t. $\sigma(y) \neq \top$ and c' is the same as c up to the variable x that is assigned the *next*-successor of the region pointed to by y. For each considered container statement $stmt \in \mathsf{Stmts}_c$, the operation δ_{stmt} is to be specified by the user. Let $p = e_1, \ldots, e_n$ where $e_i = \langle \ell_{i-1}, stmt_i, \ell_i' \rangle$, $1 \leq i \leq n$, be a sequence of edges of *cfg*. We call p a *control flow path* if $\ell_i' = \ell_i$ for each $1 \leq i < n$. The *semantics* $[\![p]\!]$ of p is the operation $\delta_{stmt_n} \circ \cdots \circ \delta_{stmt_1}$.

A *state* of a computation of a CFG *cfg* is a pair (l, c) where l is a location of *cfg* and c is a PC. A *computation* of *cfg* is a sequence of states $\phi = (\ell_0, c_0), (\ell_1, c_1), \ldots$ of length $|\phi| \leq \infty$ where there is a (unique) edge $e_i = \langle \ell_i, stmt_i, \ell_{i+1} \rangle \in E$ such that $(c_i, c_{i+1}) \in \delta_{stmt_i}$ for each $0 \leq i < |\phi|$. The path $e_0, e_1, \ldots$ is called the *control path* of ϕ.

Semantic Annotations. A *semantic annotation* of a CFG *cfg* consists of a *memory invariant* mem, a *successor relation* $\blacktriangleright$, and a *transformation relation* $\triangleright$. The quadruple $(cfg, mem, \blacktriangleright, \triangleright)$ is then called an *annotated control-flow graph* (annotated CFG). A memory invariant mem is a total map that assigns to every location ℓ of *cfg* a set $mem(\ell)$ of SPCs describing (an overapproximation of) the set of memory configurations reachable at the given location. For simplicity, we assume that sets of regions of any two different SPCs in $\mathsf{img}(mem)$ are disjoint. The successor relation is a binary relation on SPCs. For an edge $e = \langle \ell, stmt, \ell' \rangle$ and SPCs $C \in mem(\ell)$, $C' \in mem(\ell')$, $C \blacktriangleright C'$ indicates that PCs of $[\![C]\!]$ are transformed by executing $stmt$ into PCs of $[\![C']\!]$. The relation $\triangleright$ is a transformation relation on objects of configurations in $\mathsf{img}(mem)$ relating objects of C with objects of its $\blacktriangleright$-successor C' in order to express how the memory changes by executing the edge e. The change is captured in the form of the symbolic operation $\Delta_e = \{(C, \triangleright, C') \mid (C, C') \in \blacktriangleright \cap mem(\ell) \times mem(\ell')\}$. For our analysis to be sound, we require Δ_e to overapproximate δ_{stmt} restricted to $[\![mem(\ell)]\!]$, i.e., $[\![\Delta_e]\!] \supseteq \delta_{stmt}^{\ell}$ for $\delta_{stmt}^{\ell} = \{(c, c') \in \delta_{stmt} \mid c \in [\![mem(\ell)]\!]\}$.

A *symbolic trace* of an annotated CFG is a possibly infinite sequence of SPCs $\Phi = C_0, C_1, \ldots$ provided that $C_i \blacktriangleright C_{i+1}$ for each $0 \leq i < |\Phi| \leq \infty$. Given a computation $\phi = (\ell_0, c_0), (\ell_1, c_1), \ldots$ of length $|\phi| = |\Phi|$ such that $c_i \in [\![C_i]\!]$ for $0 \leq i \leq |\phi|$, we say that Φ is a *symbolic trace of computation* ϕ.

A part of the annotated CFG of our running example from Fig. 1(a) is given in Fig. 1(c), another part can be found in [7]. For each location ℓ, the set $mem(l)$ of SPCs is depicted on the right of the location l. The relation $\triangleright$ is depicted by dotted lines between objects of SPCs attached to adjacent program locations. The relation $\blacktriangleright$ is not shown as it can be almost completely inferred from $\triangleright$: Whenever objects of two SPCs are related by $\triangleright$, the SPCs are related by $\blacktriangleright$. The only exception is the $\blacktriangleright$-chain of the left-most SPCs along the control path 1, 2, 3, 4 in Fig. 1(c).

5   Replacement of Low-Level Manipulation of Containers

With all the notions designed above, we are now ready to state our methods for identifying low-level implementations of container operations in an annotated CFG and for replacing them by calls of high-level container operations. Apart from the very end of the section, we concentrate on destructive container operations whose treatment turns out to be significantly more complex. We assume that the destructive container operations to be sought and replaced are specified as sequences of destructive pointer updates, region allocations, and/or de-allocations as discussed in the last paragraph of Sect. 3.

Given a specification of destructive container operations and an annotated CFG, our algorithm needs to decide: (1) which low-level pointer operations to remove, (2) where to insert calls of container operations that replace them and what are these operations, and (3) where and how to assign the right values to the input parameters of the inserted container operations. To do this, the algorithm performs the following steps.

The algorithm starts by identifying container shapes in the SPCs of the given annotated CFG. Subsequently, it looks for the so-called *transformation chains* of these container shapes which capture their evolution along the annotated CFG. Each such chain is a sequence of sub-SMGs that appear in the labels of a path of the given annotated CFG. In particular, transformation chains consisting of objects linked by the transformation relation, meaning that the chain represents evolution of the same piece of memory, and corresponding to some of the specified container operations are sought.

The algorithm then builds a so-called *replacement recipe* of a consistent set of transformation chains that interprets the same low-level code as the same high-level container operation for each possible run of the code. The recipe determines which code can be replaced by which container operation and where exactly the container operation is to be inserted within the sequence of low-level statements implementing it. This sequence can, moreover, be interleaved with some independent statements that are to be preserved and put before or after the inserted call of a container operation.

The remaining step is then to find out how and where to assign the right values of the input parameters of the inserted container operations. We do this by computing a so-called *parameter assignment* relation. We now describe the above steps in detail. For the rest of Sect. 5, we fix an input annotated CFG *cfg* and assume that we have specified a symbolic operation Δ_{stmt} for every container statement $stmt \in \mathsf{Stmts}_c$.

5.1   Transformation Chains

A transformation chain is a sequence of sub-SMGs that describes how a piece of memory evolves along a control path. We in particular look for such transformation chains whose overall effect corresponds to the effect of some specified container operation. Such transformation chains serve us as candidates for code replacement.

Let $p = \langle \ell_0, stmt_1, \ell_1 \rangle, \ldots, \langle \ell_{n-1}, stmt_n, \ell_n \rangle$ be a control flow path. A *transformation chain (or simply* chain*)* with the control path p is a sequence $\tau = \tau[0] \cdots \tau[n]$ of SMGs such that, for each $0 \leq i \leq n$, there is an SPC $C_i = (G_i, \sigma_i) \in mem(\ell_i)$ with $\tau[i] \preceq G_i$ and the relation $\blacktriangleright_\tau = \{(C_{i-1}, C_i) \mid 1 \leq i \leq n\}$ is a subset of $\blacktriangleright$, i.e., C_i is the successor of C_{i-1} for each i. We will call the sequence $C_0, \ldots, C_n$ the *symbolic trace of* τ, *and we let* $\rhd_\tau^i = \rhd \cap (obj(\tau[i-1]) \times obj(\tau[i]))$ *for* $1 \leq i \leq n$ *denote the transformation relation between the objects of the* $i-1$*th and* i*th SMG of* τ.

An example of a chain, denoted as τ_{pb} below, is the sequence of the six SMGs that are a part of the SPCs highlighted in grey in Fig. 1(c). The relation $\blacktriangleright_{\tau_{\mathrm{pb}}}$ links the six SPCs, and the relation $\rhd_{\tau_{\mathrm{pb}}}$ consists of the pairs of objects connected by the dotted lines.

Let Δ be a specification of a container operation. We say that a transformation chain τ *implements* Δ w.r.t. some input/output parameter valuations σ/σ' iff $[\![U_\tau]\!] \subseteq [\![\Delta]\!]$ for the symbolic update $U_\tau = ((\tau[0], \sigma), \rhd_\tau^n \circ \cdots \circ \rhd_\tau^1, (\tau[n], \sigma'))$. Intuitively, U_τ describes how MGs in $[\![\tau[0]]\!]$ are transformed into MGs in $[\![\tau[n]]\!]$ along the chain. When put together with the parameter valuations σ/σ', U_τ is required to be covered by Δ.

In our example, by taking the composition of relations $\rhd_{\tau_{\mathrm{pb}}}^5 \circ \cdots \circ \rhd_{\tau_{\mathrm{pb}}}^1$ (relating objects from location 4 linked by dotted lines with objects at location 11), we see that the chain τ_{pb} implements the symbolic operation $\Delta_{\mathtt{z=push\_back(x,y)}}$ from Fig. 2, namely, its symbolic update on the right. The parameter valuations σ/σ' can be constructed as L and p correspond to x and y at location 4, respectively, and L corresponds to z at location 11.

Let τ be a chain implementing Δ w.r.t. input/output parameter valuations σ/σ'. We define *implementing edges* of τ w.r.t. Δ, σ, and σ' as the edges of the path p of τ that are labelled by those destructive pointer updates, region allocations, and/or deallocations that implement the update U_τ. Formally, the i-th edge e_i of p, $1 \leq i \leq n$, is an implementing edge of τ iff $[\![((\tau[i-1], \emptyset), \rhd, (\tau[i], \emptyset))]\!] \cap \delta_{const}$ is not an identity (the update does not talk about values of variables, hence the empty valuations).

For our example chain τ_{pb}, the edges (7,8), (8,9), and (10,11) are implementing.

Finding Transformation Chains in an Annotated CFG. Let Δ_{stmt} be one of the given symbolic specifications of the semantics of a destructive container statement $stmt \in \mathsf{Stmts}_c$. We now sketch our algorithm for identifying chains that implement Δ_{stmt}. More details can be found in [7]. The algorithm is based on precomputing sets $\widehat{U}$ of so-called *atomic symbolic updates* that must be performed to implement the effect of each symbolic update $U \in \Delta_{stmt}$. Each atomic symbolic update corresponds to one pointer statement that performs a destructive pointer update, a memory allocation, or a deallocation. The set $\widehat{U}$ can be computed by looking at the differences in the selector values of the input and output SPCs of U. The algorithm then searches through symbolic traces of the annotated CFG *cfg* and looks for sequences of sub-SMGs present in them and linked by the atomic symbolic updates from $\widehat{U}$ (in any permutation) or by identity (meaning that a statement irrelevant for *stmt* is performed). Occurrences of atomic updates are found based on testing entailment between symbolic atomic updates and symbolic updates annotating subsequent CFG locations. This amounts to checking entailment of the two source and the two target SMGs of the updates using methods of [8], augmented with testing that the transformation relation is respected. Soundness of the procedure depends on the semantics of symbolic updates being sufficiently precise, which is achieved by transparency of their semantics.

For example, for the container statement $z=push\_back(x,y)$ and the symbolic update U corresponding to an insertion into a list of length one or more, $\widehat{U}$ will consist of (i) symbolic updates corresponding to the pointer statements assigning y to the *next*-selector of the back region of x, (ii) assigning the back region of x to the *prev*-selector of y, and (iii) assigning $\perp$ to the *next*-selector of y. Namely, for the chain τ_{pb} in Fig. 1(c) and the definition of the operation $\Delta_{z=push\_back(x,y)}$ in Fig. 2, the set $\widehat{U}$ consists of three symbolic updates: from location 7 to 8 by performing Point (i), then from location 8 to 9 by performing (iii), and from location 10 to 11 by performing (ii).

5.2   Replacement Locations

A *replacement location* of a transformation chain τ w.r.t. Δ, σ, and σ' is one of the locations on the control path p of τ where it is possible to insert a call of a procedure implementing Δ while preserving the semantics of the path. In order to formalize the notion of replacement locations, we call the edges of p that are not implementing (do not implement the operation—e.g., they modify data) and precede or succeed the replacement location as the *prefix* or *suffix edges*, and we denote $p_{p/s/i}$ the sequences of edges obtained by removing all but prefix/suffix/implementing edges, respectively. The replacement location must then satisfy that $[\![\cdot p_i \cdot]\!]|_{[\![mem(\ell_0)]\!]} = [\![p]\!]|_{[\![mem(\ell_0)]\!]}$ where the notation $\delta|_S$ stands for the operation δ restricted to updates with the source configurations from the set S. The prefix edges are chosen as those which read the state of the container shape as it would be before the identified container operation, the suffix edges as those which read its state after the operation. The rest of not implementing edges is split arbitrarily. If we do not find a splitting satisfying the above semantical condition, τ is discarded from further processing.

For our example chain τ_{pb}, the edges (4,7) and (9,10) can both be put into the prefix since none of them saves values of pointers used in the operation (see Fig. 1(c)). The edge (9,10) is thus shifted up in the CFG, and the suffix remains empty. Locations 8–11 can then be used as the replacement locations.

5.3   Replacement Recipes

A *replacement recipe* is a map Υ that assigns to each chain τ of the annotated CFG *cfg* a quadruple $\Upsilon(\tau) = (\Delta_\tau, \sigma_\tau^{in}, \sigma_\tau^{out}, \ell_\tau)$, called a *replacement template*, with the following meaning: Δ_τ is a specification of a container operation that is to be inserted at the replacement location ℓ_τ as a replacement of the implementing edges of τ. Next, $\sigma_\tau^{in}/\sigma_\tau^{out}$ are input/output parameter valuations that specify which parts of the memory should be passed to the inserted operation as its input parameters and which parts of the memory correspond to the values of the output parameters that the operation should return.

For our example chain τ_{pb}, a replacement template $\Upsilon(\tau_{\mathrm{pb}})$ can be obtained, e.g., by taking $\Delta_{\tau_{\mathrm{pb}}} = \Delta_{\mathrm{z=push\_back(x,y)}}$, $\ell_{\tau_{\mathrm{pb}}} = 11$, $\sigma_{\tau_{\mathrm{pb}}}^{\mathrm{in}}(\mathbf{x}) = \sigma_{\tau_{\mathrm{pb}}[0]}(\mathrm{L})$ denoting the CS in the gray SPC of loc. 4, $\sigma_{\tau_{\mathrm{pb}}}^{\mathrm{in}}(\mathbf{y}) = \sigma_{\tau_{\mathrm{pb}}[0]}(\mathrm{p})$ denoting the right-most region of the gray SPC of loc. 4, and $\sigma_{\tau_{\mathrm{pb}}}^{\mathrm{out}}(\mathbf{z}) = \sigma_{\tau_{\mathrm{pb}}[5]}(\mathrm{L})$ denoting the CS in the gray SPC of loc. 11.

We now give properties of replacement recipes that are sufficient for the CFG cfg' generated by our code replacement procedure, presented in Sect. 5.5, to be semantically equivalent to the original annotated CFG cfg.

Local Consistency. A replacement recipe Υ must be *locally consistent* meaning that (i) every $\tau \in \mathrm{dom}(\Upsilon)$ implements Δ_{τ} w.r.t. $\sigma_{\tau}^{\mathrm{in}}$ and $\sigma_{\tau}^{\mathrm{out}}$ and (ii) ℓ_{τ} is a replacement location of τ w.r.t. Δ_{τ}, $\sigma_{\tau}^{\mathrm{in}}$, and $\sigma_{\tau}^{\mathrm{out}}$. Further, to enforce that τ is not longer than necessary, we require its control path τ to start and end by an implementing edge. Finally, implementing edges of the chain τ cannot modify selectors of any object that is a part of a CS which is itself not at the input of the container operation.

Global Consistency. Global consistency makes it safe to replace the code w.r.t. multiple overlapping chains of a replacement recipe Υ, i.e., the replacements defined by them do not collide. A replacement recipe Υ is *globally consistent* iff the following holds:

1. A location is a replacement location within all symbolic traces passing it or within none. Formally, for each maximal symbolic trace Φ passing the replacement location ℓ_{τ} of a chain $\tau \in \mathrm{dom}(\Upsilon)$, there is a chain $\tau' \in \mathrm{dom}(\Upsilon)$ s.t. $\ell_{\tau'} = \ell_{\tau}$ and the symbolic trace of τ' is a sub-sequence of Φ passing ℓ_{τ}.
2. An edge is an implementing edge within all symbolic traces passing it or within none. Formally, for each maximal symbolic trace Φ passing an implementing edge e of a chain $\tau \in \mathrm{dom}(\Upsilon)$, there is a chain $\tau' \in \mathrm{dom}(\Upsilon)$ s.t. e is its implementing edge and the symbolic trace of τ' is a sub-sequence of Φ passing e.
3. For any chains $\tau, \tau' \in \mathrm{dom}(\Upsilon)$ that appear within the same symbolic trace, the following holds: (a) If τ, τ' share an edge, then they share their replacement location, i.e., $\ell_{\tau} = \ell_{\tau'}$. (b) Moreover, if $\ell_{\tau} = \ell_{\tau'}$, then τ is an infix of τ' or τ' is an infix of τ. The latter condition is technical and simplifies the proof of correctness of our approach.
3. Chains $\tau, \tau' \in \mathrm{dom}(\Upsilon)$ with the same replacement location $\ell_{\tau} = \ell_{\tau'}$ have the same operation, i.e., $\Delta_{\tau} = \Delta_{\tau'}$.
4. An edge is either implementing for every chain of $\mathrm{dom}(\Upsilon)$ going through that edge or for no chain in $\mathrm{dom}(\Upsilon)$ at all.

Notice that Points 1, 2, and 3 speak about symbolic traces. That is, they do not have to hold along all control paths of the given CFG cfg but only those which appear within computations starting from $[\![mem(\ell_I)]\!]$.

Connectedness. The final requirement is connectedness of a replacement recipe Υ. It reflects the fact that once some part of memory is to be viewed as a container, then destructive operations on this part of memory are to be done by destructive container operations only until the container is destroyed by a container destructor. Note that this requirement concerns operations dealing with the linking fields only, the rest of the concerned objects can be manipulated by any low-level operations. Moreover, the destructive pointer statements implementing destructive container operations can also be interleaved with other independent pointer manipulations, which are handled as the prefix/suffix edges of the appropriate chain.

Connectedness of Υ is verified over the semantic annotations by checking that in the $\triangleright$-future and past of every container (where a container is understood as a container shape that was assigned a container variable in Υ), the container is created, destroyed, and its linking fields are modified by container operations only. Due to space restrictions, we refer the reader to [7] for a formal description.

Computing Recipes. The algorithm for building a replacement recipe Υ starts by looking for chains τ of the annotated CFG *cfg* that can be associated with replacement templates $\Upsilon(\tau) = (\Delta_\tau, \sigma_\tau^{\text{in}}, \sigma_\tau^{\text{out}}, \ell_\tau)$ s.t. local consistency holds. It uses the approach described in Sect. 5.1. It then tests global consistency of Υ. All the five sub-conditions can be checked straightforwardly based on their definitions. If Υ is found not globally consistent, problematic chains are pruned it until global consistency is achieved. Testing for connectedness is done by testing all $\blacktriangleright^{\text{cs}}$-paths leading forward from output parameters of chains and backward from input parameters of chains. Testing whether $[\![(S, \triangleright, S')]\!] \cap \delta_{const}$ or $[\![(S', \triangleright, S)]\!] \cap \delta_{const}$ is an identity, which is a part of the procedure, can be done easily due to the transparency of symbolic updates. Chains whose container parameters contradict connectedness are removed from Υ. The pruning is iterated until Υ is both globally consistent and connected.

5.4   Parameter Assignment

To prevent conflicts of names of parameters of the inserted container operations, their calls are inserted with fresh parameter names. Particularly, given a replacement recipe Υ, the replacement location ℓ_τ of every chain $\tau \in \text{dom}(\Upsilon)$ is assigned a variable renaming λ_{ℓ_τ} that renames the input/output parameters of the symbolic operation Δ_τ, specifying the destructive container operation implemented by τ, to fresh names. The renamed parameters of the container operations do not appear in the original code, and so the code replacement algorithm must insert assignments of the appropriate values to the parameters of the operations prior to the inserted calls of these operations. For this, we compute a *parameter assignment* relation ν containing pairs $(\ell, x := y)$ specifying which assignment $x := y$ is to be inserted at which location ℓ. Intuitively, ν is constructed so that the input parameters of container operations take their values from the output container parameters of the preceding container operations or, in case of pointer variables, directly from the access paths (consisting of a pointer variable v or a selector value $v \rightarrow s$) that are used in the original program to access the concerned memory regions. Due to space limitations, details are given in [7]. Let us just note that if we fail to find a parameter assignment, we remove some chains from Υ and restart the search.

5.5   Code Replacement

The input of the replacement procedure is the annotated CFG cfg, a replacement recipe Υ, a variable renaming λ_ℓ for every replacement location ℓ of Υ, and a parameter assignment relation ν. The procedure produces a modified CFG cfg'. It first removes all implementing edges of every chain $\tau \in \mathsf{dom}(\Upsilon)$ and adds instead an edge with a call to $\lambda_\ell(\Delta_\ell)$ at ℓ_τ, and then adds an edge with the assignment $x := y$ at ℓ for every pair $(\ell, x := y) \in \nu$. The *edge removal* is done simply by replacing the statement on the given edge by the skip statement whose semantics is identity. Given a statement *stmt* and a location ℓ, *edge addition* amounts to: (1) adding a fresh location $\ell^\bullet$, (2) adding a new edge $\langle \ell, stmt, \ell^\bullet \rangle$, (3) replacing every edge $\langle \ell, stmt', \ell' \rangle$ by $\langle \ell^\bullet, stmt', \ell' \rangle$. Intuitively, edge removal preserves all control paths going through the original edge, only the statement is now "skipped", and edge addition inserts the given statement into all control paths containing the given location.

After replacing destructive container operations, we replace non-destructive container operations, including, in particular, usage of *iterators* to reference elements of a list and to move along the list, *initialisation of iterators* (placing an iterator at a particular element of a list), and *emptiness tests*. With a replacement recipe Υ and an assignment relation ν at hand, recognizing non-destructive operations in the annotated CFG cfg is a much easier task than that of recognizing destructive operations. Actually, for the above operations, the problem reduces to analysing annotations of one CFG edge at a time. Due to space limitations, we refer an interested reader to [7] for more details.

Preservation of Semantics. It can now be proved (cf. [7]) that under the assumption that the replacement recipe Υ is locally and globally consistent and connected and the parameter assignment relation ν is complete, our code replacement procedure preserves the semantics. In particular, computations of the CFG cfg are surjectively mapped to computations of the CFG cfg' that are equivalent in the following sense. They can be divided into the same number of segments that are in the computation of cfg delimited by borders of the chains that it passes through. The two computations agree on the final PCs of the respective segments. Note also that the transformation preserves memory safety errors—if they appear, the related containers will not be introduced due to violation of connectedness.

6   Implementation and Experimental Results

We have implemented our approach as an extension of the Predator shape analyser [8] and tested it through a number of experiments. Our code and experiments are publicly available at http://www.fit.vutbr.cz/research/groups/verifit/tools/predator-adt.

The first part of our experiments concentrated on how our approach can deal with various low-level implementations of list operations. We built a collection of 18 benchmark programs manipulating NULL-terminated DLLs via different implementations of typical list operations, such as insertion, iteration, and removal. Moreover, we generated further variants of these implementations by considering various legal permutations of their statements. We also considered interleaving the pointer statements implementing list operations with various other statements, e.g., accessing the data stored in the lists.[2] Finally, we also considered two benchmarks with NULL-terminated Linux lists that heavily rely on pointer arithmetics. In all the benchmarks, our tool correctly recognised list operations among other pointer-based code and gave us a complete recipe for code transformation. On a standard desktop PC, the total run time on a benchmark was almost always under 1s (with one exception at 2.5 s), with negligible memory consumption.

Next, we successfully applied our tool to multiple case studies of creating, traversing, filtering, and searching lists taken from the benchmark suite of Slayer [1] (modified to use doubly-linked instead of singly-linked lists). Using a slight extension of our prototype, we also successfully handled examples dealing with lists with head/tail pointers as well as with circular lists. These examples illustrate that our approach can be generalized to other kinds of containers as discussed in Sect. 7. These examples are also freely available at the link above. Moreover, in [7], we present an example how we deal with code where two container operations are interleaved.

Further, we concentrated on showing that our approach can be useful to simplify program analysis by separating low-level pointer-related analysis from analysing other, higher-level properties (like, e.g., sortedness or other data-related properties). To illustrate this, we used our approach to combine shape analysis implemented in Predator with data-related analysis provided by the J2BP analyser [15]. J2BP analyses Java programs, and it is based on predicate abstraction extended to cope with containers.

We used 4 benchmarks for the evaluation. The first one builds an ordered list of numerical data, inserts another data element into it, and finally checks sortedness of the resulting list, yielding an assertion failure if this is not the case (such a test harness must be used since J2BP expects a closed program and verifies absence of assertion failures). The other benchmarks are similar in that they produce lists that should fulfill some property, followed by code that checks whether the property is satisfied. The considered properties are correctness of the length of a list, the fact that certain inserted values appear in a certain order, and correctness of rewriting certain values in a list. We used our tool to process the original C code. Next, we manually (but algorithmically) rewrote the result into an equivalent Java program. Then, we ran J2BP to verify that no assertion failures are possible in the obtained code, hence verifying the considered data-related properties. For each benchmark, our tool was able to produce (within 1 s.)

---

[2] In practice, there would typically be many more such statements, seemingly increasing the size of the case studies, but such statements are not an issue for our method.

a container program for J2BP, and J2BP was able to complete the proof. At the same time, note that neither Predator nor J2BP could perform the verification alone (Predator does not reason about numerical data and J2BP does not handle pointer-linked dynamic data structures).

7   Possibilities of Generalizing the Approach

Our method is built around the idea of specifying operations using a pair of abstract configurations equipped with a transformation relation over their components. Although we have presented all concepts for the simple abstract domain of SMGs restricted to NULL-terminated DLLs, the main idea can be used with abstract domains describing other kinds of lists, trees, and other data structures too. We now highlight what is needed for that. The abstract domain to be used must allow one to define a sufficiently fine-grained *assignment of representing objects*, which is necessary to define symbolic updates with *transparent semantics*. Moreover, one needs a shape analysis that computes annotations of the CFG with a precise enough invariant, equipped with the *transformation relation*, encoding pointer manipulations in a *transparent way*. However, most shape analyses do actually work with such information internally when computing abstract post-images (due to computing the effect of updates on *concretized* parts of the memory). We thus believe that, instead of Predator, tools like, e.g., Slayer [1] or Forester [9] can be modified to output CFGs annotated in the needed way.

Other than that, given an annotated CFG, our algorithms searching for container operations depend mostly on an *entailment procedure over symbolic updates* (cf. Sect. 5.1, [7]). Entailment of symbolic updates is, however, easy to obtain as an extension of entailment over the abstract domain provided the entailment is able to identify which parts of the symbolic shapes encode the same parts of the concrete configurations.

8   Conclusions and Future Work

We have presented and experimentally evaluated a method that can transform in a sound and fully automated way a program manipulating NULL-terminated list containers via low-level pointer operations to a high-level container program. Moreover, we argued that our method is extensible beyond the considered list containers (as illustrated also by our preliminary experiments with lists extended with additional pointers and circular lists). A formalization of an extension of our approach to other kinds of containers, a better implementation of our approach, as well as other extensions of our approach (including, e.g., more sophisticated target code generation and recognition of iterative container operations) are subject of our current and future work.

Acknowledgement. This work was supported by the Czech Science Foundation project 14-11384S.

References

1. Berdine, J., Cook, B., Ishtiaq, S.: SLAYER: memory safety for systems-level code. In: Gopalakrishnan, G., Qadeer, S. (eds.) CAV 2011. LNCS, vol. 6806, pp. 178–183. Springer, Heidelberg (2011)
2. Chilimbi, T.M., Hill, M.D., Larus, J.R.: Cache-conscious structure layout. In: Proceedings of PLDI 1999, pp. 1–12. ACM (1999)
3. Cousot, P., Cousot, R.: Abstract interpretation: a unified lattice model for static analysis of programs by construction or approximation of fixpoints. In: Proceedings of POPL 1977, pp. 238–252. ACM (1977)
4. Cozzie, A., Stratton, F., Xue, H., King, S.T.: Digging for data structures. In: Proceedings of USENIX 2008, pp. 255–266. USENIX Association (2008)
5. Dekker, R., Ververs, F.: Abstract data structure recognition. In: Proceedings of KBSE 1994, pp. 133–140 (1994)
6. Demsky, B., Ernst, M.D., Guo, P.J., McCamant, S., Perkins, J.H., Rinard, M.C.: Inference and enforcement of data structure consistency specifications. In: Proceedings of ISSTA 2006, pp. 233–244. ACM (2006)
7. Dudka, K., Holík, L., Peringer, P., Trtík, M., Vojnar, T.: From low-level pointers to high-level containers. Technical report FIT-TR-2015-03 arXiv:1510.07995, FIT BUT (2015). http://arxiv.org/abs/1510.07995
8. Dudka, K., Peringer, P., Vojnar, T.: Byte-precise verification of low-level list manipulation. In: Logozzo, F., Fähndrich, M. (eds.) Static Analysis. LNCS, vol. 7935, pp. 215–237. Springer, Heidelberg (2013)
9. Habermehl, P., Holík, L., Rogalewicz, A., Simácek, J., Vojnar, T.: Forest automata for verification of heap manipulation. Formal Meth. Syst. Des. 41(1), 83–106 (2012)
10. Haller, I., Slowinska, A., Bos, H.: MemPick: high-level data structure detection in C/C++ binaries. In: Proceedings of WCRE 2013, pp. 32–41 (2013)
11. Hendren, L.J., Nicolau, A.: Parallelizing programs with recursive data structures. IEEE Trans. Parallel Distrib. Syst. 1(1), 35–47 (1990)
12. Jump, M., McKinley, K.S.: Dynamic shape analysis via degree metrics. In: Proceedings of ISMM 2009, pp. 119–128. ACM (2009)
13. Jung, C., Clark, N.: DDT: design and evaluation of a dynamic program analysis for optimizing data structure usage. In: Proceedings of MICRO 2009, pp. 56–66. ACM (2009)
14. O'Hearn, P.W., Reynolds, J.C., Yang, H.: Local reasoning about programs that alter data structures. In: Fribourg, L. (ed.) CSL 2001 and EACSL 2001. LNCS, vol. 2142, pp. 1–19. Springer, Heidelberg (2001)
15. Parízek, P.: J2BP. http://plg.uwaterloo.ca/~pparizek/j2bp
16. Parízek, P., Lhoták, O.: Predicate abstraction of java programs with collections. In: Proceedings of OOPSLA 2012, pp. 75–94. ACM (2012)
17. Pheng, S., Verbrugge, C.: Dynamic data structure analysis for java programs. In: Proceedings of ICPC 2006, pp. 191–201. IEEE Computer Society (2006)
18. Raman, E., August, D.I.: Recursive data structure profiling. In: Proceedings of MSP 2005, pp. 5–14. ACM (2005)
19. Raza, M., Calcagno, C., Gardner, P.: Automatic parallelization with separation logic. In: Castagna, G. (ed.) ESOP 2009. LNCS, vol. 5502, pp. 348–362. Springer, Heidelberg (2009)
20. Sagiv, S., Reps, T.W., Wilhelm, R.: Parametric shape analysis via 3-valued logic. TOPLAS 24(3), 217–298 (2002)

21. Shaham, R., Kolodner, E.K., Sagiv, S.: On the Effectiveness of GC in Java. In: Proceedings of ISMM 2000, pp. 12–17. ACM (2000)

22. Vafeiadis, V.: RGSep action inference. In: Barthe, G., Hermenegildo, M. (eds.) VMCAI 2010. LNCS, vol. 5944, pp. 345–361. Springer, Heidelberg (2010)

23. White, D.H., Lüttgen, G.: Identifying dynamic data structures by learning evolving patterns in memory. In: Piterman, N., Smolka, S.A. (eds.) TACAS 2013 (ETAPS 2013). LNCS, vol. 7795, pp. 354–369. Springer, Heidelberg (2013)

Parameterized and Component-Based Systems

Regular Symmetry Patterns

Anthony W. Lin[1], Truong Khanh Nguyen[2], Philipp Rümmer[3]([✉]),
and Jun Sun[4]

[1] Yale-NUS College, Singapore, Singapore
[2] Autodesk, Singapore, Singapore
[3] Uppsala University, Uppsala, Sweden
philipp.ruemmer@it.uu.se
[4] Singapore University of Design and Technology, Singapore, Singapore

Abstract. Symmetry reduction is a well-known approach for alleviating the state explosion problem in model checking. Automatically identifying symmetries in concurrent systems, however, is computationally expensive. We propose a symbolic framework for capturing symmetry patterns in parameterised systems (i.e. an infinite family of finite-state systems): two regular word transducers to represent, respectively, parameterised systems and symmetry patterns. The framework subsumes various types of "symmetry relations" ranging from weaker notions (e.g. simulation preorders) to the strongest notion (i.e. isomorphisms). Our framework enjoys two algorithmic properties: (1) symmetry verification: given a transducer, we can automatically check whether it is a symmetry pattern of a given system, and (2) symmetry synthesis: we can automatically generate a symmetry pattern for a given system in the form of a transducer. Furthermore, our symbolic language allows additional constraints that the symmetry patterns need to satisfy to be easily incorporated in the verification/synthesis. We show how these properties can help identify symmetry patterns in examples like dining philosopher protocols, self-stabilising protocols, and prioritised resource-allocator protocol. In some cases (e.g. Gries's coffee can problem), our technique automatically synthesises a safety-preserving finite approximant, which can then be verified for safety solely using a finite-state model checker.

1 Introduction

Symmetry reduction [12,19,22] is a well-known approach for alleviating the state explosion problem in automatic verification of concurrent systems. The essence of symmetry reduction is to identify symmetries in the system and avoid exploring states that are "similar" (under these symmetries) to previously explored states.

One main challenge with symmetry reduction methods is the difficulty in identifying symmetries in a given system in general. One approach is to provide dedicated language instructions for specifying symmetries (e.g. see [22,29,30]) or specific languages (e.g. see [13,24,25]) so that users can provide insight on what symmetries are there in the system. For instance, Murφ provides a special data type with a list of syntactic restrictions and all values that belong

© Springer-Verlag Berlin Heidelberg 2016
B. Jobstmann and K.R.M. Leino (Eds.): VMCAI 2016, LNCS 9583, pp. 455–475, 2016.
DOI: 10.1007/978-3-662-49122-5_22

to this type are symmetric. Another approach is to detect symmetry automatically without requiring expert insights. Automatic detection of symmetries is an extremely difficult computational problem. A number of approaches have been proposed in this direction (e.g. [15,16,33]). For example, Donaldson and Miller [15,16] designed an automatic approach to detecting process symmetries for channel-based communication systems, based on constructing a graph called *static channel diagram* from a Promela model whose automorphisms correspond to symmetries in the model. Nonetheless, it is clear from their experiments that existing approaches work only for small numbers of processes.

In practice, concurrent systems are often obtained by replicating a generic behavioral description [32]. For example, a prioritised resource-allocator protocol [14], [Sect. 4.4] provides a description of an allocator program and a client program in a network with a star topology (allocator in the center), from which a concurrent system with 1 allocator and m clients (for any given $m \in \mathbb{Z}_{>0}$) can be generated. This is in fact the standard setting of parameterised systems (e.g. see [4,31]), which are symbolic descriptions of infinite families $\{\mathfrak{S}_i\}_{i=1}^{\infty}$ of transition systems $\mathfrak{S}_i$ that can be generated by instantiating some parameters (e.g. the number of processes).

Adopting this setting of parameterised systems, we consider the problem of formulating and generating symbolic *symmetry patterns*, abstract descriptions of symmetries that can be instantiated to obtain concrete symmetries for every instance of a parameterised system. A formal language to specify symmetry patterns should be able to capture interesting symmetry patterns, e.g., that each instance $\mathfrak{S}_i$ of the parameterised system $\mathfrak{S} = \{\mathfrak{S}_i\}_{i=1}^{\infty}$ exhibits the full symmetry S_n (i.e. invariant under permuting the locations of the processes). Ideally, such a language $\mathcal{L}$ should also enjoy the following algorithmic properties: (1) *symmetry verification*, i.e., given a symmetry pattern $P \in \mathcal{L}$, we can automatically check whether P is a symmetry pattern of a given parameterised system, and (2) *symmetry synthesis*: given a parameterised system, we can automatically generate symmetry patterns $P \in \mathcal{L}$ that the system exhibits. In particular, if $\mathcal{L}$ is sufficiently expressive to specify commonly occuring symmetry patterns, Property (1) would allow us to automatically compute which common symmetry patterns hold for a given parameterised system. In the case when symmetry patterns might be less obvious, Property (2) would allow us to identify further symmetries that are satisfied by the given parameterised systems. To the best of our knowledge, to date no such languages have been proposed.

Contribution: We propose a general symbolic framework for capturing symmetry patterns for parameterised systems. The framework uses *finite-state letter-to-letter word transducers* to represent *both* parameterised systems and symmetry patterns. In the sequel, symmetry patterns that are recognised by transducers are called *regular symmetry patterns*. Based on extensive studies in regular model checking (e.g. see [1,4,27,31]), finite-state word transducers are now well-known to be good symbolic representations of parameterised systems. Moreover, equivalent logic-based (instead of automata-based) formalisms are also available, e.g.,

LTL(MSO) [3] which can be used to specify parameterised systems and properties (e.g. safety and liveness) in a convenient way. In this paper, we show that transducers are not only also sufficiently expressive for representing many common symmetry patterns, but they enjoy the two aforementioned desirable algorithmic properties: automatic symmetry verification and synthesis.

There is a broad spectrum of notions of "symmetries" for transition systems that are of interest to model checking. These include simulation preorders (a weak variant) and isomorphisms (the strongest), e.g., see [6]. We suggest that transducers are not only sufficiently powerful in expressing many such notions of symmetries, but they are also a flexible symbolic language in that constraints (e.g. the symmetry pattern is a bijection) can be easily added to or relaxed from the specification. In this paper, we shall illustrate this point by handling simulation preorders and isomorphisms (i.e. bijective simulation preorders) within the same framework. Another notable point of our symbolic language is its ability to specify that the simulation preorder gives rise to an *abstracted system* that is finite-state and preserves non-safety (i.e. if the original system is not safe, then so is the abstracted system). In other words, *we can specify that the symmetry pattern reduces the infinite-state parameterised system to a finite-state system.* Safety of finite-state systems can then be checked using standard finite-state model checkers.

We next show how to specialise our framework to *process symmetries* [12,19,22]. Roughly speaking, a process symmetry for a concurrent system $\mathfrak{S}$ with n processes is a permutation $\pi : [n] \to [n]$ (where $[n] := \{1, \ldots, n\}$) such that the behavior of $\mathfrak{S}$ is invariant under permuting the process indices by π (i.e. the resulting system is isomorphic to the original one under the natural bijection induced by π). For example, if the process indices of clients in the aforementioned resource-allocator protocol with 1 allocator and m clients are $1, \ldots, m+1$, then any permutation $\pi : [m+1] \to [m+1]$ that fixes 1 is a process symmetry for the protocol. The set of such process symmetries is a permutation group on $[m+1]$ (under functional composition) generated by the following two permutations specified in standard cyclic notations: $(2,3)$ and $(2,3,\ldots,m+1)$. This is true for *every value of $m \geq 2$*. In addition, finite-state model checkers represent symmetry permutation groups by their (often exponentially more succinct) finite set of generators. Thus, if $\mathfrak{S} = \{\mathfrak{S}_n\}_{n=1}^{\infty}$ is a parameterised system where $\mathfrak{S}_n$ is the instance with n processes, we represent the *parameterised symmetry groups* $\mathcal{G} = \{G_n\}_{n=1}^{\infty}$ (where G_n is the process symmetry group for $\mathfrak{S}_n$) by a finite list of regular symmetry patterns that generate $\mathcal{G}$. We postulate that commonly occuring parameterised process symmetry groups (e.g. full symmetry groups and rotations groups) can be captured in this framework, e.g., parameterised symmetry groups for the aforementioned resource-allocator protocol can be generated by the symmetry patterns $\{(2,3)(4)\cdots(m+1)\}_{m\geq 3}$ and $\{(2,3,\ldots,m+1)\}_{m\geq 3}$, which can be easily expressed using transducers. Thus, using our symmetry verification algorithm, commonly occuring process symmetries for a given parameterised system could be automatically identified.

The aforementioned approach of checking a given parameterised system against a "library" of common regular symmetry patterns has two problems.

Firstly, some common symmetry patterns are not regular, e.g., reflections. To address this, we equip our transducers with an unbounded pushdown stack. Since pushdown transducers in general cannot be synchronised [5] (a crucial property to obtain our symmetry verification algorithm), we propose a restriction of pushdown transducers for which we can recover automatic symmetry verification. Secondly, there are many useful but subtle symmetry patterns in practice. To address this, we propose the use of our symmetry synthesis algorithm. Since a naive enumeration of all transducers with $k = 1, \ldots, n$ states does not scale, we devise a CEGAR loop for our algorithm in which a SAT-solver provides a candidate symmetry pattern (perhaps satisfying some extra constraints) and an automata-based algorithm either verifies the correctness of the guess, or returns a counterexample that can be further incorporated into the guess of the SAT-solver.

We have implemented our symmetry verification/synthesis algorithms and demonstrated its usefulness in identifying regular symmetry patterns for examples like dining philosopher protocols, self-stabilising protocols, resource-allocator protocol, and Gries's coffee can problem. In the case of the coffee can problem, we managed to obtain a reduction from the infinite system to a finite-state system.

Related Work: Our work is inspired by regular model checking (e.g. [1,3,4,31]), which focuses on symbolically computing the sets of reachable configurations of parameterised systems as regular languages. Such methods are generic, but are not guaranteed to terminate in general. As in regular model checking, our framework uses transducers to represent parameterised systems. However, instead of computing their sets of reachable configurations, our work finds symmetry patterns of the parameterised systems, which can be exploited by an explicit-state finite-state model checker to verify the desired property over finite instances of the system (see [32] for more details). Although our verification algorithm is guaranteed to terminate in general (in fact, in polynomial-time assuming the parameterised system is given as a DFA), our synthesis algorithm only terminates when we fix the number of states for the transducers. Finding process symmetry patterns is often easier since there are available tools for finding symmetries for finite (albeit small) instances of the systems (e.g. [15,16,33]).

Another related line of works is "cutoff techniques" (e.g. see [17,18] and the survey [31]), which allows one to reduce verification of parameterised systems into verification of finitely many instances (in some cases, ≤ 10 processes). These works usually assume verification of LTL\X properties. Although such techniques are extremely powerful, the systems that can be handled using the techniques are often quite specific (e.g. see [31]).

Organisation: Section 2 contains preliminaries. In Sect. 3, we present our framework of regular symmetry patterns. In Sect. 4 (resp. Section 5), we present our symmetry verification algorithm (resp. synthesis) algorithms. Section 6 discusses our implementation and experiment results. Section 7 concludes with future work. Due to space constraints, some details are relegated into the full version [28].

2   Preliminaries

General Notations. For two given natural numbers $i \leq j$, we define $[i,j] = \{i, i+1, \ldots, j\}$. Define $[k] = [1, k]$. Given a set S, we use S^* to denote the set of all finite sequences of elements from S. The set S^* always includes the empty sequence which we denote by ϵ. Given two sets of words S_1, S_2, we use $S_1 \cdot S_2$ to denote the set $\{v \cdot w \mid v \in S_1, w \in S_2\}$ of words formed by concatenating words from S_1 with words from S_2. Given two relations $R_1, R_2 \subseteq S \times S$, we define their composition as $R_1 \circ R_2 = \{(s_1, s_3) \mid \exists s_2. (s_1, s_2) \in R_1 \wedge (s_2, s_3) \in R_2\}$. Given a subset $X \subseteq S$, we define the image $R(X)$ (resp. preimage $R^{-1}(X)$) of X under R as the set $\{s \in S \mid \exists s'. (s', s) \in R\}$ (resp. $\{s' \in S \mid \exists s. (s', s) \in R\}$). Given a finite set $S = \{s_1, \ldots, s_n\}$, the *Parikh vector* $\mathbb{P}(v)$ of a word $v \in S^*$ is the vector $(|v|_{s_1}, \ldots, |v|_{s_n})$ of the number of occurrences of the elements $s_1, \ldots, s_n$, respectively, in v.

Transition Systems. Let ACT be a finite set of *action symbols*. A *transition system* over ACT is a tuple $\mathfrak{S} = \langle S; \{\rightarrow\}_{a \in \mathsf{ACT}} \rangle$, where S is a set of *configurations*, and $\rightarrow_a \subseteq S \times S$ is a binary relation over S. We use $\rightarrow$ to denote the relation $\left(\bigcup_{a \in \mathsf{ACT}} \rightarrow_a \right)$. In the sequel, we will often only consider the case when $|\mathsf{ACT}| = 1$ for simplicity. The notation $\rightarrow^+$ (resp. $\rightarrow^*$) is used to denote the transitive (resp. transitive-reflexive) closure of $\rightarrow$. We say that a sequence $s_1 \rightarrow \cdots \rightarrow s_n$ is a *path* (or *run*) in $\mathfrak{S}$ (or in $\rightarrow$). Given two paths $\pi_1 : s_1 \rightarrow^* s_2$ and $\pi_2 : s_2 \rightarrow^* s_3$ in $\rightarrow$, we may concatenate them to obtain $\pi_1 \odot \pi_2$ (by gluing together s_2). In the sequel, for each $S' \subseteq S$ we use the notation $post^*_{\rightarrow}(S')$ to denote the set of configurations $s \in S$ reachable in $\mathfrak{S}$ from some $s \in S$.

Words, Automata, and Transducers. We assume basic familiarity with word automata. Fix a finite alphabet Σ. For each finite word $w = w_1 \ldots w_n \in \Sigma^*$, we write $w[i,j]$, where $1 \leq i \leq j \leq n$, to denote the segment $w_i \ldots w_j$. Given a (nondeterministic finite) automaton $\mathcal{A} = (\Sigma, Q, \delta, q_0, F)$, a run of $\mathcal{A}$ on w is a function $\rho : \{0, \ldots, n\} \rightarrow Q$ with $\rho(0) = q_0$ that obeys the transition relation δ. We may also denote the run ρ by the word $\rho(0) \cdots \rho(n)$ over the alphabet Q. The run ρ is said to be *accepting* if $\rho(n) \in F$, in which case we say that the word w is *accepted* by $\mathcal{A}$. The language $L(\mathcal{A})$ of $\mathcal{A}$ is the set of words in Σ^* accepted by $\mathcal{A}$. In the sequel, we will use the standard abbreviations DFA/NFA (Deterministic/Nondeterministic Finite Automaton).

Transducers are automata that accept binary relations over words [8,9] (a.k.a. "letter-to-letter" automata, or synchronised transducers). Given two words $w = w_1 \ldots w_n$ and $w' = w'_1 \ldots w'_m$ over the alphabet Σ, let $k = \max\{n, m\}$ and $\Sigma_\# := \Sigma \cup \{\#\}$, where $\#$ is a special padding symbol not in Σ. We define a word $w \otimes w'$ of length k over alphabet $\Sigma_\# \times \Sigma_\#$ as follows:

$$w \otimes w' = (a_1, b_1) \ldots (a_k, b_k), \text{ where } a_i = \begin{cases} w_i & i \leq n \\ \# & i > n, \end{cases} \text{ and } b_i = \begin{cases} w'_i & i \leq m \\ \# & i > m. \end{cases}$$

In other words, the shorter word is padded with #'s, and the ith letter of $w \otimes w'$ is then the pair of the ith letters of padded w and w'. A *transducer* (a.k.a. letter-to-letter automaton) is simply a finite-state automaton over $\Sigma_\# \times \Sigma_\#$, and a binary relation $R \subseteq \Sigma^* \times \Sigma^*$ is *regular* if the set $\{w \otimes w' : (w, w') \in R\}$ is accepted by a letter-to-letter automaton. The relation R is said to be *length-preserving* if R only relates words of the same length [4], i.e., that any automaton recognising R consumes no padded letters of the form $(a, \#)$ or $(\#, a)$. In the sequel, for notation simplicity, we will confuse a transducer and the binary relation that it recognises (i.e. R is used to mean both).

Finally, notice that the notion of regular relations can be easily extended to r-ary relations R for each positive integer r (e.g. see [8,9]). To this end, the input alphabet of the transducer will be $\Sigma_\#^r$. Similarly, for R to be regular, the set $\{w_1 \otimes \cdots \otimes w_r : (w_1, \ldots, w_r) \in R\}$ of words over the alphabet Σ^r must be regular.

Permutation Groups. We assume familiarity with basic group theory (e.g. see [11]). A *permutation* on $[n]$ is any bijection $\pi : [n] \to [n]$. The set of all permutations on $[n]$ forms the *(nth) full symmetry group* $\mathcal{S}_n$ under functional composition. A *permutation group* on $[n]$ is any set of permutations on $[n]$ that is a subgroup of $\mathcal{S}_n$ (i.e. closed under composition). A *generating set* for a permutation group G on $[n]$ is a finite set X of permutations (called *generators*) such that each permutation in G can be expressed by taking compositions of elements in X. In this case, we say that G can be generated by X. A word $w = a_0 \ldots a_{k-1} \in [n]^*$ containing distinct elements of $[n]$ (i.e. $a_i \neq a_j$ if $i \neq j$) can be used to denote the permutation that maps $a_i \mapsto a_{i+1 \bmod k}$ for each $i \in [0, k)$ and fixes other elements of $[n]$. In this case, w is called a *cycle* (more precisely, k-cycle or *transposition* in the case when $k = 2$), which we will often write in the standard notation $(a_0, \ldots, a_{k-1})$ so as to avoid confusion. Any permutation can be written as a composition of disjoint cycles [11]. In addition, it is known that $\mathcal{S}_n$ can be generated by the set $\{(1, 2), (1, 2, \ldots, n)\}$. Each subgroup G of $\mathcal{S}_n$ acts on the set Σ^n (over any finite alphabet Σ) under the group action of permuting indices, i.e., for each $\pi \in G$ and $\mathbf{v} = (a_1, \ldots, a_n) \in \Sigma^n$, we define $\pi\mathbf{v} := (a_{\pi^{-1}(1)}, \ldots, a_{\pi^{-1}(n)})$. That way, each π induces the bijection $f_\pi : \Sigma^n \to \Sigma^n$ such that $f_\pi(\mathbf{v}) = \pi\mathbf{v}$.

Given a permutation group G on $[n]$ and a transition system $\mathfrak{S} = \langle S; \to \rangle$ with state space $S = \Sigma^n$, we say that $\mathfrak{S}$ is *G-invariant* if the bijection $f_\pi : \Sigma^n \to \Sigma^n$ induced by each $\pi \in G_n$ is an automorphism on $\mathfrak{S}$, i.e., $\forall v, w \in S : v \to w$ implies $f_\pi(v) \to f_\pi(w)$.

3   The Formal Framework

This section describes our symbolic framework regular symmetry patterns.

3.1   Representing Parameterised Systems

As is standard in regular model checking [1,4,31], we use length-preserving transducers to represent parameterised systems. As we shall see below, we will use non-length-preserving transducers to represent symmetry patterns.

Definition 1 (Automatic transition systems[1]). *A transition system* $\mathfrak{S} = \langle S; \{\rightarrow\}_{a \in ACT} \rangle$ *is said to be (length-preserving) automatic if S is a regular set over a finite alphabet Σ and each relation $\rightarrow_a$ is given by a transducer over Σ.*

More precisely, the parameterised system defined by $\mathfrak{S}$ is the family $\{\mathfrak{S}_n\}_{n \geq 0}$ with $\mathfrak{S}_n = \langle S_n; \rightarrow_{a,n} \rangle$, where $S_n := S \cap \Sigma^n$ is the set of all words in S of length n and $\rightarrow_{a,n}$ is the transition relation $\rightarrow_a$ restricted to S_n. In the sequel, for simplicity we will mostly consider examples when $|ACT| = 1$. When the meaning is understood, we shall confuse the notation $\rightarrow_a$ for the transition relation of $\mathfrak{S}$ and the transducer that recognises it. To illustrate our framework and methods, we shall give three examples of automatic transition systems (see [3,31] for numerous other examples).

Example 1. We describe a prioritised resource-allocator protocol [14], [Sect. 4.4], which is a simple mutual exclusion protocol in network with a star topology. The protocol has one allocator and m clients. Initially, each process is in an *idle* state. However, clients might from time to time *request* for an access to a resource (*critical section*), which can only be used by one process at a time. For simplicity, we will assume that there is only one resource shared by all the clients. The allocator manages the use of the resource. When a request is lodged by a client, the allocator can allow the client to use the resource. When the client has finished using the resource, it will send a message to the allocator, which can then allow other clients to use the resource.

To model the protocol as a transducer, we let $\Sigma = \{i, r, c\}$, where i stands for "idle", r for "request", and c for "critical". Allocator can be in either the state i or the state c, while a client can be in one of the three states in Σ. A valid configuration is a word aw, where $a \in \{i, c\}$ represents the state of the allocator and $w \in \Sigma^*$ represents the states of the $|w|$ clients (i.e. each position in w represents a state of a client). Letting $I = \{(a, a) : a \in \Sigma\}$ (representing idle local transitions), the transducer can be described by a union of the following regular expressions:

- $I^+(i, r)I^*$ — a client requesting for a resource.
- $(i, c)I^*(r, c)I^*$ — a client request granted by the allocator.
- $(c, i)I^*(c, i)I^*$ — the client has finished using the resource. $\square$

Example 2. We describe Israeli-Jalfon self-stabilising protocol [23]. The original protocol is probabilistic, but since we are only interested in reachability, we may use nondeterminism to model randomness. The protocol has a ring topology, and each process either holds a token (denoted by $\top$) or does not hold a token (denoted by $\bot$). Dynamics is given by the following rules:

- A process P holding a token can pass the token to either the left or the right neighbouring process P', provided that P' does not hold a token.

---

[1] Length-preserving automatic transition systems are instances of automatic structures [8,9].

– If two neighbouring processes P_1 and P_2 hold tokens, the tokens can be merged and kept at process P_1.

We now provide a transducer that formalises this parameterised system. Our relation is on words over the alphabet $\Sigma = \{\bot, \top\}$, and thus a transducer is an automaton that runs over $\Sigma \times \Sigma$. In the following, we use $I := \{(\top, \top), (\bot, \bot)\}$. The automaton is given by a union of the following regular expressions:

– $I^*(\top, \bot)(\bot, \top)I^*$ – $I^*(\top, \top)(\top, \bot)I^*$ – $(\top, \bot)I^*(\bot, \top)$

– $I^*(\bot, \top)(\top, \bot)I^*$ – $(\bot, \top)I^*(\top, \bot)$ – $(\top, \bot)I^*(\top, \top)$ □

Example 3. Our next example is the classical David Gries's coffee can problem, which uses two (nonnegative) integer variables x and y to store the number of black and white coffee beans, respectively. At any given step, if $x + y \geq 2$ (i.e. there are at least two coffee beans), then two coffee beans are nondeterministically chosen. First, if both are of the same colour, then they are both discarded and a new black bean is put in the can. Second, if they are of a different colour, the white bean is kept and the black one is discarded. We are usually interested in the colour of the last bean in the can. We formally model Gries's coffee can problem as a transition system with domain $\mathbb{N} \times \mathbb{N}$ and transitions:

(a) if $x \geq 2$, then $x := x - 1$ and $y := y$.
(b) if $y \geq 2$, then $x := x + 1$ and $y := y - 2$.
(c) if $x \geq 1$ and $y \geq 1$, then $x := x - 1$ and $y := y$.

To distinguish the colour of the last bean, we shall add self-loops to all configurations in $\mathbb{N} \times \mathbb{N}$, except for the configuration $(1, 0)$. We can model the system as a length-preserving transducer as follows. The alphabet is $\Sigma := \Omega_x \cup \Omega_y$, where $\Omega_x := \{1_x, \bot_x\}$ and $\Omega_y := \{1_y, \bot_y\}$. A configuration is a word in the regular language $1_x^* \bot_x^* 1_y^* \bot_y^*$. For example, the configuration with $x = 5$ and $y = 3$, where the maximum size of the integer buffers x and y is 10, is represented as the word $(1_x)^5(\bot_x)^5(1_y)^3(\bot_y)^7$. The transducer for the coffee can problem can be easily constructed.   □

3.2   Representing Symmetry Patterns

Definition 2. *Let $\mathfrak{S} = \langle S; \rightarrow \rangle$ be a transition system with $S \subseteq \Sigma^*$. A symmetry pattern for $\mathfrak{S} = \langle S; \rightarrow \rangle$ is a simulation preorder $R \subseteq S \times S$ for $\mathfrak{S}$, i.e., satisfying:*

(S1) *R respects each $\rightarrow_a$, i.e., for all $v_1, v_2, w_1 \in S$, if $v_1 \rightarrow_a w_1$, and $(v_1, v_2) \in R$, then there exists $w_2 \in S$ such that $(w_1, w_2) \in R$ and $v_2 \rightarrow_a w_2$;*
(S2) *R is length-decreasing, i.e., for all $v_1, v_2 \in S$, if $(v_1, v_2) \in R$, then $|v_1| \geq |v_2|$.*

The symmetry pattern is said to be complete if additionally the relation is length-preserving and a bijective function.

Complete symmetry patterns will also be denoted by functional notation f. In the case of complete symmetry pattern f, it can be observed that Condition (S1) also entails that $f(v) \to_a f(w)$ implies $v \to_a w$. This condition does not hold in general for simulation preorders. We shall also remark that, owing to the well-known property of simulation preorders, symmetry patterns preserve non-safety. To make this notion more precise, we define the image of a transition system $\mathfrak{S} = \langle S; \to \rangle$ (with $S \subseteq \Sigma^*$) under the symmetry pattern R as the transition system $\mathfrak{S}_1 = \langle S_1; \to_1 \rangle$ such that $S_1 = R(S)$ and that $\to_1$ is the restriction of $\to$ to S_1.

Proposition 1. *Given two sets* $I, F \subseteq \Sigma^*$, *if* $post^*_{\to_1}(R(I)) \cap R(F) = \emptyset$, *then* $post^*_{\to}(I) \cap F = \emptyset$.

In other words, if $\mathfrak{S}_1$ is safe, then so is $\mathfrak{S}$. In the case when $\mathfrak{S}_1$ is finite-state, this check can be performed using a standard finite-state model checker. We shall define now a class of symmetry patterns under which the image $\mathfrak{S}_1$ of the input transition system can be automatically computed.

Definition 3 (Regular Symmetry Pattern). *A symmetry pattern* $R \subseteq S \times S$ *for an automatic transition system* $\mathfrak{S} = \langle S; \to \rangle$ *is said to be regular if the relation* R *is regular.*

Proposition 2. *Given an automatic transition system* $\mathfrak{S} = \langle S; \to \rangle$ *(with* $S \subseteq \Sigma^*$*) and a regular symmetry pattern* $R \subseteq S \times S$, *the image of* $\mathfrak{S}$ *under* R *is an automatic transition system and can be constructed in polynomial-time.*

In particular, whether the image of $\mathfrak{S}$ under R is a finite system can be automatically checked since checking whether the language of an NFA is finite can be done in polynomial-time. The proof of this proposition (in the full version) is a simple automata construction that relies on the fact that regular relations are closed under projections. We shall next illustrate the concept of regular symmetry patterns in action, especially for Israeli-Jalfon self-stabilising protocol and Gries's coffee can problem.

We start with Gries's coffee can problem (cf. Example 3). Consider the function $f : (\mathbb{N} \times \mathbb{N}) \to (\mathbb{N} \times \mathbb{N})$ where $f(x, y)$ is defined to be (i) $(0, 1)$ if y is odd, (ii) $(2, 0)$ if y is even and $(x, y) \neq (1, 0)$, and (iii) $(1, 0)$ if $(x, y) = (1, 0)$. This is a symmetry pattern since the last bean for the coffee can problem is white iff y is odd. Also, that a configuration (x, y) with $y \equiv 0 \pmod 2$ and $x > 1$ is mapped to $(2, 0)$ is because $(2, 0)$ has a self-loop, while $(1, 0)$ is a dead end. It is easy to show that f is a regular symmetry pattern. To this end, we construct a transducer for each of the cases (i)–(iii). For example, the transducer handling the case (x, y) when $y \equiv 1 \pmod 2$ works as follows: simultaneously read the pair (v, w) of words and ensure that $w = \bot_x \bot_x 1_y$ and $v \in 1_x^* \bot_x^* 1_y (1_y 1_y)^* \bot_y^*$. As an NFA, the final transducer has ~ 10 states.

Process Symmetry Patterns. We now apply the idea of regular symmetry patterns to capture process symmetries in parameterised systems. We shall show how this applies to Israeli-Jalfon self-stabilising protocol. A *parameterised permutation* is a family $\bar{\pi} = \{\pi_n\}_{n \geq 1}$ of permutations π_n on $[n]$. We say that $\bar{\pi}$ is *regular* if, for each alphabet Σ, the bijection $f_{\bar{\pi}} : \Sigma^* \to \Sigma^*$ defined by $f_{\bar{\pi}}(\mathbf{v}) := \pi_n \mathbf{v}$, where $\mathbf{v} \in \Sigma^n$, is a regular relation. We say that $\bar{\pi}$ is *effectively regular* if $\bar{\pi}$ is regular and if there is an algorithm which, on input Σ, constructs a transducer for the bijection $f_{\bar{\pi}}$. As we shall only deal with effectively regular permutations, when understood we will omit mention of the word "effectively". As we shall see below, examples of effectively regular parameterised permutations include transpositions (e.g. $\{(1,2)(3)\cdots(n)\}_{n\geq 2}$) and rotations $\{(1,2,\ldots,n)\}_{n\geq 1}$.

We now extend the notion of parameterised permutations to *parameterised symmetry groups* $\mathcal{G} := \{G_n\}_{n\geq 1}$ for parameterised systems, i.e., each G_n is a permutation group on $[n]$. A finite set $F = \{\bar{\pi}^1, \ldots, \bar{\pi}^r\}$ of parameterised permutations (with $\bar{\pi}^j = \{\pi_n^j\}_{n\geq 1}$) *generates* the parameterised symmetry groups $\mathcal{G}$ if each group $G_n \in \mathcal{G}$ can be generated by the set $\{\pi_n^j : j \in [r]\}$, i.e., the nth instances of parameterised permutations in F. We say that $\mathcal{G}$ is *regular* if each $\bar{\pi}^j$ in F is regular.

We will single out three commonly occuring process symmetry groups for concurrent systems with n processes: full symmetry group $\mathcal{S}_n$ (i.e. generated by $(1,2)$ and $(1,2,\ldots,n)$), rotation group $\mathcal{R}_n$ (i.e. generated by $(1,2,\ldots,n)$), and the dihedral group $\mathcal{D}_n$ (i.e. generated by $(1,2,\ldots,n)$ and the "reflection" permutation $(1,n)(2,n-1)\cdots(\lfloor n/2\rfloor, \lceil n/2\rceil)$). The parameterised versions of them are: (1) $\mathcal{S} := \{\mathcal{S}_n\}_{n\geq 1}$, (2) $\mathcal{R} := \{\mathcal{R}_n\}_{n\geq 1}$, and (3) $\mathcal{D} := \{\mathcal{D}_n\}_{n\geq 1}$.

Theorem 1. *Parameterised full symmetry groups $\mathcal{S}$ and parameterised rotation symmetry groups $\mathcal{R}$ are effectively regular.*

As we will see in Proposition 3 below, parameterised dihedral groups are not regular. We will say how to deal with this in the next section. As we will see in Theorem 4, Theorem 1 can be used to construct a fully-automatic method for checking whether *each* instance $\mathfrak{S}_n$ of a parameterised system $\mathfrak{S} = \{\mathfrak{S}_n\}_{n\geq 0}$ represented by a given transducer $\mathcal{A}$ has a full/rotation process symmetry group.

Proof (Sketch of Theorem 1). To show this, it suffices to show that $\mathcal{F} = \{(1,2)(3)\cdots(n)\}_{n\geq 2}$ and $\mathcal{F}' = \{(1,2,\ldots,n)\}_{n\geq 2}$ are effectively regular. [The degenerate case when $n=1$ can be handled easily if necessary.] For, if this is the case, then the parameterised full symmetry $\mathcal{S}$ and the parameterised rotation symmetry groups can be generated by (respectively) $\{\mathcal{F}, \mathcal{F}'\}$ and $\mathcal{F}'$. Given an input Σ, the transducers for both $\mathcal{F}$ and $\mathcal{F}'$ are easy. For example, the transducer for $\mathcal{F}$ simply swaps the first two letters in the input, i.e., accepts pairs of words of the form (abw, baw) where $a, b \in \Sigma$ and $w \in \Sigma^*$. These transducers can be constructed in polynomial time (details in the full version). $\square$

The above proof shows that $\{(1,2)(3)\cdots(n)\}_{n\geq 0}$ and $\{(1,2,\ldots,n)\}_{n\geq 0}$ are regular parameterised permutations. Using the same proof techniques, we can also show that the following simple variants of these parameterised permutations are also regular for each $i \in \mathbb{Z}_{>0}$: (a) $\{(i, i+1)(i+2)\cdots(n)\}_{n\geq 1}$, and (b) $\{(i, i+1, \ldots, n)\}_{n\geq 1}$. As we saw from Introduction, the prioritised resource-allocator protocol has a star topology and so both $\{(2,3)(4)\cdots\}_{n\geq 1}$ and $\{(2,3,\ldots,n)\}_{n\geq 1}$ generate complete symmetry patterns for the protocol (i.e. invariant under permuting the clients). Therefore, our library $\mathcal{L}$ of regular symmetry patterns could store all of these regular parameterised permutations (up to some fixed i).

Parameterised dihedral groups $\mathcal{D}$ are generated by rotations $\bar{\pi} = \{(1, 2, \ldots, n)\}_{n \geq 2}$ and reflections $\bar{\sigma} = \{(1, n)(2, n - 1) \cdots (\lfloor n/2 \rfloor, \lceil n/2 \rceil)\}_{n \geq 2}$. Reflections $\bar{\sigma}$ are, however, not regular for the same reason that the language of palindromes (i.e. words that are the same read backward as forward). In fact, it is not possible to find a different list of generating parameterised permutations that are regular (proof in the full version):

Proposition 3. *Parameterised dihedral groups $\mathcal{D}$ are not regular.*

4 Symmetry Verification

In this section, we will present our symmetry verification algorithm for regular symmetry patterns. We then show how to extend the algorithm to a more general framework of symmetry patterns that subsumes parameterised dihedral groups.

4.1 The Algorithm

Theorem 2. *Given an automatic transition system $\mathfrak{S} = \langle S; \rightarrow \rangle$ and a regular relation $R \subseteq S \times S$, we can automatically check if R is a symmetry pattern of $\mathfrak{S}$.*

Proof. Let D be the set of words over the alphabet Σ^3 of the form $v_1 \otimes v_2 \otimes w_1$, for some words $v_1, v_2, w_1 \in \Sigma^*$ satisfying: (1) $v_1 \rightarrow w_1$, (2) $(v_1, v_2) \in R$, and (3) there does *not* exist $w_2 \in \Sigma^*$ such that $v_2 \rightarrow w_2$ and $(w_1, w_2) \in R$. Observe that R is a symmetry pattern for $\mathfrak{S}$ iff D is empty. An automaton $\mathcal{A} = (\Sigma^3, Q, \Delta, q_0, F)$ for D can be constructed via a classical automata construction.

As before, for simplicity of presentation, we will assume that $S = \Sigma^*$; for, otherwise, we can perform a simple product automata construction with the automaton for S. Let $\mathcal{A}_1 = (\Sigma^2, Q_1, \Delta_1, q_0^1, F_1)$ be an automaton for $\rightarrow$, and $\mathcal{A}_2 = (\Sigma_{\#}^2, Q_2, \Delta_2, q_0^2, F_2)$ an automaton for R.

We first construct an NFA $\mathcal{A}_3 = (\Sigma_{\#}^2, Q_3, \Delta_3, q_0^3, F_3)$ for the set $Y \subseteq S \times S$ consisting of pairs (v_2, w_1) such that the condition (3) above is *false*. This can be done by a simple product/projection automata construction that takes into account the fact that R might not be length-preserving: That is, define $Q_3 := Q_1 \times Q_2$, $q_0^3 := (q_0^1, q_0^2)$, and $F_3 := F_1 \times F_2$. The transition relation Δ consists of transitions $((q_1, q_2), (a, b), (q_1', q_2'))$ such that, for some $c \in \Sigma_{\#}$, it is the case that $(q_2, (b, c), q_2') \in \Delta_2$ and one of the following is true: (i) $(q_1, (a, c), q_1') \in \Delta_1$, (ii) $q_1 = q_1'$, $b \neq \#$, and $a = c = \#$. Observe that the construction for $\mathcal{A}_3$ runs in polynomial-time.

In order to construct $\mathcal{A}$, we will have to perform a complementation operation on $\mathcal{A}_3$ (to compute the complement of Y) and apply a similar product automata construction. The former takes exponential time (since $\mathcal{A}_3$ is nondeterministic), while the latter costs an additional polynomial-time overhead. $\qquad\square$

The above algorithm runs in exponential-time even if R and $\mathfrak{S}$ are presented as DFA, since an automata projection operation in general yields an NFA. The situation improves dramatically when R is *functional* (i.e. for all $x \in S$, there exists a unique $y \in S$ such that $R(x,y)$).

Theorem 3. *There exists a polynomial-time algorithm which, given an automatic transition system $\mathfrak{S} = \langle S; \rightarrow \rangle$ presented as a DFA and a functional regular relation $R \subseteq S \times S$ presented as an NFA, decides whether R is a symmetry pattern for $\mathfrak{S}$.*

Proof. Let D be the set of words over the alphabet Σ^4 of the form $v_1 \otimes v_2 \otimes w_1 \otimes w_2$, for some words $v_1, v_2, w_1, w_2 \in \Sigma^*$ satisfying: (1) $v_1 \rightarrow w_1$, (2) $(v_1, v_2) \in R$, (2') $(w_1, w_2) \in R$, and (3) $v_2 \not\rightarrow w_2$ Observe that R is a symmetry pattern for $\mathfrak{S}$ iff D is empty. The reasoning is similar to the proof of Theorem 2, but the difference now is that given any $w_1 \in \Sigma^*$, there is a *unique* w_2 such that $(w_1, w_2) \in R$ since R is functional. For this reason, we need only to make sure that $v_2 \not\rightarrow w_2$. An automaton $\mathcal{A}$ for D can be constructed by first complementing the automaton for $\rightarrow$ and then a standard product automata construction as before. The latter takes polynomial-time if $\rightarrow$ is presented as a DFA, while the latter costs an additional polynomial-time computation overhead (even if R is presented as an NFA).   □

Proposition 4. *The following two problems are solvable in polynomial-space: given a regular relation $R \subseteq S \times S$, check whether (1) R is functional, and (2) R is a bijective function. Furthermore, the problems are polynomial-time reducible to language inclusion for NFA.*

Observe that there are fast heuristics for checking language inclusion for NFA using antichain and simulation techniques (e.g. see [2,10]). The proof of the above proposition uses standard automata construction, which is relegated to the full version.

4.2   Process Symmetries for Concurrent Systems

We say that an automatic transition system $\mathfrak{S} = \langle S; \rightarrow \rangle$ (with $S \subseteq \Sigma^*$) is $\mathcal{G}$-*invariant* if each instance $\mathfrak{S}_n = \langle S \cap \Gamma^n; \rightarrow \rangle$ of $\mathfrak{S}$ is G_n-invariant. If $\mathcal{G}$ is generated by regular parameterised permutations $\bar{\pi}^1, \ldots, \bar{\pi}^r$, then $\mathcal{G}$-invariance is equivalent to the condition that, for each $j \in [r]$, the bijection $f_{\bar{\pi}^j} : \Sigma^* \rightarrow \Sigma^*$ is a regular symmetry pattern for $\mathfrak{S}$. The following theorem is an immediate corollary of Theorem 3.

Theorem 4. *Given an automatic transition system $\mathfrak{S} = \langle S; \rightarrow \rangle$ (with $S \subseteq \Sigma^*$) and a regular parameterised symmetry group $\mathcal{G}$ presented by regular parameterised permutations $\bar{\pi}^1, \ldots, \bar{\pi}^k$, we can check that $\mathfrak{S}$ is $\mathcal{G}$-invariant in polynomial-time assuming that $\mathfrak{S}$ is presented as DFA.*

In fact, to check whether $\mathfrak{S}$ is $\mathcal{G}$-invariant, it suffices to sequentially go through each $\bar{\pi}^j$ and ensure that it is a symmetry pattern for $\mathfrak{S}$, which by Theorem 3 can be done in polynomial-time.

4.3   Beyond Regular Symmetry Patterns

Proposition 3 tells us that regular symmetry patterns do not suffice to capture parameterised reflection permutation. This leads us to our inability to check whether a parameterised system is invariant under parameterised dihedral symmetry groups, e.g., Israeli-Jalfon's self-stabilising protocol and other randomised protocols including Lehmann-Rabin's protocol (e.g. [26]). To deal with this problem, we extend the notion of regular length-preserving symmetry patterns to a subclass of "context-free" symmetry patterns that preserves some nice algorithmic properties. *Proviso: All relations considered in this subsection are length-preserving.*

Recall that a *pushdown automaton (PDA)* is a tuple $\mathcal{P} = (\Sigma, \Gamma, Q, \Delta, q_0, F)$, where Σ is the input alphabet, Γ is the stack alphabet (containing a special bottom-stack symbol, denoted by $\perp$, that cannot be popped), Q is the finite set of control states, $q_0 \in Q$ is an initial state, $F \subseteq Q$ is a set of final states, and $\Delta \subseteq (Q \times \Gamma) \times \Sigma \times (Q \times \Gamma^{\leq 2})$ is a set of transitions, where $\Gamma^{\leq 2}$ denotes the set of all words of length at most 2. A configuration of $\mathcal{P}$ is a pair $(q, w) \in Q \times \Gamma^*$ with *stack-height* $|w|$. For each $a \in \Sigma$, we define the binary relation $\rightarrow_a$ on configurations of $\mathcal{P}$ as follows: $(q_1, w_1) \rightarrow_a (q_2, w_2)$ if there exists a transition $((q_1, o), a, (q_2, v)) \in \Delta$ such that $w_1 = wo$ and $w_2 = wv$ for some $w \in \Gamma^*$. A *computation path* π of $\mathcal{P}$ on input $a_1 \ldots a_n$ is any sequence

$$(q_0, \perp) \rightarrow_{a_1} (q_1, w_1) \rightarrow_{a_2} \cdots \rightarrow_{a_n} (q_n, w_n)$$

of configurations from the initial state q_0. In the following, the *stack-height sequence* of π is the sequence $|\perp|, |w_1|, \ldots, |w_n|$ of stack-heights. We say that a computation path π is *accepting* if $q_n \in F$.

We now extend Theorem 4 to a class of transducers that allows us to capture the reflection symmetry. This class consists of "height-unambiguous" pushdown transducers, which is a subclass of pushdown transducers that is amenable to synchronisation. We say that a pushdown automaton is *height-unambiguous (h.u.)* if it satisfies the restriction that the stack-height sequence in an *accepting* computation path on an input word w is uniquely determined by the length $|w|$ of w. That is, given an accepting computation path π on w and an accepting computation path π' of w' with $|w| = |w'|$, the stack-height sequences of π and π' coincide. Observe that the definition allows the stack-height sequence of a non-accepting path to differ. A language $L \subseteq \Sigma^*$ is said to be *height-unambiguous context-free (huCF)* if it is recognised by a height-unambiguous PDA. A simple example of a huCF language is the language of palindromes (i.e. the input word is the same backward as forward). A simple non-example of a huCF language is the language of well-formed nested parentheses. This can be proved by a standard pumping argument.

We extend the definitions of regularity of length-preserving relations, symmetry patterns, etc. from Sects. 2 and 3 to height-unambiguous pushdown automata in the obvious way, e.g., a length-preserving relation $R \subseteq S \times S$ is *huCF* if $\{v \otimes w : (v, w) \in R\}$ is a huCF language. We saw in Proposition 3 that parameterised dihedral symmetry groups $\mathcal{D}$ are not regular. We shall show now that they are huCF.

Theorem 5. *Parameterised dihedral symmetry groups $\mathcal{D}$ are effectively height-unambiguous context-free.*

Proof. To show this, it suffices to show that the parameterised reflection permutation $\bar{\sigma} = \{\sigma_n\}_{n \geq 2}$, where $\sigma_n := (1, n)(2, n - 1) \cdots (\lfloor n/2 \rfloor, \lceil n/2 \rceil)$, is huCF. To this end, given an input alphabet Σ, we construct a PDA $\mathcal{P} = (\Sigma^2, \Gamma, Q, \Delta, q_0, F)$ that recognises $f_{\bar{\sigma}} : \Sigma^* \to \Sigma^*$ such that $f_{\bar{\sigma}}(\mathbf{v}) = \sigma_n \mathbf{v}$ whenever $\mathbf{v} \in \Sigma^n$. The PDA $\mathcal{P}$ works just like the PDA recognising the language of palindromes. We shall first give the intuition. Given a word w of the form $v_1 \otimes v_2 \in (\Sigma^2)^*$, we write w^{-1} to denote the word $v_2 \otimes v_1$. On an input word $w_1 w_2 w_3 \in (\Sigma^2)^*$, where $|w_1| = |w_3|$ and $|w_2| \in \{0, 1\}$, the PDA will save w_1 in the stack and compares it with w_3 ensuring that w_3 is the reverse of w_1^{-1}. It will also make sure that $w_2 = (a, a)$ for some $a \in \Sigma$ in the case when $|w_2| = 1$. The formal definition of $\mathcal{P}$ is given in the full version. $\square$

Theorem 6. *There exists a polynomial-time algorithm which, given an automatic transition system $\mathfrak{S} = \langle S; \to \rangle$ presented as a DFA and a functional h.u. context-free relation $R \subseteq S \times S$ presented as an NFA, decides whether R is a symmetry pattern for $\mathfrak{S}$.*

To prove this theorem, let us revisit the automata construction from the proof of Theorem 3. The problematic part of the construction is that we need to show that, given an huCF relation R, the 4-ary relation

$$\mathcal{R} := (R \times R) \cap \{(w_1, w_2, w_3, w_4) \in (\Sigma^*)^4 : |w_1| = |w_2| = |w_3| = |w_4|\} \quad (*)$$

is also huCF. The rest of the construction requires only taking product with regular relations (i.e. $\to$ or its complement), which works for unrestricted pushdown automata since context-free languages are closed under taking product with regular languages via the usual product automata construction for regular languages.

Lemma 1. *Given an huCF relation R, we can construct in polynomial-time an h.u. PDA recognising the 4-ary relation $\mathcal{R}$.*

Proof. Given a h.u. PDA $\mathcal{P} = (\Sigma^2, \Gamma, Q, \Delta, q_0, F)$ recognising R, we will construct a PDA $\mathcal{P}' = (\Sigma^4, \Gamma', Q', \Delta', q_0', F')$ recognising $\mathcal{R}$. Intuitively, given an input $(v, w) \in \mathcal{R}$, the PDA $\mathcal{P}'$ is required to run two copies of $\mathcal{P}$ at the same time, one on the input v (to check that $v \in R$) and the other on input w (to check that $w \in R$). Since $\mathcal{P}$ is height-unambiguous and $|v| = |w|$, we can assume that the stack-height sequences of accepting runs of $\mathcal{P}$ on v and w coincide. That is, in an accepting run π_1 of $\mathcal{P}$ on v and an accepting run of π_2 of $\mathcal{P}$ on w, when a symbol is pushed onto (resp. popped from) the stack at a certain position in π_1, then a symbol is also pushed onto (resp. popped from) the stack in the same position in π_2. The converse is also true. These two stacks can, therefore, be simultaneously simulated using only one stack of $\mathcal{P}'$ with $\Gamma' = \Gamma \times \Gamma$. For this reason, the rest of the details is a standard product automata construction for finite-state automata. Therefore, the automaton $\mathcal{P}'$ is of size quadratic in the size of $\mathcal{P}$. The detailed definition of $\mathcal{P}'$ is given in the full version.   □

We shall finally pinpoint a limitation of huCF symmetry patterns, and discuss how we can address the problem in practice. It can be proved by a simple reduction from Post Correspondence Problem that it is undecidable to check whether a given PDA is height-unambiguous. In practice, however, this is not a major obstacle since it is possible to *manually* (or *semi-automatically*) add a selection of huCF symmetry patterns to our library $\mathcal{L}$ of regular symmetry patterns from Sect. 3. Observe that this effort is *independent* of any parameterised system that one needs to check for symmetry. Checking whether any huCF symmetry pattern in $\mathcal{C}$ is a symmetry pattern for a given automatic transition system $\mathfrak{S}$ can then be done automatically and efficiently (cf. Theorem 6). For example, Theorems 5 and 6 imply that we can automatically check whether an automatic transition system is invariant under the parameterised dihedral groups:

Theorem 7. *Given an automatic transition system $\mathfrak{S} = \langle S; \rightarrow \rangle$ (with $S \subseteq \Sigma^*$) presented as DFA, checking whether $\mathfrak{S}$ is $\mathcal{D}$-invariant can be done in polynomial-time.*

Among others, this allows us to automatically confirm that Israeli-Jalfon self-stabilising protocol is $\mathcal{D}$-invariant.

5   Automatic Synthesis of Regular Symmetry Patterns

Some regular symmetry patterns for a given automatic system might not be obvious, e.g., Gries's coffee can example. Even in the case of process symmetries, the user might choose different representations for the same protocol. For example, the allocator process in Example 1 could be represented by the last (instead of the first) letter in the word, which would mean that $\{(1, 2, \ldots, n-1)\}_{n \geq 3}$ and $\{(1, 2)(3) \cdots (n)\}_{n \geq 3}$ are symmetry patterns for the system (instead of $\{(2, 3, \ldots, n)\}_{n \geq 2}$ and $\{(2, 3)(4) \cdots (n)\}_{n \geq 3}$). Although we can put reasonable variations of common symmetry patterns in our library $\mathcal{L}$, we would benefit from a systematic way of synthesising regular symmetry patterns for a given automatic transition system $\mathfrak{S}$. In this section, we will describe our automatic technique for achieving this. We focus on the case of symmetry patterns that are *total functions* (i.e. homomorphisms), but the approach can be generalised to other patterns.

Every transducer $\mathcal{A} = (\Sigma_{\#} \times \Sigma_{\#}, Q, \delta, q_0, F)$ over $\Sigma_{\#}^*$ represents a regular binary relation R over Σ^*. We have shown in Sect. 4 that we can automatically check whether R represents a symmetry pattern, perhaps satisfying further constraints like functionality or bijectivity as desired by the user. Furthermore, we can also automatically check that it is a symmetry pattern for a given automatic transition system $\mathfrak{S}$. Our overall approach for computing such transducers makes use of two main components, which are performed iteratively within a refinement loop:

Synthesise. A candidate transducer $\mathcal{A}$ with n states is computed with the help of a SAT-solver, enforcing a relaxed set of conditions encoded as a Boolean constraint ψ (Sect. 5.1).

Verify. As described in Sect. 4, it is checked whether the binary relation R represented by $\mathcal{A}$ is a symmetry pattern for $\mathfrak{S}$ (satisfying further constraints like completeness, as desired by the user). If this check is negative, ψ is strengthened to eliminate counterexamples, and SYNTHESISE is invoked (Sect. 5.2).

This refinement loop is enclosed by an outer loop that increments the parameter n (initially set to some small number n_0) when SYNTHESISE determines that no transducers satisfying ψ exist anymore. The next sections describe the SYNTHESISE step, and the generation of counterexamples in case VERIFY fails, in more detail.

5.1 Synthesise: Computation of a Candidate Transducer $\mathcal{A}$

Our general encoding of transducers $\mathcal{A} = (\Sigma_\# \times \Sigma_\#, Q, \delta, q_0, F)$ uses a representation as a deterministic automaton (DFA), which is suitable for our refinement loop since counterexamples (in particular, words that should not be accepted) can be eliminated using succinct additional constraints. We assume that the states of the transducer $\mathcal{A}$ to be computed are $Q = \{1, \ldots, n\}$, and that $q_0 = 1$ is the initial state. We use the following variables to encode transducers with n states:

- x_t (of type Boolean), for each tuple $t = (q, a, b, q') \in Q \times \Sigma_\# \times \Sigma_\# \times Q$;
- z_q (of type Boolean), for each $q \in Q$.

The assignment $x_t = 1$ is interpreted as the existence of the transition t in $\mathcal{A}$. Likewise, we use $z_q = 1$ to represent that q is an accepting state in the automaton; since we use DFA, it is in general necessary to have more than one accepting state.

The set of considered transducers in step SYNTHESISE is restricted by imposing a number of conditions, selected depending on the kind of symmetry to be synthesised: for general symmetry homomorphisms, conditions **(C1)**–**(C8)** are used, for *complete* symmetry patterns **(C1)**–**(C10)**, and for *process symmetries* **(C1)**–**(C11)**.

(C1) The transducer $\mathcal{A}$ is deterministic.
(C2) For every transition $q \xrightarrow{(a,b)} q'$ in $\mathcal{A}$ it is the case that $a \neq \#$.[2]
(C3) Every state of the transducer is reachable from the initial state.
(C4) From every state of the transducer an accepting state can be reached.
(C5) The initial state q_0 is accepting.
(C6) The language accepted by the transducer is infinite.
(C7) There are no two transitions $q \xrightarrow{(a,b)} q'$ and $q \xrightarrow{(a,b')} q'$ with $b \neq b'$.

---

[2] Note that all occurrences of $\#$ are in the end of words.

(C8) If an accepting state q has self-transitions $q \xrightarrow{(a,a)} q$ for every letter $a \in \Sigma_\#$, then q has no outgoing edges.

(C9) For every transition $q \xrightarrow{(a,b)} q'$ in $\mathcal{A}$ it is the case that $b \neq \#$.

(C10) There are no two transitions $q \xrightarrow{(a,b)} q'$ and $q \xrightarrow{(a',b)} q'$ with $a \neq a'$.

Condition **(C2)** implies that computed transducers are length-decreasing, while **(C3)** and **(C4)** rule out transducers with redundant states. **(C5)** and **(C6)** follow from the simplifying assumption that only homomorphic symmetries patterns are computed, since a transducer representing a total function $\Sigma^* \to \Sigma^*$ has to accept the empty word and words of unbounded length. Note that **(C5)** and **(C6)** are necessary, but not sufficient conditions for total functions, so further checks are needed in VERIFY. **(C7)** and **(C8)** are necessary (but again not sufficient) conditions for transducers representing total functions, given the additional properties **(C3)** and **(C4)**; it can be shown that a transducer violating **(C7)** or **(C8)** cannot be a total function. Condition **(C9)** implies that padding $\#$ does not occur in any accepted word, and is a sufficient condition for length-preservation; as a result, the symbol $\#$ can be eliminated altogether from the transducer construction.

Finally, for *process symmetries* the assumption can be made that the transducer preserves not only word length, but also the number of occurrences of each symbol:

(C11) The relation R represented by the transducer only relates words with the same Parikh vector, i.e., $R(v, w)$ implies $\mathbb{P}(v) = \mathbb{P}(w)$.

The encoding of the conditions **(C1)**–**(C11)** as Boolean constraints is mostly straightforward. Further Boolean constraints can be useful in special cases, in particular for Example 3 the restriction can be made that only *image-finite* transducers are computed. We can also constrain the search in the SYNTHESISE stage to those transducers that accept manually defined words $W = \{v_1 \otimes w_1, \ldots, v_k \otimes w_k\}$, using a similar encoding as the one for counterexamples in Sect. 5.2. This technique can be used, among others, to systematically search for symmetry patterns that generalise some known finite symmetry.

5.2 Counterexample Generation

Once a transducer $\mathcal{A}$ representing a candidate relation $R \subseteq \Sigma^* \times \Sigma^*$ has been computed, Theorem 2 can be used to implement the VERIFY step of the algorithm. When using the construction from the proof of Theorem 2, one of three possible kinds of counterexample can be detected, corresponding to three different formulae to be added to the constraint ψ used in the SYNTHESISE stage:

1. A word v has to be included in the domain $R^{-1}(\Sigma_\#^*)$: $\exists w.\ R(v, w)$
2. A word w has to be included in the range $R(\Sigma_\#^*)$: $\exists v.\ R(v, w)$
3. One of two contradictory pairs has to be eliminated: $\neg R(v_1, w_1) \vee \neg R(v_2, w_2)$

Case 1 indicates relations R that are not total; case 2 relations that are not surjective; and case 3 relations that are not functions, not injective, or not simulations.[3] Each of the formulae can be directly translated to a Boolean constraint over the vocabulary introduced in Sect. 5.1. We illustrate how the first kind of counterexample is handled, assuming $v = a_1 \cdots a_m \in \Sigma_{\#}^*$ is the word in question; the two other cases are similar. We introduce Boolean variables $e_{i,q}$ for each $i \in \{0, \ldots, m\}$ and state $q \in Q$, which will be used to identify an accepting path in the transducer with input letters corresponding to the word v. We add constraints that ensure that exactly one $e_{i,q}$ is set for each state $q \in Q$, and that the path starts at the initial state $q_0 = 1$ and ends in an accepting state:

$$\left\{ \bigvee_{q \in Q} e_{i,q} \right\}_{i \in \{0,\ldots,m\}}, \quad \left\{ \neg e_{i,q} \vee \neg e_{i,q'} \right\}_{\substack{i \in \{0,\ldots,m\}, \\ q \neq q' \in Q}}, \quad e_{0,1}, \quad \left\{ e_{m,q} \to z_q \right\}_{q \in Q} .$$

For each $i \in \{1, \ldots, m\}$ a transition on the path, with input letter a_i has to be enabled:

$$\left\{ e_{i-1,q} \wedge e_{i,q'} \to \bigvee_{b \in \Sigma} x_{(q,a_i,b,q')} \right\}_{\substack{i \in \{1,\ldots,m\} \\ q,q' \in Q}} .$$

Table 1. Experimental results on verifying and generating symmetry patterns

Symmetry Systems (#letters)	# Transducer states	Verif. time	Synth. time
Herman Protocol (2)	5	0.0 s	4 s
Israeli-Jalfon Protocol (2)	5	0.0 s	5 s
Gries's Coffee Can (4)	8	0.1 s	3 m19 s
Resource Allocator (3)	11	0.0 s	4 m56 s
Dining Philosopher (4)	17	0.4 s	26 m

6   Implementation and Evaluation

We have implemented a prototype tool based on the aforementioned approach for verifying and synthesising regular symmetry patterns. The programming language is Java and we use SAT4J [7] as the SAT solver. The source code and the benchmarking examples can be found at https://bitbucket.org/truongkhanh/parasymmetry. The input of our tool includes a model (i.e. a textual representation of transducers), and optionally a set of finite instance symmetries (to speed up synthesis of regular symmetry patterns), which can be generated using existing tools like [33].

---

[3] Note that this is for the special case of homomorphisms. Simulation counterexamples are more complicated than case 3 when considering simulations relations that are not total functions.

We apply our tool to 5 models: the Herman self-stabilising protocol [21], Israeli-Jalfon self-stabilising protocol [23], the Gries' coffee can example [20], Resource Allocator, and Dining Philosopher. For the coffee can example, the tool generates the functional symmetry pattern described in Sect. 3, whereas the tool generates rotational process symmetries for the other models (see the full version for state diagrams). Finite instance symmetries were added as constraints in the last three examples.

Table 1 presents the experimental results: the number of states of the synthesised symmetry transducer, the time needed to verify that the transducer indeed represents a symmetry pattern (using the method from Sect. 4), and the total time needed to compute the transducer (using the procedure from Sect. 5). The data are obtained using a MacBook Pro (Retina, 13-inch, Mid 2014) with 3 GHz Intel Core i7 processor and 16 GB 1600 MHz DDR3 memory. In almost all cases, it takes less than 5 min (primarily SAT-solving) to find the regular symmetry patterns for all these models. As expected, the verification step is quite fast (<1 second).

7 Future Work

Describe the expressivity and nice algorithmic properties that regular symmetry patterns enjoy, we have pinpointed a limitation of regular symmetry patterns in expressing certain process symmetry patterns (i.e. reflections) and showed how to circumvent it by extending the framework to include symmetry patterns that can be recognised by height-unambiguous pushdown automata. One possible future research direction is to generalise our symmetry synthesis algorithm to this more general class of symmetry patterns. Among others, this would require coming up with a syntactic restriction of this "semantic" class of pushdown automata.

Acknowledgment. Lin is supported by Yale-NUS Grants, Rümmer by the Swedish Research Council. We thank Marty Weissman for a fruitful discussion.

References

1. Abdulla, P.A.: Regular model checking. STTT **14**(2), 109–118 (2012)
2. Abdulla, P.A., Chen, Y.-F., Holík, L., Mayr, R., Vojnar, T.: When simulation meets antichains. In: Esparza, J., Majumdar, R. (eds.) TACAS 2010. LNCS, vol. 6015, pp. 158–174. Springer, Heidelberg (2010)
3. Abdulla, P.A., Jonsson, B., Nilsson, M., d'Orso, J., Saksena, M.: Regular model checking for LTL(MSO). STTT **14**(2), 223–241 (2012)
4. Abdulla, P.A., Jonsson, B., Nilsson, M., Saksena, M.: A survey of regular model checking. In: Gardner, P., Yoshida, N. (eds.) CONCUR 2004. LNCS, vol. 3170, pp. 35–48. Springer, Heidelberg (2004)
5. Arenas, M., Barceló, P., Libkin, L.: Regular languages of nested words: fixed points, automata, and synchronization. In: Arge, L., Cachin, C., Jurdziński, T., Tarlecki, A. (eds.) ICALP 2007. LNCS, vol. 4596, pp. 888–900. Springer, Heidelberg (2007)

474 A.W. Lin et al.

6. Baier, C., Katoen, J.-P.: Principles of Model Checking. MIT Press, Cambridge (2008)
7. Berre, D.L., Parrain, A.: The Sat4j library, release 2.2. JSAT **7**(2–3), 56–59 (2010)
8. Blumensath, A.: Automatic structures. Master's thesis, RWTH Aachen (1999)
9. Blumensath, A., Grädel, E.: Finite presentations of infinite structures: Automata and interpretations. Theor. Comput. Syst. **37**(6), 641–674 (2004)
10. Bonchi, F., Pous, D.: Checking NFA equivalence with bisimulations up to congruence. In: The 40th Annual ACM SIGPLAN-SIGACT Symposium on Principles of Programming Languages, POPL 2013, Rome, Italy - January 23–25, 2013, pp. 457–468 (2013)
11. Cameron, P.J.: Permutation Groups. London Mathematical Society Student Texts. Cambridge University Press, Cambridge (1999)
12. Clarke, E.M., Jha, S., Enders, R., Filkorn, T.: Exploiting symmetry in temporal logic model checking. Formal Methods Syst. Des. **9**(1/2), 77–104 (1996)
13. Dill, D.L., Drexler, A.J., Hu, A.J., Yang, C.H.: Protocol verification as a hardware design aid. In: Proceedings 1991 IEEE International Conference on Computer Design: VLSI in Computer and Processors, ICCD 1992, Cambridge, MA, USA, October 11–14, 1992, pp. 522–525 (1992)
14. Donaldson, A.F.: Automatic Techniques for Detecting and Exploiting Symmetry in Model Checking. Ph.D. thesis, University of Glasgow (2007)
15. Donaldson, A.F., Miller, A.: Automatic symmetry detection for model checking using computational group theory. In: FM, pp. 631–631 (2005)
16. Donaldson, A.F., Miller, A.: Automatic symmetry detection for promela. J. Autom. Reasoning **41**, 251–293 (2008)
17. Emerson, E.A., Kahlon, V.: Reducing model checking of the many to the few. In: Proceedings of the 17th International Conference on Automated Deduction, Pittsburgh, PA, USA, June 17–20, 2000, Automated Deduction - CADE-17, pp. 236–254 (2000)
18. Emerson, E.A., Namjoshi, K.S.: Reasoning about rings. In: POPL, 85–94, (1995)
19. Emerson, E.A., Sistla, A.P.: Symmetry and model checking. Formal Methods Syst. Des. **9**(1/2), 105–131 (1996)
20. Gries, D.: The Science of Programming. Springer-Verlag (1981)
21. Herman, T.: Probabilistic self-stabilization. Inf. Process. Lett. **35**(2), 63–67 (1990)
22. Ip, C.N., Dill, D.L.: Better verification through symmetry. Formal Methods Syst. Des. **9**, 41–75 (1996)
23. Israeli, A., Jalfon, M.: Token management schemes and random walks yield self-stabilizing mutual exclusion. In: PODC, pp. 119–131 (1990)
24. Jaghoori, M.M., Sirjani, M., Mousavi, M.R., Khamespanah, E., Movaghar, A.: Symmetry and partial order reduction techniques in model checking rebeca. Acta Inf. **47**, 33–66 (2010)
25. Jaghoori, M.M., Sirjani, M., Mousavi, M.R.R., Movaghar, A.: Efficient symmetry reduction for an actor-based model. In: Chakraborty, G. (ed.) ICDCIT 2005. LNCS, vol. 3816, pp. 494–507. Springer, Heidelberg (2005)
26. Lehmann, D., Rabin, M.: On the advantage of free choice: A symmetric and fully distributed solution to the dining philosophers problem (extended abstract). In: Proceedings 8th Annual ACM Symposium on Principles of Programming Languages (POPL 1981), pp. 133–138 (1981)
27. Lin, A.W.: Accelerating tree-automatic relations. In: FSTTCS, pp. 313–324 (2012)
28. Lin, A.W., Nguyen, T.K., Rümmer, P., Sun, J.: Regular symmetry patterns (technical report). http://arxiv.org/abs/1510.08506 (cited in 2015)

29. Sistla, A.P., Gyuris, V., Emerson, E.A.: SMC: a symmetry-based model checker for verification of safety and liveness properties. ACM Trans. Softw. Eng. Method. **9**, 133–166 (2000)
30. Spermann, C., Leuschel, M.: ProB gets nauty: effective symmetry reduction for B and Z models. In: TASE, pp. 15–22 (2008)
31. Vojnar, T.: Cut-offs and automata in formal verification of infinite-state systems: Habilitation Thesis. Brno University of Technology, Faculty of Information Technology (2007)
32. Wahl, T., Donaldson, A.F.: Replication and abstraction: Symmetry in automated formal verification. Symmetry **2**, 799–847 (2010)
33. Zhang, S.J., Sun, J., Sun, C., Liu, Y., Ma, J., Dong, J.S.: Constraint-based automatic symmetry detection. In: ASE, pp. 15–25 (2013)

Tight Cutoffs for Guarded Protocols
with Fairness

Simon Außerlechner[1], Swen Jacobs[2(✉)], and Ayrat Khalimov[1]

[1] IAIK, Graz University of Technology, Graz, Austria
[2] Reactive Systems Group, Saarland University, Saarbrücken, Germany
jacobs@react.uni-saarland.de

Abstract. Guarded protocols were introduced in a seminal paper by
Emerson and Kahlon (2000), and describe systems of processes whose
transitions are enabled or disabled depending on the existence of other
processes in certain local states. We study parameterized model checking
and synthesis of guarded protocols, both aiming at formal correctness
arguments for systems with any number of processes. Cutoff results
reduce reasoning about systems with an arbitrary number of processes
to systems of a determined, fixed size. Our work stems from the observation that existing cutoff results for guarded protocols (i) are restricted to
closed systems, and (ii) are of limited use for liveness properties because
reductions do not preserve fairness. We close these gaps and obtain new
cutoff results for open systems with liveness properties under fairness
assumptions. Furthermore, we obtain cutoffs for the detection of global
and local deadlocks, which are of paramount importance in synthesis.
Finally, we prove tightness or asymptotic tightness for the new cutoffs.

1 Introduction

Concurrent hardware and software systems are notoriously hard to get correct. Formal methods like model checking or synthesis can be used to guarantee correctness, but the state explosion problem prevents us from using such
methods for systems with a large number of components. Furthermore, correctness properties are often expected to hold for an *arbitrary* number of components.
Both problems can be solved by *parameterized* model checking and synthesis
approaches, which give correctness guarantees for systems with any number of
components without considering every possible system instance explicitly.

While parameterized model checking (PMC) is undecidable in general [25],
there exist a number of methods that decide the problem for specific classes
of systems [12,14,16], as well as semi-decision procedures that are successful in
many interesting cases [9,18,21]. In this paper, we consider the *cutoff* method
that can guarantee properties of systems of arbitrary size by considering only
systems of up to a certain fixed size, thus providing a decision procedure for
PMC if components are finite-state.

We consider systems that are composed of an arbitrary number of processes,
each an instance of a process template from a given, finite set. Process templates

© Springer-Verlag Berlin Heidelberg 2016
B. Jobstmann and K.R.M. Leino (Eds.): VMCAI 2016, LNCS 9583, pp. 476–494, 2016.
DOI: 10.1007/978-3-662-49122-5_23

can be viewed as synchronization skeletons [11], i.e., program abstractions that suppress information not necessary for synchronization. In our system model, processes communicate by guarded updates, where guards are statements about other processes that are interpreted either conjunctively ("every other process satisfies the guard") or disjunctively ("there exists a process that satisfies the guard"). Conjunctive guards can model atomic sections or locks, disjunctive guards can model token-passing or to some extent pairwise rendezvous (cf. [13]).

This class of systems has been studied by Emerson and Kahlon [12], and cutoffs that depend on the size of process templates are known for specifications of the form $\forall \bar{p}.\ \Phi(\bar{p})$, where $\Phi(\bar{p})$ is an LTL\X property over the local states of one or more processes $\bar{p}$. Note that this does not allow us to specify fairness assumptions, for two reasons: (i) to specify fairness, additional atomic propositions for enabledness and scheduling of processes are needed, and (ii) specifications with global fairness assumptions are of the form $(\forall \bar{p}.\ fair(\bar{p})) \rightarrow (\forall \bar{p}.\ \Phi(\bar{p}))$. Because neither is supported by [12], the existing cutoffs are of limited use for reasoning about liveness properties.

Emerson and Kahlon [12] mentioned this limitation and illustrated it using the process template on the figure on the right. Transitions from the initial state N to the "trying" state T, and from the crit-

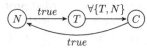

ical state C to N are always possible, while the transition from T to C is only possible if no other process is in C. The existing cutoff results can be used to prove safety properties like mutual exclusion for systems composed of arbitrarily many copies of this template. However, they cannot be used to prove starvation-freedom properties like $\forall p.\ \mathsf{A\,G}(T_p \rightarrow \mathsf{F}\,C_p)$, stating that every process p that enters its local state T_p will eventually enter state C_p, because without fairness of scheduling the property does not hold.

Also, Emerson and Kahlon [12] consider only closed systems. Therefore, in this example, processes always try to enter C. In contrast, in open systems the transition to T might be a reaction to a corresponding input from the environment that makes entering C necessary. While it is possible to convert an open system to a closed system that is equivalent under LTL properties, this comes at the cost of a blow-up.

Motivation. Our work is inspired by applications in parameterized synthesis [17], where the goal is to automatically construct process templates such that a given specification is satisfied in systems with an arbitrary number of components. In this setting, one generally considers *open systems* that interact with an uncontrollable environment, and most specifications contain liveness properties that cannot be guaranteed without fairness assumptions. Also, one is in general interested in synthesizing deadlock-free systems. *Cutoffs* are essential for parameterized synthesis, and we will show in Sect. 4 how size-dependent cutoffs can be integrated into the parameterized synthesis approach.

Contributions.

- We show that existing cutoffs for model checking of LTL\X properties are in general not sufficient for systems with *fairness assumptions*, and provide new cutoffs for this case.

– We improve some of the existing cutoff results, and give separate cutoffs for the problem of *deadlock detection*, which is closely related to fairness.
– We prove *tightness* or asymptotical tightness for all of our cutoffs, showing that smaller cutoffs cannot exist with respect to the parameters we consider.

Moreover, all of our cutoffs directly support *open systems*, where each process may communicate with an adversarial environment. This makes the blow-up incurred by translation to an equivalent closed system unnecessary. The results presented here are based on a more detailed preliminary version of this paper [4].

2   Related Work

As mentioned, we extend the results of Emerson and Kahlon [12] who study PMC of guarded protocols, but do not support fairness assumptions, nor provide cutoffs for deadlock detection. In [13] they extended their work to systems with limited forms of guards and broadcasts, and also proved undecidability of PMC of conjunctive guarded protocols wrt. LTL (including X), and undecidability wrt. LTL\X for systems with both conjunctive and disjunctive guards.

Bouajjani et al. [7] study parameterized model checking of resource allocation systems (RASs). Such systems have a bounded number of resources, each owned by at most one process at any time. Processes are pushdown automata, and can request resources with high or normal priority. RASs are similar to conjunctive guarded protocols in that certain transitions are disabled unless a processes has a certain resource. RASs without priorities and with processes being finite state automata can be converted to conjunctive guarded protocols (at the price of blow up), but not vice versa. The authors study parameterized model checking wrt. LTL\X properties on arbitrary or on strong-fair runs, and (local or global) deadlock detection. The proof structure resembles that of [12], as does ours.

German and Sistla [16] considered global deadlocks and strong fairness properties for systems with pairwise rendezvous communication in a clique. Emerson and Kahlon [13] have shown that disjunctive guard systems can be reduced to such pairwise rendezvous systems. However, German and Sistla [16] do not provide cutoffs, nor do they consider local deadlocks, and their specifications can talk about one process only. Aminof et al. [3] have recently extended these results to more general topologies, and have shown that for some decidable PMC problems there are no cutoffs, even in cliques.

Emerson and Namjoshi provide cutoffs for systems that pass a valueless token in a ring [14], which is essentially resource allocation of a single resource with a specific allocation scheme. Their results have been extended to more general topologies [2,10]. All of these results consider fairness of token passing in the sense that every process receives the token infinitely often.

Many of the decidability results above have recently been surveyed by Bloem et al. [6]. In addition, there are many methods based on semi-algorithms.

"Dynamic cutoff" approaches [1,18] support larger classes of systems, and try to find cutoffs for a concrete system and specification. These methods can find smaller cutoffs than those that are statically determined for a whole class of systems and specifications, but are currently limited to safety properties. The invisible invariants method [23] tries to find invariants in small systems, and applies a specialized cutoff result to prove correctness of all instances, including an extension to liveness properties [15].

Finally, there are methods that work completely without cutoffs, like regular model checking [8], network invariants [19,21,26], and counter abstraction [24]. They are in general incomplete, but may provide decision procedures for certain classes of systems and specifications, and support liveness to some extent.

3   Preliminaries

3.1   System Model

We consider systems $A \| B^n$, usually written $(A, B)^{(1,n)}$, consisting of one copy of a process template A and n copies of a process template B, in an interleaving parallel composition. We distinguish objects that belong to different templates by indexing them with the template. E.g., for process template $U \in \{A, B\}$, Q_U is the set of states of U. For this section, fix two disjoint finite sets Q_A, Q_B as sets of states of process templates A and B, and a positive integer n.

Processes. A *process template* is a transition system $U = (Q, \text{init}, \Sigma, \delta)$ with

- Q is a finite set of states including the initial state init,
- Σ is a finite input alphabet,
- $\delta : Q \times \Sigma \times \mathcal{P}(Q_A \cup Q_B) \times Q$ is a guarded transition relation.

A process template is *closed* if $\Sigma = \emptyset$, and otherwise *open*.

We define the size $|U|$ of a process template $U \in \{A, B\}$ as $|Q_U|$. A copy of template U will be called a U-*process*. Different B-processes are distinguished by subscript, i.e., for $i \in [1..n]$, B_i is the ith copy of B, and q_{B_i} is a state of B_i. A state of the A-process is denoted by q_A.

For the rest of this subsection, fix templates A and B. We assume that $\Sigma_A \cap \Sigma_B = \emptyset$. We will also write p for a process in $\{A, B_1, \ldots, B_n\}$, unless p is specified explicitly.

Disjunctive and Conjunctive Systems. In a system $(A, B)^{(1,n)}$, consider global state $s = (q_A, q_{B_1}, \ldots, q_{B_n})$ and global input $e = (\sigma_A, \sigma_{B_1}, \ldots, \sigma_{B_n})$. We also write $s(p)$ for q_p, and $e(p)$ for σ_p. A local transition $(q_p, \sigma_p, g, q_p') \in \delta_U$ of p is *enabled for s and e* if its *guard* g is satisfied for p in s, written $(s, p) \models g$. Disjunctive and conjunctive systems are distinguished by the *interpretation of guards*:

In disjunctive systems: $(s, p) \models g$ iff $\exists p' \in \{A, B_1, \ldots, B_n\} \setminus \{p\}: \ q_{p'} \in g$.

In conjunctive systems: $(s, p) \models g$ iff $\forall p' \in \{A, B_1, \ldots, B_n\} \setminus \{p\}: \ q_{p'} \in g$.

Note that we check containment in the guard (disjunctively or conjunctively) only for local states of processes *different from* p. A process is *enabled* for s and e if at least one of its transitions is enabled for s and e, otherwise it is *disabled*.

Like Emerson and Kahlon [12], we assume that in conjunctive systems init_A and init_B are contained in all guards, i.e., they act as neutral states. Furthermore, we call a conjunctive system 1-*conjunctive* if every guard is of the form $(Q_A \cup Q_B) \setminus \{q\}$ for some $q \in Q_A \cup Q_B$.

Then, $(A, B)^{(1,n)}$ is defined as the transition system $(S, \text{init}_S, E, \Delta)$ with

- set of global states $S = (Q_A) \times (Q_B)^n$,
- global initial state $\text{init}_S = (\text{init}_A, \text{init}_B, \ldots, \text{init}_B)$,
- set of global inputs $E = (\Sigma_A) \times (\Sigma_B)^n$,
- and global transition relation $\Delta \subseteq S \times E \times S$ with $(s, e, s') \in \Delta$ iff
  - (i) $s = (q_A, q_{B_1}, \ldots, q_{B_n})$,
  - (ii) $e = (\sigma_A, \sigma_{B_1}, \ldots, \sigma_{B_n})$, and
  - ((iii) s' is obtained from s by replacing one local state q_p with a new local state q_p', where p is a U-process with local transition $(q_p, \sigma_p, g, q_p') \in \delta_U$ and $(s, p) \models g$.

We say that a system $(A, B)^{(1,n)}$ is *of type* (A, B). It is called a *conjunctive system* if guards are interpreted conjunctively, and a *disjunctive system* if guards are interpreted disjunctively. A system is *closed* if all of its templates are closed. We often denote the set $\{B_1, \ldots, B_n\}$ as $\mathcal{B}$.

Runs. A *configuration* of a system is a triple (s, e, p), where $s \in S$, $e \in E$, and p is either a system process, or the special symbol $\perp$. A *path* of a system is a configuration sequence $x = (s_1, e_1, p_1), (s_2, e_2, p_2), \ldots$ such that for all $m < |x|$ there is a transition $(s_m, e_m, s_{m+1}) \in \Delta$ based on a local transition of process p_m. We say that process p_m *moves* at *moment* m. Configuration $(s, e, \perp)$ appears iff all processes are disabled for s and e. Also, for every p and $m < |x|$: either $e_{m+1}(p) = e_m(p)$ or process p moves at moment m. That is, the environment keeps input to each process unchanged until the process can read it.[1]

A system *run* is a maximal path starting in the initial state. Runs are either infinite, or they end in a configuration $(s, e, \perp)$. We say that a run is *initializing* if every process that moves infinitely often also visits its init infinitely often.

Given a system path $x = (s_1, e_1, p_1), (s_2, e_2, p_2), \ldots$ and a process p, the *local path* of p in x is the projection $x(p) = (s_1(p), e_1(p)), (s_2(p), e_2(p)), \ldots$ of x onto local states and inputs of p. Similarly define the projection on two processes p_1, p_2 denoted by $x(p_1, p_2)$.

Deadlocks and Fairness. A run is *globally deadlocked* if it is finite. An infinite run is *locally deadlocked* for process p if there exists m such that p is disabled for all $s_{m'}, e_{m'}$ with $m' \geq m$. A run is *deadlocked* if it is locally or globally deadlocked. A system *has a (local/global) deadlock* if it has a (locally/globally) deadlocked run. Note that absence of local deadlocks for all p implies absence of global deadlocks, but not the other way around.

---

[1] By only considering inputs that are actually processed, we approximate an action-based semantics. Paths that do not fulfill this requirement are not very interesting, since the environment can violate any interesting specification that involves input signals by manipulating them when the corresponding process is not allowed to move.

A run $(s_1, e_1, p_1), (s_2, e_2, p_2), \ldots$ is *unconditionally-fair* if every process moves infinitely often. A run is *strong-fair* if it is infinite and for every process p, if p is enabled infinitely often, then p moves infinitely often. We will discuss the role of deadlocks and fairness in synthesis in Sect. 4.

Remark 1. Why do we consider systems $A\|B^n$? Emerson and Kahlon [12] showed how to generalize cutoffs for such systems to systems of the form $A^m\|B^n$, and further to systems with an arbitrary number of process templates $U_1^{n_1}\| \ldots \|U_m^{n_m}$. This generalization also works for our new results, except for the cutoffs for deadlock detection that are restricted to 1-conjunctive systems (see Sect. 5).

3.2   Specifications

Fix templates (A, B). We consider formulas in LTL\X, i.e., LTL without the next-time operator X. Let $h(A, B_{i_1}, \ldots, B_{i_k})$ be an LTL\X formula over atomic propositions from $Q_A \cup \Sigma_A$ and indexed propositions from $(Q_B \cup \Sigma_B) \times \{i_1, \ldots, i_k\}$. For a system $(A, B)^{(1,n)}$ with $n \geq k$ and $i_j \in [1..n]$, satisfaction of $A\, h(A, B_{i_1}, \ldots, B_{i_k})$ and $E\, h(A, B_{i_1}, \ldots, B_{i_k})$ is defined in the usual way (see e.g. [5]).

Parameterized Specifications. A *parameterized specification* is a temporal logic formula with indexed atomic propositions and quantification over indices. We consider formulas of the forms $\forall i_1, \ldots, i_k.\, A\, h(A, B_{i_1}, \ldots, B_{i_k})$ and $\forall i_1, \ldots, i_k.\, E\, h(A, B_{i_1}, \ldots, B_{i_k})$. For given $n \geq k$,

$$(A, B)^{(1,n)} \models \forall i_1, \ldots, i_k.\, A\, h(A, B_{i_1}, \ldots, B_{i_k})$$

iff

$$(A, B)^{(1,n)} \models \bigwedge_{j_1 \neq \ldots \neq j_k \in [1..n]} A\, h(A, B_{j_1}, \ldots, B_{j_k}).$$

By symmetry of guarded protocols, this is equivalent (cp. [12]) to $(A, B)^{(1,n)} \models A\, h(A, B_1, \ldots, B_k)$. The latter formula is denoted by $A\, h(A, B^{(k)})$, and we often use it instead of the original $\forall i_1, \ldots, i_k.\, A\, h(A, B_{i_1}, \ldots, B_{i_k})$. For formulas with path quantifier E, satisfaction is defined analogously, and equivalent to satisfaction of $E\, h(A, B^{(k)})$.

Specification of Fairness and Local Deadlocks. It is often convenient to express fairness assumptions and local deadlocks as parameterized specifications. To this end, define auxiliary atomic propositions move_p and en_p for every process p of system $(A, B)^{(1,n)}$. At moment m of a given run $(s_1, e_1, p_1), (s_2, e_2, p_2), \ldots$, let move_p be true whenever $p_m = p$, and let en_p be true if p is enabled for s_m, e_m. Note that we only allow the use of these propositions to define fairness, but not in general specifications. Then, an infinite run is

- *local-deadlock-free* if it satisfies $\forall p.\, \mathsf{GF}\,\mathsf{en}_p$, abbreviated as $\Phi_{\neg dead}$,
- *strong-fair* if it satisfies $\forall p.\, \mathsf{GF}\,\mathsf{en}_p \to \mathsf{GF}\,\mathsf{move}_p$, abbreviated as Φ_{strong}, and
- *unconditionally-fair* if it satisfies $\forall p.\, \mathsf{GF}\,\mathsf{move}_p$, abbreviated as Φ_{uncond}.

If *fair* is a fairness notion and $\mathsf{A}\,h(A, B^{(k)})$ a specification, then we write $\mathsf{A}_{fair}\,h(A, B^{(k)})$ for $\mathsf{A}(\Phi_{fair} \to h(A, B^{(k)}))$. Similarly, we write $\mathsf{E}_{fair}\,h(A, B^{(k)})$ for $\mathsf{E}(\Phi_{fair} \wedge h(A, B^{(k)}))$.

3.3 Model Checking and Synthesis Problems

For a given system $(A, B)^{(1,n)}$ and specification $h(A, B^{(k)})$ with $n \geq k$,

- the *model checking problem* is to decide whether $(A, B)^{(1,n)} \models \mathsf{A}\,h(A, B^{(k)})$,
- the *deadlock detection problem* is to decide whether $(A, B)^{(1,n)}$ does not have global nor local deadlocks,
- the *parameterized model checking problem* (PMCP) is to decide whether $\forall m \geq n : (A, B)^{(1,m)} \models \mathsf{A}\,h(A, B^{(k)})$, and
- the *parameterized deadlock detection problem* is to decide whether for all $m \geq n$, $(A, B)^{(1,m)}$ does not have global nor local deadlocks.

For a given number $n \in \mathbb{N}$ and specification $h(A, B^{(k)})$ with $n \geq k$,

- the *template synthesis problem* is to find process templates A, B such that $(A, B)^{(1,n)} \models \mathsf{A}\,h(A, B^{(k)})$ and $(A, B)^{(1,n)}$ does not have global deadlocks.
- the *bounded template synthesis problem* for a pair of bounds $(b_A, b_B) \in \mathbb{N} \times \mathbb{N}$ is to solve the template synthesis problem with $|A| \leq b_A$ and $|B| \leq b_B$.
- the *parameterized template synthesis problem* is to find process templates A, B such that $\forall m \geq n : (A, B)^{(1,m)} \models \mathsf{A}\,h(A, B^{(k)})$ and $(A, B)^{(1,m)}$ does not have global deadlocks.

These definitions can be flavored with different notions of fairness (and similarly for the E path quantifier). In the next section we clarify the problems studied.

4 Reduction Method and Challenges

We show how to use existing cutoff results of Emerson and Kahlon [12] to reduce the PMCP to a standard model checking problem, and parameterized synthesis to template synthesis. We note the limitations of the existing results that are crucial in the context of synthesis.

Reduction by Cutoffs. A *cutoff* for a system type (A, B) and a specification Φ is a number $c \in \mathbb{N}$ such that:

$$\forall n \geq c : \left((A, B)^{(1,n)} \models \Phi \quad \Leftrightarrow \quad (A, B)^{(1,c)} \models \Phi \right).$$

Similarly, $c \in \mathbb{N}$ is a *cutoff for (local/global) deadlock detection* if $\forall n \geq c :$ $(A, B)^{(1,n)}$ has a (local/global) deadlock iff $(A, B)^{(1,c)}$ has a (local/global) deadlock. For the systems and specifications presented in this paper, cutoffs can be computed from the size of process template B and the number k of copies of B mentioned in the specification, and are given as expressions like $|B| + k + 1$.

Remark 2. Our definition of a cutoff is different from that of Emerson and Kahlon [12], and instead similar to, e.g., Emerson and Namjoshi [14]. The reason is that we want the following property to hold for any (A, B) and Φ:

if n_0 is the smallest number such that $\forall n \geq n_0 : (A, B)^{(1,n)} \models \Phi$,

then any $c < n_0$ is not a cutoff, any $c \geq n_0$ is a cutoff.

We call n_0 the *tight* cutoff. The definition in [12, page 2] requires that $\forall n \leq c.(A, B)^{(1,n)} \models \Phi$ if and only if $\forall n \geq 1 : (A, B)^{(1,n)} \models \Phi$, and thus allows stating $c < n_0$ as a cutoff if Φ does not hold for all n.   □

In model checking, a cutoff allows us to check whether any "big" system satisfies the specification by checking it in the cutoff system. As noted by Jacobs and Bloem [17], a similar reduction applies to the parameterized synthesis problem. For guarded protocols, we obtain the following *semi-decision procedure for parameterized synthesis*:

0. set initial bound (b_A, b_B) on size of process templates;
1. determine cutoff for (b_A, b_B) and Φ;
2. solve bounded template synthesis problem for cutoff, size bound, and Φ;
3. if successful return (A, B) else increase (b_A, b_B) and goto (1).

Existing Cutoff Results. Emerson and Kahlon [12] have shown:

Theorem 1 (Disjunctive Cutoff Theorem). *For closed disjunctive systems, $|B| + 2$ is a cutoff [†] for formulas of the form $A\,h(A, B^{(1)})$ and $E\,h(A, B^{(1)})$, and for global deadlock detection.*

Theorem 2 (Conjunctive Cutoff Theorem). *For closed conjunctive systems, $2\,|B|$ is a cutoff [†] for formulas of the form $A\,h(A)$ and $E\,h(A)$, and for global deadlock detection. For formulas of the form $A\,h(B^{(1)})$ and $E\,h(B^{(1)})$, $2\,|B| + 1$ is a cutoff.*

Remark 3. [†] Note that Emerson and Kahlon [12] proved these results for a different definition of a cutoff (see Remark 2). Their results also hold for our definition, except possibly for global deadlocks. For the latter case to hold with the new cutoff definition, one also needs to prove the direction "global deadlock in the cutoff system implies global deadlock in a large system" (later called Monotonicity Lemma). In Sects. 6.3 and 7.3 we prove these lemmas for the case of general deadlock (global *or* local).

Challenge: Open Systems. For any open system S there exists a closed system S' such that S and S' cannot be distinguished by LTL specifications (cp. Manna and Pnueli [22]). Thus, one approach to PMC for open systems is to use a translation between open and closed systems, and then use the existing cutoff results for closed systems.

While such an approach works in theory, it might not be feasible in practice: since cutoffs depend on the size of process templates, and the translation blows up the process template, it also blows up the cutoffs. Thus, cutoffs that directly support open systems are important.

Challenge: Liveness and Deadlocks under Fairness. We are interested in cutoff results that support liveness properties. In general, we would like to consider only runs where all processes move infinitely often, i.e., use the unconditional fairness assumption $\forall p. \, \mathsf{GF} \, move_p$. However, this would mean that we accept all systems that always go into a local deadlock, since then the assumption is violated. This is especially undesirable in synthesis, because the synthesizer usually tries to violate the assumptions in order to satisfy the specification. To avoid this, we require the absence of local deadlocks under the strong fairness assumption $\forall p. (\mathsf{GF} \, en_p \rightarrow \mathsf{GF} \, move_p)$. Since strong fairness and absence of local deadlocks imply unconditional fairness, we can then use the latter as an assumption for the original specification.

In summary, for a parameterized specification Φ, we consider satisfaction of

$$\text{``all runs are infinite''} \quad \wedge \quad \mathsf{A}_{strong} \, \Phi_{\neg dead} \quad \wedge \quad \mathsf{A}_{uncond} \, \Phi.$$

This is equivalent to *"all runs are infinite"* $\wedge \mathsf{A}_{strong}(\Phi_{\neg dead} \wedge \Phi)$, but by considering the form above we can separate the tasks of deadlock detection and of model checking $\mathsf{LTL}\backslash\mathsf{X}$-properties, and obtain modular cutoffs.

In the following, we present cutoffs for problems of the forms (i) $\mathsf{A}_{uncond} \, \Phi$, (ii) $\mathsf{A}_{strong} \, \Phi_{\neg dead}$ and no global deadlocks (and the variants with E path quantifier).

5   New Cutoff Results

We present new cutoff results that extend Theorems 1 and 2, summarized in the table below. We distinguish between disjunctive and conjunctive systems, nonfair and fair executions, as well as between the satisfaction of $\mathsf{LTL}\backslash\mathsf{X}$ properties $h(A, B^{(k)})$ and the existence of deadlocks. All results hold for open systems, and for both path quantifiers A and E. Cutoffs depend on the size of process template B and the number $k \geq 1$ of B-processes a property talks about:

	$h(A, B^{(k)})$ no fairness	Deadlock detection no fairness	$h(A, B^{(k)})$ uncond. fairness	Deadlock detection strong fairness
Disjunctive	$\|B\| + k + 1$	$2\|B\| - 1$	$2\|B\| + k - 1$	$2\|B\| - 1$
Conjunctive	$k + 1$	$2\|B\| - 2$ (∗)	$k + 1$ (∗)	$2\|B\| - 2$ (∗)

Results marked with a (∗) are for a restricted class of systems: For conjunctive systems with fairness, we require infinite runs to be *initializing*, i.e., all nondeadlocked processes return to init infinitely often.[2] Additionally, the cutoffs for

---

[2] This assumption is in the same flavor as the restriction that $init_A$ and $init_B$ appear in all conjunctive guards. Intuitively, the additional restriction makes sense since conjunctive systems model shared resources, and everybody who takes a resource should eventually release it.

deadlock detection in conjunctive systems only support 1-conjunctive systems. The reason for this restriction will be explained in Remark 4.

All cutoffs in the table are tight – no smaller cutoff can exist for this class of systems and properties – except for the case of deadlock detection in disjunctive systems without fairness. There, the cutoff is asymptotically tight, i.e., it must increase linearly with the size of the process template.

Proof Structure. To justify the entries in the table, we first recapitulate the proof structure of the original Theorems 1 and 2. The proofs are based on two lemmas, Monotonicity and Bounding. We give some basic proof ideas of the lemmas from [12] and mention extensions to the cases with fairness and deadlock detection. For cases where this extension is not easy, we will introduce additional proof techniques and explain how to use them in Sects. 6 and 7. Note that we only consider properties of the form $h(A, B^{(1)})$ — the proof ideas extend to general properties $h(A, B^{(k)})$ without difficulty. Similarly, in most cases the proof ideas extend to open systems without major difficulties — mainly because when we construct a simulating run, we have the freedom to choose the input that is needed. Only for the case of deadlock detection we have to handle open systems explicitly.

(1) *Monotonicity* Lemma: if a behavior is possible in a system with $n \in \mathbb{N}$ copies of B, then it is also possible in a system with one additional process:

$$(A, B)^{(1,n)} \models \mathsf{E}\, h(A, B^{(1)}) \implies (A, B)^{(1,n+1)} \models \mathsf{E}\, h(A, B^{(1)}),$$

and if a deadlock is possible in $(A, B)^{(1,n)}$, then it is possible in $(A, B)^{(1,n+1)}$.

Proof ideas. The lemma is easy to prove for properties $\mathsf{E}\, h(A, B^{(1)})$ in both disjunctive and conjunctive systems, by letting the additional process stay in its initial state init_B forever (cp. [12]). This cannot disable transitions with disjunctive guards, as these check for *existence* of a local state in another process (and we do not remove any processes), and it cannot disable conjunctive guards since they contain init_B by assumption. However, this construction violates fairness, since the new process never moves. This can be resolved in the disjunctive case by letting the additional process mimic all transitions of an existing process. But in general this does not work in conjunctive systems (due to the non-reflexive interpretation of guards). For this case and for deadlock detection, the proof is not trivial and may only work for $n \geq c$, for some lower bound $c \in \mathbb{N}$ (see Sects. 6 and 7). □

(2) *Bounding* Lemma: for a number $c \in \mathbb{N}$, a behavior is possible in a system with c copies of B if it is possible in a system with $n \geq c$ copies of process B:

$$(A, B)^{(1,c)} \models \mathsf{E}\, h(A, B^{(1)}) \impliedby (A, B)^{(1,n)} \models \mathsf{E}\, h(A, B^{(1)}),$$

and a deadlock is possible in $(A, B)^{(1,c)}$ if it is possible in $(A, B)^{(1,n)}$.

Proof ideas. For disjunctive systems, the main difficulty is that removing processes might falsify guards of the local transitions of A or B_1 in a given run (see Sect. 6). For conjunctive systems, removing processes from a run is easy for the case of infinite runs, since a transition that was enabled before cannot become disabled. Here, the difficulty is in preserving deadlocks, because removing processes may enable processes that were deadlocked before (Sect. 7).   □

6   Proof Techniques for Disjunctive Systems

6.1   LTL\X Properties Without Fairness: Existing Constructions

We revisit the main technique of the original proof of Theorem 1 [12]. It constructs an infinite run y of $(A, B)^{(1,c)}$ with $y \models h(A, B^{(1)})$, based on an infinite run x of $(A, B)^{(1,n)}$ with $n > c$ and $x \models h(A, B^{(1)})$. The idea is to copy local runs $x(A)$ and $x(B_1)$ into y, and construct runs of other processes in a way that enables all transitions along $x(A)$ and $x(B_1)$. The latter is achieved with the flooding construction.

Flooding Construction [12]. Given a run $x = (s_1, e_1, p_1), (s_2, e_2, p_2) \ldots$ of $(A, B)^{(1,n)}$, let $\mathsf{Visited}_B(x)$ be the set of all local states visited by B-processes in x, i.e., $\mathsf{Visited}_B(x) = \{q \in Q_B \mid \exists m \exists i. \, s_m(B_i) = q\}$.

For every $q \in \mathsf{Visited}_B(x)$ there is a local run of $(A, B)^{(1,n)}$, say $x(B_i)$, that visits q first, say at moment m_q. Then, saying that process B_{i_q} of $(A, B)^{(1,c)}$ *floods* q means:

$$y(B_{i_q}) = x(B_i)[1 : m_q](q)^\omega.$$

In words: the run $y(B_{i_q})$ is the same as $x(B_i)$ until moment m_q, and after that the process never moves.

The construction achieves the following. If we copy local runs of A and B_1 from x to y, and in y for every $q \in \mathsf{Visited}_B(x)$ introduce one process that floods q, then: if in x at some moment m there is a process in state q', then in y at moment m there will also be a process (different from A and B_1) in state q'. Thus, every transition of A and B_1, which is enabled at moment m in x, will also be enabled in y.

Proof Idea of the Bounding Lemma. The lemma for disjunctive systems without fairness can be proved by copying local runs $x(A)$ and $x(B_1)$, and flooding all states in $\mathsf{Visited}_B(x)$. To ensure that at least one process moves infinitely often in y, we copy one additional (infinite) local run from x. Finally, it may happen that the resulting collection of local runs violates the interleaving semantics requirement. To resolve this, we add stuttering steps into local runs whenever two or more processes move at the same time, and we remove global stuttering steps in y. Since the only difference between $x(A, B_1)$ and $y(A, B_1)$ are stuttering steps, y and x satisfy the same LTL\X-properties $h(A, B^{(1)})$. Since $|\mathsf{Visited}_B(x)| \leq |B|$, we need at most $1 + |B| + 1$ copies of B in $(A, B)^{(1,c)}$.

6.2   LTL\X Properties with Fairness: New Constructions

The flooding construction does not preserve fairness, and also cannot be used to construct deadlocked runs since it does not preserve disabledness of transitions of processes A or B_1. For these cases, we provide new proof constructions.

Consider the proof task of the bounding lemma for disjunctive systems with fairness: given an unconditionally fair run x of $(A, B)^{(1,n)}$ with $x \models h(A, B^{(1)})$, we want to construct an unconditionally fair run y of $(A, B)^{(1,c)}$ with $y \models h(A, B^{(1)})$. In contrast to unfair systems, we need to ensure that all processes move infinitely often in y. The insight is that after a finite time all processes will start looping around some set $\mathsf{Visited}^{inf}$ of states. We construct a run y that mimics this. To this end, we introduce two constructions. *Flooding with evacuation* is similar to flooding, but instead of keeping processes in their flooding states forever it evacuates the processes into $\mathsf{Visited}^{inf}$. *Fair extension* lets all processes move infinitely often without leaving $\mathsf{Visited}^{inf}$.

Flooding with Evacuation. Given a subset $\mathcal{F} \subseteq \mathcal{B}$ and an infinite run $x = (s_1, e_1, p_1) \ldots$ of $(A, B)^{(1,n)}$, define

$$\mathsf{Visited}_{\mathcal{F}}^{inf}(x) = \{q \mid \exists \text{ infinitely many} \quad m \colon s_m(B_i) = q \text{ for some } B_i \in \mathcal{F}\} \quad (1)$$

$$\mathsf{Visited}_{\mathcal{F}}^{fin}(x) = \{q \mid \exists \text{ only finitely many } m \colon s_m(B_i) = q \text{ for some } B_i \in \mathcal{F}\} \quad (2)$$

Let $q \in \mathsf{Visited}_{\mathcal{F}}^{fin}(x)$. In run x there is a moment f_q when q is reached for the first time by some process from $\mathcal{F}$, denoted B_{first_q}. Also, in run x there is a moment l_q such that: $s_{l_q}(B_{\mathsf{last}_q}) = q$ for some process $B_{\mathsf{last}_q} \in \mathcal{F}$, and $s_t(B_i) \neq q$ for all $B_i \in \mathcal{F}, t > l_q$ — i.e., when some process from $\mathcal{F}$ is in state q for the last time in x. Then, saying that process B_{i_q} of $(A, B)^{(1,c)}$ *floods* $q \in \mathsf{Visited}_{\mathcal{F}}^{fin}(x)$ *and then evacuates into* $\mathsf{Visited}_{\mathcal{F}}^{inf}(x)$ means:

$$y(B_{i_q}) = x(B_{\mathsf{first}_q})[1 \colon f_q] \cdot (q)^{(l_q - f_q + 1)} \cdot x(B_{\mathsf{last}_q})[l_q \colon m] \cdot (q')^{\omega},$$

where q' is the state in $\mathsf{Visited}_{\mathcal{F}}^{inf}(x)$ that $x(B_{\mathsf{last}_q})$ reaches first, at some moment $m \geq l_q$. In words, process B_{i_q} mimics process B_{first_q} until it reaches q, then does nothing until process B_{last_q} starts leaving q, then it mimics B_{last_q} until it reaches $\mathsf{Visited}_{\mathcal{F}}^{inf}(x)$.

The construction ensures: if we copy local runs of all processes not in $\mathcal{F}$ from x to y, then all transitions of y are enabled. This is because: for any process p of $(A, B)^{(1,c)}$ that takes a transition in y at any moment, the set of states visible to process p is a superset of the set of states visible to the original process in $(A, B)^{(1,n)}$ whose transitions process p copies.

Fair Extension. Here, we consider a path x that is the postfix of an unconditionally fair run x' of $(A, B)^{(1,n)}$, starting from the moment where no local states from $\mathsf{Visited}_{\mathcal{B}}^{fin}(x')$ are visited anymore. We construct a corresponding unconditionally-fair path y of $(A, B)^{(1,c)}$, where no local states from $\mathsf{Visited}_{\mathcal{B}}^{fin}(x')$ are visited.

Formally, let $n \geq 2|B|$, and x an unconditionally-fair path of $(A, B)^{(1,n)}$ such that $\mathsf{Visited}_{\mathcal{B}}^{fin}(x) = \emptyset$. Let $c \geq 2|B|$, and s'_1 a state of $(A, B)^{(1,c)}$ with

- $s_1'(A_1) = s_1(A_1)$, $s_1'(B_1) = s_1(B_1)$
- for every $q \in \mathsf{Visited}_{B_2..B_n}^{inf}(x) \backslash \mathsf{Visited}_{B_1}^{inf}(x)$, there are two processes $B_{i_q}, B_{i_q'}$ of $(A, B)^{(1,c)}$ that start in q, i.e., $s_1'(B_{i_q}) = s_1'(B_{i_q'}) = q$
- for every $q \in \mathsf{Visited}_{B_2..B_n}^{inf}(x) \cap \mathsf{Visited}_{B_1}^{inf}(x)$, there is one process B_{i_q} of $(A, B)^{(1,c)}$ that starts in q
- for some $q^\star \in \mathsf{Visited}_{B_2..B_n}^{inf}(x) \cap \mathsf{Visited}_{B_1}^{inf}(x)$, there is one additional process of $(A, B)^{(1,c)}$, different from any in the above, called $B_{i_{q^\star}'}$, that starts in $q^\star$.
- any other process B_i of $(A, B)^{(1,c)}$ starts in some state of $\mathsf{Visited}_{B_2..B_n}^{inf}(x)$.

Note that if $\mathsf{Visited}_{B_2..B_n}^{inf}(x) \cap \mathsf{Visited}_{B_1}^{inf}(x) = \emptyset$, then the third and fourth prerequisites are trivially satisfied.

The fair extension extends state s_1' of $(A, B)^{(1,c)}$ to an unconditionally-fair path $y = (s_1', e_1', p_1') \dots$ with $y(A_1, B_1) = x(A_1, B_1)$ as follows:

(a) $y(A_1) = x(A_1)$, $y(B_1) = x(B_1)$
(b) for every $q \in \mathsf{Visited}_{B_2..B_n}^{inf}(x) \backslash \mathsf{Visited}_{B_1}^{inf}(x)$: in run x there is $B_i \in \{B_2..B_n\}$ that starts in q and visits it infinitely often. Let B_{i_q} and $B_{i_q'}$ of $(A, B)^{(1,c)}$ mimic B_i in turns: first B_{i_q} mimics B_i until it reaches q, then $B_{i_q'}$ mimics B_i until it reaches q, and so on.
(c) arrange states of $\mathsf{Visited}_{B_2..B_n}^{inf}(x) \cap \mathsf{Visited}_{B_1}^{inf}(x)$ in some order $(q^\star, q_1, \dots, q_l)$. The processes $B_{i_{q^\star}'}, B_{i_{q^\star}}, B_{i_{q_1}}, \dots, B_{i_{q_l}}$ behave as follows. Start with $B_{i_{q^\star}'}$: when B_1 enters $q^\star$ in y, it carries[3] $B_{i_{q^\star}'}$ from $q^\star$ to q_1, then carries $B_{i_{q_1}}$ from q_1 to q_2, $\dots$, then carries $B_{i_{q_l}}$ from q_l to $q^\star$, then carries $B_{i_{q^\star}}$ from $q^\star$ to q_1, then carries $B_{i_{q^\star}'}$ from q_1 to q_2, then carries $B_{i_{q_1}}$ from q_2 to q_3, and so on.
(d) any other B_i of $(A, B)^{(1,c)}$, starting in $q \in \mathsf{Visited}_{B_2..B_n}^{inf}(x)$, mimics B_{i_q}.

Note that parts (b) and (c) of the construction ensure that there is always at least one process in every state from $\mathsf{Visited}_{B_2..B_n}^{inf}(x)$. This ensures that the guards of all transitions of the construction are satisfied. Excluding processes in (d), the fair extension uses up to $2|B|$ copies of B.[4]

Proof Idea of the Bounding Lemma. Let $c = 2|B|$. Given an unconditionally-fair run x of $(A, B)^{(1,n)}$ we construct an unconditionally-fair run y of the cutoff system $(A, B)^{(1,c)}$ such that $y(A, B_1)$ is stuttering equivalent to $x(A, B_1)$.

Note that in x there is a moment m such that all local states that are visited after m are in $\mathsf{Visited}_B^{inf}(x)$.

The construction has two phases. In the first phase, we apply flooding for states in $\mathsf{Visited}_B^{inf}(x)$, and flooding with evacuation for states in $\mathsf{Visited}_B^{fin}(x)$:

(a) $y(A) = x(A)$, $y(B_1) = x(B_1)$

---

[3] "Process B_1 starting at moment m carries process B_i from q to q'" means: process B_i mimics the transitions of B_1 starting at moment m at q until B_1 first reaches q'.

[4] A careful reader may notice that if $|\mathsf{Visited}_{B_1}^{inf}(x)| = 1$ and $|\mathsf{Visited}_{B_2..B_n}^{inf}(x)| = |B|$, then the construction uses $2|B| + 1$ copies of B. But one can slightly modify the construction for this special case, and remove process $B_{i_{q^\star}'}$ from the pre-requisites.

(b) for every $q \in \mathsf{Visited}^{inf}_{B_2..B_n}(x) \backslash \mathsf{Visited}^{inf}_{B_1}(x)$, devote two processes of $(A, B)^{(1,c)}$ that flood q

(c) for some $q^\star \in \mathsf{Visited}^{inf}_{B_2..B_n}(x) \cap \mathsf{Visited}^{inf}_{B_1}(x)$, devote one process of $(A, B)^{(1,c)}$ that floods $q^\star$

(d) for every $q \in \mathsf{Visited}^{fin}_{B_2..B_n}(x)$, devote one process of $(A, B)^{(1,c)}$ that floods q and evacuates into $\mathsf{Visited}^{inf}_{B_2..B_n}(x)$

(e) let other processes (if any) mimic process B_1

The phase ensures that at moment m in y, there are no processes in $\mathsf{Visited}^{fin}_{\mathcal{B}}(x)$, and all the pre-requisites of the fair extension are satisfied.

The second phase applies the fair extension, and then establishes the interleaving semantics as in the bounding lemma in the non-fair case. The overall construction uses up to $2|B|$ copies of B.

6.3 Detection of Local and Global Deadlocks: New Constructions

Monotonicity Lemmas. The lemma for deadlock detection, for fair and unfair cases, is proven for $n \geq |B| + 1$. In the case of local deadlocks, process B_{n+1} mimics a process that moves infinitely often in x. In the case of global deadlocks, by pigeon hole principle, in the global deadlock state there is a state q with at least two processes in it—let process B_{n+1} mimic a process that deadlocks in q.

Bounding Lemmas. For the case of global deadlocks, fairness does not affect the proof of the bounding lemma. The insight is to divide deadlocked local states into two disjoint sets, dead_1 and dead_2, as follows. Given a globally deadlocked run x of $(A, B)^{(1,n)}$, for every $q \in \mathsf{dead}_1$, there is a process of $(A, B)^{(1,n)}$ deadlocked in q with input i, that has an outgoing transition guarded "$\exists q$" – hence, adding one more process into q would unlock the process. In contrast, $q \in \mathsf{dead}_2$ if any process deadlocked in q stays deadlocked after adding more processes into q. Let us denote the set of B-processes deadlocked in dead_1 by $\mathcal{D}_1$. Finally, abuse the definition in Eq. 2 and denote by $\mathsf{Visited}^{fin}_{\mathcal{B} \backslash \mathcal{D}_1}(x)$ the set of states that are visited by B-processes not in $\mathcal{D}_1$ before reaching a deadlocked state.

Given a globally deadlocked run x of $(A, B)^{(1,n)}$ with $n \geq 2|B| - 1$, we construct a globally deadlocked run y of $(A, B)^{(1,c)}$ with $c = 2|B| - 1$ as follows:

- copy from x into y the local runs of processes in $\mathcal{D}_1 \cup \{A\}$
- flood every state of dead_2
- for every $q \in \mathsf{Visited}^{fin}_{\mathcal{B} \backslash \mathcal{D}_1}(x)$, flood q and evacuate into dead_2.

The construction ensures: (1) for any moment and any process in y, the set of local states that are visible to the process includes all the states that were visible to the corresponding process in $(A, B)^{(1,n)}$ whose transitions we copy; (2) in y, there is a moment when all processes deadlock in $\mathsf{dead}_1 \cup \mathsf{dead}_2$.

For the case of local deadlocks, the construction is similar but slightly more involved, and needs to distinguish between unfair and fair cases. In the unfair case, we also copy the behaviour of an infinitely moving process. In the strong-fair case, we continue the runs of non-deadlocked processes with the fair extension.

7   Proof Techniques for Conjunctive Systems

7.1   LTL\X Properties Without Fairness: Existing Constructions

Recall that the Monotonicity lemma is proven by keeping the additional process in the initial state. To prove the bounding lemma, Emerson and Kahlon [12] suggest to simply copy the local runs $x(A)$ and $x(B_1)$ into y. In addition, we may need one more process that moves infinitely often to ensure that an infinite run of $(A, B)^{(1,n)}$ will result in an infinite run of $(A, B)^{(1,c)}$. All transitions of copied processes will be enabled because removing processes from a conjunctive system cannot disable a transition that was enabled before.

7.2   LTL\X Properties with Fairness: New Constructions

The proof of the Bounding lemma is the same as in the non-fair case, noting that if the original run is unconditional-fair, then so will be the resulting run.

Proving the Monotonicity lemma is more difficult, since the fair extension construction from disjunctive systems does not work for conjunctive systems – if an additional process mimics the transitions of an existing process then it disables transitions of the form $q \overset{\text{"}\forall\neg q\text{"}}{\to} q'$ or $q \overset{\text{"}\forall\neg q'\text{"}}{\to} q'$. Hence, we add the restriction of initializing runs, which allows us to construct a fair run as follows. The additional process B_{n+1} "shares" a local run $x(B_i)$ with an existing process B_i of $(A, B)^{(1,n+1)}$: one process stutters in init_B while the other makes transitions from $x(B_i)$, and whenever $x(B_i)$ enters init_B (this happens infinitely often), the roles are reversed. Since this changes the behavior of B_i, B_i should not be mentioned in the formula, i.e., we need $n \geq 2$ for a formula $h(A, B^{(1)})$.

7.3   Detection of Local and Global Deadlocks: New Constructions

Monotonicity Lemmas. for both fair and unfair cases are proven by keeping process B_{n+1} in the initial state, and copying the runs of deadlocked processes. If the run of $(A, B)^{(1,n)}$ is globally deadlocked, then process B_{n+1} may keep moving in the constructed run, i.e., it may only be locally deadlocked. In case of a local deadlock in $(A, B)^{(1,n)}$, distinguish two cases: there is an infinitely moving B-process, or all B-processes are deadlocked (and thus A moves infinitely often). In the latter case, use the same construction as in the global deadlock case (the correctness argument uses the fact that systems are 1-conjunctive, runs are initializing, and there is only one process of type A). In the former case, copy the original run, and let B_{n+1} share a local run with an infinitely moving B-process.

Bounding Lemma (No Fairness). In the case of global deadlock detection, Emerson and Kahlon [12] suggest to copy a subset of the original local runs. For every local state q that is present in the final state of the run, we need at most two local runs that end in this state. In the case of local deadlocks, our construction uses the fact that systems are 1-conjunctive. In 1-conjunctive systems, if a process is deadlocked, then there is a set of states $DeadGuards$ that all need to be populated by other processes in order to disable all transitions of the deadlocked process. Thus, the construction copies: (i) the local run of a deadlocked process, (ii) for each $q \in DeadGuards$, the local run of a process that is in q at the moment of the deadlock, and (iii) the local run of an infinitely moving process.

Bounding Lemma (Strong Fairness). We use a construction that is similar to that of properties under fairness for disjunctive systems (Sect. 6.2): in the setup phase, we populate some "safe" set of states with processes, and then we extend the runs of non-deadlocked processes to satisfy strong fairness, while ensuring that deadlocked processes never get enabled.

Let $c = 2|Q_B \setminus \{\mathsf{init}_B\}|$. Let $x = (s_1, e_1, p_1) \dots$ be a locally deadlocked strong-fair intitializing run of $(A, B)^{(1,n)}$ with $n > c$. We construct a locally deadlocked strong-fair initializing run y of $(A, B)^{(1,c)}$.

Let $\mathcal{D} \subseteq \mathcal{B}$ be the set of deadlocked B-processes in x. Let d be the moment in x starting from which every process in $\mathcal{D}$ is deadlocked. Let $\mathsf{dead}(x)$ be the set of states in which processes $\mathcal{D}$ of $(A, B)^{(1,n)}$ are deadlocked. Let $\mathsf{dead}_2(x) \subseteq \mathsf{dead}(x)$ be the set of deadlocked states such that: for every $q \in \mathsf{dead}_2(x)$, there is a process $B_i \in \mathcal{D}$ with $s_d(B_i) = q$ and that for input $e_{\geq d}(B_i)$ has a transition guarded with "$\forall \neg q$". Thus, a process in q is deadlocked with $e_d(B_i)$ only if there is another process in q in every moment $\geq d$. Let $\mathsf{dead}_1(x) = \mathsf{dead}(x) \setminus \mathsf{dead}_2(x)$. Define $DeadGuards$ to be the set

$$\{ q \mid \exists B_i \in \mathcal{D} \text{ with a transition guarded } "\forall \neg q" \text{ in } (s_d(B_i), e_d(B_i)) \}.$$

Figure 1 illustrates properties of sets $DeadGuards$, dead_1, dead_2, $\mathsf{Visited}_{\mathcal{B} \setminus \mathcal{D}}^{inf}(x)$.

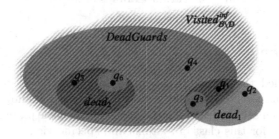

Fig. 1. Bounding lemma (strong fairness): Venn diagram for dead_1, dead_2, $DeadGuards$, $\mathsf{Visited}_{\mathcal{B} \setminus \mathcal{D}}^{inf}(x)$. States $q_1, \dots, q_6$ are to illustrate that the corresponding sets may be non-empty. E.g., in x, a process may be deadlocked in $q_1 \in (DeadGuards \cap \mathsf{dead}_1 \cap \mathsf{Visited}_{\mathcal{B} \setminus \mathcal{D}}^{inf}(x))$, and another process in $q_3 \in \mathsf{dead}_1 \cap DeadGuards \setminus \mathsf{Visited}_{\mathcal{B} \setminus \mathcal{D}}^{inf}(x)$.

In the **setup phase**, we copy from x into y:

- the local run of A;
- for every $q \in \mathsf{dead}_1$, the local run of one process deadlocked in q;

- for every $q \in \mathsf{dead}_2$, the local runs of two[5] processes deadlocked in q;
- for every $q \in DeadGuards \setminus \mathsf{dead}$, the local run of a process that reaches q after moment d.
- Finally, we keep one B-process in init_B until moment d.

The setup phase ensures: in every state $q \in \mathsf{dead}$, there is at least one process deadlocked in q at moment d in y. Now we need to ensure that the non-deadlocked processes in $DeadGuards \setminus \mathsf{dead}$ and init_B move infinitely often, which is done using the looping extension described bellow.

Order arbitrarily $DeadGuards \setminus \mathsf{dead} = (q_1, \ldots, q_k) \subseteq \mathsf{Visited}_{B\backslash D}^{inf}(x)$. Let $\mathcal{P} \subseteq \{B_1, \ldots, B_c\}$ be the non-deadlocked processes of $(A, B)^{(1,c)}$ that we moved into $(q_1, \ldots, q_k) \,\dot{\cup}\, \{\mathsf{init}_B\}$ in the setup phase. Note that $|\mathcal{P}| = |(q_1, \ldots, q_k)| + 1$.

The **looping phase** is: set $i = 1$, and repeat infinitely the following.

- let $B_{\mathsf{init}} \in \mathcal{P}$ be the process of $(A, B)^{(1,c)}$ that is currently in init_B, and $B_{q_i} \in \mathcal{P}$ be the process of $(A, B)^{(1,c)}$ that is currently in q_i
- let $\tilde{B}_{q_i} \in \mathsf{Visited}_{B\backslash D}^{inf}(x)$ be a process of $(A, B)^{(1,n)}$ that visits q_i and init_B infinitely often. Let B_{init} of $(A, B)^{(1,c)}$ copy transitions of $\tilde{B}_{q_i}$ on some path $\mathsf{init}_B \to \ldots \to q_i$, then let B_{q_i} copy transitions of $\tilde{B}_{q_i}$ on some path $q_i \to \ldots \to \mathsf{init}_B$. For copying we consider only the paths of $\tilde{B}_{q_i}$ that happen after moment d.
- $i = i \oplus 1$

Remark 4. In 1-conjunctive systems, the set $DeadGuards$ is "static", i.e., there is always at least one process in *each state* of $DeadGuards$ starting from the moment of the deadlock. In contrast, in general conjunctive systems where guards can overlap, there is no such set. However, there is a similar set of sets of states, such that *one state from each set* always needs to be populated to ensure the deadlock.

8 Conclusion

We have extended the cutoff results for guarded protocols of Emerson and Kahlon [12] to support local deadlock detection, fairness assumptions, and open systems. In particular, our results imply decidability of the parameterized model checking problem for this class of systems and specifications, which to the best of our knowledge was unknown before. Furthermore, the cutoff results can easily be integrated into the parameterized synthesis approach [17,20].

Since conjunctive guards can model atomic sections and read-write locks, and disjunctive guards can model pairwise rendezvous (for some classes of specifications, cp. [13]), our results apply to a wide spectrum of systems models. But the

---

[5] Strictly speaking, in x we might not have two deadlocked processes in a state in $dead_2$ – one process may be deadlocked, others enter and exit the state infinitely often. In such case, there is always a non-deadlocked process in the state. Then, copy the local run of such infinitely moving process until it enters the deadlocked state, and then deadlock it by providing the same input as the deadlocked process receives.

expressivity of the model comes at a high cost: cutoffs are linear in the size of a process, and are shown to be tight (with respect to this parameter). For conjunctive systems, our new results are restricted to systems with 1-conjunctive guards, effectively only allowing to model a single shared resource. We conjecture that our proof methods can be extended to systems with more general conjunctive guards, at the price of even bigger cutoffs. We leave this extension and the question of finding cutoffs that are independent of the size of processes for future research.

Acknowledgment. We thank Roderick Bloem, Markus Rabe and Leander Tentrup for comments on drafts of this paper. This work was supported by the Austrian Science Fund (FWF) through the RiSE project (S11406-N23, S11407-N23) and grant nr. P23499-N23, as well as by the German Research Foundation (DFG) through SFB/TR 14 AVACS and project ASDPS (JA 2357/2-1).

References

1. Abdulla, P.A., Haziza, F., Holík, L.: All for the price of few. In: Giacobazzi, R., Berdine, J., Mastroeni, I. (eds.) VMCAI 2013. LNCS, vol. 7737, pp. 476–495. Springer, Heidelberg (2013). http://dx.doi.org/10.1007/978-3-642-35873-9_28
2. Aminof, B., Jacobs, S., Khalimov, A., Rubin, S.: Parameterized model checking of token-passing systems. In: McMillan, K.L., Rival, X. (eds.) VMCAI 2014. LNCS, vol. 8318, pp. 262–281. Springer, Heidelberg (2014). http://dx.doi.org/10.1007/978-3-642-54013-4_15
3. Aminof, B., Kotek, T., Rubin, S., Spegni, F., Veith, H.: Parameterized model checking of rendezvous systems. In: Baldan, P., Gorla, D. (eds.) CONCUR 2014. LNCS, vol. 8704, pp. 109–124. Springer, Heidelberg (2014). http://dx.doi.org/10.1007/978-3-662-44584-6_9
4. Außerlechner, S., Jacobs, S., Khalimov, A.: Tight cutoffs for guarded protocols with fairness. CoRR abs/1505.03273 (2015). http://arxiv.org/abs/1505.03273
5. Baier, C., Katoen, J.P.: Principles of Model Checking. MIT press, Cambridge (2008)
6. Bloem, R., Jacobs, S., Khalimov, A., Konnov, I., Rubin, S., Veith, H., Widder, J.: Decidability of Parameterized Verification. Synthesis Lectures on Distributed Computing Theory, p. 175. Morgan & Claypool Publishers, San Rafael (2015). http://www.morganclaypool.com/doi/10.2200/S00658ED1V01Y201508DCT013
7. Bouajjani, A., Habermehl, P., Vojnar, T.: Verification of parametric concurrent systems with prioritised FIFO resource management. Formal Meth. Syst. Des. **32**(2), 129–172 (2008). http://dx.doi.org/10.1007/s10703-008-0048-7
8. Bouajjani, A., Jonsson, B., Nilsson, M., Touili, T.: Regular model checking. In: Emerson, E.A., Sistla, A.P. (eds.) CAV 2000. LNCS, vol. 1855, pp. 403–418. Springer, Heidelberg (2000). http://dx.doi.org/10.1007/10722167_31
9. Clarke, E., Talupur, M., Veith, H.: Proving ptolemy right: the environment abstraction framework for model checking concurrent systems. In: Ramakrishnan, C.R., Rehof, J. (eds.) TACAS 2008. LNCS, vol. 4963, pp. 33–47. Springer, Heidelberg (2008)
10. Clarke, E., Talupur, M., Touili, T., Veith, H.: Verification by network decomposition. In: Gardner, P., Yoshida, N. (eds.) CONCUR 2004. LNCS, vol. 3170, pp. 276–291. Springer, Heidelberg (2004)

11. Emerson, E.A., Clarke, E.M.: Using branching time temporal logic to synthesize synchronization skeletons. Sci. Comput. Program. **2**(3), 241–266 (1982). http://dx.doi.org/10.1016/0167-6423(83)90017-5
12. Emerson, E.A., Kahlon, V.: Reducing model checking of the many to the few. In: McAllester, D. (ed.) CADE 2000. LNCS, vol. 1831, pp. 236–254. Springer, Heidelberg (2000)
13. Emerson, E.A., Kahlon, V.: Model checking guarded protocols. In: LICS, pp. 361–370. IEEE Computer Society (2003)
14. Emerson, E.A., Namjoshi, K.S.: On reasoning about rings. Found. Comput. Sci. **14**, 527–549 (2003)
15. Fang, Y., Piterman, N., Pnueli, A., Zuck, L.D.: Liveness with invisible ranking. STTT **8**(3), 261–279 (2006). http://dx.doi.org/10.1007/s10009-005-0193-x
16. German, S.M., Sistla, A.P.: Reasoning about systems with many processes. J. ACM **39**(3), 675–735 (1992)
17. Jacobs, S., Bloem, R.: Parameterized synthesis. Logical Meth. Comput. Sci. **10**, 1–29 (2014)
18. Kaiser, A., Kroening, D., Wahl, T.: Dynamic cutoff detection in parameterized concurrent programs. In: Touili, T., Cook, B., Jackson, P. (eds.) CAV 2010. LNCS, vol. 6174, pp. 645–659. Springer, Heidelberg (2010). http://dx.doi.org/10.1007/978-3-642-14295-6_55
19. Kesten, Y., Pnueli, A., Shahar, E., Zuck, L.D.: Network invariants in action. In: Brim, L., Jančar, P., Křetínský, M., Kučera, A. (eds.) CONCUR 2002. LNCS, vol. 2421, pp. 101–115. Springer, Heidelberg (2002). http://dx.doi.org/10.1007/3-540-45694-5_8
20. Khalimov, A., Jacobs, S., Bloem, R.: PARTY parameterized synthesis of token rings. In: Sharygina, N., Veith, H. (eds.) CAV 2013. LNCS, vol. 8044, pp. 928–933. Springer, Heidelberg (2013)
21. Kurshan, R.P., McMillan, K.L.: A structural induction theorem for processes. Inf. Comp. **117**(1), 1–11 (1995)
22. Manna, Z., Pnueli, A.: Temporal specification and verification of reactive modules. Weizmann Institute of Science Technical Report (1992)
23. Pnueli, A., Ruah, S., Zuck, L.D.: Automatic deductive verification with invisible invariants. In: Margaria, T., Yi, W. (eds.) TACAS 2001. LNCS, vol. 2031, pp. 82–97. Springer, Heidelberg (2001). http://dx.doi.org/10.1007/3-540-45319-9_7
24. Pnueli, A., Xu, J., Zuck, L.D.: Liveness with $(0, 1, \infty)$-counter abstraction. In: Brinksma, E., Larsen, K.G. (eds.) CAV 2002. LNCS, vol. 2404, pp. 107–122. Springer, Heidelberg (2002). http://dx.doi.org/10.1007/3-540-45657-0_9
25. Suzuki, I.: Proving properties of a ring of finite state machines. Inf. Process. Lett. **28**(4), 213–214 (1988)
26. Wolper, P., Lovinfosse, V.: Verifying properties of large sets of processes with network invariants. In: Sifakis, J. (ed.) Automatic Verification Methods for Finite State Systems. LNCS, vol. 407, pp. 68–80. Springer, Heidelberg (1989). http://dx.doi.org/10.1007/3-540-52148-8_6

A General Modular Synthesis Problem for Pushdown Systems

Ilaria De Crescenzo$^{(\boxtimes)}$ and Salvatore La Torre

Dipartimento di Informatica, Università degli Studi di Salerno,
Via Giovanni Paolo II, 132, 84084 Fisciano, Salerno, Italy
ilaria.decrescenzo@dia.unisa.it

Abstract. The modular synthesis from a library of components (Lms) asks to compose a recursive state machine satisfying a given specification, by modularly controlling a finite set of component instances taken from the library. It combines and subsumes two synthesis problems studied in the literature: the synthesis from libraries of recursive components and the modular strategy synthesis. We consider standard specifications as reachability and safety (expressed by finite automata), and visibly pushdown automata specifications, and show that for all these classes of specifications the Lms problem is EXPTIME-complete.

1 Introduction

Component-based design is a main approach for developing configurable and scalable digital systems. In this setting, the reusability of pre-existing components plays a main role. In fact, it is current practice to design specialized hardware using some base components and programming by libraries and frameworks.

A component is a piece of hardware or software that can be directly plugged into a solution or a template that needs to be customized for a specific use. In the procedural-programming world, a general notion of component composition can be obtained by allowing to synthesize some modules from generic templates and then connect them along with other off-the-shelf modules via the call-return paradigm.

In this paper, we study a general synthesis problem for component-based pushdown systems, the *modular synthesis from a library of components* (Lms). The goal is to synthesize a recursive state machine (RSM) S [1] by composing, via the call-return paradigm, modules that are instantiated from library components such that all runs of S satisfy a given specification.

We model each component as a game graph with vertices split between player 0 (pl_0) and player 1 (pl_1), and the addition of *boxes* as place-holders for *calls* to components. The library is equipped with a *box-to-component map* that is a partial function from boxes to components. An instance of a component C is essentially a copy of C along with a local strategy that resolves the nondeterminism of pl_0. An RSM S synthesized from a library is a set of instances along with

This work was partially funded by the MIUR grants FARB 2013-15, Università di Salerno.

B. Jobstmann and K.R.M. Leino (Eds.): VMCAI 2016, LNCS 9583, pp. 495–513, 2016.
DOI: 10.1007/978-3-662-49122-5_24

a total function that maps each box in S to an instance of S and is consistent with the box-to-component map of the library.

In this paper, we give a solution to the LMS problem with winning conditions given as internal reachability objectives, or as external deterministic finite automata (FA) and deterministic visibly pushdown automata (VPA) [6]. We show that the LMS problem is EXPTIME-complete for any of the considered specifications. In particular, for reachability we adapt the algorithm from [9] that considers a special case of the LMS problem where the boxes of the components are all un-mapped (i.e., the library has no box-to-component map). The lower bound is inherited from [9]. The lower bounds for safety and VPA specifications can be obtained by standard reductions from alternating linear-space Turing machines. For safety specifications, the upper bound is based on a reduction to tree automata emptiness that is based on the notion of *library tree*: an infinite tree that encodes the library along with a choice for a total box-to-component map where both the components and the total map are unrolled. The construction is structured into several pieces and exploits the closure properties of tree automata under concatenation, intersection and union. The upper bound for VPA specifications is obtained by a reduction to safety specifications that exploits the synchronization between the stacks of the VPA and the synthesized RSM.

A solution to the LMS problem can involve arbitrarily many instances of each library component with possibly different local strategies. Such a diversity in the system design is often not affordable or unrealistic, therefore we also consider restrictions of this problem by focusing on solutions with few component instances and designs. In our setting, a natural way to achieve this is by restricting the synthesized RSMs such that: (1) at most one instance of each library component is allowed (few component instances), or (2) all the instances of a same library component must be controlled by a same local strategy (few designs). We refer to the LMS problems with these restrictions as the *single-instance* LMS problem and the *component-based* LMS problem, respectively. Note that in the *component-based* LMS there is no restriction imposed on the local strategy to be synthesized for a component and two instances of the same component can still differ in the mapping of the boxes.

The single-instance LMS problem can be reduced to the modular synthesis on recursive game graphs by guessing a total box-to-component map for the library, and thus we immediately get that the problem is NP-complete for reachability [4], and EXPTIME-complete for FA [3] and VPA [10] specifications. For the component-based LMS problem we get the same complexity as for the general LMS problem: the upper bounds are obtained by adapting the constructions given for the general case.

The LMS problem also gives a general framework for program repair where besides the intra-module repairs considered in the standard approach (see [13,14]) one can think of repairing a program by replacing a call to a module with a call to another module (*function call repairs*).

Related Work. The LMS problem strictly extends the modular synthesis on recursive game graphs [3,5,10] by allowing to synthesize multiple (possibly different) instances from each component and the call-return relation among them (i.e., the box-to-instance map). Our constructions build on the techniques used in these papers and rely on well established connections between games on graphs and tree automata. Besides that, the presented results and also the notion of library tree, which is the key of our translation to tree automata, are new.

The LMS problem also strictly generalizes the synthesis from libraries of [18,19] where there is no internal game within the components forming the library. In some sense, our problem generalizes their setting to library of infinitely many elements that are defined as instances of finitely many components.

The synthesis from libraries of components with simple specifications has been also implemented in tools (see [12] and references therein). The notion of modular strategy has found application in the automatic transformation of programs for ensuring security policies in privilege-aware operating systems [11].

Related synthesis problems concern component libraries [7,18] and weaker forms of modular strategies [8]. Modular synthesis with modules expressed as terms of the λY-calculus is captured by [21]. The synthesis problem from [20] differs from our setting in that programs and not transition systems are dealt with, and the number of functions of a synthesized program is bounded a priory but no structure of the functions is given. Deciding standard pushdown games (i.e., where strategies may be non-modular) is known to be EXPTIME-complete for reachability specifications [25], 2EXPTIME-complete for VPA specifications and 3EXPTIME-complete for temporal logic specifications [17].

2   Modular Synthesis from Libraries

For $n \in \mathbb{N}$ and $0 \leq j < n$, with $[j, n]$ we denote the set of integers i s.t. $j \leq i \leq n$ and with $[n]$ we denote $[1, n]$. Also we let Σ be a finite alphabet.

Library of Components. For $k \in \mathbb{N}$, a k-*component* is a finite game graph with two kinds of vertices, the standard *nodes* and the *boxes*, and with an *entry* node and k *exit* nodes. Each box has a *call* point and k *return* points, and each edge takes from a node/return to a node/call in the component. Nodes and returns are split into player 0 (pl_0) positions and player 1 (pl_1) positions.

For a box b, we denote with $(1, b)$ the only call of b and with (b, i) the ith return of b for $i \in [k]$. A k-*component* C is a tuple $(N_C, B_C, e_C, Ex_C, \eta_C, \delta_C, P_C^0, P_C^1)$ where N_C is a finite set of nodes, B_C is a finite set of boxes, $e_C \in N_C$ is the entry, $Ex_C : [k] \to N_C$ is an injection that maps each i to the ith exit, $\eta_C : V_C \to \Sigma$ is a labeling map of the *set of C vertices* $V_C = N_C \cup Calls_C \cup Retns_C$, $\delta : N_C \cup Retns_C \to 2^{N_C \cup Calls_C}$ is a transition function with $Retns_C = \{(b, i) \mid b \in B_C, i \in [k]\}$ (*set of C returns*) and $Calls_C = \{(1, b) \mid b \in B_C\}$ (*set of C calls*), and P_C^0 (the pl_0 positions) and P_C^1 (the pl_1 positions) form a partition of $N_C \cup Retns_C$.

We introduce the notion of *isomorphism* between two k-components. Intuitively, two components are isomorphic if and only if their game structures are equivalent, that is: the properties of standard isomorphism of labeled graphs must hold, and additionally isomorphic vertices must be assigned to the same player and be of the same kind.

Formally, the k-components C and C' are *isomorphic*, denoted $C \overset{\text{iso}}{\equiv} C'$, if there exists a bijection $iso : V_C \cup B_C \to V_{C'} \cup B_{C'}$ s.t.: (1) for all $u, v \in V_C, v \in \delta_C(v)$ iff $iso(v) \in \delta_{C'}(iso(u))$ and (2) for $u \in V_C \cup B_C$ and $u' \in V_{C'} \cup B_{C'}$, we get $u' = iso(u)$ iff u and u'

- *have the same labeling*, i.e. $\eta_C(u) = \eta_{C'}(u')$;
- *are assigned to the same player*, i.e., $u \in P_C^j$ iff $u' \in P_{C'}^j$ for $j \in [0,1]$;
- *are of the same kind*, i.e.:
  - u is an entry/box of C iff u' is an entry/box of C';
  - for $i \in [k]$, u is the ith exit of C iff u' is the ith exit of C';
  - $u = (1,b)$ iff $u' = (1, iso(b))$ and for $i \in [k]$, $u = (b,i)$ iff $u' = (iso(b), i)$ (*calls and i^{th}-returns of isomorphic boxes must be isomorphic*).

For $k > 0$, a *k-library* is a tuple $\mathcal{L}ib = \langle \{C_i\}_{i \in [0,n]}, Y_{\mathcal{L}ib} \rangle$ where:

- $\{C_i\}_{i \in [0,n]}$ is a finite set of k-components;
- C_0 is the *main component*;
- let $B_{\mathcal{L}ib} = \bigcup_{i \in [0,n]} B_{C_i}$ be the set of all boxes of the library components, $Y_{\mathcal{L}ib} : B_{\mathcal{L}ib} \to \{C_i\}_{i \in [n]}$ is a partial function (*box-to-component map*).

Running Example. We illustrate the definitions with an example. In Fig. 1(a), we give a library $\mathcal{L}ib$ of four components C_0, C_1, C_2 and C_3. Each component has two exits. In the figure, we denote the nodes of pl_0 with circles and the nodes of pl_1 with squares. Rounded squares are used to denote the boxes. Entries (resp., exits) are denoted by nodes intersecting the frame of the component on the left (resp., on the right). For example, C_0 has entry e_0 and two exits x_1 and x_2, one internal node u_1 and two boxes b_1 and b_2. With "$b_1 : C_1$" we denote that box b_1 is mapped to component C_1. The only unmapped box is b_3. To keep the figure simple, we only show the labeling of vertices with labels α, β and γ, and hide the labeling for all the remaining vertices (meaning that they are labeled with any other symbol).

Notes. For the ease of presentation, we have imposed a few restrictions. First, in the definition of library, $Y_{\mathcal{L}ib}$ can map a box to each component but the main component C_0. We observe that this is in accordance with the choice of many programming languages where the main function cannot be called by other functions and is without loss of generality of our results. Second, multiple entries can be handled by making for each component as many copies as the number of its entries, and accommodating calls and returns accordingly. Third, all the components of a library have the same number of exits that also matches the number of returns for each box. This can be relaxed at the cost of introducing a notion of *compatibility* between a box and a component, and map boxes to components only when they are compatible. We make a further assumption that is standard: in the components there are no transitions leaving from exits (assigning them to pl_0 or pl_1 is thus irrelevant).

Instances and Recursive State Machines. We are interested in synthesizing a *recursive state machine* (RSM) [1] from a library of components. Such a

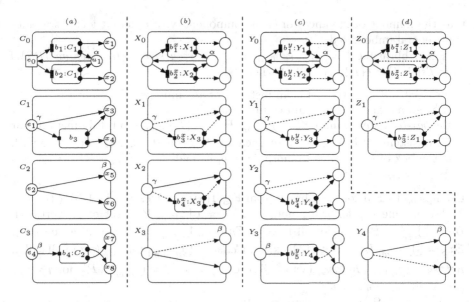

Fig. 1. A library (a) and RSMs from it: unrestricted (b), same local strategy for instances of the same component (c), and at most one instance for each component (d).

machine is formed by a finite number of *instances* of library components, where each instance is isomorphic to a library component and resolves the nondeterminism of pl_0 by a finite-state local strategy. The boxes of each instance are mapped to instances in the machine with the meaning that when a call of a box b is reached then the execution continues on the entry of the mapped instance and when the ith exit of such instance is reached then it continues at the ith return of b (as in the recursive call-return paradigm). The box-to-instance map of an RSM must agree with the box-to-component map of the library when this is defined.

We observe that our definition of RSM differs from the standard one in that (i) each finite-state machine is implicitly given by a component and a finite-state local strategy, and (ii) the nodes are split between pl_0 and pl_1. (However the last is immaterial since the nondeterminism of pl_0 is completely resolved by the local strategies).

For a component C, a *local strategy* is $f : V_C^* . P_C^0 \to Calls_C \cup N_C$ such that $f(w.u) \in \delta_C(u)$. The strategy is *finite-state* if it is computable by a finite automaton (we omit a formal definition here, see [23]).

An *instance of C* is $I = (G, f)$ where G is s.t. $G \overset{iso}{\equiv} C$ holds and f is a finite-state local strategy of G. For example, in Fig. 1, X_1 and X_2 are two instances of C_1 that differ on the local strategy (we have denoted with dashed edges the transitions that cannot be taken because of the local strategies). Also, Y_1 is an instance of C_1 and has the same local strategy as X_1. Note that, though the local strategies used in this example are memoryless, this is not mandatory and thus the number of instances of each component with different local strategies is in general unbounded.

Fix a library $\mathcal{L}ib = \langle \{C_i\}_{i \in [0,n]}, Y_{\mathcal{L}ib} \rangle$. A *recursive state machine (RSM)* from $\mathcal{L}ib$ is $S = \langle \{I_i\}_{i \in [0,m]}, Y_S \rangle$ where:

- for $i \in [0,m]$, $I_i = (G_i, f_i)$ is an instance of a component C_{j_i} from $\mathcal{L}ib$;
- I_0 is an instance of the main component C_0;
- the *box-to-instance* map $Y_S : \bigcup_{i \in [0,m]} B_{G_i} \rightarrow \{I_i\}_{i \in [m]}$ is a total function that is consistent with $Y_{\mathcal{L}ib}$, i.e., for each $i \in [0,m]$ and $b \in B_{G_i}$, denoting with b' the box of C_{j_i} that is isomorphic to b, it holds that if $Y_{\mathcal{L}ib}(b') = C_{j_h}$ then $Y_S(b) = G_h$.

Examples of RSM for the library from Fig. 1(a) are given in Fig. 1(b)–(d).

We assume the following notation: $V_S = \bigcup_{i \in [0,m]} V_{G_i}$ (set of all vertices); $B_S = \bigcup_{i \in [0,m]} B_{G_i}$ (set of all boxes); $En_S = \bigcup_{i \in [0,m]} \{e_{G_i}\}$ (set of all entries); $Ex_S = \bigcup_{i \in [0,m]} Ex_{G_i}$ (set of all exits); $Calls_S = \bigcup_{i \in [0,m]} Calls_{G_i}$ (set of all calls); $Retns_S = \bigcup_{i \in [0,m]} Retns_{G_i}$ (set of all returns); and $P_S^j = \bigcup_{i \in [0,m]} P_{G_i}^j$ for $j = 0, 1$ (set of all positions of pl_j).

A *state* of S is (γ, u) where $u \in V_{Y_S(b_h)}$ is a vertex and $\gamma = \gamma_1 \ldots \gamma_h$ is a finite sequence of pairs $\gamma_i = (b_i, \mu_i)$ with $b_i \in B_S$ and $\mu_i \in V_{Y_S(b_i)}^*$ for $i \in [h]$ (respectively, *calling box* and *local memory* of the called instance).

In the following, for a state $s = (\gamma, u)$, we denote with $V(s)$ its vertex u. Moreover, we define the *labeling map of S*, denoted η_S, from the labeling η_{G_i} of each instance I_i in the obvious way, i.e., $\eta_S(s) = \eta_{G_i}(V(s))$ for each $V(s) \in V_{G_i}$ and $i \in [0,m]$. η_S naturally extends to sequences.

A *run* of S is an infinite sequence of states $\sigma = s_0 s_1 s_2 \ldots$ such that $s_0 = ((\epsilon, e_{G_0}), e_{G_0})$ and for $i \in \mathbb{N}$, denoting $s_i = (\gamma_i, u_i)$ and $\gamma_i = (b_1, \mu_1) \ldots (b_h, \mu_h)$, one of the following holds:

- **Internal pl_1 move:** $u_i \in (N_S \cup Retns_S) \setminus Ex_S$, and $u_i \in P_S^1$, then $u_{i+1} \in \delta_S(u_i)$ and $\gamma_{i+1} = (b_1, \mu_1) \ldots (b_h, \mu_h.u_{i+1})$;
- **Internal pl_0 move:** $u_i \in (N_S \cup Retns_S) \setminus Ex_S$, $u_i \in P_S^0$ and $u_i \in V_{G_j}$ with $j \in [0,m]$, then $u_{i+1} = f_j(\mu_h)$ and $\gamma_{i+1} = (b_1, \mu_1) \ldots (b_h, \mu_h.u_{i+1})$.
- **Call to an instance:** $u_i = (1, b) \in Calls_S$, $u_{i+1} = e_{Y_S(b)}$ and $\gamma_{i+1} = \gamma_i.(b, e_{Y_S(b)})$;
- **Return from a call:** $u_i \in Ex_S$ and u_i corresponds to the jth exit of an instance I_h, then $u_{i+1} = (b_h, j)$ and $\gamma_{i+1} = (b_1, \mu_1) \ldots (b_{h-1}, \mu_{h-1}.u_{i+1})$.

An *infinite* RSM is defined as an RSM where we just relax the request that the set of instances is finite. We omit a formal definition and retain the notation. Note that the definitions of state and run given above still hold in this case.

Synthesis Problem. Fix a library $\mathcal{L}ib = \langle \{C_i\}_{i \in [0,n]}, Y_{\mathcal{L}ib} \rangle$ with alphabet Σ.

A *library game* is $(\mathcal{L}ib, \mathcal{W})$ where $\mathcal{L}ib$ is a library of components and $\mathcal{W}$ is a *winning set*, i.e., a language $\mathcal{W} \subseteq \Sigma^\omega$.

The *modular synthesis from libraries* (LMS, for short) is the problem of determining if for a given library game $(\mathcal{L}ib, \mathcal{W})$ there is an RSM $S = \langle \{I_i\}_{i \in [0,m]}, Y_S \rangle$ from $\mathcal{L}ib$ that *satisfies* $\mathcal{W}$, i.e., $\eta_S(\sigma) \in \mathcal{W}$ for each run σ of S.

As an example, consider the LMS queries $\mathcal{Q}_i = (\mathcal{L}ib, \mathcal{W}_i)$, $i \in [3]$, where $\mathcal{L}ib$ is from Fig. 1(a) and denoting $\Sigma = \{\alpha, \beta, \gamma\}$: $\mathcal{W}_1$ is the set of all ω-words whose projection into Σ gives the word $(\gamma\alpha)^\omega$, $\mathcal{W}_2$ is the set of all words whose projection into Σ gives a word in $(\gamma\beta\alpha + \gamma\beta^2\alpha)^\omega$, and $\mathcal{W}_3$ is the set of all ω-words with no occurrences of β. The RMSs from Fig. 1(b)–(d) are solutions of the LMS queries $\mathcal{Q}_1, \mathcal{Q}_2$ and $\mathcal{Q}_3$ respectively. In the figure, we use circles to denote all the nodes, this is to stress that the splitting between the two players is not meaningful any more.

3   Safety LMS

A *safety automaton* A is a deterministic finite automaton with no final states, and the language accepted by A, denoted $\mathcal{W}_A$, is the set of all ω-words on which A has a run (see [22] for a survey on ω-words automata). We denote a safety automaton by $(\Sigma, Q, q_0, \delta_A)$ where Σ is a finite set of input symbols, Q is a finite set of states, $q_0 \in Q$ is the initial state, and $\delta_A : Q \times \Sigma \to Q$ is a partial function (the transition function).

In the *safety* LMS problem the winning set is given by the set of words accepted by a safety automaton. In this section we show that deciding this problem is EXPTIME-complete. Our decision procedure consists of reducing the problem to checking the emptiness of tree automata. We assume familiarity with tree automata and refer the reader to [22] for the definitions.

Overview of the Construction. Fix a safety LMS query $(\mathcal{L}ib, \mathcal{W}_A)$ where $\mathcal{L}ib = \langle\{C_i\}_{i\in[0,n]}, Y_{\mathcal{L}ib}\rangle$ is a library and $A = (\Sigma, Q, q_o, \delta_A)$ is a safety automaton. We aim to construct an automaton $\mathcal{A}$ that accepts the trees that *encode* an RSM S synthesized from $\mathcal{L}ib$ iff S satisfies $\mathcal{W}_A$.

For the RSM encoding we introduce the notions of component tree and library tree. Intuitively, a component tree corresponds to the unrolling of a library component, and a library tree is a concatenation of component trees that encodes a choice of the box-to-instance map and of the components for the synthesis of the instances.

For a library tree t, denote with $Roots(t)$ the set of all nodes of t that correspond to a root of a component tree. A set $\mathcal{I} = \{I_x\}_{x \in Roots(t)}$ is *compatible* with t if I_x is an instance of the component corresponding to the component tree rooted at x. Such a set $\mathcal{I}$ and the total box-to-instance map defined by the concatenation of component trees in t define a possibly infinite RSM (it is infinite iff $Roots(t)$ is infinite). Denote $S_{\mathcal{I},t}$ such RSM.

Intuitively, the automaton $\mathcal{A}$ checks that the input tree t is a library tree of $\mathcal{L}ib$ and that there is a set of instances $\mathcal{I}$ that is compatible with t s.t. $S_{\mathcal{I},t}$ satisfies $\mathcal{W}_A$. For this, $\mathcal{A}$ simulates the safety automaton A on the unrolling of each component and on pl_0 nodes also guesses a move of the local strategy (in this way we also guess an instance of the component). To move across the boxes, $\mathcal{A}$ uses a *box summary* that is guessed at the root of each component tree. For $x \in Roots(t)$, denoting with C_x the corresponding component and with x_b

the child of x corresponding to a box b of C_x, the box summary guessed at x essentially tells for each such b (recall that Q is the set of states of A):

1. the associated component C_{x_b} in t, and
2. a non empty set $Q' \subseteq Q$, and for $i \in [k]$ and $q \in Q'$, sets $Q^b_{q,i} \subseteq Q$ s.t. for any run π of $S_{\mathcal{I},t}$ that starts at the entry of the instance I_{x_b} and ends at its ith exit, if the safety automaton A starts from q and reads the sequence of input symbols along π then it must reach a state of $Q^b_{q,i}$.

The above assumption 2 is called a *pre-post condition* for C_{x_b}. The correctness of the pre-post condition for each such C_{x_b} is checked in the simulation of $\mathcal{A}$ on the unrolling of C_{x_b}.

We give $\mathcal{A}$ as the composition of several tree automata: $\mathcal{A}_{\mathcal{L}ib}$ checks that the input tree is a library tree, and each $\mathcal{A}^C_{\mathcal{P},\mathcal{B}}$ checks on the unrolling of C that the pre-post condition $\mathcal{P}$ holds provided that the box-summary $\mathcal{B}$ holds.

Component and Library Trees. For a component C of $\mathcal{L}ib$, the *component tree* of C is a tree where the subtree rooted at the first child of the root is essentially the unrolling of C from its entry node and the other children of the root are leaves s.t. each box of C is mapped to exactly one of them.

Consider a library $\mathcal{L}ib = \langle \{C_i\}_{i \in [0,n]}, Y_{\mathcal{L}ib} \rangle$. Let $B_{\mathcal{L}ib} = \bigcup_{i \in [0,n]} B_{C_i}$ be the set of all boxes and $V_{\mathcal{L}ib} = \bigcup_{i \in [0,n]} V_{C_i}$ be the set of all vertices (i.e. nodes, calls and returns) of the library components.

Let d be the maximum over the number of exits, the number of boxes in each component and the out-degree of the vertices of the library components.

Denote with $\widehat{\Omega}$ the set $\{dummy, C_0, ..., C_n\} \cup B_{\mathcal{L}ib} \cup V_{\mathcal{L}ib}$. A *component tree* of some component C_i in $\mathcal{L}ib$ is an $\widehat{\Omega}$-labeled d-tree such that its first subtree encodes the unrolling of C_i and the children of its root, from the second through the $(\ell + 1)^{th}$, are leaves corresponding respectively to each of the ℓ boxes of C_i. We make use of *dummy* nodes to complete the d-tree.

Precisely, an $\widehat{\Omega}$-labeled d-tree T_{C_i} is a *component tree* of C_i in $\mathcal{L}ib$, if:

– the root of T_{C_i} is labeled with C_i;
– the subtree $T^1_{C_i}$ that is rooted at the first child of the root corresponds to the unrolling of the component C_i; the nodes of $T^1_{C_i}$ are labeled with the corresponding vertices of the component C_i; thus, in particular, the root of $T^1_{C_i}$ is labeled with e_{C_i} and the calls have as children the matching returns; a tree-node labeled with an exit has no children; in $T^1_{C_i}$ all the nodes that do not correspond to a vertex in the unrolling of C_i are labeled with *dummy*, meaning that they are not meaningful in the encoding;
– for $i \in [2, \ell + 1]$, the jth child of the root is labeled with $b \in B_{C_i}$ and for any $j, z \in [2, \ell + 1]$ with $j \neq z$ the labels of the jth child and the zth child must be different;
– the tree-nodes labeled with $b \in B_{C_i}$ have no children;
– the remaining tree-nodes are labeled with *dummy*.

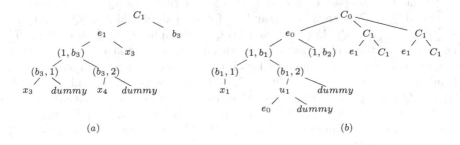

Fig. 2. Top fragments of (a) the component tree of C_1 and (b) the library tree from our running example.

As an example, in Fig. 2(a) we show a fragment of the component tree of the component C_1 from the library given in Fig. 1(a).

A *library tree* is a tree obtained by starting with the component tree of the main component and then iteratively gluing at each leaf corresponding to a box b: any component tree, if $Y_{\mathcal{L}ib}(b)$ is not defined, and the component tree of $Y_{\mathcal{L}ib}(b)$, otherwise.

One can formally define a library tree t as the ω-fold concatenation over languages of component trees. (We refer the reader to [22] for a formal definition of ω-fold concatenation). For this, let T_C be the component tree of C for each component C of $\mathcal{L}ib$ and denote $\mathbf{b} = (b_1, \ldots, b_n)$ where $B_{\mathcal{L}ib} = \{b_1, \ldots, b_n\}$ (recall that with $B_{\mathcal{L}ib}$ we denote the union of the set of boxes over all the components of $\mathcal{L}ib$). For each $i \in [n]$, we let T_i be the language $\{T_C\}$, if $Y_{\mathcal{L}ib}(b_i) = C$, and $\{T_{C'} \mid C' \text{ is a component of } \mathcal{L}ib\}$, otherwise.

A library tree for $\mathcal{L}ib$ is thus any tree $t \in T_0 \cdot_{\mathbf{b}} (T_1, \ldots, T_n)^{\omega \mathbf{b}}$ where $T_0 = \{T_{C_0}\}$.

In Fig. 2(b) we show the initial fragment of the library tree for the library from Fig. 1(a). Note that the second and the third child of the root correspond respectively to the boxes b_1 and b_2 of C_0 and thus each of them is replaced by a copy of T_{C_1} in the sample library tree.

The construction of $\mathcal{A}_{\mathcal{L}ib}$ can be obtained from the automata accepting the component trees for $\mathcal{L}ib$ using the standard construction for the ω-fold concatenation (see [22]). Thus, we get:

Proposition 1. *There exists an effectively constructible Büchi tree automaton $\mathcal{A}_{\mathcal{L}ib}$ of size linear in the size of $\mathcal{L}ib$, that accepts a tree if and only if it is a library tree of $\mathcal{L}ib$.*

Sketch of the Construction of $\mathcal{A}_{\mathcal{P},\mathcal{B}}^C$. We first formalize the notions of pre-post condition and box summary that we have informally introduced earlier in this section. Intuitively, box summaries are composed of pre-post conditions and each postcondition summarizes the states of the safety automaton A that can be reached along a play of a strategy at the exits of a corresponding component instance.

Formally, a *pre-post condition* $\mathcal{P}$ is a set of tuples $(q, [Q_1, \ldots, Q_k])$ where $q \in Q$ and $Q_i \subseteq Q$ for each $i \in [k]$, and s.t. for any pair of tuples $(q, [Q_1, \ldots, Q_k])$, $(q', [Q'_1, \ldots, Q'_k]) \in \mathcal{P}$: (1) $q \neq q'$, and (2) $Q_i = \emptyset$ implies $Q'_i = \emptyset$ for each $i \in [k]$ (i.e., for each q there is at most a tuple with q as first component and each other component is either the empty set for all the tuples or it is non-empty for all of them). For such a pre-post condition $\mathcal{P}$, each q is a *precondition* and each tuple $[Q_1, \ldots, Q_k]$ is a *postcondition*. Note that according to the above intuition, part (2) above captures the fact that all the postconditions of a pre-post condition must agree on the assumption on whether the ith exit is reachable (i.e., $Q_i = \emptyset$) or not (i.e., $Q_i \neq \emptyset$).

A *box summary* of an instance of C is a tuple $\mathcal{B}_C = \langle \hat{Y}_C, \{\mathcal{P}_b\}_{b \in B_C} \rangle$, where $\hat{Y}_C : B_C \rightarrow \{C_i\}_{i \in [n]}$ is a total map that is consistent with the library box-to-component map $Y_{\mathcal{L}ib}$ and for each box $b \in B_C$, $\mathcal{P}_b$ is a pre-post condition.

Fix a component C, a pre-post condition $\mathcal{P} = \{(q_i, [Q_{i_1}, \ldots, Q_{i_k}])\}_{i \in [h]}$ and a box summary $\mathcal{B} = \langle \hat{Y}_C, \{\mathcal{P}_b\}_{b \in B_C} \rangle$.

Denote T_C the component tree of C and T_C^1 the subtree rooted at the first child of T_C. Recall that T_C^1 corresponds to the unrolling of C from the entry node. For a local strategy f for C, a path $x_1 \ldots x_j$ of T_C^1 *conforms to* f if the corresponding sequence of C vertices $v_1 \ldots v_j$ is s.t. for $i \in [j-1]$ if v_i is a node of pl_0 then $v_{i+1} = f(v_1 \ldots v_i)$.

For each path π of T_C^1, a run of the safety automaton A on π according to box summary $\mathcal{B}$ is a run where a state q is updated (1) according to a transition of A, from a tree-node corresponding to a node or a return of C, and (2) by nondeterministically selecting a state from Q_i with $(q, [Q_1, \ldots, Q_k]) \in \mathcal{P}_b$ (i.e., a state from the postcondition for box b in $\mathcal{B}$), from a tree-node corresponding to a call $(1, b)$ to one corresponding to a return (b, i). Note that, we do not consider the case of an empty postcondition for a return. This is fine for our purposes since we need to simulate the safety automaton A only on the returns (b, i) that can be effectively reached in a play (according to the guessed box summary).

We construct $\mathcal{A}^C_{\mathcal{P}, \mathcal{B}}$ s.t. it rejects any tree other than T_C and accepts T_C iff (recall h is the number of tuples in the pre-post condition $\mathcal{P}$):

(P1) There is a local strategy f for C s.t. for each $i \in [h], j \in [k]$, and path π of T_C^1 from the root to the jth exit that conforms to f, each run of A on π according to $\mathcal{B}$ that starts from q_i ends at a state in Q_{i_j} (i.e., the *pre-post condition* $\mathcal{P}$ *holds*).

For this, we define $\mathcal{A}^C_{\mathcal{P}, \mathcal{B}}$ such that it summarizes for each precondition of $\mathcal{P}$ the states of the safety automaton A that can be reached at a given node.

The states of $\mathcal{A}^C_{\mathcal{P}, \mathcal{B}}$ are: an initial state q_s, an accepting sink state q_a, a rejecting sink state q_r, a state q_e, a state q_b for each box b of C, and summary states of the form $(R_1, \ldots, R_h)$ where $R_i \subseteq Q$ for $i \in [h]$.

$\mathcal{A}^C_{\mathcal{P}, \mathcal{B}}$ accepts on a finite path if it ends at q_a upon reading its sequence of labels. No condition is required in order to accept on infinite paths (the existence of a run suffices in this case).

At the root of T_C, from q_s the automaton enters q_e on the first child and for each box b of C, q_b on the child corresponding to b. From q_b, it then accepts entering q_a if the node is labeled with b. From q_e, it behaves as from $(\{q_1\}, \ldots, \{q_h\})$ if the current node corresponds to the entry of C (where $q_1, \ldots, q_h$ are the preconditions of $\mathcal{P}$).

In each run of $\mathcal{A}_{\mathcal{P},\mathcal{B}}^C$, for a state of the form $(R_1, \ldots, R_h)$ at a tree-node x, we keep the following invariant: for $i \in [h]$, R_i is the set of all the states that end any run of A starting from q_i on the path from the root of T_C^1 up to x (according to the box summary $\mathcal{B}$).

From a tree-node corresponding to a node or a return of C, the transitions of $\mathcal{A}_{\mathcal{P},\mathcal{B}}^C$ update each R_i as in a standard subset construction provided that there is a transition of A from all the states in $\bigcup_{j \in [h]} R_j$ (we recall that a run is unsafe if A halts), thus maintaining the invariant. The updated state is entered on all the children from pl_1 vertices, and on only one nondeterministically selected child from pl_0 vertices (this correspond to guessing a local strategy in C).

The update on tree-nodes corresponding to a call $(1, b)$ of C is done according to the pre-post condition $\mathcal{P}_b$ from the box summary $\mathcal{B}$. In particular, denoting $\mathcal{P}_b = \{(q_i', [Q_{i,1}', \ldots, Q_{i,k}'])\}_{i \in [h']}$, from $(R_1, \ldots, R_h)$ we enter q_a on the tree-node corresponding to any return (b, j) that is not reachable according to $\mathcal{P}_b$, i.e., each $Q_{i,j}' = \emptyset$ (we accept since the guessed local strategy excludes such paths and thus the condition $\mathcal{P}$ does not need to be checked). On the reachable returns (b, j), we enter the state $(R_1', \ldots, R_h')$ where $R_i' = \bigcup_{q_d' \in R_i} Q_{d,j}'$ for $i \in [h]$, i.e., according to the above invariant, for each position i in the tuple we collect the postconditions of the jth exit for each precondition of $\mathcal{P}_b$ that applies.

At a tree-node corresponding to the ith exit of C, $\mathcal{A}_{\mathcal{P},\mathcal{B}}^C$ accepts by entering q_a iff $\mathcal{P}$ is fulfilled, i.e., $\mathcal{A}_{\mathcal{P},\mathcal{B}}^C$ is in a state $(R_1, \ldots, R_h)$ s.t. $R_i \subseteq Q_i$ for $i \in [h]$.

The state q_r is entered in all the remaining cases.

By a simple counting, we get that the size of $\mathcal{A}_{\mathcal{P},\mathcal{B}}^C$ is linear in the number of boxes and exponential in the number of states of the specification automaton A. Thus, we get:

Lemma 1. $\mathcal{A}_{\mathcal{P},\mathcal{B}}^C$ accepts T_C iff property P1 holds. Moreover, the size of $\mathcal{A}_{\mathcal{P},\mathcal{B}}^C$ is linear in the number of C boxes and exponential in the number of A states.

The Construction of $\mathcal{A}$. We first construct an automaton $\mathcal{A}'$. For this, we extend the alphabets such that $\mathcal{A}_{\mathcal{P},\mathcal{B}}^C$ accepts the trees that are obtained from the component tree T_C of C by labeling the leaf corresponding to b, for each box b of C, with any tuple of the form $(\hat{Y}(b), \mathcal{P}_b, \mathcal{B}_b)$ where $\hat{Y}$ is the total map of the box summary $\mathcal{B}$ and $\mathcal{B}_b$ is any box summary for component $\hat{Y}(b)$. Denote $\mathcal{L}_{\mathcal{P},\mathcal{B}}^C$ the set of all trees accepted by any such automaton.

Let $\mathcal{P}_0 = \{(q_0, [\emptyset, \ldots, \emptyset])\}$ where q_0 is the initial state of A and Lab be the set of all labels $(C, \mathcal{P}, \mathcal{B})$ s.t. C is a component, $\mathcal{P}$ is a pre-post condition of C, and $\mathcal{B}$ is a box summary of C. For each box summary $\mathcal{B}_0$ for C_0 denote $T_{\mathcal{B}_0}$ the language $\mathcal{L}_{\mathcal{P}_0,\mathcal{B}_0}^{C_0} \cdot_{\bar{c}} (\langle \mathcal{L}_{\mathcal{P},\mathcal{B}}^C \rangle_{(C,\mathcal{P},\mathcal{B}) \in Lab})^{\omega \bar{c}}$ where $\bar{c} = \langle (C, \mathcal{P}, \mathcal{B}) \rangle_{(C,\mathcal{P},\mathcal{B}) \in Lab}$, i.e., the infinite trees obtained starting from a tree in $\mathcal{L}_{\mathcal{P}_0,\mathcal{B}_0}^{C_0}$ and then for all $(C, \mathcal{P}, \mathcal{B}) \in Lab$ iteratively concatenating at each leaf labeled with $(C, \mathcal{P}, \mathcal{B})$ a tree from $\mathcal{L}_{\mathcal{P},\mathcal{B}}^C$ until all such leaves are replaced.

By standard constructions (see [22]), we construct the automaton $\mathcal{A}'$ that accepts the union of the languages $T_{\mathcal{B}}$ for each box summary $\mathcal{B}$ of the main component.

The automaton $\mathcal{A}$ is then taken as the intersection of $\mathcal{A}_{\mathcal{L}ib}$ and $\mathcal{A}'$. Thus, from Proposition 1, Lemma 1 and known results on tree automata [22], we get that the size of $\mathcal{A}$ is exponential in the sizes of $\mathcal{L}ib$ and A. Recall that the emptiness of (Büchi) nondeterministic tree automata can be checked in linear time and if the language is not empty then it is possible to determine a finite witness of it (*regular tree*) [22]. The finiteness of a regular tree ensures both the finiteness of the local strategies and of the number of instances. Moreover, it encodes an RSM and thus starting from the automaton $\mathcal{A}$, we can use standard algorithms for tree automata to synthesize an RSM that fulfills the specification A. Note that from Proposition 1 and Lemma 1 we also get that the encoded strategy for each instance is local and, consequently, the set of synthesized strategies is modular. Further, we can show an EXPTIME lower bound with a direct reduction from alternating linear-space Turing machines. Therefore, we get:

Theorem 1. *The safety* LMS *problem is* EXPTIME-*complete.*

4   LMS with Deterministic VPA Specification

A *visibly pushdown automaton* (VPA) is a pushdown automaton where the stack operations are determined by the input symbols: a call symbol causes a push, a return symbol causes a pop and an internal symbol causes just a change of the finite control [6].

In the *VPA* LMS *problem* the specification is giving as a deterministic VPA. The labeling of the library components is synchronized with the usage of the stack of the VPA: calls are labeled with call symbols, returns with return symbols and nodes with internal symbols.

VPAs are strictly more expressive than finite state automata and they allow to express many additional specifications, as stack inspection properties, partial correctness or local properties (see [2]). For example, with a VPA we could express the requirement that along any run of an RSM M, every γ must be followed by at least an α in the same instance invocation where γ occurs. The RMS in Fig. 1(b) does not satisfy this requirement. In fact, though in any run each occurrence of γ is always followed by an occurrence of α, indeed each γ occurs during an invocation of either X_1 or X_2 while α always occurs in the only invocation of X_0 (when the invocations of X_1 and X_2 have already returned).

We give a reduction from the VPA LMS problem to the safety LMS problem. The idea is to achieve the synchronization on the stack symbols between automaton and specification using the mechanics of the game, such that the specification can be considered as a finite state automaton. The top symbol of the stack is embedded in the states of the specification automaton. Before every invocation of an instance, the adversary pl_1 has to declare the top symbol pushed by the specification automaton and the specification automaton has to verify that the adversary is honest (otherwise, pl_1 loses). After such declaration, the instance is invoked and, when its execution terminates, the adversary repeats the declared top-of-the-stack symbol such that the finite state automaton can update the simulated top symbol accordingly.

Consider a VPA LMS query with library $\mathcal{L}ib = \langle \{C_i\}_{i\in[0,n]}, Y_{\mathcal{L}ib}\rangle$ and deterministic VPA $\mathcal{A}_v$. We define a new library game $(\widehat{\mathcal{L}ib}, \mathcal{W}_\mathcal{A})$, where $\widehat{\mathcal{L}ib} = \langle \{C_i\}_{i\in[0,n]} \cup \{C_{stack_i}\}_{i\in[n]}, Y_{\widehat{\mathcal{L}ib}}\rangle$ and $\mathcal{W}_\mathcal{A}$ is the language recognized by a finite state automaton $\mathcal{A}$.

The structure of a component C_{stack_i} with $i \in [1,n]$ is given in Fig. 3 where with g we denote the number of stack symbols. Recall that k denotes the number of exits of any possible component C. Also, note that all the vertices are controlled by pl_1 and all the boxes are mapped to component C_i.

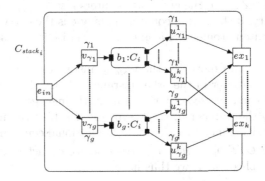

Fig. 3. The component C_{stack_i} for $i \in [n]$

The main purpose of the new components is to store the symbol that is pushed onto the stack in the $\mathcal{A}_v$ pushes. This is achieved by letting pl_1 to guess a stack symbol γ_j, then call the corresponding $\mathcal{L}ib$ component and on returning from exit x of such component, restore γ_j before exiting from the exit corresponding to x (thus reporting to the caller the exit of the callee).

We encode the stack of the specification in the library by enforcing each call to a component C_i of $\mathcal{L}ib$ to occur through a call to the new component C_{stack_i}, for $i \in [n]$. For this, we define the box-to-component map $Y_{\widehat{\mathcal{L}ib}}$, such that it preserves the original box-to-component of the input library and partially guarantees the interleaving of calls of components and calls of stack components. Namely, for $i \in [n]$, if $Y_{\mathcal{L}ib}$ maps a box b to a component C_i, then $Y_{\widehat{\mathcal{L}ib}}$ maps such box to the new component C_{stack_i}. Then, $Y_{\widehat{\mathcal{L}ib}}$ maps all the boxes of C_{stack_i} to C_i. In all the other case, i.e., if $Y_{\mathcal{L}ib}$ is undefined for a box b, also $Y_{\widehat{\mathcal{L}ib}}$ is undefined for it.

The winning condition is given as a finite state automaton $\mathcal{A}$ given as the intersection of two finite state automata $\mathcal{A}_1$ and $\mathcal{A}_2$. We embed the top stack symbol of the deterministic VPA in the states of $\mathcal{A}_1$. Moreover, the states of $\mathcal{A}_1$ simulate the corresponding states of $\mathcal{A}_v$, and the winning condition is equivalent. On calls, $\mathcal{A}_1$ must mimic a push transition t from the current state, by first storing in the control the pushed symbol γ and the next control state according to t, then, if the next input is γ, it continues, otherwise it enters an accepting sink state. Returns are handled similarly (the popped symbol occurs after the return, and the fact that this corresponds to the symbol actually pushed in the current run on the matching call is ensured by the instance of a component C_{stack_i}).

The alternation of calls to instances of components C_{stack_i} and calls to instances of the components C_i is guaranteed by the box-to-component map except for the case of the calls from unmapped boxes of instances of the input library. In fact, since these are unmapped also in the library $\widehat{\mathcal{L}ib}$, in an RSM from $\widehat{\mathcal{L}ib}$, we could map them to instances of both kinds of components C_{stack_i} and C_i. Thus, in order to enforce the alternation, and thus prevent them to be mapped directly to instances of C_i, we use the second finite state automaton $\mathcal{A}_2$. This automaton cycles on a state q_{in} until it reads a node labeled with the call of an unmapped box. Then, the automaton enters a state q_{wait} and cycles on it, waiting for an entry. If the first encountered entry e is the entry of a component C_{stack_i}, then the automaton enters again q_{in}, otherwise it enters a rejecting sink state.

Note that pl_0 has no moves in the C_{stack_i} instances, and the moves of pl_1 there are not visible to her in the other instances. Thus, the local strategies for pl_0 in the original game are exactly the same in the new game.

Denote with g the number of stack symbols. Each of the new components C_{stack_i} has $O(g\,k)$ size. Since there are only n additional components, the resulting library $\widehat{\mathcal{L}ib}$ has $O(|\mathcal{L}ib| + n\,g\,k)$ size. Also, the constructed automaton $\mathcal{A}$ has $O(g\,|\mathcal{A}_v|)$ size. By Theorem 1, we thus have:

Theorem 2. *The VPA* LMS *problem is* EXPTIME-*complete.*

5 On Modular Synthesis Problems

Modular Synthesis and Program Repair. Given a misbehaving program according to a correctness specification, the program repair looks for the fault localization and a possible small modification of the program such that the repaired program satisfies its specification. The repair problem is closely related to the synthesis problem. In [14] the fault localization and correction of the problem are achieved using infinite games: the system chooses which component is incorrect, then, if for any input sequence, the system can select a behavior of this component such that the specification is satisfied, the replacement behavior for the component can be used to make the system correct.

Consider the program in Fig. 4(a) and the correctness specifications requiring that statement (done=true) is reachable (*termination*) and condition (a[0]<=a[1]) && (a[1]<=a[2]) && (a[2]<=a[3]) holds at the end of the program execution (*correct result*). This program does not fulfill both specifications. In fact, it contains an error that causes an infinite cycle of unreturned function calls: in function MergeSort1 there is no control over the values of left and right, and no return statement before executing the recursive calls.

(a)		
| ```
1  main(){
2    const int n=4;
3    bool done=false;
4    int a[n]={7,4,5,1}
5    MergeSort1(a,0,n-1);
6    done=true;
7  }



8  void Merge(int a[],
     int left,int center,
     int right){ ...
9  //code with no errors
10 ...}
``` | ```
11 void MergeSort1(int a[],
     int left, int right){
12   int center=
       (left+right)/2;
13   MergeSort1(a,left,
       center);
14   MergeSort1(a,center+1,
       right);
15   Merge(a,left,
       center,right);
16 }
``` | ```
20 void MergeSort2(int a[],
     int left, int right){
21   if (left<left)
22     {
23     int center=
         (left+right)/2;
24   MergeSort2(a,left,
       center);
25   MergeSort2(a,center+1,
       right);
26   Merge(a,left,
       center,right);
27   }
28 }
``` |

Fig. 4. A faulty program (a) and a pre-existing function (b).

Note that this error cannot be repaired, because there is no assignment or condition on which we can set a diagnosis. However, MergeSort1 is a sorting algorithm. Thus, we could look within an available library for a different function implementing a sorting algorithm, and possibly this function is either correct or could be repaired.

In our example, suppose now that we can use a library that contains the function MergeSort2 given in Fig. 4(b). This function is faulty, but repairable, and the location of the error and its correction can be found using the approach in [14]: by assuming that in main we call MergeSort2, the algorithm suggests to change the left-hand side of the condition in Line 21 from left<left to left<right. Therefore, by fixing this error and replacing the call in Line 5 with a call to MergeSort2, the repaired program will now satisfy the given specification.

We can generalize this approach and apply it directly using the modular synthesis. Given a program P and a correctness specification, we construct a library game. Intuitively, we use the internal game to find and repair fixable faults and the external compositional game to substitute the components that can not be repaired (*function call repair*). As library we consider a given set of standard pre-existing components and the components of the program P, both modeled as game components to find and fix possible bugs as in the standard program repair approach. All the call assignments of the boxes that invoke suspected faulty functions are modeled as unassigned boxes. The correctness specification is unchanged. If there is a solution to such library game, we can obtain a repaired version of the program P that fulfills the given specification.

Other Formulations of the Modular Synthesis. We introduce two variations of the LMS problem based on the two restrictions for the RSMs that can be synthesized. The idea is to constrain our algorithms to synthesize, when possible, "simpler" RSMs. For example, in the function call repair we can imagine that it is not good to fix a fault introducing or duplicating an arbitrarily large number of new instances and we could be interested to construct a repaired system that implements at most one instance of each library component.
```

Fix a library $\mathcal{L}ib$. An RSM S from $\mathcal{L}ib$ is *component-based* if for any two S instances $I = (G, f)$ and $I' = (G', f')$ of a component C from $\mathcal{L}ib$, the local strategies f and f' *coincide* (up to a renaming). Moreover, S is *single-instance* if it has *at most* one instance of each library component.

The *component-based* (resp. single-instance) LMS problem is the LMS problem restricted to component-based (resp. single-instance) RSMs.

Denote with P_{single} (resp. P_{comp}, P_{LMS}) the set of LMS queries $(\mathcal{L}ib, \mathcal{W}_A)$ for which the single-instance LMS problem (resp. component-based LMS problem, LMS problem) admits a positive answer. Directly from the definitions, a single-instance RSM is also component-based. Thus we get that $P_{single} \subseteq P_{comp} \subseteq P_{LMS}$. These inclusions are indeed strict.

Let $\mathcal{L}ib$ be the library from Fig. 1(a). The RSM in Fig. 1(b) is not component-based (and thus not single-instance): X_1 and X_2 are instances of C_1 and use two different local strategies. The RSM in Fig. 1(c) instead is component-based but not single-instance since Y_1 and Y_2 are two instances of C_1 (note that even if they have the same local strategy, they differ on the reachable vertices because the box is mapped differently). The RSM from Fig. 1(d) is clearly single-instance.

Let $\mathcal{W}_1, \mathcal{W}_2$ and $\mathcal{W}_3$ be the winning conditions given at the end of Sect. 2. Observe that they are all expressible by safety automata. Moreover, there is no component-based RSM from $\mathcal{L}ib$ that satisfies $\mathcal{W}_1$ and no single-instance RSM from $\mathcal{L}ib$ that satisfies $\mathcal{W}_2$. Thus, we get the following lemma:

Lemma 2. $P_{single} \subset P_{comp} \subset P_{LMS}$.

The single-instance LMS problems and the synthesis of modular strategies on recursive game graphs are strictly related: a modular game is a single-instance LMS game where the box-to-component map is total. Given an instance of single-instance LMS game, we guess a total box-to-component map for the library and then we can solve all the considered single-instance LMS problems applying the algorithms proposed in [3, 5, 10]. We get:

Theorem 3. *The safety and VPA single-instance LMS problems are* EXPTIME-*complete. The reachability single-instance LMS problem is* NP-*complete.*

The construction given in Sect. 3 is based on the notion of library tree that essentially encodes the components and the box-to-instance map of an RSM. The local strategies are guessed on-the-fly by the tree automaton. To constrain the RSM to be component-based we should guess a strategy for each component C and then use it while visiting each component tree of C in the input library tree. This requires to prove first boundedness of the local strategies if there is a component-based RSM that satisfies the winning condition.

A simpler solution can be obtained by adapting the solution given in [3] for the synthesis of *modular strategies*. This problem is a particular case of the single-instance LMS problem where the box-to-component map is total, i.e., each box is pre-assigned. The solution given in [3] is based on the notion of *strategy tree* that unrolls each component as a subtree of the root and encodes in the labels of this encoding a local strategy. To adapt their automaton construction for the component-based LMS we just need to guess the mapping for the boxes that are not mapped by the box-to-component map of the library, every time a component subtree is visited.

To solve the reachability component-based LMS problem, we modify the algorithm proposed in [9] (which solves a simplified version of the reachability LMS problem), fixing the local strategy for each component.

For the VPA winning condition, the reduction proposed in Sect. 4 clearly applies also to component-based and we get the same complexity. We get:

Theorem 4. *The reachability, safety and VPA component-based* LMS *problems are* EXPTIME-*complete.*

6 Discussion and Conclusion

Synthesis is a central task in computer science that in general cannot be automatized [24]. We have presented a decidable synthesis problem for an expressive class of systems. Our decision algorithms for reachability specifications are fixed-point labeling computations and can be easily turned into an automatic synthesis of RSMs. All the other decision algorithms that we have presented are based on a reduction to tree automata, and thus also can be turned into automatic synthesis using standard results of this theory (see [22]).

Looking at the LMS as a game-graph problem the winning strategies we compute are *modular* and thus the local strategy of an instance that is called several times is oblivious of previous calls, i.e., it does not keep the memory of previous invocations. It is known that non-oblivious modular games are undecidable [5]. If we extend the class of solutions in the LMS problems by allowing to resolve the internal nondeterminism of pl_0 by a global strategy, we can show that the resulting problem is still decidable (this does not contradict the previous undecidability result since each pl_1 move is now observable by pl_0 in all the instances).

Further, the global LMS problem can be reduced to a standard pushdown game (PDG) with an exponential blow-up and vice-versa a PDG can be polynomially translated to a global LMS with a total box-to-component map (see also [1,5]). We can also show that there are LMS queries for which a global strategy exists while a modular one does not.

Nondeterministic finite automata and nondeterministic VPA specifications can be handled via determinization (since these classes are determinizable). Other common classes of specifications such as deterministic/universal Büchi/co-Büchi automata and temporal logic formulas can also be allowed in our settings by retaining decidability.

Details on all the above will be given in the extended version of this paper.

Finally, we observe that the computational complexity of the LMS problem is unlikely to improve even with simple temporal logic specifications [10] (differently from RSM model checking [16]). Also, investigating succinct representations, such as in [15], could be meaningful in the LMS settings. Further, we have given an example on how our formalism can be used to include in program repair a notion of function call repair. We believe that this direction deserves further investigation and leave it for future research.

References

1. Alur, R., Benedikt, M., Etessami, K., Godefroid, P., Reps, T.W., Yannakakis, M.: Analysis of recursive state machines. ACM Trans. Program. Lang. Syst. **27**(4), 786–818 (2005)
2. Alur, R., Etessami, K., Madhusudan, P.: A temporal logic of nested calls and returns. In: Jensen, K., Podelski, A. (eds.) TACAS 2004. LNCS, vol. 2988, pp. 467–481. Springer, Heidelberg (2004)
3. Alur, R., La Torre, S., Madhusudan, P.: Modular strategies for infinite games on recursive graphs. In: Hunt, Jr., W.A., Somenzi, F. (eds.) CAV 2003. LNCS, vol. 2725, pp. 67–79. Springer, Heidelberg (2003)
4. Alur, R., La Torre, S., Madhusudan, P.: Modular strategies for recursive game graphs. In: Garavel, H., Hatcliff, J. (eds.) TACAS 2003. LNCS, vol. 2619, pp. 363–378. Springer, Heidelberg (2003)
5. Alur, R., La Torre, S., Madhusudan, P.: Modular strategies for recursive game graphs. Theor. Comput. Sci. **354**(2), 230–249 (2006)
6. Alur, R., Madhusudan, P.: Adding nesting structure to words. J. ACM **56**(3), 1–43 (2009)
7. Aminof, B., Mogavero, F., Murano, A.: Synthesis of hierarchical systems. Sci. Comput. Program. **83**, 56–79 (2014)
8. De Crescenzo, I., La Torre, S.: Winning CaRet games with modular strategies. In: CILC. CEUR Workshop Proceedings, vol. 810, pp. 327–331. CEUR-WS.org (2011)
9. De Crescenzo, I., La Torre, S.: Modular synthesis with open components. In: Abdulla, P.A., Potapov, I. (eds.) RP 2013. LNCS, vol. 8169, pp. 96–108. Springer, Heidelberg (2013)
10. De Crescenzo, I., La Torre, S., Velner, Y.: Visibly pushdown modular games. GandALF. EPTCS, vol. 161, pp. 260–274 (2014)
11. Harris, W.R., Jha, S., Reps, T.: Secure programming via visibly pushdown safety games. In: Madhusudan, P., Seshia, S.A. (eds.) CAV 2012. LNCS, vol. 7358, pp. 581–598. Springer, Heidelberg (2012)
12. Jha, S., Gulwani, S., Seshia, S.A., Tiwari, A.: Oracle-guided component-based program synthesis. In: ICSE, pp. 215–224. ACM (2010)
13. Jobstmann, B., Griesmayer, A., Bloem, R.: Program repair as a game. In: Etessami, K., Rajamani, S.K. (eds.) CAV 2005. LNCS, vol. 3576, pp. 226–238. Springer, Heidelberg (2005)
14. Jobstmann, B., Staber, S., Griesmayer, A., Bloem, R.: Finding and fixing faults. J. Comput. Syst. Sci. **78**(2), 441–460 (2012)
15. La Torre, S., Napoli, M., Parente, M., Parlato, G.: Verification of scope-dependent hierarchical state machines. Inf. Comput. **206**(9–10), 1161–1177 (2008)
16. La Torre, S., Parlato, G.: On the complexity of LTL model-checking of recursive state machines. In: Arge, L., Cachin, C., Jurdziński, T., Tarlecki, A. (eds.) ICALP 2007. LNCS, vol. 4596, pp. 937–948. Springer, Heidelberg (2007)
17. Löding, C., Madhusudan, P., Serre, O.: Visibly pushdown games. In: Lodaya, K., Mahajan, M. (eds.) FSTTCS 2004. LNCS, vol. 3328, pp. 408–420. Springer, Heidelberg (2004)
18. Lustig, Y., Vardi, M.Y.: Synthesis from component libraries. In: de Alfaro, L. (ed.) FOSSACS 2009. LNCS, vol. 5504, pp. 395–409. Springer, Heidelberg (2009)
19. Lustig, Y., Vardi, M.Y.: Synthesis from recursive-components libraries. In: GandALF. EPTCS vol. 54, pp. 1–16 (2011)

20. Madhusudan, P.: Synthesizing reactive programs. In: CSL. LIPIcs, vol. 12, pp. 428–442 (2011)
21. Salvati, S., Walukiewicz, I.: Evaluation is MSOL-compatible. In: FSTTCS. LIPIcs, vol. 24, pp. 103–114 (2013)
22. Thomas, W.: Automata on infinite objects. In: Handbook of Theoretical Computer Science, Volume B: Formal Models and Sematics (B), pp. 133–192 (1990)
23. Thomas, W.: Infinite games and verification (Extended abstract of a tutorial). In: Brinksma, E., Larsen, K.G. (eds.) CAV 2002. LNCS, vol. 2404, pp. 58–64. Springer, Heidelberg (2002)
24. Thomas, W.: Facets of synthesis: revisiting church's problem. In: de Alfaro, L. (ed.) FOSSACS 2009. LNCS, vol. 5504, pp. 1–14. Springer, Heidelberg (2009)
25. Walukiewicz, I.: Pushdown processes: Games and model-checking. Inf. Comput. **164**(2), 234–263 (2001)

Solver Improvements

Model Checking with Multi-threaded IC3 Portfolios

Sagar Chaki[1]([✉]) and Derrick Karimi[1,2]

[1] Software Engineering Institute, Carnegie Mellon University, Pittsburgh, USA
chaki@sei.cmu.edu
[2] Carnegie Robotics, Pittsburgh, USA
derrick.karimi@gmail.com

Abstract. Three variants of multi-threaded IC3 are presented. Each variant has a fixed number of IC3s running in parallel, and communicating by sharing lemmas. They differ in the degree of synchronization between threads, and the aggressiveness with which proofs are checked. The correctness of all three variants is shown. The variants have unpredictable runtime. On the same input, the time to find the solution over different runs varies randomly depending on the thread interleaving. The use of a portfolio of solvers to maximize the likelihood of a quick solution is investigated. Using the Extreme Value theorem, the runtime of each variant, as well as their portfolios is analyzed statistically. A formula for the portfolio size needed to achieve a verification time with high probability is derived, and validated empirically. Using a portfolio of 20 parallel IC3s, speedups over 300 are observed compared to the sequential IC3 on hardware model checking competition examples. The use of parameter sweeping to implement a solver that performs well over a wide range of problems with unknown "hardness" is investigated.

1 Introduction

In recent years, IC3 [6] has emerged as a leading algorithm for model checking hardware. It has been refined [10] and incorporated into state-of-the-art tools, and generalized to verify software [8,12]. Our interest is that IC3 is amenable to parallelization [6], and promises new approaches to enhance the capability of model checking by harnessing the abundant computing power available today. Indeed, the original IC3 paper [6] described a parallel version of IC3 informally and reported on its positive performance. In this paper, we build on that work and make three contributions.

First, we formally present three variants – IC3SYNC, IC3ASYNC and IC3PROOF – of parallel IC3, and prove their correctness. All the variants have some common features: (i) they consist of a fixed number of threads that execute in parallel; (ii) each thread learns new lemmas and looks for counterexamples (CEXes) or proofs as in the original IC3; (iii) all lemmas learned by a thread are shared with the other threads to limit duplicated effort; and (iv) if any thread finds a CEX, the overall algorithm declares the problem unsafe and terminates.

© Springer-Verlag Berlin Heidelberg 2016
B. Jobstmann and K.R.M. Leino (Eds.): VMCAI 2016, LNCS 9583, pp. 517–535, 2016.
DOI: 10.1007/978-3-662-49122-5_25

However, the variants differ in the degree of inter-thread synchronization, and the frequency and technique for detecting proofs, making different trade-offs between the overhead and likelihood of proof-detection. Threads in IC3SYNC (cf. Sect. 4.1) synchronize after each round of new lemma generation and propagation, and check for proofs in a centralized manner. Threads in IC3ASYNC (cf. Sect. 4.2) are completely asynchronous. Proof-detection is decentralized and done by each thread periodically. Finally, threads in IC3PROOF are also asynchronous and perform their own proof detection, but more aggressively than IC3ASYNC. Specifically, each thread saves the most recent set of inductive lemmas constructed. When one of the threads finds a new set of inductive lemmas, it checks if the collection of inductive lemmas across all threads form an inductive invariant. Thus, in terms of increasing overhead (and likelihood) of proof-detection, the variants are ordered as follows: IC3SYNC, IC3ASYNC, and IC3PROOF. Collectively, we refer to all three variants as IC3PAR.

The runtime of IC3PAR is unpredictable (this is a known phenomenon [6]). In essence, the number of steps to arrive at a proof (or CEX) is sensitive to the thread interleaving. We propose to counteract this variance using a portfolio – run several IC3PARs in parallel, and stop as soon as any one terminates with an answer. But how large should such a portfolio be? Our second contribution is a statistical analysis to answer this question. Our insight is that the runtime of IC3PAR should follow the Weibull distribution [20] closely. This is because it can be thought of as the *minimum* of the runtimes of the threads in IC3PAR, which are themselves independent and identically distributed (i.i.d.) random variables. According to the Extreme Value theorem [11], the minimum of i.i.d. variables converges to a Weibull. We empirically demonstrate the validity of this claim.

Next, we hoist the same idea to a portfolio of IC3PARs. Again, the runtime of the portfolio should be approximated well by a Weibull, since it is the minimum of the runtime of each IC3PAR in the portfolio. Under this assumption, we derive a formula (cf. Theorem 5) to compute the portfolio size sufficient to solve any problem with a specific probability and speedup compared to a single IC3PAR. For example, this formula implies that a portfolio of 20 IC3PARs has 0.99999 probability of solving a problem in time no more than the "expected time" for a single IC3PAR to solve it. We empirically show (cf. Sect. 6.3) that the predictions based on this formula have high accuracy. Note that each solver in the portfolio potentially searches for a different proof/CEX. The first one to succeed provides the solution. In this way, a portfolio utilizes the power of IC3PAR to search for a wide range of proofs/CEXes without sacrificing performance.

Finally, we implement all three IC3PAR variants, and evaluate them on benchmarks from the 2014 Hardware Model Checking Competition (HMCC14) and the Tip Suite. Using each variant individually, and in portfolios of size 20, we observe that IC3PROOF and IC3ASYNC outperform IC3SYNC. Moreover, compared to a purely sequential IC3, the variants are faster, providing an average speedup of over 6 and a maximum speedup of over 300. We also show that widening the proof search of IC3 by randomizing its SAT solver is not as effective as parallelization. In addition, we evaluate the performance of the parallel version of IC3 reported earlier [6], which we refer to as IC3PAR2010. Experimental results indicate that our parallelization approach is a good complement to IC3PAR2010, and overall outperforms it. Complete details are presented in Sects. 6.1, 6.2 and 6.3.

Next, we note that IC3PAR is paramaterized by the number of threads and SAT solvers. We empirically show that the parameter value affects performance of IC3PAR significantly, and the best parameter choice is located unpredictably in the input space. Thus, for any input problem, the best parameter choice is difficult to compute. However, we show empirically that a "parameter sweeping" [2] solver that executes a randomly selected IC3PAR variant with random parameters is competitive with the best IC3PAR variant with fixed parameters over a range of problems. Complete details are presented in Sect. 6.4.

For brevity, we defer proofs and other supporting material to an extended version of the paper [7]. The rest of the paper is organized as follows. Sect. 2 surveys related work. Sect. 3 presents preliminary definitions. Sect. 4 presents the three variants of parallel IC3. Sect. 5 presents the statistical analysis of the runtime of an IC3PAR solver, as well as a portfolio of such solvers. Sect. 6 presents our experimental results, and Sect. 7 concludes.

2   Related Work

The original IC3 paper [6] presents a parallel version informally, which we call IC3PAR2010, and shows empirically that parallelism can improve verification time. Our IC3PAR solvers were inspired by this work, but are different. For example, the parallel IC3 in [6] implements clause propagation by first distributing learned clauses over all solvers and then propagating them one frame at a time, in lock step. It also introduces uncertainty in the proof search by randomizing the backend SAT solver. Our IC3PAR solvers perform clause propagation asynchronously, and use deterministic SAT solvers. We also present each IC3PAR variant formally with pseudo-code and prove their correctness. In addition, we evaluate the performance of IC3PAR2010 empirically, and show that our parallelization approach provides a good complement to (and overall outperforms) it in terms of speedup. Finally, we go beyond the earlier work on parallelizing IC3 [6] by performing a statistical analysis of the runtimes of both IC3PAR solvers and their portfolios. Experimental results (cf. Sect. 6.1) indicate that a portfolio of IC3PAR solvers is more efficient than a portfolio composed of IC3 solvers with randomized SAT solvers.

A number of projects focus on parallelizing model checking [1,3–5,13,17]. Ditter et al. [9] have developed GPGPU algorithms for explicit-state model checking. They do not report on variance in runtime, nor analyze it statistically like us, or explore the use of portfolios. Lopes et al. [15] do address variance in runtime of a parallel software model checker. However, their approach is to make the model checker's runtime more predictable by ensuring that the counterexample generation procedure is deterministic. They also do not perform any statistical analysis or explore portfolios.

Portfolios have been used successfully in SAT solving [14,16,19,22], SMT solving [21] and symbolic execution [18]. However, these portfolios are composed

of a heterogeneous set of solvers. Our focus is on homogeneous portfolios of
IC3PAR solvers and statistical analysis of their runtimes.

3   Preliminaries

Assume Boolean state variables V, and their primed versions V'. A verification
problem is (I, T, S) where $I(V)$, $T(V, V')$ and $S(V)$ denote initial states, transition relation and safe states, respectively. We omit V when it is clear from the
context, and write S' to mean $S(V')$. Let $Post(X)$ denote the image of $X(V)$
under the transition relation T, i.e., $Post(X) = (\exists V \cdot X \wedge T)[V' \mapsto V]$. Let
$Post^k(X)$ be the result of applying $Post(\cdot)$ k times on X with $Post^0(X) = X$,
and $Post^{k+}(X) = \bigcup_{j \geq k} Post^j(X)$. The verification problem (I, T, S) is safe if
$Post^{0+}(I) \subseteq S$, and unsafe (a.k.a. buggy) otherwise. A "lemma" is a clause (i.e.,
disjunction of minterms) over V, and a "frame" is a set of lemmas.

A random variable X has a Weibull distribution with shape k and scale
λ, denoted $X \sim \text{WEI}(k, \lambda)$, iff its probability density function (pdf) pdf_X and
cumulative distribution function (cdf) cdf_X are defined as follows:

$$pdf_X(x) = \begin{cases} \frac{k}{\lambda}(\frac{x}{\lambda})^{k-1}e^{-(\frac{x}{\lambda})^k} & \text{if } x \geq 0 \\ 0 & \text{if } x < 0 \end{cases} \qquad cdf_X(x) = 1 - e^{-(\frac{x}{\lambda})^k}$$

Let $X_1, \ldots, X_n$ be i.i.d. random variables (rvs) whose pdfs are lower bounded
at zero, i.e., $\forall x < 0 \cdot pdf_{X_i}(x) = 0$. Then, by the Extreme Value theorem [11]
(EVT), the pdf of the rv $X = \min(X_1, \ldots, X_n)$ converges to a Weibull as $n \to \infty$.
The "Gamma" function, Γ, is an extension of the factorial function to real and
complex numbers, with its argument decreased by 1, and is defined as follows:
$\Gamma(t) = \int_{x=0}^{\infty} x^{t-1}e^{-x}dx$.

4   Parallelizing IC3

We begin with a description of the sequential IC3 algorithm. Figure 1 shows its
pseudo-code. IC3 works as follows: (i) checks that no state in $\neg S$ is reachable in 0
or 1 steps from some state in I (lines 16–17); (ii) iteratively construct an array of
frames, each consisting of a set of clauses, as follows: (a) initialize the frame array
and flags (lines 18–19); (b) strengthen() the frames by adding new clauses (line
22); if a counterexample is found in this step (indicated by *bug* being set), IC3
terminates (line 24); (c) otherwise, propagate() clauses that are inductive to
the next frame (line 26); if a proof of safety is found (indicated by an empty
frame), IC3 again terminates (lines 27–28); (d) add a new empty frame to the
end of the array (line 30) and repeat from step (b). In the rest of this paper we
use the term "function" to mean a "procedure", as opposed to a mathematical
function. In particular, we use terms "pdf" and "cdf" to mean probability and
cumulative distribution functions of random variables, respectively.

```
1 //-- global variables
2 var (I,T,S) : problem (P)
3 var F: frame[] (array of frames)
4 var K: int (size of F)
5 var bug: bool (CEX flag)
6
7 //-- invariants
8 ∀i ∈ [0, K − 1], let f(i) =   ⋀        ⋀    α
                             j∈[i,K−1] α∈F[j]
9  A₁ : ∀i ∈ [0, K − 1] . I ⟹ f(i)
10 A₂ : ∀i ∈ [0, K − 2] . f(i) ∧ T ⟹ f'(i + 1)
11 A₃ : ∀i ∈ [0, K − 3] . f(i) ∧ T ⟹ S'
12 A₄ : ∀i ∈ [0, K − 2] . f(i) ∧ T ⟹ S'
13
14 //-- main function.
15 bool IC3 ()
16   if (I ∧ ¬S ≠ ⊥) ∨ (I ∧ T ∧ ¬S' ≠ ⊥)
17     return ⊥;
18   K := 3; F[0] := I; F[1] := ∅;
19   F[2] := ∅; bug := ⊥;
20   while (⊤)
21     @INV{I₁ : A₁ ∧ A₂ ∧ A₃}
22     strengthen(F, K);
23     @INV{I₂ : bug ∨ (A₁ ∧ A₂ ∧ A₄)}
24     if (bug) return ⊥;
25     @INV{I₃ : A₁ ∧ A₂ ∧ A₄}
26     propagate(F, K);
27     if (∃i ∈ [1, K − 2] . F[i] = ∅)
28       return ⊤;
29     @INV{I₃}
30     F[K] := ∅; K := K + 1;
```

```
31 //-- add new lemmas to frames. stop
32 //-- with a CEX or when A₄ holds.
33 void strengthen (F, K)
34   var PQ : priority queue
35   while (⊤)
36     if (f(K − 2) ∧ T ⟹ S') return;
37     let m ⊨ f(K − 2) ∧ T ∧ ¬S';
38     PQ.insert(m, K − 3);
39     while (¬PQ.empty())
40       (m, l) := PQ.top();
41       if (f(l) ∧ T ∧ m' = ⊥)
42         F[l + 1] := F[l + 1] ∪ {¬m};
43         PQ.erase(m, l);
44       else if (l = 0)
45         bug := ⊤; return;
46       else
47         let m₀ ⊨ f(l) ∧ T ∧ m;
48         PQ.insert(m₀, l − 1);
49
50
51 //-- push inductive clauses forward.
52 void propagate (F, K)
53   for i : 1 . . . K − 2
54     for α ∈ F[i]
55       if (f(i) ∧ T ⟹ α')
56         F[i + 1] := F[i + 1] ∪ {α};
57         F[i] := F[i] \ {α};
```

Fig. 1. Pseudo-Code for IC3. Variables are passed by reference, and arrays are indexed from 0. This holds for all the pseudo-code in this article.

Definition 1 (Frame Monotonicity). A function is frame monotonic if at each point during its execution, $\forall i \in [0, K − 1] . f(i) \implies \tilde{f}(i)$ where $\tilde{f}(i)$ is the value of $f(i)$ when the function was called.

Correctness. Figure 1 also shows the invariants (indicated by @INV) before and after strengthen() and propagate(). Since strengthen() always adds new lemmas to frames, it is frame monotonic, and hence it maintains A_1 and A_3. It also maintains A_2 since a new lemma $\neg m$ is added to frame $F[l + 1]$ (line 42) only if $f(l) \wedge T \implies \neg m'$ (line 41). Finally, when strengthen() returns, then either $bug = \top$ (line 45), or $f(K − 2) \wedge T \implies S'$ (line 36). Hence I_2 is a valid post-condition for strengthen(). Also, propagate() is frame monotonic since it always pushes inductive lemmas forward (the order of the two statements at lines 56–57 is crucial for this). Hence, propagate() maintains A_1 and A_4 at all times. It also maintains A_2 since a new lemma α is added to frame $F[i + 1]$ (line 56) only if $f(i) \wedge T \implies \alpha'$ (line 55). Hence I_3 is a valid post-condition for propagate(). Finally, note that $A_4 \equiv A_3 \wedge f[K − 2] \implies S$. Hence, after $\mathbf{K}$ is incremented, A_4 becomes A_3. Also, since the last frame is initialized to $\emptyset$, A_1 and A_2 are preserved. Hence: $\{I_3\}\mathbf{F[K]} := \emptyset; \mathbf{K} := \mathbf{K} + 1; \{I_1\}$. The correctness of IC3 is summarized by Theorem 1. Its proof is in the appendix of [7].

Theorem 1. *If IC3() returns ⊤, then the problem is safe. If IC3() returns ⊥, then the problem is unsafe.*

```
58 //-- global variables               72 bool IC3Sync (n)
59 var (I,T,S) : problem (P)           73   if (I ∧ ¬S ≠ ⊥) ∨ (I ∧ T ∧ ¬S' ≠ ⊥)
60 var ∀i ∈ [1,n].Fᵢ: frame[]          74     return ⊥;
61 var K: int (size of each Fᵢ)        75   K := 3; bug := ⊥;
62 var bug: bool (CEX flag)            76   ∀i ∈ [1,n].Fᵢ[0] := I; Fᵢ[1] := Fᵢ[2] := ∅;
63                                     77   while (⊤)
64 //-- invariants                     78     @INV{𝓘₄ : B₁ ∧ B₂ ∧ B₃}
65 ∀j ∈ [0,K − 1], let                 79     {strengthen(F₁,K);propagate(F₁,K)}
66   f(j) =  ⋀     ⋀      ⋀    α        80              ‖ ⋯ ‖
           i∈[1,n] k∈[j,K−1] α∈Fᵢ[k]   81     {strengthen(Fₙ,K);propagate(Fₙ,K)};
67                                     82     @INV{𝓘₅ : bug ∨ (B₁ ∧ B₂ ∧ B₄)}
68 B₁ : ∀j ∈ [0,K − 1].I ⟹ f(j)        83     if (bug) return ⊥;
69 B₂ : ∀j ∈ [0,K − 2].f(j) ∧ T ⟹ f'(j + 1)  84     @INV{𝓘₆ : B₁ ∧ B₂ ∧ B₄}
70 B₃ : ∀j ∈ [0,K − 3].f(j) ∧ T ⟹ S'   85     if (∃j ∈ [1,K − 2].∀i ∈ [1,n].Fᵢ[j] = ∅)
71 B₄ : ∀j ∈ [0,K − 2].f(j) ∧ T ⟹ S'   86       return ⊤;
                                      87     @INV{𝓘₆}
                                      88     ∀i ∈ [1,n].Fᵢ[K] := ∅; K := K + 1;
```

Fig. 2. Pseudo-Code for IC3SYNC(n). Functions strengthen() and propagate() are defined in Fig. 1.

We now present the three versions of parallel IC3 and their correctness (their termination follows in the same way as IC3 [6] – see Theorem 5 in the appendix of [7]).

4.1 Synchronous Parallel IC3

The first parallelized version of IC3, denoted IC3SYNC, runs a number of copies of the sequential IC3 "synchronously" in parallel. Let IC3SYNC(n) be the instance of IC3SYNC consisting of n copies of IC3 executing concurrently. The copies maintain separate frames. However, for any copy, the frames of other copies act as "background lemmas". Specifically, the copies interact by: (i) using the frames of all other copies when computing $f(i)$; (ii) declaring the problem unsafe if any copy finds a counterexample; (iii) declaring the problem safe if some frame becomes empty across all the copies; and (iv) "synchronizing" after each call to strengthen() and propagate().

The pseudo-code for IC3SYNC(n) is shown in Fig. 2. The main function is IC3Sync(). After checking the base cases (lines 73–74), it initializes flags and frames (lines 75–76), and then iteratively performs the following steps: (i) run n copies IC3 where each copy does a single step of strengthen() followed by propagate() (lines 79–81); (ii) check if any copy of IC3 found a counterexample, and if so, terminate (line 83); (iii) check if a proof of safety has been found, and if so, terminate (lines 85–86); and (iv) add a frame and repeat from step (i) above (line 88). Functions strengthen() and propagate() are syntactically identical to IC3 (cf. Fig. 1). However, the key semantic difference is that lemmas from all copies are used to define $f(j)$ (lines 65–66). Global variables are shared, and accessed atomically. Note that even though all IC3 copies write to variable bug, there is no race condition since they always write the same value ($\top$).

Correctness. The correctness of IC3SYNC follows from the invariants specified in Fig. 2. To show these invariants are valid, the main challenge is to show that if $\mathcal{I}_4$ holds at line 78, then $\mathcal{I}_5$ holds at line 82. Note that since strengthen()

and `propagate()` are frame monotonic, they preserve B_1 and B_3. This means that $B_1 \wedge B_3$ holds at line 82. Now suppose that at line 82, we have $\neg bug$. This means that each `strengthen()` called at lines 79–81 returned from line 36. Thus, the condition $f(\mathbf{K} - 2) \wedge T \implies S'$ was established at some point, and once established, it continues to hold due to the frame monotonicity of `strengthen()` and `propagate()`. Since $B_4 \equiv B_3 \wedge (f(\mathbf{K} - 2) \wedge T \implies S')$, we therefore know that $B_1 \wedge B_4$ holds at line 82. Also, B_2 holds at line 82 since a new lemma α is only added to frame $F_i[j+1]$ by `strengthen()` (line 42) and `propagate()` (line 56) under the condition $f(j) \wedge T \implies \alpha'$. Note that once $f(j) \wedge T \implies \alpha'$ is true, it continues to hold even in the concurrent setting due to frame monotonicity. Finally, the statement at line 88 transforms $\mathcal{I}_6$ to $\mathcal{I}_4$. The correctness of IC3SYNC is summarized by Theorem 2. Its proof is in the appendix of [7].

Theorem 2. *If* `IC3Sync()` *returns* $\top$, *then the problem is safe. If* `IC3Sync()` *returns* $\bot$, *then the problem is unsafe.*

```
89  //-- invariants
90  ∀j ∈ [0, max(K₁,...,Kₙ) − 1], let
91     f(j) =  ⋀       ⋀         ⋀   α
              i∈[1,n] k∈[j,Kᵢ−1] α∈Fᵢ[k]
92
93  C₁ : ∀j ∈ [0, Kᵢ − 1] . I  ⟹  f(j)
94  C₂ : ∀j ∈ [0, Kᵢ − 2] . f(j) ∧ T  ⟹  f'(j + 1)
95  C₃ : ∀j ∈ [0, Kᵢ − 3] . f(j) ∧ T  ⟹  S'
96  C₄ : ∀j ∈ [0, Kᵢ − 2] . f(j) ∧ T  ⟹  S'
97
98
99
100 //-- top-level function
101 bool IC3Async (n)
102    if (I ∧ ¬S ≠ ⊥) ∨ (I ∧ T ∧ ¬S' ≠ ⊥)
103       return ⊥;
104    bug := ⊥;
105    IC3Copy(1) ◇ ··· ◇ IC3Copy(n);
106    return bug ? ⊥ : ⊤;
```

```
107 //-- global variables
108 var (I, T, S) : problem (P)
109 var ∀i ∈ [1, n] . Fᵢ : frame []
110 var ∀i ∈ [1, n] . Kᵢ : int (size of Fᵢ)
111 var bug : bool (CEX flag)
112
113 void IC3Copy (i)
114    Kᵢ := 3; Fᵢ[0] := I;
115    Fᵢ[1] := ∅; Fᵢ[2] := ∅;
116    while (⊤)
117       @INV{I₇ : C₁ ∧ C₂ ∧ C₃}
118       strengthen(Fᵢ, Kᵢ);
119       @INV{I₈ : bug ∨ (C₁ ∧ C₂ ∧ C₄)}
120       if (bug) return;
121       @INV{I₉ : C₁ ∧ C₂ ∧ C₄}
122       propagate(Fᵢ, Kᵢ);
123       if (∃j ∈ [1, Kᵢ − 2] . ∀l ∈ [1, n] . Fₗ[j] = ∅)
124          return;
125       @INV{I₉}
126       Fᵢ[Kᵢ] := ∅; Kᵢ := Kᵢ + 1;
```

Fig. 3. Pseudo-Code for IC3ASYNC(n). Functions `strengthen()` and `propagate()` are defined in Fig. 1.

4.2 Asynchronous Parallel IC3

The next parallelized version of IC3, denoted IC3ASYNC, runs a number of copies of the sequential IC3 "asynchronously" in parallel. Let IC3ASYNC(n) be the instance of IC3ASYNC consisting of n copies of IC3 executing concurrently. Similar to IC3SYNC, the copies maintain separate frames, interact by sharing lemmas when computing $f(i)$, and declare the problem unsafe if any copy finds a counterexample. However, due to the lack of synchronization, proof detection is distributed over all the copies instead of being centralized in the main thread.

Figure 3 shows the pseudo-code for IC3ASYNC(n). The main function is `IC3Async()`. After checking the base cases (lines 102–103), it initializes flags (line 104), launches n copies of IC3 in parallel (line 105) and waits for some copy to terminate (the $\diamond$ operator), and checks the flag and returns with an appropriate result (line 106). Function IC3Copy() is similar to IC3() in Fig. 1. The key difference is that lemmas from all copies are used to compute $f(j)$ (lines 90–91).

Correctness. The correctness of IC3ASYNC follows from the invariants specified in Fig. 3. To see why these invariants are valid, note that C_1 and C_3 are always preserved due to frame monotonicity. If strengthen() returns with $bug = \bot$, then it returned from line 36, and hence $f(\mathbf{K}_i - 2) \wedge T \implies S'$ was true at some point in the past and continues to hold due to frame monotonicity. Together with C_3, this implies that C_4 holds at line 119. Also, C_2 holds at line 119 since a new lemma α is only added to frame $F_i[j+1]$ by strengthen() (line 42) and propagate() (line 56) under the condition $f(j) \wedge T \implies \alpha'$. Note that once $f(j) \wedge T \implies \alpha'$ is true, it continues to hold even under concurrency due to frame monotonicity. Hence, $\mathcal{I}_8$ holds at line 119. Since bug is never set to $\bot$ after line 104, this means that $\mathcal{I}_9$ holds at line 121 even under concurrency. Finally, the statement at line 126 transforms $\mathcal{I}_9$ to $\mathcal{I}_7$. The correctness of IC3ASYNC is summarized by Theorem 3. Its proof is in the appendix of [7].

Theorem 3. *If* IC3Async() *returns* $\top$, *then the problem is safe. If* IC3Async() *returns* $\bot$, *then the problem is unsafe.*

```
127 //-- global variables
128 var (I,T,S) : problem (P)
129 var ∀i ∈ [1,n].Fᵢ,Pᵢ: frame[]
130 var ∀i ∈ [1,n].Kᵢ: int (size of Fᵢ and Pᵢ)
131 var bug,safe: bool (CEX and proof flags)
132
133
134 void IC3PrCopy (i)
135     Kᵢ := 3; Fᵢ[0] := I;
136     Fᵢ[1] := ∅; Fᵢ[2] := ∅;
137     while (⊤)
138         @INV{I₇ : C₁ ∧ C₂ ∧ C₃}
139         strengthen(Fᵢ,Kᵢ);
140         @INV{I₈ : bug ∨ (C₁ ∧ C₂ ∧ C₄)}
141         if (bug) return;
142         @INV{I₉ : C₁ ∧ C₂ ∧ C₄}
143         propProof(Fᵢ,Kᵢ);
144         if (safe) return;
145         @INV{I₉}
146         Fᵢ[Kᵢ] := ∅; Kᵢ := Kᵢ + 1;
```

```
147 bool IC3Proof (n)
148     if (I ∧ ¬S ≠ ⊥) ∨ (I ∧ T ∧ ¬S' ≠ ⊥)
149         return ⊥;
150     bug := ⊥; safe := ⊥;
151     IC3PrCopy(1) ◇ ··· ◇ IC3PrCopy(n);
152     return bug ? ⊥ : ⊤;
153
154 void propProof(F,K)
155     for j : 1...K − 2
156         for α ∈ F[j]
157             if (f(j) ∧ T ⟹ α')
158                 F[j+1] := F[j+1] ∪ {α};
159                 F[j] := F[j] \ {α};
160             if (F[j] = ∅)
161                 Pⱼ := ⋃_{j<k≤K−1} F[k];
162                 Π := ⋃_{{i|1≤i≤n∧j<Kᵢ}} Pᵢ;
163                 if (Π ∧ T ⟹ Π')
164                     safe := ⊤; return;
```

Fig. 4. Pseudo-Code for IC3PROOF(n). Function strengthen() is defined in Fig. 1. Formulas $f(j), \mathcal{I}_7, \mathcal{I}_8$, and $\mathcal{I}_9$ are defined in Fig. 3.

4.3 Asynchronous Parallel IC3 with Proof-Checking

The final parallelized version of IC3, denoted IC3PROOF, is similar to IC3ASYNC, but performs more aggressive checking for proofs. Let IC3PROOF(n) be the instance of IC3PROOF consisting of n copies of IC3 executing concurrently. Similar to IC3ASYNC, the copies maintain separate frames, interact by sharing lemmas when computing $f(i)$, and declare the problem unsafe if any copy finds a counterexample. However, whenever a copy finds an empty frame, it checks whether the set of lemmas over all the copies for that frame forms an inductive invariant.

The pseudo-code for IC3PROOF(n) is shown in Fig. 4. The main function is IC3Proof(). After checking the base cases (lines 148–149), it initializes flags (line 150), launches n copies of IC3 in parallel (line 151) and waits for at least one copy to terminate, and checks the flag and returns with an appropriate result (line 152). Function IC3PrCopy is similar to IC3 in Fig. 1, but calls propProof() instead of propagate() where, once an empty frame is detected (line 160), we check whether a proof has been found by collecting the lemmas for that frame (lines 161–162), and checking if these lemmas are inductive (line 163).

Correctness. The correctness of IC3PROOF follows from the invariants (whose validity is similar to those for IC3ASYNC) specified in Fig. 4. It is summarized by Theorem 4. The proof of the theorem is in the appendix of [7].

Theorem 4. *If* IC3Proof() *returns* $\top$, *then the problem is safe. If* IC3Proof() *returns* $\bot$, *then the problem is unsafe.*

5   Parallel IC3 Portfolios

In this section, we investigate the question of how a good portfolio size can be selected if we want to implement a portfolio of IC3PARs. We begin with an argument about the pdf of the runtime of IC3ASYNC(n).

Conjecture 1. The runtime of IC3ASYNC(n) converges to a Weibull rv as $n \to \infty$.

Argument: Recall that each execution of IC3ASYNC(n) consists of n copies of IC3 running in parallel, and that IC3ASYNC(n) stops as soon as one copy finds a solution. We can consider the runtime of each copy of IC3 to be a rv. Specifically, let rv X_i be the runtime of the i-th copy of IC3 under the environment provided by the other $n - 1$ copies. Recall that the pdf of X_i has a lower bound of 0, since no run of IC3 can take negative time. Also, for the sake of argument, assume that $(X_1, \ldots, X_n)$ are i.i.d. since the interaction between the copies of IC3 is logical and symmetric. Finally, let X be the random variable denoting the runtime of IC3ASYNC(n). Note that $X = \min(X_1, \ldots, X_n)$. Hence, by the EVT, $X \sim \text{WEI}(k, \lambda)$ for large n. $\square$

A similar argument holds for IC3SYNC and IC3PROOF, and therefore their runtime should follow Weibull as well. Indeed, despite the assumption of $(X_1, \ldots, X_n)$ being i.i.d., we empirically find that the runtime of IC3PAR(n) follows a Weibull distribution closely for even modest values of n. Specifically, we selected 10 examples (5 safe and 5 buggy) from HWMCC14, and for each example we:

1. Executed IC3ASYNC(4) "around" 3000 times (we actually ran each example 3000 times but some timed out – the exact number of timeouts varied across examples);
2. Measured the runtimes;

Example	IC3SYNC (4)				IC3ASYNC (4)				IC3PROOF (4)			
	k	λ	μ,μ^*	σ,σ^*	k	λ	μ,μ^*	σ,σ^*	k	λ	μ,μ^*	σ,σ^*
6s286	4.07	1119	1015,1015	280,274	4.44	990	902,903	230,220	4.35	980	892,892	232,228
intel026	2.71	49.0	43.6,44.2	17.3,14.6	3.70	50.2	45.3,46.2	13.6,10.1	3.70	50.1	45.2,46.1	13.6,10.3
6s273	3.80	26.1	23.6,23.6	6.93,6.57	4.11	23.5	21.3,21.4	5.85,5.36	4.17	23.3	21.2,21.3	5.73,5.29
intel057	6.58	16.0	14.9,15.1	2.66,2.11	7.31	17.2	16.1,16.1	2.60,2.46	7.52	17.8	16.7,16.9	2.63,2.07
intel054	7.82	24.3	22.8,23.0	3.46,2.94	8.69	26.1	24.6,24.8	3.38,2.84	9.26	26.1	24.7,24.8	3.20,2.92
6s215	2.38	7.69	6.82,7.03	3.05,2.34	4.71	6.75	6.17,6.21	1.49,1.34	4.72	6.38	5.84,5.90	1.41,1.21
6s216	1.95	35.1	31.1,31.0	16.6,16.9	3.56	27.5	24.8,24.9	7.74,6.97	2.78	28.1	25.0,25.1	9.74,9.05
oski3ub1i	5.98	54.9	50.9,51.4	9.90,7.90	7.02	52.3	48.9,49.2	8.20,6.71	4.78	54.8	50.2,50.8	11.9,9.53
oski3ub3i	5.71	52.4	48.5,48.9	9.84,8.00	5.51	52.2	48.2,48.6	10.1,8.51	5.66	52.2	48.2,48.5	9.87,8.39
oski3ub5i	5.08	66.8	61.4,61.9	13.8,11.6	4.94	67.2	61.6,62.0	11.4,12.4	4.93	66.2	60.7,61.1	14.0,12.1
SAFE	5.00	246	224,224	62.1,60.2	5.65	221	202,202	51.1,48.3	5.80	219	200,200	51.4,49.7
BUG	4.22	43.4	39.7,40.0	10.6,9.37	5.15	41.2	37.9,38.2	8.36,7.20	4.58	41.5	38.0,38.3	9.42,8.07
ALL	4.61	145	131,132	36.4,34.7	5.40	131	120,120	29.7,27.7	5.19	130	119,119	30.4,28.9

Fig. 5. Fitting IC3PAR(4) runtime to Weibull. First 5 examples are safe, next 5 are buggy; SAFE, BUG, ALL = average over safe, buggy, and all examples; $\mu, \mu^* = $ predicted, observed mean; $\sigma, \sigma^* = $ predicted, observed standard deviation.

3. Estimated the k and λ values for the Weibull distribution that best fits these values (using maximum likelihood estimation and the R statistical tool); and
4. Computed the observed mean and standard deviation from the data, and the predicted mean and standard deviation from the k and λ estimates.

We repeated these experiments with IC3SYNC and IC3PROOF. The results are shown in Fig. 5. We see that in all cases, the observed mean and standard deviation is quite close to the predicted ones, indicating that the estimated Weibull distribution is a good fit for the measured runtimes. IC3ASYNC and IC3PROOF have similar performance, are and slightly faster overall than IC3SYNC, indicating that additional synchronization is counter-productive. The estimated k and λ values vary widely over the examples, indicating their diversity. Note that smaller values of λ mean a smaller expected runtime.

Determining Portfolio Size. Consider a portfolio of IC3PARs. In general, increasing the size of the portfolio reduces the expected time to solve a problem. However, there is diminishing returns to adding more solvers to a portfolio in terms of expected runtime. We now express this mathematically, and derive a formula for computing a portfolio size to achieve an runtime with a target probability. Consider a portfolio of m IC3PAR solvers run on a specific problem. Let Y_i denote the runtime of the i-th IC3PAR. From previous discussion we know that $Y_i \sim \text{WEI}(k, \lambda)$ for some k and λ. Therefore, the cdf of Y_i is: $cdf_{Y_i}(x) = 1 - e^{-(\frac{x}{\lambda})^k}$. Note that Y_i refers to an instance of IC3PAR, whereas X_i, used before, referred to a single thread (executing a copy of IC3) within an instance of IC3PAR.

Let Y be the rv denoting the runtime of the portfolio. Thus, we have $Y = \min(Y_1, \ldots, Y_m)$. More importantly, the cdf of Y is:

$$cdf_Y(x) = 1 - (1 - cdf_{Y_1}(x)) \times \cdots \times (1 - cdf_{Y_m}(x))$$

$$= 1 - (e^{-(\frac{x}{\lambda})^k})^m = 1 - e^{-m(\frac{x}{\lambda})^k} = 1 - e^{-(\frac{xm^{\frac{1}{k}}}{\lambda})^k}$$

Note that this means Y is also a Weibull rv, not just when $m \to \infty$ (as per the EVT) but for all m. More specifically, $Y \sim \text{WEI}(k, \frac{\lambda}{m^{\frac{1}{k}}})$. Recall that if $m = 1$, then the expected time to solve the problem by the portfolio is $E[Y_1]$. We refer to this time as t^*, the expected solving time for a single IC3PAR. Recall the Gamma function Γ. Since $Y_1 \sim \text{WEI}(k, \lambda)$, it is known that $t^* = \lambda \Gamma(1 + \frac{1}{k})$. Now, we come to our result, which expresses the probability that a portfolio of m IC3PARs will require no more than t^* to solve the problem.

Theorem 5. *Let $p(m)$ be the probability that $Y \leq t^*$. Then $p(m) > 1 - e^{-\frac{m}{e^{\gamma}}}$ where $\gamma \approx 0.57721$ is the Euler-Mascheroni constant.*

Proof. We know that:

$$p(m) = cdf_Y(t^*) = 1 - e^{-m(\Gamma(1+\frac{1}{k}))^k} = 1 - (\alpha(k))^m, \text{ where } \alpha(k) = e^{-(\Gamma(1+\frac{1}{k}))^k}$$

Next, observe that $\alpha(k)$ increases monotonically with k but does not diverge as $k \to \infty$. For example, Fig. 11 in the appendix of [7] shows a plot of $\alpha(k)$. Since we want to prove an lower bound on $p(m)$, let us consider the limiting case $k \to \infty$. It can be shown that (see Lemma 2 in the appendix of [7]): $\lim_{k \to \infty} \alpha(k) = e^{-\frac{1}{e^{\gamma}}}$. In practice, as seen in Fig. 11 in the appendix of [7], the value of $\alpha(k)$ converges quite rapidly to this limit as k increases. For example, $\alpha(5) > 0.91 \cdot e^{-\frac{1}{e^{\gamma}}}$, and $\alpha(10) > 0.95 \cdot e^{-\frac{1}{e^{\gamma}}}$. Since $\forall k \, . \, \alpha(k) < e^{-\frac{1}{e^{\gamma}}}$, we have our result:

$$p(m) > 1 - (e^{-\frac{1}{e^{\gamma}}})^m = 1 - e^{-\frac{m}{e^{\gamma}}} \qquad \square$$

Achieving a Target Probability. Now suppose we want $p(m)$ to be greater than some target probability p. Then, from Theorem 5, we have:

$$p = 1 - (e^{-\frac{1}{e^{\gamma}}})^m \iff 1 - p = e^{-\frac{m}{e^{\gamma}}} \iff \ln(1-p) = -\frac{m}{e^{\gamma}}$$
$$\iff \ln(\frac{1}{1-p}) = \frac{m}{e^{\gamma}} \iff m = e^{\gamma} \ln(\frac{1}{1-p})$$

For example, if we want $p = 0.99999$, then $m \approx 20$. Thus, a portfolio of 20 IC3PARs has about 0.99999 probability of solving a problem at least as quickly as the expected time in which a single IC3PAR will solve it. We validated the efficacy of Theorem 5 by comparing its predictions with empirically observed results on the HWMCC14 benchmarks. Overall, we find the observed and predicted probabilities to agree significantly. Further details are presented in Sect. 6.3.

Speeding Up the Portfolio. To reduce the portfolio's runtime below t^*, we must increase m appropriately. In general, for any constant $c \in [0, 1]$, the probability that a portfolio of m IC3PAR solvers will have a runtime $\leq c \cdot t^*$ is given by:

$$p(m, c, k) = 1 - e^{-m(c \cdot \Gamma(1+\frac{1}{k}))^k}$$

For $c < 1$ we do not have a closed form for $\lim_{k \to \infty} p(m, c, k)$, unlike when $c = 1$. However, the value of $p(m, c, k)$ is computable for fixed m, c and k. Figure 6(a) plots $p(m, c, 4)$ for $m = \{1, \ldots, 100\}$ and $c = \{0.4, 0.5, 0.6\}$. Figure 6(b) plots

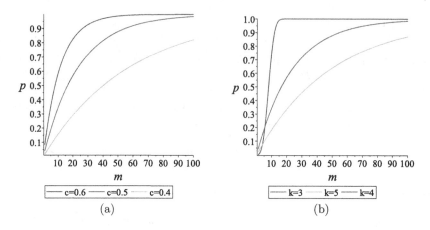

Fig. 6. (a) $p(m, c, 4)$ for different values of c; (b) $p(m, .5, k)$ for different values of k.

$p(m, .5, k)$ for $m = \{1, \ldots, 100\}$ and $k = \{3, 4, 5\}$. As expected, $p(m, c, k)$ increases with: (i) increasing m; (ii) increasing c; and (iii) decreasing k. One challenge here is that we do not know how to estimate k for a problem without actually solving it. In general, a smaller value of k means that a smaller portfolio will reach the target probability. In our experiments – recall Fig. 5 – we observed k-values in a tight range (1–10) for problems from HWMCC14. These numbers can serve as guidelines, and be refined based on additional experimentation.

6   Experimental Results

We implemented IC3SYNC, IC3ASYNC and IC3PROOF by modifying a publicly available reference implementation of IC3 (https://github.com/arbrad/IC3ref), which we call IC3REF. All propositional queries in IC3 are implemented by calls to MINISAT. We refer to the variant of IC3REF that uses a randomized MINISAT as IC3RND. We use IC3RND to introduce uncertainty in IC3 purely by randomizing the backend SAT solver. We performed two experiments – one to evaluate the effectiveness of the IC3PAR variants, and another to validate our statistical analysis of their portfolios. All our tools and results are available at http://www.andrew.cmu.edu/~schaki/misc/paric3.tgz.

Benchmarks. We constructed four benchmarks. The first was constructed by preprocessing the safe examples from HWMCC14 (http://fmv.jku.at/hwmcc14cav) with IIMC (http://ecee.colorado.edu/wpmu/iimc), and selecting the ones solved by IC3REF within 900 s on a 8 core 3.4 GHz machine with 8GB of RAM. The remaining three benchmarks were constructed similarly from the buggy examples from HWMCC14, and the safe and buggy examples (without pre-processing) from the TIP benchmark suite (http://fmv.jku.at/aiger/tip-aig-20061215.zip). We refer to the four benchmarks as HWCSAFE, HWCBUG, TIPSAFE and TIPBUG, respectively.

SAT Solver Pool. The function f (cf. Fig. 1–4) is implemented in IC3REF by a SAT solver (MINISAT). A separate SAT solver S_i is used for each $f(i)$. Whenever $f(i)$ changes due to the addition of a new lemma to a frame, the corresponding solver S_i is also updated by asserting the lemma. To avoid a single SAT solver from becoming the bottleneck between competing threads in IC3PAR, we use a "pool" of MINISAT solvers to implement each S_i. The solvers are maintained in a FIFO queue. When a thread requests a solver, the first available solver is given to it. When a lemma is added to the pool, it is added to all available solvers, and recorded as "pending" for the busy ones. When a busy solver is released by a thread, all pending lemmas are first asserted to it, and then it is inserted at the back of the queue. We refer to the number of solvers in each pool as $SPSz$.

6.1   Comparing Parallel IC3 Variants

These experiments were carried on a Intel Xeon machine with 128 cores, each running at 2.67 GHz, and 1TB of RAM. For each solver selected from $\{\text{IC3ASYNC}(4), \text{IC3SYNC}(4), \text{IC3PROOF}(4), \text{IC3RND}\}$ and each benchmark $\mathcal{B}$, and with $SPSz = 3$, we performed the following steps:

1. extract all problems from $\mathcal{B}$ that are solved by IC3REF in at least 10 s; call this set $\mathcal{B}^*$; the cutoff of 10 s was a tradeoff between problem complexity and benchmark size; our goal was to avoid evaluating our approach on very simple examples to limit measurement errors, and also to have enough examples for statistically meaningful results;
2. solve each problem in $\mathcal{B}^*$ with IC3REF and also with a portfolio of 20 solvers, compute the ratio of the two runtimes; this is the speedup for the specific problem;
3. compute the mean and max of the speedups over all problems in $\mathcal{B}^*$.

Figure 7(a) shows the results obtained. In all cases, we see speedup. On this particular run, IC3PROOF performs best overall, with an average speedup of over 6 and a maximum speedup of over 300. As in the non-portfolio case

$\mathcal{B}$	$|\mathcal{B}^*|$	IC3SYNC		IC3ASYNC		IC3PROOF		IC3RND	
		Mean	Max	Mean	Max	Mean	Max	Mean	Max
HWCSAFE	31	1.30	5.61	1.58	5.47	1.60	4.08	1.17	4.64
HWCBUG	14	2.49	18.7	14.3	151	25.1	309	1.07	1.49
TIPSAFE	14	1.28	4.50	2.61	11.1	2.29	12.8	1.37	3.80
TIPBUG	9	2.23	5.35	2.82	7.32	3.50	12.1	1.16	2.17
SAFE	44	1.30	5.61	1.93	11.1	1.83	12.8	1.24	4.64
BUG	23	2.38	18.7	9.58	151	16.3	309	1.11	2.17
ALL	67	1.67	18.7	4.74	151	6.79	309	1.19	4.64

$\mathcal{B}$	$|\mathcal{B}^+|$	IC3PAR2010	
		Mean	Max
HWCSAFE	20	2.67	14.40
HWCBUG	15	1.62	3.91
TIPSAFE	14	.89	1.82
TIPBUG	7	1.32	1.67
SAFE	34	1.94	14.40
BUG	22	1.52	3.91
ALL	56	1.77	14.40

(a)   (b)

Fig. 7. (a) Speedup of IC3SYNC, IC3ASYNC, IC3PROOF and IC3RND compared to IC3REF; (b) Speedup of IC3PAR2010 compared to IC3REF2010.

(cf. Fig. 5) IC3PROOF and IC3ASYNC have similar performance, and are better than IC3SYNC. The pattern is followed for both safe and buggy examples. Finally, IC3RND provides mediocre speedup (not just on the whole, but across all examples) indicating that parallelization enables better search for shorter proofs/CEXes compared to randomizing the SAT solver.

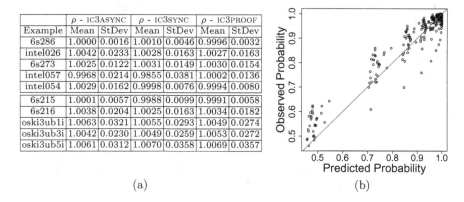

	ρ - IC3ASYNC		ρ - IC3SYNC		ρ - IC3PROOF	
Example	Mean	StDev	Mean	StDev	Mean	StDev
6s286	1.0000	0.0016	1.0010	0.0046	0.9996	0.0032
intel026	1.0042	0.0233	1.0028	0.0163	1.0027	0.0163
6s273	1.0025	0.0122	1.0031	0.0149	1.0030	0.0154
intel057	0.9968	0.0214	0.9855	0.0381	1.0002	0.0136
intel054	1.0029	0.0162	0.9998	0.0076	0.9994	0.0080
6s215	1.0001	0.0057	0.9988	0.0099	0.9991	0.0058
6s216	1.0038	0.0204	1.0025	0.0163	1.0034	0.0182
oski3ub1i	1.0063	0.0321	1.0055	0.0293	1.0049	0.0274
oski3ub3i	1.0042	0.0230	1.0049	0.0259	1.0053	0.0272
oski3ub5i	1.0061	0.0312	1.0070	0.0358	1.0069	0.0357

(a)   (b)

Fig. 8. Validating Theorem 5; (a) mean and standard deviation of ratios of predicted and observed probabilities; (b) scatter plot of predicted and observed probabilities.

6.2   Comparing IC3PAR2010

We compared the parallel version of IC3 reported in the original paper [6], which we refer to as IC3PAR2010, with our IC3PAR variants. We first downloaded the source code[1] of IC3PAR2010. It comes with its own version of IC3 implemented in Ocaml, which we refer to as IC3REF2010. The parallelization in IC3PAR2010 is implemented via three Python scripts that invoke the IC3 binary. We modified these scripts to implement a solver with four copies of IC3 running in parallel. This was done for a fairer comparison with our IC3PAR results presented earlier which also used four copies of IC3 per solver. In addition, we made other changes to the scripts to make the solver more robust (e.g., replacing hard coded TCP/IP port numbers with dynamically selected ones). All experiments were done on the same machine as in Sect. 6.1.

While IC3REF was quite deterministic in its runtime, IC3REF2010 demonstrated random behavior in this respect. One source of this randomness is that IC3REF2010 randomizes the backend SAT solver. However, there could be other sources of randomness due to the management of the priority queue during strengthen(). We were unable to eliminate the randomness satisfactorily via command line options. Instead, we accounted for it by running experiments multiple times and computing the average. We computed the speedup of IC3PAR2010 using a similar process as for the IC3PAR variants. Specifically, we performed the following steps:

---

[1] http://ecee.colorado.edu/~bradleya/ic3/ic3.tar.gz.

1. extract all problems from $\mathcal{B}$ that are solved by IC3REF2010 in at least 10s; call this set $\mathcal{B}^+$; note that $\mathcal{B}^+$ differs from $\mathcal{B}^*$ since the underlying solvers – IC3REF2010 and IC3REF – have different solving capability.
2. solve each problem in $\mathcal{B}^+$ with IC3REF2010 twenty times and compute the average runtime (call this t_s) and also with IC3PAR2010 twenty times and compute the average runtime (call this t_p); compute the ratio $\frac{t_s}{t_p}$; this is the speedup with IC3PAR2010 for that specific problem;
3. compute the mean and max of the speedups over all problems in $\mathcal{B}^+$.

Figure 7(b) shows the results obtained. Comparing with Fig. 7(a), we see that all three of our IC3PAR invariants provided considerably better speedups compared to IC3PAR2010 on the three benchmark groups HWCBUG, TIPSAFE and TIPBUG. Indeed, for the TIPSAFE group as a whole, IC3PAR2010 does not provide a speedup. However, for the HWCSAFE group, IC3PAR2010 provided better speedups. If we look at all the safe examples, then IC3PAR2010 edges out IC3PAR marginally. In contrast, for unsafe examples IC3PAR provides much better speedups. Overall, IC3PROOF performs best. In summary, portfolios of IC3PAR variants appear to be a good complement to IC3PAR2010, and a better option for unsafe examples.

6.3   Portfolio Size

These experiments were done on a cluster of 11 machines, each with 16 cores at 2.4 GHz, and between 48 GB and 190 GB of RAM. To validate Theorem 5, we compared its predictions to empirically observed results as follows (again using $SPSz = 3$):

1. Process each problem from Fig. 5 as follows.
2. Solve the problem b (≈ 3000) times using IC3PAR(4). This gives a set of runtimes $t_1, \ldots, t_b$. Fit these runtimes to a Weibull distribution to obtain the estimated value of k (the same as the second column of Fig. 5).
3. Compute $\tilde{t} = \text{mean}(t_1, \ldots, t_b)$. This is the estimated average time for IC3PAR(4) to solve the problem.
4. Pick a portfolio size m. Start with $m = 1$.
5. Divide $t_1, \ldots, t_b$ into blocks of size m. Let $B = \lfloor \frac{b}{m} \rfloor$. We now have B blocks of runtime $T_1, \ldots, T_B$, each consisting of m elements. Thus, $T_1 = \{t_1, \ldots, t_m\}$, $T_2 = \{t_{m+1}, \ldots, t_{2m}\}$, and so on. For $i = 1, \ldots, B$, compute $\mu_i = \min(T_i)$. Note that each μ_i is the runtime of a portfolio of m IC3PAR(4) solvers.
6. Let $n(m)$ be the number of blocks for which $\mu_i \leq \tilde{t}$, i.e., $n(m) = |$ $\{i \in [1, B] \mid \mu_i \leq \tilde{t}\}|$. Compute $p^*(m) = \frac{n(m)}{B}$. Note that $p^*(m)$ is the estimate of $p(m)$ based on our experiments. Compute $p(m) = 1 - (\alpha(k))^m$ (use k from Step 2). Compute $\rho(m) = \frac{p^*(m)}{p(m)}$. We expect $\rho(m) \approx 1$.
7. Repeat steps 5 and 6 with $m = 2, \ldots, 100$ to obtain the sequence $\rho = \langle \rho(1), \ldots, \rho(100) \rangle$. Compute the mean and standard deviation of ρ.

Figure 8(a) shows the results of the above steps for each IC3PAR variant. We see that for each example, the mean of ρ is very close to 1 and its standard deviation is very close to 0, indicating that $p(m)$ and $p^*(m)$ agree considerably. Figure 8(b) shows a scatter plot of all $p^*(m)$ values computed against their corresponding $p(m)$. Note that most values are very close to the (red) $x = y$ line, as expected.

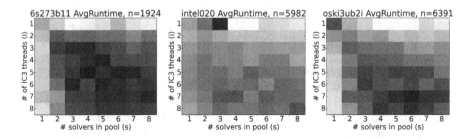

Fig. 9. Heatmap of IC3PROOF runtimes for three examples. Deeper color of cell (i, s) indicates that IC3PROOF(i, s) solves the benchmark faster; n = total number of runs of IC3PROOF over all 64 values of (i, s).

6.4 Parameter Sweeping

IC3PAR has two parameters: number of IC3 threads and $SPSz$. We write IC3PAR (i, s) to mean an instance of IC3PAR with i IC3 threads and $SPSz = s$. Thus, IC3PAR$(4, 3)$ was used is all previous experiments. We observed in Sect. 6.1 that different IC3PAR variants perform the best for different benchmarks. We now evaluate the performance of IC3PROOF by varying i and s. These experiments were also done on our cluster (cf. Sect. 6.3). We begin with a conjecture about the relationship of runtime and parameter values.

Conjecture 2. The parameter value affects performance of IC3PAR significantly, and the best parameter choice is located unpredictably in the input space.

To investigate Conjecture 2, we measured the runtime of IC3PROOF(i, s) for each $(i, s) \in I \times S$ where $I = S = \{1, \dots, 8\}$. We selected 16 examples from $\mathcal{B}$. For each example η, and each $(i, s) \in I \times S$, we executed IC3PROOF(i, s) on η "around" 3000 times (again, the exact number varied across examples due to timeouts) and computed the average runtime. This gives us the entry at (i, s) for the "heatmap" for η. The heatmaps in Fig. 9 summarize our results for three of the benchmarks that we found to be representative. They support Conjecture 2, as average runtimes (indicated by the color depth of cells in the heatmaps) across the parameter space are varied. The depth of cells show no discernable pattern (e.g., do not increase with i or s), and the deepest cells are significantly more so than the lightest ones. This implies that: (i) selecting the best parameters for IC3PROOF would be quite beneficial; but (ii) this is a non-trivial problem.

As a preliminary step to address this challenge, we ran portfolios of a solver that uses parameter sweeping [2]. Specifically, the solver (denoted IC3SWEEP) executes a randomly selected IC3PAR variant with a random (i, s) selected from

Example	Time IC3REF	Speedup				Example	Time IC3REF	Speedup			
		Sync	Async	Proof	Sweep			Sync	Async	Proof	Sweep
6s286	947.6	1.54	1.57	1.66	1.77	6s215	12.20	2.47	2.57	2.61	2.36
intel026	78.33	2.61	2.77	2.85	2.58	6s216	67.24	4.33	4.35	4.30	4.29
6s273	31.06	1.84	1.88	1.90	1.65	oski3ub1i	83.64	1.90	1.97	1.94	1.96
intel057	31.33	2.45	2.49	2.49	2.66	oski3ub3i	79.41	1.90	1.94	1.99	1.94
intel054	55.89	3.52	3.51	3.52	3.92	oski3ub5i	127.3	2.66	2.65	2.67	2.76
Mean		2.39	2.44	2.48	2.52	Mean		2.65	2.70	2.70	2.66

Fig. 10. Parameter sweeping; Sync, Async, Proof, Sweep = average speedups over IC3REF for portfolios of 20 IC3SYNC (4,3), IC3ASYNC (4,3), IC3PROOF (4,3), and IC3SWEEP, respectively.

$I \times S$. We compared the average speedup (over 50 runs) of a portfolio of 20 IC3SWEEPs with the average speedup (over 50 runs) of portfolios of 20 of each of the three IC3PAR variants with fixed $(i, s) = (4, 3)$. Figure 10 summarizes our results. We observe that in general IC3SWEEP is competitive with each of the IC3PAR variants (indeed, it performs best for the hardest examples from the safe and buggy categories). We believe that parameter sweeping shows promise as a strategy for real-life problems where good parameters would be difficult (if not impossible) to compute.

7 Conclusion

We present three ways to parallelize IC3. Each variant uses a number of threads to speed up the computation of an inductive invariant or a CEX, sharing lemmas to minimize duplicated effort. They differ in the degree of synchronization and technique to detect if an inductive invariant has been found. The runtime of these solvers is unpredictable, and varies with thread-interleaving. We explore the use of portfolios to counteract the runtime variance. Each solver in the portfolio potentially searches for a different proof/CEX. The first one to succeed provides the solution. Using the Extreme Value theorem and statistical analysis, we construct a formula that gives us a portfolio size to solving a problem within a target time bound with a certain probability. Experiments on HWMCC14 benchmarks show that the combination of parallelization and portfolios yields an average speedups of 6x over IC3, and in some cases speedups of over 300. We show that parameter sweeping is a promising approach to implement a solver that performs well over a wide range of problems of unknown difficulty. An important area of future work is the effectiveness of parallelization and portfolios in the context of software verification via a generalization of IC3 [12].

Aknowledgment. We are grateful to Jeffery Hansen and Arie Gurfinkel for helpful comments and discussions. This material is based upon work funded and supported by the Department of Defense under Contract No. FA8721-05-C-0003 with Carnegie Mellon University for the operation of the Software Engineering Institute, a federally funded research and development center. This material has been approved for public release and unlimited distribution DM-0002752.

References

1. Albarghouthi, A., Kumar, R., Nori, A.V., Rajamani, S.K.: Parallelizing top-down interprocedural analyses. In: Vitek, J., Lin, H., Tip, F. (eds.) Proceedings of the ACM SIGPLAN 2012 Conference on Programming Language Design and Implementation (PLDI 2012), pp. 217–228. Association for Computing Machinery, Beijing, China, June 2012
2. Ansel, J., Kamil, S., Veeramachaneni, K., Ragan-Kelley, J., Bosboom, J., O'Reilly, U., Amarasinghe, S.P.: OpenTuner: an extensible framework for program autotuning. In: Amaral, J.N., Torrellas, J. (eds.) Proceedings of the 23rd International Conference on Parallel Architectures and Compilation (PACT 2014), pp. 303–316. Association for Computing Machinery, Edmonton, AB, Canada, August 2014
3. Barnat, J., et al.: DiVinE 3.0 - an explicit-state model checker for multithreaded C & C++ programs. In: Sharygina, N., Veith, H. (eds.) CAV. Lecture Notes in Computer Science, vol. 8044, pp. 863–868. Springer, Saint Petersburg (2013)
4. Bingham, B., Bingham, J., Erickson, J., de Paula, F.M., Reitblatt, M., Singh, G.: Industrial strength distributed explicit state model checking. In: Proceedings of the 9th International Workshop on Parallel and Distributed Methods in verifiCation (PDMC 2010), Twente, The Netherlands, September-October 2010
5. Blom, S., van de Pol, J., Weber, M.: LTSMIN: distributed and symbolic reachability. In: Touili, T., Cook, B., Jackson, P. (eds.) CAV 2010. LNCS, vol. 6174, pp. 354–359. Springer, Heidelberg (2010)
6. Bradley, A.R.: SAT-Based model checking without unrolling. In: Jhala, R., Schmidt, D. (eds.) VMCAI 2011. LNCS, vol. 6538, pp. 70–87. Springer, Heidelberg (2011)
7. Chaki, S., Karimi, D.: Model Checking with Multi-Threaded IC3 Portfolios (2016), Extended version of this paper. http://www.contrib.andrew.cmu.edu/~schaki/publications/VMCAI-2016-Extended.pdf
8. Cimatti, A., Griggio, A.: Software model checking via IC3. In: Madhusudan, P., Seshia, S.A. (eds.) CAV 2012. LNCS, vol. 7358, pp. 277–293. Springer, Heidelberg (2012)
9. Ditter, A., Ceska, M., Lüttgen, G.: On parallel software verification using boolean equation systems. In: Donaldson, A., Parker, D. (eds.) SPIN 2012. LNCS, vol. 7385, pp. 80–97. Springer, Heidelberg (2012)
10. Eén, N., Mishchenko, A., Brayton, R.K.: Efficient implementation of property directed reachability. In: Proceedings of the 11th International Conference on Formal Methods in Computer-Aided Design (FMCAD 2011), pp. 125–134. IEEE Computer Society, Austin, TX, October-November 2011
11. de Haan, L., Ferreira, A.: Extreme Value Theory: An Introduction. Springer, New York (2006)
12. Hoder, K., Bjørner, N.: Generalized property directed reachability. In: Cimatti, A., Sebastiani, R. (eds.) SAT 2012. LNCS, vol. 7317, pp. 157–171. Springer, Heidelberg (2012)
13. Holzmann, G.J.: Parallelizing the spin model checker. In: Donaldson, A., Parker, D. (eds.) SPIN 2012. LNCS, vol. 7385, pp. 155–171. Springer, Heidelberg (2012)
14. Kadioglu, S., Malitsky, Y., Sabharwal, A., Samulowitz, H., Sellmann, M.: Algorithm selection and scheduling. In: Lee, J. (ed.) CP 2011. LNCS, vol. 6876, pp. 454–469. Springer, Heidelberg (2011)

15. Lopes, N.P., Rybalchenko, A.: Distributed and predictable software model checking. In: Jhala, R., Schmidt, D. (eds.) VMCAI 2011. LNCS, vol. 6538, pp. 340–355. Springer, Heidelberg (2011)
16. Malitsky, Y., Sabharwal, A., Samulowitz, H., Sellmann, M.: Boosting sequential solver portfolios: knowledge sharing and accuracy prediction. In: Nicosia, G., Pardalos, P. (eds.) LION 7. LNCS, vol. 7997, pp. 153–167. Springer, Heidelberg (2013)
17. Melatti, I., Palmer, R., Sawaya, G., Yang, Y., Kirby, R.M., Gopalakrishnan, G.C.: Parallel and distributed model checking in eddy. In: Valmari, A. (ed.) SPIN 2006. LNCS, vol. 3925, pp. 108–125. Springer, Heidelberg (2006)
18. Palikareva, H., Cadar, C.: Multi-solver support in symbolic execution. In: Sharygina, N., Veith, H. (eds.) CAV 2013. LNCS, vol. 8044, pp. 53–68. Springer, Heidelberg (2013)
19. Ppfolio website. http://www.cril.univ-artois.fr/~roussel/ppfolio
20. Weibull, W.: A statistical distribution function of wide applicability. ASME J. Appl. Mech. **18**(3), 293–297 (1951)
21. Wintersteiger, C.M., Hamadi, Y., de Moura, L.: A concurrent portfolio approach to SMT solving. In: Bouajjani, A., Maler, O. (eds.) CAV 2009. LNCS, vol. 5643, pp. 715–720. Springer, Heidelberg (2009)
22. Xu, L., Hutter, F., Hoos, H.H., Leyton-Brown, K.: Satzilla: Portfolio-based algorithm selection for SAT. J. Artif. Intell. Res. (JAIR) **32**, 565–606 (2008)

Automatic Generation of Propagation Complete SAT Encodings

Martin Brain[1], Liana Hadarean[1], Daniel Kroening[1], and Ruben Martins[2(✉)]

[1] Department of Computer Science, University of Oxford, Oxford, UK
{Martin.Brain,Liana.Hadarean,Daniel.Kroening}@cs.ox.ac.uk
[2] University of Texas at Austin, Austin, USA
rmartins@cs.utexas.edu

Abstract. Almost all applications of SAT solvers generate Boolean formulae from higher level expression graphs by encoding the semantics of each operation or relation into propositional logic. All non-trivial relations have many different possible encodings and the encoding used can have a major effect on the performance of the system. This paper gives an abstract satisfaction based formalisation of one aspect of encoding quality, the *propagation strength*, and shows that propagation complete SAT encodings can be modelled by our formalism and automatically computed for key operations. This allows a more rigorous approach to designing encodings as well as improved performance.

1 Introduction

Almost all industrial applications of SAT solvers translate from a higher level language into propositional logic. Many of these translations are *modular* in the sense that each sub-expression is encoded into a set of clauses whose structure is independent of how the expression is used. For example, an SMT solver can use the same template to generate clauses for every occurrence of a 64-bit multiplication operation.

For most non-trivial expressions, there are many different encodings available. For example, there are several ways to encode cardinality constraints [1,4,37]. These may use different clauses and possibly introduce auxiliary variables to simplify and compact the encodings. The choice of encoding can have a significant impact on the performance of the solver [35]. This difference can be large enough that identifying a bad encoding from the CNF it generates and then replacing it with a better one *within the SAT solver* can give a net improvement in solver performance [34]. Despite the importance of choosing a good encoding there remain open questions about why some encodings perform better than others. A common rule of thumb is that smaller encodings (primarily in terms of number clauses but also in the number of variables) are preferable. For some kinds of encoding, for example cardinality constraints, arc consistency [24] is regarded to be a desirable property. Another desirable property is being propagation complete [11]. Encodings with this property are considered extremely important since constraint solvers can benefit from the increase in inference power. However, its use is not yet wide spread in encoding design within the SMT community.

B. Jobstmann and K.R.M. Leino (Eds.): VMCAI 2016, LNCS 9583, pp. 536–556, 2016.
DOI: 10.1007/978-3-662-49122-5_26

These issues are particularly relevant in encodings of bit-vector and floating-point operations. Often the only way to tell if an encoding might be better than another is to implement it and then compare system level performance on a 'representative' set of benchmarks. Furthermore, the encodings commonly used are frequently literal translations of circuits designs used to implement these operations in hardware. These designs were created to minimise signal propagation delay, to reduce area or for power and layout concerns. It is not clear why a multiplier hardware design with low cycle count should give a good encoding from bit-vector logic to CNF.

This paper advances both the theory and practice of the creation of encodings through the following contributions:

- Section 3 uses and extends the framework of abstract satisfiability [19] to formalise one aspect of encoding quality: *propagating strength*. We show that propagation complete encodings [11] are modelled by our framework and can serve as a basis for comparing encodings.
- An algorithm is given in Sect. 4 which can be used to determine if an encoding is propagation complete, strengthen it if it is not or generate a propagation complete encoding from scratch with and without auxiliary variables.
- In Sect. 5 we show that using our propagation complete encodings improves the performance of the CVC4 SMT solver on a wide range of bit-vector benchmarks.

2 Abstract Satisfaction

The *abstract satisfaction* framework [19] uses the language of abstract interpretation to characterise and understand the key components in a SAT solver [17]. One advantage of this viewpoint is that it is largely independent of the concrete domain that is being searched (sets of assignments) or the abstract domain used to represent information about the search (partial assignments). This allows the CDCL algorithm to be generalised [18] and applied to a range of other domains [12, 20, 27]. Another important feature of the abstract satisfaction framework is that it allows the *representation of a problem* and the *effects of reasoning* to be cleanly formalised. As we show later, this allows us to characterise propagation algorithms, such as unit propagation, as a map from representation to effect. In this section we recall some background results required to formalise this idea.

The foundation of abstract interpretation is using an *abstract domain* to perform approximate reasoning about a *concrete domain*. This requires a relation between the two domains; with Galois connections being one of the simplest and most popular choices.

Definition 1. *Let $(C, \subseteq)$ and $(A, \sqsubseteq)$ be sets with partial orders. The pair $(\alpha : C \to A, \gamma : A \to C)$ form a* Galois connection *if:*

$$\forall c \in C, a \in A \, . \, \alpha(c) \sqsubseteq a \Leftrightarrow c \subseteq \gamma(a)$$

C *is referred to as the* concrete domain *and* A *is the* abstract domain. *It is sometimes useful to use an equivalent definition of Galois connection:* α *and* γ *are monotone and*

$$\forall c \in C \centerdot c \subseteq \gamma(\alpha(c)) \qquad \forall a \in A \centerdot \alpha(\gamma(a)) \sqsubseteq a$$

If, additionally, $\gamma \circ \alpha = id$, *then the pair is referred to as a* Galois insertion *and each element of the concrete domain has one or more representations in the abstract domain.*

Given the domain that we want to reason about and the abstraction that will be used to perform the reasoning, the next step is to characterise the reasoning as *transformers*.

Definition 2. *A* concrete transformer *is a monotonic function* $f : C \to C$. *Many of the transformers of interest are* extensive, reductive *or* idempotent, *respectively defined as:*

$$\forall c \in C \centerdot c \subseteq f(c) \quad \forall c \in C \centerdot f(c) \subseteq c \quad f \circ f = f$$

A function that is extensive, monotonic and idempotent is referred to as an upper closure *while a reductive, monotonic, idempotent function is referred to as a* lower closure.

Finally, we will need a means of approximating the transformer on the abstract domain using an *abstract transformer*. This gives a key result: the space of abstract transformers (for a given concrete transformer) forms a lattice with a unique *best abstract transformer*.

Definition 3. *Given a transformer* f *on* C, $f_o : A \to A$ *is an* (over-approximate) abstract transformer *if:*

$$\forall a \in A \centerdot \alpha(f(\gamma(a))) \subseteq f_o(a)$$

Proposition 1. *Given a reductive transformer* f *on a lattice* $(C, \subseteq)$, *the set of abstract transformers on lattice* $(A, \sqsubseteq)$ *form a lattice with the bottom element, referred to as the* best abstract transformer, *is equal to:*

$$\alpha \circ f \circ \gamma$$

3   Characterising Propagating Strength

While the framework we introduce in this section generalizes to other domains, we will focus on CNF encodings targeting CDCL-style SAT solvers [9]. We only consider unit propagation, but other propagation algorithms, such as generalised unit propagation [33], can be treated in the same way.

A number of attributes can be used for evaluating encodings. Some of these are algorithmic such as how much information it can propagate, how it affects the quality of learnt clauses, how it interacts with the branching heuristic or what effect it has on preprocessing. Others are more implementation-oriented: how many variables it uses, how many clauses it contains and how many are binary, ternary, how quickly it propagates, etc. In this work we will be characterising one of the major algorithmic properties: the amount of information that can be propagated.

Informally, this can be thought of as the proportion of facts that are true (with respect to the current partial assignment and encoding) that can be proven with unit propagation. If E is an encoding, l is a literal and p is a partial assignment expressed as a conjunct of all of the assigned literals, then it is the degree to which:

$$\mathsf{p} \wedge \mathsf{E} \models l \quad \text{implies} \quad \mathsf{p} \wedge \mathsf{E} \vdash_{up} l,$$

where $\models$ represents logical entailment and $\vdash_{up}$ stands for unit propagation.

We formalise this intuition using the viewpoint of abstract satisfaction. Figure 1 gives a visual summary of the formalisation; the key steps are:

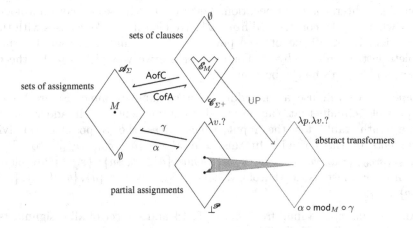

Fig. 1. A graphical presentation of the results in Sect. 3

a	b	c_{in}	c_{out}	s
1	1	1	1	1
1	1	0	1	0
1	0	1	1	0
1	0	0	0	1
0	1	1	1	0
0	1	0	0	1
0	0	1	0	1
0	0	0	0	0

(a) Truth table

(b) A basic adder circuit

Fig. 2. A nest of adders

1. Present syntax as an abstraction of semantics and define the space of encodings of a set of assignments as a substructure of the syntax lattice (Subsect. 3.1).
2. Show that partial assignments, the information about possible models that is manipulated during the search, is also an abstraction of the semantics (Subsect. 3.2).
3. Express the *effects of reasoning* as abstract transformers and characterise propagation algorithms such as unit propagation as *maps from representations of a problem to the effects of reasoning* (Subsect. 3.3).

3.1   Syntax and Semantics

We first fix a set of *variable names* Σ. This will include the 'input' and 'output' bits of the encoding, plus any auxiliaries. Let Σ^+ be the set of *literals* constructed from these variables (i.e. $\Sigma^+ = \{v|v \in \Sigma\} \cup \{\neg v|v \in \Sigma\}$). For simplicity we will assume double negation is always simplified $\neg\neg v = v$.

A *clause* is a disjunction of one or more literals. For convenience we will identify clauses with the set of literals they contain. A clause is a *tautology* if it contains a literal and its negation. Let $\mathscr{C}_{\Sigma^+}$ be the set of non-tautological clauses which can be constructed from Σ^+. We identify sets of clauses with their conjunction. Let $2^{\mathscr{C}_{\Sigma^+}}$ denote the powerset of $\mathscr{C}_{\Sigma^+}$ and note that it forms a complete lattice ordered by $\supseteq$. For convenience we will pick $\emptyset$ to be the top element and $\mathscr{C}_{\Sigma^+}$ to be the bottom.

Example 1. We will use a full adder as a running example. Figure 2 shows one possible circuit that can be used to implement a full adder as well as the truth table for the input which gives the 8 possible satisfying assignments of the formula. In this case $\Sigma = \{a, b, c_{in}, s, c_{out}\}$ so $\Sigma^+ = \{a, b, c_{in}, s, c_{out}, \neg a, \neg b, \neg c_{in}, \neg s, \neg c_{out}\}$. Thus $\{a\}$, $\{b, \neg a\}$, $\{s, \neg s\}$ are clauses and only the last is a tautology. Also $\mathscr{C}_{\Sigma^+} = \{\emptyset, \{a\}, \{b\}, \{\neg a\}, \{a, b\}, \{a, \neg b\}, \dots\}$.

An *assignment* is a map from Σ to $\{\top, \bot\}$ and the set of all assignments is denoted by $\mathscr{A}_\Sigma$. Similarly $2^{\mathscr{A}_\Sigma}$ forms a powerset lattice. Following usual convention (and the opposite of the syntax lattice), the top element will be $\mathscr{A}_\Sigma$ and $\emptyset$ the bottom. With a slight abuse of notation, we use assignments to give literals values: $\mathsf{x}(\neg a) = \neg\mathsf{x}(a)$.

The *models* relation, denoted using an infix $\models$, is a relationship between $\mathscr{A}_\Sigma$ and $\mathscr{C}_{\Sigma^+}$, defined as follows:

$$\mathsf{x} \models c \Leftrightarrow \exists l \in c \bullet \mathsf{x}(l) = \top$$

An assignment is a *model* of a set of clauses if the models relation holds for all of the clauses in the set.

Example 2. An assignment for the full adder example would be:
$\mathsf{x} = \{(a, \top), (b, \top), (c_{in}, \bot), (c_{out}, \top), (s, \bot)\}$.
From this we can see that $\mathsf{x} \models \{a\}$ and $\mathsf{x} \models \{a, \neg c_{in}, c_{out}\}$ but $\mathsf{x} \not\models \{\neg b, \neg a\}$. So x is a model of $\{\{a\}, \{a, \neg c_{in}, c_{out}\}\}$.

This relation gives maps $\mathsf{AofC} : 2^{\mathscr{C}_{\Sigma+}} \to 2^{\mathscr{A}_{\Sigma}}$ and $\mathsf{CofA} : 2^{\mathscr{A}_{\Sigma}} \to 2^{\mathscr{C}_{\Sigma+}}$:

$$\mathsf{AofC}(C) = \{\mathsf{x} \in \mathscr{A}_{\Sigma} | \forall c \in C \centerdot \mathsf{x} \models c\}$$
$$\mathsf{CofA}(A) = \{c \in \mathscr{C}_{\Sigma+} | \forall \mathsf{x} \in A \centerdot \mathsf{x} \models c\}$$

$\mathsf{AofC}(C)$ is the set of assignments which are models of C, while $\mathsf{CofA}(A)$ is all of the clauses that are consistent with all of the assignments in A. Both maps are monotonic, $\mathsf{AofC}(\mathsf{CofA}(A)) = A$ and $\mathsf{CofA}(\mathsf{AofC}(C)) \supseteq C$ so they form a *Galois insertion* between $2^{\mathscr{A}_{\Sigma}}$ and $2^{\mathscr{C}_{\Sigma+}}$. *A set of clauses is a representation, or abstraction, of its set of models.*

Example 3. Given $C = \{\{a, \neg b\}, \{\neg a\}\}$, the set of all models of C is $\mathsf{AofC}(C) = \{\mathsf{y} : \Sigma \to \{\top, \bot\} | \mathsf{y}(a) = \bot \wedge \mathsf{y}(b) = \bot\}$. Conversely, $\mathsf{CofA}(\{\mathsf{x}\}) = \{\{a\}, \{a, b\}, \{a, \neg b\}, \dots\}$ is the set containing all of the clauses consistent with the assignment x from Example 2. When multiple assignments are given this is all of the clauses that are consistent with *all* of the assignments.

In the SAT field, similar Galois connections to the one presented in this section have been studied in [32]. Although we have presented this result with Boolean valuations (the "concrete" domain) and CNF (the "abstract" domain), the construction is much more general and can be applied to SMT, CSP, ASP,

$$\begin{array}{lll}
\{\neg a, \neg b, \neg c_{in}, \neg c_{out}, s\} & \{\neg a, \neg b, \neg c_{in}, c_{out}, \neg s\} & \{\neg a, \neg b, \neg c_{in}, c_{out}, s\} \\
\{\neg a, \neg b, c_{in}, \neg c_{out}, \neg s\} & \{\neg a, \neg b, c_{in}, c_{out}, \neg s\} & \{\neg a, \neg b, c_{in}, c_{out}, s\} \\
\{\neg a, b, \neg c_{in}, \neg c_{out}, \neg s\} & \{\neg a, b, \neg c_{in}, c_{out}, \neg s\} & \{\neg a, b, \neg c_{in}, c_{out}, s\} \\
\{\neg a, b, c_{in}, \neg c_{out}, \neg s\} & \{\neg a, b, c_{in}, \neg c_{out}, s\} & \{\neg a, b, c_{in}, c_{out}, s\} \\
\{a, \neg b, \neg c_{in}, \neg c_{out}, \neg s\} & \{a, \neg b, \neg c_{in}, c_{out}, \neg s\} & \{a, \neg b, \neg c_{in}, c_{out}, s\} \\
\{a, \neg b, c_{in}, \neg c_{out}, \neg s\} & \{a, \neg b, c_{in}, \neg c_{out}, s\} & \{a, \neg b, c_{in}, c_{out}, s\} \\
\{a, b, \neg c_{in}, \neg c_{out}, \neg s\} & \{a, b, \neg c_{in}, \neg c_{out}, s\} & \{a, b, \neg c_{in}, c_{out}, s\} \\
\{a, b, c_{in}, \neg c_{out}, \neg s\} & \{a, b, c_{in}, \neg c_{out}, s\} & \{a, b, c_{in}, c_{out}, \neg s\}
\end{array}$$

(a) Naïve truth table encoding

$$\begin{array}{llll}
\{\neg a, \neg b, c_{in}, \neg s\} & \{\neg a, b, \neg c_{in}, \neg s\} & \{a, \neg b, \neg c_{in}, \neg s\} & \{a, b, c_{in}, \neg s\} \\
\{\neg a, \neg b, \neg c_{in}, s\} & \{\neg a, b, c_{in}, s\} & \{a, b, \neg c_{in}, s\} & \{a, \neg b, c_{in}, s\} \\
\{\neg a, \neg b, c_{out}\} & \{\neg a, \neg c_{in}, c_{out}\} & \{\neg b, \neg c_{in}, c_{out}\} & \\
\{a, b, \neg c_{out}\} & \{a, c_{in}, \neg c_{out}\} & \{b, c_{in}, \neg c_{out}\} &
\end{array}$$

(b) Eén and Sörensson's basic encoding

$$\begin{array}{llll}
\{c_{in}, \neg s, \neg c_{out}\} & \{a, \neg s, \neg c_{out}\} & \{b, \neg s, \neg c_{out}\} & \{a, b, c_{in}, \neg s\} \\
\{\neg a, \neg b, \neg c_{in}, s\} & \{\neg c_{in}, s, c_{out}\} & \{\neg a, s, c_{out}\} & \{\neg b, s, c_{out}\} \\
\{\neg a, \neg b, c_{out}\} & \{\neg a, \neg c_{in}, c_{out}\} & \{\neg b, \neg c_{in}, c_{out}\} & \\
\{a, b, \neg c_{out}\} & \{a, c_{in}, \neg c_{out}\} & \{b, c_{in}, \neg c_{out}\} &
\end{array}$$

(c) A propagation complete encoding

Fig. 3. A nest of adder encodings

etc. For more discussion of the Galois connection between syntax and semantics, see [21].

Given a set of assignments $M \subset \mathscr{A}_\Sigma$, an *encoding (of M)* is any set of clauses $C \subset \mathscr{C}_{\Sigma^+}$ such that $\mathsf{AofC}(C) = M$. We shall denote the set of encodings of M as $\mathscr{E}_M = \{C \subset \mathscr{C}_{\Sigma^+} | \mathsf{AofC}(C) = M\}$. If C and D are both encodings (of the same set of models), then so is $C \cup D$; this is the basis for redundant encodings in CSP. It also implies that the encodings of a set of models form a meet semi-lattice with a minimum element, $\mathsf{CofA}(M)$, the most verbose encoding. There can be multiple, incomparable, least verbose encodings. For example if $M = \emptyset$, then $\{a, \neg a\}$ is a least verbose encoding (as there are no proper subsets which are encodings), but so is $\{b, \neg b\}$. This notion of encoding has been studied is the SAT field (e.g. [23]) and has recently been formalised as a formula that has the same satisfying assignments as the set of assignments of a given specification [26].

Example 4. Continuing our example of a full adder, let M be the set of eight models described by the truth table in Fig. 2a. There are many possible encodings, some of which are given in Fig. 3. All of these are subsets of $\mathsf{CofA}(M)$, all the clauses consistent with M, in effect, the 'theory' of the full adder. However, not every subset of $\mathsf{CofA}(M)$ is an encoding, as they are required to have the same models as M. Possible encodings include the naive encoding (Fig. 3a) in which all full assignments that are not models are removed, the basic encoding given by [23] (Fig. 3b) and a propagation complete encoding (Fig. 3c). Notice that the first two encodings are not propagation complete.

To formally define propagation strength, we will need a notion of what kind of information we are propagating and to relate the encoding to the action of propagation.

3.2 Representing Information During Search

Some propositional logic tools, such as BDDs, represent sets of models directly. For solving SAT problems this is not really viable — as soon as you have a model that you could represent, you have solved the problem. Thus SAT algorithms need a way of representing partial information about models. For example if an encoding contains the clause $\{\neg a\}$ then the SAT solver needs a way of recording "there are no models that assign a to $\top$". The most common approach is to use *partial assignments*.

Following [17] we characterise a partial assignment over Σ ($\mathscr{P}_\Sigma$ denotes the set of all of them) as an abstraction of $2^{\mathscr{A}_\Sigma}$. Partial assignments are maps from Σ to $\{\top, ?, \bot\}$, where ? denotes an unknown or unassigned variable. They can be ordered by:

$$\mathsf{p} \sqsubseteq \mathsf{q} \Leftrightarrow \forall v \in \Sigma.\mathsf{q}(v) \neq ? \Rightarrow \mathsf{p}(v) = \mathsf{q}(v)$$

Allowing an additional 'contradiction' partial assignment, $\bot^{\mathscr{P}}$, ordered below all other partial assignments, makes $\mathscr{P}_\Sigma$ a complete lattice, where $\top^{\mathscr{P}} = \lambda v.?$ is the partial assignment that does not assign any variables. The discussion below generalises to other abstractions; we use partial assignments as they are a popular and simple choice.

Example 5. In our running example, p and q are partial assignments:

$$p = \{(a, ?), (b, \bot), (c_{in}, \bot), (s, \top), (c_{out}, \top)\}$$
$$q = \{(a, ?), (b, ?), (c_{in}, ?), (s, \top), (c_{out}, \top)\}$$

with $p \sqsubseteq q$ because where q assigns a variable to $\top$ or $\bot$, p agrees.

To use $\mathscr{P}_\Sigma$ as an abstraction of $2^{\mathscr{A}_\Sigma}$, we need to define a Galois connection between them. Let $\alpha : 2^{\mathscr{A}_\Sigma} \to \mathscr{P}_\Sigma$ denote the map from models to the most complete partial assignment that is consistent with all of them and $\gamma : \mathscr{P}_\Sigma \to 2^{\mathscr{A}_\Sigma}$ denote the map from a partial assignment to the set of models that is consistent with it:

$$\alpha(A) = \bigsqcup_{x \in A} x \qquad \gamma(p) = \{x \in \mathscr{A}_\Sigma | \forall v \in \Sigma \,.\, p(v) \neq ? \Rightarrow x(v) = p(v)\}$$

Example 6. Let x_1, x_2, x_3 and x_4 be (full) assignments:

$$x_1 = \{(a, \top), (b, \top), (c_{in}, \bot), (s, \bot), (c_{out}, \top)\}$$
$$x_2 = \{(a, \top), (b, \bot), (c_{in}, \top), (s, \bot), (c_{out}, \top)\}$$
$$x_3 = \{(a, \top), (b, \top), (c_{in}, \top), (s, \bot), (c_{out}, \top)\}$$
$$x_4 = \{(a, \top), (b, \bot), (c_{in}, \bot), (s, \bot), (c_{out}, \top)\}$$

then:

$$\alpha(\{x_1, x_2\}) = \{(a, \top), (b, ?), (c_{in}, ?), (s, \bot), (c_{out}, \top)\}$$
$$\gamma(\alpha(\{x_1, x_2\})) = \{x_1, x_2, x_3, x_4\}$$

3.3 Effects of Reasoning

Having defined partial assignments as the 'units' of information that propagation uses, the next step is to formalize what kind of reasoning we are performing. In a SAT solver the role of reasoning is to add to a partial assignment p (i.e., reduce the set of assignments that is being considered) that is consistent with all of the models in $\gamma(p)$. Formally, this is expressed in two steps: a *models transformer* on the concrete domain, $2^{\mathscr{A}_\Sigma}$, which captures the kind of reasoning that we are approximating and abstract transformers on $\mathscr{P}_\Sigma$, which express the actual changes to the partial assignments.

In slight variation from [18] we define the *models transformer*, $\mathrm{mod}_M : 2^{\mathscr{A}_\Sigma} \to 2^{\mathscr{A}_\Sigma}$, as parameterised by a set of assignments rather than a formula:

$$\mathrm{mod}_M(A) = M \cap A$$

This is a downward closure function on $2^{\mathscr{A}_\Sigma}$ and expresses the ideal reasoning, or, conversely, the limit of what is sound.

Example 7. In the full adder example, let M be the set of assignments described in the truth table in Fig. 2a. If $A = \{x_1, x_2, x_3, x_4\}$, then $\mathrm{mod}_M(A) = \{x_1, x_2\}$ as these are the only two assignments in A that are also models of the full adder.

As $2^{\mathscr{A}_\Sigma}$ is not directly representable for problems of significant size, we use $\mathscr{P}_\Sigma$. Likewise, we cannot directly implement mod_M so instead we must use over-approximate transformers on $\mathscr{P}_\Sigma$. Let $\mathscr{T}_{\mathsf{mod}_M}$ denote the set of abstract transformers that over-approximate mod_M and recall from Proposition 1 that they can be ordered point-wise to form a lattice with id as the top element and $\alpha \circ \mathsf{mod}_M \circ \gamma$ as the bottom. The *effect* of a sound propagator or other form of reasoning should be an abstract transformer, as they soundly add to partial assignment.

The final link is to connect the encoding used to the effect of reasoning. To do this we consider the unit propagation algorithm as a map from UP : $\mathscr{E}_M \rightarrow (\mathscr{P}_\Sigma \rightarrow \mathscr{P}_\Sigma)$ that uses a set of clauses to add assignments to a partial assignment.

Definition 4. *Let* $\mathsf{up} : \mathscr{C}_{\Sigma+} \rightarrow (\mathscr{P}_\Sigma \rightarrow \mathscr{P}_\Sigma)$ *map clauses to functions on partial assignments.*

$$assign(l) = \lambda k. \begin{cases} \top & k = l \\ \bot & k = \neg l \\ ? & otherwise \end{cases}$$

$$\mathsf{up}(c) = \lambda p. \begin{cases} p \sqcap assign(l) & \exists l \in c . p(l) =? \wedge \forall k \in c . k \neq l \Rightarrow p(k) = \bot \\ p & otherwise \end{cases}$$

Define UP *as the (greatest) fix-point of applying* $\mathsf{up}(c)$ *for each clause in the encoding:*

$$\mathsf{UP}(C)(p) = GFP\left(\lambda q.p \sqcap \left(\prod_{c \in C} \mathsf{up}(c)(q) \right) \right)$$

Example 8. Given the set C clauses in Fig. 3b we have:

$$\mathsf{UP}(C)(\{(a, \top), (b, \top), (c_{in}, \top), (s, ?), (c_{out}, ?)\}) = \\ \{(a, \top), (b, \top), (c_{in}, \top), (s, \top), (c_{out}, \top)\})$$

as the clause $\{\neg a, \neg b, c_{out}\}$ assigns c_{out} to $\top$ and $\{\neg a, \neg b, \neg c_{in}, s\}$ assigns s to $\top$.

Formalised in this manner, UP has a number of useful order-theoretic properties:

Proposition 2. *Given* $C, D \subset \mathscr{C}_{\Sigma+}$, $\mathsf{UP}(C_i)$ *is a closure function as:*

$$\mathsf{UP}(C) \leqslant id \quad C \leqslant D \implies \mathsf{UP}(C) \leqslant \mathsf{UP}(D) \quad \mathsf{UP}(C) \circ \mathsf{UP}(C) = \mathsf{UP}(C)$$

Note that UP is neither injective ($\mathsf{up}(\{\{a\}, \{b\}\}) = \mathsf{up}(\{\{a\}, \{b\}, \{\neg a, b\}\})$) nor surjective. Furthermore, UP does not preserve meets (well defined on encodings) or joins (partially defined on encodings, fully defined on supersets of a given encoding). A propagation algorithm that preserves joins would give a Galois connection between supersets of an encoding and abstract transformers, thus giving a unique, minimal encoding required to give a certain amount of inference.

The final step is to show that the closure functions given by $\mathsf{UP}(C)$ are abstract transformers and that they include the best abstract transformer.

Theorem 1. *Let $M \in 2^{\mathscr{A}_\Sigma}$ be a set of assignments then:*

$$\{\mathsf{UP}(C)|C \in \mathscr{E}_M\} \subseteq \mathscr{T}_{\mathsf{mod}_M} \qquad \mathsf{UP}(\mathsf{CofA}(M)) = \alpha \circ \mathsf{mod}_M \circ \gamma$$

Thus an encoding $C \in \mathscr{E}_M$ is a propagation complete encoding *(PCE) [11] when:*

$$\mathsf{UP}(C) = \alpha \circ \mathsf{mod}_M \circ \gamma$$

Propagation complete encodings (PCEs) are not unique and there may be many, incomparable PCEs. One goal of encoding design can be the creation of PCEs with other desirable properties, such as using a minimal number of clauses or auxiliary variables. As with clauses, assignments and partial assignments, the discussion above is more general than unit propagation alone. Using our abstract satisfaction framework we can model PCEs. In the next section we present an algorithm for automatically generating PCEs.

4   Generating Propagation Complete Encodings

The previous section defined the notion of propagation complete encodings (PCEs) within our framework. Next, we present an algorithm (Algorithm 1) that can be used to determine if an encoding is propagation complete, strengthen it if not, and generate a PCE that is equisatisfiable to a reference encoding. Algorithm 1 takes as input a set of variables Σ that will serve as the encoding vocabulary, an initial encoding E_0 and a reference encoding $\mathsf{E}_{\mathsf{Ref}}$ (over a vocabulary including Σ), such that $\mathsf{AofC}(\mathsf{E}_{\mathsf{Ref}}) = M$. Note that, if $\mathsf{E}_0 = \emptyset$, then the algorithm will build a PCE over Σ from scratch that is equisatisfiable to $\mathsf{E}_{\mathsf{Ref}}$. In practice $\mathsf{E}_0 = \emptyset$, and $\mathsf{E}_{\mathsf{Ref}}$ can be any encoding of the circuit.

The algorithm traverses the fix-points of the best abstract transformer $\alpha \circ \mathsf{mod}_M \circ \gamma$, i.e. partial assignments where no new facts can be deduced. To achieve this, the algorithm uses a priority queue (PQ) of partial assignments sorted by partial assignment size. For each element of PQ, we examine the variables v that unit propagation cannot infer from E and pa (line 5). We then check if the reference encoding $\mathsf{E}_{\mathsf{Ref}}$, along with the current partial assignment pa logically entail either v or $\neg v$. This check is done via a call to a SAT oracle at line 8 (in our implementation this is a call to a CDCL SAT solver). If the query returns *sat*, the variable is not entailed and the extended partial assignment is added to the queue. Otherwise, l was a missed propagation and the encoding is strengthened by adding a clause that blocks the partial assignment pa.[1]

---

[1] As an optimization we add the negation of the minimal unsatisfiable core of $\neg$pa$'$: MUS(pa$'$).

Algorithm 1. Generating a propagation complete encoding of a CNF formula

---

Input: $\langle \Sigma, \mathsf{E}_0, \mathsf{E}_{\mathsf{Ref}} \rangle$

1    $\mathsf{E} \leftarrow \mathsf{E}_0$

2   PQ.push($\lambda v.?$)

3   **while** *not* PQ.empty() **do**

       // $\forall q_1, q_2 \in PQ \,.\, UP(\mathsf{E})(q_1) \neq UP(\mathsf{E})(q_2)$ and $\perp^{\mathscr{P}} \notin PQ$

4   pa $\leftarrow$ PQ.pop()

5   **foreach** $v \in \{x | x \in \Sigma \text{ and } UP(\mathsf{E})(\mathsf{pa})(v) = ?\}$ **do**

6   **foreach** $l \in \{v, \neg v\}$ **do**

7   pa$'$ $\leftarrow$ pa $\sqcap$ *assign*(l)

8   **if** SATSolver($\mathsf{E}_{\mathsf{Ref}}$, pa$'$) $= sat$ **then**

9   PQ.push(pa$'$)

10   **else**

11           $\mathsf{E} \leftarrow \mathsf{E} \cup \{\neg \mathsf{MUS}(\mathsf{pa}')\}$

12   PQ.compact()

       // $UP(\mathsf{E})(\mathsf{pa}) = (\alpha \circ \mathrm{mod}_M \circ \gamma)(\mathsf{pa})$

13 **return** E

If two partial assignments q_1 and q_2 unit propagate the same literals ($UP(\mathsf{E})(q_1) = UP(\mathsf{E})(q_2)$) we only need to explore extensions of one of them. Therefore, the push operation on line 9 only adds pa$'$ to PQ if $\forall q \in PQ \,.\, UP(\mathsf{E})(q) \neq UP(\mathsf{E})(\mathsf{pa})$. In other words we cache assignments that become equal when extended by unit propagation. Because we are potentially strengthening the encoding E with each iteration of the for-loop the amount of information unit propagation can infer from E increases. The PQ.compact call on line 12 iterates over the queue elements and removes queue elements that UP-extend to the same partial assignment. This ensures the invariant at the beginning of the while-loop. Furthermore, at the end of the while loop the current encoding E is strong enough to unit propagate all literals entailed from pa. The continuous strengthening of E also reduces the number of unassigned variables explored at line 5.

The algorithm is not always guaranteed to generate subset-minimal encodings. The order in which the partial assignments is considered may lead to the learning of redundant clauses. A clause c is redundant w.r.t. a PCE E_{PC} if for all literals $l \in c$ unit propagation can infer l from $\mathsf{E}_{\mathsf{PC}} \setminus c$ assuming the negation of the other literals $\neg(c \setminus \{l\})$. For example, in the presence of a chain of implications, $v_1 \Rightarrow v_2 \Rightarrow \ldots \Rightarrow v_k$, the algorithm may learn the redundant clause $c = \{\neg v_1, v_k\}$. Note that c is redundant since $v_1 \wedge (\mathsf{E}_{\mathsf{PC}} \setminus c) \vdash_{up} v_k$ and $\neg v_k \wedge (\mathsf{E}_{\mathsf{PC}} \setminus c) \vdash_{up} \neg v_1$. For this reason, after running Algorithm 1 we use the minimisation procedure described in [11] to remove redundant clauses while maintaining propagation completeness.

Auxiliary Variables. The algorithm we described so far only works on a fixed vocabulary Σ consisting of the input and output variables of the encoding. For certain operators, there no polynomially-sized CNF encodings if we restrict

---

Algorithm 2. Greedy algorithm for introducing auxiliary variables

---

1 E ← genPCE(E_0, E_{ref}, Σ)
2 **while** Aux $\neq \emptyset$ **do**
3   best ← undef
4   **foreach** aux $\in$ Aux **do**
5   E' ← genPCE(E_0, $E_{ref} \wedge$ Def(aux), $\Sigma \cup \{aux\}$)
6   **if** $|E'| < |E|$ **then**
7   E ← E'
8   best ← aux
9   **if** best = undef **then** **return** E
10   Σ ← $\Sigma \cup \{best\}$
11   E_{ref} ← $E_{ref} \wedge$ Def(best)
12   Aux ← Aux $\setminus \{best\}$
13 **return** E

---

ourselves to the input/output variables only. For this reason, we extended our algorithm to further reduce the size of the encoding while maintaining propagation completeness by heuristically adding auxiliary variables. Given a set of auxiliary variables Aux, we extend the reference encoding E_{Ref} by adding the definitional clauses Def(aux) for each auxiliary variable aux $\in$ Aux: Def(aux) $\wedge E_{Ref}$. For example, to introduce an auxiliary variable $a \equiv x \wedge y$ for inputs x, y, we add the clauses corresponding to the formula $a \Leftrightarrow (x \wedge y)$ to E_{Ref} and run Algorithm 1 on $\Sigma \cup \{a\}$.

We implemented a greedy algorithm that iteratively repeats this process as shown in Algorithm 2. We denote by genPCE the procedure of generating a propagation complete encoding from a reference encoding given in Algorithm 1. We denote by $|E|$ the size of an encoding as the number of clauses. The algorithm takes as input a reference encoding E_{Ref}, a fixed alphabet Σ as well as a set of auxiliary variables Aux. It initially computes the PCE over the input/output variables Σ. For each auxiliary variable aux in the current set of auxiliary variables, it computes the PCE over the alphabet $\Sigma \cup \{aux\}$ from reference encoding $E_{Ref} \wedge$ Def(aux), where Def(aux) is the set of definitional clauses for aux. It then chooses the auxiliary variable best that minimises the encoding the most, and adds it to the reference encoding. The process is repeated on the remaining auxiliary variables Aux $\setminus \{aux\}$ until no minimisation is achieved. Note that this is a greedy algorithm, and does not guarantee finding a minimal size encoding w.r.t. the given auxiliary variables. For the set of potential auxiliary variables Aux, we generate Boolean combinations over the input/output variables up to a limited depth. As a heuristic, we also add to the set Aux the auxiliary variables used by the reference encoding.

Generating Propagation Complete Encodings. Algorithm 1 solves an inherently hard problem and may call a SAT solver an exponential number of times. It is intended to be used as a tool to support encoding design rather than generating complete encodings.

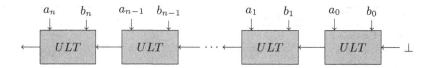

Fig. 4. Composition of encoding primitives to build a n-bit less than comparator.

To explore the feasibility of generating PCEs, we analysed the propagation completeness of encodings used in the CVC4 SMT solver [5]. CVC4 uses small circuit primitives to build more complex encodings of word-level bit-vector operators. Figure 4 shows an example of how small circuits for unsigned less than $(a < b)$ primitives can be composed to build a more complex encoding to compare n-bit bit-vectors. Each unsigned less than comparator (ULT) has three input bits (a, b, r) and one output bit (o). There are different ways that this primitive can be encoded into CNF. A possible PCE is: $\{\{o, \neg b, a\}, \{o, \neg b, \neg r\},$ $\{a, \neg r, o\}, \{\neg o, b, \neg a\}, \{\neg o, r, \neg a\}, \{\neg o, r, b\}\}$. If r has value $\bot$, then o will be $\top$ iff $a < b$. Otherwise, if r has value $\top$, then o will be $\top$ iff $a \leq b$. This structure allows the ULTs to be chained together to form an n-bit PCE for the ULT comparator. A similar construction can be done for other encoding primitives and is common in circuit design. For example, full-adders can be chained to form a ripple-carry adder. Note that, if the encoding primitives are not PC, then their composition will not be PC. However, the converse does not necessarily hold.

Table 1 shows the size of the encodings generated by Algorithm 1 and by introducing auxiliary variables compared to the size of the reference encoding $\mathsf{E_{Ref}}$, starting with an empty initial encoding $\mathsf{E_0}$. As encoding primitives $(prim)$, we have considered the if-then-else operator (ite-gadget), an unsigned less than comparator (ult-gadget), a signed less than comparator (slt-gadget), the full-adder (full-add), adder with base 4 (full-add-base4), bit-count circuits (bc3to2, bc7to3), 2 x 2 multiplication circuit (mult2), and multiplication by a constant (mult-const3, mult-const5, mult-const7). These encoding primitives are then composed $(comp)$ to build n-bit bit-vector operators.

These experiments were run on Intel Xeon X5667 processors (3.00 GHz) running Fedora 20 with a timeout of 3 h and a memory limit of 32 GB. In case of timeout of the greedy algorithm, we present the smallest encoding found until the timeout. The reference encodings used were the default implementations in CVC4. From the encoding primitives presented in Table 1, ite is the only encoding primitive that is propagation complete in CVC4. This scenario is not restricted to CVC4, and most state-of-the-art SMT solvers do not build PCEs (see Sect. 5 for further details).

For small primitives our algorithms can easily find PCEs with small size even when restricting the set of variables to inputs and outputs. For more complex circuits, as mult-4bit, the PCE can be much larger than the non-PCE. When generating PCEs with Σ containing auxiliary variables, we can obtain considerably smaller encodings. For example, for the addition operator add-4bit the number of clauses decreased from 336 to 43 by only adding 3 auxiliary variables. In this case, the auxiliary variables that are added by our greedy algorithm correspond

Table 1. Generation of PCEs for small encoding *prim*itives and their *comp*osition

Benchmark	Type	Original enc.		PCE			PCE w/ aux. vars		
		#Vars	#Cls	#Vars	#Cls	#time (s)	#Vars	#Cls	#time (s)
ite-gadget	prim	4	6	4	6	<0.01	4	6	<0.01
ult-gadget	prim	5	10	4	6	<0.01	4	6	<0.01
slt-gadget	prim	4	6	4	6	<0.01	4	6	<0.01
full-add	prim	8	17	5	14	<0.01	5	14	<0.01
full-add-base4	prim	33	74	10	120	0.31	12	86	140.40
bc3to2	prim	20	46	8	76	0.03	10	57	5.32
bc7to3	prim	27	68	10	254	0.49	14	136	769.50
mult2	prim	30	66	8	19	0.02	8	19	0.50
mult-const3	prim	16	33	6	20	<0.01	6	20	0.03
mult-const5	prim	25	50	9	24	0.01	9	24	0.21
mult-const7	prim	38	105	9	32	0.01	9	32	0.62
ult-6bit	comp	33	68	13	158	27.73	15	38	timeout
add-3bit	comp	18	39	9	96	0.09	11	29	10.05
add-4bit	comp	26	58	12	336	3.89	15	43	1,607.50
bc3to2-3bit	comp	38	78	12	1,536	11.72	16	69	timeout
mult-4bit	comp	36	97	12	670	5.26	12	670	298.95

to the carry bits from the chained adders. Note that the PCE for add-4bit formed by chaining the propagation complete full-adder results in an encoding with 20 variables and 60 clauses, which has a similar size to the PCE found by our greedy algorithm.

Even though the algorithm can take a considerable amount of time to find small PCEs with auxiliary variables, our goal is not to apply such algorithm to large formulae but only to find PCEs of primitives. This process is done once, offline. Afterwards, the encoding primitives can be chained together to form larger encodings for any bit-width. We verified with our algorithm that for small bit-widths the composition of PCEs for adders and comparators is propagation complete, while for the multiplier is not. We conjecture that the existence of a reasonably-sized propagation complete multiplier is unlikely, as this would help to efficiently solve hard factorization problems.

5   Experimental Evaluation

To explore the impact of propagation strength on performance, we implemented the PCE primitives generated in Sect. 4 in the CVC4 SMT solver [5]. CVC4 is a competitive solver that ranked 2nd in the 2015 SMT-COMP bit-vector division. We instrumented the solver's bit-blasting procedure to use the primitives to build more complex encodings of word-level bit-vector operators.

We focused on the following bit-vector operators: comparison, addition and multiplication. The rest of the bit-vector operations were either already propagation complete (e.g. bitwise and), or could be expressed in terms of other operations. We implemented n-bit circuits using the primitives described in Sect. 4. For addition, we used the propagation complete full-adder (cvcAO) and for comparison the ult-gadget and slt-gadget (cvcLO). For multiplication we implemented variants that use PC primitives: shift-add multiplication (cvc vs cvcMO), tree reduction (cvcT vs cvcTO) and multiplication by blocking (cvcB2 vs cvcB2O).

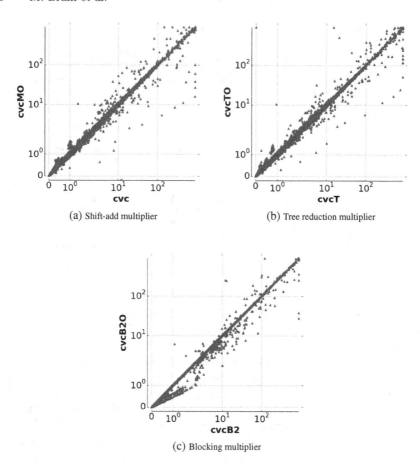

(a) Shift-add multiplier

(b) Tree reduction multiplier

(c) Blocking multiplier

Fig. 5. The impact of using PC primitives in various kinds of multiplication circuits

We append O to the solver's name to denote that the propagation complete sub-circuits are enabled. All implementations of multiplications that use propagation complete sub-circuits use the PC full-adder for adding the partial products, while blocking multiplication also uses the propagation complete 2 by 2 multiplication sub-circuit mult2.

We used 31066 quantifier-free bit-vector benchmarks from SMT-LIB v2.0 [6]. Experiments in this section were run on the StarExec [38] cluster infrastructure on Intel Xeon E5-2609 processors (2.40 GHz) running Red Hat Enterprise Linux Workstation release 6.3 (Santiago) with a timeout of 600 s seconds and a memory limit of 200 GB.

Figure 5 quantifies the impact of the PC components in the various kinds of multiplication circuits we implemented. The scatter plots are on the entire 31066 set of benchmarks, and are on a log-scale. Each point is a benchmark, and the x and y-axis represent the time (seconds) taken by CVC4 to solve the benchmark with the given configuration. Using the propagation complete

Table 2. Comparison of performance of propagation complete encodings in CVC4

set	cvc		cvcMO		cvcAMO		cvcALMO	
	solved	time (s)	solved	time (s)	solved	time (s)	solved	time (s)
VS3 (11)	**1**	**145.3**	0	0.0	0	0.0	0	0.0
bmc-bv (135)	**135**	**641.4**	135	665.6	135	669.7	134	527.0
brummayerbiere2 (65)	57	2866.9	62	2852.9	62	2870.2	**62**	**2847.9**
brummayerbiere3 (79)	40	3570.4	39	3527.6	40	3369.3	**44**	**5546.3**
bruttomesso (64)	38	3143.2	38	3145.7	**41**	**4876.7**	41	4904.5
calypto (23)	**8**	**5.5**	8	6.5	8	7.6	8	6.3
fft (23)	**8**	**981.4**	8	1053.9	7	59.1	7	190.7
float (213)	159	14550.6	158	13233.2	158	12004.4	**159**	**12190.9**
log-slicing (208)	67	23828.9	66	23426.5	70	27087.5	**70**	**26871.2**
mcm (186)	78	8674.2	78	8646.3	**80**	**7387.8**	80	8182.2
rubik (7)	6	623.2	6	619.0	6	615.8	**7**	**1371.7**
spear (1695)	1690	28046.5	1690	28603.8	**1690**	**22731.4**	1690	23357.9
	2287	87077.4	2288	85780.9	2297	81679.5	**2302**	**85996.6**

primitives (cvcMO, cvcTO and cvcB2O) consistently improves performance over their default implementations. Although the performance improvement is not dramatic, we believe it is consistent enough to show that propagation strength is an important characteristic of encodings. Since cvcMO had the best performance between multiplication circuits that use propagation complete sub-circuits, we considered this encoding for further evaluation.

Table 2 gives the number of problems solved and the time taken to solve them for CVC4 without propagation complete primitives (cvc) and with propagation complete primitives, namely: shift-add multiplier (cvcMO); shift-add multiplier and full-adder (cvcAMO); and shift-add multiplier, full-adder and comparison (cvcALMO). Due to space constraints we removed rows where the number of problems solved by all configurations was the same (see Appendix for full table). Table 2 shows that adding each PC primitives increases performance, with the configuration using PC primitives for addition, comparison and multiplication (cvcALMO) solving the most.

We believe this improvement is not limited to CVC4 but will translate to other solvers as well. We examined the source code of other competitive SMT solvers, such as boolector [13], stp2 [28], yices2 [22] and z3 [15], and their implementation of addition is not propagation complete. Therefore, although the notion of propagation complete encodings is not new, it is not widely applied to solver encoding design. Preliminary results from implementing the PC full-adder in the CBMC model-checker [14] also showed an improved performance. The improvement is also not limited to constraint solvers that use CDCL SAT solvers but is also expected for look-ahead SAT solvers [29]. These solvers are geared towards propagation and are even more likely to take advantage of the increased inference power than CDCL SAT solvers.

We have shown that the propagation complete encoding primitives our algorithm generated can be used to build encodings of bit-vector operators in an SMT solver. The results are promising considering we are only strengthening a small part of the overall problem. Furthermore the propagation complete encodings have been automatically generated from scratch, while the existing encodings had been optimized by hand. This highlights the importance of propagation complete encoding in encoding design and that our proposed framework can help practitioners improve encodings.

6 Related Work

The notion of propagation strength has been explored under various names such as unit refutation complete [16] and propagation complete encodings (PCEs) [11] in AI knowledge compilation. A formula is unit refutation complete [16] iff any of its implicates can be refuted by unit propagation. Here we refer to refutation as being the process of proving the implication $E \models l$ by proving $E \wedge \neg l \models \perp$. Bordeaux et al. [10] consider variations of unit refutation complete encodings, such as its disjunctive closure and a superset of unit refutation complete encodings where variables can be existentially quantified and unit refutation concerns only implications from free variables. Gwynne and Kullmann [25] introduce a general hierarchy of CNF problems based on "propagation hardness" and generalise the notion of unit refutation complete encodings.

PCEs are a proper subset of refutation complete encodings [25] and have been introduced by Bordeaux and Marques-Silva [11] for finding encodings where only using unit propagation suffices to deduce all the literals that are logically valid. The authors reduce the problem of generating PCEs to iteratively solving QBF formulas. We consider PCEs using an abstract satisfaction framework and rely on a SAT solver's efficient UP routine to check whether a clause is empowering. Since QBF is a PSPACE-complete problem, it is unclear that the approach from [11] would scale better than ours. Because [11] has no implementation that we are aware of, we cannot compare against them. Their framework can also support adding auxiliary variables to PCEs but this approach was not explored by the authors. Our approach supports generating encodings over a limited alphabet of auxiliary variables and includes an implementation and extensive experimental results that show performance gains. The work in [2] shows that checking whether a clause is *empowering* (it is entailed by the given CNF formula and it increases the propagation power of the formula) is co-NP complete. It also shows the existence of operations that have only exponential PCEs. This supports our targeting of small encoding primitives as opposed to n-bit circuits which is likely intractable.

Propagation completeness has also been considered in CSP (e.g. [3,8]) because of its connection to Domain Consistency, also known as Generalised Arc Consistency (GAC): when a constraint is encoded into SAT over some Finite-Domain variables, if the encoding of the constraint is propagation complete, then unit propagation on the SAT encoding effectively finds the same implications as Domain Consistency. In CSP it is common to consider GAC over procedural propagators [3] of specific constraints. Propagators can also be decomposed into primitive constraints that can be translated to SAT [8]. GAC has been adopted in SAT [24] and many encodings have this property [1,4,37]. However, GAC is usually only enforced on input/output variables and not on auxiliary variables.

PCEs consider a stronger notion of propagation strength since GAC is enforced on both input/output variables as well as on auxiliary variables.

Trevor Hansen's PhD [28] (independently) touches on many of the techniques we have used. He considers both 'bit-blasting' encodings and forward propagators (algorithms that implement abstract transformers directly), but treats these as independent approaches, omitting the link we show in Sect. 3. Although he tests the propagators for propagation completeness and even generates clauses to improve the propagators, he does not use this approach to generate complete encodings, nor does he perform minimisation. The SMT solver Beaver [30] also computes pre-synthesised templates for bit-vectors operators which are optimised offline using logic synthesis tools such as the ABC logic synthesis engine [7]. However, these templates are only computed for predefined bit-widths and are not PC. Hansen makes use of Reps' et al. [36] work on computing best abstract transformers via a lifted version of Stalmarck's algorithm. Algorithm 1 similarly uses breadth-first traversal, but the key difference is in how and when the algorithms are used. In [36] and most applications of their work [31], the *result* of the best abstract transformer is computed on-line as part of a search. We compute an *encoding* that gives the best abstract transformer off-line as part of solver development.

7   Conclusion

By using the abstract satisfaction framework we can characterise the space of encodings, the effects of reasoning and the link between them. Propagation complete encodings allow an increase of inference power that can be exploited by CDCL SAT solvers. We have showed that these encodings are captured by our abstract satisfaction formalism which allows us to reason about them and their extensions (Sect. 3). It is possible to compute subset-minimal propagation complete encodings and for various key operations these are tractably computable and often smaller than conventional encodings. For more complex encodings, we have shown that greedily introducing auxiliary variables can generate significantly smaller propagation complete encodings (Sect. 4). Implementing these in the CVC4 SMT solver gives performance improvements across a wide range of benchmarks (Sect. 5). It is hoped that this work will contribute to a more theoretically rigorous approach to encoding design.

Linking encodings to abstract transformers has many possible applications. Abstract transformers are functions on ordered sets and are therefore partially ordered. This gives a way of comparing the propagation strength of different encodings or investigating the effects of pre and in-processing techniques. This is particularly important as for certain operators there are no polynomially sized PCEs. A quantitative measure of propagation strength is a useful practical alternative. Proof-theoretic measures can be expressed as properties of the syntactic representation lattice, for example proof length becomes path length. Likewise solver run-time is bounded by the length of paths in $UP(2^{\mathscr{C}_{\Sigma^+}})$. Finally, the abstract satisfaction viewpoint provides a means of exploring many interesting questions about composition of encodings and when they preserve propagation strength.

Acknowledgments. This research was partially supported by ERC project 280053 (CPROVER) and by DARPA MUSE award #FA8750-14-2-0270. The views, opinions, and/or findings contained in this article are those of the authors and should not be interpreted as representing the official views or policies of the Department of Defense or the U.S. Government.

References

1. Asín, R., Nieuwenhuis, R., Oliveras, A., Rodríguez-Carbonell, E.: Cardinality networks: a theoretical and empirical study. Constraints **16**(2), 195–221 (2011)
2. Babka, M., Balyo, T., Čepek, O., Gurskỳ, Š., Kučera, P., Vlček, V.: Complexity issues related to propagation completeness. Artif. Intell. **203**, 19–34 (2013)
3. Bacchus, F.: GAC via unit propagation. In: Bessière, C. (ed.) CP 2007. LNCS, vol. 4741, pp. 133–147. Springer, Heidelberg (2007)
4. Bailleux, O., Boufkhad, Y.: Efficient CNF encoding of boolean cardinality constraints. In: Rossi, F. (ed.) CP 2003. LNCS, vol. 2833, pp. 108–122. Springer, Heidelberg (2003)
5. Barrett, C., et al.: CVC4. In: Gopalakrishnan, G., Qadeer, S. (eds.) CAV 2011. LNCS, vol. 6806, pp. 171–177. Springer, Heidelberg (2011)
6. Barrett, C., Stump, A., Tinelli, C.: The SMT-LIB standard: Version 2.0. In: Workshop on Satisfiability Modulo Theories (2010)
7. Berkeley Logic Synthesis and Verification Group: ABC: A System for Sequential Synthesis and Verification, Release 70930, http://www.eecs.berkeley.edu/alanmi/abc
8. Bessiere, C., Katsirelos, G., Narodytska, N., Walsh, T.: Circuit complexity and decompositions of global constraints. In: International Joint Conference on Artificial Intelligence, pp. 412–418. AAAI Press (2009)
9. Biere, A., Heule, M.J.H., van Maaren, H., Walsh, T. (eds.): Handbook of Satisfiability, Frontiers in Artificial Intelligence and Applications, vol. 185. IOS Press, Amsterdam (2009)
10. Bordeaux, L., Janota, M., Marques-Silva, J., Marquis, P.: On unit-refutation complete formulae with existentially quantified variables. In: Principles of Knowledge Representation and Reasoning. AAAI Press (2012)
11. Bordeaux, L., Marques-Silva, J.: Knowledge compilation with empowerment. In: Bieliková, M., Friedrich, G., Gottlob, G., Katzenbeisser, S., Turán, G. (eds.) SOFSEM 2012. LNCS, vol. 7147, pp. 612–624. Springer, Heidelberg (2012)
12. Brain, M., D'Silva, V., Haller, L., Griggio, A., Kroening, D.: An abstract interpretation of DPLL(T). In: Giacobazzi, R., Berdine, J., Mastroeni, I. (eds.) VMCAI 2013. LNCS, vol. 7737, pp. 455–475. Springer, Heidelberg (2013)
13. Brummayer, R., Biere, A.: Boolector: an efficient SMT solver for bit-vectors and arrays. In: Kowalewski, S., Philippou, A. (eds.) TACAS 2009. LNCS, vol. 5505, pp. 174–177. Springer, Heidelberg (2009)
14. Clarke, E., Kroning, D., Lerda, F.: A tool for checking ANSI-C programs. In: Jensen, K., Podelski, A. (eds.) TACAS 2004. LNCS, vol. 2988, pp. 168–176. Springer, Heidelberg (2004)
15. de Moura, L., Bjørner, N.S.: Z3: an efficient SMT solver. In: Ramakrishnan, C.R., Rehof, J. (eds.) TACAS 2008. LNCS, vol. 4963, pp. 337–340. Springer, Heidelberg (2008)

16. Del Val, A.: Tractable databases: how to make propositional unit resolution complete through compilation. In: Principles of Knowledge Representation and Reasoning, pp. 551–561. Morgan Kaufmann (1994)
17. D'Silva, V., Haller, L., Kroening, D.: Satisfiability solvers are static analysers. In: Miné, A., Schmidt, D. (eds.) SAS 2012. LNCS, vol. 7460, pp. 317–333. Springer, Heidelberg (2012)
18. D'Silva, V., Haller, L., Kroening, D.: Abstract conflict driven learning. In: Symposium on Principles of Programming Languages, pp. 143–154. ACM (2013)
19. D'Silva, V., Haller, L., Kroening, D.: Abstract satisfaction. In: Symposium on Principles of Programming Languages, pp. 139–150. ACM (2014)
20. D'Silva, V., Haller, L., Kroening, D., Tautschnig, M.: Numeric bounds analysis with conflict-driven learning. In: Flanagan, C., König, B. (eds.) TACAS 2012. LNCS, vol. 7214, pp. 48–63. Springer, Heidelberg (2012)
21. D'Silva, V., Kroening, D.: Abstraction of syntax. In: Giacobazzi, R., Berdine, J., Mastroeni, I. (eds.) VMCAI 2013. LNCS, vol. 7737, pp. 396–413. Springer, Heidelberg (2013)
22. Dutertre, B.: Yices 2.2. In: Biere, A., Bloem, R. (eds.) CAV 2014. LNCS, vol. 8559, pp. 737–744. Springer, Heidelberg (2014)
23. Eén, N., Sörensson, N.: Translating pseudo-boolean constraints into SAT. J. Satisfiability Boolean Model. Comput. 2(1–4), 1–26 (2006)
24. Gent, I.P.: Arc consistency in SAT. In: European Conference on Artificial Intelligence, pp. 121–125. IOS Press (2002)
25. Gwynne, M., Kullmann, O.: Generalising unit-refutation completeness and slur via nested input resolution. J. Autom. Reasoning 52(1), 31–65 (2014)
26. Gwynne, M., Kullmann, O.: On SAT representations of XOR constraints. In: Dediu, A.-H., Martín-Vide, C., Sierra-Rodríguez, J.-L., Truthe, B. (eds.) LATA 2014. LNCS, vol. 8370, pp. 409–420. Springer, Heidelberg (2014)
27. Haller, L., Griggio, A., Brain, M., Kroening, D.: Deciding floating-point logic with systematic abstraction. In: Formal Methods in Computer-Aided Design, pp. 131–140. IEEE (2012)
28. Hansen, T.: A Constraint Solver and its Application to Machine Code Test Generation. Ph.D. thesis, University of Melbourne (2012)
29. Heule, M., van Maaren, H.: Look-ahead based SAT solvers. In: Handbook of Satisfiability, pp. 155–184. IOS Press (2009)
30. Jha, S., Limaye, R., Seshia, S.A.: Beaver: engineering an efficient SMT solver for bit-vector arithmetic. In: Bouajjani, A., Maler, O. (eds.) CAV 2009. LNCS, vol. 5643, pp. 668–674. Springer, Heidelberg (2009)
31. King, A., Søndergaard, H.: Automatic abstraction for congruences. In: Barthe, G., Hermenegildo, M. (eds.) VMCAI 2010. LNCS, vol. 5944, pp. 197–213. Springer, Heidelberg (2010)
32. Kleine Büning, H., Kullmann, O.: Minimal unsatisfiability and autarkies. In: Handbook of Satisfiability, pp. 339–401. IOS Press (2009)
33. Kullmann, O.: Upper and lower bounds on the complexity of generalised resolution and generalised constraint satisfaction problems. Ann. Math. Artif. Intelli. 40(3–4), 303–352 (2004)
34. Manthey, N., Heule, M.J.H., Biere, A.: Automated reencoding of boolean formulas. In: Biere, A., Nahir, A., Vos, T. (eds.) HVC. LNCS, vol. 7857, pp. 102–117. Springer, Heidelberg (2013)
35. Martins, R., Manquinho, V., Lynce, I.: Exploiting cardinality encodings in parallel maximum satisfiability. In: International Conference on Tools with Artificial Intelligence, pp. 313–320. IEEE Computer Society (2011)

36. Reps, T., Sagiv, M., Yorsh, G.: Symbolic implementation of the best transformer. In: Steffen, B., Levi, G. (eds.) VMCAI 2004. LNCS, vol. 2937, pp. 252–266. Springer, Heidelberg (2004)
37. Sinz, C.: Towards an optimal CNF encoding of boolean cardinality constraints. In: van Beek, P. (ed.) CP 2005. LNCS, vol. 3709, pp. 827–831. Springer, Heidelberg (2005)
38. Stump, A., Sutcliffe, G., Tinelli, C.: StarExec: a cross-community infrastructure for logic solving. In: Demri, S., Kapur, D., Weidenbach, C. (eds.) IJCAR 2014. LNCS, vol. 8562, pp. 367–373. Springer, Heidelberg (2014)

Author Index

Printed in the United States
By Bookmasters